THE ULTIMATE
Book of Shadows
FOR THE
NEW GENERATION

About the Author

"The best way for a magickal person to be accepted is to let people get to know you," recommends Silver. "Once they understand your personal values and principles, their attitudes about your alternative religion interests tend to be more positive. Let them know you for the work that you do." Silver RavenWolf is a true Virgo who adores making lists and arranging things in order. The mother of four children, she celebrated her twenty-second wedding anniversary in 2002. Silver extensively tours the United States, giving seminars and lectures about magickal religions and practices. She has been interviewed by the *New York Times*, the *Wall Street Journal,* and *US News & World Report*. It is estimated that Silver has personally met over 25,000 magickal individuals in the last five years. Silver is the Clan Head of the Black Forest Family that includes 28 covens in 19 states and 1 in Canada. Visit her website at:

HTTP://WWW.SILVERRAVENWOLF.COM

To Write to the Author

If you wish to contact the author or would like more information about this book, please write to the author in care of Llewellyn Worldwide and we will forward your request. Both the author and publisher appreciate hearing from you and learning of your enjoyment of this book and how it has helped you. Llewellyn Worldwide cannot guarantee that every letter written to the author can be answered, but all will be forwarded.

Silver cannot answer letters that request private counseling on matters of the heart, nor is the information in this book to be used in place of standard practices, such as relationship, medical, or psychiatric counseling, by a qualified professional or the necessity for consulting a qualified attorney. Please write to:

Silver RavenWolf
℅ Llewellyn Worldwide
2143 Wooddale Drive
Woodbury, MN 55125-2989

Please enclose a self-addressed stamped envelope for reply,
or $1.00 to cover costs. If outside U.S.A., enclose
international postal reply coupon.

Many of Llewellyn's authors have websites with additional information
and resources. For more information, please visit our website:

HTTP://WWW.LLEWELLYN.COM

THE ULTIMATE
Book of Shadows
FOR THE
NEW GENERATION

Solitary Witch

Silver
RavenWolf

Llewellyn Publications
Woodbury, Minnesota

FIRST EDITION
Twenty-first Printing, 2015

Book editing and design by Rebecca Zins
Cover design and interior illustrations by Gavin Dayton Duffy
Cover image © Photodisc Background

Library of Congress Cataloging-in-Publication Data
RavenWolf, Silver, 1956–
    Solitary witch : the ultimate book of shadows for the new generation / Silver RavenWolf.
        p.   cm.
    Includes bibliographical references and index.
    ISBN 13: 978-0-7387-0319-0
    ISBN 10: 0-7387-0319-2
    1. Witchcraft.   2. Teenagers—Miscellanea.   I. Title.

    BF1571.5.T44 R38 2003
    133.4'3—dc21

                                                                                2002030106

Llewellyn Worldwide does not participate in, endorse, or have any authority or responsibility concerning private business transactions between our authors and the public.
    All mail addressed to the author is forwarded but the publisher cannot, unless specifically instructed by the author, give out an address or phone number.
    Any Internet references contained in this work are current at publication time, but the publisher cannot guarantee that a specific location will continue to be maintained. Please refer to the publisher's website for links to authors' websites and other sources.

Llewellyn Publications
A Division of Llewellyn Worldwide Ltd.
2143 Wooddale Drive
Woodbury, MN 55125-2989
www.llewellyn.com

Llewellyn is a registered trademark of Llewellyn Worldwide Ltd.
Printed in the United States of America

Other Books by Silver RavenWolf

To Ride a Silver Broomstick

To Stir a Magick Cauldron

To Light a Sacred Flame

Teen Witch

Angels: Companions in Magick

American Folk Magick

Beneath a Mountain Moon (fiction)

Witches' Runes Kit (with Nigel Jackson)

Halloween: Customs, Recipes & Spells

Murder at Witches' Bluff (fiction)

Teen Witch Kit

A Witch's Notebook

Hexcraft

MindLight

HedgeWitch

In the *Silver's Spells* Series

Silver's Spells for Prosperity

Silver's Spells for Protection

Silver's Spells for Love

Silver's Spells for Abundance

In the *Witches' Night Out*
Teen Fiction Series

Witches' Night Out

Witches' Night of Fear

Witches' Key to Terror

This book is dedicated to

Ronald Hutton, Professor, University of Bristol
Thank you for helping me bring magick, history, and people together.

Tempest Smith
Gone but not forgotten.

Contents

Witchcraft, practiced honorably,
gives you power beyond your imagination.

The basic modern scholarly definition of religion
was provided in 1871 by Sir Edward Tylor,
who suggested that its essential component
was a belief in the existence of spiritual beings and in
the need of humans to form relationships with them.
—*Ronald Hutton*[1]

Preface

The Ultimate Book of Wiccan Shadows for the New Generation Solitary Witch

This book represents a collection of magick, spells, rituals, and definitions related specifically to modern Witchcraft, yet it is grounded in the magickal work of people who lived in the ancient world. In this book you will read about and practice the magick of many ages, collected and combined in a user-friendly way that can bring about the same results today as they did many thousands or hundreds of years ago.

Even though the early Egyptians, Greeks, or Celts didn't have lockers, cafeterias, school bells, cheerleaders, guys on skateboards, the Internet, the stock market, or the prom, they still had debt, malicious gossip, bullies, parties, homework, a social pecking order, street gangs, sickness, poverty, troubles at home, the need to find love (and keep it), and the driving question, "Why am I here in the first place?"

This tells us that the old adage is true—the more things change, the more they stay the same. Believe it or not, magick has always been around to help solve our problems and give us mental tools that can allow us to shape our lives into what we want them to be; all we have to do is provide the faith.

What You'll Find in This Book of Shadows

Like a medieval magickal book, this one is a collection of neat and nifty spells, charms, formularies, rituals, and all manner of enchantments. Unlike a textbook, it doesn't build toward closure—that's your job. Take the bits and pieces of information and put them together the way it feels comfortable for you. If you've ever seen *The Grimoire of Lady Sheba* or other unpublished works of the Witch famous, magickal lodges, or European cunning-folk, you'll discover this same disjointed effect. In many Books of Shadows, especially in some of the German ones I've looked at, the student was given a main spell format and a main ritual structure, to avoid repetition in every spell or ritual in the book. At one time, getting paper wasn't like popping over to the nearest store and picking up a few reams. You will find some of that format here, where several of the rituals can be used for a variety of spells and conjurations.

Solitary Witch honors what has gone before and what is new. It is a vehicle of personal interpretation, magick, and faith. It's a magickal

cookbook, encyclopedia, dictionary, and more, and is alphabetized under five distinct categories. Part I, Shadows of Religion & Mystery, discusses the religion of Witchcraft, its ceremonies, and common practices associated with the religion. Part II, Shadows of Objects & Tools, talks about the tools and objects commonly found in modern Witchcraft and where their use most likely came from. Part III, Shadows of Expertise & Proficiency, is where we look at things like auric programming, dreaming, the Tarot, and other occult-related subjects. Shadows of Magick & Enchantment, Part IV, covers general forms of magick and items associated with it, ranging from the discussion of holographic quantum physics to medieval ideas. The last part, Part V, Shadows of Magick & Real Life, hits human-related subjects: eating disorders, dating, sex, suicide, peer pressure, anger, stalkers, shopping, family difficulties, grades—magick and real life combined. There's fun stuff and serious stuff, and plenty to keep you amused. Finally, as much as possible, all categories are not only discussed in modern terms, they are also associated with their historical roots so that when you are called on to take the plunge and seriously discuss the history of your religion, you have a wide array of research to rely on.

New to this type of Book of Shadows are the endnotes that cite sources or are used for further clarification. Some of you may groan at this and I apologize, but the research is important. Besides, think of them as our secret code.

At the bottom of many categories in this book I have given you a selected reading list for that topic, or web addresses. This doesn't mean you have to rush right out and buy the book or wrench the computer from your brother or sister, husband or wife to surf to that site immediately. This is simply my way of telling you what books or sites on the 'Net that I think might be of further interest if you wish to study more on that particular topic.

How You Use This Book . . .

is entirely up to you. Feel free to skip over the parts you already know, or read each section in alphabetical order—doesn't matter. Not every topic has its own category, as some Wiccan terms or magickal applications blend or support each other, so check the index if you can't find what you're looking for. If one section requires the support or information of another, I've tried to let you know which part to go to so you can flip there. The book is designed for both the beginner and intermediate student, so if you don't understand something, try reading the passage again.

On the other hand, if you feel the information is too basic, I beg your indulgence—it isn't my desire to insult your intelligence, I'm simply trying to find a happy medium. If you are unfamiliar with Witchcraft, you may wish to start with this basic reference list:

Teen Witch by Silver RavenWolf. Teen, first level.

Teen Witch Kit by Silver RavenWolf. Teen, first level.

To Ride a Silver Broomstick by Silver Raven-Wolf. Adult, first level.

The Witch Book: The Encyclopedia of Witchcraft, Wicca and Neo-Paganism by Raymond Buckland. Adult, first level.

Wicca: A Guide for the Solitary Practitioner by Scott Cunningham. Adult, first level.

The Truth About Witchcraft Today by Scott Cunningham. Adult, first level.

Positive Magic by Marion Weinstein. Adult, first level.

The Complete Book of Witchcraft by Raymond Buckland. Adult, first level.

Above all, I have tried to make this book a training companion to those of my titles listed above, designing it to fit in my overall series of New Generation Witchcraft books. This being the case, there are a few instances where I have referred the student to my previous books in an effort not to repeat material. It is my sincere hope that this work answers questions and gives the student an in-depth look at the Craft of the Wise.

The Essence of Witchcraft . . .

is transformation. The idea is to take the "you" currently present and accounted for and change your essence into something better, greater, stronger, and incredibly dynamic. Being a Witch means to *want* to work every day to be a better person. When you change yourself,

then the world around you cannot help but change. There's no getting around it. All this changing can be a lot of hard work—and there are certain aspects of the path that require time, effort, and energy. Although many of the things you truly want can be achieved in a short time with the techniques presented in this book, there are other issues in your life that will require patience, effort, and practice to reach your ultimate goals. That's okay. If you didn't have to work at some things, then the study wouldn't seem worthwhile. To be a Witch, you must be brave enough to face everything inside of you, and have the courage to change the things you do not like. Being a Witch has nothing to do with spells, rituals, and unusual clothing—they are the fun stuff. To be a Witch is to desire personal transformation.

Where to Go from Here

Wherever Spirit moves you. Good luck, and happy zapping! Just remember, don't get stuck in anybody's dogma (including mine).

Special thanks to Ronald Hutton,
Professor of History at the University of Bristol,
for reviewing this work and making such helpful suggestions
in the avenue of historical accuracy.
Any mistakes on historical content are my own.

shadows
of
Religion
&
Mystery

Blessings

Whether you can believe you can do a thing or believe you can't—you are right.
—*Henry Ford*

Although today many of us don't think about the power of words, sound, or touch, those who have gone before us knew that all these things carried an energy of their own, and to give that positive energy to another was a gift more precious than gold. To bless is to remove any negative energy around a person, animal, place, or thing and instill them with positive energy. To bless another is to empower them. By sound, touch, and thought, we can help the sick, lighten the heart of the troubled, or open a pathway for a better life by removing negative blockages. The mere utterance of a blessing can change the course of a person's life. In our modern world, people often scoff at this idea, not believing that such power could be contained in anything so simple. Many of us are independent individuals, and to think that someone else (by mere word or physical proximity) could alter our pattern of living may seem unthinkable.

But they can.

In many cultures, past and present, it is customary to leave a blessing at an individual's home when saying farewell. It was believed that a magickal person could make words turn into flesh, meaning by uttering words with one's magickal voice (SEE PART III, UNDER POW WOW) you could create a physical manifestation. To have your house blessed in such a way by a magickal/religious person ensured health and prosperity for the occupants for months to come. You too can give such a gift. Don't be shy about it. If you believe you can do it, so shall it be. Sometimes the mere presence of magickal individuals can change the course of one's fate. The more spiritual the person, the more pure the environment. I've also noticed that if a magickal

person is involved in a particular type of study, that study can affect those around him or her. One Witch who steadfastly worked on building her prosperity realized after a few months that every time she walked into a store, especially a deserted one, her energy attracted paying customers off the street. Another Witch who worked on protection experienced the same phenomenon. He could walk into any establishment and if there were negative people around, they would quickly disperse. What you work on in the magickal world *will* affect the world around you.

The mechanism of a blessing is very easy:

- Think of a white light so powerful that it encompasses your mind, body, and spirit.

- Move the white light into a mental picture of the person, place, or thing.

- In your mind, allow the white light to burst through the object (no, this won't hurt anyone).

- Intone words of blessing or touch the person, animal, or thing.

- Seal the blessing with a hand motion of your choice while pronouncing aloud "It is done."

The Thirteen Powers of the Witch

When you truly take the power of Witch training into your being and strive to do the best that you can regardless of the situation, the thirteen powers of the universe are given to you. These are either transferred through a religious ceremony by those who have been gifted before you, or they can come about at their own pace as you grow and learn on your own. If a power is abused, it is thought that the gift is taken from you, either for a period of time or permanently. The powers speak of blessings that you can give to others or use for yourself to enhance your own life as well as the lives of those around you.

Thirteen powers do the Witches claim
their right of lineage by (say the name of
your patron god or goddess here)'s name.
Tie a knot and say the words
or hand on head—the blessing conferred.
A Witch can give success in love
curse or bless through God/dess above.
Speak to beasts and spirits alike
command the weather; cast out a blight.
Read the heavens and stars of the night
divine the future and give good advice.
Conjure treasure and bring fortune to bear
heal the sick and kill despair.

This poem can be said as a blessing when giving something to another, and can be included in any spell by adding:

This is my birthright to have and to share
blessings upon you, (the person's name),
may the spirits be fair.

This poem itself is very powerful and *will* create change. Just be careful what you wish for.

Bedtime Blessing

Close your eyes and breathe deeply three or four times until you feel relaxed and at peace. Imagine that your entire body is filled with brilliant, white light. If you like, hold your hands over your heart, and say:

In the still of the night
while the world around me sleeps
may the angels smile upon me
and the Lady bring me peace.
Blessings upon (list those whom you would
like to remember in your prayers).
I know that You will care for them
and bring them what they need.

Instill in me great harmony
in thought and word and deed.
So mote it be.

Gift Blessing

Hold the object in your hands. Take several deep breaths, inhaling and exhaling slowly. Visualize the object glowing with white light. Connect your mind to Spirit and try to think of nothing else. Imagine the gift capturing the pure perfection of the universe. Then say:

Perfect love and perfect peace
the world will dance as one.
I dream the wish to make it real
the magick now is done.

Seal your work by drawing an equal-armed cross (+) in the air over the object. You can also empower birthday, get well, and sympathy cards in this same manner.

Meal Blessing

Hold your hands over the food, and say each line below three times. This can be worked into a fun blessing for the whole family if chanted in a round.

The table round contains the Earth
and thus becomes the Mother.
We share her bounty in this hour
and bless and love each other.
So mote it be.

Personal Journal/Book Blessing

These words herein are mine alone
fashioned deep inside my bones
each picture, thought, and quote you see
are all reflections of what is me.
Beware the urge to take this book

or read it in some private nook
because its magick isn't blind
and I will know you've touched what's mine.

Charge of the Goddess

The Charge of the Goddess is one of the most popular ritual invocations in modern Wicca. The foundation of the work comes from a book titled *Aradia: Gospel of the Witches (Vangelo delle-Streghe)*, written by Charles Leland and published in 1899. Sometime after 1955, Doreen Valiente, one of the most gifted poets and priestesses of Wicca in our time, used the information in poetry while assisting Gerald Gardner in compiling the material later used for Gardnerian instruction. The version written here appeared in *The Grimoire of Lady Sheba*, first published in 1972. In later years, the Charge was broken into two parts, with the second section standing alone and titled "The Charge of the Star Goddess."

Depending upon personal or coven choice, the Charge is read:

- At the beginning of a ritual. Members of the coven may practice deep breathing, grounding and centering, or meditation.

- Before communion.

- At the end of a ritual, as a closure.

- At some point during an initiation rite.

- During daily devotions.

- During personal spellworking.

The Charge (Part I)

Listen to the words of the Great Mother, who was of old, called amongst men, Artemis, Astarte, Dione, Melusine, Aphrodite, Cerridwen, Diana, Arionhod, Bride, and by many other names.

At mine Altar, the youths of Lacedemon in Sparta made due sacrifice. Whenever ye have need of anything, once in the month and better it be when the Moon is Full, then shall ye assemble in some secret place and adore the Spirit of Me, who am Queen of all the Witcheries. There shall ye assemble, who are feign to learn all sorceries who have not as yet won my deepest secrets. To these will I teach that which is as yet unknown. And ye shall be free from all slavery and as a sign that ye be really free, ye shall sing, feast, and make music, all in my presence. For mine is the ecstasy of the Spirit and mine is also joy on earth. For my Law is love unto all beings. Keep pure your highest ideals, strive ever towards them. Let none stop you or turn you aside. For mine is the secret that opens upon the door of youth and mine is the Cup of the Wine of Life and the Cauldron of Cerridwen, which is the Holy Grail of Immortality. I am the Gracious Goddess who gives the gift of joy unto the heart of man upon earth. I give the knowledge of the Spirit Eternal, and beyond death I give peace and freedom and reunion with those that have gone before. Nor do I demand aught or sacrifice, for behold I am the Mother of all things, and my love is poured out upon the earth.

The Charge of the Star Goddess (Part II)

Hear ye the words of the Star Goddess. She, in the dust of whose feet are the Hosts of Heaven, whose body encircleth the universe.

I, who am the beauty of the Green Earth and the White Moon amongst the stars and the mystery of the Waters, and the desire of the heart of man; I call unto thy soul to arise and come unto me. For I am the Soul of Nature who giveth life to the universe; from me all things proceed an unto me all things must return. You, beloved of the Gods and men, whose innermost divine self shall be enfolded in the raptures of the Infinite, let my worship be in the heart. Rejoiceth, for behold, all acts of love and pleasure are my rituals; therefore, let there be beauty and strength—power and compassion—honor and humility, mirth and reverence—within you. And thou who thinkest to seek me, know that thy seeking and yearning avail thee not, unless thou knowest the mystery—that if that which thou seekest thou findeth not within thyself, thou wilt never find it without thee. For behold! I have been with the from the beginning, and I am that which is attained at the end of desire!

Circlecasting

Spirit is a circle whose center is everywhere
and whose circumference is nowhere.

—*Hermes Trismegistus*

From cave paintings to crowns, halos, and Stonehenge, circles and spirals figure prominently in all walks of ancient life, spanning a multitude of cultures with religious and magickal significance. Magicians were casting magick circles in the Middle East during the Assyrian reign from 883–612 B.C.E., and a fellow by the name of Honi cast a circle and successfully called in rain during a drought to save the people around 65 B.C.E.,[1] as noted in Jewish rabbinical literature. The story of Honi the Circle Maker is interesting because it gives us several clues to your heritage of ancient magick, and how it is still taught today.

Honi and the Rain[2]

Since Honi's story occurred more than 2,000 years ago, there is debate on what he actually represented in his society. Was he just a plain old magician, or was he a part of the priesthood? Some feel that his miracle was remarkable enough to write down (which they did) but too dangerous to let the reader think he was operating outside of the current religious structure of the day, therefore Honi (in successive tellings of his story) became part of Jewish rabbinical society. Honi's story gives us important clues as to how magick works and why, 2,000 years later, we continue to use the magick circle.

In the spring, the people desperately needed rain, but it did not come. They approached Honi the Circle Maker and said, "Pray so that the rains will fall." Honi told the people to find sufficient cover for the mud and clay Passover ovens because they would melt in the rain. In magick, this is the mental preparation needed to set the stage for the working. In making the people move the ovens, Honi was mentally encouraging them to believe in the magick. Once the ovens had been covered, Honi prayed, but it did not rain. He then realized that he had made an error: he forgot to cast the circle! No wonder the rains would not come—he had not created a stable platform for the work to manifest. Honi then cast a magick circle (possibly with a staff or rod in the dirt, though the text does not say), and stood within it.

What is interesting about this story is that Honi then talked to God as if he were talking to anyone. He said, "Master of the universe, your children have turned their faces to me because I am like a son of the house before you. I swear by your great name that I am not moving from here until you have mercy on your children." In essence, he gets a bit feisty.

So far, Honi has done four important things. He's moved the bake ovens to indicate his faith in his ability to make rain, a physical act which, by involving the people, makes them expectant of a miracle. He's cast a magick circle to purify the area because when he "just" prayed, nothing happened, therefore someone in the crowd probably wanted to see him fail, and (more than likely) he wasn't centered and cast the circle to put himself in the correct frame of mind. The next thing he does is connect with deity. Then he tells Spirit his magickal intent, and very firmly too. Is he threatening God with that last statement? Actually, no. Again, looking at this from a magickal point of view, he's telling *himself* that he's going to succeed, no matter what. He's putting his conviction into the magickal mix and giving himself a verbal booster at the same time. He's being firm, like a Victorian lady who won't take no for an answer, yet it is not God he is pressing, but himself. Honi has been trained that he must touch the unmanifest to manifest, which has nothing to do with threatening God and everything to do with believing in himself. Evidently, he needed the extra verbal push that day. And with that push, the rains began to drip.

As dripping was not what he had in mind, Honi says, "I did not ask for this, but for rains of sufficient amount to fill cisterns, ditches, and caves." Honi has just added visualization to the proceedings. Those who are unmagickal think that Honi is continuing to talk to God, but he isn't. His dialog is meant for himself. He's matching the word to the visualization.

The rains fell with a vehemence. Oops, too much visualization! Honi isn't at all happy. It's raining too hard, so he says, "I did not ask for this, but for rains of benevolence, blessing, and graciousness!"—fine-tuning that visualization and adding the proper wording.

The rain fell precisely as he ordered it.

Finally, Honi says, "I know you will do this for me," which magickally turns out to be the most important statement he can make. He is affirming his belief with utter conviction, removing all doubt from his mind with the force of the statement.

Did Honi order God to make it rain? No. In actuality, Honi was ordering rain from the collective unconscious like you order fries from McDonald's. He did, however, ask for God's involvement by stating the need and calling God by a title and thus touching upon what everyone inherently believes—the perfection and order of the universe. Therefore, divine energy was definitely in the mix because, to Honi, that divine energy was "all that is good" and the basis for successful manifestation. Was Honi acting like a spoiled child in circle? Some people may read it this way, but I think it shows us that even great magicians become irritated with themselves. They are human, after all.

Honi's family, and his sons after him, were all rainmakers, which means that Honi's magick worked successfully on more than one occasion to become a family tradition. What is lost in this story, unfortunately, are any other incantations and specific motions he may have done, but what we do have works quite well. The story itself is enough to let us know that (*a*) real magickal people in history were not a figment of our imagination or characters in a fairy tale, they lived and breathed and practiced magick all the time; (*b*) they were not necessarily a part of any religious structure (though afterward they are sometimes claimed to be so, especially if, like Honi, they were at least sympathetic to the religious regime at the time); and (*c*) for Honi's magick to work that day, he had to have a magick circle. The story also shows that the universe has a sense of humor, and that when you ask for something, you better be specific and you darned well better not forget to cast that circle.

Does Honi's method work? Absolutely! In the Honi tradition, add this to any spell:

1. Ground and center.

2. Cast the circle.

3. Pronounce the Honi conjuration (below).

4. Continue on with your working.

5. Release the circle.

6. Ground and center.

Here's how the conjuration works.

"Master/Mistress of the universe!"—you are calling on the perfection and order of the universe. *"I am* (state your name), *your magickal son/daughter"*—here, you are activating your pathway to deity, and you are melding your entire being with the perfection of the universe that you called in the first line above. If you are working for someone else, state his or her name as well, much like Honi did, "like a son of the house before you." State your request and add *"for all that is good."* Finish with *"I know you will do this for me"*—the affirmation of faith.

Walking the Circle

Walking the circle occurs often in European folktales and religious ceremonies to break evil spells, to transform oneself or the area into something sacred, and to acquire power. This walking the circle was called circumambulation, which means to walk around an object, person, or place with the right hand toward the subject either in religious ceremony, in an act of reverence, or in magickal practice.[3] One walks sunwise (clockwise) to bring good luck, destroy evil, cure disease, and in some cultures to ensure that the sun will rise the following day. These circumambulations were especially used in ceremonies of birth, marriage, and death, whether we are talking about Tibet, Europe, South America, or the Inuit culture. Knowing this, we understand that the magick circle does not belong solely to Witches, but is another ancient practice that has touched all cultures and all faiths, and is still practiced by many of them today. As with many other antiquated practices, it is the modern Witch that gives Western civilization a taste of our ancient, magickal birthright by remembering and practicing such things as the circlecasting in daily life and reminding our brothers and sisters of other faiths where many of these applications actually came from. To deny one's history is to deny knowledge.

This clockwise, sunwise movement in the Craft is called deosil (pronounced *jess-el*). The original spelling, *deiseal*, is of Irish descent, and it's also called "the holy round." Dances, processions, and parades—even riding around the battlefield one turn for good luck before the clash of axes and swords—are embedded in our history. When someone says, "Gee, I hope this goes right," they are actually invoking the ancient power of the magick circle.

Although there are numerous ways in the Craft to cast a magick circle, most of them involve walking the circle one to three times with the finger of the right hand (or the chosen tool) held out from the body and pointing down while reciting a verbal invocation.[4] Some individuals draw the circle on the ground with chalk or use corn meal that can be easily swept away; however, the drawing does not take the place of raising the circle unless you are experienced and can conjure while you are making the symbol. Two additional popular symbols are the Spirit circle and the pentacle.

The circlecasting is recommended for most magickal activities, rites, and rituals in the Craft. Yes, I've heard that a few individuals don't cast circles for folk magick applications, but it's sort of like gas. If you want the magickal engine to

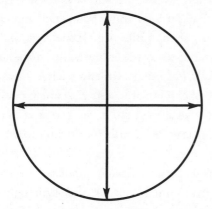 

Some magickal individuals paint the Spirit circle (left) on a large terra-cotta plate and use the dish for a mini altar. The same procedure can be done with the pentacle (right). This is a safe way to burn candles and incense (in their appropriate holders) and it protects expensive altar cloths.

run pure, then cast a circle. If you think that dirty gas is an okay thing, so be it—however, you may not achieve your intended goal. Granted, the longer you work in the Craft (usually years) and have practiced meditation and other sacred practices faithfully, you won't always need the magick circle for every little thing, but until you reach this point in your spiritual training, I always suggest casting the magick circle for all Craft- and spiritual-related activities. Just remember Honi.

Once the circle has been cast, most Witches seal it by saying: "As above, so below—this circle is sealed. So mote it be!" (SEE SECTION AS ABOVE, SO BELOW IN PART IV.) At this point, the practitioner usually stomps their foot on the floor (or ground) to indicate the seal has been activated.

In your visualization of a circle, think of a bubble, rather than a flat circle. As the words indicate, "as above, so below"—the circle is all around you, over your head, and under your feet. While in circle, one never, ever walks widdershins (counterclockwise) unless you are releasing the circle at the end of the ritual, and if

you break this rule in traditional Witch training, you are certainly told about it—pronto! This goes back to the ancient belief that to walk counterclockwise in circle brings bad luck and breaks the power of the magick. Whether this is true or not, the clockwise movement in the circle is one of the standard Wiccan policies, and there are some Wiccan groups that will not even take up the circle by moving widdershins (which is a common practice) at the end of a ritual. These groups, usually with strong Celtic associations, dismiss the circle by moving clockwise. However, if you participate in a spiral dance (which is truly a fun thing to do), the entire group dances clockwise to the center, but as they return they move counterclockwise—moving in to build the magick, spiraling out to release the magick. Therefore, there are exceptions to the rule.

Once the spell, magick, or ritual is over, the circle is released. If you leave a magick circle in place and allow the energy to hang there, it has a habit of causing chaos as it breaks down on its own, and if you have forgotten to release the quarters, the energies there aren't too happy about that, either. Most Wiccans move widdershins to release the circle (one pass around), and usually draw the energy into a tool or into their hands. A few transfer the energy of the circle to the sacred altar. Once the movement is complete, they may say, "The circle is open, but never broken. Merry meet and merry part until we merry meet again. So mote it be!"[5] and then stomp their foot one time to indicate that the circle is now open.

The magick circle has two main functions: to provide you with a sacred area in which to raise energy until you are ready to release it, and to give you protection from things seen and unseen while you work your magick. Granted, years ago, individuals at the quarters also helped to guard those within the circle, and often an elder or the "man in black" kept an eye on what was going on outside of the circle area while the high priest, high priestess, and other coven members concentrated on the work going on inside. The man in black was the high priestess' right-hand man, and had numerous responsibilities within the coven hierarchy.

Magick containing circular symbols is also prominent in modern Craft practice. For example, you might lay a small circle of stones, gems, or crystals around the picture of a loved one, asking for protection. A small circle of salt around a photograph also works in the same way. To remove the threat of unwanted spirits or thoughtforms, use crushed eggshells around a white candle placed on top of a person's picture. Words written on paper in a circular pattern to gain success is another easy yet powerful spell. Most ceremonial magick involving talismans and amulets are prepared in circular form, either on paper or fashioned in metal. A circle inside a square represents the divine spark from which material can manifest from the realm of Spirit into the daily workaday world.[6]

How the Circle Works

Real science (case in point: new physics) can tell us a lot about how and why magick and related concepts, such as the magick circle, work. Once you realize that the universe is made up of processes, not things, you are really on a roll, for what makes life truly interesting are the connections between events. The sum total of our lives is the change from one connection to another, which becomes a process. Therefore, when magickal people stress the importance of change in their teachings, debates, and studies, they are scientifically discussing the process of moving from one connection to another that will eventually create their desired goal, whatever it may be. Life is change because nothing really *is*, except in a very temporary sense, because everything changes. Our chant, "She changes everything She touches, and everything She touches changes," often done in a round in magickal workings, expresses this thought on a very basic level and uses words to create the circle. Therefore, casting a magick circle allows us to control the process of change and modify what we want, the way we want it.

In the Craft you are taught that every cause has an effect, and that every event can provide a variety of choices in which we can orchestrate the change we desire. In new physics, this is called the relational universe—where all energies are connected and related to each other. As you can see, the "we are one" statement expounded in Hermeticism (SEE PART IV, ALCHEMY) and many Craft teachings falls right in line with modern science. The energy of one event will travel and affect the energy of a future event. This process is called the future light cone[7] and explains why we need the magick circle and the Cone of Power (SEE PAGE 17) in our magickal workings. To understand this concept better, I've created the drawing on the next page for you.

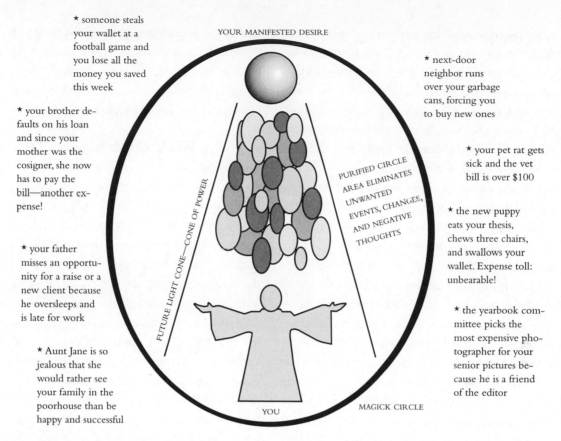

★ someone steals your wallet at a football game and you lose all the money you saved this week

★ your brother defaults on his loan and since your mother was the cosigner, she now has to pay the bill—another expense!

★ your father misses an opportunity for a raise or a new client because he oversleeps and is late for work

★ Aunt Jane is so jealous that she would rather see your family in the poorhouse than be happy and successful

YOUR MANIFESTED DESIRE

★ next-door neighbor runs over your garbage cans, forcing you to buy new ones

★ your pet rat gets sick and the vet bill is over $100

★ the new puppy eats your thesis, chews three chairs, and swallows your wallet. Expense toll: unbearable!

★ the yearbook committee picks the most expensive photographer for your senior pictures because he is a friend of the editor

FUTURE LIGHT CONE—CONE OF POWER

PURIFIED CIRCLE AREA ELIMINATES UNWANTED EVENTS, CHANGES, AND NEGATIVE THOUGHTS

YOU

MAGICK CIRCLE

★ This symbol represents events and energies that would disrupt your working, if you had not cast a circle.

Let's say you want to cast a spell to bring more money into the home. By casting a circle when working your magick, you will be removing random events that could affect your working and destroy your goal.

Now, this means that the operation of the circle and the cone of power, or controlled future light cone, keep on working even though you will conclude your ritual and release your circle. You have already set the process of change in motion and chosen which causal events you want to keep and which you want to remove. If, however, you doubt yourself or your desire, the risk of "dematerializing" your outcome can be very real. Visually this diagram shows you why the magick circle is so necessary in spellwork, ritual, and even meditation.

Cutting the Door

Every now and then you will need to "cut a door" in an erected circle. This may occur because you forgot something and it's sitting there outside of the circle, taunting you to come get it, and you can't go on with the ritual or spell without it. In group format, a circle might be cast by what I call the "bone people" (high priestess, high priest, and representatives of the four quarters), who in turn cut the door so that others outside of the circle may enter. Those inside the circle concentrate on keeping the circle up because every moment the door is open weakens the circle (especially if you are just learning—SEE PART III, DOWSING, for tips on how to check the strength and breadth of your circle). By looking at the circle diagram again, you can see how random events and energies can enter the circle if it is broken, which will in turn affect your working. Keeping the circle strong is very important; therefore, if you are working solitary and are new at this, you may want to forgo whatever you forgot until you are more confident about holding the circle in place.

Should you feel ready to cut a door, you can use the athame or your hands to create the opening. The athame gives a smoother line, where your hands move as if you are parting a curtain. Take your time making the shape of the door or portal that you will walk through. As soon as you step over that boundary, turn and close the opening either with your hands or by reversing the action you used with the athame. Retrieve the object, then cut the door again, turn, and close the door. Take your time. In a ritual with several people, crossed brooms at the door are ritually opened to allow individuals to enter and then crossed to signify the portal has been closed after all are inside. This visual representation allows all circle members to participate in sealing the portal.

Those individuals who have done a great deal of energy work, including circlecastings, can meld with the circle and therefore move freely in and out of the circle environment without damaging the energy. However, just because this feat can be accomplished doesn't mean that you should utilize the practice all the time, for several reasons. First, you must be able to do this on a repetitive basis, which can be checked by using the previously mentioned dowsing rods. Secondly, if you are training students, barging in and out of the circle encourages them to disregard their own training. Finally, every circle is based on process—meaning each is different, depending on the person who cast the circle, the location, the weather, your emotions, and a variety of other factors. My personal advice (take it or leave it) is to practice melding so that you can use it in

case of severe emergency, but not to do it in public or in training circles on a regular basis. Melding, like other forms of transformation, takes time and practice and is not a common phenomenon among current Craft practitioners.

Triple Circle Magick

In antiquity, the idea of using three circles in magick invoked the three Fates, or Goddesses of Life, Growth, and Death. In the Nordic pantheon, these triple goddesses were Skuld, Verdandi, and Urd, who wove the tapestry of your destiny. The Roman Fates were Fortunae, and the Greeks called them the Moerae. Symbolic offerings to the three Fates, such as bread and milk, were said to guarantee prosperity and long life, and could even bring one's future husband knocking at the door (or at least a dream or vision of him). From the Greek triad of body, mind, and shadow came the primitive Christian corpus, anima, and spiritus (body, mind, and spirit), which was based on oriental and Hebrew foundations known as the magick of the triple circle.[8] As I mentioned earlier, many Wiccan traditions cast a triple circle in their spellworking and rituals to magnify the power of the body, mind, and spirit.

Here is an example of the conjuration for a triple circlecasting. You will find additional circlecasting instructions in my books *To Stir a Magick Cauldron* and *To Light a Sacred Flame*.

Triple Circlecasting
by Lady MorningStar[9]
(Recite as you walk the first
time around the circle)
In this place, this circle round
I consecrate the sacred ground
with golden light this space surround
all power here contained and bound.

(Second pass around the circle)
From earth, the things that manifest
from air, the things of mind
from fire, the things that motivate
from water, the souls refined.

(Third pass around the circle)
And yet no place or time there be
between the worlds, my word and me
welcome, Ancient Ones, and see
this place is sealed, so mote it be!

Witches know that their perception of the world is based on how each individual personally views and processes emotions and events. If you always see the negative side, then that's what you will become. If, on the other hand, you work to change your perceptions, and try to see

The triple ring design (top), and the triceps.

all things with equal clarity, then harmony within your life has a chance to grow. Your emotions are based on your perceptions of what is happening to you. If you perceive something as frightening, then that's what it will be to you. If you perceive something as inspirational, then the fullness of life has a chance to expand. When we cast the ritual circle using the number three, we are linking into the triple aspect of the Goddess (Maiden, Mother, and Crone) and the God (Father, Son, and Sage) in an effort to bring purification and clarity into our lives. If you seek healing of body, mind, and soul for yourself or for another individual, carve the triple ring design on a candle or draw it on a piece of paper, then write the person's name over top.

If you are seeking a boost in prosperity (let's say Mom has to pay a bill and she just doesn't know where the money is going to come from), try using the diamond or triceps variation, which also belongs to the Nordic pantheon.

The triceps (earth diamonds) invokes the powers of Earth (earth, sky, and sea—often found in Druidic teachings as well) by using three diamonds. The four sides of the diamonds stand for earth, air, water, and fire. This symbol can be used for weather magick as well as prosperity work. These diamonds literally mean "the gifts of the Earth." Write the amount needed inside each diamond with the triple ring emblem on top. Keep until you have obtained the amount needed. Burn when the amount is received.

Note: Although Witches a hundred years ago would have written directly on the dollar bill in the United States, defacing our currency with any wording or sigils is against the law in this country; therefore, place a drawing of the triple triceps over the currency rather than writing directly on the bill. It is also illegal to burn the currency, therefore burn only the drawing when the spell is completed.

Communion

The idea of eating and drinking a sacred liquid in celebration of one's deity choice is another practice we find in antiquity and does not belong specifically to any particular religion. In the modern Craft there are two kinds of communion—that which we celebrate in circle with each other (meaning communion of fellowship) and that which is given to the gods in offering of thanksgiving. The act of communion (food and beverage offerings to the gods) can be done by the solitary Witch or can be celebrated by a group of Witches. Many traditions have special chalices and plates that are set aside only for the rite of communion. This rite is often called "cakes and ale."

For ritual purposes, breads are made in the likeness of women, animals, flowers, and birds; examples have been found as early as 5000 B.C. According to Marija Gimbutas, a prominent women's studies scholar, the bread oven itself was a prehistoric symbol for the incarnation of the grain mother.[10] Today, sabbat cakes used in ritual communion may be in various shapes, the most prevalent being the crescent moon and stars, though there is no end to the imagination of the baker! Many groups no longer use wine or ale in respect for those who may be battling alcoholism or because the laws in the United States do not permit children to drink alcoholic beverages (if children are present in circle) and prefer fruit juices instead. If alcohol is used, as each member only takes a sip of the drink, the possibility of creating a bunch of drunk Witches over communion is highly unlikely. Everyone with half a brain knows you cannot do adequate magick if you are inebriated, as alcohol impairs your ability to mentally and physically function.

You can't focus on a single candle flame if you are seeing twenty of them spinning around your head.

Solitary Communion— Cakes and Ale

Originally called cakes and ale, the Wiccan communion rite is normally done after any operation of magick or ritual drama/celebration. It is the last major block of activity before the circle is closed. The tradition of the participants usually decides which item is blessed first, the cakes or the ale/juice. Depending on the tradition, the high priest may bless the cakes, and the high priestess the juice, or they may switch, or do the blessings together. The activity of blessing the food is meant to put you in sync with the divine.

The tray containing the cakes and juice is usually set out of the way of the working altar until you are ready to perform this rite. Most Wiccans cover both the chalice and the cakes with a white cloth until they are ready to use them. When you are ready for the rite, set the tray on your altar and remove the cloth coverings.

Hold your hands over the chalice (or cup), and say:

> *From the sun to the vine*
> *from the vine to the berry*
> *from the berry to the wine*
> *this brew is blessed in the sacred names*
> *of our Lord and Lady.*
> *So mote it be.*

As this is said, the Witch visualizes the energy of the sun feeding into a vine, which grows into the berry, which in turn becomes the juice.

In most traditions, the athame is now lowered into the chalice, and the Witch says:

As the rod is to the God
so the chalice is to the Goddess
and together they are one![11]

The Witch visualizes divine energy pulsating from the blade into the cup, and the entire cup filling with white light.

When taking a drink from the chalice, visualize pure, divine energy entering your body, pushing out any negativity. When you are finished, say: "May you never thirst." If someone is in circle with you, repeat the statement as you pass the cup to them, and they are to answer with the same blessing—"May you never thirst." In this way, you are passing the positive energies of Spirit on to the next person. If you are alone, you are affirming that you have taken this blessing for your own.

Next, hold your hands over the cake(s), and say:

From the moon to the stalk
from the stalk to the grain
from the grain to the bread
this bread is blessed in the sacred names
of our Lord and Lady.
So mote it be!

Take a bite from the cake (or eat the entire cake). When you are finished, say: "May you never hunger." If someone is in the circle with you, say the blessing as you pass them the cakes, and then they are to repeat the same sentence back to you, acknowledging the blessing.

In some groups everyone waits until all have the item in hand—for example, the cup of juice. When the high priestess raises her cup to drink, then everyone takes communion at the same time and says "May you never thirst" in unison. In other groups the high priest holds the cup for the high priestess while she takes a drink, and

she does the same for him. Again, practices differ, so if you are visiting a group for the first time, don't assume anything. Watch. Listen.

The next part of the ceremony is the Offering to Spirit.

Giving the Offering

There are several types of offerings, including that of the libation performed in the communion rite. If the ceremony is held outside, the libation is given to the gods near the end of the rite by pouring some of the juice and scattering a bit of cake on the ground. If you are indoors, the remainder of the cakes and juice are poured in a cleansed and consecrated libation bowl, then carried outside after the ritual is over and poured on the ground. You may speak your own words of thanksgiving, or you may use the following:

I honor the spirits of the north.
(hold the bowl to the north)
I honor the spirits of the east.
(hold the bowl to the east)
I honor the spirits of the south.
(hold the bowl to the south)
I honor the spirits of the west.
(hold the bowl to the west)
I honor the spirits of my ancestors.
(hold the bowl out in front of you)
I honor the Lord and Lady.
(hold the bowl slightly above your head)
I honor the spark of all life.
(hold the bowl out in front of you)
From perfection to perfection
this gift is given.
So mote it be.

Bring the bowl down to the ground and pour out the contents.

Those Wiccans following a more shamanic path may give food offerings when petitioning the gods in spellworking. Write your request on a piece of paper and place it underneath the dish containing the food. Set a white household emergency candle firmly upright in the center of the food dish. If the candle burns clean with little mess, it is believed the offering has been accepted, and the food is then removed in twenty-four hours. If the candle does not burn well, then the food is immediately removed and something else is put in its place. Although the Santerían and Voudon belief systems have a list of what types of food their deities require that includes various taboos, Wicca has no such list and you are free to choose what you feel will meet the needs of the gods should you incorporate this practice into your work.

Food offerings can also be given to the ancestral dead. In this case, the foods chosen would match what they enjoyed the most while living on the earth plane.

Moon Cookies Recipe

These may be used as cakes in communion. Bless all ingredients before using. Hold your hands over the ingredients while visualizing purifying white light, and say:

Golden energy of sun-kissed grain
precious drops of cleansing rain
beams of moonlight from stem to bud
bringing joy from up above.
Blessings of the Mother
strength of the Father
unity of Love
so mote it be.

1   cup shortening

2   cups sugar

2   eggs

1   cup oil

½   teaspoon salt

1   teaspoon vanilla

5   cups flour

2   teaspoons baking soda

2   teaspoons cream of tartar

    Powdered or colored sugar

    Cinnamon

Cream shortening, sugar, eggs, oil, salt, and vanilla together. Mix flour, baking soda, and cream of tartar in a separate bowl. Add slowly to wet mixture until thoroughly mixed. Roll into one-inch balls, then shape into half-moons or stars. Flatten a bit with fork. Bake at 350 degrees for 10 minutes. After cookies have been baked, sprinkle with powdered or colored sugar, and top with cinnamon. Makes 8 dozen.

Silver's Witch's Brew Recipe

This may be used as ale in communion.

1   gallon apple cider (love)

1   orange (love)

1   apple (love)

3   cinnamon sticks (love, psychic powers)

⅛   teaspoon nutmeg (fidelity)

1   handful rose petals (love)

Pour apple cider into a large kettle. Peel orange, reserving the peel, and squeeze its juice into the cider, discarding the pulp. Tear the orange peel into one-inch strips and add to mixture. Core apple and cut into ¼-inch slices. Add to mixture. Break the cinnamon sticks in half. Add to mixture with nutmeg. Warm over low heat for two hours. Do not bring to a boil. Sprinkle with rose petals before serving.

Cone of Power

The cone of power occurs when the Witch, working in a magick circle alone or with others, raises the energy inside the circle to a point of focus. Once the energy is raised through drumming, chanting, or meditation, it is released toward the goal of focus. Some Witches use the athame, wand, or other pointing device to aid them in their visualization of lifting the energy and sending it toward the desired outcome. Others (like me) use only their hands. The choice is yours.

In the Craft, energy work through visualization, prayer, and touch are of prime importance, whether you are working alone or in a group setting. Teachers begin instructing students to see, think about, and manually control energy immediately, and this training never ceases. Long after students have progressed through the levels that any course has to offer, they will continue to work with energy, honing their skills, until the day they pass to the Summerland. The longer a person practices energy manipulation, the more adept he or she becomes. There is no substitute for continual repetition. Learning to create this energy (or draw it from other sources) is the basic building block for the cone of power.

The modern Wiccan musical chant "We are a circle, within a circle, without beginning, and never ending" (author unknown) tells us why the circle is so important in the Craft environment—it reminds us that we are all one, and that if we work together in a circle (rather than sitting on pews in a straight line), we can raise more power by linking together in this shape, physically and mentally. The circle stands for the Wheel of the Year and the cycles of life. The uroborus is an alchemical symbol that appears in various cultures (Egyptian, Greek, Roman, Chi-nese), showing a snake swallowing its own tail. In animal form, this image presents the circle as the embodiment of the eternal return—that in every end there is a beginning—a cycle of endless repetition. In alchemy, the uroborus (sometimes written *ouroboros*) symbolizes the cyclical process of heating, evaporation, cooling, and condensation of a liquid in the process of purifying a substance.[12] The uroborus can mean "the One, the All,"[13] reminding us that we are all connected and that we are all, ultimately, one energy in the divine dance of life, death, and rebirth. In many cultures, the world serpent of uroborus encircles the cosmic egg, protecting it (us) from ultimate destruction, meaning that which has no ending cannot be destroyed. The Great Round, which is another name for the uroborus, symbolically reminds us of our primordial parents, the Great Mother and the Great Father (as mentioned in our Craft creation myth).[14]

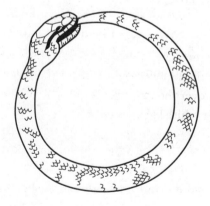

The uroborus symbol (above) can be drawn on candles, petitions, or other magickal items to draw forth the power of the circle and the unity of all beings. It is an excellent protective device. Sometimes you will see the uroborus drawn in a figure-eight design, impressing us with the idea of infinity. Magickal themes for the uroborus include wisdom; infinity; divine parents; self-sufficiency; the cycle of life, death, and rebirth; time;

protection; order from chaos; alpha and omega symbolism; potential of birth; and immortality.

Ball Energy Exercise

One of the first energy exercises taught to Wiccan students is how to make a ball of energy with their hands. The exercise requires your imagination. Rub your hands together until your palms are warm, then slowly pull your palms apart, visualizing a ball of energy growing between them. Students are taught to expand and then contract the ball, using their hands and their imaginations.

After the student gets the hang of the energy ball, the fun begins. The balls are passed to other students, thrown across the room at each other, and dropped like water balloons on top of the head. If you catch the ball, you'll feel a tingling sensation in your hands.

Once this is accomplished, the student now puts a thought into the ball. The easiest thought transference is love (which should tell us something). Think of the universal love from Spirit, and you've just moved light-years into magick. This is the first step in learning to take what is in the mind and transferring that thought into energy created by the friction of rubbing the hands together.

Once accomplished, you can transfer the love energy to any object or person through the vehicle of touch. Now you know how empowerment is done and how Witches heal people either by touch or from long distance. When my children were young and got into squabbles (try having four kids all arguing at the same time and see what a circus your life becomes), I would stand in the doorway (unobserved) and throw love balls into the center of the fray. The kids would break down into giggles every time, the argument forgotten. Hey, it pays to be a Wiccan mother. If you have several siblings, you might

teach your mother how to conjure balls of love energy—I'm sure she will be forever grateful.

Once you have learned to create energy balls, the next step is to learn to share them with others by passing them around the circle. This movement of energy is the next step (in a group environment) when creating the cone of power. The energy moves around the circle, building a faster momentum. You no longer have to use your hands to move the energy, only your mind, which is why Witches link hands in the magick circle. Once sufficient momentum is built, and all are focused through meditation or chant to the desired point of release (for example, healing for a specific person), then the high priestess tells everyone when to release the energy. When you are working alone, you choose when to "let go." In a group environment, a visual clue as to how hard to push the energy and when to release it is the slow raising of hands as the chant or drumming builds to a crescendo.

Hint: Although it doesn't sound particularly magickal, when working with others, you can make an agreement that the leader counts down from five to one once he or she believes that enough energy has been raised, and that everyone releases when they hear "one."

Creation Story

The basic creation story tells of the birth of the cosmos. It explains how a no-thing became a some-thing. Every culture, religion, and civilization has, somewhere within its history, the myth of creation. These symbolic narratives often recognize specific teachings that are sacred to that generation and contain metaphors to explain how the society sees itself within its worldview.[15] Our creation story can be read during a dedication ceremony, at a Samhain ritual, or at any other event where the seeker is to be reminded of his or her roots and the decision he or she has made to become one with the Spirit of the Witches. It can also be performed in ritual drama with the addition of musical instruments, singing, and drums.

Long, long, ago, there was only darkness—a deep, ebony ocean of empty infinity—the void that was no place. From this place of nothingness, Spirit drew in upon itself and, with a mighty burst of joyful vibration, our Lady of Light exploded into being, Her essence the totality of perfect love and perfect trust. In Her heart She held the presence of Spirit, and there was no part of Her that was not of the divine.

In delight, our Lady began the Great Work. She danced among the heavens, Her bare feet beating out the rhythm of all creation, giving birth to every pattern of energy as sparks of light catapulted from Her flying hair and extended fingertips. She created the stars and planets, and bid them to dance with Her. As they began to move, so the cycle of the year was born, and the divine symphony of the universe came into form. She gave them names of power, each unto their own. These things moved from the void, into the thought, given the breath of life, and then into the world.

Our Lady chanted the words of perfect love and perfect peace and, as these sounds fell to the Earth, the trees, flowers, and grasses took root in the fertile soil of Gaia. From the pure, white light of Her breath came the colors of the universe, turning all things to vibrant beauty. From the bubbling laughter in Her throat sprang the sounds of the clear, running water of the streams, the gentle lapping vibrations of the lake, and the roaring of the oceans. Her tears of happiness became the rains of our survival. Our Lady was the Presence, and the Presence our Lady.

And when Her dancing slowed, the Lady sought a companion to share the wonders of the many worlds. As the Holy Spirit, She created the God as Her soulmate. Because our Lady so loved the Earth, the energy pattern of the God contained both the essence of the Presence and the Divine energy of the Earth—and He was known by many names: Green Man; Lord of the Forests; King of the Fields; and Father, Son, and Sage.

Together, the Lord and Lady created all the beings of Earth. The Lord's power moved through Her, and She showered the Earth and all upon it with Her blessings. Together, They designed the birds, animals, fishes, insects, reptiles, and people of our world. To protect and guide the humans, the Lord and Lady fashioned the angels, guides, and spirits of power. These energies still walk with us, although we often cannot see them.

To each being our Lady gave a unique vibration in which to communicate, and the Lord bestowed to each the fire of passion and the burning instinct to survive. As a gift for His magnificent handiwork and caring for the creatures of Earth, our Lady gave our Lord a crown of stag antlers, which He wears upon His great head. This aspect of half man, half animal would forever show His joy in both the human and animal creations of the Presence. The crown will always be a symbol that people can spiritually work with the duality of their own natures to reach into the core of Spirit.

Together, the Lord and Lady blessed the first humans with free will. "We are of the gods, and the gods are us!" the people cried. And the Lord and Lady smiled. "We are all one," said our Lady, and through a web of silver light She connected each human to the other, and then linked the humans to all other energy patterns on the planet. When this was done, She wove Herself and Her Lord into the divine tapestry of pulsating energy.

"Love is the law, honor is the bond," said the Lord as He empowered the tapestry of life.

Our Lady has many names: Isis, Astarte, Bride, Diana, Aradia, Innana, Hecate, Mitzu Gami, and thousands more. The Lady walks within and beside each woman and man of every race in every place. She is the Maiden, Mother, and Crone. She is the sacred trinity of all religions. Indeed, She is the Holy Ghost.

The Lord has many faces, from the strong Cernunnos to the delightful Pan, and Osiris, Tyr, Anubis, Ra, Apollo, Odin, and thousands more. He guards and guides us and resides in each man and woman of every race in every place. When thunder roars in the heavens and lightning cracks from the ground, the Lord and Lady dance the divine myth of creation so that we may remember Them and know that we are never alone, and that we are one. When the sun rises each morning, we bask in the joy of His love for us, and when the moon moves through Her phases, we understand the cycle of birth, growth, death, and rebirth, as is the nature of all things, and we honor Her power.

But as the humans began to grow and prosper, they forgot about their divine parents. Although the Lord and Lady called to Their children, they did not listen. They were lost, fighting the demons they themselves had created. Not wishing to abandon Their children, the Lord and Lady decided to create healers and workers of harmony among the humans to remind them of the divine source and to show them the way home to the arms of the Mother. Within each special soul would be the remembrance of the Great Work: to love, create, and move in harmony. And so the Lord and Lady drew forth energy from the realm of angels, the realm of power animals, the realm of the dead, and the realm of humans, instilling these special souls with the divine energy of the Presence through miracles of magick. These beings of power were called Witches.

Our Lady taught the Witches the wisdom of the universe. They were instructed how to cast the circle of art and how to communicate with Spirit, because the humans of Earth had forgotten. She taught them to talk to the dead, how to honor their ancestors and succession of teachers, and how to focus the mind and cast a spell. In each brain She imprinted the patterns of all the energies in the solar system, and how to work magick by the moon and the stars. The Lord taught the Witches how to meld with the elements and spirits of air, fire, earth, and water, and to commune with the animal and plant kingdoms. He taught them weather magick and the healing arts with energy and plants—and, most of all, like their ancestors before them, He taught them how to protect themselves and how to survive. Each Witch was given the rites of purification and the ability to tap into his or her lineage of creation.

Together, the Lord and Lady gave the humans the Witch's Pyramid: To Know, To Will, To Dare, and To Be Silent, because They knew that not all the humans on Earth would welcome these special beings of magick and love. The instruction complete, the Witches were sent to every culture and every tribe on the planet Earth, being born of the people but carrying the mission of the divine. In this way they have been known by many names and many races, yet, in soul, Witches they remain. Above all, they were given the message that the Goddess lives.

Even with the Great Work of the magickal people, perfect love and perfect trust did not come easily. Many religions rose among the people to honor the Mother and Father, but each, in turn, cast out our Mother, thinking that worshipping the God alone would bring them the riches and strength they needed. In His disappointment of their actions, the Lord abandoned each religion, allowing them to crumble and die in the dust of the earth. Rather than create beauty and joy, the humans sought to destroy one another, to spread the sickness of greed and despair among their own. They forgot that the power within is greater than the power over one another.

The people would not listen to the Witches. Instead, they burned them.

Thus, over times of great trial and suffering, the Witches became the hidden children, conducting their rites in secret lest they risk capture and death at the hands of the fearful humans and their terrible dogma. As the world grew dark with the ignorance and hate created by the humans, and evil arose like black steam from the cauldron of their minds, covering the planet with negative energy, the Lady whispered to the Witches that they should draw power from Her body of the moon, and the Lord enchanted the vibrant rays of the sun to instill them with strength. "The moon and the sun," They said, "are beacons of the Great Work. As long as they shine, you may draw from them whatever energy you may need, and when you look to these symbols in the heavens you will know that We are within you. There is no part of you that is not of the gods."

And so it was that once a month, when the moon grew full, the Witches celebrated in secret and remembered the blessings our Mother bestowed upon them, and worked magick to fulfill their divine mission of the Great Work. In these rites, the Witches called forth the essence of the Lord and Lady to help them take care of themselves, their families, the planet, and their friends. Four times a year, as the cross-quarters (Samhain, Candlemas, Beltane, and Lammas) blossomed with bonfires across the land, the Witches celebrated the festivals of fire in honor

of our Lord and His love and protection for all the children of the Earth as well as the birth of our Mother from the Void and the divine dance that brought all humans into creation. At the four quarters of the seasons (Yule, Ostara, summer solstice, and Mabon), the Witches honored the solar cycle of life and the gifts of the Earth through celebrations of thanksgiving. For 8,000 years we have done this, for our essence is in every shaman, every magi, every priest, and every priestess who carries the hidden truth of perfect love and perfect trust within their souls. We are the Craft of the Wise.

When it is our time to leave the Earth plane, our Lady sends a guide to escort us to the Summerland. From the Presence that moves and flows through the Lord and Lady, we continue to learn the mysticism of the universe so that we may return, life after life, to serve our brothers and sisters—to remind them that they are only visiting here, and that each action, not each piece of gold garnered, is the way, the truth, and the light. In each lifetime, Spirit guides us through learning experiences, preparing us along the way for our individual missions. Sometimes we are born among our own kind, but more often than not, we are born among the unbelievers—we are born to show them the way home. It is by our actions, not our preaching, that the journey is made.

We are the Witches, the representatives of wisdom's growth on our planet. Because the religions of the world have failed to recognize the Great Work and to see our Mother in all things, the Lord and Lady gave us our own religion. This is our greatest test.

We are the hidden children. We are the people, the power, and the change—and we have incarnated in every race and in every culture, and will continue to do so until the end of time. We are the weavers, and we are the web. We cannot be stopped, because we are the Presence and the

Presence is us. We are the divine angels of Earth. We are the heavens and the stars. We are the earth, the air, the fire, and the water.

We are the Spirit. We are one. And . . .

We have come to guide you home.

For we are the Witches, back from the dead. So mote it be.

If done in ceremony, this story has the most impact if only a blue light shines in the center of the circle and the remaining area stays in darkness. A drummer can begin with a soft and slow drum beat, speed up at various areas, and slow down again, which will move the energy of the story about the room. At the end of the story—"And . . . we have come . . ."—thirteen individuals within the group (if it is a large one) may simultaneously light their candles and hold them aloft as the remaining lines are read by the narrator.

Esbat

The words "esbat" and "sabbat" are thought to come from the French word *s'esbattre*, which means "to joyfully celebrate."[16] During the 1920s, British anthropologist Margaret A. Murray postulated that a group of Witches, which included both peasants and nobles, celebrated the eight major fire festivals (sabbats) and met at regular gatherings, called esbats. Murray also indicated that these Witches gathered themselves into thirteen-member covens. Although some scholars feel that her conclusions came from reading the transcripts of the Inquisitions, other historians feel that her research did not extend that far. To quote from private correspondence from Ronald Hutton, historian at Bristol University, dated 9 August 2002:

The only records of trials at which she looked were nineteenth-century printed versions of earlier Scottish depositions (and Scotland never had an Inquisition). Her information on sabbats and esbats came instead from the treatises of continental deomonologists—that on esbats from just one, Pierre de Lancre, whose text is also our sole source of information for the Basque Witches. De Lancre was not a Basque himself, but a highly imaginative French magistrate, reworking reports of what Basques were supposed to believe.

Margaret Murray additionally indicated that Witchcraft could be traced to "pre-Christian times and appears to be the ancient religion of Western Europe."[17] Although in subsequent years much of Murray's work has been trashed by students of history, her ideas were so stunning that they did, indeed, affect what we now practice as modern Witchcraft. Whether or not there were "real" esbats and sabbats does not change the fact that we celebrate both now.

To the modern Witch, an esbat is a moon ceremony. It's also called a working night, where two or more Witches gather together to practice magick for the good of all in the group. Many times these gatherings coincide with a particular moon phase or other planetary alignment. Depending upon the group, the meetings might be held once a month, or as often as every week. Training and tradition have a heavy influence on the esbat. Where some groups follow set rituals by rote with no deviation, others allow more spontaneity and creativity within the ritual format. Others use esbat nights as training classes, where lessons are taught or a guest speaker is present. With the aid of the computer generation, long-distance training between a daughter coven and a mother coven can be done on videocam. Dedications, initiations, crossings, and wiccanings may also be performed when the esbat coincides with the full moon. If a special ceremony is not planned, most full moon esbats include the "Drawing Down the Moon" (DDM) rite somewhere in the ritual (SEE PART III, MOON). Still others meet only for the sole purpose of the DDM.

A sabbat, on the other hand, is normally relegated to the eight High Holy Days, and is designed to honor the god/dess, followed by a feast of some kind. Ritual drama during the sabbat ritual is normally seen as the high point of the festivities, where a small play or other scene from legend that is associated with the group or tradition takes center stage. (SEE PART I, WHEEL OF THE YEAR.)

Modern solitary Witches—a Witch who works alone, without the support of a cohesive group—also incorporate esbats in their religious practices, though the ceremonies are often not as long as those practiced in the group format (which ideally run forty-five minutes to one hour). These Witches use the evening to meditate; pray; grind herbs; mix powders; make tinctures and holy water; weave magickal cords; craft amulets, talismans, and poppets; repair or make magickal tools; and spellcast and/or perform ritual, depending on their personal preference. An esbat for the solitary Witch is a time to stock up on items that may be needed throughout the month. In ritual, some may follow a formal outline, where others write their own. Solitary Witches write their rituals by studying ritual books and other magickal works. Most new Witches like to begin by using the information straight out of the books and then going on to use their own creativity as time passes. Learning ritual, like learning magick, is a process of skill building.

Thirteen–Step Solitary Esbat[18] (Basic Ritual Structure)

SUPPLIES: Altar and setup (earth, air, fire, water, illuminator candles). The altar setup is described in Part II. Tools such as the athame or wand are up to you. Candles or other representations are positioned at the four quarters (east, south, west, and north)—colors are your choice.

INSTRUCTIONS:

Step One: Cleanse the ritual space by carrying a representation of the four elements around the area in a clockwise movement, working with one element at a time.

Step Two: Open altar energies by blessings with the four elements (or devote the altar as explained in *To Stir a Magick Cauldron*).

Step Three: Light the illuminator candles.

Step Four: Cast the magick circle (clockwise).

Step Five: Light the quarter candles and call the quarters.

Step Six: Invoke deity.

Step Seven: State intent of ritual aloud.

Step Eight: Draw Down the Moon (if this is a full moon esbat).

Step Nine: Perform the magickal work, which may include drawing and raising energy, then sealing the spellwork.

Step Ten: Take communion (optional).

Step Eleven: Thank deity, thank quarters, release, and extinguish quarter candles.

Step Twelve: Release magick circle (counterclockwise). Seal altar energies, extinguish illuminator candles.

Step Thirteen: Clean up and offer libation bowl (if you took communion) out-of-doors.

Esbat Flavors of the Moon

Every two and one-half days the moon moves into a new sign, which means that in her 28.5 (or so)-day cycle from new to full, she visits all of the signs. She isn't full, of course, in every sign every month. Therefore, each month she is full in a different sign of the zodiac. Our present calendar and the cycles are not entirely compatible. There are twelve months with varying numbers of days, where the moon steadfastly sticks to her own 28.5-day cycle. This means that once in approximately every two and a half calendar years, there will be a month that has two full moons. The second full moon in that month is called a blue moon, and is used by Witches for goal planning, special wishes, or unique ceremonies of their own design.

When planning your esbats, you'll want to keep an eye on what sign of the zodiac the moon is currently visiting, and then structure your magick accordingly. For a new moon, the signs will be the same—both the sun and the moon will be in the same sign. Although I've provided the following table for esbat planning, you can also use it for other ceremonies and magicks as well. No matter the phase, check in your almanac to see what sign the moon is in if you feel you need a helpful boost in any situation. The phases of the moon, something else you need to know when working magick, are covered under the Moon section in Part III.

Below are two tables. The first is for planning magick and ritual for the new moon esbat, and the second is designed for the full moon esbat. These tables are guidelines to help you choose when to do what, according to the flavor of the moon. However, they are by no means the last word on the subject.

New Moon Esbats

ARIES

Basic energy: Power, energy, force, expression, self-reliance, assertiveness, spontaneousness, fearlessness, enthusiasm.

Zodiac color association: Red.

Primary element: Fire.

Suggested magickal operations: Rituals and spells for gaining confidence, learning new things, sports, controlling your fear or anger, winning, starting a project, being a pioneer, making announcements, boosting your reading level, taking calculated risks.

Avoid: Skipping over ritual steps, or hurrying through ritual.

Be careful: Of your own temper.

Note: Remember that Aries energy is not long-haul. Follow up with another spell later on to keep this energy rolling.

TAURUS

Basic energy: Stability, peace, affection, responsiveness, saving, artistic ability, devotion, harmony.

Zodiac color association: Red-orange.

Primary element: Earth.

Suggested magickal operations: Rituals and spells for prosperity, saving money, holding on to something you already have (like a grade point average), building and keeping harmony in the home, investing time and money in a project, long-term goal planning, spells for people you love, spells for long-term healing, meditations for peace.

Avoid: Missing a good opportunity.

Be careful: Of your own stubbornness.

GEMINI

Basic energy: Intellect, awareness, agility, adaptability, multitasking.

Zodiac color association: Orange.

Primary element: Air.

Suggested magickal operations: Rituals and spells for any type of learning or research. Spells to finish the old and move on to the new; to help you juggle the many projects you are working on at once without failing; or for finding a new car or new job. Spells for any of the mental arts, including meditation, learning a divination tool, pathworking, and telepathy. Magick for learning to understand and deal with siblings.

Avoid: Trying to pack too many magickal operations into one ritual.

Be careful: Of self-denial.

CANCER

Basic energy: Emotions, maturity, psychism, peace, protection, magnetism, sympathy, maternal.

Zodiac color association: Amber.

Primary element: Water.

Suggested magickal operations: Rituals and spells for women, maturing without losing your mind in the process, peace in the home, protection of yourself or loved ones, your mother, psychism, transforming negative emotions into positive ones, dream spells, divination, and telepathy. Spells to draw positive things toward you or protect a friend or family member through pregnancy.

Avoid: Thinking that Spirit owes you.

Be careful: Of being too emotional.

LEO

Basic energy: Strength, positivity, leadership, confidence, generosity, kindness, success.

Zodiac color association: Yellow.

Primary element: Fire.

Suggested magickal operations: Rituals and spells for courage, strength, thinking in a positive way, winning, success, and learning to be a good leader, kind, loyal, and generous. Spells for drama and acting, fun at the beach or on vacation, wealth in the home, and for making your talents shine. Spells to find the perfect pet for you, or to help you realize your talents.

Avoid: Overspending on ritual and spell supplies.

Be careful: Don't brag about your magick. Remember the Witch's Pyramid: To Know, To Dare, To Will, and To Be Silent.

VIRGO

Basic energy: Examination, analysis, brilliance, making choices with head, not heart; precision, finding solutions.

Zodiac color association: Yellow-green.

Primary element: Earth.

Suggested magickal operations: Rituals and spells for solving problems and finding information, things, or people. Spells where you must make a difficult choice, maintain accuracy in research, get good grades on tests, eliminate mistakes, analyze yourself so that you can be a better person, or uncover an illusive medical problem that has the doctors stumped. Spells for improving your ritual or spellcasting techniques. Understanding the meaning of service to others or finding a person who can help you with a particular task.

Avoid: Getting lost in ritual detail.

Be careful: Of being overly critical.

LIBRA

Basic energy: Beauty, love, sociability, cooperation, originality, courtesy, responsiveness.

Zodiac color association: Emerald.

Primary element: Air.

Suggested magickal operations: Rituals and spells for sharing the arts (music, painting, dance, writing) where you seek the approval of others. Spells for love, friendship, and romance, and for conflict mediation. Spells to ensure you are treated fairly, to enjoy beauty, and to learn to cooperate with others. Spells to improve communication between yourself and a teacher or parent. Partnerships of any kind.

Avoid: Making open enemies.

Be careful: Of indecisiveness.

SCORPIO

Basic energy: Intensity, rebirth, transformation, illumination, wisdom, karma, instinct.

Zodiac color association: Green-blue.

Primary element: Water.

Suggested magickal operations: Rituals and spells for a situation that needs ultimate power, must transform, or is karmically related. Spells to hone your instincts, or to get to the bottom of a messy situation. Spells for wisdom, to renew an old project, to stop aggressive action (cold), to bring down a criminal, and to stop gossip or other unhealthy emotional situations. Spells to sign documents where you will get the best deal. Spells to end things (though a waning Scorpio moon is best for this). Understanding

the cycle of birth, life, death, and rebirth. Reincarnation and past-life regression.

Avoid: Creating a secret agenda.

Be careful: Of your resentment.

SAGITTARIUS

Basic energy: Expansion, generosity, faith, optimism, understanding, mercy, charity, hope.

Zodiac color association: Blue.

Primary element: Fire.

Suggested magickal operations: Rituals and spells to expand any project or talent, and to find understanding in a difficult situation. Spells to give yourself or friends hope. Spells to strengthen your personal faith, to expand your awareness, and to learn generosity when dealing with yourself and others. Spells to borrow money, make travel plans, or visit a foreign country. Learn and study world religions.

Avoid: Sloppy ritual.

Be careful: Of running from commitment.

CAPRICORN

Basic energy: Structure, patience, thrift, diplomacy, sincerity, restraint, endurance, justice/law, order, self-discipline.

Zodiac color association: Indigo.

Primary element: Earth.

Suggested magickal operations: Rituals and spells to learn to work with authority figures, rules, and business or school organizational structure. Spells to help you build your savings account, call for divine justice, or to work for a promotion on your job. Spells to create order out of a chaotic situation, to learn self-discipline, and to create the underlying structure of anything (even the video game you are creating). Perfect moon phase for political science majors.

Avoid: Depressing rituals.

Be careful: Of your own ruthless ambition.

AQUARIUS

Basic energy: Independence, originality, progressive ideas, reformation, universal love, inventiveness, heightened perception, resourcefulness, individualism.

Zodiac color association: Violet.

Primary element: Air.

Suggested magickal operations: Rituals and spells for independence, finding new ways to look at the world, changing structures that you think are wrong (school dress code), finding universal love. Spells to boost new ideas, or finding yourself and defining yourself as an individual. Rituals and spells to help you learn mathematics, science, or astrology.

Avoid: Ritual interruptions.

Be careful: Of feeling too detached.

PISCES

Basic energy: Visionary outlook, inspiration, psychism, compassion, creativity, devotion, universal peace.

Zodiac color association: Crimson.

Primary element: Water.

Suggested magickal operations: Rituals and spells for improving your imagination, visualization techniques, dreaming, astral projection, telepathy, and divination. Spells and rituals for the dead. Spells for finding compassion within yourself or seeking compassion in others. Spells for universal peace, or peace among friends and yourself. See the big picture rather than getting lost in the details.

Avoid: Self-doubt when focusing.

Be careful: Of illogical reasoning.

If this all seems complicated at first, don't worry about it. After you work with the moon in each of the signs, you'll understand better and there will come a time when you will instinctively know which energies are present and useful and which are not.

Remember that a full moon is actually an opposition to the sun (astrologically speaking). To obtain the most out of these two energies, we need to find the middle ground. Let's look at how we might use these energies to our best advantage over a full moon by keeping in mind the flavor of the moon and the flavor of the sun. Remember, the moon represents emotions, and the sun stands for your will in any situation. The sun is force, the moon is form.

Full Moon Esbats

FULL MOON IN ARIES

Sun is in: Libra.

Full moon element association: Fire.

Sun element association: Air.

Suggested ritual theme: Advance social situations, find new friends, add passion to your romance. Work on music or use your favorite music in ritual. Rise to a challenge in a fair and honorable way.

FULL MOON IN TAURUS

Sun is in: Scorpio.

Full moon element association: Earth.

Sun element association: Water.

Suggested ritual theme: Bring success for any type of investment (time, money, energy). Find serenity, or find unique ways to save money.

FULL MOON IN GEMINI

Sun is in: Sagittarius.

Full moon element association: Air.

Sun element association: Fire.

Suggested ritual theme: Work on magickal studies, sending long-distance messages or healings, and learning about cultures, religions, and pantheons. Compose spells and rituals.

FULL MOON IN CANCER

Sun is in: Capricorn.

Full moon element association: Water.

Sun element association: Earth.

Suggested ritual theme: Stability for the home; protection for yourself and family.

FULL MOON IN LEO

Sun is in: Aquarius.

Full moon element association: Fire.

Sun element association: Air.

Suggested ritual theme: Work to bring humanitarian issues out into the open. Personal goal fulfillment. Issues that have to do with groups or organizations.

FULL MOON IN VIRGO

Sun is in: Pisces.

Full moon element association: Earth.

Sun element association: Water.

Suggested ritual theme: Find answers to problems in a visionary way. Tackle situations using your intuition and divinatory tools.

FULL MOON IN LIBRA

Sun is in: Aries.

Full moon element association: Air.

Sun element association: Fire.

Suggested ritual theme: Breathing new life into social situations. Making decisions. Asking for fair, swift justice.

FULL MOON IN SCORPIO

Sun is in: Taurus.

Full moon element association: Water.

Sun element association: Earth.

Suggested ritual theme: Directing energy toward growth in your resources. Use drumming for transformation. Crossing (funeral) ceremonies.

FULL MOON IN SAGITTARIUS

Sun is in: Gemini.

Full moon element association: Fire.

Sun element association: Air.

Suggested ritual theme: Expanding your knowledge and ability to communicate in a positive way.

FULL MOON IN CAPRICORN

Sun is in: Cancer.

Full moon element association: Earth.

Sun element association: Water.

Suggested ritual theme: Restructuring home, school, or magickal life to meet your needs.

FULL MOON IN AQUARIUS

Sun is in: Leo.

Full moon element association: Air.

Sun element association: Fire.

Suggested ritual theme: Work on courage, loyalty, and leadership skills to bring about personal independence and a sense of self-worth.

FULL MOON IN PISCES

Sun is in: Virgo.

Full moon element association: Water.

Sun element association: Earth.

Suggested ritual theme: Analyze your dreams and meditations. Practice service to others in a magickal way (reading cards, working on healings, etc.).

Gods, Goddesses, and Pantheons

All the gods are one god; and all the goddesses
are one goddess, and there is one initiator.
—Dion Fortune, *Aspects of Occultism*[19]

The concept of what God is to every Wiccan becomes a deep, philosophical, and precious subject. If you are into science and quantum physics, then you probably believe that God is the perfection of the universe, and to give it a name and a personality, to build myth and dogma around such a concept, may seem pretty silly. Indeed, all the blood, death, and horrible things done in the name of a god (any god, mind you) becomes more than ludicrous. But we are humans, after all, and we need that personal touch—which is how all great religions are born. The religion of Witchcraft allows people to believe what they want in respect to "what runs the universe." It is this freedom of faith that makes the religion so powerful, and although you may find us arguing—about which quarter comes first, how one properly casts a circle, historical information (everyone argues about that!), or whose lineage is valid (or not)—you'll not find us quibbling over the validity of one's personal concept of god/dess (unless, of course, you try to draw dogma from another re-

ligion into it—dogma, in this sense, means established doctrine, code, or opinion concerning faith formally dictated by a religious body, like the Christian church). Most Wiccans believe that there is a single source of positive energy or force that runs the universe. Because it is hard to connect in times of trial with a "source," we've divided it into the Lord and the Lady—male and female. Sometimes They are called the Master and Mistress of the Universe. That's why, when we say "and together They are one," we see the combined force of the Lord and the Lady as the totality of all that is positive and good. When you reach the study of alchemy in this book (SEE PART IV), you will notice that we find our current concept of the world-soul (that is sometimes split between the female divine of the starry heavens and the god of earth who protects and cares for us all—and together they are united) in the Hermetic doctrine. From the Greeks comes the idea of just the opposite—that the sky becomes the divine masculine and the earth is the divine feminine. Again, these two heavenly powers are united as one.

Some historians believe that it was Charles Kingsley in his novel *Hypatia* (1852) that gave rise to the idea that the Greek philosophy recognized the existence of the one true deity, of whom Pagan goddesses and gods were merely aspects;[20] Ronald Hutton, in private correspondence dated 9 August 2002, agrees that "Kingsley was quite correct, for virtually all Greek philosophers taught this, especially Platonists, Stoics, and Neoplatonists"—(which have affected modern Craft practices more than you know—it is interesting that we put more stock in this triumvirate than those who lived at the time)—"The problem for historians is that there is no sign that the vast majority of ancient Greeks and Romans paid attention to what the philosophers said, and desisted from believing in

THE GOD
The Lord
Father, Son, Sage
Male Deities

THE GODDESS
The Lady
Maiden, Mother, Crone
Female Deities

many deities." In modern Craft lingo, you will hear about the theory of aspecting, which is where the Witch becomes either divinely feminine or divinely masculine by drawing deity into him- or herself in ritual—known in some alternative Christian circles as the concept of "I am." Aspecting, in this case, is divine possession by deity—and no, last I checked, no one rolls on the ground or froths at the mouth in a Wiccan circle. It just ain't done.

For some Crafters, the idea of all-deities-as-one provides the power and unity they psychologically need to connect them to all of nature. It is certainly true that today's Wiccans and Pagans, in their effort to reconstruct and revitalize ancient ideas, have been influenced by those who have gone before, especially in the body of work presented by the Romantic movement in the late eighteenth century in the form of literature and poetry. It is also true that the over-

whelming majority of ancient Pagans genuinely believed that the different goddesses and gods were separate personalities, and that in only one ancient text appearing at the end of the Pagan period did the author declare that his favorite goddess was the embodiment of all other goddesses.[21] Although you may think this incredibly confusing, modern Wicca has managed to open its arms (and keep them open) in regard to one's personal deity choice and the hierarchy or pecking order that they represent.

In researching various coven dynamics in England, Ronald Hutton wrote the following:

Among Witches I have found people who think of their goddess and god as archetypes of the natural world or of human experience, others who regard them as projections of human need and emotion which have taken on a life of their own, others who see them merely as convenient symbols, and yet others who have a belief in them as independent beings with whom relationships can be made. . . . More remarkable, and significant, I have encountered all those viewpoints within a single coven, co-existing in perfect harmony because the members never felt the need to . . . debate them.[22]

He's absolutely right.

Another interesting ancient deity concept often favored by Witches is the trinity. The idea that "three make one" isn't a foreign construct in the major religions of today; in Christianity, we see Father, Son, and Holy Ghost. Here, the Father and Son are male, and the Holy Ghost is female (although this information isn't often discussed). In the Jewish Kabbalah, there are several manifestations of three-to-make-one, including the daughter, bride, and mother of Malkhut (the feminine presence of God, sometimes referred to as the Shekinah) to combine the energies of the Tree of Life in various sequences of three that can be used for meditation and raising one's spiritual purpose.

Most of today's Crafters agree that within every god and every goddess is the energy of the "single source"—and what that source may be is part of the Great Mystery. Many Wiccans use pantheons (family trees of gods and goddess linked by cultural belief) as representations of the single source—with personality. That means that if you plan to use a particular pantheon, or choose a specific god or goddess to work with, you must research his or her entire mythos, or story.

Many times you will discover that the gods and goddesses of a particular pantheon pick you, you don't pick them. Each has its own energy pattern, and you will be drawn to those that best match your cosmic construction. When this occurs—through meditation, an event, or other situation—the Crafter often relates to others that this particular god or goddess is his or her patron

deity, meaning that, above all others, this deity is often the main focus of the Crafter's work. This is not to say that they don't use other deity forms in ritual and worship, or that he or she might balance the patron with another equally powerful deity, which often occurs. For example, if you work with a dark goddess as your patron deity, at some point you will be required to work with her balance (in male form and in light) and vice versa.

Traditional Wiccan groups normally have a single, chosen pantheon used by all the members for sabbats, esbats, group workings, initiations, circlecasting, and quarter calls. Everything matches. This doesn't mean that these Witches don't work with other deities and pantheons on their own, outside of the group. Many do. The idea of everyone following the same pantheon "tune" is, above all, a question of focus. If three people are thinking of a Celtic goddess, and four are calling Isis, and another person throws an Aztec war god in there, you've got quite a muddy mix. Experienced Witches have also learned that, just as all should be focusing on the same deity or set of deities, all deity representations should be from the same pantheon for any single ritual. Here, you are also working with cultural energy patterns. If you try to mix them (e.g., Celtic at one quarter, Roman at another, American Indian at the third, and Norse at the fourth, then invoke a Chinese goddess for aid in the magickal working itself), the cultural patterns won't blend well, and it is highly possible that one (or all of them) won't show up or, worse, will throw a tantrum. (When I said deity "with personality," I wasn't kidding.)

When first entering the religion of the Craft many students work with the concept of the Lord and the Lady before tackling the research required in using pantheons and their associated deities. Others may call this duo divinity the

Master and Mistress of the Universe. Focusing on only two basic energies isn't a bad idea, and gives you time to work with the three-in-one concept (male, female, and unity of the two) in a new way. When you are ready to examine pantheons, many groups want you to write five- to ten-page papers on each deity in the group's selected pantheon before you use them, hoping that your efforts in research will bring you a wider understanding of the deity energy. Where do you find this information? At the library, in books on history, religion, and archeology. There's no other way around it. Every deity has its own personality, which will affect your magickal working. It's up to you to choose which personality and legend serves you best. In Witchcraft, your history in relationship to the gods is not laid out for you in one nifty, neat-o book. It is expected that you will go digging under your own steam, allowing Spirit to guide you to the information that will serve you best at a particular time in your life. In time you will probably collect statues and pictures of your favorite deities. When a Witch says, "I am a priestess (or priest) of . . . " and names a particular deity, it is often because he or she has had a life-altering experience (called an epiphany) that involves that deity energy, and has chosen that deity as his or her patron. Magickal groups also have patron deities, wherein one single deity "rules" the clan or group. In the Black Forest, for example, the patron deity is the Morrigan. The concept of a deity as patron stems from pre-Christian Roman times and is very much a product of that culture's hierarchy.

What if you don't want to do all that work and research? Stick with the Lord and the Lady, or Master and Mistress of the Universe. Eventually you will read something about a particular god or goddess that interests you, and off you'll go on a quest to find out as much as you can.

Over time, you'll amass quite a library of your own and have lots of notes from research you've done. You can put this information into your personal Book of Shadows until it gets too thick (it will happen), and then you can break the information out into its own book.

In the Craft, there are no middlemen to God. It's you and the divine. In a coven environment, a high priest and a high priestess are facilitators of the group government. Yes, they do aspect the divine. And yes, they do try very hard (usually) to be a proper conduit for the need at hand, but they cannot substitute themselves in your life as your god or goddess. They aren't any better than the other members of their group, and they don't get favors from deity because they hold that rank (which, by the way, is a heck of a lot of work). Every Witch, regardless of whether they belong to a group or not, is a Witch alone. In the eyes of divinity, each stands on his or her own two feet in ritual, magick, and learning. The only difference between a high priestess and a new Witch should be knowledge and maturity, and even then there are always exceptions to the rule.

Up until this point, you may have noticed that I haven't talked about Satan at all. That's because Witches don't believe in him. He belongs in the Christian pantheon, and he can stay there (which is why most Witches don't use the Christian pantheon). Witches believe that to give evil a name is to create that evil. Why bother to do that? Humans manage to manufacture enough evil in the world on their own, without slapping it on the shoulders of a mythical beastie. Most Witches believe that there wouldn't be any evil in the world if humans didn't keep creating it by their own dastardly deeds, whether they are done in the name of a religion or for one's own personal gain.

If we use other pantheons, why don't most of us work with the Christian one? There's more than one answer to this question, and I think it partially depends on who you are talking to, their personality, their educational background (as far as history and magick are concerned), and the experiences they have had in other religious structures. The pantheons, as most of us work with them today, do not single out evil by giving it a name and personality. Each god and goddess has their own personality, and in that personality they have a dark side and a light side, order and chaos, animal and spiritual—just like people. That's why we study their legends. How you use this energy is extremely important. In the Christian pantheon, the dark side is given individual power through the idea of Satan and his many demons (thanks to early Christian clerics playing with the Arabic Zoroastrian system, which predates Christianity). Some magickal people feel that by separating this darkness and allowing it to stand on its own, the Christian religion weakened their own pantheon, leaving the door wide open for a person to rationalize away his or her own responsibility to themselves and to the world. For some people it is easier to look to a new system (or pantheon), rather than bear the weight of negative dogma.

When one of my daughters was interviewed by a reporter writing for a major parental webpage last year, she was asked, "Do you worship Satan?" Her response was, "I wouldn't be that stupid." Many Wiccans today find this question not only irritating, but insulting. My daughter continued by saying, "It is the major religions of this world that play with Satan, not us. You are trying to equate my religion to yours, and that's not fair." Angered, the reporter never printed the story.

For others, it is the history of the Christian church that makes it so unappealing. One Wiccan teen, standing at the threshold of a Protestant church on Girl Scout Sunday, said, "I can't go in there." When her mother asked her why not, she replied, "Because if the people who go to this church every Sunday knew the amount of blood spilled and horrors done in the name of Christianity over the last 2,000 years so that this building could stand here, I would like to think that they wouldn't go in either. I can't go in a place that tells me they are preaching the truth, when they are lying through their teeth about their own history." She, along with five other girls, spent the hour during the service in the church garden.

Another reason why many don't use the Christian pantheon is the absence of male/female balance. Christianity is a patriarchal religion, or male-dominated faith, and many women and men find this idea equally offensive. Although some Wiccans learn to "plug in" female divinity somewhere in the Christian pantheon, relying on old information from Gnostic texts and other areas, the system itself, and many of its current practitioners, continue to view the presence of women as something that must be tolerated, not celebrated, and certainly within the system as it now stands the female principle will never be elevated to equal divine status. The Witch who also practices Christianity, then, will at some time have to come to a personal truce on the subject and look beyond the confines of the Christian dogma that grips its adherents so tightly. Can he or she work with a pantheon that says, depending upon the sect, women aren't as good as men, or that relies on dogma rather than truth? You will find even fewer Wiccans working with the Islamic pantheon because of the cultural (not necessarily religious) attitude of degradation toward women in certain areas of the world today.

Does this mean that Christianity is a bad religion, and that you can't work magick or advance spiritually within its ranks? Remember, I was giving you the reasons why many Wiccans don't work with the pantheon, which doesn't mean that you can't work magick, be spiritual, or become what you desire in the confines of that belief system. Ceremonial magicians, who use Christianity, Judaism, and magick together, seem to get along quite well. Some of these magickal people also use Pagan pantheons, particularly the Egyptian one. Just as in other practices, there are many different groups under the ceremonial umbrella. There are also a few European Druid groups that have not let go of the Christian dogma—it is simply too ingrained in their cultural practices. If you want to work this way, take your time to choose which is right for you. Just remember that you are working with your own construct, and in view of some (not all) Wiccan circles, you will not be considered either a Witch or a Wiccan. To pique your historical interest, there was another time in history where people wanted to practice the magick of Witches but didn't want to use the religion of the Craft or play with the expense and literacy required of the ceremonial crew. These people were known in towns and villages as "cunning folk," and much of their magickal material included bits and pieces of Pagan magick melded into the Christian mythos. Unfortunately, their desire to take and not to respect led to the deaths of thousands of people and the degradation of the name of Witchcraft, wherein lies another reason that many Witches today find the idea of a Christian Witch not only an oxymoron, but an insult as well.

Where ceremonialists may borrow from other pantheons, so, too, have Wiccans borrowed from the ceremonialists, as you can see from many of the historical roots of various magickal practices discussed in this book. The title Ceremonial Witch does not mean that the Witch is using the Christian pantheon, rather that the Witch likes lots of bells and whistles in ritual, follows a structured format (rather than a spontaneous one), and often tends toward more erudite studies. For some Witches, then, religious practice is ceremonial minus the Christian and Judaic influence, specifically Alexandrian and Gardnerian (to name two). For others, Wicca is a not so much a trip into erudition and devout structure as it is a free-flowing journey to the divine through nature's way—a more shamanistic approach to finding God. Still other groups mix the two (shamanistic and ceremonial) for different rituals or for group government purposes. As mentioned, ceremonial Wicca does not use the Christian or Judaic dogma, but may rely heavily on Arabic or Judaic mysticism mixed with a Pagan pantheon.

Finally, some Wiccans like to use pantheons because the religious leaders and rule makers of those cultures are dead. They can't tell you what to do, or that you are doing something "the wrong way," or that you are a bad person because you don't think like the rest of the cultural pack. The pantheons of the Greeks, Norse, Egyptians, Celts, and Romans (the ever-present favorites) cannot exclude us just because somebody said so. This doesn't mean, however, we won't get smacked if we use the energies of the pantheon in a less than honorable way—although the culture is dead, the patterns of energy are not.

Buzzwords

You'll hear these on Internet discussion boards in relation to deity and religion.

Animism: The belief that the forces of nature are inhabited by spirits.

Canon: Rule, law, model, or standard; often used by the early Christian church to squash people's rights, especially in dictating what they could and could not believe.

Culture: The sum total of those things (including traditions, techniques, material goods, and symbol systems) that people have invented, developed, and transmitted to each other.

Karma: A Sanskrit word that means "deed"—the law says that one's deeds determine one's future life.

Monotheism: The belief in only one god.

Pantheism: The belief that a divine spirit encompasses all things in the universe.

Polytheism: The belief in many gods.

Prehistory: The study of history before written records.

Theocratic Monarch: A human being who rules as the representative of a god or gods, and believes that he or she is the divine made flesh (and therefore better than the common rabble).

Pantheons Most Used in Modern Witchcraft

Listed on the following pages are five of the most-used pantheons in the religion of Witchcraft. This collection is only meant to get you started, and does not represent the thorough research you should do before working with any deity. Pantheons are tricky. For example, the Celtic pantheon, when you get deeper into it, has a three-tiered classification—the first, the children or subjects of Danu, were the Irish pantheon, a divine society of beings associated with each other and dwelling in a parallel world with its own politics, customs, and functions,[23] yet they also had children (sometimes the heroes

and heroines of epic proportions and who represent the second tier), who encountered not only humans, but nature spirits (the third tier). The Norse tradition is much the same, and the Grecian and Roman pantheons also have lesser deities that are half-human and half-god. With the Egyptian pantheon, all kings or pharaohs were considered god in human form, and therefore they were to be worshipped as well (usually only as long as they were in power, though a few turned into gods later on, much like the Voodoo Lwa and the concept that Marie Laveau—a deceased New Orleans Voodoo priestess who is credited with major contributions to her faith and to her people—can be considered a goddess/Lwa in her own right because she earned it). Also floating through all these pantheons are the errors of history in mistakes never corrected or information that was lost.

Greek Pantheon

Zeus: Divine god

Hera: Wife of Zeus, Mother Goddess

Apollo: God of prophecy, archery, and music

Aphrodite: Goddess of love

Ariadne: Goddess of the labyrinth

Aries: God of action and war

Artemis: Goddess of the hunt and protection

Athena: Goddess of war and wisdom

Calliope: Muse of epic poetry (female)

Clio: Muse of history (female)

Demeter: Earth goddess

Dionysus: God of wine and ecstasy

Eileithia: Goddess of childbirth

Erato: Muse of love poetry (female)

Eros: God of love

Euterpe: Muse of music (female)

Gaia: Primal earth goddess

Hecate: Goddess of Witchcraft, ghosts, and the dead

Hades: God of the underworld

Helios: God of the sun

Hephaistos: God of sun, fire, and forge

Hermes: Messenger to the gods (male)

Hestia: Goddess of hearth and home

Melpomene: Muse of tragedy (female)

Metis: Wisdom

Moerae: Three goddesses of fate—Clotho, Lachesis, and Atropos

Mnemosyne: Goddess of memory, mother of Muses

Nike: Goddess of victory

Pan: God of the forests

Persephone: Queen of the underworld

Phoebe: Goddess of the moon

Polyhymnia: Muse of singing (female)

Poseidon: God of the sea

Psyche: Goddess of the soul

Terpsichore: Muse of dance (female)

Tethys: Goddess of the sea

Thalia: Muse of comedy (female)

Theia: Goddess of light

Urania: Muse of astronomy (female)

Roman Pantheon

Jupiter: Great God; storms, thunder, and lightening

Juno: Queen of Gods; women, marriage, childbirth, household prosperity

Apollo: God of the sun, music, poetry, fine arts, prophecy, eloquence, and medicine

Bacchus: God of liquid spirits, fruits, and parties

Ceres: Goddess of harvest, agriculture, fertility, and fruitfulness

Cupid: God of love and passion

Diana: Goddess of the moon, hunting, children, and Witches

Fanus: God of the woodlands

Fates: Three goddesses of destiny; daughters of the night

Flora: Goddess of nature

Furies: Goddesses of vengeance

Janus: Two-faced god of beginnings

Mars: God of war and action

Mercury: Messenger of the gods, trade and commerce, travelers

Minerva: Goddess of wisdom, practical arts, and war

Neptune: God of the sea, earthquakes, and horses

Pluto: God of the underworld

Saturn: God of harvest and golden ages in history

Venus: Goddess of love

Vesta: Goddess of the hearth, home, and community

Vulcan: God of fire, craftspeople, metalworkers, and artisans

Celtic Pantheon

Dagda: Father God (the good god)

Danu (Anu)/Don: Mother Goddess

Abarta: Warrior energy (Irish)

Aine: Goddess of love and fertility (Irish)

Amaethon: God of agriculture (Welsh)

Aonghus: God of love (Irish)

Badb: Goddess of battle—one of the three faces of the Morrigan (Irish)

Belenus: Sun god (Welsh/Irish)

Bran: God of sea voyages

Bran the Blessed: God of the underworld (British)

Brigantia: Goddess of the water, war, healing, and prosperity

Brigid: Goddess of healing, fertility, poetry, and the forge (Irish)

Ceridwen: Goddess of fertility (Welsh)

Dian Cecht: God of healing (Irish)

Dylan: God of the sea (Welsh)

Epona: Goddess of sweet water, fertility, and horses (Welsh)

Lir: God of the sea (Irish)

Lugh: God of the sun (Irish)

Macha: Goddess of war—one of the three faces of the Morrigan

Morrigan: Goddess of war; original goddess of the earth and agriculture

Nemain: Goddess of war (Irish)

Nodens: God of healing (British)

Nuada: God of valor

Ogma: God of eloquence (British)

Rhiannon: Goddess of suffering and patience (Welsh)

Scathach: Goddess of martial arts and warrior-princess of the Land of Shadows

Taliesin: Prophet and bard (Welsh)

Tuatha de Danann: People of the Goddess Dana

Norse/Germanic Pantheon

Aegir: God of the sea (Germanic)

The Aesir: The younger branch of the family of the gods (Germanic)

Baba Yaga: Avenger of women (Slavic)

Buri: Ancestor of the gods (Germanic)

Dazhbog: God of the sun (Slavic)

Forseti: God of justice (Germanic)

Freyja: Goddess of fertility (Germanic)

Frigg: Queen of the gods

Gefion: Goddess of fertility (Germanic)

Hel: Goddess of the underworld and the dead (Germanic)

Huginn and Muninn: Ravens—Thought and Memory—belonging to Odin; messengers (Germanic)

Idun: Goddess of youth and apples (Germanic)

Jumala: Creator god of Finnish mythology

Kied Kie Jubmel: Lord of the herds, stone god (Lapp)

Leib-Olmai: Lord of the bears (Lapp)

Loki: God of fire (Germanic)

Luonnotar: Creatrix goddess (Finnish)

Madder-Akka and Madder-Atcha: Divine couple who created humankind (Lapps)

Mati Syra Zemlya: Moist Earth Mother (Slavic)

Menu: Moon god (Baltic)

Nerthus: Mother Goddess (Germanic)

Njord: God of the sea (Germanic)

Norns: Goddesses of Fate—Urd (Past), Verdandi (Present), Skuld (Future) (Germanic)

Odin: Father of the gods; gifted in eloquence

Perunu: God of thunder (Slavic)

Potrimpo: God of fertility (Slavic)

Rig: Watchman of the gods (Germanic)

Saule: Goddess of the sun (Slavic)

Skadi: Goddess of vengeance and the hunt (Germanic)

Svarazic: God of fire (Slavic)

Tapio: God of the forest (Finnish)

Thor: God of thunder (Germanic)

Tuoni: God of the dead (Finnish)

Tyr (Tiwaz): God of the sky and bravery (Germanic)

Valkyries: Female battle and shield maidens who take brave warriors to Valhalla, the idyllic abode of Odin's ghostly army (Germanic)

The Vanir: The older of the two branches of the Germanic family of gods

Vidar: God of justice (Germanic)

Egyptian Pantheon

No overall male and female figures that equate to the Lord and Lady are given, as the Egyptian civilization was the longest in human history. Gods and goddesses changed or gained or lost prominence over the centuries.

Amon: First worshipped as a fertility god; rose to prominence for a time as the most important god of Egypt

Anath: Mistress of heaven, protector of the king; known for her ferocity

Anubis: God of the dead and protection; Input is his female counterpart

Anukis: Goddess of water

Apis: The Black Bull, symbol of fertility and the undying soul

Aten: Sun god who turned into a monotheistic entity, then lost his footing among the other gods and goddesses

Bastet: Goddess of cats, fertility, music, the moon, and protection from evil (associated with Sekhmet)

Bes: God of good fortune and protection of pregnant women; Beset is the female side of Bes

Geb: God of the Earth

Hathor: Goddess of business, beauty, joy, love, harmony, children, and the all-seeing "Eye of Ra"

Horus: God of the sky, divine child

Hauhet: Goddess of boundless infinity; Hu is her male counterpart

Hekat: Goddess of midwifery and childbirth, associated with water

Isis: Goddess of All; Divine Mother; partnered with God Osiris

Ius-a'as: Goddess of creation

Ma'at: Goddess of truth

Mehet-Weret: Goddess of sky and floods

Merit: Goddess of music

Min: God of roads, fertility, and agriculture; protector of travelers

Neith: Goddess of destiny, war, and the mother of Ra; protector of the dead; bisexual

Nekhbet: Primal Mother Goddess; divine nurse

Nephthys: Goddess of secrets, initiation, and the dead

Nut: Goddess of the sky

Osiris: God of vegetation and the dead; rules with Isis

Ptah: God of learning, architecture, and building

Ra: God of the sun

Renenet: Goddess of prosperity and the home

Sekhmet: Goddess of protection

Selket: Goddess of scorpions; protector of the dead, travelers, and weather

Seshat: Goddess of writing and patron of libraries

Seth: God of storms and chaos; although unfriendly and cruel, he was respected

Shu: Goddess of moisture

Sobek: Crocodile God of lakes and protection

Taweret: Hippo goddess of childbirth

Tefnut: God of air

Thoth: God of knowledge, wisdom, and the moon

Wadjet: Serpent goddess of protection, children, and the land

Wenut: The "swift one"—moves things quickly; hare or serpent

Wosret: The powerful woman

Where Did Our Goddess Come From?

The Great Mother Goddess took shape in the mind of man during the Paleolithic Age (5 million to 10,000 B.C.E.). Perceived as the life-giver and identified with the mysterious powers of procreation, her exalted form carried importance in the prehistoric community, which is confirmed by the great numbers of female statuettes uncovered by archeologists throughout the world.[24] The Neolithic or New Stone Culture lasted from 8000 to 4000 B.C.E. Here, too, we find real indications that the Mother Goddess moved with the growth of the human mind into this era. The overwhelming evidence of female statuettes found in Neolithic graves contin-

ues to suggest that the belief in the Earth Mother may have become even more important in the transition from food gathering to food production, when fertility and agricultural abundance were vital to the life of the community.[25]

When we look at creation stories (SEE PAGE 18), we discover that in many ancient cultures, references to the Goddess come first. She is the darkness from which light came, the void from which all things were born; She is the beginning. When we examine the Charge of the Goddess (SEE PAGE 5), we see this affirmed in our own Wiccan religion—"from me all things are born, and to me all things shall return." Yet our Goddess, as we know Her, can take a great deal of credit for Her entrance into our culture through the works of three distinct individuals: Jane Ellen Harrison, Sir Edmund Chambers, and Sir Arthur Evans. Chambers, a civil servant and a scholar of the medieval stage of human development, declared in 1903 that prehistoric Europe worshipped a Great Earth Mother in two aspects, creatrix and destroyer, who was known by many names.[26] Ronald Hutton notes:

> *Chambers was not the main influence on the entrance of the Goddess into modern culture. That honor should go to his immediate contemporary, Jane Ellen Harrison of Cambridge University, who promoted the concept where it most mattered, among classicists and ancient historians. What Chambers did was introduce it subsequently to scholars of English literature, while it was prominently promoted among archeologists by Sir Arthur Evans, the person who made the discoveries in Crete.[27]*

It was Evans' discoveries in 1901 in Crete that led to a plethora of work on the subject by scholars of his time. Through this time period, the Goddess rose from the archeological dead. In 1948, a fellow by the name of Robert Graves fired the public with his rendition of *The White Goddess.*

> *Using his full tremendous talents as a poet, his excellent knowledge of the Greek and Roman classics, and a rather slighter acquaintance with early Irish Welsh literature, Graves developed the icon of the universal ancient European deity beyond the point at which it had been left in the 1900s. He took the imagery of . . . the three aspects and related them to the waxing, full, and waning moons to represent the One Goddess most potently as a bringer of life and death in her forms as Maiden, Mother, and Crone. He divided her son and consort into two opposed aspects of his own, as God of the Waxing and of the Waning Year, fated to be rivals and combatants for her love. An especially important function of the Goddess, for Graves, was that she gave inspiration. . . .*[28]

Whether or not She had been complete before is not an issue; what *is* important is that She emerged fully functional in the Year of the Goddess, 1948, and She was ready for a new twist on religion—modern Witchcraft. She was indeed a countercultural deity who was to place a delicate but firm foot on the neck of patriarchy, Christianity, and the industrial world.

If this is so, how did She get buried in the first place? The birth of unified civilization, as we understand it today, seems to have put the first major dent in the idea of the supremacy of the Goddess, digging a grave from which most believed She would never rise. As Neolithic villages gave way to city-states—as mankind strove to conquer, tame, and control the environment as well as his own kind—so the strength and power of the Goddess (and Her human female counterparts) fell victim to the violence constructed by a male-dominated society. A good look at Afghanistan today (I write this as the conflict has been thrown full force into the media eye of the

world) shows us how, as women become degraded and abused, so their divine archetype is slowly strangled. The Goddess of the ancients, however, didn't go easily into that dark night of modern, structured religion. For thousands of years She continued to speak from many faces—Astarte in Babylon and Sumeria; Isis (and others) from Egypt; Danu of the Celts; and Mary, Sophia, and Brigid of medieval Europe, to name a few. It is, unfortunately, our modern culture that stares at ancient history like a rabbit caught in the headlights of a truck.

Goddess? What goddess?

Of course there is a great deal more to learn about the history of the Goddess and how She has floated in and out of our cultural and social models throughout history. And where there is history, there will be controversy on "the facts." Case in point: Mary Magdalene was not a prostitute, and indeed many of the stories about Mary Magdalene are nothing more than a collection of many Marys (as Mary was the predominant female name in Christ's time) jumbled into one mythos. Indeed, according to historians today, Mary Magdalene was considered the most spiritually aggressive of the disciples, and it was her dollars that funded the rest of the male crew while they romped around the Holy Land spreading their message of hope for the future. Ain't it always the way. (Just kidding.) I still want to know how she turned that white egg to red (but I digress) . . .[29]

Regardless of such stories, we know that the supremacy of the Goddess even existed in early Christianity, until She was tossed out. Let's face it, if the women of the time were treated like baggage, enslaved, and considered property, how could one employ a female divinity in one's religion? If She really existed, wouldn't She be a bit testy on the treatment of Her energy made flesh? Let's just ignore Her, they said, and maybe She will go away.

Or not.

The point here is to tell you that the belief that She exists isn't something new, strange, or anti-religious. She was here first, and She will be the last to go, no matter what anyone tries to tell you, simply because everyone needs the perfect mommy.

Recommended Reading

Drawing Down the Moon by Margot Adler

The Triumph of the Moon: A History of Modern Pagan Witchcraft by Ronald Hutton

The Goddesses and Gods of Old Europe: Myths and Cult Images by Marija Gimbutas

Green Man

When someone explains Wicca or Witchcraft, they almost always indicate that our belief system is a "nature-oriented religion." This means that we follow the cycle of the seasons in our religious practices, respect life in all its forms on our planet, and often link our magick and love of deity with the many facets of Earth. Whether we live in the city or the country, this important tie is never broken. It isn't surprising that the earth-related customs of our ancestors are very much a part of the rites and celebrations of modern Witchcraft. Those that came before us lived closely to the land, and depended on a prosperous harvest to survive. Our ancestors learned to read the stars, till the earth, follow the signs of nature, and commune with the animals to bring harmony into the household. Although the cultivation of soil has been practiced for thousands of years, the garden as we understand it today, with a variety of vegetables, herbs, and flowers, did not begin in Europe until the 1500s. Those who had farms and gardens fol-lowed the phases of the moon and the moon in the signs for practical, daily living. Many bibles at the turn of the nineteenth century contained astrological information for animal husbandry, farms, and gardens. Indeed, what we view as "magick" today (in farm and garden lore) was simply considered practical advice in those times, yet by 1872 city folks sneered at the very thought that the moon could affect agriculture, relegating many sound practices as superstition for the simple minded.[30]

Magickal people of this century have realized the importance of living *with* the seasons rather than struggling against them, and in that understanding we have cultivated a rich and harmonious lifestyle. Many have made the effort to dig through local historical records to find reference to agricultural practices of their region, especially if they have their own farms or gardens. Others investigate community customs in an attempt to revitalize the magick of earth, sea, and sky as our ancestors enjoyed them in their personal rituals. If you work magick and ritual for any length of time at home, you cannot help but learn in which direction the sun rises and sets, the natural currents of the winds in your locale, what type of storm comes from which direction, what plants are native to your area, and which flowers, birds, trees, small animals, herbs, and weeds find sanctuary in your magickal stomping grounds. The more you commune with nature, the more balanced your lifestyle will become.

There is another upside in working with nature, and that falls within the realm of your pets (should you have any). As you work with nature by celebrating the seasons, paying attention to the weather, and enjoying the beauty of our planet, you will begin to intuit the health of your pets. Symptoms that may go unnoticed by others in the household will be obvious to you.

In some cases your heightened sensitivity will literally save the life of your pet, where in more normal circumstances you will be able to ensure that the animal receives medical care that can prevent an illness from becoming something more drastic.

Deities and Nature

Pagan deities also have a rich and vibrant attachment to nature in the form of animal husbandry, agricultural, and seafaring myths. Indeed, all Pagan deity pantheons are closely tied to the planet and her seasons. You just have to dig through history to find those associations. Therefore, when you call a deity into the magick circle, you are also inviting the seasonal energy and any nature power related to that god/dess.

Although modern Witchcraft is tempered by various myths, from those who are completely immersed in Celtic history to those who celebrate the highlights of Egyptian flair and enchantment (to name only two), there is a strong line of belief that runs through all areas of the Craft: the cycle of the seasons as it relates to male and female energy, and the combining of the two to create the fluid energy of life on this planet. What is often confusing to the new Witch are the various myths attached to any given season. Unlike (for example) the Christian religion, which has only one legend for a given day, the Pagan religions may have several, each believed to be as important as the other. The age-old battles of the Oak and Holly Kings, held twice a year at Midsummer and Yule, are a traditional reminder in some Wiccan groups of our Pagan root system, where others might celebrate the divine wedding of the Lord and Lady at Midsummer (or Lughnasadh) instead. The myths used may depend upon the pantheon of the practicing Witch. Some like a smorgasbord of ideas and exercise them all! What never changes

is the idea that we are tied to the land, and the land is tied to us.

More About the Green Man

When studying the Craft you will, at one point, stumble on our beloved Green Man. Once you meet him, you won't forget him, and he will speak to you often—from the trees, the grass, the desert sands, in flowers, bushes, and even seaweed. He is the ultimate god of vegetation, symbolizing fertility, bounty, and harvest; the Green Man "appears and seems to die and then comes again after long forgettings at many periods in the past two thousand years. He is much older than our Christian era, and in his appearances he is an image of renewal and rebirth."[31] The Green Man constantly reminds us that the Earth is a single, living organism, of which we are only a part.

Throughout history the most common image of the Green Man is that of a male head surrounded by leaves and branches, as if the face and the vegetation are as one (see above). Visit almost any lawn and garden shop in the United States and you're bound to find at least one, if not several, of these faces cast in stone, pewter, bronze, or ceramic, ready for placement in the most fashionable American gardens. In Europe we find him in churches, shrines, secret alcoves, government buildings, statuary, castles, and private gardens. The Green Man touches all, regardless of religious choice. In myth he is Jack in the Green, Robin Hood, King of the May, the Oak and Holly Kings, the Wild Man, and the garlands woven among the ribbons in a May Day celebration. Europe is not alone in the legend of the Green Man—he is the feared Curupira in Brazil; Ixpe Totec, the Aztec corn god of spring; Tammuz, lord of the wood of life, of Mesopotamia; Min, the fertile god of the fields in Egyptian lore; and Osiris (of the same pantheon) who, like Christ, was resurrected, matching his myth to the birth, growth, death, and rebirth of the seasons. Osiris is often represented with drawings of corn, wheat, vines, and tree branches. The Green Man is an ever-present theme across the world, and he is associated many times over with the sacred Tree of Life. Some feel that "the remote origins of the Green Man are found in the religion of Old Europe—the matriarchal religion of the Neolithic period of the first farmers centered on and around the Danube Basin."[32] Indeed, the divine, sacrificed god who attains resurrection is not a new plot line, but thousands of years old, dating well before the story of Christ.

A Green Man Ritual for Blessings and Prosperity

The following ritual can be performed on the first day of spring, when you plant your garden, when the farm household prepares for the coming growing season, honor the harvest on August 2 or September 21, or to bless a barn, animal shelter, or home. The ceremony has three distinct parts.

PART ONE: Using your magickal basket, take a walk in the woods, fields, by the beach, or along a creek or river. Collect small items from nature that you would like to include in your ritual— an acorn, an interesting small stone, flowers, and so on. Before you remove anything living, ask the universe for permission. If you feel uncomfortable, don't take the item—look for something else. Thank nature and deity each time you put something in the basket, asking for blessings and prosperity. At some point on your walk, rest and close your eyes. Talk to the Green Man (as he represents nature) in your mind. Does he have a message for you?

PART TWO—SUPPLIES: Modeling clay of your choice; a collection of earth-related objects, large and small; incense; salt; and holy water.

INSTRUCTIONS: Following the instructions on the clay package, fashion the face of the Green Man with your own hands. When modeling the face, take your time. It doesn't have to look gorgeous—what is important is the energy you use and the thoughts you have while you are building your Green Man. As your fingers move through the clay, think of the thousands of years of history that belong to the figure. Work some of the items you collected into your design. When you are finished, cleanse and consecrate the image with incense, salt, and holy water. Finish by holding the Green Man image in the sunlight for a few minutes, asking for the cleansing and blessing of heavenly fire. Finally, hold your hands over your work and ask that the Green Man instill the image with the positive energy of harmony and abundance. Place the Green Man in a basket filled with sweet-smelling leaves, plants, and flowers of the season until you are ready to perform the ritual.

PART THREE—SUPPLIES: Sacred oil; illuminator candles for the altar; basket with Green Man.

INSTRUCTIONS: Prepare for ritual by setting up your sacred space, followed by taking a spiritual bath or shower. As the water pours over you, think of your body, mind, and spirit casting off all negative energy. Towel dry and dress in ritual clothing or something loose—stay away from dragging sleeves or overly voluminous material if you are working with fire of any kind. If you are not permitted to work with candles, substitute solar lights or flashlights.

Light the illuminator candles on your altar. Place the basket containing your Green Man project on the center of your altar. Cast the circle. Carry the basket to the north quarter, hold it out toward that quarter, and say:

> *I call to the Green Man*
> *who resides in the north.*
> *I am the son/daughter of Earth*
> *who summons you forth.*
> *From caves and deep forests*
> *from fields and their flowers*
> *bring abundance and joy in this sacred hour.*

Move to the east, and say:

> *Green Man with the knowledge*
> *who sits in the east*
> *please hear my wishes and bless my pleas.*
> *Bring abundance and joy on eastern breeze*
> *from over the land and across the seas.*

Walk to the south, and say:

> *Green Man with the fire*
> *from out of the south*
> *remove from my life negativity and doubt. Instill in this circle courage and growth.*
> *Bring blessings and joy; abundance of both.*

Walk to the west, and say:

> *Green Man who governs the love*
> *and the rain*

> *come from the west*
> *and push away pain.*
> *With each movement I make*
> *and breath that I take*
> *bring blessings, abundance, and gain.*

Remove the Green Man image from the basket and place in the center of the altar. Set the basket aside. Anoint the eyes and mouth of the Green Man, and say:

> *May your eyes be focused on prosperity.*
> *May your mouth utter blessings*
> *upon this household. So mote it be.*

Hold your hands over the image, and say:

> *I saw you in the forest,*
> *your eyes so deep and green.*
> *I saw you in the fields, dancing there unseen.*
> *I heard your breath of life*
> *as you tickled leaf and blade*
> *I wondered at your rippling skin*
> *of amber, gold, and jade.*
> *I banish smog and poisons*
> *as I bring you in my life.*
> *I release all pain and suffering*
> *I refuse to live in strife.*
> *Your gifts of joy and bounty*
> *are welcomed in this place.*
> *Pray bring blessings to each season*
> *and touch this sacred space.*

Repeat the words "Blessings, abundance, and gain" nine times, beginning softly and growing louder, concentrating on positive energy surrounding you. After the ninth time, clap your hands three times. Say loudly:

> *It is done! So mote it be.*
> *From this day forward*
> *I enjoy blessings, gain, and harmony!*

Close the quarters and release the circle. Place the Green Man image wherever you like. Scatter the leaves and flowers from the basket outside to the four quarters, asking for continued blessings for your home from the winds of each direction. Re-empower the statue every six months, or on the Craft's High Holy Days.

Enchanted Green Man Harvest Candle

Wiccans celebrate three harvest festivals: Lughnasadh (August 1 or 2), Fall Equinox (around the September 21), and Samhain (October 31 to November 7, depending on the tradition). You can make three candles with three different themes:

Lughnasadh: Grain harvest and sacred wedding theme

Fall Equinox: Garden harvest

Samhain: Fruit harvest and honoring the cycle of death and loved ones in particular

The purpose of the candle is to:

- Bring unsolved issues to a natural closure.
- Celebrate the season and honor the Green Man energy.
- Bring deserved rewards to fruition and harvest.
- Place you in sync with the energies of the season.

SUPPLIES: Dried herbs and flowers of your choice (SEE PAGE 283 FOR INSTRUCTIONS); one white pillar candle (or candle color of your choice); an old candle of the same color or paraffin; sauce-pan; old, heatproof bowl; water; blow dryer; 2 pieces of plain white paper; scissors; old paint brush. Choose a ritual format.

INSTRUCTIONS: Cleanse, consecrate, and bless all items in the name of the Green Man. Should you be making the candle as a gift, ask for blessings upon the intended household.

Take your time and arrange the dried herbs and flowers on one of the pieces of paper the way you would like them to be on the candle. Cut away any excess leaves or stems with scissors.

Heat the surface of the new white pillar candle with the hairdryer (one section at a time) until the wax is slightly sticky. Gently press the herbs or flowers onto the heated wax of the candle with your fingertips (or the eraser of a pencil). Do not overheat the wax. As soon as you apply a leaf or flower, wrap a white sheet of paper around the candle and roll on a smooth surface. This is done each time you add an herb or flower to make sure the leaves stay attached to the pillar candle. Be careful, if you press too hard when rolling you will crush or break stems and delicate petals. Continue this process until the design is complete.

Boil water in saucepan, then reduce heat to simmer. Put paraffin or old candle in a heatproof bowl, and place bowl in saucepan. Leave in the bowl in the simmering water until the wax melts completely. Remove from heat. Exercise caution with simmering water and hot wax. You can never be too careful! With an old paint brush, quickly paint your decorated pillar candle with the liquid wax. (If you take too long, the wax will cool and gum up on the brush.) Do not touch the hot wax with your fingers. Allow candle to cool completely.

If you can, begin your chosen ritual format outside at dusk. Empower the candle, repeating the four intentions given at the beginning of this spell. Follow ritual closure format. As we are moving to the dark of the year, we choose dusk because it symbolizes closure of the day, yet birth of the night (day symbolizing spring and summer, and night symbolizing fall and winter). Use the candle in holiday ritual or give to a friend as a spectacular autumn gift.

Note: Candles containing herbs, flowers, and assorted natural items will burn differently than other candles. Sometimes the natural ingredients will catch fire in unusual ways, producing a hotter flame, which increases the burning time, or an overabundance of melted wax, or a double flame. Although this doesn't happen all the time, the candle should be set in a fireproof metal pan to ensure safety, and positioned well away from curtains, wall hangings, altar decorations, or living plants. When giving the candle as a gift, you can place information about the Green Man and what he stands for on a decorated card along with instructions for safe burning.

Group Mind and the Witches' Coven

The ancient mystery traditions taught the student that "we are all one," that all forms of energy are interconnected, and that therefore we are all a part of the great whole sometimes referred to as the divine dance or the collective unconscious. Our society, however, is stuck on individualism—that we are separate from each other, and that our differences are so wide we can never find ultimate peace with each other. Not true. Do you remember the old adage *Together we stand—divided we fall*? It's more accurate than you think.

If we begin with the idea of believing that we are all a part of the universal mind (the collective energy of the universe) and that we are never truly "unplugged" from that mind, it puts a whole different twist on reality as we understand it. This would mean that our enemy is a part of us. If they are part of us, then are they an enemy? Heavy stuff, I agree.

What leads us into the idea that we are separate is our individual conscious choices (and we make millions, maybe even billions, of these choices each day). We all work with the same energy, yet we each choose to use it differently. If the choices prevent perfect love and perfect trust, thereby attempting to destroy unity, then they are in error and the collective unconscious will take steps to balance the situation and restore harmony. These choices are based on our emotions, our body chemistry, our goals, what we have learned by past experience, and what we continue to learn. Even when our choices are in error (and we all make bad decisions), we are always connected through Spirit. We are never alone. This universal mind is a storehouse of information to which we all have a key, and that living energy never depletes and never dies.

How do we know that this overall group mind (or collective unconscious) exists? Telepathy, for one: the ability to speak with the deceased (although we haven't been able to slice and dice this idea with pure science quite yet), remote viewing (used successfully by the U. S. government), and the gift that some of us have to communicate with animals (to name just a few). There is another way of knowing that this collective unconscious exists: we can watch groups of people tied together by like interests or skill (like a soccer team, a science club, a political party, your family, or a clique). When the group is successful and their actions work to restore or hold harmony, they are thinking as one. When they fail, then—whether they know it or not—they are mentally divided by choice: their own. When you hear someone say that a group of people is only as strong as their weakest member, this actually factors down to an occult idea. In this case we're not talking about physical strength, but mental fortitude. The weakest member is the person who is constantly practicing negative self-talk, engaging in gossip, or who is just an all-around weenie who sabotages the group for the sake of a personal agenda. By choice, this person (or persons) try to refute the unity of the collective unconscious. If this seems confusing, don't worry about it. After you work magick and ritual for awhile, it will all become clear to you.

To help you understand the idea of the collective unconscious and how groups draw from it, let's practice two occult exercises.

Group Mind Exercise 1

For the next two days to one week, carry a notebook with you and write down all the different groups you see around you, and your impressions of those groups. Don't let anyone read your impressions. These are private feelings. If you must, write your ideas in code. Next to the group, write who you think is the strongest and the weakest member of that group, and why you think the group is successful or not. At the end of your experiment, meditate on what you have found. Think about the universal mind. Write down what you have learned from observing with your eyes and what you have discovered in meditation. Keep these notes because we will use them again.

Group Mind Exercise 2

Go back and read the Charge of the Goddess (PAGE 5). Pay particular attention to the words "From me all things are born, and to me all things will return." What is the Goddess energy telling you? She wants you to know that, in order to be the best you can be, you need to see the big picture before you can make little ones for yourself. She wants you to understand the concept of unity. You are one with every person and animal that lives, and you are one with god/dess already. You don't have to do any hard work to get there, you just have to remember. You are one with every form of life and energy. Everything (including you) came from the same energy, and

everything will return to that energy, regardless of the choices you make (I detect that little bugger called quantum physics here, do you?). How you use this energy is what is important, to yourself and to your community. One person *can* change the world, yet when these changes occur, the resource is that of the infinite, creative energy, which is the unity of all things. To hammer this point home, the Witches act out this journey through celebrating their eight High Holy Days, and calling them the Wheel of the Year. When they look at the holidays as interconnected, and celebrate each one in its turn, they are acknowledging the magick of birth, death, and rebirth in the lives of everyone (not just the Witches), as well as honoring the total unity of that creative energy that never dies.

The unity of all energy (people, place, animals, things, and deity) has been an occult maxim for a very long time, and many famous people in history have tried to explain it to those who would care to listen—Buddha, Confucius, Lao Tze, Muhammad, Dion Fortune, Israel Regardie, and Jesus, to name just a few. Personally, I will never forget Lord Serphant leaning close to me not long after my third-degree initiation, and whispering in my ear, "There is only one secret—we are all one."

The Modern Coven

What, then, does all this have to do with the coven environment? A coven is a group of Witches who have chosen to work magick, healing, and learning together, and normally acknowledge some type of internal government. Yes, that means they have rules. These rules vary from group to group. Not all Witches work in covens. Some use the word "circle" and others use the word "groves." A few use the word "church" and have been incorporated under the laws of state and country government (where such laws provide them the freedom of religion). The internal government of a coven, grove, or circle may be loose or very strict—this all depends on who started the group and what they saw as an adequate way to work together. Many Witches work solitary and don't belong to a group, where others work solitary but join a community Pagan-sponsored function to celebrate the moons (esbats) and High Holy Days (sabbats). Covens who follow the same teachings with an organized system of rules are called a tradition, if and only if the person who began the entire system is dead (as in Gardnerian Wicca). If, however, the original organizer is not deceased, the grouping of covens is called a "clan" (as in my own clan of twenty-eight covens). These covens may not have a central government (as in the case of Gardnerians), although several may communicate with each other for various reasons, or they may have a hearthstone concept where the covens never hive off but remain a part of the original organization (like the Black Forest), governed by a single person (queen/clan head), two people, or a council of elders. Once a single clan becomes too large to be governed properly, some groups allow significant sections to disengage, create their own queen or clan head, yet remain affiliated in the way most members feel is satisfactory. Some may choose to separate from the mother group entirely. What makes the network of covens confusing is that not all of them follow the same rules, and some groups call themselves traditions right from the get-go. To an outsider wading through the buzzwords and the coven behaviors, it is enough to make your eyeballs go wacky in your head; yet this is not unlike other religious groups where one denomination does one thing, but a group five miles away does something different. Certainly there are innumerable Christian denominations. Why would

the Craft, the fastest-growing, grass-roots religion in the United States, be any different?

A group mind is a pocket of like-minded individuals that come together in the whole of collective unconsciousness. It is a microcosm of the universal mind that tries, through human effort, to reflect the macrocosm of the collective whole (*As above, so below*). Each organization, small or large, has a group mind—people who link their thoughts and behaviors together to reach a certain goal. The difference between a cheerleading squad or a football team and the coven is that the magickal people know they are linked to the divine source, and through that "knowing" make a group effort to work with that source for healing, success, and happiness. The cheerleading squad, unless it has a strong and charismatic leader and plenty of individuals who practice positive thinking, does not understand the full impact of unity, and therefore only uses a small portion of the creative mind that links them all together. Your family also has a group mind. You are linked together by blood (DNA, genetics) and possibly living conditions, as well as any family traditions. Covens, then, and sometimes clans are often referred to as "family." They aren't necessarily your blood family, but they call themselves brothers and sisters from a spiritual viewpoint—the idea that we are linked together by choice, by practice, and by the ultimate creative energy that everyone shares. This type of grouping is not to be mistaken for a cult, which in this day and age refers to an organization that attempts to wholly destroy individuality and forces people, through a variety of means, to act in a manner that is unfitting to their spiritual path and the constructs of society as a whole.

In the Craft there is a method used to connect the individual to the group mind that is not designed to override the individual's personal choices. That connection is called an initiation. The primary focus of an initiation into a group is to link you to that group mind and, through their assistance, remove any psychic blockages to help you prepare the way for increased spirituality. Therefore, you are connecting to the energy of the present group, the energy that members of the group carry with them from past associations within that group, and the energy of members who are deceased that worked within the confines of that group. One's Craft lineage, then, is a listing of all who have gone before you litanized by the names of the individual(s) who orchestrated your personal initiation rite, and who have orchestrated their initiation rites, and so on. If you leave such a group once you have experienced the initiation ceremony, and do not desire to be connected to the group mind, then you should participate in a separation ritual, or one will be sometimes be done for you by the group after you are gone. The group mind is never to be taken lightly; never underestimate the power of the older groups or their members who have gone through years of training. A skilled high priestess can swing the sword in ritual and cut you from the group mind in less than five minutes, should she deem it necessary, and you will forever believe that you made the choice to leave all on your own. This tells you that there is a difference between a newly formed group and one that has functioned for several years—something that you will want to keep in mind if and when you decide you are ready for group work.

The really tricky thing about any group mind is that it is never stagnant. If a person leaves a group, the group mind will close ranks and change to recover from the loss of energy. Sometimes this is a sad moment and other times everyone in the group heaves a collective sigh of relief. For a moment, think of a group mind like a state. If you live in the state of Texas, you are a member of that state and also a member of the collective whole—the United States. If you leave Texas and move to Montana, you are no longer attached to the Texas group, but you are still a part of the United States. If you leave the United States you are still a part of the world group. You never leave the ultimate collective whole, you just move around within it.

If a person joins a group, then the group mind will expand and try to work this new energy into the whole. If this new energy does not vibrate at the same frequency as the whole, the group mind will expel the new member or the new member will destroy the group mind. If the new member refuses to go, things will get dicey for everyone. It doesn't matter what kind of group mind we are talking about, the debate club or a coven—harmony will always try to prevail. In the Craft there is a standing joke called "high priestess/priest fever," which is not so funny at all. This is a person who enters a group with the main focus of being the center of attention, and who will consciously or subconsciously sabotage the group mind in order to rule it. More than one coven has crashed and burned because of such an individual. An entire organization of over two hundred people or more can be ground into the dust through the selfishness or bad behavior of one person who makes a concerted effort to split the clan, hoping to capture the attention he or she needs. Usually this individual has been elevated to a trusted position and the blindsiding effect of his or her antics can literally rock the group's world. At times such as these, one wonders what happened to perfect love and perfect trust.

The group mind, then, is an ever-changing environment. Although we may recognize and try to cope with the physical reality of someone leaving or joining, we often don't consciously recognize this change beyond the physical, though our subconscious (which is always hooked up to the collective unconscious) does try to let us know—we just don't always listen.

The group mind always tries to imitate the unity of the collective unconscious. The problems that arise within any group are in direct relation to choice: When the group as a whole moves away from harmony, or when one or two group members try to upset the harmonious balance already established by the group, there will be an energy flux. If a group gathers together under the banner of negativity (such as a hate group), those within are destined to destruction. However, because the collective unconscious is not affected by time (like we are), this implosion may take longer than we'd like and many innocent people can be affected. Karmically, those who worked in error will pay, but you won't always see the method of payment as the universe (Spirit, God, the gods and goddesses) decides when and where those dues will be exacted. When you have suffered at the hands of such group activity, it is incredibly hard to have faith that perfect love and perfect peace will prevail because you cannot always be present when justice occurs.

The word *coven* means an assembly or meeting, and is related to *convent* and *covenant*, both speaking of an agreement or pact among people. In a coven the members agree to work together for the welfare of themselves and of the group. They may also agree on general rules, which gods and goddesses will be the patrons of the group, and what types of magick they like to do best. They may agree to learn together, and eventually to teach others. Craft covens are often small, with anywhere from three to thirteen members. Although the number thirteen can have occult significance, the smaller the coven, the tighter the group mind. I can tell you from experience that over thirteen members takes a leader skilled in diplomacy, with undying patience and an incredible amount of time and energy. Because the coven environment can have political pitfalls, many teens (and adults, too) choose to work "in circle"—meaning they simply come together to do magick and ritual, but don't want all the responsibilities that go along with regular coven work, or to be bothered with group government. There is no pact of behavior, only an agreement of what can (and can't) be done at any particular sabbat or esbat. In this case, the group mind only has "power" while the magick is in progress. Yes, it could be considered a loose group mind, but then we're splitting hairs and we don't need to worry about that at the moment. How do I know this is true? Because as my husband and I travel across the country and visit various areas, we hold what is called a "healing circle." Every time we do this ritual different people are involved, yet working together in that moment in time they are incredibly powerful and they always get the job done. We share one thing in common: faith.

Earlier I mentioned that the group mind is not stagnant. It will evolve or disintegrate as is needed by the group members and the collective unconscious. If you are a history buff (or even forced to read history for school), you'll notice that certain groups of people rise (or fall) in history as their energies are needed. Although we may say, "Gee, weren't we lucky that so-and-so was involved," in essence, so-and-so was called to be there by the collective unconscious. That person had the choice of whether or not to become involved. Had they not, the collective mind would have called someone else into service. Why does the collective unconscious choose a particular individual? To ensure that ultimate harmony will prevail. Why does the collective unconscious (god/dess) have to do this? Because humans create the circumstances they deal with by thought, choice, and free will.

Most covens do not accept members under the age of eighteen or twenty-one for several reasons. First, many are looking for a specific level of maturity because every time they bring a new member into a magickal group, the group mind changes. If that group mind is not prepared to deal with teen or early adult energy, it can and might disrupt the group mind. There is also the question of the laws of the state in which the coven is operating and how your parents feel about your participation in a magickal group. This doesn't mean that being a teen is bad. There are also covens operating that require a specific level of pre-training, or self-study. If you haven't studied in advance, you may not be permitted to join the coven. Others require that you have hearth and home, meaning a stable job and a secure place to live. You don't have to be a rocket scientist or live in a mansion. In this case the leader is looking for personal stability and the assurance that you will have the necessary time to study. Some will not admit an individual who is going through a personal crisis, such as a divorce, until that individual has given the necessary time required to that challenge and can now turn their sights on something new and exciting. Others will not take college students or newlyweds because the demand for their personal time might become too strenuous for the student.

When in a crisis or going through a major life change, one cannot focus on several issues at the same time—something has to take precedence. As you should not be forced to choose between your spirituality and your income (college, as an example), several teachers will suggest that you wait until a more appropriate time in your life to begin. Many covens now have application forms that are prerequisites for entry. Some people feel that this type of exclusiveness is a bad thing. Yet, if your group has been running well for three

years, and you are mindful of the impact of how a person's energy can change the group, you may make your choice to exclude someone to protect the group and the person who has made an application. In many magickal groups, the candidate must serve a year and a day before entrance is granted and the ceremony of connection is solidified. This gives both sides a chance to bow out if one or the other feels this is not the right situation for them.

Even if no new members are admitted and no one leaves the group mind, changes will continue to occur for a variety of reasons, including personal growth and our missions in life. Most magickal groups last less than three years; at the most, five. A few go beyond fifteen, and even less make it to twenty. Some groups totally remake themselves, with only a handful of the original members still involved, past that twenty-year mark, and there are some where the name has continued but the original founder is long gone and the group mind has morphed into something completely different. If you are a teen, you are familiar with the short life span of the group mind. You are in middle school and involved in those activities for a finite period of time. High school is the same thing. In college you may remain an alumni, but once you are no longer active at the core of the group, you may lose interest or only pay your dues for the networking the group might provide at a later date.

Finally, various covens have different goals. Some are purely for socialization, others focus on training in general or training for what is called the priesthood (which includes both women and men). Those who focus on the priesthood are usually structured and require that you devote four years or more to training within the organization.

If you are interested in forming a coven with your friends or are looking to join a coven, it is important that you write down what you desire from this relationship with your magickal peers and how you plan to fit that group mind into your lifestyle. My best suggestion is that before you make any decisions, you read the book *Coven Craft* by Amber K. This excellent book discusses the joys, pitfalls, and various structures you can choose when forming your own coven. I also have a section on Tradition Guidelines in my book *To Light a Sacred Flame*.

Invocation and Evocation

SEE CHARMS IN PART IV FOR A COMPLETE DIS-CUSSION OF INVOCATIONS AND EVOCATIONS. Please note that evocation in Wicca and evocation in ceremonial magick differ in philosophy, depending upon the training of the individual. Normally, invocations and evocations are done once the circle has been cast and the quarters called, and before any magickal working is performed.

Invocation: Calling upon the presence or power of deities or positive energy.

Evocation: To call positive energy up from within yourself.

Evocation of the Witch
I am one with the universe.
I am no-thing and I am everything.
I am the stars and the moon
the seas and the storms
the breath of life
the alchemical change
the living and the dead.
I am!

I am the power and the joy.
I am the spirit that dances.
I am the magick and the priest
the Witch and the sorceress
the angels and the elements
omnipotent
omnipresent
I am!

I am the past, the present, and the future.
I am the void
and I am the manifestation of my desire.
I am!

Invocation of the Goddess
I call thee down, O my great Queen
to enter my body
and commune with my spirit.
Be with me now as I fulfill my destiny
and work magick
in accordance with your will.
So mote it be.

Prayer

One of the questions I am most asked by interviewers is "Do Witches pray?" Of course they do, and when I answer, "Yes, absolutely," they look at me as if I have gone crazy. This is because the interviewer is equating prayer as only belonging to the religion that they are most familiar with (which isn't Wicca).

Granted, Witches are more focused than most people about prayer. We concentrate on the purity of the area and the purity of the mind before we begin to pray. Indeed, most spellcasting activities are nothing more than focused prayer with tools conducted in sacred space. Like other religions, we have prayers and rituals of adoration, devotional prayers, prayers for holidays, and prayers for when we are sad. We have prayers in which we are asking for help, and prayers of thanks. The only difference that I have ever seen is that Wiccan prayers do not grumble or cry out "Why me?" Instead, our prayers are designed to help us take action rather than stand around and wallow in the dirt with self-pity. Our religion also encourages people to speak to Spirit from the heart. Be honest and forthright. Don't mince words—be specific.

The following are Wiccan prayers that you can use as they stand, or rewrite them to fit your circumstance. Prayers work best if you pray in sacred space, ground and center (SEE PART III, BREATHING, FOR THESE TECHNIQUES), and meditate a bit before you begin; however, some of the most powerful prayers are those you will say in times of great need on the spur of the moment. If at all possible, pray aloud using your magickal voice (SEE PAGE 312), and repeat the prayer at least three times.

Prayer for When You Are in Financial Distress

Great Mother, hear me, your Wiccan son/daughter (say your name), *who is in financial distress. I call upon Thee in my hour of need.* (List specific needs. For example: Almost all the food in the house is gone and my family has no money to buy more, I don't have the money to pay for my pet's medicine, my father cannot pay for the dental appointment he needs so badly, my mother has no money to send me to the karate tournament, bill collectors are hounding my parents and I fear we will lose our home, etc.) *I ask Thee to relieve our emotional stress over this (these) issue(s) and bring to us what we need to fulfill our obligations and receive what we need and more.* (Always add the "and more" in case you've forgotten something. Spirit has a better memory than we do, especially when we are upset.) *I know that the universe is a*

place of abundance, and that if I allow that energy of abundance to enter my life, all my needs will be met; therefore, I open my arms to that abundance now and thank You for Your gifts. I know that You will answer my prayer and I am certain of success. In the name of the Lord and the Lady, so mote it be.

Note: In this prayer the knowledge and certainty is not an aloof assumption that you are so special that Spirit will come to your rescue, but a statement of your faith that anything is possible. Also, if you have brought this problem onto yourself, such as overspending or not managing your money wisely, be open and honest about that fact. Don't beat yourself over the head with your own failings, but do make sure you haven't drifted into the would of illusion and denial. Ask for assistance that, in the future, you gain the ability to manage your money wisely.

Prayer for Healing

Great Mother, You of infinite love and grace, I, your Wiccan daughter/son (say your name), *call upon You in the name of* (person you are praying for) *so that he/she may be healed as quickly as possible. Give him/her spiritual assistance to mentally overcome this medical problem, lift his/her spirits, and give him/her hope and confidence so that he/she can be well again. Bless his/her body with restorative energy and lighten the stressful load, and calm his/her emotional pain. Bring harmony to body, mind, and spirit. Ensure that he/she receives the right medical care from the right people at the right time. I know that You will do this for him/her and I am confident that he/she will receive what is needed, and more. In the name of the Lord and Lady, so mote it be.*

Prayer in the Face of Disaster

It doesn't happen often, but from time to time we find ourselves confronting a disaster, whether it be in our family, in our community, or even in our country. Say this prayer each night for at least six weeks or until the crisis is over.

Most Gracious Mother, She whose compassion reaches every corner of the universe and beyond, hear me, (say your name), your son/daughter of the Craft of the Wise, as I call out to You in our desperate time of need. We are facing a powerful force that threatens to bring (or has brought) destruction to our door, and I call upon Your great influence to put an end to this terror. Hear me, O Mother, as I pray for the sick and injured, for those who are trapped with little hope of survival, for those who feel frightened and alone, for those who are angry and filled with hatred, for those who are so emotionally distraught that they cannot find the wisdom to make sound decisions, for those who have lost loved ones, for those who are tirelessly working in rescue efforts—and protect the people from those who would misuse their power, both personal and greater, to harm the innocent. Allow no magicks to be impenetrable to Your hand, and sweep away those magicks that protect the guilty and hide them from Your justice. Gather all the positive energies from all the prayers across the world and bind them together to create a powerful vortex of love and harmony, peace and joy, protection and solace to those in need. And I pray for myself, my Mother, so that I may rise above this crisis and put my energies to where they will do the most good, that I not be self-serving, and that I not, in any way, add to the negativity or evil that has befallen us. I know that You will do this for (state the purpose), and I have confidence that You will immediately assist all those in need. In the name of the Lord and Lady, so mote it be.

Prayer Ribbons

A prayer ribbon can be used for any type of spiritual request. The ribbon(s) are activated at your altar, and then placed outside the home with the idea that as the ribbons dance in the wind, so your prayers are sent to Spirit. These prayers can be for protection, health, wisdom, success, and so on. The type of prayer used is entirely up to you.

SUPPLIES: Wooden dowel; ribbons (your choice of color, based on the type of prayer you are sending); anointing oil or holy water.

INSTRUCTIONS: Cast a magick circle. Call the quarters. Beginning with the north quarter, present the ribbon(s) and indicate your request. Ask for blessings of the elements on your wish. Sprinkle the ribbons with holy water or anoint with sacred oil, once again stating your request.

Sit in the center of your magick circle and hold the ribbon(s)—use one prayer for each ribbon, if you have more than a single ribbon. Hold the ribbon in your hand and intone your prayer. Repeat until your fingers grow warm and you feel as if you are enveloped with spiritual peace and happiness. Seal your prayer by kissing the ribbon. When you are finished with your prayers, tie the ribbon(s) to the dowel. Thank Spirit and the quarter energies, then release the quarters. Draw the circle energy into the dowel by walking counterclockwise around the circle one to three times, then saying: "The circle is open, but never broken," knowing that the circle energy is now in the dowel.

Take the dowel outside and stick it upright in the ground. As you do this, think of boosting the prayer with Earth energy so that it can travel to the heavens like a rocket. Run your hand up the dowel, beginning with the closest point to the ground, letting your hand continue traveling up off the stick and toward the heavens. As you do this, say:

Sacred Goddess, Mother Earth
Thou from whose immortal bosom
gods, and men, and beasts, have birth
leaf and blade, and bud and blossom[33]
from the earth to the sky
my prayers travel high
and the ear of my Mother is listening.

Quarter Calls

Although quarter calls can have a variety of associations, they are basically linked to the four directions and the four elements (SEE PART IV, ELEMENTS, FOR EXERCISES AND DISCUSSIONS OF THE ELEMENTS). The most simple call, and perhaps the most well-known, is the following, said at the respective quarter after the circle is cast:

Hail guardians of the north, element of earth, and all ye in the realm of Faery, I, (say your name), do summon, stir, and call you forth to witness this rite and protect this sacred space.
So mote it be.

Hail guardians of the east, element of air, and all ye in the realm of Faery, I, (say your name), do summon, stir, and call you forth to witness this rite and protect this sacred space. So mote it be.

Hail guardians of the south, element of fire, and all ye in the realm of Faery, I, (say your name), do summon, stir, and call you forth to witness this rite and protect this sacred space. So mote it be.

Hail guardians of the west, element of water, and all ye in the realm of Faery, I, (say your name), do summon, stir, and call you forth to witness this rite and protect this sacred space.
So mote it be.

Quarter calls are designed to call only that energy you will allow in your magick circle. For all others, there is a No Trespassing sign. Nothing can come into your circle unless you, yourself, invite it, which is why there are so many different types of quarter calls that address various kinds of energy. There are calls that invoke the elements, angels, totem animals, deities of a particular pantheon, dragons, airts, winds, the dead, ancient archetypes, one's lineage, and/or the Watchtowers (stellar/ceremonial).[34]

The quarter call creates a one-way passage into the circle for that which you have called to enter. It must wait in the circle until you are finished, and you must provide a way home for that energy. Therefore, you can't forget to release the quarters when you are done. Think of it this way: it's like asking your best friend to meet you at a party. She says, "That's cool, but I don't have a ride." You tell her that's not a problem, you'll provide the transportation. When the party is over, you can't just leave your best friend sitting there. You gave your word that you would provide the transportation both ways—that's the essence of a quarter call. You agreed to bring the energy in, and it is your responsibility to make sure that the energy returns to whence it came. There's no "Gee, I forgot" allowed!

In the standard quarter call above, you are inviting the following into your circle:

- Summoning the element related to that quarter.

- Stirring your ancestral dead in a positive way.

- Calling deity energy related to that quarter.

Once the four quarters are called (beginning at the north for those who practice shamanic Wicca, or beginning at the east for those who like more of a ceremonial flavor), the circle energy is fine-tuned, cleaner than before, and prepared for the entrance of deity, which occurs when you speak the invocation you've chosen aloud.

Quarter calls are often accompanied by physical motions and visualization. Some magickal people draw pentagrams in the air with their wands, athames, or fingers, where others simply hold the tool pointing toward the quarter. In both cases, the center of the circle is at their

The God (left) and the Goddess (right) positions.

back. If you want a smoother opening and transition of energy, stand with your feet apart, facing the appropriate direction, with the center of the circle at your back. Cross your arms over your chest. Bow your head (this is the God position). As you say the quarter call, slowly raise your head and open your arms, as if you are parting a curtain. Visualize a portal opening through which what you have called can enter, and visualize your concept of them coming into the circle. With the last words of the quarter call, your arms should be like a *Y*, with palms facing toward the quarter (this is the Goddess position). Other Witches open the quarters by lighting a candle that matches the quarter color while intoning the quarter call. Colors are governed by tradition (what the group has chosen). Standard colors are green for north, yellow for east, red for south, and blue for west.

Unless they are fortunate enough to have a ritual room (a room used only for magick), most Witches do not have a shrine at each quarter to represent the elements and other energies they normally call into their circles. Decorations at quarters are often temporary, put in place before the circle is cast and removed when the circle is released. Quarter decorations can include candles, items that relate to the specific energies called at that quarter (a bowl of water in the west quarter), or things important to the type of ritual they are doing (for example, seasonal decorations that match a sabbat).

Each type of quarter call (angelic, dragon, etc.) has its own release that matches the original call. For example, the standard release to be said at each quarter is:

Guardians of the (direction)*, element of* (element)*, thank you for participating in my circle this night* (day)*. Go if you must, stay if you like. Hail and farewell.*

Again, some sort of hand motion is often involved. If you used the crossed arms, you would begin with your arms open, then slowly cross them as you visualize the portal through which they traveled closing. Quarters are released after deity has been thanked and before the circle is released, and you always begin with the last quarter opened. This means that if you opened with the north, then called east, south, and west, you would close first with west, then move to south, east, and finally north. If you began in the east and moved to south, west, and then north, you would begin in the north, then move to west, south, and finish with east. Quarters are conjured clockwise, and released counterclockwise. If this is confusing, think of a spring—you tightened it up (clockwise) going into the ritual, now you are going to release it by letting the energy go back the way it came, which means it would travel counterclockwise when allowed to follow its original path. Remember, in Wicca clockwise is deosil, and counterclockwise is widdershins.

What happens if you forget to release the quarters? The energy begins to decay and, in that breakdown, causes chaos—sometimes minor, sometimes not so minor, depending on how many people worked within that circle environment. Although some people say, "Oh, heck, I forgot. It's an hour later, I'll just forget it," this is considered by some to be magickally irresponsible. You might want to go back and release those quarters no matter when you realize you've made the error. In doing so you will not be so apt to forget next time, and you will also be cleaning up your own mess. To avoid forgetting, some Witches call the quarters within their cir-

clecasting. That way, when the circle goes down, the quarters automatically close. However, separating the circlecasting and quarter calls is standard procedure within the current community because each action requires its own visualization, and separating them eliminates the possibility of error, especially if you are working with individuals new to the faith.

Why must you call the quarters in the first place? If you remember that calling the quarters is an act of fine-tuning the energies in your circle and asking for reinforcements in your work, then you can make the decision whether or not you wish to use them. In most magickal training programs, students are required to learn all about quarter energies and use them in every spell and ritual they conduct for at least a full year. If you skip this repetition, the work eventually suffers. Once you've been studying for a while, you might want to open only one quarter in a spell or ritual. For example, maybe you are working on personal transformation and letting go of upsetting emotions. You may feel that west quarter energy is all you need for that working. By this time, however, since you have been working with all four quarters for over a year, you will naturally compensate for that which you haven't called. Here is a list of when quarters are definitely called in almost every Wiccan tradition:

- Sabbats.
- Esbats.
- Wiccanings (baptisms).
- Handfastings (marriages).
- Crossings (funerals).
- Dedications, initiations, and elevations.
- All magicks for first- and second-year students.

Rites of Passage

Sometimes you feel like an alien, whether you are sixteen or sixty-six—like you don't belong, like nobody understands you, or that it seems as if everyone is out to get you. I bet you wonder how the heck you got on this planet, or whether those adults in your house are really your parents, or if your children were plopped here by some unseen force, or that you've been dumped on this planet for the purpose of one big cosmic joke. When people talk to you it sounds like gibberish. For some kids and adults it feels like you've always been out of sync with the rest of the world, or perhaps lately you've felt like disaster has turned your self-esteem upside down and inside out. Regardless of your age, your body is changing, your mind is changing, and the world around you is changing. You want to scream and make it stop! Not only are you changing inside out, you are also changing from the outside in—when I was a kid, I used to think that it would have been far better if I'd just been born an adult and skipped all those years between one and twenty-one. The older I got, the more I considered dropping some more years—say, birth occurs at thirty, a nice magickal number. Unfortunately, the world doesn't work that way.

Magickal parents know how tough these levels of change can be. In the Craft, depending on the group, rites of passage are written and performed for the growing child and young adult. (From my ancient standpoint, a young adult can be as old as twenty-six.) The cycle begins with a wiccaning or saining (like a baptism) soon after the birth of the baby. In this ceremony the baby is blessed with the four elements and Spirit is asked to watch out for the child through his or her growing years. When puberty graces you with its presence, a second ceremony is performed, called a rite of passage. There is more than one kind of rite of passage, which means that these three words are a catch-all phrase for special ceremonies written and performed for certain events in your life from puberty to death.

Rites of passage ceremonies can be long or short, flowery or serious, ceremonial or tribal. They can be quiet and solemn or noisy and filled with drums and shouts of delight. Again, this depends upon the personality of the child and the family environment. The main purpose of this type of ceremony is simple: to help you cope with what you've already done, what's happening now, and what is waiting for you around the bend of your future. For young adults, rites of passage can include puberty, when you reach middle school, when you reach high school, when you turn eighteen, or when you reach the golden ring of twenty-one.

If you decide to become a magickal person, you are always going to be different. Let's face it, the world as we know it contains people that don't understand who or what we are, and don't want to, either, which hurts sometimes. You will be able to do things naturally that others can't even imagine. If you stick with your magickal studies, you may always feel that you are a member of some obscure, alien nation. I know I do sometimes, and I've been in the Craft a long while. In adulthood you may pick and choose your friends related to your interests, but you will still have to associate with the rest of the world, and even adults have trouble letting go of people who don't support them.

Feeling like you are different from everyone else is normal, whether you are magickal or not. People do crazy or subtle things to be noticed. The important point here is that we need to funnel this urge to be different and be accepted in a positive way. Gossip, bullying, or violence isn't the answer, especially if you are a magickal person, regardless of your age. The adage *Ever* mind the rule of three, *what you put out comes back to thee* is a very real lesson in the Craft. It means that what you do (in your thoughts, words, and actions) affects in a positive or negative way what you will receive. The adage is a reminder of what you can expect if you screw up.

What happens if you don't live in a magickal family or aren't part of a magickal group, which means there isn't anyone to help you out by performing a rite of passage? How can you reap the advantages and protection provided by such a rite? Do it yourself.

This section contains a belly blessing (for a pregnant mom) and a wiccaning (for a newborn or young child). The teen rite of passage for young adult can be used whenever you feel appropriate. I have also included a discussion on death and the crossing ceremony. Finally, I have added a graduation ceremony that can be used for any type of advancement, like leaving middle school, high school, college, or even graduating from Army boot camp! Immediately after this rites of passage section is a complete discussion on ritual; therefore, if you are new to the Craft, you may wish to read over those passages as well before actually performing any of the rites of passage ceremonies.

Belly Blessing Ceremony

I've included this ceremony in the hope that this book grows with you over the course of your magickal life, and to encourage your family to celebrate together, regardless of everyone's individual religious choice. This ceremony is for the pregnant mother and the protection of her forthcoming child. In some Wiccan circles the belly blessing is the equivalent of a baby shower plus ritual. Perhaps your mom is going to have another baby, or your older sister would like to do something really special to honor the conception of her child; or you may wish to throw a magickal shower for a friend.

SUPPLIES: One large white pillar candle and one smaller blue votive candle (to signify mother and child); five white votive candles (for the points of the pentacle); holy water; a red candle; incense (your choice); masking tape; gifts for the prospective mother.

INSTRUCTIONS: Before the ritual, cleanse the area with the four elements. Stack gifts for the mother by the altar and cleanse with burning sage or other incense. Place the white pillar candle in the center of the altar with other supplies close by. Set the red candle in the south section of your altar. Light. With the masking tape, make a large pentacle on the floor, with the pentacle pointing up toward the altar. Place a white votive candle on each point of the pentacle. Cast the circle, call the quarters, invoke deity, then cut a door and bring the mother into the circle, anointing her head and saying:

> *May you be cleansed, consecrated,*
> *and regenerated in the names of*
> *our Lord and Lady. So mote it be.*

Remember to seal the door and take care that no flowing hemlines touch the candle flames on the pentacle.

Have the mother light the white pillar candle (the mother candle) and tell her to utter a silent prayer to Spirit for a safe, successful birth and for continued protection for her child. The blue candle represents the baby. Have her light the blue candle from the white candle, asking for special gifts and protection for the unborn. With the blue votive candle in her hand, lead her to the points of the pentacle. Ask deity for a blessing for the mother and baby, then light the pentacle candles from the blue candle, visualizing the exchange of energy from deity to mother. The points of the pentacle represent Love, Good Health, Strength, Harmony, and Wisdom. ***Note:*** You may wish to print these words on a tent card and place them near the respective candles so that everyone, including the mother, knows what you are asking for.

Return to the center and ask for blessings from deity by holding the blue candle toward the heavens. Place the blue candle on top of the white candle, saying:

As we are one with the Lord and Lady,
so this mother and baby are one.

Hold both hands on the stomach of the mother, and say:

May they remain healthy and safe throughout
the birthing process. May no evil, real or
imagined, penetrate the sanctity of the love be-
tween mother and child, and may they
be protected in this world and
in the worlds we cannot see.

If there are others present, they can also add their blessings.

At this point you may wish to read the Charge of the Goddess (PAGE 5) or you may like to recite the Thirteen Powers of the Witches (PAGE 3). Give the mother the gifts. Close the circle in the normal way. Allow the blue candle to burn continuously until it goes out, or snuff it out with your fingers and give to the mother to continue burning at home.

Wiccaning Ceremony

A wiccaning/saining ritual welcomes a newborn into the "world family," providing protection for the infant as he or she grows in the material world. A wiccaning ceremony can be done soon after the child is born or can occur later in the year. Sometimes when parents join the Craft they ask the high priest or priestess to perform a wiccaning ceremony for children anywhere from birth to ten years old. You may live in a household where your mom and dad would be delighted if you do a wiccaning for your new sibling. If this is the case, here is a simple ritual that the family can do.

SUPPLIES: General altar setup of the four elements; illuminator candles; a new baby blanket; and eight thirteen-inch-long ribbons. Carefully sew the ribbons onto the blanket, thinking of what they stand for as you sew. Each ribbon's color stands for a special gift:

White: The gift of spiritual success and free will, and the purification of Spirit.

Silver: The gift of psychism and the love of the Goddess.

Blue: The gift of communication and intelligence.

Green: The gift of healing and attunement with nature.

Yellow: The gift that all needs will be met in a positive way and that joy be a constant companion.

Gold: The gift of wisdom and discernment.

Red: The gift of courage, laughter, and right action.

Purple: The gift of communication with your guardian.

Choose the ritual format in which you feel your family would be most comfortable.

INSTRUCTIONS: Cleanse the area with the four elements. Stack any physical gifts for the baby by the altar. At the core of the ritual, bless the baby with holy water (just a touch), saying:

May you be cleansed, consecrated, and regenerated
in the name of our Lord and Lady (or Spirit).
May your feet always walk the path of love
and enlightenment. So mote it be.

The pass the four elements over the baby, asking each for love and empowerment in his or her forthcoming life.

Place the blanket around the baby, saying:

> *Welcome back, little one!*
> *May the Mother's blessings shower thee*
> *with the love of family and friends*
> *by my hand on your head I empower thee*
> *in this Circle that never ends.*[35]
> *I give you these gifts of life*
> *and enchantment—*

Touch each ribbon as you repeat the gift, then hold your hands over the baby and envision all the gifts coalescing into a ball of light that surrounds the baby. Draw an equal-armed cross over the baby, saying:

> *These gifts are yours to keep or to discard*
> *when you come of age to understand them.*
> *May you use them wisely. So mote it be.*

If there are other gifts to be given to the baby, do so now, then close the ritual in the normal way.

Teen Rite of Passage

SUPPLIES: One full-length mirror; your favorite incense; water; salt; a single white candle; soft music; a gift for yourself. I realize there are all sorts of tools we could use here (the chalice, the wand, the athame, etc.), but the most important idea in a rite of passage is your communion with Spirit. Tools are an earthly thing and fun to use, but here we are focusing on raising your personal vibratory level to create a positive future life path. Besides, you can't always have your tools with you (like in the gym locker room), so learning to work with what you have (your own true self) is not a bad thing.

PREPARATION: As much as you probably don't want to, please clean the room where the ritual will take place. Dust and dirt harbor negative energy. Sit down and think about the gifts that you feel you need to manifest a positive future for yourself. Write these things on a piece of paper. You will ask for them in the ritual. A note on the blessings: Asking to win the lottery is not an option. This ritual is designed for requests such as raising your self-esteem, finding courage, learning to like yourself, helping your talents to grow, walking in wisdom, and so on.

TIMING: New moon.

INSTRUCTIONS: There are three segments to this ritual, the beginning (which is preparatory in nature), the middle (which is the guts of what you want to do), and the end (which closes things up in a magickal way). If you have read other books about the Craft, or are involved in a magickal group, you might discover that rituals and ways to do things are different. If you are more comfortable with what you have learned somewhere else, by all means incorporate those practices into this ceremony. The most important backdrop for any spell or ritual is the necessity for undisturbed privacy. This can be really tough, especially if you share a room with a sibling or your family feels that your personal space is really Grand Central Station, meaning what's yours is a free-for-all. If this is the case in your house, you may want to perform this ritual outside by a lake or a stream (which means you don't need the mirror or you can take a small one with you). That's okay, too. Whatever works for you is what is important here. If you do choose to work outside, follow the normal rules of safety—don't go wandering around in the dark alone (daylight will be just fine) and stay away from places that you know are dangerous. If you have a magickal friend, you might want to take them with you. Perhaps you could perform the ceremony together.

Set the mirror and all the elements either in the center of the room or at the north corner of the room (both are acceptable). Take a bath or shower, which cleanses the mind and spirit as well as the body, then practice a grounding and centering exercise before you begin (SEE PAGE 238).

Part One: One by one, carry the four elements around the room in a clockwise direction beginning with the salt (representing earth), followed by the lit incense, then the lit candle, and finally the bowl of water. As you walk, say the following:

The Witch, the magick, the fire (or earth, or air, or water, matching the element you are carrying), *the power—be one, be one, become.*

A bit of explanation here. With this chant and the pattern of movement, you have done the following:

- Created sacred space.
- Called the elements.

This might be different than what you have learned elsewhere. In some ceremonies, creating sacred space and calling the elements may be two different functions, with calling the elements (or quarters) occurring after you cast the circle.

From the north quarter at the outside edge of the room, walk clockwise in a spiral until you reach the center of the circle (use at least three passes or up to seven to reach the center of the room). As you are walking, hold your index finger out and down as if you are drawing a circle in the air as you move. The only problem with this visualization is if you think of the circle as a line (which it isn't)—rather, the circle will en-

compass you like a bubble, above your head and below your feet. As you move, say:

*The Witch, the Spirit, the circle of power—
transform, transmute, become!*

As you reach the center of the circle, say the chant one more time in a loud (if you can) and powerful voice as you raise your arms to the ceiling (or sky). Stamp your foot on the ground, and say: "This circle is sealed!"

A few things might happen here, so let's talk about that. You may experience any of the following:

- A rush of hot or cold energy from head to toe.

- The jitters (like you get before a big game or a school play).

- A tingling sensation in the limbs or fingers.

- A neat, peaceful feeling.

- Sweaty palms.

- An empowered feeling, like you can take on the world.

None of these reactions are bad and none of them lead to something scary. All of them are natural. You can ground and center if you feel wobbly or nervous. Take nice, deep, even breaths before you move to part two of the ritual.

Part Two: Set the candle in front of the mirror so that you can see your reflection and that of the candle clearly. Look in the mirror and say:

Lord and Lady (or Spirit), *one comes seeking a rite of passage* (name what sort of passage you desire, for example: into the world of puberty, middle school, high school, adulthood, etc.).

Look at yourself hard in the mirror.

That seeker is myself. I bring my hands (hold them out), *my heart* (cover your heart with both hands), *and my own true self* (open your arms out and hold palms faceup as if you are carrying something). *I ask your blessings upon this journey of change* (lift your arms, still palms up, toward the sky).

Close your eyes and allow yourself to feel the love of the universe around you. When you feel you are finished, open your eyes.

Now look at the reflection of the candle in the mirror, and ask Spirit (or the Lord and Lady) for the blessings you listed earlier. Take your time. Say them one by one. Will them to happen as you stare into the flame. When you are finished, take a deep breath and relax. Hold your hand over the gift you've prepared for yourself. Ask for the blessings of Spirit upon the gift, that it may be imbued with the special power of universal love.

Part Three: Thank Spirit (or the Lord and Lady) for their presence and their gifts. Starting at the center of the circle, walk in a counter-clockwise direction, spiraling out of the center, and say:

Return from the center, return to beyond,
return to the elements, return to the dawn.
With blessings of peace, with joy, and with love,
return to our Lady, who smiles from above.

A note here about mirrored reflections. Sometimes we are afraid to look into a mirror at ourselves because we don't like what we see (like that zit on your nose) or because you're not built like a movie star or an action figure. Rather than wishing to be something that we aren't, know that you chose that body, those eyes, and that hair for a darned good reason before you ever got to the Earth plane. Yes, yes, I know about genes and all that stuff, but many Witches believe that you had far more control over who and what you are rather than being stuck with the luck of the genetic draw. If you chose those hips, you must have had a good reason. If you decided on straight hair rather than curly, that, too, was a part of your inner wisdom. Considering that each set of parents can create over 10,000 variations to their genetic code, this isn't as far-fetched as you might think. It's okay to want to improve yourself—after all, that's why we're here in the first place—to learn and grow, change and become in a special way; however, mentally beating yourself up because you aren't as handsome as Harold or as beautiful as Lisa isn't in the game plan. You've got more important things to do! Besides, did it ever occur to you that the cute dip in your nose, or those freckles, or your unusual ears are there so that the most important people in this life will recognize you? No kidding. Some magickal people believe that we choose certain physical traits as prearranged symbols so that we can find each other on the Earth plane. It's okay if you don't believe this, but it sure is interesting to think about, isn't it?

Death

Witches believe that when a person or pet passes away, they still have the ability to hear you and be with you. This doesn't mean they are "stuck" and can't go on, it just means that Spirit provides the deceased with the ability of lending love and support to those who are still living until they realize in their hearts that death is not the final chapter, only a new one. Most Witches believe that once the deceased individual has given some type of farewell, the spirit of the person goes to a truly wonderful place beyond our realms of understanding called the Summerland. In the Summerland we grow strong again, re-view what we did in the last life, learn new things, and choose (or not) to return to the Earth plane once again. This belief is called reincarnation, where we are born, live, die, and are born again—the sacred cycle of life and death.

When dealing with death, the people left behind need some type of closure, especially if the death was a sudden one. It is thought by some that there is a resting time from death until the person is able to communicate with you, and for some this time will be longer than others. The condition of your emotions also has a lot to do with their ability to communicate with you. If you are extremely upset, or believe that dead is dead is dead, with no hope of a message, then they may not be able to get through for quite a while.

The American public does not deal well with death, although we watch giant-screen movies of murder and mayhem, read mystery books by the truckload, and never miss *America's Most Wanted*. When it comes into our own back yard, however, we seem to be at a loss as to what to do. Some Wiccans have ancestral altars or shrines where they honor deceased friends and relatives on a regular basis. Mine is a shelf on my desk that contains several photographs. On Samhain and other times of the year when I feel moved to do so, I will light a candle and say a prayer for their continued growth and love in the spirit world. Sometimes I just look at the pictures and honor their gifts to me, or place a favored candy or flower next to a particular picture. I am forever reminded that the only thing that is constant are the good things that we do, the love in our hearts, and the way we conduct ourselves in daily life.

Wicca is a religion of freedom and you will find this in our funerary rites and crossing rituals. There is no one specific way to conduct either. And where other religions require the wearing of black, Wiccans normally wear white, which means that we honor Spirit and we honor the new birth of the individual who has passed away.

Although the funeral and the crossing can be the same thing, they can also be separate ceremonies. The funeral is conducted for the grief of the living and the crossing is done to ensure that the loved ones find their way safely to the other side of the veil. The reason for separate ceremonies, sadly, is that although the deceased may be Wiccan, his or her family may follow a different faith and insist on doing it their way. When this occurs, the crossing is a separate matter done by coven members and close friends who had no problem with the faith of the Witch. Sometimes Wiccans are buried with their measure taken at the time of their initiation, the original candle ends from that ceremony, and a few of their favorite tools.

Crossings are also done in honor. For example, your aunt may not have been Wiccan, but you would like to do something to honor her passing in a way that is separate and private.

The ritual below is designed to help you and your family or friends deal with the separation that you have experienced by the loss of a loved one (including pets). If you need a full funeral rite, or a crossing format, you will find them in my book *Halloween*.

Ceremony of Remembrance

WHEN TO PERFORM: This is entirely up to you and should be done when you feel ready. Some covens prefer the full moon, where others find the new moon more appropriate. If you are really into magickal timing, you might want to think about the following:

1. When the moon is in Pisces (ruled by Jupiter and Neptune; both are considered spiritual energies).

2. In the hour of Jupiter, Venus, or the moon. (See the planetary hour section in part III under Astrology to learn how to calculate planetary hours.)

3. On Monday (the moon), Thursday (Jupiter), or Friday (Venus).

SUPPLIES: A bell (or drum); a candle (of the person's favorite color) for the altar; eight votive candles for the positions of the eight holidays on the Wheel of the Year (SEE DIAGRAM ON PAGE 104); a needfire candle (which will be the first lit); the deceased's favorite flowers; a picture; a cauldron; a bottle of holy water; the person's favorite drink and favorite food. Have a box of tissues handy (it is perfectly healthy to cry). Music, if you think this is appropriate. If possible, dress in white. Make a list of your deceased relatives and friends (this will be explained further in the body of the ritual). **Optional:** Illuminator candles.

PREPARATION: Cleanse the room with the four elements. Set up the altar with your choice of Wiccan tools. Set the cauldron (for transformation) in the center of the circle or the altar. Place the flowers, candle to the deceased, fire candle, picture, and food on your altar or on a table. Place the votive candles in their appropriate places around the room (you can put place cards by them if you forget which holiday goes where), or you can place everything on a large table (like a dining room table), turning the table itself into the altar. Devote the altar through prayer, light the fire candle, then mix the energies on the altar with your hands. Seal with an equal-armed cross.

THE RITUAL: Light illuminator candles. Cast your magick circle and call the quarters. If there are others in the room, stand in a circle holding hands. Invoke the Lord and Lady using any of the invocations in this book or one you have written yourself.

Stand in front of the picture, and say:

As the sacred Wheel of the Year spins slowly, blessing us with the gifts of transformation, so does the cycle of life, death, and rebirth also turn, allowing us to fulfill our destiny.

Say the person's name three times loudly. Then say:

Even though you have gone beyond the veil, we know that we can send these blessings to you.

Light each of the sabbat candles, repeating the name of the sabbat aloud, and then saying a gift that you are sending to the loved one—such as love, peace, harmony, rest, happiness, safe journey, and so on—with the flame of that candle, with the following procedure: Light the Yule candle from the fire candle. Carry the fire candle clockwise around the circle and place on the altar. Stand in front of the Yule candle and give the Yule blessing (below), then light the Candlemas candle from the Yule candle. Carry the Yule candle around the circle in a clockwise direction and replace in the Yule position. Stand in front of the Candlemas candle, give the blessing, then move to the Ostara candle, and so on. In this way each sabbat candle is lit from the last, beginning with Yule and moving around the circle in a clockwise direction, which builds the energy to send to the deceased. Blessings might include:

Yule: May the love of the divine be with you.

Candlemas: May your guide light your journey.

Ostara: May you find joy in your rebirth.

Beltane: May you receive our love and blessings.

Midsummer: May you find wisdom and empowerment.

Lammas: May you find forgiveness for all things.

Mabon: May you be purged of all unhappiness.

Samhain: May you rest in peace.

Pick up the Samhain candle and stand before the altar. In your own way, ask Spirit to carry your blessings to the individual. In the case of a pet, you might also ask that the spiritual caretaker of animals also be present to ensure the safety of the animal's spirit. Say the deceased's name three times, then light the pillar candle in front of their picture with the Samhain candle, and envision all the energy and blessings built into the ritual being released into their arms.

If you wish to move the deceased individual into the realm of your personal ancestral dead, you will now make the first offering by verbally listing your lineage and adding the person's name to the list. Each time you say a person's name, you will sprinkle holy water into the cauldron. If you do not wish to add them to your ancestral pantheon, you will still state the names of your ancestors but you will not add the deceased person's name—you will say their name later. If you are facilitating this ceremony for someone else (say the family of a friend), they need to give you a list of beloved friends and family who have passed away. It is this list you would intone during this portion of the ritual. The litany might go as follows:

I honor my great grandfather, Harold Crossing.
I honor my great grandmother, Mabel Crossing.
I honor my great grandfather, Charles Taylor.
I honor my great grandmother, Lucy Taylor.
I honor my grandmother, Christine Crossing.
I honor my grandmother, Louise Taylor.
I honor my uncle, Patrick Taylor.

I honor my pet, Joey.
I honor the Lord and Lady.
May they continue to bless the living
as well as the dead.

Add the deceased's favorite drink to the cauldron, honoring the newly deceased (this would be a second time you said their name if you added them to the ancestral pantheon). For example, "I honor my friend, Randy Boyer. May Spirit carry this act of honor to him. So mote it be."

When you are finished, thank Spirit (and the caretaker of pets, should the deceased be an animal), release the quarters, and then release the circle. Lay the food and flowers outside. Pour the contents of the cauldron on the ground. If you can, allow the candle(s) to burn completely. If your parents say that you aren't allowed to have candles in the house, then perhaps they will sit with you while you perform the ceremony. If you are in a college where there is a chapel, perhaps you could petition for use of the area.

Are They Really Gone?

Well, no. Sort of, but not exactly. Obviously they aren't here in the physical anymore, but that doesn't mean they can't communicate with you and can't help you if you've managed to dig a massive pit for yourself. Eventually, you may have a dream that they are okay, or receive a gift that reminds you of the deceased, smell their favorite perfume or aftershave in the room, or suddenly think of them out of the blue. In truth, they *are* communicating with you. If you open your mouth and start talking to them, they will hear you. The best book I have ever read on the subject is *Journey of Souls* by Dr. Michael Newton, and I recommend this book to individuals of every faith when they have lost someone dear. It is an amazing read.

Death of a Pet

The passing of a beloved pet is difficult to bear, and often occurs in the home. At first you would say, "Of course it would happen there"—however, this creates circumstances with which the humans of this century are not necessarily familiar. Many times, when people pass, they are in the hospital or they have been taken from us as a result of an accident, and the dying process may occur elsewhere. A pet, especially if he or she has a social personality, will most likely choose to leave while you or someone in the household is present and aware that the time for the journey has come. Even though extremely ill, some pets have been known to wait until their human friends have returned from vacation. The experience of watching a pet pass to the next world can be frightening and certainly emotionally upsetting. Our connections to our pets are so deeply ingrained that it feels like we have lost a beloved friend, sibling, or, in the case of adults, a child, and can be just as painful as if a person has died. You know there is nothing more you can do, and anger and frustration can rise to the surface that may result in an unexpected emotional avalanche that can affect you for days, months, or even years, depending on how much time you have spent in this world with your pet. Everyone must work through the passing at their own pace. There is no right way to deal with death. Each of us must come to terms with the cycle of life in their own time.

Many parents shield their children from the passing of both people and pets, but now that you are older you may choose to be present at the passing. Today, many veterinarians have arrangements that include coming to your house to help a pet on the journey, if they have been really sick. The most important thing you can do is mentally (or verbally, if you can talk) tell the pet that it is okay to go to the next world, send him or her loving energy, and have the courage to say good-bye. Crying is not babyish or stupid. Some Witches sage the area to create sacred space, and light white candles to help the pet move on; however, if you feel you are too upset to do these things, that's okay too. They will go to the right place regardless of what you do. If you feel very weak or like you are totally going to lose it, take a deep breath and mentally ask for help. When my beloved sheltie died I thought I would go insane, but I wanted to be strong for my kids. I took a deep breath and asked Spirit to help me—I really needed something right then! Immediately I was filled with the most pure, loving energy I have ever experienced, which enabled me to get a grip on my emotions and help my children through that difficult time.

Your family might be very helpful, or appear totally unfeeling. If they are not sympathetic it is probably because they may not understand the depth of your despair, or because they, too, don't know how to handle the passing of a beloved friend. All sorts of reactions may occur, from tears to arguments over silly things or dumb comments from siblings like, "Gee, Richard, it's only a stupid rat." There is nothing you can do about another person's response to death, but know in your heart that the passing was beautiful and filled with light and love. Death didn't come with a face of horror, but with splendor and peace, because death is the transition, not the event.

When the pet has gone on, you will want to bury him or her. Parents will often whisk the animal away for several reasons, and you might want to be aware of their logic before you lose your cool. Above all, they want to protect you and your feelings. The longer the animal is visible, the harder this emotional moment is for you, hence the more emotional it is for the parent. Not only are they upset at the loss, they are upset that you are upset. Their basic instinct is to protect you, and they will assert their right to do so. Too, since younger children are so used to holding stuffed animals, some find no difficulty in hanging on to the deceased pet. Therefore, if your younger sibling loses a pet, you might want to keep this in mind. Gently reassure them that the spirit of the animal is no longer there and give them time to physically and emotionally let go. Although you may think this strange, I believe that Spirit made the body in such a way as to decompose quickly on purpose so that we will not want to try to mistake it for the essence of the person. This is another reason that parents may wish to remove larger animals (cats and dogs) immediately. Your parents may insist on handling the burial, or they may allow you to participate. It helps to put toys and other favored objects with the body, and close the box (if you can) by yourself while saying goodbye. At this point you can hold a private ceremony or allow the burial to take place and then perform a ceremony. It all depends on how you feel.

Sometimes your pet will return a few days or weeks later in the form of very clear memories, a familiar sound, or you may think that you see your pet in one of his or her favorite places. You may have vivid dreams of seeing your pet in a happy situation. Although most individuals put such an experience down to wishful thinking, many magickal people believe that your pet is letting you know that he or she is okay.

Simple Passing Ceremony for a Pet
(In honor of Buddy the rat)

SUPPLIES: One purple candle; holy water; an Oreo cookie; one favored pet toy; stalks of fresh mint. ***Note:*** Purple is the color associated with the dead. The Oreo cookie, with its white and black coloring, stands for the darkness before the First Mother and the light of Spirit. (It also hap-

pened to be Buddy's favorite food.) Mint is used to banish negative energy as well as provide protection for the spirit of the deceased during his or her journey to the Summerland.

INSTRUCTIONS: Band the stalks of the mint together with string or a rubber band. Lightly crush the mint, once, in your hand. Dip the mint leaves in the holy water and sprinkle over the altar, then sprinkle around the area in a clockwise direction. Return to the altar. Sprinkle the candle (avoiding the wick). Hold the candle in your hands and close your eyes. Think of your pet being happy in an environment that he or she loved. In your mind, surround your pet with favorite toys and food. Know that your pet is safe and in the arms of the Goddess and God. Focus loving energy into the candle. Take a deep breath, relax, and open your eyes. Place the candle back on the altar and light, saying:

I love you and I release you to the happy, loving place where your spirit belongs.

Allow the candle to burn completely. Bury mint, candle end, food, and toy on your property, or place on the grave.

The day after your pet has passed away, you may not feel so good physically. You might experience a headache or an upset stomach, feel listless, want to sleep a lot, or be just plain sad. You may feel like you are walking in a dream world. All these things are natural and will pass quickly.

I'll leave you with a parting thought on this subject, and you can do with it what you like. Given the research of Dr. Michael Newton and his newest book *Destiny of Souls*, it is highly possible that you were there, on the other side, to welcome your pet. Dr. Newton believes that although a large part of our spiritual essence is in the physical body here on Earth, there is a portion of our spirit on the other side that does function, and provides a connection between the part of us here and the part of us there. He came to this conclusion by interviewing hundreds of subjects while they were under hypnosis and discovered that husbands, wives, and relatives still living will sometimes be present to welcome us on the other side at our own passing. If this is indeed the case, then your pet has not lost your loving energy at all, and he or she was not alone when crossing the veil. You were there.

Graduation Ritual

SUPPLIES: Choose a pillar or taper candle in either your favorite color or, if you are into astrology, you might want to match the color of the planet that ruled the day you were born. I was born on Tuesday, so my power color is red. If you know the day you were born, you can find your power color on pages 188–190. You will also need something that signifies your advancement—something you have earned. This could be a certificate, a badge, a hat, and so on. Other supplies include two sheets of laminating plastic (you can buy this at an office supply store) that are used to protect papers, photos, cards, etc.; a card wishing yourself success; one dried flower that matches either your power color or the desire for success and honor (SEE FLORAL TABLE BEGINNING ON PAGE 280); a photograph of yourself; a cornmeal or painted pentacle on a large ceramic dish, or a picture of a pentacle on a piece of 8 by 11-inch paper; your favorite incense; scissors.

TIMING: Full moon (representing harvest) or the new moon (representing beginnings).

SETUP: Cleanse, consecrate and empower all supplies (SEE PART IV). If you are using cornmeal, then you will most likely want to perform this ritual out-of-doors, where you can draw a large pentagram on the ground with it. If you are using the pentacle plate or the pentacle on a

piece of paper, you can set either of these items on your indoor altar. Place what you have earned in the center of the pentacle (this would be the hat, sash, certificate, etc.). Set the power candle at the top point of the pentacle. With careful thought, write a secret wish to yourself on the inside of the graduation card.

RITUAL: Light the incense and carry around the room or sacred area. Cast the circle and call the quarters. Walk to the center of your pentacle and stand in the God position.

Concentrate on your image of the God in your mind and feel yourself filling with the power and strength of the Master of the Universe. Take a deep breath and open your eyes. Stand in the Goddess position, opening your arms to the gifts and enchantments of the Mistress of the Universe. Feel Her move through your body. Take a deep breath and lower your arms, welcoming your connection to all that is.

Hold the power candle in your hands and think about your wondrous accomplishment. Be proud of yourself! Believe that the pathway ahead will be filled with joy and opportunity. Light the red candle in honor of your present success and to draw future positive energies toward you.

Peel the backing off of one of the laminated sheets. Artfully place the card of congratulations, flower, and your picture on the sticky side of the sheet. Once you are satisfied with the arrangement, peel the backing off the second laminated sheet and place it on top of your creation (sticky-side down and smooth side on top) to form your magickal success packet. As you smooth out the bubbles, believe that this smoothing process is helping to level out the road ahead. When you are finished, trim your new success packet and put in a safe place. Thank deity for all that you have accomplished and the help that you have received along the way. Be sure to ask for future success for yourself and for anyone who has assisted you. Dismiss the quarters and release the circle. If possible, allow the candle to burn completely, then bury the cool end somewhere on your property. After the ritual, store any memorabilia from the recent past and carefully pack it away.

When you reach the next milestone in your life, repeat the ceremony and make a new packet. With a paper punch, punch a hole in the top of both packets and tie them together with a ribbon that matches your power color. As your successes continue to grow, these packets can work together to launch you into the type of lifestyle that you imagine for yourself in the future.

Ritual

A ritual is a set of thoughts and movements geared to a single purpose. For example, many people have a morning ritual that includes a shower, choosing what clothes to wear, eating breakfast, and brushing their teeth (hopefully)— all this to prepare themselves for the day's activities. Rituals can become fond memories, something to hang on to when the going gets tough. For example, my husband often talks about his grandmother and her morning ritual—toast with a bit of jelly, a cup of tea, and the crossword puzzle in the paper. Remembering a ritual like this gives us security that all is right with the world (or at least it was when the event occurred). In religion, when you attend a ritual, you are combining a set of actions with the thoughts of God and spirituality. When you or your parents attend a church service, you are in essence taking part in the rituals of that faith. In Wicca, rather than saying, "I'm going to church

today," we say, "I'm attending ritual," or "I'm going to circle"—here, the words "ritual" and "circle" mean the same thing.

One part of ritual observed by most Wiccans is that of alternating joy and reverence in the circle. This technique—one moment light and amusing, the next solemn and thoughtful—gives balance to the proceedings. As a solitary, this balance isn't as obvious, as there isn't a group to dance with, or someone to make an amusing comment. For the solitary, inserting something he or she likes to do (singing, playing a musical instrument, even finding levity in one's own errors) can be akin to the mirth portion that one might experience in a group ritual. I know one solitary who spends about an hour taping songs to match portions of his ritual. One may be light, like a Celtic jig, followed by something that is a bit quieter and thought provoking. Not all groups, especially those that are particularly stuffy in their proceedings, allow laughter within the circle environment; therefore, if it is your first time visiting a group ritual, it's best to watch the others and follow their lead. Even if there is laughter and some of the members speak out with a joke or two, it is best if you remain silent at least the first time you attend because your humor may come at the wrong time without you realizing it. Hey, don't get all huffy on me—it can happen. At least if you read it here, you are forewarned.

Ritual Bath

When studying various magickal traditions, past and present, we find a common denominator in the ritual or cleansing bath often performed by practitioners before spellcasting or ceremony. The bath (or shower, if for some reason a bath isn't possible) is a process of cleansing body, mind, and spirit before walking into sacred space.

SUPPLIES: Scented soap to cleanse the body and hair; sponge or washcloth; a clean white towel; two white votive candles in holders; scented oil or perfume; clean clothing to put on after the bath or a clean robe. You can also mix cleansing herbs, put them in a coffee filter and staple it shut, then add this magickal packet to the bath water.

INSTRUCTIONS: The bath should not be so hot that you become ill, but it should be warm enough that you can at least soak for ten minutes. Draw a banishing pentagram with your finger over the water. Light the votive candles; be very careful of fire hazards, and keep them away from shower curtains. Turn out the bathroom lights. Say a prayer before you enter the water, asking Spirit to cleanse body, mind, and soul. Relax in the water. Close your eyes and allow all the frustrations of the day to seep out of your body. Take three deep breaths, imagining that as you exhale you are pushing negativity away from you and removing all blocks. Meditate for at least five minutes on issues you would like to cleanse from your life. Don't stress over them, just work on letting these things go. Open your eyes and cleanse your body with the soap and sponge, visualizing that, as you are washing your body, you are also cleansing your mind and spirit. Don't forget to wash your hair. Rinse body thoroughly. Leave tub and pat dry. Say a prayer of thanks as you put on your clothes/robe. Watch as the water drains from the tub, visualizing that all the negativity in your life is going down the drain with the water. Turn on the bathroom lights. Extinguish the candles. Clean out the tub, removing any oils, herbs, or other dirt deposits.

Ritual Clothing

When I was a kid, folks wore their "Sunday best" to church. Ritual attire included nice shoes, a good dress (or pants and shirts for the boys), a Sunday hat and Sunday gloves (okay, so I'm showing my wrinkles). The minister wore a robe (so you could tell him apart from the rest of the men). Dads wore suits. Moms were dressy. People had special clothing for baptism and confirmation. This, for that era and in that religion, was ritual dress.

In the Wiccan community today, there is no standard dress code, although different traditions may have guidelines. For example, black robes for initiations and elevations, and white robes for funerals. The idea of changing from street clothes to ritual garb is both psychological and practical; moving from daily life to the spiritual life through the act of altering one's attire touches on the psyche and wearing clothing that is cleansed and consecrated (after your spiritual bath) ensures that you won't carry any excess negativity into the circle. Where some groups require that you wear special cords and jewelry, other groups insist that all be equal within the circle environment and only the high priest/priestess may wear something different or unusual. There are groups where rank is not an issue and everyone wears what they like, or all wear the same color but in different styles, and therefore you really have no idea what rank anyone is. Then there are groups where individuals of different elevations wear matching colors indicative of their status. As robes are not always practical, there are also magickal people who may wear something different or special for ritual, but it doesn't flap around and threaten to snare every candle flame in the room. Finally, there are those that don't wear anything at all, called skyclad. Although prominent in Gardner's time due to his influence, skyclad has fallen out of favor in most Wiccan groups. Like other Wiccan magickal tools, robes, cords, vestments, and jewelry should be cleaned frequently, then cleansed, consecrated, and blessed before use.

Ritual Structure

Wiccans perform rituals for two basic reasons:

- Acts of honor.

- Working magick.

Acts of honor include wiccanings (baptism), handfastings (marriages), crossings (funerals), dedications, initiations, and elevations in one's group, and the eight High Holy Days (called sabbats).

Working magick might include healing circles,[36] esbats, training classes, and spellcasting.

Just like other religions have prayer books and formats on how to conduct their services, Wiccans also have a vast collection of rituals from which they can draw ideas. When they find a ritual they like, they often write it down in their own Book of Shadows (BOS) (SEE PART II). However, with today's standards in copyright protection, many teachers are training their students to write their own rituals, using a basic ritual outline and building from there.

There are two main ritual formats, structured and spontaneous. A structured ritual is one that is preplanned and written out in a step-by-step procedure that the seeker can follow while doing the ritual. These structured rituals also include prep work—what supplies are needed, a statement of purpose, the best timing for performance, and so on. A spontaneous ritual follows basic ritual structure (SEE PAGE 23); however, songs, poems, or other work comes from the heart, and a written format is unnecessary. Although this book does not cover Craft group government in-depth, you do need to know that covens often have standard rituals that they have chosen to perform on a repetitive basis, especially when celebrating acts of honor. For example, all dedication, initiation, and elevation rituals might follow the same format and structure, no matter how many times they are performed. The repetition of these ceremonies ensures that everyone is on the same page, which helps to solidify the group mind and builds an unbroken line of energy from the earliest initiate to the most recent. This line of energy is called lineage, and many initiated Crafters are required to know their lineage, or who has gone before them, by heart, back to the individual who began the tradition.

In this book, you will find several rituals, including rites of passage like belly blessing for pregnant mothers, wiccaning, teen rite of passage, the crossing, graduation ceremony, esbat, sabbat, and spellcasting, and so on. In the Seeker Ceremonies section (SEE PAGE 89), you will find the teen seeker ceremony and the self-dedication ceremony. If you already have *Teen Witch*, then the teen seeker ceremony isn't new to you; however, to ensure this book is complete, I have reprinted it below. Also, the dedication ceremony provided here is a bit different than the one given in *To Ride a Silver Broomstick*.

Sabbats

The modern sabbat ritual (representing one of the eight High Holy Days) can be as intricate or as simple as you desire. The ceremony's main function is to honor the season and the gods, and to ask for their harmonious intervention in our lives in the coming months. Each ritual celebrates one portion of the cycle of life:

- Yule and Candlemas are inception.

- Beltane and Ostara are birth and growth.

- Midsummer is maturity.

- Lammas and Mabon are harvest.

- Samhain is death and its subsequent spiritual transformation.

These holidays are both original and reconstructionist, depending upon the mythos (legends) you choose, which is sometimes confusing to the new student. Each sabbat can have several stories attached to it, some ancient and others relatively modern. In large Wiccan groups, ritual drama may be a significant portion of the ritual, where members act out characters or deities, much like in a play, complete with props and techno-marvels. I have witnessed sabbats where the sets, costumes, props, and other devices cost well into the thousands, and a Georgian group did so well when performing in Texas that many in the audience really thought that the death of the god included the demise of the actor (my husband and I can attest to the fact that he was alive and breathing an hour later, quite happy in the company of his wife). Conversely, I've been to celebrations where the only expense entailed a jug of apple juice, a box of cookies, and a few candles—the mind and imagination of the Witch being the primary focus. Neither type of ritual could be considered better than the other, as both were most fulfilling and both the rituals in some way or another focused on raising energy. You will also find differences in altar placement. Where some groups keep their altar in the same area all year long, others move the altar to match the holiday (as on the wheel pictured at the beginning of this section). There are those Witches who dispense with all that movement and simply place the altar in the center of the circle. Quarter calls may also differ. For example, a single group may always start at the north to open the quarters for esbats, but choose the quarter that most matches the season from which to begin their sabbat ceremonies.

Most sabbats are followed by a feast, where each member brings something to eat. This can be as extravagant as a full meal or as simple as a collection of munchies. Where esbats are performed primarily at night (lunar workings), many sabbat celebrations (solar holidays) are done during the daylight hours, if the group has the opportunity to meet at that time, save for Samhain, which is primarily done in the evening. Though, again, there is no "right" time to perform a sabbat celebration, unless you are following astrological correspondences and timing your ritual to the moment that the sun crosses over the fifteen-degree mark of the appropriate sign:

Samhain: Sun is at 15 degrees Scorpio (water)

Candlemas: Sun is at 15 degrees Aquarius (air)

Beltane: Sun is at 15 degrees Taurus (earth)

Lammas: Sun is at 15 degrees Leo (fire)

Notice that these are the four fixed signs of the zodiac, with each of the elements represented in the festival year. The idea here is to hold on to one's fortune, happiness, and love, making it last as long as possible. These festivals are also known as the fire festivals, and some call them the cross-quarter festivals. They are best known in history for their association with people lighting bonfires atop hills in the hope of kindling the light of Spirit within people's hearts and warding off any negativity through the purification of the fire. The other four holidays are definitely solar driven:

Winter Solstice (Yule): December 21 (or around that time) when the sun is at 1 degree Capricorn (earth)

Spring Equinox (Ostara): March 21 (or around that time) when the sun is at 1 degree Aries (fire)

Summer Solstice (Midsummer): June 21 (or around that time) when the sun is at 1 degree of Cancer (water)

Fall Equinox (Mabon): September 21 (or around that time) when the sun is at 1 degree Libra (air)

Notice that these are the cardinal signs of the zodiac, and are each (in their own way) considered festivals of beginnings, especially related to any work regarding their element (earth, air, water, fire). Again, there is one festival for each element. These celebrations are sometimes called the quarter festivals.

After you have worked with both types of High Holy Days (fire festivals and quarter festivals), you will begin to see unique differences in the categories. The fire festivals occur during midsign (in the middle of an astrological sign) and seem to demand that you make changes and adjustments in your life (work on the "old"), where the quarter festivals fall in sign transition (when the sun is leaving one astrological sign and entering another) and encourage changes toward the "new." Quarter festivals bring their energy into your home environment approximately one full week before the astrological occurrence actually takes place. For example, you may buy a new computer when the sun is in Gemini (communication) and place it in your dining room for family use as the sun moves into Cancer (home environment) without even realizing it. The human condition is very much tuned to these eight High Holy Days, even though you may not recognize the influences.

Although there are a few groups in the Craft that use the same ceremony for every sabbat, most delight in researching history to discover what "neat new thing" they can incorporate into their ceremonies, lending variety to the seasonal celebrations as well as introducing historical trivia to coven members. Some groups require beginning students to take on this challenge. In cohesive groups that have many covens in one sect (such as the Black Forest), covens may actually compete to see who can come up with the most inventive sabbat of the year. Where esbats may be single-coven oriented, sabbats may become clan gatherings. The sabbats are also conducive to public rituals. Where you may not be invited to attend a local group's esbat or moon rituals, they may open the doors for the High Holy Days. Check your local magickal or occult shop to see if they hold open celebrations.

The remainder of this section includes a basic solitary sabbat ritual format, and briefly covers the eight High Holy Days with minimal historical information that matches the ritual provided. There is such an abundance of lore that could be incorporated in any one ceremony, there just isn't room enough here. At the end of this section is a suggested reading list, if you would like to investigate these holidays further. Please note that in some traditions the day "officially" celebrated may be different, and I've tried to make note of that under each holiday. In reality, many of the holiday celebrations historically spanned several days. In the Wheel of the Year, the Craft shows its agrarian roots by matching the seasons to agricultural practices and climate with teachings of inception, birth, growth, maturity, transformation, harvest, death, and rebirth. It is this cycle that I have tried to present here.

Basic Solitary Sabbat Ritual Format

SUPPLIES: Altar and setup (earth, air, fire, water, illuminator candles). Tools such as the athame or wand are up to you. Candles or other representations positioned at the four quarters (east, south, west, and north)—colors are your choice. Additional supplies will depend on the amount of time you have and how creative you wish to make your ceremony.

STEP ONE: Sweep area with a broom. Cleanse the ritual space by carrying a representation of the four elements around the area in a clockwise movement, working with one element at a time. Place any object of seasonal honor on the altar, along with the communion vessels and your Book of Shadows.

STEP TWO: Open altar energies by passing the four elements over the altar and intoning a personal blessing, then tap the altar five times—once for each element, and once for Spirit.

STEP THREE: Light the illuminator candles on the altar.

STEP FOUR: Cast the magick circle (clockwise) using the following sabbat circlecasting or one of your choice.

Tides of the season, ebb and flow
(Tap the altar once, stating the name of
the holiday energy to be invoked.)
From spring's first light to autumn's glow.
(Hold your hands over the altar.)
Deosil around from birth to death
(Begin at the north and start to walk
clockwise around the circle.)
Legends, myths, and lore connect.
(You should be back at the north.)
Solar fire, sun's bright burning
(Lift the red fire candle on the altar
and look skyward.)
Purify the Great Wheel turning.
(Return candle to altar.)
Winds of north to carry the flame
(Begin walking from the north
to the east.)
The mists of eons, call the name.
(Say the name of the holiday aloud.)
East and south, the west inspire
(Pause the wording at each direction as
you continue around the circle.)

Energy spirals ever higher!
(Return to the north.)
The circle rises and marks rebirth
(Begin the third pass around the circle.)
As seasons change and kiss the earth.
(Return to the north.)
From seed and plough to harvest home
(Hold your hands over the altar.)
To starry vault and standing stone
(At the north, point upward.)
This sabbat circle thrice around
(Visualize the complete circle.)
I seal thee now from sky to ground!
(Bring your arm down and
stamp the floor with your foot.)

STEP FIVE: Light the quarter candles and call the quarters.

Winds of the (name of holiday) *north,*
attend, acknowledge, and proclaim!
Winds of the (name of holiday) *east,*
attend, acknowledge, and proclaim!
Winds of the (name of holiday) *south, at-*
tend, acknowledge, and proclaim!
Winds of the (name of holiday) *west, at-*
tend, acknowledge, and proclaim!
Winds of the (name of holiday) *Spirit,*
fill this circle with thy love and protection![37]

STEP SIX: Read the Charge of the Goddess (PAGE 5).

STEP SEVEN: Invoke your ancestors by reading their names and declaring your honor for them.

STEP EIGHT: Read the sabbat invocations given under the individual sabbats in this section.

STEP NINE: State intent of ritual aloud, along with your personal understanding of the holiday you are celebrating. This can be through poetry, a story, or even through meditation, and adds your own individual creativity to the ritual.

STEP TEN: Draw down the sun (optional). However, do not stare directly into the sun. Lift your head with eyes closed.

STEP ELEVEN: Perform any magickal work.

STEP TWELVE: Take communion (see page 14).

STEP THIRTEEN: Perform the offering to the gods. This is the sabbat fire offering:

Upon the wings of fiery flame
I give this offering in Goddess' name.
(Pour offering into fire.)

STEP FOURTEEN: Thank deity.

STEP FIFTEEN: Thank and release the quarters, extinguish quarter candles at the release of each quarter—remember to begin in the west if you started in the north, moving widdershins (counterclockwise).

Winds of the Spirit of (name the holiday), *blessings upon you! I release thee upon thy way till next we meet again! Winds of* (name the holiday) *west, blessings upon you! I release thee upon thy way till next we meet again! Winds of* (name the holiday) *south, blessings upon you! I release thee upon thy way till next we meet again! Winds of* (name the holiday) *east, blessings upon you! I release thee upon thy way till next we meet again! Winds of* (name the holiday) *north, blessings upon you! I release thee upon thy way till next we meet again!*

STEP SIXTEEN: Release magick circle (counterclockwise).

O Great Circle of Sabbat Art, attend me no more this day but be released into—(most likely into the objects made in the spellworking if they

were designed to draw things to you. If you have no items, and you do not wish to put the energy into wand, rod, staff, or athame, then simply say *"released back to Spirit"*).

STEP SEVENTEEN: Seal altar energies by tapping once on the altar and extinguishing illuminator candles.

STEP EIGHTEEN: Clean up and offer libation bowl out-of-doors.

Samhain / Celtic New Year

Other names: Hallowmas, All Hallow's Eve, Halloween, Samhuinn.

Date: October 31, November 2, November 4, or when the sun is at 15 degrees Scorpio.

Meaning of the word: Celtic, meaning "Summer's End." There is no historical record of a Celtic God called Samhain or Lord of the Dead—this was erroneously coined by researchers in the 1700s.

Primary focus: Transformation, regeneration, honoring the dead, divination, honoring the harvest, preparing for the winter.

Age of holiday: Second oldest unbroken holiday in the European world—approximate age is 6,000 years.[38]

Popular mythos: Cerridwen's Cauldron of Transformation; Feeding the Morrigan; Sniggling the Cailleach; Festival of the Dark Goddess.

Astrological sign: 15 degrees Scorpio.

Planetary ruler: Pluto (modern) or Mars (classical).

No one has described Samhain better to the public than Ronald Hutton, professor at the University of Bristol. With his kind permission, the following is taken from his excellent book, *The Stations of the Sun:*

Hallowe'en developed from the Celtic feast of Samhain (pronounced "sow-in"), which marked the end of summer and the beginning of winter. For the Celts, Samhain was the beginning of the year and the cycle of the seasons. Samhain was a time when the Celts acknowledged the beginning and the ending of all things. As they looked to nature, they saw the falling of the leaves from the trees, the coming of winter and death. It was a time when they turned to their Gods and Goddesses seeking to understand the turning cycles of life and death. Here, on the threshold of the cold barren winter months, it was also a time of feasting and celebration as the weakest animals were culled to preserve valuable foodstuffs, and provide food to last until the following spring. . . . For the Celts, Samhain was a time when the gates between this world and the next were open. It was a time of communion with the spirits of the dead, who, like the wild autumnal winds, were free to roam the earth. At Samhain, the Celts called upon their ancestors, who might bring warnings and guidance to help in the year to come.[39]

SAMHAIN INVOCATION

*Forests misty, dark and deep
the door between the worlds release
loved ones, family, favored pets
to join me in this evening's fest.
The birth of new, the death of old
I will this cycle to unfold.
Each leaf that drifts upon the ground
will bury all that is unsound
and in its place will rise anew
the gift of love the whole year through.
With harvest gold and autumn sun
I reap the best that I have done.
And as the days grow shorter still
with longer nights and winter's chill*

*I'll work to build a better place
for every soul and human race.
Wild autumn winds and crone's dark voice
speak to me of wisdom's choice
let me hear your words of fate
so I know which path to take!
Those of you who went before
speak to me from crossroad's door
whisper words of love and care
let me know that you are there.*

Insert divinatory work here, then continue with the remainder of the ritual.

MAGICKAL IDEAS FOR YOUR SAMHAIN SABBAT RITUAL

- Carve a pumpkin and empower it to repel negativity.

- Build or erect a shrine to your ancestors.

- Add divination to your ritual.

- Fill a small plastic pumpkin with gold-wrapped candy and empower for prosperity.

- Research your family history and make a litany out of the names for your ritual.

- Make a family photo album or poster to place in your room. Bless during ritual for family harmony.

- Set a place at the dinner table for the recently deceased. If the lost one is a pet, place their favorite food on a plate and put where their bowls used to be.

- Place small jack-o'-lanterns at the four quarters.

- Place crossed brooms at the four quarters.

- Build your altar out of hay bales.

- Visit the cemetery and place flowers on the graves of deceased loved ones.

- Remember that Samhain is a fire festival that signals personal closures and occurs in Scorpio, a mutable, watery sign that has the ability to rebuild what is needed and toss what is not. Ruled by Pluto and Mars (modern and classical planetary rulers of the sign, respectively), there is much you can accomplish during this time period.

Yule / Winter Solstice

Other names: Mean Geimhridh, Alban Arthuan, Modranicht (Mother Night).

Date: December 20, 21, or 22, depending upon the calendar. Sun at 1 degree Capricorn.

Meaning of the word: *Yule* means "wheel" (Scandinavian derivation); *solstice* means "the sun stands still."

Primary ritual focus: Rebirth and renewal, "saining" or "blessings" in ritual form, burning of the Yule log.

Age of holiday: Wooden pillars throughout Europe aligned with the rising sun of the winter solstice have been recently dated to 3200–3000 B.C. (Newgrange in Ireland, Maes Howe in Scotland, Stonehenge and the Dorset Cursus in Britain), enabling us to currently calculate this this holiday to be at least 5,000 years old.

Popular mythos: Battle of Oak and Holly King (Oak King wins), Divine King, the Stag and the Wolf; Festival of the Dark God as seen in the German Belsnickle.

Astrological sign: 1 degree Capricorn; earth; cardinal.

Planetary Ruler: Saturn.

It was a custom of the Pagans to celebrate on the same 25 December the birthday of the sun, at which they kindled lights in token of festivity. In these solemnities and revelries the Christians also took part. Accordingly, when the doctors of the Church perceived that the Christians had a leaning to this festival, they took counsel and resolved that the true Nativity should be solemnized on that day—Scriptor Syrus, fourth century A.D.[40]

Thus Christmas began, and the Dark God of the Pagans, represented by the first stranger to set foot in one's house bearing gifts, is the surrogate for Cernunnos, Herne the Hunter, and Old Nick, who grew into the character of Santa Claus. Yet the celebration of winter solstice is far older than the fourth century.

The word "Yule" is of Scandinavian origin, and the Yule log is the domestic counterpart of the communal Yule bonfire.[41] Normally made of oak (sometimes ash), the log was originally dedicated to the Teutonic Thor, god of courage and fire. It was his job to dispel the cold and dark of the harsh northern winters and bring the warmth of the sun back to the people. The Yule log, therefore, was burned in sympathetic magick, hoping to inspire the god to share his blessings and bring back the sun. Decorated with ivy, ribbons, and evergreens, the log was then blessed with holy water, ale, or wine (the blood of the mother) to bring manifestation. The log was lit with a piece of last year's log to close the cycle of the season from one Yule to the next. Never allowed to burn completely, pieces were saved as a charm against misfortune over the coming months.

YULE INVOCATION

*Morning light will flood the chamber
—winter solstice sun.
Energy unfolding,
Saturn's rule has just begun.
Crystals formed of ice and frost
freeze field and forest green.*

While Mighty Oak and Holly
fight for favors from our Queen.
The Great Wheel brings conception,
birth, and death as days of yore.
Each bonfire on a leyline
honors what has gone before.
Seven planets, seven spheres,
seven gates swing open.
I lift my arms and call the charge
the incantation spoken!
I conjure water spirits,
pour forth the sacred winds
come hither, O great fire!
The magick now begins!
Solar vapors, starry heavens
clouds and earth and waves
unite in your perfection
on this shortest solstice day!
I hold the key of secrets
and the phantoms will avail
the crossroads shimmer open
as the rod connects to grail.
Seven planets, seven spheres,
seven gates swing open.
I lift my arms and call the charge
the incantation spoken!
Beribboned Yule logs burning
each spark a blessing brings.
Red and green, the sacred blood
of past and future kings.
Mistletoe and bayberry,
winter's leaves and resin.
Spice and myrrh and evergreen
connect the Earth to heaven.
Through scented smoke and sacred prayer
I manifest good will.
Bring peace and joy to hearth and home

and every wish fulfill.
Seven planets, seven spheres,
seven gates swing open.
I lift my arms and call the charge
the incantation spoken!

MAGICKAL IDEAS FOR YOUR YULE SABBAT RITUAL

- Make your own Yule log. (If you don't have a fireplace, you can carve holes in a log and insert metal tea candle cups.) Decorate with evergreens, ribbons, and ivy.

- Empower mistletoe for healing and prosperity.

- Make puppets or statues to represent the Oak and Holly Kings. Place them on the altar or put on a skit for younger members of your household.

- Research the history of St. Nick (*When Santa Was a Shaman* by Joseph Cusamano is a good start) and the Christmas/Yule tree.

- Empower Yule and Christmas cards with loving energy.

- Empower Yule tree ornaments for prosperity.

- Empower all gifts you give this season with love and happiness.

- Build a Yule altar to honor the spirits of the wolf and the stag.

- Find out what the Belsnickle is and how he fits into the magickal German Yule.

- Recognize that Yule is a time of closure, especially in relation to solar-driven activities in your life—groups and organizations, major work projects, corporations, etc. Gracefully let go of those things that are no longer needed. Add meditation and prayer, tuned to the lowest ebb of solar energies, to your daily activities over this period.

- Begin or keep family traditions associated to the season.

- Yule occurs at the transition of Sagittarius to Capricorn—from a mutable fire sign to an earthy cardinal one. Capricorn, ruled by Saturn, gives us the authority, strength, and business acumen to make wise decisions about our future.

Imbolc

Other names: Candlemas, Oimealg, Imbolg, Brigantia, Lupercus, Disting, Lupercalia.

Date: February 2, or when the sun is at 15 degrees Aquarius.

Meaning of the word: *Imbolc* means "in milk."

Primary ritual focus: New growth, end of winter, rituals of purification, offerings to deity, candle rituals.

Age of holiday: Unknown.

Popular mythos: Pouring milk on the ground, associated with the goddess Brigit; laying the Cailleach to rest; Lupercus (wolf god in Italian Witchcraft).

Astrological sign: 15 degrees Aquarius.

Planetary ruler: Saturn (classical astrology), Uranus (modern astrology).

In Celtic legend, the months from Hallowmas to Candlemas (called the "months of the little sun") were ruled by the Cailleach or, as she is sometimes called, the Cailleach Bheur, a Scottish female deity that begins winter by washing her plaid in a whirlpool. The Cailleach is not a lady to tangle with, as she is depicted as a wild hag with a venomous temper who hurries about with a magick wand in her hand, switching the grass and blasting vegetation to unite the forces of sun, dew, and rain.[42] Her rages are the spring storms. At Imbolc she leaves by raising the tempests in her wake. Bried, or Brigit, on the other hand, a far more sensible goddess of healing, poetry, and the forging of fire, extends her blessings on this day, and it is to her that most generic and traditional Wiccan groups pay homage.

IMBOLC/CANDLEMAS INVOCATION

Coronet of candles, each flame a golden jewel
Saturn Lord withdraws his cloak
yet retains his rule.
Lambs bleat season's greetings
spring's essence on their breath
the sun pays homage to the sky
in Aquarius.
The Lord and Lady dance the waltz
within the magick round
to banish all that isn't pure
and prime the sacred ground.
The Cailleach swirls her tempest skirts
to raise the season's storms
that which lies within her wake
will surely be reborn.
The time has come for tilling
to arrange for harvest's gain
the right amount of seed and skill
of wind and sacred rain
are needed to perform the task
of planning for my future
I conjure such by Breid's bright word
and nothing will refute her.
The cat that leaps is not
the cat that lands upon the stair
I conjure things that others think
appear from thinnest air
yet superimposition reigns
my choice a pattern set.
(Insert what you wish for here.)
My power grows, the light ignites
desires manifest!

MAGICKAL IDEAS FOR YOUR IMBOLC SABBAT RITUAL

- Add a circle of white candles to the altar setup, each one representing a goal you would like to achieve in the coming year. Empower, then light during ritual.

- Banish winter by burning paper snowflakes (carefully, of course).

- Empower ice to banish negativity. As the ice melts, so the negativity will drain away. Pour water off your property.

- Plant seeds to be cared for indoors, or buy an indoor plant and make friends!

- Bless your pet and give him or her a safe amulet for his or her collar, or place in a protected area on the cage (for smaller animals).

- Purify the house with a house blessing ritual incorporated into the sabbat, or do one separately.

- In ritual, offer milk to the gods, then pour outdoors on the ground, or leave in a bowl for the animals.

- Do a visionquest/meditation on the wolf totem.

- Imbolc is a fire festival falling in the fixed astrological air sign of Aquarius. The magick that you do during this time period will have long-lasting consequences. Uranus and Saturn (modern and classical planetary rulers, respectively) bring the ability to make sudden changes, reach for rewards, and learn how to interact with authority figures.

Ostara/Spring Equinox

Other names: Ostara, Ostre, Mean Earraigh, Alban Eiler, Pasch, Caisg, Pesse.

Date: March 20, 21, or 22, depending upon the calendar. When the sun reaches 1 degree Aries.

Meaning of the word: Germanic dawn deity meaning "the month of beginnings or the month of openings."[43]

Primary ritual focus: Fertility, sunrise ceremonies, offerings to the goddess of spring.

Age of holiday: 3000 B.C. or older.

Popular mythos: Return of the goddess from the underworld (Persephone).

Astrological sign: 1 degree Aries; fire; fixed.

Planetary ruler: Mars.

The custom of giving eggs on Ostara was known to the early Egyptians, Persians, Greeks, Romans, and Gauls. The symbol of life, the egg stands for our cosmic universe. The practice of coloring these eggs also dates back to ancient civilizations. The Persians dyed theirs red, where folks in other countries chose a variety of colors obtained by boiling the eggs with flowers or vegetables to achieve unique coloring.[44] From foodstuff and symbol of new life to courtly art object to household decoration to focus for juvenile games, the Easter egg has traveled a very long way.[45]

OSTARA INVOCATION

Ouroborus tells us the beginning has no end
Alpha and Omega—all reside within.
Pisces swims beyond the veil
Aries on the rise.
Mars becomes the focal point
capturing the prize.
The moon slips through her mansions
dancing in the signs
stars are fixed yet activate
the treasures of the mind.

The air is filled with harmony
of plant and bloom and bud
each egg foretells the birthing
of peace, and joy, and love.
Persephone emerges as winter falls away
Mother Earth rejoices—
her daughter's come to stay.
As days grow long and nights are warm
the Goddess reigns supreme
Her power rises in my blood
I command all things unseen!
Magick symbols, knots and cords
wand and staff and blade
earth and water, fire and air
become the Witch's trade.
I am the ground, the sea, the sky
the breezes springtime sweet
gods and spirits dance the round
within this circle meet.
I conjure thee, O leaves of spring
hyacinth and myrtle
roses, lilacs, lavender
black earth, warm and fertile.
Gifts of Gaia, Green Man rule
my wishes come to form
good fortune roots within my world
prosperity is born!

MAGICKAL IDEAS FOR YOUR OSTARA SABBAT RITUAL

- Color and empower Oestre eggs for health, wealth, and prosperity.

- Celebrate the return of the Goddess by conjuring potted plants and giving them to friends and loved ones.

- Incorporate chocolate into your Ostara ritual.

- Review the items in your magickal cabinet or box and replace what is needed. Empower the supplies during the Ostara ritual.

- Bless seeds for the garden.

- Hold your ritual at dawn.

- Ostara (spring equinox) is solar driven. The sun moves from mutable, watery Pisces to cardinal, fiery Aries. Aries is a great "starter" sign, but it manages to poop out along the way. Any magick done while the sun or moon is in Aries should be supplemented with other workings later on.

Beltane/May Day

Other names: Valpurga, Mean Earraigh, Bealteinne, Beltaine, Beltainne, Roodmas, Calin Mai.

Date: May 1 or when the sun is at 15 degrees Taurus.

Meaning of the word: Beltane means "bright fire" or "lucky fire."

Primary ritual focus: Appearance of the matured Horned God, fertility, protection of animals and gardens, leaping the fire for a fortunate summer, love magicks.

Age of holiday: Said to be the oldest known holiday.

Popular mythos: Maypole dancing,[46] tenuous link to the Celtic Belenus.

Astrological sign: 15 degrees Taurus; earth; fixed.

Planetary ruler: Venus.

Of the seasonal European festivals, Beltane and Samhain, the two great fire festivals, seem to have held the most cultural and religious focus. May Day observances are thought to be drawn from two sources: the fire rites from Celtic tradition, and the flower rites from the Roman Floralia.[47] In Celtic tradition, the night before Beltane, all the fires in the land were doused. A little before dawn the people would gather the nine sacred woods and prepare them for the birthing of the new fire, which was thought to purify the air of all evil forces. In many areas, a predawn procession began that reached its culmination on the hilltops. As the people watched, the fires were kindled at the rising of the sun, and as the flames leapt, the people walked deosil around the bonfire three times. Farm animals were sometimes paraded between the fires to remove any curses or sickness and protect them over the summer season. In some areas of Europe, people would leap over the flames of a small fire so that they, too, could be purified. Torches lit from the Beltane fire were taken home to light the new fires of the year. Libations of milk, butter, eggs, and bread (*bonnach Bealltain*) were offered to the fire with incantations (pre-Christian) or prayers (during the Christian reign) in hopes that the growing season would be a good one.[48]

European practices included tying a wand of rowan and hanging it above the door, and collecting ashes from the Beltane fire and placing them on the forehead to purify the body and bring good luck. Water collected from wells or cupped stones to catch the morning dew, called May dew, was believed to be especially powerful for holy water, and was sprinkled about the home to ensure good fortune, health, and happiness. Today, in some group rituals, the sacred fire is made to dance in a deosil spiral in honor of the Beltane purification rite.

BELTANE INVOCATION

Light a fire in a cauldron. Turn to the east, and say:

Out of the east the sun wells and whitens, the darkness trembles into light, and the stars are extinguished like the lamps of a human city. The whiteness brightens into silver, the silver warms into gold, the gold kindles into pure and living fire, and the face of the east is covered with elemental scarlet. The day draws its first breath, steady and chill, and for leagues around, the woods and valleys will sigh and shiver. From every side the shadows will leap from their ambush and fall prone. The day of prosperity has come![49] *This I give to thee, O sacred fire, so that I and my family shall be spared from all evil.*

Walk around the cauldron three times, then repeat the following invocation:

Maypole rises to the heavens
lengths of colored ribbon
flutter in the morning sunlight
tokens kept and given.
Costumed lords and ladies
step quick in deosil round
weaving love and harmony
as the sun goes down.

Circle in to touch the sky, and out to manifest
spiral dance around the ring
grant me my request!

Venus rules, her passions deep
in love and games of war
Taurus vows that he will keep
great riches at the door.
Cupid's bow is pointed to shoot
right through the heart
Aphrodite's scented lips breathe
"Romance is an art."

Circle in to touch the sky, and out to manifest
spiral dance around the ring
grant me my request!

The maypole is the World Tree
Poteau Mitan of lore
that draws from ebony oceans
stars to earthen shore
and carries power to the dance
through streamers of each hue
the spark of life that is required
to make a Witch's brew.

Circle in to touch the sky, and out to manifest
spiral dance around the ring
grant me my request!

The first dew of the morning
and rowan on the ledge
are secrets of the season
renewing each year's pledge
of joy and peace within my home
prosperity and more
magick thunders from my palms
and penetrates the core.

Circle in to touch the sky, and out to manifest
spiral dance around the ring
grant me my request!

Deosil thrice around the bonfire
leap the roaring flame
cast off the old and birth the new
in God and Goddess' name.
Protection for the animals
good fortune, healing too
Bonnach Bealltain, an offering
to make my dreams come true.

Circle in to touch the sky, and out to manifest
spiral dance around the ring
grant me my request!

MAGICKAL IDEAS FOR YOUR BELTANE RITUAL

- Erect your own maypole using a Christmas tree stand and a large pole. Decorate with ribbons.

- Hang prayer ribbons on the trees and bushes on your property.

- Sew ribbons onto a white handkerchief, then empower each ribbon for a different goal or wish. Keep the handkerchief safe until all the wishes are granted.

- Collect the morning dew for magickal use.

- Hang a branch of rowan tied with red thread above your bedroom door for protection.

- Add spells for self-esteem and self-love to your Beltane ritual.

- Bless your garden or the nearest field.

- Beltane occurs when the sun is in the earthy, fixed sign of Taurus. Any magick done now will last (and work hard) for a long time. This is an excellent time of the year for prosperity work, for adding to the stability of your lifestyle, and making those needed repairs around the home.

Midsummer/Summer Solstice

Other names: Litha, Alban Heruin, Mean Samhraidh.

Date: June 20, 21, or 22, depending upon the calendar. When the sun is at 1 degree Cancer.

Meaning of the word: *Litha* means "moon."

Primary ritual focus: Love, marriage, divination.

Age of holiday: Counterpart of Yule; at least 10,000 years old.

Popular mythos: Primary festival of the Horned God, Battle of Oak and Holly King (Holly King wins), Scandinavian Baldur (god of light), the descent of the God or Goddess.

Astrological sign: 1 degree Cancer; cardinal; water.

Planetary ruler: Moon.

In Aberdeen in 1745, a reverend wrote, "I never saw so many bonfires . . ."[50]

At Midsummer the sun is at the height of its strength and, as with the other quarter festivals, the main element used in popular custom was fire, which has especially strong roots with the Teutonic peoples (German, Norse, Scandinavian, and so on). Reports of bonfires on the hilltops and even in the streets were prevalent during European medieval times, and the celebration gave a great excuse for a major party.

> *They wore splendid costumes and carried pails of fire hung from poles. By the early sixteenth century the local parades had grown into one grand consolidated procession 4,000 strong, including the corporation and the livery companies and featuring morris dancers, model giants, and pageants. They carried so many torches that, according to a later writer, they released "A thousand sparks dispersed throughout the sky/ Which like to wandering stars about did fly/ Whose wholesome heat purging the air/consumes the Earth's unwholesome vapours, fogs, and fumes."*[51]

In keeping with Teutonic magicks, water also features prominently in the Midsummer festival (fire and ice = fire and water), and whether we are talking about the Greek Persephone descending into the underworld, Egyptian Isis going there to save Osiris, or Baldur's descent into the lower worlds from Asgard, the theme of descent is extremely prominent in this festival. In the Craft, the descent is our journey into ourselves in an effort to see our inner being clearly and change the things about ourselves that we feel should be different or better. The second-degree ceremony in many traditional groups is primarily about this type of descent and our desire to be the best that we can be.

In keeping with the ritual given here, the wheel itself was a major focus of public ceremonies and was often set afire, as well as the practice of gathering the dew of the morning (as on Beltane) for health and continued happiness. Again, we see the elemental representations of fire and water. Branches of birch were also cut down and hung over doorways to ensure protection of the household. A mixture of yarrow, vervain, fern, and St. John's Wort was dried, powdered, and thrown into the fire. The length, breadth, and color of the flames were considered before the future was foretold.

MIDSUMMER INVOCATION

Gemini to Cancer
the moon becomes the Queen
mighty Herne pursues her
in the forests dark and green.
Summer's bright enchantment
workings of my will
"I know" begins the power
that turns the magick mill.

Oceans glitter in the heat
as passions raise the tide
the Oak and Holly navigate
for the favors of the bride.

Summer's bright enchantment
workings of my will
"I know" begins the power
that turns the magick mill.

Faeries dance upon the air
making circles round
luring humans to the earth
beneath the sacred mound.
Summer's bright enchantment
workings of my will
"I know" begins the power
that turns the magick mill.

Roman Fanus plays the flute
the notes a binding spell
of love and healing conjured
from the waters of the well.
Summer's bright enchantment
workings of my will
"I know" begins the power
that turns the magick mill.

Shakespeare's night of potions
bright world of in between
where gnomes hide buried treasure
and devas dance unseen.
Summer's bright enchantment
workings of my will
"I know" begins the power
that turns the magick mill.

Crossroads vibrate open
the dead no longer rest.
I am a Witch and I know how
to conjure up the best!
Summer's bright enchantment
workings of my will
"I know" begins the power
that turns the magick mill!

MAGICKAL IDEAS FOR YOUR MIDSUMMER SABBAT RITUAL

- Collect morning dew, use in Midsummer ritual, and empower for holy water.

- Begin your ritual at dawn.

- Work magicks for partnerships and unions.

- Incorporate the legend of descent into your ritual.

- Study hex signs and paint one, adding its empowerment in your ritual.

- Build your own circle of stones.

- Glue eight candle cups to a wheel and use as a centerpiece for your ritual. Empower each candle for special wishes or overall good fortune.

- Midsummer is a solar holiday that recognizes the passage of Gemini, a mutable air sign, into Cancer, a cardinal water sign. It is the one solar holiday that strives to meld the outside world in which you function to the workings inside your family environment.

Lammas

Other names: Lughnasadh, Lunasdal.

Date: August 1 or 2.

Meaning of the word: *Lammas*, or "Hlaf-mass," is the Feast of the Bread; *nasadh* means "to give in marriage," and *Lugh* is the name of a Celtic god; therefore, *Lughnassadh* means "to give in marriage to Lugh."

Primary focus: Bread harvest, first harvest, grain harvest, games of sport, blessing and saining rites, payment of debts, weather magick.

Age of holiday: Unknown.

Popular mythos: Marriage of Lugh to the Goddess (goddess varies), sacrifice of fruits to the soil (depending on your area), season of handfasting.

Astrological sign: 15 degrees Leo; fire; fixed.

Planetary ruler: Sun.

Lammas is most associated with the first of the harvest celebrations encompassing hay, grain, and cereal yields, and appears to be best known for its festival atmosphere and temporary handfastings (marriages that lasted one year at the consent of both parties) in medieval documentation.

LAMMAS INVOCATION

The King and Queen are wed at last
while summer's kiss turns fields and grass
to harvest gold, and garden gifts
find sacrifice on earthen lips.

Witches gather hand to hand
power raised along the band.
Vortex spiral in its quest
force to form I manifest!

Debts repaid and games of sport,
weather magick—Thor's retort
blessing babies, baking bread
stocking up for winter's stead.

Witches gather hand to hand
power raised along the band.
Vortex spiral in its quest
force to form I manifest!

Bonfires, dancing, circle round
fruits and produce from the ground
offer up a feast of praise
while shadows lengthen in the maze.

Witches gather hand to hand
power raised along the band.
Vortex spiral in its quest
force to form I manifest!

August sun turns all to bronze
golden children singing songs
fireflies flitter in the dusk
touching all with faery dust.

Witches gather hand to hand
power raised along the band.
Vortex spiral in its quest
force to form I manifest!

Dark Lord[52] *melts into the night*
taking with him summer's light
merging wishes, law, and might
removing evil from our sight.

Witches gather hand to hand
power raised along the band.
Vortex spiral in its quest
force to form I manifest!

MAGICKAL IDEAS FOR YOUR LAMMAS SABBAT RITUAL

- Bake bread or pretzels.
- Bless marriages, babies, and homes.
- Have an outdoor picnic.
- Make a wreath out of grain to honor the harvest.
- Go camping and perform your ritual in the woods.
- Use the photographs taken over the summer to honor harvest home, or spend the week before Lammas taking pictures in the country or mountains to make a magickal collage of thanksgiving.
- The sun in fixed, fiery Leo rules this season. Use your magicks to "set" patterns for the coming winter months.
- Design an outdoor scavenger hunt for younger family members. Each item can represent the celebration of the season. Use the things found to create a simple spell for ongoing prosperity and health through the winter months. Use the tables of correspondences in this book to assist your choices—for example, white clover for prosperity, and a creek stone for flow, purification, and stability.

Mabon/Fall Equinox

Other names: Harvest Home, Alban Elued, Mean Fomhair.

Date: September 20, 21, or 22 (depending upon calendar); sun is at 1 degree Libra

Meaning of the word: "Divine youth."

Primary focus: Second Harvest, offering of vegetable and fruit harvest, corn festival

Age of holiday: 3000 B.C. or older

Popular mythos: Death of the Harvest Lord (although some attribute this to Samhain), King and Queen of the Harvest.

Astrological sign: 1 degree Libra; air; cardinal.

Planetary ruler: Venus.

Mabon is the second of the three harvest festivals concentrating on the fruits and vegetables (as opposed to the grains of the first harvest).

> *A seventeenth century poet, Robert Herrick, in "The Hock-cart, or Harvest Home," depicts the cart carrying the last load from the fields, dressed up with all the country art, and followed by adults crowned with ears of corn and a whooping group of children accompanied by a piper playing a harvest-home song. "Some bless the cart, some kiss the sheaves; some prank them up with oaken leaves."* [53]

All the world over, great reverence has always been paid to the last sheaf of corn to be cut on the harvest field, which was believed to embody the spirit of the corn. To ensure good harvests it was necessary to keep this spirit alive, and thus the sheaf became the center of a remarkable ritual, which, in spite of its Pagan character, has persisted in many countries, notably in Scotland.[54] Corn dollies[55] and other talismans and amulets were fashioned at this time in the hope that the family would be blessed with good fortune. The last sheaf of corn was not necessarily made to look like a human being—braided or bound wreaths, brooms, and other handicraft objects were also made. There is one thing for certain in the mind of the modern Wiccan: the Corn Mother has always ruled Mabon, whether she is Demeter, Bried, the Cailleach, or Maighdean-Bhuana.

MAGICKAL IDEAS FOR YOUR MABON SABBAT RITUAL

- Dip leaves in paraffin and use in your ritual. Bless them and give as gifts.

- Make a corn dolly.

- Perform your ritual in a harvested field.

- Visit a local orchard to find deity offerings.

- Thank a field for rendering its harvest.

MABON INVOCATION

Mabon brings the scent of autumn
Golden glow and sun's soft kiss.
Magick swirls and eddies onward
Season's end demands all this.

The wheel is turning, ever forward
Calling for your act of closure,
Fill the cauldron, light the fire
Cast the magick ever higher!
Find the laughter, make ye merry
Touch the heartbeat of our Mother.

Libra brings an air of beauty
Gracing all with harvest lore
Listen closely wisdom's duty
Look within to find the door.

(repeat second stanza)

The fruits are heavy on the trees
Yellow, gold, and orange leaves
Nature's show of alchemy
Ever clear to you and me.

(repeat second stanza)

Seeker Ceremonies

When information on the Craft became publishable, Wiccan groups found themselves at a loss as to how to handle the large numbers of individuals who were curious about Witchcraft and wanted to try it, but weren't sure they wanted to immerse themselves totally in the religion. Up until that point, an individual came into the Craft as a dedicant, served a year and a day, and was then initiated or, in some groups, were initiated immediately without a waiting period (the idea of immediate initiation has been almost completely dropped in modern Craft, with groups opting for the waiting period of the year and a day). From the point of initiation, they worked through various stages of development until they reached clergy status, which took approximately four to seven years, depending upon the group, and the power of the lineage was passed. Although most Craft children were wiccaned (baptized) when young and then dedicated around the age of sixteen, they were not *initiated* until the age of twenty-one, or the age at which the parents felt that the child understood the nature of the religion and it was felt that the child could make an informed choice for him- or herself. The age was not the important factor—maturity was the basis for the decision. Witchcraft, remember, is a religion, not something cool to try on for a few months and then discard when you're bored. Once you take your vow at your initiation, that's it—there is no turning back.

Widespread publication of Wiccan material brought a new phenomena to the Craft world: the solitary Witch. This new kind of Witch—one who learns on their own, using material found in books, without the benefit of a living, breathing teacher or a group that can provide adequate training—presented a few problems in the hierarchy of the then-Craft structure. Granted, the definition of the solitary practitioner has since expanded, but right now, for the sake of keeping explanations short and reasonable, this is as far as I'm going to take it. As the solitary practitioner did not have a teacher who could initiate them into the Craft, Wiccan writers sort of drummed their fingers, thinking, "What to do. What to do." Raymond Buckland published the first dedication ceremony that showed readers how, without the help of a teacher or group, one could dedicate themselves to solitary Craft training. The initial portion of the dedication covered the standard year-and-a-day timeframe. Once the individual had "done the time," he or she could rework the same ritual to dedicate themselves for life. My book *To Ride a Silver Broomstick* also contains a self-dedication ritual, as do several others currently on the market. However, self-dedication for life by an individual is not like an initiation ritual provided by a group that connects you to a specific lineage and the group mind of that coven, tradition, or clan, as I explained earlier in this book—though both ceremonies are designed as an opening to power and your acceptance of that link to deity.

This idea worked very well until the advent of *Teen Witch*, which publicly opened Craft training to teens. As readers would be coming from different backgrounds and various levels of maturity, the dedication ceremony was not tailored to fit the wide range of differences among readers—differences that included age, religious background, parental preferences and guidelines, educational level, and something very new to be considered: culture. Because *Teen Witch* is published in several languages and is read by people all over the world, something else had to be written—a prelude to the dedication, something just for teens that didn't sign, seal, and deliver them permanently to Witchcraft.

The seeker ceremony is much like that of the dedication—it is a declaration of intent, provides a protective net while one studies, is totally spiritual in nature, and holds for one year and a day. The difference lies in the wording. Where a Wiccan dedication focuses totally on the religion of Witchcraft, the seeker ceremony is more liberal, allowing the student to move toward the Craft philosophy at a pace selected for the growing teen. If the teen truly loves Witchcraft, then he or she can progress with a self-dedication ceremony when he or she feels ready to do so. At the teen seeker level, the individual has not taken the steps to cement him- or herself into the life of a Witch. For some that occurs at the dedication ceremony, and for others at the time of formal initiation.

Teen Seeker Ceremony

WHEN TO PERFORM: When you feel ready. You might like to choose a special day, such as your birthday, a Wiccan holiday (Beltane is a good one), or other day that has importance to you. Some teens like to wait for a full moon, a new moon, or a Sunday. Your timing doesn't matter as much as your intent.

WHERE TO PERFORM: Wherever you wish. Some teens like to go to the beach, the forest, a favorite fountain, etc., or you could stay in your back yard, or do the ritual in your room.

SUPPLIES: These depend a great deal on the permissiveness of your parents and your living environment (such as a dorm room). In reality, you don't need any supplies to tell Spirit that you feel you are ready to walk the path of spiritual enlightenment, but humans like to use things to represent important moments in their lives. You may like to put a little cauldron on your altar with a tea candle (as this ritual does), or use a particular kind of incense. The choice of

supplies will be up to you. You might like to buy yourself a small token to represent the ceremony—a necklace, bracelet, or small item to carry in your pocket.

WHAT TO SAY AND WHAT TO DO: This, again, is up to you. Although I provide a ritual outline here, I recommend that you say what comes from the heart—that's the best way to talk to Spirit, whether you choose to do the seeker ritual or a ritual of healing for a friend. The seeker ceremony follows a basic Wiccan structural format.

THE DAY OF THE CEREMONY: Gather all of your things together, such as your incense, what you would like to wear, the token for yourself, any items you will use to place at the quarters or on your altar, etc. Place everything on your altar and ask for the blessings of the elements. You can pass incense over the items to represent east, a red candle for the south, holy water for west, and a bit of salt for north, saying:

I cleanse and consecrate these items in preparation for my seeker ceremony. May no evil or negativity abide in thee. May the blessings of the Lord and Lady (or Spirit) descend upon this altar and these things. So mote it be.

If you plan to transport your props to another site, pack them carefully in a picnic basket, a duffle bag, backpack, or other type of carrying item. Include something to eat and drink for communion.

THE RITUAL: Set up the ritual site and your altar. Remember that your altar can be temporary. Don't forget to check the quarter alignments with a compass, and place markers at the quarters so you know exactly where they are. If you have chosen to do your ritual outside, be sure to walk the area and ask the faeries and devas of the land to accept and protect you while you perform the ritual. When you feel ready, devote the altar by passing the four representations of the elements, one by one, over the altar surface, cleansing and consecrating the area as you have been taught. Take your time and enjoy this sacred moment. You are about to take a very big step in your life—a leap toward personal spirituality. Don't forget to ground and center before you begin.

When you are ready, cast your circle, saying:

I conjure thee, O circle of power, so that you will be for me a boundary between the world of humans and the realms of the mighty ones—a meeting place of perfect love, trust, peace and joy, containing the power I will raise herein. I call upon the elements of the east, the south, the west, and the north to aid me in this consecration. In the name of the Lord and the Lady thus do I conjure thee, O great circle of power!

Remember that you can cast the circle by walking clockwise three times around while reciting the words, or walking around only once. When finished, tap the ground and say: "This circle is sealed!"

Move to the north quarter (don't forget the hand motions I taught you earlier, in Quarter Calls), and say:

Guardians of the north, element of earth, welcome to my seeker ceremony. Powers of earth, lend your strength and stability to this ritual, gift me with your special abilities. Enter here and welcome on this momentous occasion.

Move to the east quarter, and say:

Guardians of the east, element of air, welcome to my seeker ceremony. Powers of air, lend your strength and stability to this ritual, gift me with your special abilities. Enter here and welcome on this momentous occasion.

Move to the south quarter, and say:

Guardians of the south, element of fire, welcome to my seeker ceremony. Powers of fire, lend your strength and stability to this ritual, gift me with your special abilities. Enter here and welcome on this momentous occasion.

Move to the west quarter, and say:

Guardians of the west, element of water, welcome to my seeker ceremony. Powers of water, lend your strength and stability to this ritual, gift me with your special abilities. Enter here and welcome on this momentous occasion.

Move to the center of the circle, and stand in the God position. Close your eyes and feel the power of the God enter your body. Now take the Goddess position stance, and say:

Holy Mother, Divine Lord, I welcome you into this circle cast for my seeker ritual. Come to me and bless me with thy divine presence. Gift me, please, with your special powers. I have come this day (eve) to proclaim my interest in spirituality and the Craft of the Wise.

Kneel, place your hands on the altar, and say:

I, (your full name), do solemnly swear by my Mother's lineage and by all that I hold sacred and holy that I will honor and respect Spirit and the brothers and sisters of the Craft of the Wise. I will work hard to serve Spirit in every way, and I will try to learn all aspects of the Craft. I will not use my knowledge of the Craft to purposefully cause harm, nor will I require the payment of money, goods, or services when I pray for people or work magick for them beyond a fair exchange of energy. When I have learned sufficiently, I may choose to dedicate myself to the Lord and Lady, or I may walk away and follow another spiritual path. I will do my best to work in harmony for myself and for others, always. I will respect other religions as I respect my own. Spirit has now witnessed my oath. On this day, (name the day), I claim my power! So mote it be.

Stand up and light the tea candle in the cauldron. Take the token you have purchased or found for yourself and hold the item over the altar, saying:

Lord and Lady, please bless this token of my faith. May it provide protection as I walk the path of the Wise.

Take the token to each quarter and ask for the energies of that quarter to bless and energize the object. Return to the altar, hold out the token again, and say:

This object represents my testament to this day and to my vow. I will wear it in honor of the Lord and Lady. So mote it be.

As you put the token on your person, say:

At this moment I am reborn in body, mind, and spirit. So mote it be!

Seal the ceremony with your personal communion. Hold your hands over the drink, and say:

From the moon to the land, from the land to the vine, from the vine to the berry, from the berry to the juice, I consecrate this drink in the name of the Lord and the Lady. May their blessings shower upon me through eternity. So mote it be.

Drink some of the juice, then pour the rest on the ground (or into a bowl if you are in your room) as a libation to Spirit, saying: "To the gods!"

Hold your hands over the cake, cookies, or bread, and say:

From the sun to the land, from the land to the stalk, from the stalk to the grain, from the grain to this bread, I consecrate this food in the name of the Lord and Lady. May their blessings shower upon me through eternity. So mote it be.

Eat some of the cake and drop the rest to the ground (or in the bowl) as libation to Spirit, saying: "To the gods!"

When you are finished, spend some time in meditation. To close, move to the center of the circle, and say:

Great Mother, Divine Father, I thank you for attending my seeker ceremony. Guard and guide me until I decide to become part of the community of the Craft of the Wise, or choose to seek another path. Help me to do the divine work given to me, and help me in all of my choices.
So mote it be.

Move to the western quarter, and say:

Guardians of the west, element of water, thank you for your participation in my seeker ritual. Peace be with you and harm none on your way. Powers of water, thank you for your special gifts. Go if you must, stay if you like. Hail and farewell!

Move to the southern quarter, and say:

Guardians of the south, element of fire, thank you for your participation in my seeker ritual. Peace be with you and harm none on your way. Powers of fire, thank you for your special gifts. Go if you must, stay if you like. Hail and farewell!

Move to the eastern quarter, and say:

Guardians of the east, element of air, thank you for your participation in my seeker ritual. Peace be with you and harm none on your way. Powers of air, thank you for your special gifts. Go if you must, stay if you like. Hail and farewell!

Move to the northern quarter, and say:

Guardians of the north, element of earth, thank you for your participation in my seeker ritual. Peace be with you and harm none on your way. Powers of earth, thank you for your special gifts. Go if you must, stay if you like. Hail and farewell! Everything comes from the north!

Begin at the west, releasing your circle as you walk widdershins around the circle area. When you finish, pound the ground with your hand, and say:

This circle is open, but never broken. Merry meet and merry part until we merry meet again. For we are the people, the power, and the change. So mote it be!

You have just completed one of the most important ceremonies of your life! Be proud of the step you have made toward personal spirituality. It's time now to clean up the ritual area, making sure that nothing remains of your presence (especially if you are outside). If you did your ceremony inside, take the libation bowl outside and pour the contents on the ground, saying: "To the gods!"

The Self-Dedication Ceremony

Okay, you've gone beyond the teen seeker ceremony and you are ready to make a commitment to the Craft of the Wise and practice Witchcraft (not some other religion) for a year and a day. This means that you fully wish to integrate the art, science, and religion of Witchcraft into your life in every way possible for twelve full months and one day. After that, you intend to seek initiation into a group or permanent dedication

through the repetition of the ceremony given here. *Note:* If you find this ceremony confusing or bothersome in any way, then you are not ready to take your dedication. Give yourself time. The Lord and Lady will always be there. Rushing yourself only causes problems later on. Also, I have not listed the supplies necessary for this ritual, as I feel you should be able to go through the ritual and make a list of what you will need. If you plan to become a Witch, you will have to learn how to do this at some point—might as well begin now.

PHASE ONE: For nine weeks prior to your selected date, you should burn a white candle every Sunday (or the day that matches the day you were born), saying the following prayer:

Guardian of the Gates, I welcome you. Protect me on my path toward dedication and initiation and by your will, open the gates between the worlds so that my request may be heard and acted upon without harm to myself. Guardian angel, come to me, come to me. I need you. I invite you. Protect and guide me on my path toward dedication and initiation. Whatever I need for the ceremony, provide the way for me. So mote it be.

Special note: If you forget to perform this function on the given day, then you must start all over again because you have broken the momentum toward this special future event.

These nine weeks are to be used for setting up your sacred space, building/erecting your altar, collecting and making the sacred tools of the art, stocking your magickal cabinet with necessary supplies, choosing your permanent magickal name, and sewing or purchasing a ritual robe (you will find a great deal of the preliminary information needed for your dedication in my book *To Ride a Silver Broomstick*). You should spend at least fifteen minutes a day in meditation throughout this time period. These ceremonies are often performed on a new moon; however, you can choose a date for your dedication that will mean something special to you—perhaps your birthday or the first day of spring. During the nine weeks you should buy a new Book of Shadows and copy the dedication ritual given below in the book. Take your time. It doesn't have to be done all in one night. Copying the ritual in your "own hand of writ" helps to prepare you for the acceptance of the divine energies you will receive during the ceremony, especially if you plan to work as a solitary Witch. A week or two before the ceremony (possibly sooner), you will feel a "quickening" of your spirit. It is hard to explain—a sort of a fluttery, expectant feeling. Some people feel a slight pressure on the top of their head. Don't worry, this is normal. Energies are moving into place to set the stage for this new life choice.

PHASE TWO: On the night of the ceremony, take a spiritual bath. Towel-dry with a fresh towel. Dress in your ritual robe (no jewelry). If you plan to transport your props to another site, pack them carefully in a picnic basket, a duffle bag, backpack, or other type of carrying item. Include something to eat and drink for communion. Use the basic altar setup (SEE PART II, ALTARS) as your guide. Place your favorite jewelry in the north section of the altar. Turn off the phone and lock your doors (if you are staying home) to ensure that you will not be disturbed. Spend at least a half hour meditating before you go further. Think hard about why you want to do this, what benefits you wish to derive, and what positive changes you desire to make in your life. Immediately before beginning the ceremony, cleanse, consecrate, and empower all supplies that will be used. Pass the four elements over the items, saying:

I cleanse and consecrate these items in preparation for my dedication ceremony. May no evil or

negativity abide in thee. May the blessings of the Lord and Lady descend upon this altar and these things. So mote it be.

Set your Book of Shadows by the altar where you can clearly read it. Using a book light is acceptable during the ritual.

PHASE THREE: Create sacred space by carrying a representation of each of the elements around to the four quarters in a clockwise direction. Sweep the area with a new, empowered broom in the same manner (clockwise). Place a votive candle at each quarter along with flowers or appropriate items (your choice) that match the quarter. Once you have cast the circle for the self-dedication, it is best not to cut a door. Double-check your altar setup. Do you have everything you need? Did you remember the items for communion? The lighter?

PHASE FOUR: Begin the ritual by casting the circle and calling the quarters, as you did in the teen seeker ritual.

I conjure thee, O circle of power, so that you will be for me a boundary between the world of humans and the realms of the mighty ones—a meeting place of perfect love, trust, peace, and joy, containing the power I will raise herein. I call upon the elements of the east, the south, the west, and the north to aid me in this consecration. In the name of the Lord and the Lady thus do I conjure thee, O great circle of power!

Remember that you can cast the circle by walking clockwise three times around while reciting the words, or walking around only once. When finished, tap the ground and say: "As above, so below. This circle is sealed!"

Tap your foot or your staff on the ground three times. Stand in the center of the circle, and say:

Guardian of the Gates of Dedication, I welcome you. Protect me during my dedication ceremony and by your will, open the gates between the worlds so that my request may be heard and acted upon without harm to myself. Guardian angel, come to me, come to me. I need you. I invite you. Protect and guide me on during this dedication ritual. So mote it be.

Move to the north quarter, and say:

Guardians of the north, element of earth, and all ye in the realm of Faery, I, (state your name), do summon, stir, and call you forth to witness this rite and protect this sacred space. Welcome to my dedication ceremony. Powers of earth, lend your strength and stability to this ritual, gift me with your special abilities. Enter here and welcome on this momentous occasion.

Move to the east quarter, and say:

Guardians of the east, element of air, and all ye in the realm of Faery, I, (state your name), do summon, stir, and call you forth to witness this rite and protect this sacred space. Welcome to my dedication ceremony. Powers of air, lend your strength and stability to this ritual, gift me with your special abilities. Enter here and welcome on this momentous occasion.

Move to the south quarter, and say:

Guardians of the south, element of fire, and all ye in the realm of Faery, I, (state your name), do summon, stir, and call you forth to witness this rite and protect this sacred space. Welcome to my dedication ceremony. Powers of fire, lend your strength and stability to this ritual, gift me with your special abilities. Enter here and welcome on this momentous occasion.

Move to the west quarter, and say:

Guardians of the west, element of water, and all ye in the realm of Faery, I, (state your name), do summon, stir, and call you forth to witness this rite and protect this sacred space. Welcome to my dedication ceremony. Powers of water, lend your strength and stability to this ritual, gift me with your special abilities. Enter here and welcome on this momentous occasion.

Move to the center of the circle, and stand in the God position. Close your eyes and feel the power of the God enter your body. Now take the Goddess position stance, and say:

Holy Mother, Divine Lord, I, (state your real name, followed by your magickal name), welcome You into this circle cast for my dedication ritual. Come to me and bless me with Thy divine presence. Gift me, please, with Your special powers. I have come this day (eve) to proclaim my desire to dedicate myself to the Craft of the Wise.

I desire to learn and study to be a practicing Witch. Help me in this year and a day to understand what it means to be a spiritual person and give me the strength I will need to continue on this sacred path, for I know and understand that I have much to learn.

Walk to the north quarter, and say:

Hail, guardians of the north, I, (state your real and magickal name), come to you seeking dedication into the Craft of the Wise. I invoke the powers of earth to teach me what I must know.

Light the votive candle that you placed in that quarter. Visualize the energies of the north filling your body, helping you to prepare for your sacred journey. Walk to the east quarter, and say:

Hail, guardians of the east, I, (state your real and magickal names), come to you seeking dedication into the Craft of the Wise. I invoke the powers of air to teach me what I must know.

Visualize the energies of the east filling your body, helping you to prepare for your sacred journey. Walk to the south quarter, and say:

Hail, guardians of the south, I, (state your real and magickal names), come to you seeking dedication into the Craft of the Wise. I invoke the powers of fire to teach me what I must know.

Visualize the energies of the south filling your body, helping you to prepare for your sacred journey.

Walk to the west quarter, and say:

Hail, guardians of the west, I, (state your real and magickal names), come to you seeking dedication into the Craft of the Wise. I invoke the powers of water to teach me what I must know.

Visualize the energies of the west filling your body, helping you to prepare for your sacred journey.

Walk to the altar. Repeat the blessing below as you dab holy water on each of the eight points of your body:

Blessed be my feet that walk the path of spiritual service. Blessed be my knees that kneel at the sacred altar. Blessed be my womb (phallus) that gives forth life. Blessed be my heart formed in beauty and strength. Blessed be my lips that speak only the truth and wisdom of the Lord and Lady. Blessed be my eyes so that I may see the abundance of the earth. May I be cleansed, consecrated, and regenerated in the service of the Craft of the Wise. So mote it be!

Take three deep breaths and visualize yourself filled with holy, divine light. Kneel at your altar. Place your Witch's blade on the center of the altar. Place your hands over the blade and repeat the oath below:

I, (your full name), do solemnly swear by my Mother's lineage and by all that I hold sacred and holy that I will honor and respect the Lord and the Lady and the brothers and sisters of the Craft of the Wise. I will work hard to serve the Lord and Lady in every way, and I will try to learn all aspects of the Craft in preparation for my initiation. I will not use my knowledge of the Craft to purposefully cause harm, nor will I require the payment of money, goods, or services when I pray for people or work magick for them beyond a fair exchange of energy. When I have learned sufficiently, I may choose to seek initiation or permanent dedication, or I may walk away and follow another spiritual path. I will do my best to work in harmony for myself and for others, always. I will respect other religions as I respect my own. I will not disrespect the work of those that have gone before me, and I honor each individuals' contribution to my faith and learning. I will not reveal those brothers and sisters who are forced to practice in secret and, should I break this oath, I shall with full knowledge suffer the consequences. I will reach for the perfection in the universe and I shall obtain it. Thus said,
I give myself to the religion of Witchcraft.
Spirit has now witnessed my oath. On this day, (name the day), I, (say your magickal name), claim my power! So mote it be.

Stand up and light the tea candle in the cauldron. Take the token you have purchased or found for yourself and hold the item over the altar, saying:

> *Lord and Lady, please bless this token*
> *of my faith. May it provide protection*
> *as I walk the path of the Wise.*

Take the token to each quarter and ask for the energies of that quarter to bless and energize the object. Return to the altar, hold out the token again, and say:

> *This object represents my testament to this day*
> *and to my oath. I will wear it in honor of the*
> *Lord and Lady. So mote it be.*

As you put the token on your person, say:

> *At this moment I am reborn in body, mind,*
> *and spirit! So mote it be!*

Seal the ceremony with your personal communion. Hold your hands over the drink, and say:

> *From the moon to the land, from the land to the*
> *vine, from the vine to the berry, from the berry to*
> *the juice, I consecrate this drink in the name of*
> *the Lord and the Lady. May their blessings*
> *shower upon me through eternity. So mote it be.*

Drink some of the juice, then pour the rest on the ground (or into a bowl if you are in your room) as a libation to Spirit, saying: "To the gods!"

Hold your hands over the cake, cookies, or bread, and say:

> *From the sun to the land, from the land to the*
> *stalk, from the stalk to the grain, from the grain*
> *to this bread, I consecrate this food in the name of*
> *the Lord and the Lady. May their blessings*
> *shower upon me through eternity. So mote it be.*

Eat some of the cake and drop the rest to the ground (or in the bowl) as libation to Spirit, saying: "To the gods!"

When you are finished, spend some time in meditation. To close, move to the center of the circle, and say:

> *Great Mother, Divine Father, I thank you for at-*
> *tending my dedication ceremony. Guard and*
> *guide me until I decide to become part of the*
> *community of the Craft of the Wise, or choose to*
> *seek another path. Help me to do the divine*
> *work given to me, and help me in all of my*
> *choices. So mote it be.*

Move to the western quarter, and say:

> *Guardians of the west, element of water, and all*
> *ye in the realm of Faery! Thank you for your*
> *participation in my dedication ritual. Peace be*
> *with you and harm none on your way. Powers of*
> *water, thank you for your special gifts. Go if you*
> *must, stay if you like. Hail and farewell!*

Move to the southern quarter, and say:

> *Guardians of the south, element of fire, and all*
> *ye in the realm of Faery! Thank you for your*
> *participation in my seeker ritual. Peace be with*
> *you and harm none on your way. Powers of fire,*
> *thank you for your special gifts. Go if you must,*
> *stay if you like. Hail and farewell!*

Move to the eastern quarter, and say:

> *Guardians of the east, element of air, and all*
> *ye in the realm of Faery! Thank you for your*
> *participation in my dedication ritual. Peace be*
> *with you and harm none on your way. Powers of*
> *air, thank you for your special gifts. Go if you*
> *must, stay if you like. Hail and farewell!*

Move to the northern quarter, and say:

*Guardians of the north, element of earth, and all
ye in the realm of Faery! Thank you for your
participation in my dedication ritual. Peace be
with you and harm none on your way. Powers of
earth, thank you for your special gifts. Go if you
must, stay if you like. Hail and farewell!
Everything comes from the north!*

Begin at the west, releasing your circle as you walk widdershins around the circle area. When you finish, pound the ground with your hand, and say:

*This circle is open, but never broken.
Merry meet and merry part, until we merry meet
again. For we are the people, the power,
and the change! So mote it be!*

Congratulations, you have made a definitive step toward becoming a Witch. Just remember, it is the journey, not the path, that is important.

Helpful Ritual Hints

I've been practicing magick and ritual since my teen years and I've learned a few helpful hints I'd like to pass along to you. Granted, you don't have to follow them, but if you do take the time to try them out, I think you'll find that your magickal applications will move along a little smoother.

- Ritual and magick are personal, therefore it is a good idea to practice in a private area where you will not be disturbed. I felt really silly when I first started because I wasn't sure if the magick would work, and I didn't want anybody to see me doing something that they might think was dumb. After a while, you won't feel self-conscious, but it is still a good idea to keep your activities to yourself. If someone makes fun of

you, it is disrespectful and it will lower your self-esteem.

- Gather everything you need ahead of time, rather than running around looking for something you've forgotten in the middle of a ritual or spellcasting procedure. That way, you don't scatter the energies or the focus of what you are doing.

- Never work magick or ritual when you are angry. Count to ten. Wait a few hours. Cool off. Think about it. Later on in the book, I'll give you positive ways to work out anger (SEE PART V, ANGER AND CONFLICT RESOLUTION).

- If you mess up a spell or ritual, don't worry about it. Some students are afraid that if they do something wrong, then bad things will happen. Nope. The worst thing that could occur is that your goal simply won't manifest. The walls of the house will not crumble, the basement will not flood, demons will not crawl out from under the bed and snatch your sister from her crib, Poe's telltale heart will not beat beneath the floorboards, nor will a tornado blow through the trailer park and whisk you away to Oz because you made a boo-boo. Everybody makes mistakes. Acknowledge the error and go on.

- Fear is your worst enemy. A long time ago, I read a book called *A Course In Miracles* from the Foundation of Inner Peace, currently published through Viking Press. Their motto is: "Nothing real can be threatened. Nothing unreal exists. Herein lies the peace of God." Study those words and think about them. Write them down on a 3 by 5-inch card and tack them to your bedroom mirror. Never forget them; they will serve you well. When you read the section on magick and holographic quantum physics, these words will leave you much to ponder.

Do rituals work? Absolutely! Whether we are talking about now or a thousand years ago, the drama and complexity of ritual clearly functions as an excellent antidote to feelings of depression, persecution,[56] loneliness, and fear, regardless of the magickal components. In a way, ritual is just as psychological as it is spiritual, and indeed is a melding of quantum physics and mental health.

Modern Witchcraft Ritual

If you study formal Craft ritual (of which not all sects participate), you will learn of the parallels also found in Freemasonry and their initiation and celebratory rituals. I happened upon this fact about fifteen years ago when I read a 1920 copy of the Masonic Rites found in someone's attic. These parallels include initiation; the degree system; challenge; admission; presentation; oath-taking; ritual tools, each with their own symbology; geometric glyphs; code words; station acknowledgement (we call them quarters); the five-fold kiss; and a system of governmental hierarchy. Indeed, I was a member of the Rainbow Girls, which is the teen female faction of the Masons, and these elements were also in our rituals. In fact, we lived for ritual because it was so beautiful. Oh, my station? I was the chaplain. Now some of you quick thinkers are saying, since she was a Rainbow Girl, then her father had to be a Mason. Yes, he was and still is, but he wasn't the one that gave me the book, and the book did not belong to him. Indeed, their oath of secrecy is so strong that he was extremely chagrined when I waved the book under his nose. Is there anything bad in that book? Nah. Here again, the Masons and the Crafters have something very important in common—their oath of secrecy to their individual orders, which permeates training, ritual, and socialization within the group mind.

Modern ritual ceremonial magick (of which you will find some elements in modern Craft) owes much of its current format to a Frenchman by the name of Alphonse Louis Constant, better known as Eliphas Zahed Levi,[57] born in 1910. It is from Levi that we have the word "occult," which has gone in and out of fashion in response to social temperatures. He also postulated something I told you in the very beginning of this book—you don't "get" powers, you already *have* them. The Craft merely provides a mode of study, encourages practice, and provides triggers that may work for you. Levi believed that over time we allowed many of our true gifts to take a back seat in our lives, and that we needed only training and study to enhance what we already had. Our scientists today actually agree (in part) to Levi's theory when they tell us that humans use only a small percentage of their brain power and, if we encouraged ourselves to expand our thinking, we would be able to accomplish many times more than what we currently achieve. It is the Golden Dawn, however, that placed the four ceremonial "elemental weapons"[58] (the chalice, the pentacle, the dagger, and the wand) on the Craft altar. For more information about ritual, read the sections on Esbats (PART I), Spellcasting (PART III), and the Wheel of the Year (PART I).

Spirit Guides and Angels

Before we get started on this topic, let's make sure we cover a few very important points about spirit guides and angels:

- Neither belong to any particular religious system. The belief in angels/guides predates modern religious structures.

- You can't own an angel or a guide. They aren't your personal property.

- Angels/guides don't discriminate on religious faith.

- Angels/guides create bridges between various religions.

- To call on an angel/spirit guide is to rise above religious dogma and touch the universal Spirit.

Now that we've got that out of the way, and you know you can keep your belief in angels and guides if you want to work magick, let's dig a little deeper into the subject. Just as there is no "one right way" to practice a religion, there aren't any rules when it comes to angels/guides, though many people will tell you that there are. To some people, angels/spirit guides simply don't exist. To others, they are rather authoritarian in nature—Archangel Michael comes to mind, with dashing good looks and slashing sword; or perhaps you would prefer the John Travolta version? (If you are a bit macabre, Christopher Walken should do.) If we lean a little more on Babylonian representations, then angels have many heads, lots of eyeballs, and razor-sharp teeth. (Well, cut them a break—the people in those days couldn't fulfill the need to be scared at the local movie theater, so they *had* to come up with something . . . no Wes Craven for them!)

Most of the written information we have today does not come from the orthodox scriptures of the four Western religions that believe in the existence of these heavenly beings (Christianity, Judaism, Zoroastrianism, and Islam). Over the centuries, ideas about the angelic hosts have changed, depending on who wrote about them.

Many scholars believe that angels are the result of mixing belief systems that include Egyptian, Sumerian, Babylonian, and Persian myths. Through further research we find that belief in angelic hosts and spirits is far older than any of the religions practiced today, which supports the idea that they aren't tied to what humans want them to be.

Angels and spirit guides simply are. And they aren't *just* Christian, or *just* Jewish, or *just* Islamic. After a bit of digging into history, we learn that angels are "thoughts" that predate all the religions mentioned previously, stemming back into our tribal cultures, our genetic memories, and our spiritual recall. Angels/guides do not exist to serve a particular religion. They *do* exist to help humans and other inhabitants of this plane—and that, by the way, includes the Witches. The idea of a guardian angel most likely comes from the ancient philosophers, who claimed to have invisible companions who protected them for life. Both Plotinus and Socrates declared that they had *daemons* who acted not only as guides, but as guardians as well. Magicians of their time also maintained that they had such helpers, called *parhedros* (divine companions), and many historians feel that these protectors were adopted by the early Catholic church in the form of saints.[59] "Plato refers to spirits *(daemones)* and gods, jointly by name, either because the gods are 'daemones,' meaning 'gifted of knowledge of the future,' or as Posidonius writes . . . because their nature springs from and shares in the heavenly substance—this word for spirits being then derived from *daiomenos*, which may mean either 'burning' or 'sharing.'"[60] Throughout history it wasn't (and isn't) uncommon for a religious body to absorb magickal acts, reinvent their origins, and claim them for their own—angels being a case in point.

If you really want to stretch that brain power of yours, think of this: Witches are angels in disguise. Now, before you get carried away and think that Witches have all those powers you see on television or can do the things that Buffy can —hold that thought. Witches are angels on earth in that they have taken an oath of service to help themselves deal with life in a positive way, and once they've got their own lives running fairly smooth (nothing is perfect, you know), they can reach out and help others, functioning as guardians of a sort. *Service* is the keyword here. It is cool to imagine yourself with big, fluffy wings and a serene personality. You get more done that way. (Just don't try to jump off a building. Imaginary wings are just that—imaginary.) As a note, one of the first rites a ceremonial magician might perform is the acknowledgement of his or her guardian angel in his or her life and work. In Santería, the head is blessed with a guardian spirit in a long, sacred ceremony that never leaves the individual until the moment of death. Spiritualism and Voodoo have much the same ceremonies. Having a guide to call your very own in magickal practice is not new or unusual.

The neat thing about angels/guides is that they always listen to you. You are never, ever alone. Just because you can't see them doesn't mean that they aren't there. As you grow, their presence will sort of float in and out of your life (or so it will seem). Sometimes you think of them and ask them for help, other times you are so busy with cheerleading practice, dates, the prom, or summer fun that they are the furthest thing from your mind—but they're there. And the really neat thing about angels is that you don't need a big ritual, a lot of tools, or to be in a special place to contact them. Nope. All you have to do is simply open your mouth and start talking. It's that simple!

There are lots of people who have angel altars or shrines in their homes (or bedrooms) because it makes them feel better, and because the visual aids help them to relax and talk to the angels. That's okay, too. Whatever you need is fine. You can find really cool angel statues, especially around Christmas time, and giving a friend a gift of angel love when you buy any sort of gift that has angels on it is one of the best gifts you can give (besides your love, a smile, and a helping hand, of course). Some people think that believing in angels/guides takes away your love from God, but I just don't see how that can be, as we are all creatures of Spirit, even angels and guides. If you believe in angels/guides, then you believe that something nice and friendly runs the universe. What's so bad about that? Angels are great friends because they will never make fun of you, won't drink and drive, and aren't into drugs. So you can't see them—big deal. There are worse things in the world than being invisible.

Requesting the assistance of angels/guides in magick is an extremely old practice. However, you'll see Witches working more with spirits, such as the spirit of a tree, flower, crystal, and so on, and not specifically saying they are *angels*, where in ceremonial magick you'll read about the angels that govern the planets, the winds, the days, and so on. Basically (with a few exceptions), we're dealing with the same type of energy, and you will find crossovers (especially with the angels of the days and planetary hours) where most magickal people are at least familiar with the energy. It does get sticky, however, when we start poring over medieval texts. One angel may be a good guy to one religion and a bad guy to another (I'm thinking of Metatron as I write this). Then there's the argument about what is a spirit and what is an angel, especially if you start reading about the *Greater or Lesser Keys of Solomon* or dance those peepers of yours over books of questionable ethics. The old occult adage of *Don't call up what you can't put down* fits here. My advice here is, if you haven't researched it, *don't touch it*. If what you are reading is unappealing, then work with something else, especially in dealing with medieval information. Life for the medieval cleric (from whence most of these books come) was a heck of a lot different than life for you. Let's face it, an elevator or an automatic door, which is commonplace to you, would be mysterious and magickal to them. Get it? Things are what we make them, after all.

Guardian Angel Ceremony to Call Your Guardian to You

SUPPLIES: Four white pillar candles; one white bowl filled with spring water; one empty white bowl (to mix the herbs); one pillar candle that matches the color of the planetary ruler of the day you were born; seven herbs that match the planetary energies of the hour you were born (SEE PART III, UNDER ASTROLOGY); incense of your choice; a white sheet; one lodestone; a small white purse with a drawstring; and a chair with a straight back.

TIMING: First or second quarter of the moon, preferably on the day that matches the day you were born. For example, if you were born on a Monday, then you would perform the ceremony on a Monday. No pets are allowed in this ritual, due to the open candle flames.

RITUAL: Cleanse and consecrate all the supplies. Take off your shoes (if you are wearing any). Place the white sheet on the floor of your magickal working area. Place the chair in front of the altar, on the sheet. Cast the circle and call the quarters. Invoke deity. Place the four white candles around the chair in firesafe holders and on firesafe plates. Please be careful not to knock them over or catch the hem of pants or skirts on

the flames when they are lit. You could even place them on stepstools at a safe distance. For now, leave them dark. Carry the lit incense around the room in a clockwise direction. Light the guardian candle (the colored one) and place on the center of the altar. In your own words, ask your guardian angel to come to you. Mix the herbs together in the white bowl without the water. Conjure the herbs as instructed on page 381. Place the lodestone in the bowl of spring water. Put that bowl in front of the chair (but not so close that you will knock it over). Scatter the herbs on the sheet around the base of the bowl. You will need to collect them later, so don't throw them all over the place.

Moving clockwise, light the four white candles around the chair. Sit on the chair with your feet flat on the floor, your back straight, and your palms up, relaxed in your lap. Take seven deep breaths. Repeat the following softly until you begin to grow drowsy:

> *Guardian angel, come to me, come to me.*
> *I need you, I invite you.*

Now switch the chant to "I am," repeating these two words until you drift into a meditative state. Be patient. You may see something in your mind, or you may see nothing. A slight pressure on your head is a good indication that your guardian is coming through to you. If you have a special request, now is the time to make it. When you feel you are finished, thank your guardian, count from one to five, and open your eyes. Take three deep breaths. Remain seated for at least three minutes, considering your experience.

Rise from the chair and extinguish the candles clockwise around the chair. Take the lodestone out of the water and dry it thoroughly. Gather up the herbs. Place the lodestone and the herbs in the white bag. Place the white bag on the altar. Let the bag remain there until the candle is finished burning, or you can extinguish the candle and use it again when you wish to commune with your guardian. Thank deity, close the quarters, and release the circle. Put the guardian bag in a safe place or carry with you on a daily basis. Make a fresh bag once a year.

Wheel of the Year

The Wheel of the Year is best known in modern Witchcraft as representing the cycle of the seasons throughout one calendar year. This symbolic wheel is divided into eight parts, with each spoke of the wheel representing a particular season. Although Witches consider the Wheel of the Year to be a Celtic/European symbol, it actually appeared in Greek references as early as 600 B.C. Once again we see the threads of Craft history shooting back into the realms of the ancient civilizations in the Mediterranean world.[61]

There is equal debate on the origin of the word "sabbat."[62] Most feel it was birthed in the Witch Trial era, then coined by Margaret Murray (1862–1963), an anthropologist who tried desperately to put the pieces of the historical Witchcraft puzzle together.[63] Although Margaret's work was received well by the public and the scholars of her time, it has since been torn to shreds; however, we cannot dispute the basic kernel of Margaret's theory: (1) Pagan earth- and fertility-centered celebrations did exist for thousands of years; (2) magickal practices in the populace weren't something new, these applications had been around for thousands of years; and (3) Pagans had religion—ergo our ancestor's celebrations were magickal as well as religious and cultural, with dividing lines between the three intensely blurred, which leaves us to the question . . .

Where Do Witches Come From?

How much was magick, how much was religion, and how much was cultural in the above-mentioned celebrations is still up for debate. Scholars and Witches alike will continue to theorize, argue, and research this issue until the end of time. When ancient and medieval history is involved there is never a definitive answer. Did Witches exist before Gerald Gardner? Of course they did—the Basque Witches are one example, and there are hundreds more in our history from all over the world. Just look at some of the archeological tribal studies still conducted today in remote areas that shed light on what type of magick and ritual people employed thousands of years ago. Did the Witches of old practice like we do in the modern Craft? No. Were they organized? Possibly in some areas, but more than likely not in the way they are today, unless we take into account tribal functions and then once again we are back to what is religion, what is magick, and what is tradition. Certainly, a great deal of what we call the Craft as it stands now can be attributed to Gardner's organization of a revitalized idea in the twentieth century. There are even major differences in the way the Craft was practiced thirty years ago as opposed to what is done today.

The Craft changes and grows to meet the needs of its people. The twentieth century provided us with several gifted individuals who helped to solidify the various aspects of religion, magick, and culture into modern Witchcraft. Doreen Valiente gave us our history and our poetry. Raymond Buckland carried the Craft to the New World. Sybil Leek established covens on the eastern seaboard of America. StarHawk and Laurie Cabot brought us psychology and led us into the political arena (and they continue to do so) insofar as making definitive statements that we are here, we exist, and we want to be

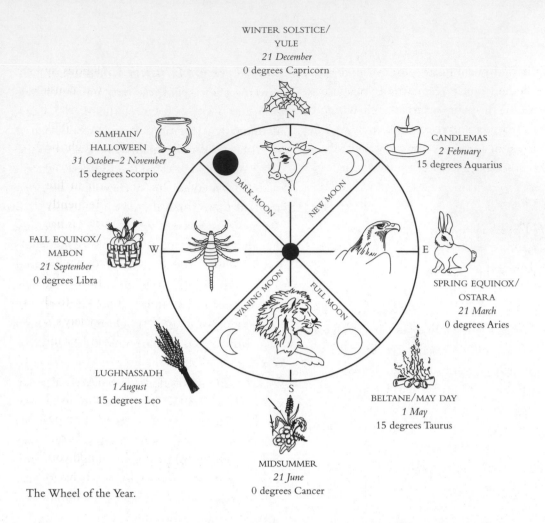

The Wheel of the Year.

treated fairly, and that we can be helpful to society. The Farrars opened up the Wiccan rituals to thousands of people. Z. Budapest gave us the belief that we could have personal power and succeed. Scott Cunningham made the Craft incredibly simple for us to understand and practice, giving us small bites of easily digested theory and folklore, all the while improving our lives without undue headache. There are literally hundreds of others, some whose participation glimmered only throughout their lifetimes and whose works faded into history, especially where there was no one to record their positive "nameless deeds," and others who continue to work in an effort to educate Wiccan practitioners and the general public alike. I could go on listing these strong individuals, but you get the idea.

Modern Witchcraft, like all the other religions on the planet, is a blended one—meaning it combines ancient history, cultural practices, and social models of the past and present. Unlike other religions, it carries little dogma, though as the religion ages this may change (I hope not—it's the dogma that always gets you into trouble). It is difficult to say when any religion began, and it is equally tough to determine which practice belongs to what religion. Which brings us back to our discussion on the Wheel of the Year. As an example, the eight High Holy Days of the modern Craft religion are rooted in the practices of ancient civilizations that were carried by the people through medieval times and into the present, especially in the European segment of the population, and the Norse/Germanic influence on the eight sabbats cannot be denied. Unique to the Craft is that although many sects choose various pantheons, most stick with the European High Holy Days for their major sabbats (though there are groups that also celebrate specific holidays that match a particular pantheon in addition to what we now label as "generic" Wiccan holidays). We need to note, however, that although the timing may be much the same, there is more than one name attributed to each sabbat, depending upon the Craft group that you belong to and the history from which they draw their legends and lore. For example, where some may use generic names (such as Winter Solstice), others will say Yule.

Wiccan Rede/ Witch's Creed

You will hear the following statement often in your study of magickal spirituality: *Eight words the Wiccan Rede fulfill; an' it harm none, do what ye will.* Although Gerald B. Gardner claimed that the creed came from the words of legendary good King Paulsol—"Do what you like as long as you harm no one,"[64] it is highly likely that, like other forms of Gardnerian material, the Rede may have been borrowed from Crowley's Law of Thelema—"Do what thou wilt shall be the whole of the Law"—who gathered this snippet of wisdom from European magickal lodges popular in the late eighteen and early 1900s, and *they* got it from ancient Egyptian magickal texts dated around 3000 B.C.E.[65] However, there is a debate on the time frame. Some historians date this information from 1600 B.C., where others may be adding the Pyramid Texts of 2500 B.C., which in turn may well draw on even older concepts. Even with the 1600 B.C. timing, that's pretty darn old.

In the Egyptian magickal/religious system, magick itself (as in the Craft) was considered neither good nor bad, and if one was called upon, one met difficulties head-on with like energy without the worry that you might be condemned for it later. *Do what thou wilt* meant that you were to follow your mission in life. The Egyptians also gave us another frequently used Craft adage: *There is no part of us that is not of the gods.* Greek Pagans originated the saying *To the pure, all things are pure,* meaning that when you have reached a high stage of spiritual enlightenment, you have evolved past petty day-to-day irritations, religious dogma, and society's sometimes misguided decrees to understand the meaning of one's true will.[66]

The only problem with taking "an' it harm none" in a literal sense is that if you lived by it fundamentally, you couldn't grow up to be a police officer, join the military service, sit on a jury of your peers, or be a judge, nor could you work against disease, stop discriminatory behavior, halt abuse, or make sure that the yo-yo who smashed your car window gets caught.

Many new students in the Craft stub their toe on this rule. Indeed, a few never seem to overcome the worry that every time they do magick, they are somehow tinkering with the universe in a way they shouldn't. Everyone's thoughts already tinker with the universe (the collective unconscious and quantum physics), therefore doing focused magick is actually more intelligent then letting your thoughts fly all over the place. People are here to create; they have their individual talents for a good reason. I don't think anyone was born to be a couch potato. There are people who buy loads of books on Witchcraft, the occult, and magick, and read, read, read, but never find the courage to lift one magickal pinky, even when a tornado threatens to squash their home, because they are afraid that they will do something wrong. This is a victim's mentality, not that of a real, practicing Witch. The word *Rede* comes from Old English, meaning "to guide or direct"—it doesn't mean "to lie down and allow life to run over you."

"An' it harm none" is a moral, spiritual sound bite. (I read that somewhere on the Internet—whomever said it, kudos to you.) Think of a karate student who is trained to walk away from a fight, and to only use the skills he or she has learned if there is ultimately no other choice for survival of the home, family, or friends. In the old laws of the Craft, the student was instructed that they could not attack, but they had every right to defend themselves if the necessity arose in a manner in which they felt would get the job done most efficiently, and if in that defense harm occurs, they weren't going to wring their hands and fret over the positive or negative balance in their karma bank. They were also taught that they may never, ever harm the innocent on purpose in their workings, which meant every precaution possible was taken before any work was done.[67] However, if you lived by the "an' it harm none" rule to the letter, you couldn't even work against disease! Now that's a silly thought, isn't it?

How the Rede Works

Let me give you an example, to be sure you understand how this rule works. Let's say you and Alicia are running for student government president—college, high school, doesn't matter. If you zap Alicia because she's pretty, has everything, and is most likely going to win because she is a good person, you have just broken the "an' it harm none" rule, and you will pay for it. However, if Alicia is running a dirty campaign by spreading lies about you, accusing you of tearing down her campaign posters when you didn't, and telling the teachers you smoke dope, which you don't, then you have every right to

do something about this nasty predicament. If you *don't* do anything, then you are breaking the "an' it harm none" rule because you are allowing yourself to be hurt. Even in this circumstance there are rules of Craft behavior. Here, rather than just blast Alicia (which could have karmic repercussions), you might first do a ritual of protection for yourself, and then you might choose to work a spell or ritual that concentrates on exposing the truth.

Have your magickal actions harmed Alicia? No. As she is the one who started the negativity in the first place, she gets to keep it. You are just kindly sending back her own package of glop, magickally marked "undeliverable." In the Craft, you make it—you own it. You are always responsible for your own actions and you cannot blame your behavior on someone else (living, dead, or myth). Unlike Christianity and Judaism, which have their own boogymen (Satan and assorted demons), the Craft belief system identifies all negativity as human driven, putting responsibility for one's actions right where it belongs: in one's own lap. In this scenario, Alicia may very well win the election (especially if you didn't move fast enough, or just let it go to see what might develop); however, she will reap the consequences of her actions further down the line. Magick doesn't always move as quickly as we'd like, which tells us that Spirit has a divine plan, despite our impatience. Years later you may learn that Alicia did get her just rewards. I've found that Spirit does somehow inform you, especially when you consciously or subconsciously need closure—just don't stop your life to wait for the message or stew over a situation that you should have released a long time ago.

There are other Witches who follow the Wiccan Rede by working the magick and giving the problem up to Spirit, thereby releasing themselves from incurring karmic debt (where every action has an equal reaction). This is especially so in healing magicks (which we'll cover under that section). They still work the magick and do the ritual, but rather than targeting Alicia by name, they focus on harmony in Spirit with Spirit on the subject, and let Spirit handle all the tough decisions—which is not a bad thing, and ties into the alchemical transformation you'll read about in this book. Looking at this alchemically: Chaos (the problem) meets your thoughts on the subject, and is challenged by purification (the Spirit-guided magick) to create positive change (the best manifestation possible) because you know for certain that the change in a positive direction can occur. (SEE PART II, WAND, ROD, STAFF, AND STANG, FOR MORE INFORMATION ON HOW THIS IS DONE.) Therefore, if you use the alchemical formula of manifestation in your magick, you will not have to worry about ethics because you have purified all intent by incorporating Spirit after you created the thought. If this is confusing to you, be sure to read the sections in Part IV on Alchemy and As Above, So Below before you continue.

Finally, the Wiccan Rede also applies to how you treat people of other belief systems.[68] According to my understanding of religion (meaning ritual and reverence), the idea isn't to trash someone else's belief to make oneself feel better, stronger, or secure. Religion should be a set of practices that supports one's spiritual needs. Being nasty to someone of a faith different from yours isn't supporting your spiritual requirements—indeed, such a negative practice cripples the soul, and spirituality flounders and drowns. I will always believe that Witches are among the physical angels of the Earth plane, and their job is not only to enhance their own lives but to be of service to those around them, regardless of their (or those they help) religious preference. Likewise, to dishonor a fellow Crafter over petty

differences, jealousies, or greed is considered in many magickal circles to be the epitome of disrespect, and eventually you will lose your gifts as well as any standing you have gained in the community. If you turn on your own, then you don't deserve to belong.

Many of today's Craft students were introduced to the Rede through the poetry of Doreen Valiente titled *The Witches' Creed*, which can be recited after the circlecasting of a sabbat ritual. However, what most modern Wiccan students do not see are Doreen's obvious references to alchemy. Once you've read about alchemy, the Emerald Tablet, and the Great Work in this book, you will thoroughly understand what she was saying, and in that moment you will never again argue over ethics. (Notes to Doreen's poem are in brackets.)

The Witches' Creed (Annotated)

Hear now the words of the Witches,
the secrets we hid in the night,
when dark was our destiny's pathway,
that now we bring forth into light.

Mysterious water and fire
[Primal energies of water and fire;
ice and fire in some groups]
the earth and the wide-ranging air,
by hidden quintessence
[Spiritual energy—the fifth element,
first used in the alchemical sciences]
we know them,
and will and keep silent and dare.
[The Witch's Pyramid]

The birth and rebirth of all nature,
[The Wheel of the Year]
the passing of winter and spring,
we share with the life universal,

rejoice in the magical ring.
[The magick circle]

*Four times in the year the Great Sabbat
returns, and the witches are seen
at Lammas and Candlemas dancing,
on May Eve and old Hallowe'en.*

When day-time and night-time are equal
[Solstices]
*when sun is at greatest and least,
the four Lesser Sabbats are summoned,
and again gather Witches in feast.*

Thirteen silver moons in a year.
[Ancient lunar calendar where
there were 13 months following
the moon rather than 12]
*Thirteen is the coven's array.
Thirteen times at Esbat make merry,
for each golden* [solar] *year and a day.*

The power was passed down the ages
[Lineage]
*each time between woman and man,
each century unto the other,
ere time and the ages began.*

*When drawn is the magickal circle,
by sword or athame of power,
its compass between the two worlds lies
in land of the Shades for that hour.*

*This world has no right then to know it,
and world of beyond will tell naught.
The oldest of Gods are invoked there,
the Great Work* [Alchemy]
of magic is wrought.

For two are the mystical pillars
[Chaos vs. Order; Force and Form]

*that stand at the gate of the shrine,
and two are the powers of nature,
the forms and the forces divine*
[Occult Kabbalah].

*The dark and the light in succession,
the opposites each unto each*
[Full Moon]
*shown forth as a God and a Goddess:
of this did our ancestors teach.*

*By night He's the wild wind's rider,
the Horn'd One, the Lord of the Shades.
By day he's the King of the Woodland,
the dweller in green forest glades.*

*She is youthful or old as She pleases,
She sails the torn clouds in Her barque*
[Boat (see the Four Adorations)]
*the bright silver lady of midnight,
the crone who weaves spells in the dark.*

*The master and mistress of magic,
they dwell in the deeps of the mind*
[Psychology and the science of magick]
*immortal and ever-renewing,
with power to free or to bind.*

So drink the good wine to the Old Gods
[Communion]
*and dance and make love in their praise,
till Elphame's*
[Summerland; Faeryland]
*fair land shall receive us
In the peace at the end of our days.*

*And do what you will be the challenge,
so be it in love that harms none,
for this is the only commandment.
By magic of old it be done!*

Then take up the pentacle, and walk with it clockwise around the circle, holding the symbol up at the four quarters, east, south, west, and north, repeating each time:

> *Eight words the Witch's Creed fulfill:*
> *If it harms none, do what you will!*[69]

Witch's Pyramid

In some Craft circles, the Witch's Pyramid is known as the Four Powers of the Magus or the Four Secrets of the Sphinx, whose energy is considered to be the foundation and four pillars of all practical and esoteric magick. Whether you are conjuring the weather for a great day at the beach or concentrating on empowering the Witch within, the basic building blocks are always the same: To Know, To Dare, To Will, and To Be Silent, known in some Craft circles by their Latin names as Noscere (to know), representing the element of air; Audere (to dare), designated by the element of water; Velle (to will) stands for the element of fire; and Tacere (to be silent) linked to the element of earth.[70] Together they become *voces mysticae,* discussed in the Magickal Alphabets section in Part IV. The most difficult lesson to learn of the four corners is the last, to be silent. There are Crafters who have been in magick for twenty years and still haven't learned that one. When the four powers are gathered together, then the fifth sacred power occurs—that of quintessence, or Spirit, which represents the top of the pyramid, sometimes called *ire*, meaning "to go"—the movement of energy toward manifestation guided by the hand of the Witch. Without this solid foundation (the four corners of magick, not to be mistaken for the four elemental quarters, though the associa-tion can be considered), the cone of power will stutter and fall and the enchantment will break apart before it can reach your desire. The oath you take upon seeking entry into the Craft, whether you are doing the seeker ceremony, a dedication, or an initiation, rests entirely on the foundation of the Witch's Pyramid.

To Know means that you will strive to learn as much as you can in this lifetime and that you will apply this knowledge to your daily life. It also means that you will seek truth in all things and be willing to change your perceptions to meet your awakening spirituality.

To Dare says that you have pushed fear behind you and that you will be courageous and proac-tive in all that you do. You will believe in your-self and have faith in the universe and in your own abilities.

To Will means that you will learn to focus your thoughts and practice meditation and visu-alization in order to reach your goals. It means that you won't sit back and let the world pass you by—you will work toward your dreams. You will meet obstacles and find positive solu-tions to overcome them.

To Be Silent is, perhaps, the most important. It means that you will keep your mouth shut about the magick that you do, lest your friends and others destroy the magick with their negativity before it ever manages to manifest. It also means that you will think before you speak, and that you won't throw pearls before swine (which means don't give good information to bad peo-ple). Finally, it means that you will follow the etiquette of the Craft and not blab about what happened in ritual circle (if you work with a group), carry gossip about the other members, nor harm others intentionally through your words. For adults and teens, this is by far the most difficult promise to keep.

To Go means that you will master the four pillars (energies) of the base of the pyramid and use them in a positive way to help yourself as well as others. To Go is the ultimate meaning of the Witch's Oath of Service.

If we trace the pentacle with our finger beginning at To Know, moving up at To Dare, over at To Will, down at To Be Silent, and then up to Spirit, then finish by moving back down at To Know, not only have we made a pentacle, we have also worked through the four corners before moving to Spirit. Coming back down again at To Know, we have the occult maxim *As above, so below*. Not only must you begin by studying and believing you can do anything, you must end that way as well—faith followed by magick followed by faith.

Witch's Pyramid Meditation

Study the above diagram. Now close your eyes. Take three deep breaths. Ground and center. In your mind, begin at To Know. Let your mind wander. What do you see? How do you feel? To Know represents the element of air. Breath in and out slowly. Connect with the element of air. Ask for wisdom and it shall be given.

Now move to the To Dare position. This is the element of water. Is there something you are afraid of? Cleanse it from your mind. Open your heart to transformation. Feel the universal love.

Take a deep breath and travel over to the To Will point of the star. This is the element of fire. What courage do you feel you need right now? Are you using your creativity to your best advantage? Fire also purifies. Let any negativity within you turn to ash and drift away.

Take a deep breath and move on to the To Be Silent point. What does this mean to you? Touch the still point of the universe, where everything is one, where everything is at total peace and harmony. In silence you will find truth.

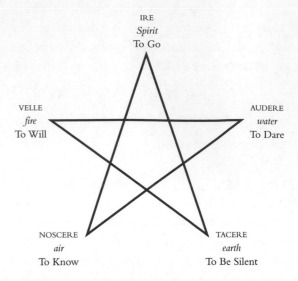

The Witch's Pyramid.

Take a deep breath and move up to Spirit, the point of manifestation. Reach out and touch deity with your mind. What are you trying to manifest in your life? What are your goals? Visualize them.

Take a deep breath and travel back down to the To Know point of the star. As your mind moves down to this point, imagine that Spirit has granted your wishes and that they are even now moving toward you on the material plane. Will you be ready to recognize these gifts when they materialize? Do you feel you deserve what you have asked for? If you don't, then your will won't take form.

Have faith that what you have asked for will be brought to you. Know that Spirit has granted your request. Feel that certainty, that knowing, deep inside. Take another deep breath and let any visualizations go. Count from one to five, then open your eyes. Practice this meditation for at least two weeks to get the feel of it, then use it before ritual, spellcasting, or in your daily devotions.

Ritual of the Sphinx

Draw a large pentacle, about the size of a dinner plate, on a piece of poster board. Cut out the pentacle and place it on the center of your altar. Place white illuminator candles or electrical candles on either side of the pentacle. Write out specifically what you want to manifest. Place the paper with your desire on top of the pentacle. Cast a magick circle. Light the illuminator candles, saying: "Out of the darkness our Mother emerged, bringing health, wealth, love, and harmony to her people." Take three deep breaths, then ground and center. Place your hands on the altar and leave them there for a few moments to activate the energies there.

In this spell you will not follow the compass points for the directions. Instead you are going to walk the pentacle to manifest your desire; therefore, you will not call the quarters in the usual manner. Next, light a red candle and place in a safe candleholder that can be carried. As you carry the candle from point to point, it will gather the energy you build. As you light the candle, say: "Spirit of fire, bring to me my heart's desire."

Using your altar as the point of Spirit, take the candle and walk clockwise around the circle until you reach the point of To Know as given in the Witch's Pyramid diagram, repeating the word "Noscere" in your magickal voice. As you walk, visualize walking toward the element of air, and believe that you are gathering wisdom with every step. When you reach the To Know point, face outward, with your back to the center of the circle, hold the candle high with both hands, and say:

Element of air, I seek your blessings here.
I invoke the power of wisdom and knowledge.
I know that you will do this for me.

Turn and face the center of the circle. Begin chanting the word "Audere" as you walk to the To Dare point in your circle. As you walk, visualize yourself transforming into the most powerful magickal person in the world. Feel that confidence grow with each step. When you reach the To Dare point, face outward, with your back to the center of the circle, hold the candle high with both hands, and say:

Element of water, I seek your blessings here.
I invoke the power of love and transformation.
I know that you will do this for me.

Turn and face the center of the circle. Begin chanting the word "Velle" as you walk to the To Will point in your circle. As you walk, visualize divine light before you. Straighten your shoulders. Walk proudly forward. Think of this point as the one that will sling your spell into forward motion, where the spark of life will be added to your work. When you reach the To Will point, face outward, with your back to the center of the circle, hold the candle high with both hands, and say:

Element of fire, I seek your blessings here.
I invoke the power of action and creativity.
I know that you will do this for me.

Turn and face the center of the circle. Begin chanting the word "Tacere" as you walk to the To Be Silent point of the circle. Imagine the mystery of your work surrounding you as you walk—the essence of the meaning of "the hidden children." Walk toward that still point of the universe where perfect harmony exists. When you reach the To Be Silent point, face outward, with your back to the center of the circle, and say:

Element of earth, I seek your blessings here.
I invoke harmony and balance in my work.
I know that you will do this for me.

Turn and face the center of the circle. Following the diagram, walk to the Spirit portion of the circle (located at the altar), chanting "Ire" as you make your way there. As you walk, visualize that you have gathered blessings from all of the elements and that you are taking these combined energies to the point of manifestation, where their pattern will form on the astral plane under the guidance of Spirit. If it helps to visualize, think of these energies as collected in the candle flame that you hold out before you. Once you reach the Spirit point, face the altar and hold the candle up over the altar, and say:

> *The power is gathered*
> *the energies one.*
> *The elements are summoned*
> *the magick begun.*

Place the candle on top of the paper that contains your desire. Beginning with your hands at your side, slowly raise them as you chant, "Noscere, Audere, Velle, Tacere, Ire!" until your palms are pointed at the heavens and you feel amazingly good inside. Run through the chant one more time, and on the last word stretch your arms toward the heavens and utter the last sound as loud as you can. You should feel an emotional release. Before you lower your hands, inhale deeply from your nose and exhale slowly from your mouth.

At this point, you can burn the paper in a fire-safe cauldron or keep it until your wish has been granted. Allow the candle to burn completely, if at all possible (meaning if you can monitor it safely while it burns, do so; if not, extinguish with a candlesnuffer, not your breath.) Thank deity. Thank the elements. Release the circle.

Note: The condition of this spell is that you must keep it secret or it won't work.

Solitary Power Exercise (Silver's Secret)

The following exercise can be used in any ritual, spell, or in daily life. It is an exercise of the mind that, once practiced, will bring you health, happiness, and prosperity—but you must believe. If you do not have faith, it won't work. I call this exercise/energy-raising technique Silver's Secret. The name will become a keyword for you, though you may wish to change it to your name—for example, Ted's Secret, or Angela's Secret, or David's Secret. Try saying your name with the word "secret" behind it. Sounds magickal already, doesn't it? That's good. A little pizzazz never hurt anybody.

ONE: Choose what you will work for. This is the planning phase. All the doubts, worries, ideas, and possible solutions should be removed from your mind. The only thing that should be left is the desire.

TWO: Close your eyes. This allows you to shut out the world around you and focus on the exercise. In time, you will be able to use your secret with your eyes open, but for now, close them.

THREE: Take three deep breaths. This brings more oxygen to the brain and other areas of the body, relieves stress, urges relaxation of the muscles, and helps to put you in the "alpha" state.

FOUR: Let go of time and space. Say "release" as you breathe out. When your eyes are closed, it is easy to forget that time and space exist. Spirit does not need time or space to perform miracles, and neither do you when you mentally release those thoughts of restraint and touch deity energy, which is the next step. If it helps, think of opening your hands (or physically allow your hands to slowly open) while you say the word "release."

FIVE: Touch deity energy. Say the word "unity." In the Craft we teach that you and deity are one, and that you share creative force with every manifestation of energy in the universe. This is a given. Of course, you have to acknowledge this fact, which isn't easy for everyone to do. When you speak the word "unity," you are affirming that we are all one and that you have the power to become one with everything. If you don't believe this, the secret won't work. If it helps, as you say the word "unity," think of yourself moving into your conception of god/dess—losing, for a moment, your conscious thought of separateness.

SIX: Conceive the form. Visualize the thing. Say the word aloud. Surround the thing with pure white light. For some, this will be the most difficult part of the exercise. It is why the Craft teaches you to learn how to visualize people, places, and things. There are also ideas that do not have a physical form: love, compassion, success, happiness, joy, and so on. For these, or if you cannot visualize the object desired (but keep practicing), substitute the feeling. How do you feel when you are happy? Are you all smiles? Or maybe happiness to you is security, pleasant surroundings, a good joke? You need only hold on to this thought for a short period of time (a count to five is a good start; if it's shorter, that's okay, but longer is even better). There are other ideas that are not an emotion, yet not necessarily a specific physical object either. The word "information" comes to mind; "time" is another. If you can't link the idea into a mental picture, just firmly say the word aloud and fill your mind with pure, white light. The birth of the visualization in your mind, holding it, affirming the word aloud, and surrounding the object with white light is a simple one, two, three operation once you get used to the process. You might want to practice this part of the secret before you do the whole technique for the first time.

SEVEN: Accept success. This is important. If you don't mentally accept success, your "secret" will bomb. You must want it, and welcome it.

EIGHT: Know beyond a shadow of a doubt that this will be done. Suspend disbelief. This is a toughie, but you only have to hold onto this knowing for a few seconds. (The longer you practice, the better at this you'll get.) However, just getting to that knowing can be hard, depending upon your personality, how much work you've done in the Craft already, and what you've learned about life in the past. You're one up on adults because childhood, where you believed in things unequivocally because someone told you so, is not that far behind you.

So, let's talk about how you feel when you know something to be true (through whatever method, scientific or otherwise). For example, at noon on any given day the sun rose in the east and is now overhead, even if it is hidden by clouds and you can't see it. Close your eyes and think about how you feel about knowing that the sun is overhead. There is no gap in your thought process. No indecision, like, "It's there—no, maybe not." You didn't debate in your head how it got there in the first place. You immediately *know* (from past experience, science, and other good stuff) that the sun is overhead. Try that again. That *knowing* was a nanosecond, wasn't it? And there wasn't any effort, was there? You didn't grunt, or groan, or make wild gestures with your hands to *know* that the sun was overhead. You didn't dance around a fire, call a demon, or spit in the wind. Nor was there any emotion. The sun is overhead. Big deal. Hold that thought.

Ever been to a really great movie with cool special effects, and the script was so wonderful that you lost yourself completely in the story and you believed everything that happened to the character, even though you know for a fact that in real life (as you know it) those things on the screen couldn't possibly be true? Yet while you are watching the movie you believe those things are true for that character. In writing and screenplays this phenomenon is called "suspension of belief"—where the audience lets go of what they know to be true to enhance their enjoyment. This is what every actor, writer, publisher, and movie company hopes you will do, because when you suspend your belief (and like that feeling), they count their work a success. There are other activities where you are already familiar with this process—when reading a book and when watching a magician (to name two). Where else might you try to suspend belief? How about when working with things of an artistic nature—that zone your mind goes to when you listen or create music, sculpt a statue, paint a picture, take the perfect photograph, write a poem, or dance? When you do these things you are tapping into the creative unconsciousness of the universe.

If this is something we already know how to do, how come we don't do it all the time? Because there are environments where we believe it is safe and appropriate to let go, and environments where we believe it is not safe to let go, because if we did, our survival would be seriously threatened. Therefore, the question is not whether you can "let go and believe," but in what environment you allow yourself to let go. Now, when we talk "environment," what exactly are we referring to? Here, we mean the material and the nonmaterial. Let's start with the material.

The material environment most conducive to magick and raising power is the place where you feel most safe and secure. It is a place that is devoid of negative energy, which is why Witches are taught to physically cleanse an area, to create sacred space with the elements, and to cast the magick circle. This physical area is then thought to be suitable for physical, mental, and spiritual magickal work. The creation of this place, by you, represents your permission to yourself that it's okay to work with magick here. These exercises (cleansing, sacred space, and circlecasting) fulfill other criteria for magick, but for what we're discussing here, that is as far as we need to take it.

The nonmaterial environment is your mind, which takes us back to the sun in the sky explanation, and the discussion on what it feels like to know something, and how quickly we are able to grasp any thought, and how quickly we can suspend belief. Doesn't take much, does it? Since you are capable of knowing and capable of suspending belief, then you are capable of absolutely anything and everything. So what stops you? Fear. (Which we'll get to in step number nine.)

If you are still confused on how to exercise this knowing thing, let's try one more example. Set a glass of water in front of you. You know it's there because you put it there. Close your eyes. Is the glass still there? Of course it is. You know it is there. How long did it take you to process the feeling that you know the glass is there? Less than a hiccup. You didn't need to go through the long mental process of how you put that glass in front of you. Analyze the knowing feeling. Calm. Certainty. Aha! That's the feeling we're talking about, and you need only hold on to that feeling for a nanosecond, even in magick, provided you're using this entire sequence. In magick, we must always believe that what we want will happen, and the key to finishing out the process is knowing it. Belief plus knowing equals magick.

NINE: Reject any thoughts of failure, now and in the future. Will your mind to think only of success. Fear will ruin any ritual, spell, goal, or focused thought, whether your fear is frivolous or has logic behind it. You must banish fear to win.

You cannot debate the finer points of what you want in the middle of any magickal process, and you cannot choose the way in which Spirit will grant your request, just as you cannot live another person's life for them (magick always follows the path of least resistance). Either you want to succeed, or you don't. If you don't, then don't use your secret because it won't work. If Spirit thinks that your request is not precisely in harmony with your life path, Spirit will accommodate your choices as long as you legitimately feel you are working in harmony with the universe and not intentionally trying to hurt anyone. Spirit expects you to make boo boos. If you don't trust yourself, then trust in Spirit. When you connected with deity in step five and welcomed pure, positive energy into this technique, you banished any inadvertent mistakes. What if you think that your request is too fantastic to take form in your life? If you believe this, your secret will fail. You will have thought your failure into reality because you believed, by acknowledging that thought in the first place, that it's easier to fail than to succeed. In magick and daily life, negative thoughts are the enemy. If you give them power by dwelling on them, they will win and you will be miserable. Every time a defeatist or negative thought comes into your brain, blow it away! At first, this will be easier said than done, but eventually you'll get the hang of it. The human brain is incredibly creative.

TEN: Keep your mouth shut. Yeah, for some of you this is going to be a problem and you're just going to have to work on that; but for others, no sweat. However, if you want to succeed, remember this: the procedure is called "Silver's *Secret*," or, in your case, *your* secret. When you tell others about magick, especially those who don't believe in the process, you are allowing that person to work against you. No, they're probably not going to run out there and light up a black, jumbo candle and sing a song of mojo by the light of the big, fat moon, but more than likely they'll just laugh at you, and make you feel small and stupid, which sets in motion your fear of failure (because we all have subconscious buttons people can push that relate to defeat, and this is especially so of close friends and family members because we usually care what they think). This does not infer that you shouldn't talk to reliable people about your problems, and if your mind went there right away, shame on you. Magick is never meant to be harmful—not the casting of it nor the practicing of it.

Now that you've read the entire sequence on your special secret, let's put it in outline form. You might want to copy this down on a small piece of paper or on a 3 by 5-inch card so that you can carry it with you.

YOUR SECRET SUCCESS FORMULA

To Dare

To Release

To Connect

To Conceive

To Accept

To Know

To Believe

To Will

To Be Silent

Some of you are saying, *Awww, Silver, I know what this is. This is the Witch's Pyramid!* So it is. If we factored out the steps I've given you to make the process more streamlined, you'd get To Dare, To Know, To Will, and To Be Silent. For our purposes, though, we don't want to remove any of the steps until you have used your secret so much that you can blend the steps together in your own time, should you so desire. As you can see, there is more to the formula than how it is normally presented in most books on the Craft.

Let's make your secret formula into a chant: "Release, Connect, Conceive, Accept, I Know, Believe!" Try saying this about ten times, and see how it rolls off the tongue. What kind of rhythm did you come up with? This is your signature rhythm for this formula. Try drumming out the beat on the table. Give it a go, twenty times or so, until the drumming is fluid with the chant. How does that make you feel? Empowered? Good! I left out "Dare" because that's the setup and you wouldn't be working the magick in the first place if you weren't a little daring. "Will" and "Silence" were removed from the chant because they are after the fact, and represent the rules to follow to ensure success, but if you would prefer to add them, that's just fine. If this chant doesn't feel comfortable, try: "Let Go, I Am, Conceive, Accept, I Know, Believe!" and see if that works better for you.

Okay, you've read the formula, you understand the explanations, you practiced some of the steps, worked with a chant, and added your own rhythm of drumming to set up a familiar vibration. Now it's time to put the formula to good use. We're going to do a dry run. Pick something you want to work for (smaller is best since this is a new experience for you). With your eyes open, read through the outline, doing each step in your mind. Good. Now, let's get a little creative. Think of your desire, then say:

One, let go (and do that in your mind).
Two, I am (and connect with deity).
Three, I conceive (and visualize
the desire).
Four, I accept (and welcome success).
Five, I know (and bring that nanosecond
of certainty into your mind).

Six, I believe (and say it like you
darned well mean it!).
So mote it be! (this is the "will" part)

That wasn't so tough, was it? Excellent! Let's go further. After declaring each number and the intention, follow with your chant and drumming, like this:

One, let go!
(let go, I am, conceive, accept, I know, believe!)
Two, I am!
(let go, I am, conceive, accept, I know, believe!)
Three, I conceive!
(let go, I am, conceive, accept, I know, believe!)
Four, I accept!
(let go, I am, conceive, accept, I know, believe!)
Five, I know!
(let go, I am, conceive, accept, I know, believe!)
Six, I believe!
(let go, I am, conceive, accept, I know, believe!)
So mote it be!
(let go, I am, conceive, accept, I know, believe!)

Tricky, huh? What if you do not want to drum? Try tying a knot in a string or cord as you say your chant (rather than drumming). "Let go" (tie the knot and say the chant), "I am!" (tie the knot and say the chant), and so on. Carry the cord with you until your desire has reached you. Don't forget to thank Spirit. Think of other creative ways that you can use your secret formula. Once you have practiced this technique a long time, you won't need the words anymore. Instead, the formula will compact in your mind into a set of feelings, and then into a single feeling. When this occurs, you will know that you have become an adept.

shadows of Objects & Tools

Altars

Some scholars think that the first altars were actually tombs of the dead where offerings were made to a deified ancestor. Others believe that the idea of the altar came from the Pagan belief that the newly deceased were gathered on the borders of the sky, under the constellation called Ara, meaning "the altar."[1] Ara lies in the Milky Way, south of Scorpius, and is well to the south of the celestial equator. The ancient Greeks visualized it as the altar on which their gods swore an oath of allegiance before challenging the Titans for control of the universe.[2] The word "altar" comes from a Latin word that translates to "on high." We could put a variety of meanings to this terminology—from a physically high place, to a seat in the stars, to the more esoteric meaning of consecrating a sacred area that sits between the worlds of human and deity, enabling the human to work with deity on the deity's level from where the Witch physically stands. Ancient altars were often made of stone or, if constructed of wood, held some type of stone surface in the center. Many were carved or painted with symbols of animals and deities. It was during the various Inquisitions that the Witch altar took on a more lurid, negative role —an inappropriate and inaccurate representation of the Craft altar—that was reflected in many horror movies from the 1940s through the 70s, feeding the inaccurate, sensationalist information to the general public. During a few modern Craft ceremonies, a person's body may become the altar for a few moments to meld them with the elemental and divine energies so that in the future they may work easily through space and time; however, sacrifices and rampant sexual excursions, as shown in the movies, are *not* part of Wiccan dogma.

Altar Designs

For as many magickal people as there are in the world, there are an equal number of altar designs. A magickal altar is normally a flat surface that becomes the focus of spells, rituals, and daily devotional activities. The altar is a place of power; over time, it will collect all the positive energy that manifests while doing magickal work. An altar can be made out of any material, and quite a few magickal people use the furniture they already have in their homes rather than buy or build a new altar (especially when they are first learning). Your altar can be the top of your bedroom dresser, a coffee table, or nightstand. A home entertainment center with compartments of various sizes and moveable shelves is an excellent choice, as long as you remember to watch burning candles. You need at least three feet of air space from any flame to the next shelf. If not, you can scorch the wood and set the furniture on fire. You may choose to use a portable altar instead, something that can be packed away when not in use, such as the top of a trunk, a flat board, or a piece of flagstone that you can push under your bed.

Altars can be decorated in a variety of ways, including the use of an altar cloth to cover the surface, special candle holders, statues of gods and goddesses, or your favorite totem animal. Depending on your personality, you may wish to keep your altar bare and only use it when you have a special working in mind. How you place items on your altar is called an altar setup. Those Witches who belong to a coven or larger group are taught to set up their altar a traditional way common to the training of the group.

Your primary concern should be that the altar is fire safe, as most magickal people work often with candles, oils, and flame. You may wish to keep a fire extinguisher close to the altar surface. I know I do. I've never had the occasion to use it, but my entire family has had accidents and, although they are amusing now, they weren't when the flames were jutting up to the ceiling! I literally blew up my dining room table because I wasn't careful with a bag of Vesta powder (a special effect for cauldron flame), and once a glass seven-day candle exploded all over my altar and the flames began to crawl up my dining room curtains. Luckily, several members of the family were in the room, so disaster was averted. Had no one been present, my whole house would have gone up. You can never be too careful with fire.

Before activating your altar, you should clean the surface of any dirt or grime, then perform a cleansing ceremony, followed by an empowering and blessing ceremony, to activate the magnetic properties of the altar. Once activated, the altar surface should contain only those things relating to your religion and magick—no dirty socks, tennis balls, soda bottles, car keys, or wads of chewing gum. Anything that doesn't belong there clutters the pure, positive energy that you have created.

Magickal Things You Need to Know About Your Altar

- Your altar becomes a focus of positive power once activated—yours and that of Spirit.

- The altar was originally designed to request the presence of deity.

- Where you put your altar isn't as important as how you use it.

- The shape of your altar is a personal choice.

- You can have more than one altar.

- Having an altar for spiritual reflection isn't against any religious dogma.

- Before use, your altar should be sprinkled with holy water and salt, infused with incense smoke, blessed with holy oil, and empowered in the name of Spirit (SEE ALTAR CLEANSING).

Altar Ideas

- Dresser, nightstand, or bureau in your room.

- A flat piece of stone that is portable.

- A skateboard.

- Empty closet.

- Desk drawer (not recommended for burning candles).

- Cinderblocks.

- Steppingstone (can be purchased at a garden store, or you can make one yourself from materials purchased at a craft store).

- Bookshelf (not recommended for burning candles—even though you think the flame is far enough away from the next shelf, it will warp and eventually burn the shelf above. I almost lost my dining room hutch that way when someone placed a candle on a shelf.)

- Top of a filing cabinet.

- A large mirror.

- A cookie sheet.

- A serving tray.

- A camping tripod, sold in most camping sections of large department stores. (Be careful, these can wobble.)

- An old steamer trunk or other trunk with shelves from an antique store or flea market. (Be careful of open candle flames and take appropriate precautions.)

- A window sill (however, don't put burning candles there).

- In your imagination. Some people scoff at this, but there are people who are not permitted to have altars for a variety of reasons. Perhaps your parents or guardians are afraid that you're religiously going down the tubes and have put their foot down on the issue of an altar. College students, due to living conditions, may not be allowed to have an altar. Individuals in the military service at boot camp can't have one either. Maybe you are visiting Grandma for the summer and you know that she'll find the idea of an altar offensive. If your family goes on an extended vacation, where luggage is a factor, Mom and Dad might not be too happy if you bring a twenty-ton suitcase with all your altar stuff, even though they don't mind your altar at home. Learning to build an altar in your imagination helps you to enhance your visualization skills. You really never know when you might need those mental powers. When people complain to me that they can't have an altar, I tell them they are lucky. Not having one forces you to train your mind, where you might have been lazy before.

Altar Placement

Now that you have chosen your altar, where should you put it? Is there a "right place"? Um, no. Just as there are various ways to cleanse and consecrate an altar, there is no one right place for the altar to go. Some magickal people prefer the altar to sit in the east, corresponding to the dawn, intelligence, and the rising sun. Others like the north, considering this direction to be the energy of manifestation into the physical world ("everything comes from the north"). A third grouping places their altar in the center of

the magick circle, where they can walk around it. This is a wise move if you have a big altar. Reaching across a vast surface is an accident waiting to happen. Finally, there are a few magickal people that move their altars with the movement of the seasons (SEE PART I, WHEEL OF THE YEAR), matching a compass-point direction (north, northeast, east, southeast, south, southwest, west, northwest) to the eight High Holy Days.

Don't worry if you can't move your altar. For example, I know one woman that keeps her altar in the top drawer of her desk—in fact, her altar *is* the top drawer of her desk. When she isn't using it, she simply closes the desk drawer. There are a few drawbacks to this type of altar. First, she can't put anything too heavy on the drawer because the weight would pull out the drawer. Secondly, she has to be careful that she doesn't close the drawer by mistake while working with lit candles! This idea, however, does allow her the privacy she desires and keeps the dust off her magickal tools.

Altar Setup

I'm a big supporter of Keep It Simple. Altar setups that are overflowing with magickal goodies seem to collect a ton of dust, and dust is a magnet for negativity. If you're a busy person, with friends staying over, siblings or children running through your room, and the cat jumping on and off your altar surface at will, collecting a bunch of stuff to set on your altar may not be such a good idea. If you are in college, especially in a dorm room, there's no telling what might happen to your magickal items. We tend to form an attachment to our magickal tools, and a missing wand or cauldron can send anyone into a tizzy. If a magickal tool of yours should decide to "walk off," don't despair. If the item does not return, abide by the old magickal adage *If it's gone,*

Example of an altar setup. Clockwise from top center: (1) statue of deity, (2) illuminator candle, (3) incense, (4) wand, (5) fire candle, (6) cakes, (7) sword, (8) anointing oils, (9) water bowl, (10) salt cup, (11) BOS, (12) illuminator candle, and (13) chalice. A broom rests on the altar's eastern quarter.

it's supposed to be gone. Sometimes magickal things leave us for a good reason. Perhaps something better is coming your way.

In the last few years, the idea of having a personal altar has gained popularity outside of the Craft environment. However, often what people are calling "altars" are actually shrines dedicated to a deity or a particular energy the person would like to bring into the home. The altar, for a Crafter, is a working magickal surface, where a shrine is more of a representation of your spirituality and a place for daily, weekly, or monthly offerings. In some Craft traditions the shrine is called the high altar, and the separate, working surface is called the low altar. Where prayers and petitions are given at the high altar, the messy

work (such as grinding herbs, working with wax, or spellwork that requires you to make and then put together a particular object) is done on the low altar.

A basic altar setup requires only the four elements. The beginning Craft altar adds a statue of deity; two illuminator candles (one for the God and one for the Goddess); a flat centerpiece for focus (usually a geometric symbol: pentacle, hexagram, lunar crescent, the zodiac ring, and so on); the wand; and, if your family environment supports it, the athame (SEE ATHAME, PAGE 124).

If you have more space and plenty of privacy, you may wish to use the traditional altar setup[3] used by most Wiccan students when they first learn about the tools of the Craft of the Wise.[4]

Altar Cleansing

SUPPLIES: Holy water; scented oil; incense; miniature broom (you can find these at craft stores); salt; two bowls (one for the salt and one for the water—any small, waterproof container is acceptable, many teens like to use seashells); red candle (taper or votive); candle holder; inspirational music. *Note:* If you are not permitted to burn candles or use a lighter, it is okay to think of something else that represents fire to you. For example, you may use a picture of a candle, an electric candle (which are sold around Halloween and Christmas), or a combination of red, yellow, and orange tissue paper fashioned into your idea of fire. You could even wrap colored tissue paper over the head of a flashlight to help you visualize that fiery glow. I wholeheartedly agree that nothing beats the real thing, but if your parents say no, then no it is and we need to use our imaginations to think of something that will be acceptable to them.

TIMING: Full moon or new moon.

INSTRUCTIONS: The most important aspect of any magick or ritual is that you take your time, and perform the working without interruption. If your brother keeps knocking on your bedroom door, or your aunt insists on repeatedly walking through the room while you are working, you will most likely become frustrated and lose your concentration. As focus is a major part of magick, you need to choose a time when you will not be disturbed, especially for the very serious things, like cleansing and consecrating your altar.

Place your supplies on a tray or on the floor by your altar. Before you begin, take three deep breaths. As you breathe out, release any negativity or unhappiness you may feel. Now close your eyes and rub your hands lightly together. The deep breathing helps you relax and the friction you create with your hands activates the chakra points (energy fields) in your palms. Closing your eyes helps you to ground and center, and prepare for a magickal working. Say:

> *I feel the power of Spirit in and around me.*
> *So mote it be.*

Open your eyes. Hold the red candle in your hand, and say:

> *May you be cleansed, consecrated, and blessed*
> *in the name of Spirit*
> *(or "in the name of the Lord and Lady").*

Light the candle, then hold the candle out in front of you, over the altar, saying:

> *From the black and formless void, light blossomed*
> *into existence. By igniting this candlewick,*
> *I bring the grace of Spirit (or "our Mother")*
> *into my life and into my altar. Element of fire,*
> *work your will by my desire.*

Pass the flame three times in a counterclockwise (widdershins) direction over the altar, saying:

> *I banish all negativity from this (wood, stone).*
> *Nothing evil or nasty, real or imagined,*
> *can ever abide here.*

Set the burning candle safely to the side. You will be using it again.

Hold your hands over the incense, and say:

> *Element of air, may you be cleansed, consecrated,*
> *and blessed in the name of Spirit.*

Light the incense from the candle flame. Pass the incense smoke over the surface of the altar three times in a counterclockwise direction, saying:

> *Element of air, work your will by my desire.*
> *I banish all negativity from this (wood, stone).*
> *Nothing evil or nasty, real or imagined,*
> *can ever abide here.*

Set the burning incense safely to the side. You will be using it again.

Hold your hands over the salt, and say:

Element of earth, may you be cleansed,
consecrated, and blessed in the name of Spirit.

When your palms begin to tingle or grow warm, sprinkle the salt lightly over the top of the altar surface. Just a little will do. Say:

I cleanse this altar with the salt of the earth.
Element of earth, work your will by my desire.
I banish all negativity from this (wood, stone).
Nothing evil or nasty, real or imagined,
can ever abide here.

Set the bowl aside. Pick up the bowl of water, and say:

Element of water, may you be cleansed,
consecrated, and blessed in the name of Spirit.

Place the bowl of water in the center of the altar. Add three pinches of salt, stirring clockwise with your finger after each addition to the water. Imagine the water glowing with a soft blue or white light. Pick up the small broom and sprinkle with both salt and water, saying:

Besom (means "broom"), *may you be cleansed,*
consecrated, and blessed in the name
of Spirit. Work the magick by my desire.

Dip the broom into the consecrated water, and begin sprinkling tiny drops of the liquid onto the altar in counterclockwise (widdershins) circles, saying:

I banish all negativity from this (wood, stone).
Nothing evil or nasty, real or imagined,
can ever abide here. So mote it be!

Altar Blessing and Empowerment
(to follow altar cleansing)

SUPPLIES: In addition to those used above, scented oil or perfume.

INSTRUCTIONS: Pass the four elements (red candle, incense, salt, and water) over the altar three times in a clockwise direction. Imagine that you are stirring positive energies into action. Once this is done, place the incense in the east, the fire in the south, the water in the west, and the salt in the north. Dab the scented oil on each corner of the altar, and then in the middle, saying:

I bless and consecrate thee, O sacred altar, in the
name of Spirit. May you repel negative energy
and collect positive energy from this day forward
until the end of time. So mote it be.

Draw an equal-armed cross in the air over the altar surface to seal the positive energies to the stone/wood. Tap the edge of the altar four times, once for each direction. Then say:

As above, so below. This altar is sealed.
So mote it be!

You are now ready to work any kind of magick!

Athame, Bolline, Dagger, and Sword

(Better known as the sharp, pointy stuff.) Pottery from ancient Rome (about 200 B.C.) shows two people drawing down the moon, one holding a wand and another a short sword, telling us that the use of tools in ritual practices flows from ancient civilizations.[5] In today's Craft, an athame is a type of double-edged dagger, usually constructed with a steel blade and a black handle, used only for non-cutting ritual purposes (meaning the blade doesn't cut anything physical, and if it does, the metal is considered tainted). Most Craft traditions use the athame as a symbol of either air (the whistling sound it makes when one makes hand motions calling the east quarter) or fire (because the blade was forged in fire).[6] Although some Witches claim that an iron blade is best, others draw back in horror, believing that iron will destroy one's magickal intent. And if you plan on working with faery energy, iron is definitely a no-no—they hate it.

Ritual knives can be used to cast a circle, open and close circle quarters, cleanse and empower items, or command astral energies (to name a few examples). In many traditions, specific symbols are carved into the handle that tie the magickal intentions of the blade to the practitioner, the elements, and to the group mind. These sigils can also be used together or separately in other types of magick, such as candle spells, petition magick, and general ritual. (CHECK THE SIGILS, SYMBOLS, AND MAGICKAL ALPHABETS SECTION OF THIS BOOK IN PART IV FOR COMPLETE INFORMATION ABOUT SYMBOLS AND SIGILS.)

Some Witches empower the athame by rubbing a magnet, crystal, or lodestone over the steel blade several times to magnify its power. It was believed that the sharp point of the athame could direct energy to repel negativity, where the wand was used to guide magickal current for other matters. The logic, as I understand it, matched the point of the blade with incisive current, where the blunt end of the wand and its construction of wood was considered not as effective for magickal defense activity. However, in ancient Egyptian magick, rods (made of wood or other natural materials) were used in defense of the lady of the household. These rods were used to turn negative energy into positive current.[7]

Where the word "athame" comes from and how the ritual knife appeared on the Wiccan altar is historically debatable. Some feel that the word "athame" comes from the Arabic *adhdhame*, meaning "blood-letter" in symbolic form;[8] however, this definition leaves many modern Wiccans running for PR cover as our knives are never used to draw blood. In the Craft, the athame represents the will, not the physical association with weaponry intended to hurt an animal or individual. Many feel that Gerald Gardner (father of modern Wicca) took the athame straight from Mathers' *The Key of Solomon*, a ceremonial text used in the magickal lodges of his time (and still available today); however, as Ronald Hutton explains in *The Triumph of the Moon*:

> . . . there are seven different versions of this text in the British Museum and the number and functions of the ritual weapons varies significantly between these, and only one of them gives the black-handled knife a name of arclavo or arclavum. The closest to Gardener's version is arthame, which appears in Paris (France) . . . Some historians feel that the word is not of Arabic derivation, but French (attame), which means to cut.[9]

Given the other ceremonial associations in the Craft contributed by Gardner from these same organizations, and his limited association with Crowley, it is highly possible that he added the blade from ceremonial, not Craft-related, sources. However, we do know from Celtic history that, for a time, their weaponry through the use of iron was far superior than their contemporaries, and that they were feared because of it. We also know that such folklore practices as hanging a knife above a door to cut any negativity that might enter the home (which means the knives were not used to physically cut, but to defend on the astral plane) were highly popular in that culture. It is possible that Gardner simply melded the local tribal/folklore history (wherein the knife is used to banish malevolent faeries and other unwelcome astral nasties) with the more modern ceremonial practices as his reasoning for placing the blade on the Wiccan altar. The Scottish Highlander's *skean-dhu*, which means "black knife," has a hilt of this color, and may give us another hint of part of the athame's origin in Wiccan lore.[10]

Of all the Craft tools, the athame, bolline (small, white-handled knife used for cutting herbs), and sword (basically those things with sharp, pointy ends) have fallen out of favor in some Wiccan traditions (notice I say "some") due to the possibility of accidents and society's current view on things that can hurt you. Although most ritual blades are dull, if you stumble you can still hurt yourself (or someone else) in ritual circle. In some cases your environment will dictate whether or not you can own a blade. You can't take an athame to school, carry it on a plane, or (depending upon the rules) have a blade in your dorm room. Likewise, if you are the parent of curious, rambunctious children, leaving a sword lying around the house would be a bad idea. Transporting blades in a car is also tricky—some states have laws on the length of a blade that you can have on your person or in your vehicle. To the police, a blade is a weapon—they will not view it as a sacred tool and will confiscate it. Where athames continue to be relatively popular, the sword is normally found in ceremonial groups rather than shamanic ones.

Craft tradition on blades in circle may also extend to the medieval belief that only a free person could carry a double-edged dagger, and therefore since all in the ritual circle are free, he or she has the right to show this symbol of freedom. If the sword is used in circle, only one sword is present, usually wielded by the master of the circle (high priest), though the high priestess can also "strap on the sword," meaning she can use the implement to cast the circle and call the quarters. Again, we look to medieval times, when owning a sword meant you were a cut above normal society (class distinction). In the hierarchy of a coven, the high priest and high priestess are considered the leaders, and therefore, as leaders, have the right to work with the sword in a magickal environment. The two-edged sword or athame symbolizes the dual powers and opposite currents in manifestation (positive and negative; male and female; as above, so below; creation and destruction; life and death), invoking opposites that compliment each other.[11]

In the Craft today, teens of Craft parents are not given a blade until that parent or guardian feels that he or she can handle the responsibility and understand the ritual significance of the tool. Traditional ages differ—presenting the blade at the age of sixteen, eighteen, or twenty-one—in honor of the teen's rite of passage into adulthood.

Now, some of you are saying, "I want to be a real Witch, and so if *real* Witches have blades, then I want one." Not so fast. First, if you are a teen, let's think about your parents. You know, those people that love you? Unless the knife is in the kitchen cutting vegetables, most parents would take a dim view of Witchcraft if you trotted around the house brandishing a blade while muttering unintelligible words. I can see my Baptist mother now—"And *what* do you think you are doing?" Nope. Not worth it. Church camp for you, kid. Secondly, you don't need any tools to be a Witch. Just your own, true self will do.

If you feel you must have a ritual blade, then my advice would be to discuss this with your parents. For some of you who are old enough to own a blade, it probably won't be that big of an issue, but for those of you in the younger crew, your parents' permission is a necessity. If your parents say no, then that's the answer. Use your ingenuity instead. There are lots of other representations for air or fire in the magick circle, and one can always cast a circle with one's finger or hand rather than a blade (I still do). My own children were not permitted to own a ritual blade until the age of fifteen, and then the knife was kept locked in a cabinet and only taken out for ritual. A few of the younger teens I've known have used a butter knife with the handle wrapped in black electrical tape until they were permitted to own a regular blade, where others chose not to work with a blade at all. My first blade was actually a carved wooden one made by my father when I was thirteen.

This entire discussion on blades leads us into a very important realm of Craft training: The object isn't the power of change, *you* are. Granted, any item you use in magick will collect some of your energy and be attached to your desires, however the tool itself isn't going to get up and dance around, cast the circle, call the quarters, and do a little jig without you. It all goes back to that *As above, so below* maxim; since Dion Fortune seems to have said it best, I'm going to paraphrase her:

For whatever reason, beginning magickal students often attach great importance to the number, color, sound, and form of a given object, thinking that the spiritual associations of that object will somehow make one's desire manifest. It is true that all these correspondences provide a link and are important in the learning process, but the link is only a trigger for your mind. The uninitiated, writes Fortune, believe that the force invoked comes through the object, where the initiated know that the material object isn't used to make the energy come down, but to help the mind of the magickal person go up along a particular line of thought. It is only through yourself (not the object) that the desired

change occurs. The value, then, lies within you, not within the object.[12]

So! If the powers that be at home say no blades for you, don't sweat it. It's only a tool (not the magick), after all.

Awakening the Tool

Many magickal people believe that once the tool has been cleansed, consecrated (dedicated to Spirit), and blessed (asking Spirit to fill the object with positive energy), the tool should also be "awakened" before each use. This activation process is often governed by the group that the Witch belongs to, meaning one coven may have a special chant, while another group may "alert" the tool by tapping it one to three times on the altar, or they may simply pass hands over the tools, and say: "Waken ye unto life."[13] No matter how it is achieved, this process serves as a trigger to the mind that the time for magick has begun.

Basket

Although not included as a standard Craft tool, many magickal people have a favorite basket that they use to collect herbs, stones, or other magickal objects from nature. Normally made from natural materials, the basket is also used in ritual to carry objects to the quarters for placement during the ceremony, or when offering an object to the quarters for blessings. You can decorate your basket with ribbons, bells, and other magickal items. The basket is cleansed, consecrated, and blessed in a short ritual before use.

In magick, the basket becomes a reminder of our responsibility to nature, to other people, and to ourselves. The cupped shape of the basket tells us that if we give our problems and cares to deity in prayer, deity will hold that energy and surround your request with love, regardless of what you have asked. This doesn't mean that you will always receive what you work for, but it does mean that your request is always heard. Many Witches have a basket on their altar that contains the requests of others for help. Some magickal people call this the prayer basket. When a person asks for assistance, the Witch writes the request on a piece of paper, passes that paper through incense, then drops it in the basket, asking divinity for help. Once a month the magickal person may go through the slips of paper and burn those prayers that have been answered. Those that have not are re-empowered and dropped back into the basket. If, after time, a request has not been answered but is no longer relevant, you should think about why what was asked for did not come to pass. Over time, you will see the wisdom behind the silence, if you truly seek an answer.

Bell

Bells were known in China before 2000 B.C. and were also found in Egypt, India, Greece, Rome, and other ancient cultures, to name a few. From earliest times they were used as signaling devices, as ritual objects, as magical and often protective amulets (hung in doorways or around the necks of animals), fertility charms, to summon god/desses and spirits, as well as a purely musical instrument. Bells of gold were worn on the hem of the high priest's garment in Israel so that the sound could protect him from nasty energies that were believed to hang around doors and thresholds. In China, bells were rung to call the rain, and some cultures matched the pitch of the bells to the season. The use of bells in churches spread through Europe in the sixth to eleventh centuries and were first used in eastern Christ-

ian churches in the ninth century. Bells were publicly baptized, named, and dedicated to specific saints. Magickal powers were attributed to church bells especially because of their position, hanging in the steeple "between heaven and earth"; this is the traditional place of Pagan magick, between the worlds.[14] Some bells were said to ring by themselves and oodles of myths and legends attached themselves to the care, transport, and ringing of the bells in medieval history. The term "bell, book, and candle," often playfully associated with modern Witches and the title of a popular 1958 movie staring James Stewart and Kim Novak, came from a literary expression in the Roman Catholic church for the ceremony they might perform to throw you out. As a bell tolled in ritual ceremony, twelve priests carried candles and then threw them to the ground as the sentence of condemnation was read. Today there are many magickal shops across the United States that have proudly taken the name of Bell, Book, and Candle.

In modern Witchcraft, bells are employed for a variety of reasons. Much like our Pagan ancestors, they are used to banish negativity (especially during healing work), to prepare sacred space, in house blessings, as charms for fertility and protection, to call the dead, invoke deity, and to work weather magick.

- One ring denotes the beginning of a spell or ritual.

- Three rings are for a pause and for clearing items of negativity.

- Four rings seal a magickal act.

- Five rings invoke quarter energies.

- Seven or twenty-one rings call the dead.

- Nine rings invoke deity.

The custom of ringing bells in the face of a thunderstorm to disperse the energy dates to medieval times, when bell ringers were paid for their service during particularly nasty storms. Many bells from that time bear the inscription "Lightning and thunder, I break asunder."[15] The ringing of the bells and intoning these words to break a violent storm is still used by modern-day Witches, as well as ringing bells to bring rain and curtail a drought. The number for such weather magick is a combination of 3, 7, and 9, tolled three times. The number of rings and the time you spend outside ringing the bell is in direct proportion to the severity of the weather.

Bells, like other ritual objects, should be cleansed, consecrated, and empowered. They can be dedicated to general magickal work or given a specific task, such as weather magick, protective amulet for a child, or specifically employed to call deity. A bracelet of bells can give you an idea of who might be spiritually attuned and who may carry a lot of negativity. Generally, those who enjoy the sounds of the bells are (at the moment) in a "good place" mentally, and those who find the bells irritating have consciously or subconsciously collected a lot of negativity around them. If someone tells you to "take those stupid bells off," then you can bet they're certainly not in a happy frame of mind. A bell bracelet (or anklet) constantly clears the air of negativity as you move, especially if you have empowered the bells for protection.

Book of Shadows

Most practitioners of Witchcraft have what is called a Book of Shadows. In modern times this book normally has a black cover and is written in the owner's own hand. The practice of keeping such a book shoots deep into the shadows of early human development, when the written word took form. Before this, and during the many changes in world cultures (wars, famine, politics, and so on), the power of magick was passed down orally, sometimes within one's family, in a student-teacher environment (called mystery schools), or through priestly training. Memorized information, rituals, and recipes, however, can be lost for a number of reasons. Eventually, fearing this oral information would be irretrievably misplaced, those that could write (depending upon the area in which they lived and their station in life) began to copy what they knew into book form.

Egypt, the land of mystery and enchantment, is thought to be the cradle of much of the written occult knowledge shared through the centuries. In Egypt, the use of amulets goes back as far as the early fourth millennium B.C., while magickal books were found from the late third millennium B.C. until the fifth century C.E.[16] If we do a bit of quick math, this means that magick was in evidence six thousand years ago, and books of magick were in existence five thousand years ago. That's a heck of a long time!

Three thousand years ago, Clement of Alexandria made reports that the Egyptians had forty-two secret books of wisdom, written by Hermes (also known as Thoth, the Egyptian god of wisdom), which were kept in the temples (we'll talk more about who probably wrote what later on in this book). These books included laws, hymns, rituals, information on how to train priests and priestesses, and information about the deities, astrology, geography, medicine, talking to the dead, spells, the invocation of deity, doll magick, and cosmology[17]—the same types of subjects you will find in a modern Book of Shadows. And the same idea of reverence was applied to those books, just as is taught in current Craft circles—the emphasis on secrecy and copying such information in your own "hand of writ," to name just two. It is also interesting that even then, thousands of years ago, these books of magick were not the product of a single culture, but of many peoples as they collided in the arms of Egypt through slaves, royalty, travelers, scholars, and even the retired military who flocked to the Queen of the Nile for rest and recuperation. That means that any magick you practice today is somehow multicultural in content.

The Egyptians, however, are not the only ancient peoples with the lore of magickal books. In *Folklore in the Old Testament*, J. G. Frazer notes that Noah learned how to make the ark from a holy book, which had been given to Adam by the angel Raziel. This book contained within it all knowledge, human and divine, including astrological secrets, and was made of sapphires.[18] Noah enclosed the book in a golden casket when he took it with him into the ark, where it served as a timepiece to distinguish night from day. Sounds like a magickal book to me! And no, it wasn't the Bible, it is known today as Sepher Rezial, and is mentioned in several historical texts and research. Noah was not the only biblical person to have this information; it is said that King Solomon learned much of his magick from the Sepher Rezial.[19]

Through the centuries, most Books of Shadows or magickal books appear to be a mixed collection of all sorts of stuff jumbled together with little or no order. They are, after all, magickal notes, and therefore don't read like the textbook system that you're used to, and more often than not (when first written) reflected the personality of the author. Think about Grandma's recipe book and you've got a good idea of how these books appeared. As some of the books were handed down from person to person, things were added, and sometimes removed —also a product of the personality of the indi-

vidual who had possession of the book. More often than not, however, someone in a family or clergy line would come along and feel it was their duty to destroy what they didn't understand. Even in the first century A.D., magickal books were often burned, especially if they had to do with divination and prophecy (as they were considered a threat to church and state). Hey, if you were going to fiddle while Rome burned, would you want everyone to know it beforehand and try to stop you? I think not.

The eleventh century and the advent of the Crusades brought a flood of magickal information from the Arabic/Muslim community, often spirited over the Spanish borders (remember your history) and into the whole of Europe. One of these books was called the *Ghayat Al-Hakim*, meaning "The Aim of the Wise One," an Arabic work translated into Latin under the title *Picatrix*. The Arab author carefully concealed his identity—understandably, as the book makes Lovecraft's *Necronomicon* look like *Winnie the Pooh*. You will find additional reference to this work when we cover the Lunar Mansions.

The Sepher Rezial (Noah's magickal book) emerged in the thirteenth century, the translation attributed to Eleazer of Worms. By the fifteenth century, there were several kinds of magickal books floating around Europe that mostly included magickal beliefs and practices from the classical cultures (Greeks and Romans who borrowed from the Egyptians and who knows who else) mingling with the beliefs and practices of the Germanic and Celtic peoples. Early Christian magicians borrowed heavily from the Neoplatonians as well as the Jews and Muslims. All this makes it super hard to figure out what came from where! Regardless, we have to keep in mind that these books were written by people just like you. They weren't greater or better.

They were seekers, just as you are today. Some of these books were written by people in their late teens and early twenties.

In fifteenth-century manuscripts we find two distinct types of magickal books—one used for the running of a regular household (from the Wolfsthurn Castle in the Tyrol) that deals with natural magick (plants, elements, healing, finding the love of a nice lady, and so on) as well as household affairs, and a more sinister jumble now kept in Munich that involves some nasty conjurations that historians feel were written by underground Christian clergy, and which may give us a hint on what fueled the Burning Times in Europe (compounded by moblike hysteria, the desire of the church to acquire money and property as well as control the people by using fear tactics).[20] Some of the magickal books, such as the Wolfsthurn manuscript and the Munich collection, were called *grimoires*, a French word meaning "a magician's manual." Unfortunately, the word *grimoire* stems from the Witch trials, and therefore wasn't seen in a particularly fair or pleasant light. In fact, medieval clergy treated books like people, and would sometimes put a book on trial (as if it were a person), and then burn it if they didn't like it—hence the idea for book burning by present-day fundamentalists.

In seventeenth-century Europe, there is mention of a magickal book in the records of the Venetian Inquisition concerning a woman named Laura Malipero, who was accused of practicing Witchcraft. Upon searching her home, agents of the Inquisition found a copy of the Key of Solomon, along with a private, handwritten book of spells and rituals into which Laura had copied portions of the Key.[21] In other records of the Witch persecutors (I hesitate to actually say "Witch persecutors," because they weren't killing Witches, they were murdering just about anybody that took their fancy) there is mention of a black book in one's own hand of writ—hence the tradition of one's Book of Shadows being bound in black was born. According to many historical records, magickal books actually had a variety of color covers, including red, green, and purple.

In studying the history of Witchcraft, it is sometimes difficult to ascertain what is fact and what is fiction. Some of the terminology we use today comes directly from the persecution era—such words or ideas may not have been used before the persecutions ("sabbat," for example) but if you've been stretched on the rack you'll say just about anything, and hence a whole new vocabulary (medieval buzzwords, if you will) took form. A wondrous number of words appeared to describe things that previously didn't have definitions at all. The Inquisition and the church, in their desire to eradicate what wasn't there, made up words and copious definitions to support their fantasies so that the world in general wouldn't know they were offing people just for the fun of it ("grimoire" being another such word). Modern Witches kept some of these words (now that they were there, they might as well use them) and discarded others. "Familiar" and "warlock" were discarded completely by the year 2000.

Tinkering with words (something people love to do) causes a lot of confusion all around the magickal town and in the regular one, too. As you enter the study of Witchcraft you'll begin to see what a mess people have made of words and what they stand for, which is why when you are learning a particular type of magick you need to know all about the culture that produced that magick. Relying on modern interpretation will only confuse the issue. Finally, you'll discover that "living it" brings understanding and helps you navigate through all those definitions—and this, like all things of serious study, takes time.

Practicing Wiccans will probably tell you that the Book of Shadows is normally bound in black to keep out the negativity of the "real world" and to protect the contents therein — which isn't exactly wrong, but I'll bet you that most of the common people in Europe didn't have access to fuchsia-colored covers for their books in medieval times, and a sky-blue cover with pink polka dots in an Irish village would have probably drawn unwanted attention, if such a thing could be had. We know that one of the reasons students are told that the cover of a Book of Shadows should be black directly relates to the information produced during the Inquisition (under pain and torture, I might add). In honor of the innocent, then, is another reason why the cover of a Book of Shadows might be black in color. Keeping the book in your own penmanship also comes from the Inquisition—especially considering they didn't have a printing press before that.

The printing press brought a new age of enlightenment, where superstitions peeled away and science began to surge forward, opening up new territory for the masses. What had been kept for the chosen few was now passed around like an Internet joke. Those magickal books that hadn't been destroyed by the zealous fanatic found a whole new set of hungry eyes to please. With the advent of the printing press, rather than sitting laboriously copying from thick volumes of faded lettering, one could get magick hot off the press! Granted, there was still a lot of secrecy involved (church and state hunted you down like a ravenous dog), but at least you could share this good stuff with more than just a student or two. By the early 1900s, individuals like Dion Fortune were happily spreading their magickal information with hundreds of students in newsletter form.

The wording "Book of Shadows" in regard to Wicca is attributed to Gerald Gardner, who is considered to be the founder of modern Witchcraft (though there were other prominent magickal individuals during his time who could also lay claim to this title). Doreen Valiente, a member of his group (and whose poetry binds all modern Wiccans together) believed that the idea of the Book of Shadows first came into being in 1949, when Gardner thought of calling a Witch's book of rituals and magickal information a Book of Shadows[22] to replace the traditional and functional "grimoire." Valiente discovered that the term was borrowed from an article published in *The Occult Observer* in 1949, about an ancient Sanskrit manual of that name which taught how to tell a person's destiny from the length of their shadow.[23] Gardner's book was originally titled *Ye Bok of Ye Art Magical*, which went through various phases of reproduction. The renaming of this grimoire to Book of Shadows occurred soon after his groundbreaking work *High Magic's Aid* was published in 1949 (cited as fiction). Portions of *High Magic's Aid* were taken from *Ye Bok of Ye Art Magickal*. When the Witchcraft laws in England were repealed in 1951, *High Magic's Aid* became the first how-to magickal book on Witchcraft available to the general public in modern times.

By the end of the 1900s, there were over 1,000 titles available on Witchcraft (with the breakdown of ⅓ fiction, ⅓ nonfiction historical, and ⅓ nonfiction how-to), and there are even Books of Shadows on the World Wide Web! Which just goes to show you that magick never dies, it just changes with the times.

In the past, many of the magick books used symbols (like an equal-armed cross typed three times) to let the reader know where a specific format, or a certain set of words, should be included. If you didn't know the code, then the book would be fairly useless, which is why some historians have a habit of saying "followed by nonsensical gibberish" when they are trying to explain (historically speaking) what things meant. For the most part I tried to stay away from that practice in this book, however you will find a code or two. If, two hundred years from now, a future historian finds this book and portions are torn out, he or she might not know what "SMIB" or "BB" means. To him or her it would look like silly letters, but you know that SMIB means So Mote It Be and that BB means Blessed Be (okay, so maybe you didn't know before, but you know now). BOS means Book of Shadows. Codes can be used for longer passages, like "Insert COTG"—which means in this ritual (or spell), insert the Charge of the Goddess here. If ever in your magickal training you are required to copy a Book of Shadows in "your own hand of writ," you will completely understand why the codes are important—they saved time, soothed your aching hand, and helped to lend some type of secrecy to the work.

Ceremony for Empowering Your Personal BOS

SUPPLIES: Holy water; cleansing incense of your choice; two white candles; a white sheet; a large, hand-drawn pentacle; your altar; a cord nine feet long (in the color of your choice); your personal BOS; and, if you like, this book as well.

INSTRUCTIONS: On a full or new moon, place the white sheet over your altar. Set the pentacle in the center. Place your Book of Shadows on top, opened to the first page. Place the white candles on either side of the book. Drape the cord on the book and over the altar. Take a spiritual bath (SEE PART I, RITUAL) and dress in something loose and nonflammable of a solid color (white for purity, black to repel negativity, green for growth of spirit, and so on). Create sacred space in the room by cleansing it with the four elements (a representation of earth, air,

water, and fire). Fumigate the pages with incense. Pass the candle flame over the book three times. Sprinkle book with holy water. Follow the basic esbat format in Part I, under Esbat. When you get to step nine, do the following:

Light the white candles, asking Spirit to bless this sacred rite. Hold your hands over the book, and say:

Gracious Lord and Lady, who guide the universe ever toward peace and harmony, who guard and protect your hidden children of the Craft of the Wise, who bring transformation and joy to all serious seekers, hear me. Bless and consecrate this book in your names that I may always walk in the path of the light, that the words written here take shape and form in this world and in the worlds beyond so that they may ever function in the service of peace, love, prosperity, protection, happiness, and harmony. With the utterance of each syllable in the direction of the light, may my power and wisdom grow. Please protect this book of magick so that it will not be taken from me and destroyed, and if circumstances remove it from my possession, I ask that the power be returned to Spirit. If it is taken without my permission, burned, or destroyed, may that person know your names for lifetimes to come, and may their ignorance be stripped from them. I know you will do this for me. As I will, so mote it be.

Draw an invoking earth pentagram (SEE PAGE 396) in the air over the pages, then blow softly on the book three times, visualizing the sacred breath of divinity entering the pages. Seal by drawing an equal-armed cross in the air over the book. Close the book and wrap loosely with the cord. Again draw the seal.

Finish the basic ritual format.

When you work with the book, wear the cord to symbolize your connection to the essence of Spirit. The first words in your book should be the Personal Journal/Book Blessing, which you will find in Part I under Blessings. Anytime you work with the book, you can use the blessing and consecration prayer, which helps to build the power of your working.

Broom

Jumping the broom in a modern Wiccan marriage ceremony relates to the same custom as performed by the gypsies. Midwives of ancient Rome used special brooms to sweep the threshold of the house after childbirth[24] to cut the ties between the world of the living and the realm of the dead, as it was believed that the child had entered from the world of the dead and the pathway should not be made easy for a quick return. As a part of the Athenian festival, the souls of the dead visited the houses of the living and were received hospitably, but then driven out by a thorough sweeping of the house with a broom.

In ancient Mexico, a broom festival called Ochpaniztli was dedicated to the old Earth Goddess Teteo-innan (Tlazolteotl), who swept away disease and harm.[25] In her rites, priests burned black incense and laid brooms made from rushes across the fires.[26] Her totem was the snake and the owl.

In Chinese folk belief, the Goddess of Fine Weather—"the girl who sweeps the weather clear"—named Sao Ch'ing Niang lives on the Broom Star, Sao Chou. During great rains, little girls cut a human figure representing the goddess out of paper and hang the figure near a gate with a request that the goddess bring clear weather and sunshine.[27] She is also called upon in times of great drought and invoked at the New Year for fine weather.

It wasn't until the various Inquisitions that Witches became associated with brooms, which may have occurred from the European Pagan custom of riding a broom like a hobbyhorse over freshly turned fields to promote the fertility of land, sweeping away death (last year's old crops) and preparing the way for rebirth. The broom-ends were thought to have their own life-force, and were capable of warding bad weather away from the crops. A popular name for medieval Witches was "broom Amazons."[28]

In Italian Witchcraft, the Witches' broom is made from three woods: an ash handle, a birch twig for the brush, and willow for the binding string. These three parts are symbolic of the triple aspect of the Goddess. Ash represents one's ability to work with four elements, the birch draws spirits to one's service, and the willow is connected to Dark Goddess energy.[29] In other lore, magickal brooms contained six different woods—birch, broom, hawthorn, hazel, rowan, and willow.[30]

It is highly possible that the broom is the oldest of magickal tools. In modern Craft practice, a large broom, used for sweeping, cleanses the area before the circle is cast, yet this practice dates back to 1336 B.C. when Egyptian priests swept the ritual area with brooms, then sprinkled the ground with blessed water.[31] A small, hand-held broom may be used to sprinkle those who enter the circle with holy water as a rite of purification. Sometimes, a broom is lain across the edge of the circle to serve as a temporary closure. Crossing brooms at quarters, and then symbolically uncrossing them, has been used to allow quarter energies into the cast circle area, while nailing crossed brooms to your front door or on a wall in the home are said to guard the house and disperse any negative energies.[32]

Early American magickal practitioners, especially women, used the broom for quite another purpose—as a form of communication. Without answering machines or phones at their disposal, a broom positioned in a particular way outside of the house apprised friends and neighbors of one's whereabouts. A broom leaning close to the front door with bristles up meant "I've gone visiting." With the bristles down, "I'm home." A broom lying down meant "I'm busy, please call another time." If the broom sat bristles up over a window, then the lady of the house was not home, but would be back shortly, and visitors were welcome to come in and wait. Messages meant for everyone were tied onto the broom with various colored ribbons. These messages indicated if someone was sick, in labor, had a baby, got married, or needed some type of assistance. With the advent of the telephone, broom communication was no longer needed and faded out of existence; however, Crafters trained thirty years ago still use this type of communication among themselves.

Brooms can be handmade or store-bought, depending upon the choice of the magickal individual; however, brooms with metal handles are not recommended for magick. As you've seen by the history, brooms are used to banish unwanted energies, send the dead back to the Summerland (SEE PART I, UNDER RITES OF PASSAGE), and work weather magick. Amazing, isn't it, what powerful enchantment lies in a simple household tool!

Banishing Negativity
from Your Home

SUPPLIES: One skein of red yarn (the color of life); one small onion; one broom; holy water (SEE PART IV, UNDER ELEMENTS).

INSTRUCTIONS: Wrap the yarn around the onion. You don't have to use all the yarn, but enough so that the onion is thoroughly covered and, when used, will not unravel.

At dawn, stand outside facing the sun. Close your eyes and feel the warm rays on your face. Take three deep breaths and find that still point, discussed in Grounding and Centering (PART III, UNDER BREATHING). Hold the broom and the onion ball toward the sun, and say:

Blessings upon me, O Spirit. Instill my work
with joy and harmony. Let thy golden rays
fill every facet of my being. May I dance
in the love of the divine.

Begin on the top floor of the house. Scoot the ball of yarn along the floor with the broom, covering as much of the floor in the first room as possible. Repeat the following as you push the ball around with the broom:

Love, harmony, joy, and peace. Therefore I say
unto you, anything you pray for and ask,
believe that you will receive it, and it will be
done. Love, harmony, joy, and peace.

As you leave the room, sprinkle a bit of holy water at the threshold. Continue to the next room. Go through the entire house in this manner. The onion and the yarn are picking up negativity as you go along. Make sure that the last room you sweep contains an outside exit. After you finish this room, open the door, and say:

I am surrounded by the forces of divine
creation—love, harmony, joy, and peace.
There is no room for evil here.

Hit the ball of yarn outside. As you watch it leave the house and fly through the air, repeat: "Love, harmony, joy, and peace." Sprinkle holy water at the threshold of the exit. Push the ball out to the gutter. Pick it up with a piece of plastic (do not touch the ball), then dispose of it and the plastic off your property. Sprinkle the broom brush with holy water to cleanse.

If you live in an apartment, where there are lots of halls and stairs before you reach the outside, guide the ball along the hall and down the stairs, then outside to the gutter. If for some reason you can't do this, then be sure to at least push the ball out into a public hallway before you pick it up with the plastic. As the onion rots in the trash, so will the negativity dissipate, so don't bring the ball back inside the house, trailer, or apartment.

Candles and Wax

Used in magick, religious worship, in community processions, and for daily household needs, the candle has been with us for over 5,000 years. Candles made of beeswax were used in Egypt and Crete as early as 3000 B.C. Relief carvings in ancient Egyptian tombs at Thebes show cone-shaped candles on dishlike holders, or candle-sticks.[33] In Roman times, candles were lit in honor of Juno Lucina (Mother of Light), who was said to govern the sun, moon, and stars. Her Festival of Lights became the Christian feast of Saint Lucy.[34] Pliny wrote that these candles were made of flax rope and soaked in pitch and wax. The oldest-known archaeological finding of a candle fragment in Europe was near Avignon, France, dating from the first century C.E.,[35] which tells us that by the beginning of the Common Era, the use of candles had traveled from the Middle East to the European continent.

Perhaps one of the easiest enchantments to perform, candle magick has always been highly symbolic of the sacred light of Spirit, dispelling the darkness and bringing forth positive power through working with divinity. The ancient rite of plunging a lit candle into holy water and asking for divine blessings is a magickal activity associating the candle with the first god birthed from the body of the first goddess. Once this rite has been performed, the water is used to cleanse and consecrate people, homes, and magickal tools.

Over the last two thousand years, like the bell and the broom, the candle has gathered tales of myth, superstition, and legend. Honey, wax, and wine, all byproducts of the industrious bees, were considered blessings from the Goddess and, if you listened closely, you could hear Her voice in the steady drone of the bee. In the Middle Ages, if a girl could re-spark a dying flame, she was considered pure and untouched. If she couldn't, this nasty reputation could cause the fortunes of her home to be ruined, as she was considered an unsuitable match for any gentleman.[36] Candles were even used as divination tools, and it is said that wise folk could read the shapes and patterns of melted wax floating upon cold water. Even today pillar candles encased in glass can tell the Witch if someone is working against her family in thought, word, or deed. If the glass clouds and grows black, nasty business is afoot.

Extremely popular in our modern culture, candle magick is used by individuals of all faiths (although some don't exactly call it "magick," choosing to avoid the word as much as possible). Still, using candles to make petitions, light altars, or to hold them up in a protest is symbolic of bringing the light of Spirit into the darkness of our world. Here is a brief list of how candles may be used in the Craft (I say "may" because all traditions and groups are not the same).

- As representations of the Lord and Lady on the altar, sometimes called illuminator candles.

- To mark the four quarters of a circle (sometimes the candle colors match the quarter colors, and other times not).

- To represent the element of fire on the altar (called the fire candle, different from the illuminator candles).

- To represent a sacred triangle within the circle wherein the God and Goddess are called.

- To represent a particular person, place, or thing, aiding in the focus of a spell. In this case a person's name may be carved on the candle, or perhaps a desire, such as "success," written in a magickal alphabet. Other times a person's name might be written on a piece of paper and placed under the candle holder.

- As a magickal timing device, where notches are carved on the candle associated with the increment of days or months to complete the work. For example, a candle with seven markings would be burned on the first day to the first mark, to the second mark on the second day, and so on (popular in seven-day spells).

- As a magickal working within themselves, where the candle is dressed with oil and/or loaded by carving a small space out of the bottom, where herbs are inserted.

- As an offering to Spirit, or to the ancestors.

- To repel negativity. In medieval times it was believed that evil could not pass through a circle of flame.

In most spells and magickal workings, the shape and the size of the candle isn't important, unless you are working with novelty candles. These candles come in the pre-molded forms of ani-mals, people, and objects, and for the beginning practitioner may be difficult to find in the more rural areas. Although useful, novelty candles are not required to cast a successful candle spell. Unfortunately, many chap-book-style spell books call for these novelty candles; however, you can always substitute what you have available and still work the spell. The shape of the novelty candle is designed to help you focus on your intent, but don't be swayed into thinking that something like a skull candle or a devil candle should be automatically associated with harming someone. For example, a green skull candle works well for healing the mind and body, and a red skull candle might be lit to turn unwanted negative attentions away from you. The devil candle can be burned to combat evil and break hexes, though most Wiccans don't use them because of their distaste for anything linked to Satan.

Candles and Purposes

7-KNOBBED CANDLE

Green: Release bound money or property.

Black: Release someone's hold on you.

Red: Remove blocks to love.

Yellow: Remove bad luck.

Purple: Remove negative magick.

Blue: Remove confusion.

Orange: Remove blocks to creative success.

Purpose: Burn one "knob" each day to bring about your desired intention, to undo a serious situation, or to remove blocks one at a time. Dual colors (black and red) are to undo and banish by burning the black wax first, then switch to activation as the red wax begins to burn.

BLACK CAT CANDLE

Purpose: Shaped like a black cat, this candle is burned to bring good luck or to entreat the assistance of the Egyptian goddess Bast (Bastet) for protection of oneself, property, and pets.

DEVIL-BE-GONE/SATAN CANDLE

Purpose: Image of the devil is burned to rid the house or a person of evil influences. As the candle burns, evil flees.

DOUBLE ACTION OR REVERSING CANDLES

White and black: Reverse a bad spell.

Red and black: Stop someone from destroying your love life.

Green and black: Stop someone from taking your money or dispel gossip that has affected your good name or fortune.

Purpose: Come in two colors, one on top of the other in a single seven-day pillar candle or a thick, one-inch taper. Where glass is not used, the second color is hand dipped over the original pillar color. These candles are designed to reverse ill fortune. If tapers are used, as the wax drips down the shaft of the candle, the situation is trapped or neutralized by the positive energy.

CEREMONIAL CANDLE/ MEMORIAL CANDLE

Purpose: White pillar candle in glass tumbler. Used to celebrate a special day, give thanks, or commemorate an event. Light at dawn. Burns twenty-four to thirty hours.

FRUIT OR VEGETABLE IMAGE CANDLES

Purpose: Ears of corn, apples, and other novelty shapes are burned to bring food into the home or to harvest the fruits of a long-term project.

IMAGE CANDLE/ADAM & EVE

Purpose: Is in the form of a male or female and comes in a variety of colors. Used to draw information and people to you, or push them away from you. The figure candles are moved on the altar as they burn, either toward each other, or away. They can also be used alone for healing purposes.

SEPARATION CANDLE

Purpose: Red pillar candle dipped in black wax. Burned to liberate yourself from the bondage of another person or situation. To literally break someone's hold on you, inscribe a snake from the top to the bottom of the candle.

SKULL CANDLES

Black: To banish death and evil.

Green: Healing and bringing money.

Red: Activate a situation, push negativity away.

Purpose: Shaped like a skull to get to the "head" of the matter. Used for a variety of purposes, including banishing death in patients with terminal illnesses.

TRIPLE ACTION CANDLES— HOUSE BLESSING

Purpose: Pillar candles in glass with three colors, often red, white, and blue or red, white, and green. Used to bless the house, dispel arguments between family members, and bring harmony into the atmosphere.

Those Wiccans who have had additional training in Santería, Voudon, Hoodoo, or who may have come from traditional Catholic backgrounds may also use saint candles in their magickal workings. As ancient deities were pushed further into the background, the number of Christian saints increased, beginning with the martyrs. Equating these people with ancient gods and goddesses became a common practice both in Europe and then again in America as the Afro-magico-religious systems of the slaves melded with Catholicism.[37] Although some Wiccans peel off the saint wrappers on the seven-day glass candles, others don't mind at all and leave the wrapper on, believing that all religions lead to the same universal source. Some of the more popular saint candles for Wiccan spells are:[38]

Our Lady of the Miraculous Medal: Aid to restore health, to break bad habits, for special favors, protection of motorcyclists, and general blessings.

Saint Barbara: Drives away evil, protects women, clears your path of obstacles, for protection during a storm, and helps in legal difficulties.

Saint Anthony: For special requests, miracles, to find lost articles, and to overcome financial problems.

Guardian Angel: For protection of children, to gain spiritual strength during difficult times, for guidance in work, school, and play.

St. Francis of Assisi: For greater understanding and peace, to detect gossip and plots against you, helps with ecology and conservation as well as any magick involving the care of wild animals and pets.

Most Witches dress their candles prior to using them in magick or ritual by rubbing scented oil on the taper (or around the top layer of wax of a seven-day glass candle). The oil chosen has a symbolic meaning that matches the working, which is why you'll see names like "Altar Oil," "Sabbat Oil," "Blessing Oil," and "Divination Oil" in magickal shops across the country. I've seen two ways to dress a candle.

1. To bring something toward you, rub the oil lightly (not too much) on the candle from the top down. To send something away from you, rub the oil lightly on the candle from the bottom up.

2. To bring something toward you, begin at the top of the candle and rub oil only to the middle, then rub the oil from the bottom to the middle. To send something away from you, rub from the center of the candle up, and then from the center of the candle down.

Either practice works. If you don't have oil, a little bit of perfume will do, or you can use any natural living food oil, like olive oil or canola oil—normal vegetable oils are called "dead oils." I began using bottled Florida Water (SEE PART IV, UNDER ELEMENTS) years ago to cleanse all of my candles, then follow with the oil dedicated to the specific purpose.

The most important thing to remember about candle magick is that *fire burns!* Fire is a living element: it breathes and it eats things, like tables, chairs, drapes, whole houses, animals, and people. It doesn't have picky taste buds, and it can move faster than you ever imagined. Add several candles together in a cauldron with a little paper and you could very well have an inferno. Flames like to go high, go wide, and go big. Count on it. Accidents can happen, even to the most experienced practitioners. Although all the elements (earth, air, fire, and water) carry tremendous power, fire is by far the most cantankerous and unforgiving in a ritual setting, because only a little bit can explode into disaster.

Handling Fire

- Any candle holder will *not* do. Yeah, I know, there's some really neat ones out there to buy, but they may not be safe. Glass candle cups and candle holders will explode if the flame burns next to the glass for any length of time. When they explode, bits of glass, flame, and sparks will ignite altar cloths, ritual robes, and hair, not to mention drapes and the occasional curious cat. Ceramic candle holders aren't any safer, and those that aren't glaze fired but just painted will also catch fire. The paint, especially if it is metal based, will smolder and create hazardous fumes. Honestly, it's best not to use glass or ceramic at all. Leave those for decoration only. Metal candle holders are much safer. And, of course, never leave a burning candle unattended.

- Be careful of special effects, such as flash paper, flash cotton, sparklers, explosive powders, and firecrackers. In all honesty, it's best not to use them. I literally blew up my dining room table using Vesta powder. I found out too late that flame crawls across a flat surface faster than our pet rat. One adult male Witch that we know blew pieces of his nose off trying to be fancy with legalized firecrackers. He spent the whole night in the hospital rather than at the ritual feast.

- Although a metal cauldron is normally a safe container for fire, too much of anything can cause an accident. Many of the magickal books written for adults have all sorts of recipes in them for self-made incenses, special effects, and ways to burn things. Problems occur when the magickal person tries to "soup up" some of those ingredients. If you are allowed to use those books, please follow the directions. If you

have a candle in the center of your cauldron, and you are using petition magick (burning small pieces of paper), be very careful. The pieces of the paper that don't burn right away can become coated with melted wax. Too many pieces like this will cause a flare-up in the flame, as much as several feet, especially if the base of the candle catches fire. This can happen in an instant, singeing eyelashes and eyebrows if you've got your face too close to the open cauldron, or can ignite curtains and clothing.

- Be careful when using taper candles. If the taper does not fit securely in the candle holder you have, don't use it. Sometimes you can wrap the bottom of the candle with foil so that it fits tighter, but this does not always work, especially if the cup of the holder isn't deep. If the candle taper is the least bit wobbly, think of something else. Unusual things happen in ritual and it isn't out of the norm for an unsteady taper candle to topple over and set the altar cloth on fire, especially if you are using ritual dance, martial arts movements, or simply walking the circle. Also, the more people you have in your circle, the fewer candles you should use, unless you have a person designated as the fire guardian, whose sole responsibility is to make sure no one steps near a candle, drags an arm across a flame, and so on. In an adult ritual circle, this job normally falls to the elder of the coven or clan, as he or she has done hundreds, maybe even thousands, of rituals, and is content to look out for the safety of the younger members of the group. Even in solitary ritual, never leave candles burning unattended and be careful if you choose to wear a robe with long sleeves, or if you have long hair. All can easily burn.

- Be careful of those charcoal bricks that are designed specifically for loose incense. It's best to use one of those long-handled lighters designed for outdoor grilling to get them started because they contain highly flammable material. Sometimes they are extremely difficult to light, but when they finally get going they'll bite your fingers faster than the time it takes to put them down safely. Cones and sticks are much safer and easier to light.

- Do not use your outdoor grill in the house and definitely don't use grilling charcoal (like the stuff your parents use to make those steaks and burgers in the summertime) inside. The charcoal used for this kind of fire contains hazardous fumes. Families have died from trying to grill food inside the house using this kind of charcoal.

Many Witches prefer to use a stone surface for burning candles, not only to connect with the element of earth, but also to prevent accidents. Keep either water or a fire extinguisher nearby at all times. If your parents or guardians do not approve of burning candles, cut them a break. Everything they own can be lost in a matter of minutes and not all parents can afford fire insurance. This is especially so with apartment living, where fire insurance is not required (unlike the insurance required when you buy a home). Some magickal shops in larger cities will allow you to burn your candles there if you tell them about home or dormitory restrictions.

To help you match candle colors to your magickal intentions, use the chakra table on page 240 or the color list on page 235.

Extinguishing Candles

Generally, the magickal practitioner never blows out a candle, believing that one creative force (your breath, symbolizing the breath of life) should not darken another (the flame, symbolizing the spark of life). You can use a candlesnuffer, a small metal or stoneware cup, or even a piece of tinfoil. (Fingers are not recommended.) Clapping your hands sharply over a flame can also create an extinguishing downdraft. There are various candle spells that can span more than one day. For example, some spells require that you burn the same candle every night at the same time for five minutes, then use the candlesnuffer to extinguish the flame and seal the work until the following evening.

General Candle-Burning Invocations

Recite the following while you carve your choice of sigils or words into the candle that matches your desire. Dress the candle with your favorite oil. Light the candle. Repeat any of the following chants.

FALCON'S INVOCATION

Keepers of the sun
keepers of the sea
keepers of the forests and spirits in the trees.
Keepers of the earth
keepers of the fire
keepers of the heavens and music in the lyre.
Lend to me your energy
hear my spoken word!
(State what you wish here).

Light the candle and repeat the spell as you focus on the flame. Finish with: "I know you will do this for me. SMIB."

ECHO'S INVOCATION

The candle, the taper, the wick, the flame
The ribbons of magick unfurl again.
The words, the sound, the will, the spell
To know, to dare, and not to tell.

Repeat three times, light the candle, state your intent, repeat three times again. Finish with: "I know you will do this for me. SMIB," then seal with an equal-armed cross in the air over the lit candle.

Candle Spell to Help Choose Your Classes

In most schools, you are required to choose your classes for the next year, or semester. Although there are counselors available, the ultimate choice of what you will take will be yours. Whether you are picking classes for high school or college, it's a good idea to talk to students who have already gone through a class with a particular teacher or professor before you make your final decision. Find out which classes are considered by your peers tougher than others, and be sure to leave yourself enough free time to help to alleviate the stress of those more difficult classes. Talk to your parents (or guardian) to determine their opinion. This can be the hardest hurdle. Your parents may want you to do one thing, and your heart is telling you to go another way. Always remember that you can compromise and add the more pleasurable classes to a strong core of learning, rather than relying on just one or the other (all play and no work, or all work and no play). The spell below can serve more than one function: to help you choose all your classes, to assist you in picking the right path, or to simply help you make the final decision of one class over another.

SUPPLIES: Sidewalk chalk; a flat piece of stone (at least one foot by one foot); and a white candle. The choice you need to make written on a piece of paper (or the choices you have made, if you are merely asking for blessings on your decision). Choose your favorite ritual format.

INSTRUCTIONS: Put the papers under the stone. With the chalk, draw a circle on the face of the stone. Draw a square within the circle. Dress the candle with your favorite oil. Place the candle in the center of the square. Cast a magick circle. Invoke deity (SEE PART I, INVOCATION AND EVOCATION). Hold your hands over the candle and chant the word "wisdom" as you ground and center. Light the candle and then repeat the following words:

Rise up for me, O flame of love.
Bring blessings—hundreds—from above.
Help me make this difficult choice
put magick in my form and voice.
Clear my path with light so bright
let not confusion blind my sight.
My tasks in life will shine with fire
and wisdom sung from angel choirs
Will circle 'round this task of art
as truth resides within my heart.
The road is long and paths are many
I'll find mine own, there won't be any
wrong turns or red lights that shouldn't be there
I'll finish in excellence with love to spare.

Thank deity. Release the magick circle. Allow the candle to burn completely. Make your choice (if you have not already), then find a copy machine and make a copy of the paperwork. Hand the original in and keep the copy with the candle end in a safe place. If you have used a seven-day glass candle, keep the copy in the empty glass throughout the school year. When you need help with a particular course of study, empower a penny and throw it in the glass holder, asking for additional blessings on your choices.

Jumbo Candle Spell

SUPPLIES: One jumbo candle (large, fat pillar candle) in your color choice; magickal oil to match your desire; a pencil; a safe place to burn the candle; drum or other musical instrument; candlesnuffer. Choose your favorite ritual format.

INSTRUCTIONS: Think of your desire. Mark the candle in seven equal increments with the pencil. Dress with oil. Each day at the same time, light the candle. Meditate on the flame as you drum, sing, chant, or play a musical instrument of your choice for fifteen to twenty minutes. When you are finished, say: "As I desire," then repeat your intention. Say: "So mote it be!" as you snuff out the candle. At the end of the seventh meditation/drumming session, extinguish the candle, and say: "My will is done." Once the candle ends cool, bury in a white handkerchief.

Rather than seven days, you can also have a drumming session each weekend with your friends for three weeks. In that situation, do not mark the candle, simply put it out at the end of each session.

Wax Talismans

Mentioned in both the *Picatrix* and Agrippa's *Three Books of Occult Philosophy*, talismans are nothing new and were often created in conjunction with planetary or general astrological magicks.

INGREDIENTS: Scented wax, paraffin, or potpourri wax; small, magickal objects of your choice (natural items such as an acorn or a crystal, or manmade objects of clay or wood); herbs to match your intent; candy molds; medicine dropper. (**Optional:** Essential oil of your choice.) Wax potpourri burner or old double boiler. Choose ritual format.

INSTRUCTIONS: Cleanse, consecrate, and empower all ingredients to match your intent. Melt wax in potpourri burner or in double boiler. Carefully use the medicine dropper to slowly add the melted wax to the mold. Halfway through, add magickal item and herbs, then continue filling the mold with the wax. Place mold in freezer to harden. When completely cool and solid, pop talisman out of the mold. Empower for specific purpose in ritual circle. Wax talismans can be carried on the person, or added to gris-gris bags, cloth poppets, or other magickal applications. They can be timed and then melted at a specific point in ritual to release their magick, or they can be given as magickal gifts. If you study any of the medieval classical astrological literature, you will discover that wax talismans were a mainstay of magickal expertise in that time period, especially when working magick by the Lunar Mansions (SEE PART III UNDER MOON).

Cauldron

The central image of Celtic Craft shamanic tradition is the cauldron, the vessel of heat, plenty, and inspiration. Notable Celtic cauldrons include the cauldron of the Dagda, which leaves no one unsatisfied; the cauldron of Diwrnach, which will not serve cowards; the cauldron of Bran the Blessed, which confers rebirth; and the cauldron of the goddess Cerridwen, which confers knowledge.[39] Folks from ancient Gaul (modern France, Belgium, and part of Germany) had a similar deity, Sucellus, associated with the hammer and the pot of plenty.[40] These properties are also found in the cauldron's later manifestation as the Grail, conferring plenty, healing, and spiritual wisdom. The Gundestrup cauldron, a huge silver cauldron discovered in Denmark and dated at 400 or 300 B.C., gives us proof that such ritual pots existed over 2,000 years ago in Europe.[41] In fact, cauldrons as big as a person were common among the ancient Celts. Sometimes they made the cauldrons themselves, and other times they would buy them from traders from as far away as Egypt and Greece. These pots were often buried with the owner when they died. The Egyptian picture-writing of the great Female Deep that gave birth to the universe and to the gods was a design consisting of three cauldrons, and in Norse legend, the three cauldrons stood for the female power of cosmic creation. Here, the cauldron represents the birthing process. Greek history gives us the Cauldron of Medea, a priestess of Hecate (goddess of the moon), and you'll find her famous soliloquy in Part III, under Moon. Where the Celts often spoke of buried cauldrons beneath water in the underworld, the Romans referred to sacred cauldrons hidden in caves. Scandinavian folklore holds that the "Roaring Cauldron" was the source of all rivers.[42] In checking history, then, we see that the cauldron was associated with both male and female divinity, and appeared to be an important ritual item throughout many cultures. Legends about the Christian evangelist Saint John claimed that he was birthed from a boiling cauldron and had spiritual powers.[43]

If we really think about it, the cultural significance of the cauldron is an exact replica of modern-day new physics, where the unmanifest (seen in this instance as liquid form) becomes manifest through the transformation of light (the heated cauldron). The bubbling sound of the liquid as it heats is the "pop" that occurs from "no-thing" to "some-thing." Isn't it amazing that myths from all over the world lead back to the same scientific principles? The basis for all new science is explained differently in each ancient culture, yet these mythos lead to the same understanding.

Most modern Witches have both a cauldron and a chalice somewhere in their magickal tool box, and use them for various purposes. Much like the beliefs of the ancient Celts, the cauldron is used to heat things (or contain the fire itself), seen in ritual as the representation of inspiration and transformation (Celtic Goddess Cerridwen), and is associated with plenty, or abundance, sometimes through the Celtic god Dagda. For the solitary Witch or those with small groups, the chosen iron cauldron is usually small (six to twelve inches in diameter), called a gipsy pot. Larger groups who have been practicing for several years might invest in the bigger iron kettles (two to three feet in diameter), many times discovered at flea markets and auctions. The chalice (the more refined version of the cauldron) is associated with our holy communion.

In the Craft, cauldrons with three legs represent the three faces of the Goddess—Maiden, Mother, and Crone. Cauldrons with four legs are associated with the four elements, the four airts (magickal winds), the four watchtowers (astrologically related), and the four major fire festivals (Wheel of the Year). Other keywords connected with the cauldron are water, transformation, death, and rebirth.

Cauldron Ritual: A Time to Move On

Some people think that it's brave to keep your feelings locked away, but when you bottle your emotions inside of you, they *will* find a way to get out—sometimes into sickness and sometimes into altered behavior patterns—they do not just go away. This ritual is titled "A Time to Move On," meaning that although you acknowledge the pain or sorrow of a particular event, you also realize that life keeps going and that there are better times ahead. This ritual is to help you start on your way with peace and the blessings of Spirit, and it can also be performed the day you realize you aren't a child anymore, the day before starting high school or college, or the day of your graduation. You can even reformat this ritual for the opening of a bridal shower.

SUPPLIES: One cauldron; spring water; your favorite skin-safe magickal oil; white rose petals; one new wooden spoon; and thirteen white votive candles. (**Note:** If you are not allowed to have candles, make them out of construction paper.) One white taper candle on which you will inscribe the name of what is lost (this could be the name of a person, the name of a pet, the loss of an important friend who has moved away, the defeat you experienced in a physical challenge, the idea of graduation, growing up, moving to a new home or apartment—even the loss of a prized possession) and set it aside. One box of tissues to wipe away the tears; thin red, white, and black ribbon, measuring a yard long; black cloth. Choose your favorite ritual format.

INSTRUCTIONS: Cast a magick circle and call the quarters. Place the cauldron and all supplies in the center of the circle. Surround the cauldron with the thirteen unlit candles. As you lay out the candles, say:

The first for the blessings of Spirit.
The second for combined energy
of the Lord and Lady.
The third for the unity of the sacred triad.
The fourth for love that never dies.
The fifth for all the elements—
earth, air, water, fire, and Spirit.
The sixth to honor memories past.
The seventh for the safe journey forward
and changes I will encounter.
The eighth to build for the future.
The ninth to grant all wishes.

The tenth for endings free of pain.
The eleventh to master all fear.
The twelfth to bring happiness near.
The thirteenth to dispel all evil.
So mote it be.

Tie the ribbons onto the handle of the spoon, saying:

Red for the blood of life, white for the purity
of Spirit, black to repel all negativity.

Pour the water into the cauldron, saying:

Water cleanses and renews. Water washes
away pain and sorrow. Water blesses
and creates harmony.

With the oil, draw a pentacle on your forehead, then put three drops into the water. Stir the water three times with the spoon in a clockwise direction, saying:

Once for love, twice for joy, three times for
harmony. The cauldron is blessed.

Add the rose petals to the water, then stir the water with the spoon in a clockwise direction three times, repeating:

Once for love, twice for joy,
three times for harmony.

Recite the Charge of the Star Goddess (PAGE 5), which invokes the energy of deity, as you hold your hands over the cauldron. Once finished, light the candles, one at a time, remarking again what each is for ("The first is for the blessings of Spirit . . ."). Light the taper candle and say:

Bring forth, Great Lady, a new day, a time of
laughter and joy, a time of happiness and love.
May the blessings of Spirit be ever upon me now,
and in times to come. So mote it be.

If you are in an area where the burning candles can safely remain lit, you can let them burn out. If this is not the case, then, with the back of the spoon, snuff each of the thirteen original candles, again repeating what they are for. Allow the inscribed candle to burn completely. Thank deity, release the quarters, release the circle, and pour the water outside off your property. If you have had to put out the candles, wrap them and the spoon with ribbons in black cloth. Place under your bed. If this has been a particularly bad time for you, repeat the spell with the same materials in thirty days. If you have done this ritual as a gift for someone else, give them the spoon with instructions for its safekeeping.

Poppets and Dollies

Poppets are doll-like representations of the human form used for magickal and spiritual purposes. They appear in the history of almost every culture throughout the world. The ancient Egyptians believed that magickal powers resided in certain persons, and the greater the person, the greater the life-force: *mana,* or magick. As the Egyptians had theocratic monarchs (SEE PART IV, MAGICK), this belief makes sense—their king was the representation of God on Earth. To make a statue of him and put it in your living area was to bring the divine light to the supper table. The Egyptians also believed that if you were to make a statue of a powerful person, then you could share in that power, too, because the image formed a link between the worshipper and the divine energy of the universe as manifested in that person. In the fertile area of the Nile, images (or statues) were treated as living, active beings whose occult powers could affect the natural world,[44] and herein lies all the grumbling about "graven images" and "worshipping

idols" that comes directly from the ancient Jewish belief system that taught its followers that God was so vast that he/she had no form. They were so adamant about this fact that they forbade any images (governmental or deity) to be erected in their cities and had to pose a sit-down strike more than once against the Roman government to prove their point. Sometimes they won and sometimes they lost. Masada, in Jewish history, is the ultimate bloody conclusion of such a strike.

Ancient Egyptians used soft substances such as clay, wax, animal fats, and bread doughs to create figures of gods and enemies alike. One of the earliest discussions on poppet magick occurs in an Egyptian text of the Middle Kingdom—2133–1786 B.C.[45]—which means that the formal use of poppet magick is at least four thousand years old. These small images were stuffed with herbs or tiny magickal scrolls, indicating the spellcaster's intent. In some cases, the desire was written on papyrus and attached to the neck of the doll with a cord. Later in the ancient world, Greek city officials in the fourth century B.C. used poppets in public binding ceremonies in an effort to psychologically gather the people together to overcome their enemies[46]—and yes, this is a good look at early propaganda.

The legendary Nectanebo is said to have repelled invasions by making wax models of his own ships and men and those of the invaders. After placing them all in a bowl of water, Nectanebo would wave his ebony rod and invoke gods to animate the wax models and sink the enemy ships.[47] However, it is important to note that in Egyptian society, as in the structure of Witchcraft, the use of magick rarely took the place of more practical action. Animal poppets also figured in Egyptian magick, including a spell for a scorpion bite that required the wax image of a cat to be placed onto a person who had been bitten by the scorpion. As cats were the natural enemies of the scorpion (and the snake), and sacred to the Egyptian pantheon, it was believed that the cat would destroy the dangerous venom and assist in the healing of the patient.[48] Life was breathed into the poppet through the use of sacred breath and various incantations.

In other cultures, poppets were made from cloth, straw, corn husks, willow fronds, and vegetable material including carrots, turnips, potatoes, and mandrake root, or fruits such as lemons, oranges, mangos, and apples. Who hasn't seen the dried apple dolls so popular in American harvest celebrations? Items used to fill such objects included a taglock (something belonging to the person the doll represents), herbs associated with the magickal intent, magickal symbols or objects, or small pieces of paper containing the name of the person as well as a simple rhyme or spell (just like the ancient Egyptian practice). Today's Witches often use photographs in place of a poppet, where others believe that the energy spent handcrafting the poppet is as important as the photograph and use both. Skill in sewing is not required as the intent is more important than the quality of the finished product. If you don't want to venture into needle and thread territory, you can always visit an arts and crafts shop that carries material for doll making, or purchase the small, ready-made variety for under five dollars. In modern Witchcraft, poppets are used primarily for healing and workings of harmony and personal success. Corn dollies figure prominently in harvest festivals as representations of the Lord and Lady (depending upon the tradition you follow).[49]

It is important to note (since you want to be an expert on magick) that the Voodoo doll is a direct product of Hollywood and the tourist trade of New Orleans. You will not find this interesting little beastie in other forms of Voodoo

(of which there are several popular varieties). However, you will find Money Dollies and paquettes (stuffed geometric objects representing the gods, covered with sequins) in Haitian and Louisiana Voodoo.

General Rules of Poppet Magick

- You should have a taglock (something belonging to the individual for whom you are working the magick). If you can't get your hands on something, use a photograph. Last ditch: use their name, and be sure it is correctly spelled and you have spent time holding the paper and visualizing the face of your friend or family member in an effort to make a good connection.

- Choose herbs, oils, and incenses that match the intent of the working (love, money, health, protection, and so on).

- Always work in a magick circle, especially if you are performing healing magicks. The cleaner the area, the purer the magick.

- If you are working on a chronic condition or long-term medical care, remember that the person did not get sick in a day, therefore they will most likely not get well in a day. Continue to work with the same poppet, renewing the spellwork on critical days as well as every thirty days thereafter.

- Once the link has been forged between the person and the poppet, keep the poppet in a safe place. Finding it in your pet rat's nest would not be a good thing.

- When your magick has reached the desired end, de-magick the poppet by cutting the tie between the person and the poppet and sprinkling the doll with holy water. Dismantle the doll and burn everything, asking that harmony and healing continue for that person.

- Well Dollies—poppets empowered only for healing without attachment to a person or animal—can be given as get-well gifts to friends and family members. Use Well Dollies in place of taglocked poppets if there is any possibility that the doll might be torn, lost, or given to the family pet as a play-toy.

- Birthing Dollies contain a taglock from both prospective parents, and are empowered with seven gifts to the prospective newborn (love, intelligence, compassion, discernment, health, wealth, and protection). Many women take these fertility dollies into the delivery room with them, and then hand the doll over the bed of the newborn child for added protection.

- Money Dollies are stuffed with at least three pieces of paper money and one each of the coinage used in your country, as well as your name, herbs associated with money and success, and a lodestone or magnet. Each week (or month), the doll should be reactivated with incense and prayer, and a fresh piece of paper money should be safety-pinned to the body of the doll. This doll should also be hidden for two basic reasons: To protect the integrity of your work, and to keep people from tearing off the bills when they desperately need money. If someone does take the money off the doll, you will have to dispose of that doll and make a new one.

- Animal toys (such as catnip mice and dog chews) can be empowered for the health and safety of your favorite pet. As they will be destroyed, don't link the animal's energy to the toy; rather, empower it to release healing energy as it naturally disintegrates.

Ritual to Empower a Poppet or Dolly

SUPPLIES: Two white illuminator candles; the poppet; herbs and incense of choice; representations of the four elements; taglock; perfume; needle and thread; scissors; picture of the individual you are working for as well as a small piece of paper with their complete name on it.

INSTRUCTIONS: Based on your choice of moon phase and moon flavor (or perhaps the day of the week), gather together all your supplies and place them on the altar. Ground and center. Sprinkle the illuminator candles lightly with the perfume. Light the illuminator candles, saying:

> *Out of the darkness came the birth of creation,*
> *just as I will create* (state your purpose)
> *this night* (day).

Cast the magick circle and call the quarters. Cleanse and consecrate the doll with the four elements. Conjure the herbs using the conjuration in Part IV, under Charms. If you have any doubt on the ritual format, check the one listed as Silver's Spellcasting Ritual in Part III's Spells section. Stuff them in the doll, along with the taglock and the person's name on the paper. Sew the doll shut. With each stitch, repeat your intent (for example, healing, prosperity, and so on) and visualize the person for whom you are making the doll.

Hold the photograph of the person and the doll together in both hands (you can lightly tie the doll and picture together with colored ribbon matching the intent). Pass the doll and photo through the four elements again, saying:

> *Earth links you to* (say the person's name).
> *Air links you to* (repeat the name). *Fire links*
> *you to* (name). *Water links you to* (name).

Hold the doll in both hands over the altar, and say:

The bond is forged. The doll and (person's name) are one, the link cannot be broken until I so choose or, in Spirit's eyes, the work is complete.

Breathe slowly on the doll three times, saying each time:

The breath of life around you The breath of life within you. So mote it be!

Carry the doll and picture to the center of the circle. Hold the doll high and ask for blessings of Spirit (or your patron deity) on your intention. Take the doll to each quarter, beginning in the north, asking that each elemental energy bless this working. Return the doll to your altar. Ground and center. Thank deity. Release the quarters in a counterclockwise direction, and then release the circle in the same manner. You can take the energy from the circle and place it in the doll, if you desire.

Wand, Rod, Stang, and Staff

Four tools, all made of wood, and all used in some way to direct magickal current, usually within the ritual circle.

Wand

Most of us think of a wand as being a straight stick, but some of the earliest wands, both in Egyptian[50] and Teutonic[51] (Norse) cultures, were fairly flat and shaped in a semicircle, carved with all manner of magickal symbols and mythical beasties. These wands, called "magic knives," were used to turn back evil. The earliest known wands in the Egyptian culture were made out of hippopotamus ivory and date to around 2800 B.C. with points ending in exotic animal heads, like a panther or a jackal. Around 2100 B.C., the head was dropped in favor of the multitude of decorations. Archeologists and historians believe that the curved shape of the wand might have come from a type of throw stick used to kill birds and small animals. The curved stick moved from a practical application to a magickal one, symbolizing order over chaos. Personal wands even appeared as symbols and sigils painted on makeup pots, headrests, and other household ornaments.

Today's wand measurement is elbow to wrist or elbow to thumb. The wood chosen is usually picked in association with the magickal correspondence of the tree type. Not all wands are made of wood. Some consist of copper tubes wrapped with leather and topped with a crystal, or constructed of hand-blown glass or glass crystal inset with copper, silver, precious, and semiprecious stones. The type, size, and shape of the wand that you use should ultimately please you, as this is your magickal tool.

Rod

Egyptians, Babylonians, Sumerians, Greeks, and Romans also carried rods and staffs as symbols of authority in daily life as well as in magickal practice. Some rods were made for specific purposes, such as protection for women during childbirth, and were consecrated to Bes. The rod is a particularly interesting magickal tool with symbolism linked to power, authority, and the World Tree (Tree of Life/Yggdrasil/Pole Star), and appears in stories of Egyptian, Greek, Jewish, and Islamic magick. If one carried a rod, he or she had the power to settle all disputes, especially if empowered during a storm that carries both thunder and lightening. In European lore, a rod empowered on the Halloween full moon carried great authority over the spirits of heaven and earth. Ancient civilizations believed that the rod was thought to command all types of spirits and send messages to god/dess. Its measurement is approximately three feet in length, or from shoulder to fingertips. Modern magickal rods are either painted in the color of a Wiccan tradition or group, or are carved or painted with magickal symbols and sigils of the magickal person's choice. Long-handled wooden spoons (with a handle at least three feet long) can also be carved, painted, empowered, and used in the same manner as the magickal rod.

Stang

The stang is a straight branch with a fork or *Y* at one end, and is most used in ritual circle as a type of centerpiece representing the magick of the three[52]—the trinity—in the following ways: Earth, Sea, and Sky; Body, Mind, and Spirit; God, Goddess, and Unity; the three faces of the God; the three faces of the Goddess; and the crossroads of life. Stangs used today are normally five to six feet in height and are often decorated with ribbons and flowers that match the seasonal ritual. The stang also relates to the legend of the World Tree, and in some ritual groups it is the pole of libation, where gifts of food and liquid are arranged or poured by the base in honor of the gods. This is similar to the pole erected in the center of a Voodoo rite, dedicated to Damballah, called the Ponteau Mitan. The stang is normally placed at the north (the seat of all power) or directly behind the altar. A few groups, often with Druidic leanings, place the stang in the center of the circle.

Staff

Today's staff is either chosen in accordance with your height, or by how it feels when used as a walking stick. Where some Witches prefer a shorter staff, others like the extended length. Of all the wooden tools, the staff is often seen as a symbol of honor and authority, and is normally decorated with magickal symbols, talismans, bells, amulets, and trinkets given as gifts to the bearer tied with leather strips or sturdy cord, and other unusual magickal bits that relate to its owner. In a group environment the staff of the high priest or high priestess may have symbols that relate to how many covens they have under their direction and how many members they have initiated. Like the wand and the rod, the staff is used to direct magickal current, often out-of-doors, but also used indoors if space permits. In more shamanic groups, the staff has replaced the sword. A staff carved with knobs and topped with a wooden replica of a human skull is specifically used at Samhain to honor the dead, or in other rituals where ancestors play a pivotal role: a duo derivation from Canadian Indian tribes and Haitian Voudon traditions, though ancient Celts did put the heads of their enemies on poles to capture their power and honor their valor. Obviously the Witches of today don't carry reconstructionism that far.

Over time you may gather quite a collection of wands, rods, staffs, and stangs. Where some will be all-purpose, others may work well for one type of magick over another, depending upon how and when it was originally empowered and the type of wood chosen. On occasion a tool will come to you that is not meant for you, and you will know this by the way the tool feels to you. It is not uncommon in the magickal community for an individual to say to another, "I received this as a gift, but I know that I was just part of the journey; this tool was meant for you." They may also say, "I have worked with this tool for many years, but now I know it is time for it to be a part of someone else's life." When the appropriate person comes along, they will be gifted with the tool. Recycling gifts in this way is not an insult; it means that the bearer understands the transient mechanics of the earth plane and acknowledges the value of sharing during the limited time in which we spend here. In the Craft community, to have something previously owned by a teacher, mentor, or close friend is the epitome of pride and honor. Such things are highly valued and treated with respect.

You can use the following list to choose what type of wood matches the intent of your work.

Magickal Woods and Their Uses

Apple: Love, healing, immortality.

Apricot: Love.

Ash: Protection, prosperity, health, the sea.

Bamboo: Protection, luck, hex-breaking.

Birch: Protection, banishing, purification.

Cherry: Love, divination.

Chestnut: Love, strength, money, healing.

Cypress: Longevity, healing, comfort, protection.

Dogwood: Wishes, protection.

Elder: Banishing, protection, healing, wards off attackers, prosperity, sleep. **Note:** Some Wiccan traditions believe that the elder is sacred to the Goddess and therefore should not be cut or used; however, the leaves and berries are used in spells.

Elm: Love.

Fig: Divination, fertility, love.

Hawthorn: Fertility, happiness.

Hazel: Luck, protection, wishes, anti-lightning.

Hickory: Longevity, legal matters.

Holly: Protection, luck, dream magick.

Juniper: Protection, love, banishing, health, anti-theft.

Magnolia: Fidelity, enjoyment, riches.

Maple: Love, money, longevity.

Mesquite: Healing.

Mimosa: Protection, love, dreams, prophecy, purification.

Mulberry: Protection, magickal focus, strength.

Oak: All-purpose.

Orange: Love, money, luck, divination.

Peach: Love, fertility, wishes, banishment, longevity.

Pear: Love.

Pine: Healing, protection, banishment, money, anti-hunger.

Plum: Healing.

Poplar: Money, success, personal riches.

Rowan: All-purpose.

Walnut: Health, mental powers, wishes.

Willow: Divination, love, protection, healing.

Collecting and Preparing a Magickal Wood

Most Witches prefer to use a fallen branch rather than cutting a limb from a tree, feeling that taking from the tree with a blade is disrespectful. Others believe that if you ask the tree and indicate your purpose, you can tell if the tree gives permission by laying your hand softly on the bark. If you feel unhappy, sad, or like you're being brushed off, permission is not granted. If, however, you feel a warm, flowing sensation, then the tree has given its permission.

An offering should always be left at the base of the tree if a branch is taken in this way.

The wood should be left in a warm, dry place and allowed to cure, if it was living when taken. Fallen branches may already be sufficiently dried. If in doubt, treat it as living wood. Some Witches prefer to leave the bark on the wood, where others peel away the bark with a pocket knife, then sand the surface with sandpaper until smooth to the touch. The soft surface takes paint and wood-burning techniques better than the bark. The choice is yours. As a final touch you may wish to wrap the handle portion with leather or other soft cloth. Some Witches add crystals and gems to the point that will direct the current, either gluing or wiring the stone into place with thin copper or silver wire.

Empowerment Ceremony for Wands, Rods, Staves, Stangs, and Brooms

TIMING: New moon (unless the item will be used to specifically to banish, then choose dark moon, or moon in Scorpio).

SUPPLIES: One red candle; holy water or Florida Water (SEE RECIPE, PAGE 414); salt; empowering oil; incense of your choice; a carving tool or wood-burning tool; a selection of magickal symbols; a pencil (to trace the designs before you carve or use the wood-burning tool); thirteen bricks or white stones; one cauldron.

PRE-RITUAL PREPARATION: Choose and carve the magickal symbols you desire on the piece. Build your circle with the bricks or stones. When you are finished, sprinkle both wooden tool and circle with holy water or Florida Water. Libation to the Gods.

THE RITUAL: Cast your circle (SEE PAGE 6) around the stone circle, which will be in the center. Place the cauldron in the stone circle. Light the fire candle and place inside the cauldron. Call the quarters. Invoke deity. Place the wooden ritual piece inside the stone circle. Pass the four elements over the item (fire, incense, salt, and holy water). Stand over the circle, raise your arms to the heavens, and say:

Mistress (Master) of the Universe! I call thee forth to cleanse and consecrate this (name item). Empower this (name item) in the name of universal perfection!

Outstretch both hands toward the item.

(Name item), I conjure thee in the name of the Mistress (Master) of the universe to work all forms of magick for me! Ye shall conjure, banish, empower, or cast aside negative energies as I so dictate. Ye shall overcome all obstacles in the performance of these tasks. At my very touch ye shall awaken into life in preparation for any and all magicks and respond with perfection to my very will, and you shall retain your power in fallow days when magick is not required. As I will, so shall it be!

Rub the item with the holy oil, then draw an equal-armed cross in the air over the item to seal your work. Complete the ritual by offering a libation to the gods. Thank deity. Close the quarters. Take up the circle with your finger and place the circle energy in the tool by directing your finger at the tool and envisioning the energy leaving your finger and entering the tool. Leave the item in the light of the following full moon for at least one hour.

Witch's Bottle

The first containers on record for "holding" magick come from an Egyptian document where names and incantations were copied onto papyrus, then sealed within a box or small pot, which was buried in a cemetery to entreat the dead for their assistance. This method of control seems to be a forerunner of the Islamic tradition of sealing a djinn in a bottle[53] and is considered by modern scholars to fall under the category of defixiones (SEE PART IV UNDER TALISMANS, AMULETS, AND DEFIXIONES). Other Egyptian pot magick included the Ritual of the Red Pot (see Part V, under Enemies), where the pot is actually broken. In Australia, Aborigines made a small clay vessel, no larger than an inch in diameter, called a cous-cous. The magician whispers a spell into the bottle, then caps and buries it. A cous-cous handled in this manner is said to protect all secrets. The cous-cous also works as a timing device. A spell, regardless of intent, is placed in the small clay jar and hung by a thin piece of twine on a tree. When the twine breaks and the bottle crashes to the ground and breaks open, the spell will be released. In the sixteenth and seventeenth century, English Witches used bellarmine jugs and bottles as magickal containers. These vessels took their names from the fierce faces molded into them at the time of kiln firing.[54] They were used to banish energies as well as protect the Crafter's home and property.

Witches today use bottles and jars of all shapes and sizes for a variety of magickal purposes. Although a few have faces and animals on them, and some are unique in design, most are plain, taken from cabinet or cupboard whenever the need arises. If the bottle surface is relatively flat and you have a computer, you can scan any design you like onto a large label and then affix it to the bottle. If you don't have a computer, you can always look through magazines, find a picture you feel fits the intent of your spell, and glue or tape it to the container.

Finally, the twenty-first century brought us food sealers—machines that vacuum-pack a variety of foods in different-sized bags as well as jars. Readily available at most inexpensive department stores, this unique tool can serve several magickal purposes, from protecting your prized books, sealing ritual items, keeping herbs fresh, and for using quite effectively in lieu of the Witch's bottle. The vacuum action can be used to remove negativity from an individual by placing their name in a bag and therefore becoming a protective device (so as you remove the air from the bag, so, too, is the negativity removed). If you suck the air out of 'em and then pop 'em in the freezer, they are as good as gone—trust me on this one.

The number of ingredients (or things) in a Witch's bottle can be chosen by the magickal significance of the number.

Ingredient Numbers and Their Significance

ONE

Meaning of the number: Unity in spirit; independence; creativity.

Astrological symbol: Sun.

Color: White.

TWO

Meaning of the number: Balance; home life.

Astrological symbol: Moon.

Color: Silver.

THREE

Meaning of the number: Creative power and growth; any trinity.

Astrological symbol: Mars.

Color: Red.

FOUR

Meaning of the number: Building; order; justice.

Astrological symbol: Saturn.

Color: Black.

FIVE

Meaning of the number: Change and insight; love; the Witch's Pyramid.

Astrological symbol: Venus.

Color: Pink

SIX

Meaning of the number: Harmony and the work done to create it; fertility.

Astrological symbol: Mercury.

Color: Gold.

SEVEN

Meaning of the number: Mysticism; safety; defensive magicks; protection.

Astrological symbol: Neptune.

Color: Purple.

EIGHT

Meaning of the number: Transformation and renewal; the intellect.

Astrological symbol: Pluto.

Color: Orange.

NINE

Meaning of the number: Triple triad: supreme spiritual power; healing.

Astrological symbol: Jupiter.

Color: Green.

TEN

Meaning of the number: Turning point: ultimate manifestation; universal laws; fate.

Astrological symbol: Uranus.

Color: Blue.

ELEVEN

Meaning of the number: Self-mastery; success.

Astrological symbol: All.

Color: Aquamarine.

The type of ingredient is up to you—herbs, oils, tiny gems, a magnet, spells written on parchment, small clay amulets or talismans, and a taglock are just a few ideas. Ingredients should be chosen to match your desire.

Once the ingredients are mixed in a magick circle and empowered for a specific purpose, they are dropped or poured into the bottle. The entire bottle is then "conjured" (empowered) and the contents mixed by a slow, swirling motion while visualizing your intent. Pass your wand, athame, or hands over the top of the bottle or jar, and say:

> *In the name of Aradia,*
> *Queen of the Witches,*
> *I conjure thee, O magick bottle,*
> *to be of service to me.*

Tap the side of the bottle the same number of times as the number of ingredients. If you put five things in, then tap the side of the bottle five times. Follow with your verbal statement of intent. Then say: "Thou will not fail. So mote it be!" Close the bottle or jar tightly with the cap. Seal with hot wax of the color that matches the magickal number of ingredients. ***Note:*** Matching the color with the number and intent also helps you to tell which spell is in what bottle, if you have several of the same type of bottles or jars working at once.

Once sealed, a Witch's bottle is normally not reopened unless, for some reason, you wish to break the spell, you want to use the bottle for a magickal catalyst and therefore it will be broken, or if you want to renew a general (not specific) protection spell. If you are working to pull something toward you, you can keep the bottle on your altar and swish it every now and then to keep it activated. When the desire has been obtained, then bury on your property or stick under the eaves of the attic or in a cupboard in the basement to bring additional good luck. If you are absolutely sure that the bottle can no longer be of service, then you can throw it away. If you are working to push something away from you, bury off of your property or by a crossroads. Like the Egyptians, you can leave the bottle by a loved one's grave, asking for their assistance; however, check the rules of the cemetery as to what can and cannot be placed within the cemetery environment. Southern states are far more liberal on this issue than the Northern ones. If the bottle has been designed to protect the home, such as the bellarmine jug mentioned earlier, place it just inside the front door, facing the door or on the porch step. Clean out and renew at the solstices and equinoxes. Finally, a Witch's bottle can be thrown into a fire during the course of a spell to explode its power into the universe. It is suggested that you do this outdoors and with great caution.

shadows
of

Expertise

&

Proficiency

Affirmations

Affirmations are sentences filled with a bunch of good words that say nice things about what sort of future we want to have, or what type of person we want to be. The study of psychology tells us that if we repeat words, thoughts, or visualizations (fantasy pictures in our minds) often enough, what we speak or think will manifest in the material world. In essence, thoughts are things, and you are what you think! Most magickal people, past and present, will agree that when we speak aloud, we are activating our throat chakra energy (SEE CHAKRAS) as well as sending sound vibrations into the universe to create what we desire. Scientists say we are using our right brain—a gold mine of manifestation.

Too often we pay more attention to the nasty things people say about us than the nice comments. When we do this, we are opening the door to negative programming. After a while, we just might believe that we're a loser because someone (whom we think is important) tells us we are. Don't you believe it! Affirmations are a positive magickal defense mechanism against our worries, doubts, and the garbage other people sometimes throw at us. Deceptively simple, many people forget just how much power these affirmations have!

Daily Affirmations

Daily affirmations are repetitive sentences that we write or say to ourselves with the intent to improve or change our condition in a positive way on a day-to-day basis. They are a plan of action to reach a specific, intended goal. These statements are normally written or said (or both) at least ten times each morning and evening for thirty days (or from moon to moon). Anything less, and you will have to start all over again! You can't skip a day if you really want the change to happen. Larger changes, such as a complete personal makeover, may take sixty or even ninety days. That's okay. I know you can do it. If you have been meditating for a while, the affirmations you choose to recite may begin to take form quickly, perhaps within the first few days or the first week. If you haven't been practicing meditation or visualization techniques, you may wait longer to see some sort of progress. No matter. Your motto should be: Don't give up, and don't give in! Just because you are now a magickal person doesn't mean that everything is going to come easy for you. We all have lessons to learn, and sometimes patience is the most valuable goodie you will ever have in your cauldron of enchantments.

Spellcasting Affirmations

These are a bit different. Spellcasting affirmations are sentences we write that match the idea of what we want to accomplish in the spell we plan to use. This means that we have to sit down and think about what we truly want, and then put those thoughts into words before we start the magick. If we follow quantum physics, then this would be the effort to set the pattern that we wish to unfold. If we aren't specific, then anything could pop out! These sentences are repeated anywhere from three to nine times during a spell. Not every spell contains an affirmation (also called a statement of intent), though most spells have at least one sentence that describes what we want to happen, which can be separate from or be a part of an affirmation that we use at other times. According to the spell, it may be necessary to say the same affirmation while doing a physical act several days in a row—a seven-day candle spell comes to mind. Once the magickal working is completed, you might not use that affirmation again until the next time you cast the spell, either for the original intent or for a new one. Sometimes affirmations turn into magickal charms simply because we like the way they sound and they have worked for us before (SEE PART IV, CHARMS). Although magickal word charms usually rhyme, I have several in my own Book of Shadows that don't.

There is a term sometimes used in magickal work that we need to cover before you delve further into affirmations. It's called "resentment of result," and means that if you worry endlessly over an issue, even though you have worked magick, the strength of your worry will overcome the strength of your magickal work, and in the end you will reap what you most feared. This is why the old teachers taught that you should do a spell and forget about it—if you worry, or try to force the issue by skipping steps, ignoring basic universal laws and blundering blindly on, you will fail as a result of your own actions. This doesn't mean that affirmations don't work (because they are spoken in a positive way), but if you say the affirmations and then think the opposite, it's like pulling the plug on your internal computer. No electrical juice means no access. Positive change cannot occur.

In magickal training, affirmations support the various exercises, rituals, and spellwork we do by helping to purify the field of intent. For example, if you did a spell to stop gossip but allowed the gossip to lower your self-esteem by mentally agreeing with what is being said (or worrying about who said what), the spellwork or ritual you employ to stop the problem could be negated or severely hampered. Affirmations help to put you in the zone of success and keep you there, despite any negativity that decides to wend its way toward you. In every negative situation you encounter, learn to pick one positive statement that can be said when the negativity hits, no matter how many times it hits. The statement can be composed for the specific in-stance at hand, or can be something more all-encompassing. Years ago I bought a set of excellent tapes from Sun Valley Publishing in Arizona. One particular statement, "I am at peace with the world and everything in it," has stuck with me and I've used it numerous times when I'm really angry or upset at someone's negative behavior. A more simple statement, "Cancel that," works well when you worry too much, think frightening scenarios, or have no desire to continue a particular train of thought. I learned this one in college dictation class (something they don't even have anymore—boy, am I showing my age!).

Positive Thinking Exercise

How many times have you said, "I can't do that," "I won't make the grade," "I'm lousy at Spanish," or other negative comments about yourself and your future? Every time you think negatively and say negative stuff, you are planning a negative future for yourself. For the next week, remove ALL negative words about yourself from your thinking process and don't say anything negative about your future aloud. To help stop this bad habit, think of a silly keyword, like "banana," a magick word, like "abracadabra," or a power word, like "Isis," or the simple statement, "Cancel that." When the negative thought comes, yell your keyword out loud if you have to! You'll be surprised how much your life changes in just one week. Now stretch this practice to two weeks, then three. It's amazing just how powerful your mind can be.

Exam Affirmation

With so many adults going back to school for specialized training, teens are no longer among the ranks of individuals that must suffer through written examinations. Psychologists tell us that choosing and implementing a lucky item for studying and test taking is actually a good idea. Whether it be a particular shirt, belt, or lucky pencil, you are to use or wear the item while studying for the examination. On the examination day, you should wear the lucky piece (or use it) during the test. In this spell, we are going to use a lucky pencil.

SUPPLIES: A current calendar (any kind will do) that you will use only for magick; a new pencil (and a spare in case you lose it); a piece of clean, white paper; a small red bag or piece of cloth.

TIMING: New moon, full moon, on your birthday, or as otherwise mentioned.

INSTRUCTIONS: Cleanse and consecrate all supplies with the four elements in a magick circle. Pick a key affirmation, such as "Success, success, success!" Empower the calendar and the pencils with this affirmation. Dedicate the pencils and the calendar to Hermes (FOR A LISTING, SEE PART I, GODS, GODDESSES, AND PANTHEONS). On the piece of paper, write the following:

Every time I use these pencils while studying
or for an examination, I will be filled with
confidence and poise and I will be able to retain
and recall any and all necessary information
that is applicable to the work at hand. I will
confidently know what to study and I will pass
any and all examinations with great success.
SMIB.

Wrap the paper around the pencils and secure with a rubber band. Place in the red bag. Thank deity (Hermes, in this case), close the quarters (if you have called them), and release the circle.

HOW TO WORK THE SPELL: Okay, so you know that you have a history exam on Tuesday, or you know you have finals next week. You also understand that magick can't take the place of studying. (You *do* know that, right?) Each evening open the red bag and remove the paper from the pencils. Read the paper aloud and set aside. Use the pencils while studying. When you are finished studying for that time period, place your magick calendar on top of your notes. Find the date of the exam. Circle that date with a blue or purple pen. (Blue, purple, and silver are the colors of mental activity.) Hold your hands over the date, and say:

I will be calm, cool, and collected
before, during, and after the exam.

That's statement number one. Nobody wants exam jitters. Statement number two is as follows:

I will pass the exam with
an excellent grade, or better.

Choose the grade you are shooting for, and write that down on the calendar day. We always add the "or better" in our affirmations or spells because sometimes we have a bad habit of stopping our success by thinking too small. Say both statements out loud ten times while you hold your hands over that calendar date.

Complete this process by once again reading the spell intent affirmation on the white paper. Roll the pencils in the paper, secure, and place in the red bag until you are ready to study again. On the day of the exam, repeat all affirmations in this spell before you leave the house. Remember to take your lucky pencils with you and use them during the exam. Do not lend your pencils to someone else, as their energy might taint your magickal work.

So what happens if you don't make the grade you visualized the first time you try this spell? If you were only a few points off, don't sweat it. Keep up the same study practice, as you can count this a success. If you were way off, first determine if your study habits need to be improved and make adjustments accordingly. Did you not give yourself enough time? Did you not pay attention in class when the instructor indicated the span of information to be covered? Were you absent and missing a large section of notes? Did you stay up too late studying the night before? Did you cram rather than studying a little bit each day? Are you worried about something else—a looming, life sort of thing? If so, you need to work on it rather than worry about it. Then do the spell again, choosing two new pencils.

Magick is the process of practice. This is assuming, of course, that you studied enough and that you truly believed you could do it—and you'll know in your heart whether you studied or not and whether you were serious when doing the spell. Failure also comes from lack of focus and worry, or sleep deprivation. The more magick you do, the better at it you'll get because once you've had one success, you can build on that one to create more.

Almanacs

An almanac is an annual publication that contains moon phases, gardening tips, predictive weather forecasting, and articles that the publisher feels will be of interest to the reader. A magickal almanac, also produced on a yearly basis, includes moon phases, moon in the signs, planetary information, important historical dates of interest to the magickal community, planting and harvesting dates, Pagan holidays, and articles geared toward magickal readers.[1] Most magickal people learn to rely on a magickal almanac for choosing the best day and time for planning rituals, spellcasting, divination, and other mystical endeavors.

Magickal tip: Sit down with your magickal almanac and a set of colored highlighters. Choose one color to represent the full moon, one to represent the new moon, one to represent whenever a planet goes retrograde or direct, one for eclipses, one for when the moon goes void of course, and one for Pagan holidays—or you can just use one highlighter color for all these important timing mechanisms as a simple "heads up" reminder. Go through each page of the almanac for the coming year and highlight the appropriate category with the color you've chosen. This way, throughout the year, you will know at a glance when the holidays are, when the moon is full or new, if an eclipse is coming up, or if the moon is void, etc. (SEE MOON SECTION FOR INFORMATION ON MOON VOIDS). The ideal almanac is one where there is enough space to keep track of when you cast what spell and how long your work took to manifest. Once you have worked with your almanac and have played with magickal timing for about a year, you may want to extend your highlighted entries to the following:

- Major positive aspects that involve Venus (fast cash), the sun (representing the forward motion of the will), and Jupiter (long-term financial planning). Or, you may wish to take note of all aspects less the moon (there are many of these).

- Sun cycles—when the sun moves from sign to sign.

Of all the highlighted categories, I've found the moon voids reminder to be the most helpful in daily activities that may not include spellwork. If someone offers you something or has a great idea on a moon void, it will most likely fall flat on its face. A quick glance can tell you volumes when you must make hurried decisions, plan doctor's appointments, or begin major projects.

Understanding Almanac Terminology

Almost all books on general Wicca talk about the moon and her eight phases, yet most almanacs do not list moon phases. Instead, they use a different set of moon-related terms (quarters and the lunation cycle, to name a few). This is confusing to the magickal student who first reads about moon magick from the pen of an alternative religious writer (Druid, Wiccan, etc.) and then reaches for the almanac, where a compendium of new buzzwords appear. You'll also come across terms like "hot" and "barren," as well as read how the moon behaves in each astrological sign as that energy relates to agricultural interests. Before you throw up your hands and say, "I don't need to know this stuff, I've never grown so much as a marigold in a cup and I don't intend to start now. I just want more power and lots of it!"—think again. If a farmer or gardener can apply this information successfully to something physical, like a field of wheat, then we can use these same methods on, say, cultivating your career, choosing classes for next semester, or pushing away a negative habit in the same way. In magick, paying attention to the moon and what the heck she's doing up there is called "astrological timing."

In any almanac, the lunation cycle is the circuit from new moon to full moon, then back to new moon, which takes approximately twenty-nine-and-a-half days. In the Craft this twenty-nine-and-a-half day cycle is sometimes called moon to moon; however, when some Witches say "moon to moon" they mean full moon to full moon, where others mean new moon to new moon. And then there are those that take "moon to moon" to mean "same phase twenty-nine-and-a-half days from now." Confusing, I know—but there you have it.

To avoid bewilderment, just remember that there are two distinct ways to divide that twenty-nine-and-a-half day cycle:

- By *phases* (of which there are eight; each increment is approximately 3.7 days long; see Moon for a complete description of the phases).

- By *quarters* (of which there are four; each increment is approximately 7.3 days long).

Just remember that the cycle remains the same, it is only how the cycle is divided and the buzzwords that change. I included the numbers for those of you that are mathematically minded (and these are only approximations).

Most almanacs will kindly tell you what quarter (or phase) you're in on any given day, which is one of the reasons we use the almanacs in the first place, but who came up with terms like "barren" and "fruitful" in regard to the moon in the signs? And what does that quarter stuff mean?

Your wish is my command.

One of the oldest books on record in which such words as barren and fruitful appear in regard to astrology and daily life was written by a fellow named Marcus Manilius, a Roman who lived at the birth of the Common Era (that's about 2,000 years ago). The book was titled *Astronomica*[2] and is actually considered a poem in four parts (though some argue five). Granted, this is not the only book on astrology that has emerged from our distant past, echoing down the corridors of time, but it does supply proof for our purposes that following the moon, the sun, and the planets as a form of serious science for planning daily activities isn't something somebody plopped into print last Sunday, and that almanacs (of a sort) existed even then. If the practice of following the moon (planets, stars, comets, etc.) has lasted this long, there's got to

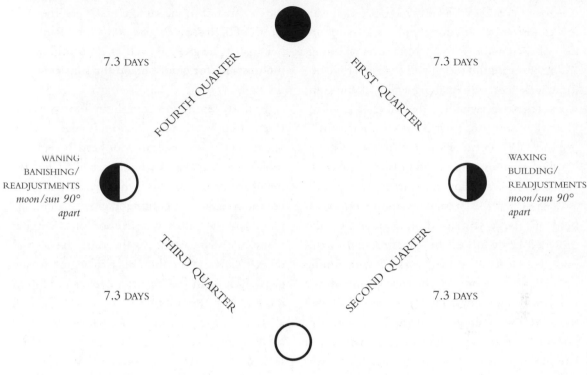

BEGINNINGS/0°
new moon/conjunction of sun and moon

7.3 DAYS

FOURTH QUARTER

FIRST QUARTER

7.3 DAYS

WANING
BANISHING/
READJUSTMENTS
*moon/sun 90°
apart*

WAXING
BUILDING/
READJUSTMENTS
*moon/sun 90°
apart*

THIRD QUARTER

SECOND QUARTER

7.3 DAYS

7.3 DAYS

FULL MOON/OPPOSITION OF SUN AND MOON
harvest/sun and moon 180° apart

The quarters of the moon.

be something to it. (YOU WILL FIND A DISCUSSION OF THESE TERMS ON PAGE 226.)

The Quarters of the Moon

Before we get rolling on this subject, I'd like to make clearer to you something that's a bit confusing. As I mentioned earlier, there are two ways to divide the movements of the moon, *quarters* and *phases*. There are four quarters in one system, eight phases in the other system. What can really be mystifying is that these two systems share a single terminology that does not represent the same thing. This terminology is *first quarter*—which means one thing in the quarterly separation and another in the phase system. In this section I am explaining the quarters (not the phases). (SEE PAGE 295 TO LEARN ABOUT PHASES.)

The first quarter begins at the new moon, when the sun and moon look like they are in the same place in the sky. They aren't really, of course, but it appears that way from our position on the Earth. In fact, the moon is in front of the sun (because its orbit falls between us Earthlings and that of the sun) so, therefore, the moon doesn't appear to be visible at all. For those of you that are into astrology, this phenomenon is called a *conjunction*—when one planet occupies the same degree of the same astrological sign (if you were looking at a horoscope chart). Conjunctions are usually considered pretty cool things in astrology because that's when two planets (or the sun and moon) mix their energies together and give a fairly nice magickal wallop to just about anything you do. A conjunction always stands for the birth of something, and in this case the moon and the sun are dancing cheek-to-cheek, making will and emotions work together (whether they like it or not). How they work together is easy to figure out—just look at the astrological sign they are visiting. This information is included in your almanac, so you don't have to know more than the keywords associated with each sign to figure out what kind of energy you are dealing with. I've also provided keywords in the Esbat section of this book (SEE PART I). When working with timing of any kind for a project, the first quarter always stands for beginnings. This first quarter (where the new moon slowly gains light) is your Go button. Press it. According to this timing, you have approximately 7.3 days to use this energy. Follow your almanac. To help you out, I've created a New Moon Esbats list (SEE PAGES 24–27) that will give you some ideas on how to use this energy in each of the astrological signs.

The second quarter begins halfway between the new moon and the full moon. Another word for this time period is *waxing*. This half moon rises around noon and sets around midnight, which is why if you look toward the western sky you'll see it floating there. This moon is going full tilt with the energy you gave it during its new cycle. It's still considered to be growing. In astrological terms, it is *square* the sun. Squares in zodiac lingo mean "challenges"—and if you want to get technical, the moon is now 90 degrees away from the sun (if you viewed a horoscope chart that represents this placement on paper). In magick, now's the time to take care of any hidden stumbling blocks that appear to be interfering with your magick. More power in the right place is the key. How do you know

what kind of power? By this time the moon and the sun are not in the same sign. Check the keywords of both signs to give you a hint. Remember that in magick, as well as in astrology, the moon stands for emotion and the sun stands for the will.

If this is getting too complicated for you, just take a deep breath and plow on. It takes a while to get the terms straight in your head. It certainly took me longer than I would have liked. Just remember that in most cases the second quarter of the moon stands for continued growth, development, and the pathway to fruition of something you've already started. By the time the second quarter ends and the third quarter begins, we are halfway through the lunation cycle and plop in the middle of the full moon. In magick (as well as daily life), most things that you want to increase are worked on or done in the first and second quarters of the moon. Once you become experienced at moon energy, you'll be able to determine which signs apply to what you want to do on your own. Again, many almanacs will give you this information, so it won't be too much of a head trip.

The third quarter begins at the full moon. Its energy represents the beginning of the harvest of what you planned at the new moon. This energy will culminate right before the moon is declared new and the next lunation cycle begins. If it helps, think of a pendulum that begins on one side and swings to the other, then back again. That "back again" is heading to its starting place, that of the new moon. It is here that we experience the full joy of the moon's light. She rises in the east at sunset and sets in the west at dawn a little later each day. In astrological terms, the moon is *opposite* the sun. The moon appears to glow because she is receiving the full effect of the sun's rays. She reflects the light of the sun, and we on Earth are the happy recipients of this heavenly magick. In all honesty, however, it isn't magick (per se), it's science! This is one of the reasons that Witchcraft is often described as the art and the science of magick. The art part is how we use science to make magick. As you study Witchcraft, you will learn that there is a great deal of Craft lore, as the moon relates to the Goddess and the sun relates to the God, in the use of a full moon. This information is covered at various places in this book. In magick and everyday stuff, the full moon stands for fulfillment, completion, power, expressing oneself emotionally in all forms of art and daily circumstances, maturity, and fruition. It is here that you'll get a clue (one way or another) if your spellwork is on track or if it's pooped out on you. Never fear, adjustments can always be made. Scientifically, during a full moon, the sun is opposite the moon (they are 180 degrees apart). This means that the moon and sun do not share the same sign. For hints on what type of magick to do, given the signs they might be in, see pages 27–29 (Full Moon Esbats).

The full moon is also a heads-up about life in general. Just because your eyeball says it's so doesn't mean you are interpreting what you are seeing the way it really is. As a child I believed that the moon glowed on its own, just like the sun did. It never occurred to me that I was looking at a giant mirror in the sky. Go figure. In technical Witch language, one-and-a-half days after this full moon is the beginning of the waning moon. This is when it is cool to start banishing stuff.

The fourth quarter moon begins halfway between the full moon (that's just passed) and the upcoming new moon. If you're into numbers, that's about 7.3 days past the full moon and 22.5 days past the original new moon (the start of the lunation cycle). We are definitely into the waning cycle of the moon. This decreasing moon

rises at midnight, so if you look eastward after midnight, you'll see what's left of her (visually) glowing there. As the sun is rising in the east, the moon is now directly overhead. This is why you can sometimes (depending on weather and placement) see the moon during the day. It's as if she forgot to go to bed at her appointed time. About midday, then, she disappears over the western horizon. In magick, this phenomenon can be useful, allowing you to visually incorporate both the sun and moon as they chase each other across the heavens from sunrise to midday. In astrological terms, the moon is once again in a square position, letting you know (energy-wise) what challenges may remain in that original magick you did at the new moon, or what energy you may wish to apply (if any) to reap your final rewards as the moon nears that conjunction with the sun to begin a new lunation cycle. This is not the same square as in the second quarter. Yes, the amount of degrees is the same (90) but the placement is different. In the second quarter, the moon has passed the sun (as she moves faster) and, in our minds, is now racing ahead of the sun. With this square, she is coming up behind the sun (buzzing through the heavens to pass the sun again), so she is on the other side and in a different sign than she was at the second quarter. Again, your almanac will tell you what sign she's currently in.

To really understand the quarters of the moon, I recommend that you keep a short journal from new moon to new moon. Watch your family, your friends, your own life, and the news on television. In the first quarter, you'll most likely see heightened activity and people wanting to start new things (whether they do or not depends on their personality, their situation, and the sign the moon was in during the new moon quarter). During the second quarter this pace may continue for a while, and then begin to slow down around the full moon. Family members may pull out old projects and work on them during this second quarter, or friends might push you to get something done, or press you to fulfill a promise you made. The full moon often brings emotional upsets. People think with everything but their brains, and hasty behavior can lead to unexpected occurrences now and later on. The fourth quarter is a time of pulling apart. You'll see breakups between friends, parents, and lovers. Many people unconsciously begin to reorganize anything that either isn't working or seems to be getting out of hand. Your mother may ground you for a simple offense when normally she simply would have given you a lecture and been done with it. Some people may appear pensive or moody because they need time to reflect, yet they override this gut feeling and bravely blunder on. Granted, the moon alone isn't the only thing with input into life—personal habits, family structure, ingrained behavioral patterns, and even other planets and their placement in the heavens (especially retrograde ones) can all affect the individual—but, again, the choice on how this energy is used is their own. None of these things makes anyone do anything if they don't want to.

Once you've reviewed your journal, have another go at it the next month. Pretty soon you'll be able to spot patterns without checking your almanac. You'll also be able to adjust your behavior, as well as understand the actions of others who are experiencing the same energy, but possibly in a different way because they have a different personality than your own, and you will be able to "feel" the lunar energies. Following the quarters (or the phases) of the moon in daily life allows you to control your life in a way that pleases you. Things can, with a little planning, run smoother than you ever thought possible. You will read more about the moon in the signs and using the moon's quarters and signs under the Farming section in Part IV.

For the Expert

Now, if you are really the technical sort, the ancient astrologers left us with an interesting tidbit: Always perform the most important magick either three degrees before ("before" meaning "applying") the conjunction, or when the moon has moved three degrees beyond the conjunction (separation). Normally, any planet in what is called the "combust" window is overtaken by the sun's energy; however, because of the moon's reflective qualities, she doesn't behave the way other planets do. So how would you know this if you don't have a computer program? What most people who are not into astrology don't know is that the moon can be considered fast or slow in its speed (the rate at which it is moving through the heavens). Taking the midpoint between fast and slow, we come up with the moon's average movement through the heavens at .5 degrees per hour. This means that (according to ancient astrologers) magickal work is best done six hours before a conjunction between the moon and sun (new moon) or six hours after the conjunction between the moon and the sun (new moon). Your almanac will give you the time of the conjunction, so all you have to do is count six hours before or six hours after the time given to pinpoint a specific time.

Does the speed of the moon affect your magickal applications? Yes, it does. Spells cast when the moon is fast seem to manifest quickly; when the moon is average, so is the time to complete the manifestation. When the moon is slow, we have noticed that the working takes much longer to complete than originally anticipated. To know the speed of the moon you will need an astrological software program or an ephemeris. An ephemeris is a book that gives the location of all the planets, including the sun and the moon, on any given day, at any given time, as well as their current speed.

Moon magick figures prominently in many Craft applications. Most Witches begin by learning the phases and quarters, then move on to the moon in the signs, the motion of the moon, lunar mansions,[3] and finally the dialog it may have with other planets at any given time. This study process can take as little as six months or as long as two years, depending on the individual and their interest in the subject. Some magickal astrologers believe that the moon in the signs packs more punch than simply working with the quarters or phases in magickal workings. Only you can decide.

Animals

As animals and humans have had to exist together from time immemorial, it is not surprising that animals have taken such prominence in our history, our religions, and in our concept of spirituality. Animism is the belief that all things carry life energy—this includes people, animals, rocks, and plants—and that within their own spheres, each grouping can communicate with its own. "Dumb as a rock" takes on new meaning, doesn't it? If we pay attention and try hard enough, we can communicate with plants and animals, and even work with gems and stones! The Drachenlock caves in Switzerland show altars dedicated to the bear that are 70,000 years old,[4] and in the Lascaux caves in France, there are paintings 13,000 years old, and a statue of a ceremonial bear's body can be found at Montespan. Some historians feel that findings such as these tell us that people have attuned themselves to animal energy in their religious and cultural ceremonies for thousands of years. Others, however, have a different view, especially on the issue of the bear altar found at Drachenlock. In private correspondence, dated 9 August 2002, historian Ronald Hutton states:

> The consensus among experts such as Trinkhaus and Stringer is that the bear skulls and altars in the Drachenloch cave were probably rolled together by flood action rather than human beings. There is now no agreement between them as to whether the Neanderthals had any ritual or artistic life at all, and these activities are only clearly apparent from c. 35,000 years ago. By contrast, the paintings of animals at Lascaux are excellent evidence for both art and ritual.

Witches believe that because everything is made up of energy it has a life force, and that the life force of all things is interconnected. In the world's collective tribal history we used fetishes (objects fashioned of feathers, skins, and bones) in ceremonies to honor our animal brothers and sisters, and in an effort to communicate and bridge the gap between animal and human, human and divine. It was believed that the fetish put you in sympathy with the animal energy. *Sympathy*, in occult terminology, means "making a connection" or "using items of like mind." Today, many humans are too busy to pay attention to the gifts of the animals, much less communicate with them on a serious level. The Witch realizes that because we are interconnected, the survival of the planet and of the animals is directly related to our own spiritual welfare.

Native Americans studied nature and learned profound spiritual lessons from her. By studying the connected threads of a spider's web, they understood that there is one web of life, within which everything is related. Nothing exists alone. They saw that the threads of the web are drawn out from within the spider's very being, just as Spirit creates the natural world from within itself, and we create our own worlds within our minds.[5]

Our predecessors, shamans, spirit keepers, magi, priests, and priestesses studied plants and animals not only for mystical purposes but also to learn which plants were safe to eat, and which could be used as medicines. The Native American Indians followed the bear to learn which plants would cure what ailment. The bear was considered the giver of medicine. Animal movements in any area could also warn a tribe of impending danger, and today we know that mass animal movement spells trouble in the environment.

Unlike humans, animals are always in the brain-wave known as alpha, a semi-psychic state. This is why they can sense when you are unhappy, can know when you are on your way home, or even see ghosts! Humans, on the other hand, experience several levels of the mind, and we are in the alpha state only when we are meditating, relaxed, or bored. When you daydream, eat, or watch television, you are usually in the alpha state, which is why you are susceptible to commercials!

It is from our love of animals and the attunement that magickal people seek with them that brought about the Christian belief that Witches have familiars, and during the dark days of the European Inquisition[6] many ridiculous stories were extracted from innocent people under torture about their animal friends. Yet in every tribal history we find groups of people gravitating to a particular animal energy, and claiming that animal as a representation of the people. Even in medieval times figures of animals were placed on shields and banners of the most royal, and four of the eight Wiccan and Druid High Holy Days (the fire festivals) are associated with the protection and raising of animals and crops. For over six thousand years, community activities and celebrations on Candlemas (February 1,

lambing and calving), Beltane (May 1, leading the animals out to high pasture), Lughnasadh (August 1, agricultural harvest), and Samhain (November 1, depending on the tradition—bringing the animals in from the pasture to protected areas for the winter) involved the honor and care of animals.

Many tribes in Scotland and Ireland claimed to have been descended from the animal energies they revered.[7] Tribes (and family lines later on) carried representations of the favored animal, called a totem animal. In modern Witchcraft and Druidry, animals still hold important roles in religious ceremonies and, depending upon the group, certain quarters of the magick circle may be attributed to them. In the Black Forest Clan, our overall totems are the Wolf and the Raven, yet each quarter also has a totemic animal representation, and each of our twenty-nine covens has chosen a coven totem of their own. We believe that the animal energy helps us to bridge the gap between the physical realm and the spiritual worlds. Rather than wearing a Witch's garter,[8] I wear a charm bracelet with each of the coven animals represented. When studying deities you will notice that most of them have an animal association, combining the animal energy with the spiritual energy of the divine. These animals serve as protectors as well as extend admirable traits such as courage, peace, intelligence, grace, and so on. When the deity energy is called in ritual circle, the associated animal energy is also present, even though you may not acknowledge it.

In magick, Witches may call upon the energy of a particular animal to help them in their work. We might place a statue or picture of the animal on the altar to help us focus, or we may invite our pets into ritual circle (animals love magick), or ask our personal totem animal to carry a message to the collective oversoul of a particular species. Animal energy is especially helpful in work for the environment, healing, and protection. As you can see from the following list, animals, birds, reptiles, and insects are associated with their natural life patterns and instincts. When and if you choose a totem animal for yourself, you should study that animal's normal behavior by reading all about them and, if you can, by visiting them and spending time with them in their natural habitat. If you have a domesticated animal, it's time to give him or her more attention and care. Now that you are magickal, animals will sense changes in you and will expect you to pay closer attention to their needs, especially if they require additional protection or medical care. Healing charms and chants aren't just reserved for people—they work well on animals, too.

Animals and Their Associations

Aardvark: Finding hidden things

Alligator/Crocodile: Initiation; power; patience; basic earth energy; hold on to your money

Apes: Communication; group government

Armadillo: Personal protection; empathy

Badger: Courage; bold self-expression

Barracuda: Making it on your own

Bat: Initiation; intuition; revealing secrets; transition

Bear: Healing; medical diagnosis; strength

Bee: Community; clan; work; industry; organization

Blackbird: Enchantment; between-the-worlds work

Black Widow Spider: Weaving a new fate

Boar: Strength; family protection; warrior spirit; leadership

Bobcat: Solitary magick; psychic warning; secrets

Bull: Wealth; creativity; ability to expand opportunities

Butterfly: Transformation; dance; artistic endeavors

Camel: Survival during lean times

Cat: Magick; mystery; independence; psychic warning; grace

Chameleon: Changing environment; camouflage

Cheetah: Speed; flexibility

Chipmunk: Finding treasures in the earth; working for the future

Cicada: Happiness; joy

Clam: Closing ranks for protection

Cobra: Swift, decisive action

Copperhead: Aggressive healing; psychism

Cougar: Power; agility

Crab: Good luck; protection; success

Cricket: Luck; faith; intuition

Crocodile: Primal strength; creation; patience; Great Mother; balance

Daddy Longlegs Spider: Invisibility

Deer: Nature

Dog: Guidance; protection; loyalty; friendship

Dingo: Relentless pursuit of goals

Dolphin: Intelligence; psychism; community; protection

Dragonfly: Dreams; psychism; artistry

Eagle: Intelligence; courage; decision making; carrier of prayers

Earthworm: Reworking old projects; investigation

Elephant: Prosperity; power; strength

Ferret: Stealth; agility; uncovering the truth

Firefly: Hope; inspiration; beginnings; ideas; creativity

Fox: Shapeshifting; transformation; cunning; diplomacy

Frog: New beginnings; abundance; medicine; hidden beauty

Garter Snake: Activity; opportunity

Gecko: Overcoming strife

Goat: Reaching success; confidence

Goose: Protection; parenting; perseverance

Goldfish: Peace; prosperity

Guinea Pig: Group mind

Hawk: Cleansing; nobility; remembering; clarity; spirit messenger

Hippopotamus: Transformation; initiation; creative power

Horse: The Goddess; travel between the worlds; rebirth; grace

Hummingbird: Repair relationship difficulties; healing

Hyena: Family/clan life; group mind; heightened perception

Impala: Grace

Jackal: Protection from hidden dangers; guidance

Jaguar: Reclaiming power; strength; speed; ability

Kangaroo: Forward movement

Koala: Serenity; peace; removing sickness

Komodo Dragon: Long life; survival

Lady Bug: Wish fulfillment; luck; protection; prosperity

Lemur: Heralds ghosts

Leopard: Ghost buster; overcoming bad habits; destroying jealousy; intuition

Lion: Courage; strength; loyalty

Lizard: Patience; dreaming

Loon: Creative inspiration; fidelity

Lynx: Visionquesting; visionary work; cutting-edge mentality

Mole: Luck

Moth: Sending and receiving messages

Mouse: Attention to detail

Muskrat: Navigating through tricky situations

Mussels: Filtering information

Octopus: Creative center; intelligence; power

Otter: Sharing; playfulness; grace in the water; learning to swim

Owl: Wisdom; heightened perception; discernment; female magick; messages to and from the dead

Panda: Nourishment; finding the heart of a problem

Panther: Regaining one's power; protection; finding information; Dark Mother

Pig: Abundance; fertility; intelligence

Polar Bear: Supernatural power; guides between the worlds

Praying Mantis: Finding solutions to problems; dreaming; using the higher mind

Rabbit: Balance; rebirth; intuition; messages from the Spirit world

Raccoon: Dexterity; glamouries; secrecy

Ram: Achievement; strength; success

Rat: Intelligence; socialization; success

Rattlesnake: Transformation; healing; cycle of life and death

Raven: Healing; initiation; protection; messages; wisdom; balance

Rhinoceros: Ancient wisdom

Salamander: Inspiration; help; creativity; inspiration

Scorpion: Transformation; success; cycle of life and death; protection; weather

Sea Horse: Honor; codes of conduct; creativity

Seal: Dreaming; the collective conscious; birth; imagination

Shark: Relentless ferocity; intuition

Siberian Tiger: Creativity; power; passion; unpredictable

Snake: Initiation; wisdom

Spider: Weaving strong magick; fate; spiral energy

Stag: The God; independence; purification; protection of forests

Starfish: Working toward your desires; regeneration

Stick Bug (Walkingstick): Camouflage; focus

Squirrel: Preparation; saving money; collecting

Swan: Love; beauty; healing; dreaming

Tiger: Strength; power; new adventures; family magick

Toad: Inner strength; protection

Turkey: Increase material abundance

Turtle: Faith; patience; rewards; wisdom; creation

Wolf: Family; clan; teaching; protection; intuition; strength

Wolverine: Boldness; ferocity

Zebra: Agility; finding individuality within a group

When working with animals (either spiritually or physically), magickal people follow rules of conduct—a type of etiquette. We don't order animals to help us, we ask nicely, and then we remember to say thank you. Offerings, or gifts, to the animals are considered a normal Craft practice (and you'll find this in Druidism and Native American spirituality as well). An offering is a physical way of saying "thank you" to our animal friends. The best kind of thank you is leaving food or milk in the wild, or helping out at a local shelter. There are rules, however, about leaving food in state parks or other nature preserves, so be sure you ask permission from those in authority first because you don't want to upset the animal's natural diet. Giving your own pet attention and good care can be considered an offering. By taking care of the physical animal, you are also giving assistance to the spiritual counterpart.

How Totem Animals Work in Real Life

Most magickal people begin working with totem animals by choosing their favorite creature—one that has fascinated them for most of their lives. You will find, however, that once the animal kingdom feels the positive vibration of your interest in communication, others will step forward at different times in your life to lend you aid or to simply allow you to feel the harmony of the worlds as they work together on another plane. Your only requirement is to pay attention and honor that communication. A simple "thank you" from your lips once you have received the information will often suffice. For example, whenever I am worried about something and I am away from home, ravens and crows will show up to let me know that everything is okay. They've also warned me of auto accidents and other hazards on the road, repeatedly. In books about omens, this is exactly the opposite of what such a flock is supposed to mean, so be careful and don't let old superstitions color the communication the animals may have for you. While writing the animal section for this book, a family of baby squirrels played under my feet on the back porch, reminding me that it is okay to take time away from work to watch their activities, and that taking time to enjoy the antics of animals can be a fun, meditative experience. For over a week my entire family, from fourteen to seventy-eight, spent many hours enthralled with those squirrels.

Sometimes your favorite animal is not necessarily your strongest totem animal. If this is the case, the animal energy closest to yours will show up in the oddest places. Eventually you'll get the hint. Don't feel bad if you tire of a particular animal and move on to something else. They won't be offended. Just like people, each animal has its own individual energy. As your spirituality heightens, you may grow into communication with a different species— something that better matches your vibratory patterns.

Totem Animals and Meditation

One of the easiest ways to meditate on your totem animal is to watch it in real life. If you can, take a trip to the zoo, aquarium, or animal habitat, and spend time gazing at your chosen totem. Sometimes this is hard to do, especially if an adult or other family members are with you. They want to see the rest of the sights! If you can, ask them to take a break close to the animal you like best. If you're older and allowed to visit the animals by yourself or with magickal friends, this won't present a problem. Before you enter and upon leaving the habitat, ask that Spirit bless all the animals with health and harmony. The time spent viewing the animal will leave a lasting impression. You can use what you've seen at the preserve when meditating on the animal energy at home. Simply sit quietly and contemplate the animal. It's okay to hold a conversation with the animal energy. In your mind, leave its favorite food and make sure you've created a happy men-

tal place for it to roam as you finish the meditation. I've discovered that it isn't the length of time you meditate on an animal but the number of times you connect that holds the key to powerful animal energy. The more you think of the animal, the stronger the connection becomes.

Animal Spell for Protection of Your Room, House, or School Locker

SUPPLIES: One statue or plastic figure of your favorite animal; a small amount of protection oil or holy water; one red votive candle; a bell; your favorite incense. Remember to check your divination tool.

INSTRUCTIONS: Cast a magick circle and call the quarters. Carry the animal image to each of the four quarters, asking for power, protection, and blessings from that quarter. Take the image to your altar and set the statue in the center. Light the incense and swirl the smoke around the image, saying:

Smoke is the prayer of fire. I cleanse and consecrate thee in the name of the Lord and Lady.

Light the red votive candle, and say:

Fire is the spark of life. I invoke protection, blessings, and power, and transfer this energy into (say the name of the animal).

Pass the candle over the statue. Sprinkle salt over the image and say: "Life is the gift of the gods." Ring the bell three times over the statue, saying:

Sound is the voice of Spirit. I infuse this image with the blessings and protection of the Lord and Lady. May I be protected night and day.

Place the holy water or oil on the feet of the statue. Hold your hands over the statue and say nine times:

Smoke is the prayer of fire.
Fire is the spark of life.
Life is the gift of the gods.
Sound is the voice of Spirit.

After the ninth verse, solemnly say aloud exactly what the animal energy is to protect—your room, the contents of your school locker, etc., or you can be more specific, saying exactly what you want protected. Visualize the strength and power of the animal in your mind. When you are finished, say:

As I will, it shall be done.
Oil seals the spell.

Thank the collective animal energy. Close the quarters and release the circle. Place the statue pointing toward the nearest door or outside window (depending on what kind of protection you feel you need). If you must wait to place the statue (for example, if you are taking it to school to put in your locker), wrap it in black cloth for transport. When you set the image in place, repeat the words of the spell softly. Do not move the statue once you've chosen where it should stand. Renew every three months or sooner if there is a great deal of chaos where you have placed the statue.

OTHER IDEAS FOR THIS SPELL: Almost all spells can be tailored to your own needs. Let's say you don't have a statue or plastic animal that represents your favorite protective animal energy. You can use a photograph, a picture from a magazine, a postcard or greeting card, or a drawing that you have created. If you want to carry protection with you all the time, you can use a silver or gold charm in the shape of the animal and wear it around your neck or keep it in your pocket. For years, my girls protected their school

books from theft by drawing or pasting pictures of their favorite totem animals on brown paper bag covers they made themselves. Even if the books were lost or stolen, they all managed to filter back into their hands before the end of the school year.

Mythical Beasts

Mythological animals, sometimes called alchemical animals, have been used in magickal and religious settings for thousands of years. Each beastie was considered to have its own realm of expertise, and mythical animals in various cultures stood for a variety of enchantments as well as physical and psychological issues unique to that grouping of people. The sylphs, salamanders, and undines sometimes used at the quarters of a magickal circle (SEE PART IV, ELEMENTS) are considered alchemical animals (the fourth, gnomes, relates to mythical people). Sometimes standard animals were given mythical powers, in the case of the lion, the eagle, the bull, and the serpent, and they are sometimes used at the quarters of ceremonial circles. In these instances the powers of the animals are considered much larger than life and have alchemical as well as normal associations. You will often find the alchemical animals depicted on The World card of the Tarot. If you plan to work with any fabled beast, in-depth research will be required, and meditation is also recommended. The list below represents only a small portion of mythical animals.

Centaur: Healing; shapeshifting; music; divination; teaching

Chinese Lion Dog (Fu-Dog): Guardians against evil; will drive any evil from the home

Gargoyles: Protection of house or property; psychism; removing negative people

Griffin: Protection; spiritual wisdom; enlightenment

Horned Snake: Cures illness; kundalini energy; wisdom

Phoenix: Transformation; spiritual growth

Rainbow Serpent: Magick; rain; life; procreation

Sphinx: Initiation; elemental magick; wisdom; mystery

Unicorns: Good will; fame; prosperity; success; wisdom

Winged Horse: Aids in astral travel; fame; eloquence; visiting the dead

Winged Serpent (Buto): Wisdom; protection; teaching; guide to ancient knowledge

Recommended Reading

Animal-Speak by Ted Andrews

Animal-Wise by Ted Andrews

The Druid Animal Oracle by Philip and Stephanie Carr-Gomm

Magickal Mystical Creatures by D. J. Conway

Astral Projection

Descriptions of ancient astral travels have come from Egypt, India, China, and Tibet. In Tibet, people who traveled astrally were called *delogs*, which means "those who return from beyond."[9] Astral projection is also called an out-of-body experience (OBE) or soul travel, which occurs when the nonphysical or astral body (SEE AURA) takes a short trip from the physical body and then returns. Ancients believed that, when traveling, the astral body is connected to the physical body with a silver cord, and that all people on the planet are bound together with silver strands of light (which is where I got my first name). Years ago I actually saw this web, before I read anything about it. Some describe this tapes-

try of light as a web of silver,[10] and that's exactly what it looks like. In the Druidic tradition, there is an old story about Mog Ruith, a Druid from West Munster, who was able to fly over the heads of an opposing army and bring back details of the enemy while wearing a bird costume—an obvious account of astral travel.[11]

What most people don't realize is that OBEs are, for many individuals, a natural part of the sleep cycle, and that your astral body is a regular little traveler throughout the universe and you don't need a passport (or your conscious mind) to do it! Controlled OBEs (when you are consciously trying to have an OBE experience) are sometimes called remote viewing (also known as bilocation), and our federal government has done a heck of a lot of experimenting on that with a great deal of success.

Although you can plan OBEs, some of our most profound experiences will most likely happen when we aren't expecting them or trying to make them happen. These events are normally very spiritual and they occur as part of Spirit's overall plan to help us reach another level of spirituality, or when it is time for our perception on a particular subject to drastically change. These vivid OBEs are normally full of sharp color and unusually loud sounds—Spirit's way of making sure we don't forget the experience. Such spontaneous episodes often relate to critical times in our lives when we are under stress or must make an important decision. It is as if Spirit says, "You've got this great but little-used tool in your magickal toolbox, and it's time to use it!" OBEs can also occur when we are sick or when we have experienced a loss. In this case, the OBE helps to create a positive event from which we can gain healing and find the courage to go on.

Many people think that astral projection involves making your astral body get up and move around by conscious direction in the physical world. Although this can happen with practice (for some it's easier than others), the range of OBE experiences tells us that there's more to it than that, and that OBEs occur with various degrees of consciousness while daydreaming, meditating, sleeping, when you are ill, or when you are simply resting after a particularly stressful day. Some OBEs may be extremely dramatic, and others not. Some may appear to take place in the physical world with familiar surroundings, where others will happen in foreign places and even other worlds! These other worlds are called the astral planes.

There are a few negative side-effects from OBEs, and we should talk about them in case you have any such experiences (or have had them before and didn't know what they were). Have you ever been half asleep and half awake and your body feels like it is frozen and you have no control over your limbs? Talk about panic! This happened to me all the time when I was a kid, and it occurs because your astral body hasn't fully connected to the physical one. Sometimes the sensation takes place right before you go to sleep, or when you've been suddenly awakened. Don't have heart failure, this will pass quickly. Have you ever felt like you've fallen back into your body with the speed of a freight train? That's another one. For some reason your astral body has been told that it is imperative that it return, and so it does. Normally, if you follow a simple induction procedure when trying for an OBE, you won't have these experiences, and if they happen naturally, you'll know exactly what they are. The most common reason for failure in conscious OBE work is your own fear that somehow if you go, you won't be able to get back, or that something bad might happen to you while you are gone; however, there has never been a recorded instance of either of these things occurring.[12] In several instances it has been proven that a portion of your conscious

ness does remain behind, that it can tell the difference between friend or foe near your physical body, and that it would rouse you should you be in physical danger. According to Richard Webster, a highly skilled teacher on the subject, you are actually a great deal safer on the astral plane than in the physical one![13]

You'll be surprised who and what you may meet during an OBE exercise—famous people, mythical animals, angels, loved ones who have gone beyond the veil, and even archetypes (gods and goddesses). My most exhilarating experience found me running smack into the Morrigan (the Celtic goddess who was first an Earth goddess and then through legend graduated into a war goddess) in the middle of my dining room. The ancients say that you don't pick the gods and goddesses, they pick you, which was absolutely the case in my experience. I've never experienced anything so real in my life. She was wearing a black and white animal skin, and she was unutterably beautiful and extremely frightening at the same time. I re-entered my body like a derailed Ferris wheel. I've had other experiences as well. When one of my daughters went through a sudden and serious operation, I fell asleep, exhausted, in her hospital room. I had the most uplifting and assuring dream and I knew that everything would be okay. Many times I've spoken with deceased loved ones in very vivid dreams. When I awake, I burn a white candle as acknowledgement of their message and as a gift of loving energy. I have no doubt that life continues beyond this plane of existence.

Sometimes people will say, "I had a dream about you last night." If you were doing nonsensical things, they were probably working something out from their own memory storehouse, but if you have given them some wisdom or helped them with a serious problem, then you most likely met together on the astral plane. In most cases you won't have any memory of giving such assistance, but now and then something will "ring true." When people are connected by the activities of a group mind (SEE GROUP MIND IN PART I), they often assist each other on the astral plane during the dream state.

If you practice daily devotions and meditations, or keep a dream diary, you'll begin to pick out what is an OBE occurrence and what isn't. Just as in magick, practice (the experts agree) is the key. Conscious OBEs appear to occur more often for those who are unafraid, where people who think something bad might happen to them (which it won't) are less likely to experience a conscious out-of-body experience.

How to Take Your First Astral Trip

PREPARATIONS: Place a bowl of water and a bowl of salt by your bed. Bless both, then sprinkle a little of both in the four corners of the room. This assures you that the area from which you will start is purified. Choose a time and place where you know you will not be disturbed. Most folks do their astral voyages right before they go to sleep, when the rest of the family has settled down for the night, though you can choose any time of day as long as you are positive you won't be bothered. When first learning, many individuals take a ritual bath before traveling, and some add a bit of salt or a magickal herb to the water. If you are permitted to have candles, you may wish to light at least one white candle before your journey; however, be sure that it is in a fire-safe holder and away from curious pets (cats seem to love batting the heck out of candles). Make sure your clothing isn't too tight, that you haven't eaten heavily the hour before, and that the temperature is comfortable. Some people (like me) get very cold during meditation, self-hypnosis, auric imprinting (SEE AURAS), and astral travel. I always have a sheet or blanket handy.

For your first trip, you will need a purpose. Experts advise that you should stay in the same room and not venture elsewhere until you get the hang of how astral travel works (from a conscious point of view).

INSTRUCTIONS: Lie down in a comfortable position, with arms and legs uncrossed. Take three deep breaths (in through the nose, out through the mouth) and imagine yourself surrounded by a pure, white light. Silently, tell each part of your body to relax; for example, "My forehead is relaxing, loose and limp. The muscles around my eyes are relaxing, loose and limp." Work through your whole body. When you feel you are completely relaxed, focus on your forehead, right between your eyes (the place of the third eye), and imagine yourself moving out of your body from that point.

It is possible you will feel a "floaty" sensation (I do), or you may tingle, feel some sort of inner vibration, or a tickling on your face—these are all natural experiences. Sometimes I feel like something "snaps" lightly and then the floating sensation occurs. Try to go with the flow. If you jerk, brush your face, or physically move to "relieve" the sensation, then you will have to start all over again. To be honest, this is the most difficult part, learning to let go, and it may take you several tries, or even several nights, until you can get past this stage. Any mental resistance now and lift-off will not occur in this semi-conscious state.

Once you have succeeded, then you are over the biggest hurdle. Each time you practice astral projection, it will get easier. If you continue to fail, don't lose heart. Practice every day until one day, when you are least expecting it, off you will zoom! Once you are out of your body, spend time exploring your own room. Go no further. Finally, visualize yourself returning to your body. Once you have returned, lie as still as possible for a few minutes. Count from one to five, then open your eyes. Even though you've just had the coolest experience of your life, wait at least twenty-four hours before you take your next trip. This is to give your total body time to recuperate. Once you have been practicing, you will be able to take several trips per day.

Astral Travel and the Magickal Person

As with many things in the world of magick, there is a type of etiquette that goes along with astral travel. Peeking in someone's home and spying on the activities there is considered poor taste. It is one thing to run experiments with your friends with their consent and at an appointed time; it is quite another to go brandishing about someone's home uninvited. Magickal people often set up defenses against those who might take it upon themselves to cross the etiquette/ethics line. Here are some of them:

- Surrounding the house with a ring of pickling salt (be careful, though, or you'll ruin the grass).

- Planting specific plants, such as lobelia, around the home to keep out unwanted intruders, physical and otherwise.

- Blessing all the doors and windows, then sealing them with a banishing pentacle in the air over all windows and exits.

- Drawing an equal-armed cross with clove oil on all window frames and exits.

- Setting an astral "guard dog" (usually a mythical beast or a predator from the animal kingdom) on a constant twenty-four-hour tour around the perimeter and outside of the home, supported by a shrine or statue inside the home. Visualization is renewed every month and an offering of thanks is made to the physical animal kingdom.

- Reinforcing a weekly visualization of a deep thicket that grows around the house (as in the fairy tale *Sleeping Beauty*). Others visualize the outside of the house as looking like a thick fortress (spikes, turrets, moat, and all). To keep the visualization firm, they may keep a picture of such a scene hanging inside the home.

A note of caution: When people first learn to astral travel, they get so excited they want to rush right out and tell everyone. Even though both practices have been around a long time, and have gone through spurts of popularity over the last thirty years, not everyone will understand what you are talking about. Some people will make fun of you, others will simply scoff and walk away. A few of the unenlightened ones will try to tell you that you are doing something wrong or evil. Over the years I've discovered that those people who are the best at these things don't share, or only discuss such subjects with people of like mind. Although astral travel and reading auras are natural to all humans, not everybody wants to acknowledge this fact. Until you know that you are on firm ground with your friends, you might like to practice the ever-faithful Wiccan rule of To Know, To Dare, To Will, and To Be Silent, otherwise known as the Witch's Pyramid (SEE PART I).

Recommended Reading

Flying Without a Broom by D. J. Conway

Astral Travel for Beginners by Richard Webster

Astrology

Astrology, we are told, is the oldest science (as astronomy and astrology were once wed as a single entity), and it has had an incredible impact on human history. Given this information, we can easily assume that both astronomy (the study of the heavenly bodies in defining weight, speed, mass, and how that body interacts with the other bodies of the universe) and astrology (the study of the movements of the heavenly bodies and how these movements relate to human activity and consciousness) have enormously changed over centuries of study because they are no longer seen as one entity.

In magickal studies, having a sense of our history is important as we build for the future. We are living history and the choices we make for our future are often made on the experiences of our past (or on the experiences of someone else's past). In astrology, a snapshot in time becomes the living history of the birth of a person, place, or thing. Even though all things are destructible, that point in time will live on. This is why charts of famous people can still be read for present-day occurrences in their personal chronicle of pain and pleasure. For example, the release of the story of William Wallace through the movie *Braveheart* would be apparent in Wallace's astrological chart, even though his physical existence passed from this Earth centuries ago. More recently, Princess Diana's chart will continue to reflect media releases about her life, times, and family. So, too, your natal chart will reflect your past, your present, and your future opportunities for *choice*.

The study of natal astrology is the contemplation (called *delineation*) of patterns of energy brought into this dimension by your birth, and the manipulation of that energy by yourself throughout your life. When we view astrology in this manner, we realize that nothing is fixed or fated, save what we make it that through past, present, and future choices. A life lesson can be learned through many approaches. It is our actions and our reactions that will determine what type of experience we will manifest in order to grasp this lesson. Sometimes we must go through several experiences of the same nature until we get it right! Our natal astrological chart is a mystery puzzle, and only we, the individual who massages the energies in the chart through daily choices, are the Chart Master. Indeed, we hold the keys to the secrets of ourselves and the brass ring of our success. An event chart, in the same manner, shows your upcoming energy patterns—and by your own choice, you can be there or be square! (Pun intended.) Your higher self, for all intents and purposes, is still in control, and if you let your conscious mind analyze the data of the chart, you can manifest the best choice possible for you. You have only two main requirements: making the effort to learn the language of astrology and, once integrated into your head, using the information to create a better lifestyle for yourself and those around you. Sounds just like real magick, doesn't it?

In the occult, the student is taught "the mysteries," which vary from group to group, order to order, and teacher to teacher; however, many of the building blocks of these teachings have remained the same over the centuries. Astrology is (and always will be) a part of the mysteries. We can trot it out into a new arena, slap politically safe words on it, gussie it up and make it acceptable to even the most discriminating of minds (and I don't mean minds of good taste), and it will still be a *mystery* teaching. We can make it scientific, we can make it psychological, or we can make it spiritual. A rose by any other name is still a rose. And a mystery, by the very nature of it, is created with the sole purpose of being solved, and in that resolution comes enlightenment. A mystery teaching is named so not because the information is special, but because the information is not mass taught. Think about it. Christianity and other standard religions began as mystery teachings, but are not considered as such in our current lifestyle.

The guts of today's astrological study focuses on eight of the known planets—Mercury, Venus, Mars, Saturn, Jupiter, Uranus, Neptune, and Pluto—our moon (which is a satellite), and our sun (which is the only star in our solar system). Although astrologers speak of the ten planets (as listed above, including the sun and the moon), don't say that to an astronomer or in science class! The sun and moon are not scientifically classified as planets, yet they are seen as such for the purposes of astrology. (You still need to know the difference!) The sun and moon are sometimes called the Greater and Lesser Lights (the sun associated with the "greater" and the moon with the "lesser"). In many ancient religious teachings, the sun and moon were likened to the illumination of god/dess, gracing our world with light and life—two halves of a whole—the will and emotion married to create ultimate, positive energy. Does not our own Pagan spiral dance reflect the birth of the universe? We spiral in to focus, and we move out in a circular pattern to manifest the joy of the human soul as it marries the heavenly divine. From the physical to the spiritual, illumination carries enlightenment.

Religion aside for the moment, most historical accounts of astrology agree on the following:

Various studies of astronomy/astrology birthed out of different areas of the world independently. One of the first to surface was the Chaldeans (then Babylonia, now Iraq), developing around 3000 B.C. By 2000 B.C., the Chinese had their own variety of astrology. Others included India and the Maya of Central America. This affirms my belief that astrology is a gift from Spirit, introduced into the minds of different cultures to make sure everyone got a copy.

Around 500 B.C., astrology became a part of Grecian study, with philosophers such as Pythagoras and Plato incorporating their own expertise into the subject. Although condemned by some individuals in the Christian church (not all), astrology continued to be practiced through the Middle Ages and was often used by royalty for planning events and studying the possible ups and downs of favorite notables. Natal astrology was not the favorite study of the day, as few people knew the exact time of their birth (only the rich people or, in tribal times, the sons and daughters of the ruling hand had that privilege); therefore, if you wanted to know something about your life path, you relied on horary or electional interpretations.

Pliny the Elder (23 C.E.–79 C.E.), a Roman scholar, wrote an amazing number of texts, including the great *Encyclopedia of Nature and Art* (thirty-seven books). The volumes covered a compendium of subjects covering astronomy, geography, human physiology, etc., and it is felt by some that he was the foremost authority on science and history in ancient Europe. Pliny indicates that the Chaldeans were moon worshippers, and that their system of astrology was based on the movements of the moon—a zodiac system known as the houses of the moon (lunar mansions) and of which some information can be found today in the *Picatrix*. He further stated that the study of the heavens was "traditionally the business of women."[14] There is evidence that the astrology of Babylon and Egypt was moon-oriented and, even in Roman times, the Emperor Augustus used not his sun sign but his moon sign, Capricorn, on his coinage.[15]

Between 161 C.E. and 139 C.E., a man by the name of Claudius Ptolemaeus (Ptolemy) set about the task of writing down that which had been studied for centuries. Encompassing a four-volume series, the *Tetrabiblos* was the first material available in book form on astronomy/astrology. He also catalogued over 1,022 stars called *paranatellonta*, which were first seen as a device for locating objects in the heavens, and then grew into points that carried their own significance. When studying aspect sets (of which there are several), you will find that the Ptolemaic set of aspects is a favorite among modern astrologers, and the starting point for most beginning students. The Ptolemaic aspects also allow experienced astrologers to "get back to basics" when they hit the mind-clutter syndrome after several years of advanced study. (And yes, it happens to everyone.) In a chapter titled "On the Influence of the Stars," Ptolemy wrote that by using astrology "we may await the future with dignity."

Astrology was introduced to the Greeks by Alexander, who brought the study from Babylon and Egypt. It soon gained tremendous popularity. Not only was the hour of birth considered important because of its astrological influence, but horoscopes were cast for many important decisions. Chaldean astrologers settled in Athens and won wealth and favor. Berosus, a Babylonian, founded a college for astrology. He was so successful that the Athenians erected his statue in their gymnasium symbolizing divine prophecy.[16] In Rome, however, emperors tended to be hypocritical of magick and astrology. Nero, for example, felt that the common man shouldn't be able to read the stars because the stars could predict conspiracies (and considering what Nero had in store for them, it isn't any wonder). As an aside, we see this pattern repeated often by European royalty, including Queen Elizabeth. On the other hand, both Nero and his wife and Queen Elizabeth employed the astrologers of the day, meaning it was okay for the elite few to have astrological foreknowledge, but the common populace could wither and die. In Rome, being an astrologer did not assure fame and fortune. You could read for the emperor and his court, but you'd best keep your trap shut to anyone else. If your predictions were wrong, or found disfavor with a particular project, into the dungeon you would go, or you would perhaps share your

evening meal with a passel of lions—you, of course, being the entrée.

The fall of Toledo (Spain) in 1085 placed the richest philosophical library in Europe at the disposal of Western scholars. The work of translation began soon afterward, coordinated by scholars from Italy, Germany, and Britain, but was dependent on the expertise of Spanish Arabs and Jews.[17] This bit of trivia is important because it tells us where medieval astrologers gathered much of the astrological information that is still used today in a variety of magickal applications. Although most Witches don't realize it, the magick they currently practice carries a great deal of medieval and Renaissance influence, including work from Guido Bonatti, Michael Scot, Roger Bacon, the patronage of Cosimo de Medici, Kepler, Newton, Paracelsus, Bruno, Thomas Campanella, Cornelius Agrippa, John Gadbury, William Ramsey, and William Lilly. It is Roger Bacon who said, "There is no fatal necessity in the stars; they incline but do not compel," which has been paraphrased by numerous astrologers and magickal practitioners alike for hundreds of years—and which supports the concept of free will and the control you have over the energies you brought with you into this lifetime.

The study of astrology and astronomy was considered one practice until the 1600s, when Copernicus blew everyone out of the water by insisting that the Earth was *not* the center of the universe—that regal spot belonged to our sun. Hence, we now have two types of astrological study: *heliocentric* (the study of the planets from the position of the sun), and *geocentric* (the study of the planets from the position of the Earth). Geocentric astrology appears to be the current popular favorite in astrological studies.

Now, why is this history stuff so important? A great deal of the information that astrologers and magickal practitioners use in timing and correspondences still used today comes from the centuries of observations by astronomers/astrologers before them. It is also important to understand the nature of astrology within the framework of ancient religions. There was a good reason why the two were melded together. Naturally, some of the conclusions drawn so long ago were based on superstition, and we are forever grateful to the modern study of astronomy for correcting such errors; however, we are also finding that many of the conclusions postulated by ancient astronomers are returning to us through modern satellite transmissions. (See the works of Stitchen, published through Bear and Company, if you are interested in this phenomena.) In late Grecian history, and eventually in Rome, we hear the warning notes of the schism coming between magick and astrology. In the drive to consolidate authority, the Romans, and later the Christian church, would wade in blood and politics, almost obliterating magick and grievously wounding astrology.

Today, many astrologers believe that it was the work of Carl Jung, through his advanced studies of the human mind, which rescued astrology for the modern practitioner, melding the two sciences of psychology and astrology together to bring about healing mechanisms for the human psyche—which restructures the collective unconscious, which in turn breathes new life into the study of astrology, which can be used as a positive healing tool. If he had not done this, it is highly likely that all of the classical texts on astrology would still be moldering in some museum somewhere. Today we are lucky enough to have at least a few.

But what does all this have to do with the study and practice of magick? Most ancient mystery traditions, from what we can tell, were based on the study of nature, human behavior, the chosen religion of the tribe or order, and the movement of the heavens. By bringing astrology back into our lives, we give ourselves another avenue in which to operate, hopefully more efficiently than we did before. By granting ourselves the right to practice magick, we unfetter the human mind and allow our goals to manifest in a positive way. The mind *is* magick. To me, anyone that denigrates magick is purposefully choosing to destroy the inherent abilities of each and every human.

No longer bound by the fear and control mechanisms of the Middle Ages (you're not, right?), we can move beyond superstition and into the science and art of positive human development. I have discovered that most, if not all, of the problems we wrestle today are merely illusions of our own perception. How frightening, and yet . . . how simple. Astrology and magick allow us to adjust those self-imposed perceptions and create that elusive win/win situation. Faith is our own construct of a positive energy pattern that allows us to produce a better individual reality. By being the best that we can be, we affect those around us in a positive way, which in turn affects the people around them. If we drop a pebble in the water, the reaction moves outward in a widening circle, creating a different reality (even if it is just a moment in time) for the pebble and the water. You are that pebble. What type of reality are you creating for yourself, and for others?

There are, however, a few stumbling blocks for the magickal astrologer. Without trying to purposefully border on the negative, it is necessary for you to know that there are those in the modern astrological community who have fought long and hard to remove the magick from astrology. I can understand this. We are still, even in this modern age, a superstitious species. Any "woo-woo" stuff and some people run for cover, while others loudly choose to erroneously disclaim the benefits of the system in question (let's take the attacks on alternative medicine for an example) and do their best to drive the more intuitive among us deep into the bowels of the Earth. These people choose to ignore the magickal history attached to the subject of astrology because they are afraid. I agree that modern astrology is not fortunetelling, but I disagree that the astrologer's intuitive process is left dormant while analyzing a chart. To me, our intuitive selves are an inherent part of our psychological and spiritual construction. We need only open the door of acceptance to take advantage of such a gift. Whether we admit it or not, every time we look at a person's chart and begin the process of delineation (or analysis), we are actively applying a mystical energy, just as the ancients did before us. We are employing the building blocks of shamanistic and ceremonial study by seeking this process for the betterment of the human situation. We are the masters to a better future. And if that ain't positive magick, I don't know what is.

So what am I trying to tell you? Astrology is open to your interpretation. Yes, you can find guidelines in books, or teachers to help you, or software programs to make the calculations easier and provide pretty pictures at the same time, but in the end you need to formulate how you will use what you learn all by your little lonesome while attempting to keep an open mind. This also means that you are going to make mistakes. What you thought was a "hmmm" might only be a brain fart. That's okay. This simply means that you are human and have not reached deity status. Join the club. This is also where accurate record keeping comes into play. Over time you will learn how you react to "segments" of a particular energy pattern by watching your own actions (and recording them) while that energy pattern is active, or when you activate that energy pattern through choice. Once you understand your personal as-

trological profile, you can adjust or improve your behavior to flow in a positive way with any energy pattern. This doesn't mean that there won't be any surprises, but planning and understanding how the energy might manifest in your life helps you to work with, rather than against, necessary change (those lessons in life provided by Spirit for our growth and amusement) or guide your actions in a harmonious way to create the changes that you desire. At the same time, by learning astrology and applying what you discover to your own life path, you will also have the added bonus of learning to understand the actions and behavior of those around you. It's sort of fun to know that even though Aunt Bess is screaming that it's an earthquake in her life, you've seen her chart and you know it's only a chuck hole.

Natal astrology is so vast a subject that we can't possibly cover it in this book; however, you will work with the planetary and sign energies throughout this material.

The Heptagram and the Magickal Days

Although the heptagram (a seven-pointed star, above) is often used by the Faery traditions to represent their spirituality, it appears that its original basis had much to do with astrology, timing, and the advent of the seven-day week used throughout the Hellenistic world of mixed cultures (Egyptian/Greco-Roman). For some, the design represents the magick in the number seven, and various cultural deities, including the Seven Faces of Hathor (Egyptian), the Seven Pillars of Wisdom (Middle East), and the Seven Mothers of the World (Southeast Asia).[18] In general magick you can place this symbol on any object as a defense against penetration—for example, private papers (your diary or magickal journal). If your mom or dad is a police officer or construction worker, where they face danger every day, you can write his or her name in the center of the star and empower the drawing as a protective device. Make sure the person puts the paper in a pocket or wallet, or something they wear or carry close to their body.

You will also find the heptagram in several old grimoires, where it is associated with the speed of the planets moving through the heavens, and matches the energies of the planets to the seven days of the week.

The diagram above, on the right, can be read two ways and gives us two interpretations. First, if we begin with the moon and move counterclockwise, we see that the planets are listed from the fastest-moving body in the heavens to the slowest of the known planets in classical times, which are as follows: the moon, Mercury, Venus, sun, Mars, Jupiter, and Saturn. If we put our finger on the moon, then trace down to Mars, over to Mercury, up to Jupiter, down to Venus, up to Saturn and down to the sun, we have just traced the planetary energies of our calendar week:

Monday: Moon

Tuesday: Mars

Wednesday: Mercury

Thursday: Jupiter

Friday: Venus

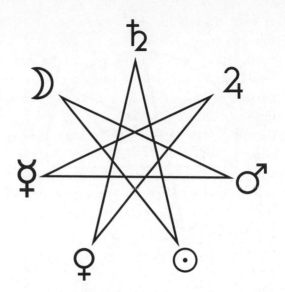

Saturday: Saturn

Sunday: Sun

. . . and this continuous line moves clockwise around the diagram. In some magickal traditions, the heptagram begins with the sun placed at the highest point.

The diagram on the next page works the same way. If we want to remember which planet moves faster, then we start with the moon and move counterclockwise to Mercury, to Venus, to the sun, and so on. If we want to know what rules which day of the week, we start with the sun (Sunday), trace the line down to the moon (Monday), up to Mars (Tuesday), down to Mercury (Wednesday), over to Jupiter (Thursday), up to Venus (Friday), and down to Saturn (Saturday). As with the first diagram, these are the seven classical planets of the ancient world.

To modern magicians, the heptagram stands for the distribution of the planetary energies through the seven days of the week, and is associated with the seven colors of the rainbow, the Egyptian Goddess Isis, and is sometimes called the Symbol of Venus or Star of Venus because Venus is both the rising and setting star (SEE

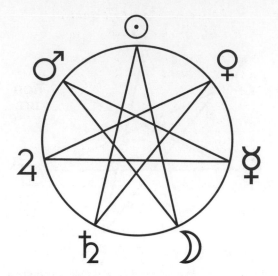

PENTAGRAM). At certain times of the year she rises at dawn, and other times of the year she rises at twilight—therefore some called her the Gateway to the Stars. The heptagram is also used for calculating planetary hours, a fine-tuning device used in magick and ritual.

The Planets

In Witchcraft, planetary and astrological sign energies are used in making incense, oils, potions, timing, ritual, spellcasting, and numerous other facets. In an effort not to be redundant, you will find the following list includes scientific and general information about the planets. The energies these planets represent and what they can be used for will fall in the weekly associations, and in the planetary hour table on page 197. However, if you are new to astrology, don't skip over this first list. You may find it incredibly invaluable in the future when reading your planetary guide, astrological almanac, trying to figure out the astrological software program you just bought, or trying your hand at event planning. And if you are very brave, you will need these rough calculations for the study of horary astrology.

Miscellaneous Information About the Inner Planets

TIME IT TAKES TO CIRCLE AN ASTROLOGICAL CHART (360 DEGREES IN CIRCUMFERENCE), WHICH ALSO EQUALS THE PLANET'S ORBIT AROUND THE SUN

Sun: 365 Earth days and spends approx. 30 days in each sign.

Moon: 27 days and 7 hours and spends 2.3 to 2.5 days in each sign.

Mercury: 88 Earth days—moves around the chart approx. 4 times each year and spends about 7.5 days in each sign (not including retrograde periods).

Venus: 225 Earth days and spends approx. 18.7 days in each sign (not including retrograde periods).

Mars: 687 Earth days or 1.9 years (almost two years) and spends approx. 57.3 days in each sign (not including retrograde periods).

RETROGRADE PERIODS

Sun: None.

Moon: None.

Mercury: Three times per year for 3 weeks per retrograde period.

Venus: Retrogrades every 18 months for approx. 40 days.

Mars: Retrogrades every 26 months for 10 weeks (70 days).

NUMBER OF SATELLITES (MOONS AND ASTEROIDS)[19]

Sun: (blank).

Moon: None, though she does go "void" as she moves from sign to sign. A void period can last from a few minutes to two days.

Mercury: None.

Venus: None.

Mars: Two moons, Phobos and Deimos (diameter of fourteen miles and seven miles, respectively).

DEGREES THIS PLANET MOVES ON AVERAGE PER DAY

Sun: Approx. one degree.

Moon: Approx. .5 degrees per hour, or twelve degrees per day.

Mercury: Approx. 4 degrees per day.

Venus: Approx. 1.6 degrees per day.

Mars: Approx. .5 degrees per day, which would be a movement of 30 minutes.

CONSISTENCY[20]

Sun: Star ball of incandescent gas of average size and brightness compared to other stars.

Moon: No air and no liquid water. No weather. Landforms are a result of meteoric impact.

Mercury: Less than half the diameter of Earth. No air or water.

Venus: Covered in bright clouds of sulfuric acid. Atmospheric pressure is 90 times that of Earth. Most of the surface is covered by undulating plains.

Mars: Has a 24-hour day, a pattern of seasons, and polar ice caps. Temperatures on Mars rarely rise above freezing. Called the red planet because it is covered by red deserts. Some think Mars is the precursor of Earth and was destroyed by war.

ASTROLOGICAL SIGN RULERSHIP

Sun: Leo.

Moon: Cancer.

Mercury: Gemini and Virgo.

Venus: Taurus and Libra.

Mars: Aries and Scorpio (classical).

Miscellaneous Information About the Outer Planets

TIME IT TAKES TO CIRCLE AN ASTROLOGICAL CHART (360 DEGREES IN CIRCUMFERENCE), WHICH ALSO EQUALS THE PLANET'S ORBIT AROUND THE SUN

Jupiter: Approx. 11.9 Earth years (usually rounded to 12 years), spending approx. one full year in each sign.

Saturn: Approx. 29.5 Earth years to complete its cycle around the chart. Spends approx. 2.4 years in each sign.

Uranus: Approx. 84 Earth years to complete a cycle. Spends approx. 7 years in each sign.

Neptune: Approx. 165 Earth years to complete a cycle. Spends approx. 13.8 years in each sign.

Pluto: Approx. 248 Earth years to complete a cycle. Spends 20.6 years in each sign.

RETROGRADE PERIODS

Jupiter: Once per year for 120 days or approx. 4 months.

Saturn: Once per year for 140 days or approx. 5 months.

Uranus: Once per year for 148 days or approx. 5 months.

Neptune: Once per year for 150 days or approx. 6 months.

Pluto: Once per year for approx. 6 months.

NUMBER OF SATELLITES (MOONS AND ASTEROIDS)[21]

Jupiter: 16 known satellites that fall into three groups: inner eight, including the four Galilean moons; the middle four, and the outer four. The Galilean moons are the largest: Io, Europa, Ganymede, and Callisto.

Saturn: 18 moons, of which the largest is Titan and is the second largest moon in the solar system (smaller only than Ganymede). Other moons are Rhea, Tethys, Dione, Iapetus, Enceladus, and Mimas.

Uranus: 21 known moons. Titania is the largest. Cordelia and Ophelia are shepard moons straddling the Epsilon ring.

Neptune: 8 moons with Triton as the largest, which is actually bigger than Pluto and moves in retrograde motion.

Pluto: 1 moon, Charon.

DEGREES THIS PLANET MOVES ON AVERAGE PER YEAR

Jupiter: 30 degrees per year, or .08 degrees per day.

Saturn: 12.5 degrees per year, or .03 degrees per day.

Uranus: 4.3 degrees per year, or .01 degrees per day.

Neptune: 2.1 degrees per year, or .005 degrees per day.

Pluto: 1.4 degrees per year, or .003 degrees per day.

CONSISTENCY[22]

Jupiter: Largest planet in the solar system, weighing more than any other planet—it spins faster than any other planet and its constantly changing cloud formations form bands parallel to the equator. The planet is made primarily of liquid hydrogen and helium.

Saturn: Second largest planet in the solar system—broad, bright rings made of icy chunks that encircle equator; cloudy atmosphere that covers an interior of liquid hydrogen and helium.

Uranus: Gas giant and third largest planet in solar system. Axis of rotation makes it look like it is orbiting on its side. Covered in methane clouds that absorb red light. Also has eleven rings.

Neptune: Gas giant, faint ring system; atmosphere consists of hydrogen, helium, and methane. Stormy atmosphere. Crust is icy water, methane, and ammonia.

Pluto: Actually a double heavenly body with the other half (sometimes referred to as a moon) known as Charon. Where Pluto is covered with frozen methane, Charon is covered with frozen water.

ASTROLOGICAL SIGN RULERSHIP

Jupiter: Sagittarius and Pisces (classical).

Saturn: Capricorn and Aquarius (classical).

Uranus: Aquarius.

Neptune: Pisces.

Pluto: Scorpio.

Magickal Days and Basic Timing

In modern Wicca, the heptagram is one of the first timing devices we learn, although you'll find a table of correspondences like the one below in most books rather than the geometric symbol (SEE PAGE 184).

SUNDAY

Symbol: ☉

Planet: Sun.

Basic energy: Will.

Basic magick: Success.

Element: Fire.

Color: Yellow or gold.

Rules: Leo.

Energy keywords: Aggressive, authority, confidence, courage, determination, dignity, egocentric, faith, fortitude, individualism, leadership, loyalty, optimism, overbearing, poise, power, reliance, stubborn, vitality, willful.

MONDAY

Symbol: ☽

Planet: Moon.

Basic energy: Emotion.

Basic magick: Protection, psychism.

Element: Water.

Color: White or blue.

Rules: Cancer.

Energy keywords: Creativity, domestic, feeling, flexible, growth, imagination, impressionable, intuition, kindness, magnetism, masculine, maternal, matter, mother, peace, plasticity, protective, psychism, receptive, sensitive, sympathy, visionary.

TUESDAY

Symbol: ♂

Planet: Mars.

Basic energy: Action.

Basic magick: War, change.

Element: Fire.

Color: Red.

Rules: Aries, Scorpio.

Energy keywords: Assertive, combative, constructive, courage, defiant, destruction, dynamic, energy, expressive, fearless, force, frank, heroics, impulsive, leadership, passion, self-reliant, spontaneity, violent.

WEDNESDAY

Symbol: ☿

Planet: Mercury.

Basic energy: Speed.

Basic magick: Communication.

Element: Air.

Color: Blue or silver.

Rules: Gemini, Virgo.

Energy keywords: Active, adaptable, agility, alert, analytical, articulate, aware, brilliant, changeable, critical, dexterous, diffusive, discriminatory, duality, efficient, expressive, indecisive, intelligent, irresponsible, precise, reason, restless, sensory, skeptical, verbose, versatile.

THURSDAY

Symbol: ♃

Planet: Jupiter.

Basic energy: Expansion.

Basic magick: Money.

Element: Fire.

Color: Purple.

Rules: Sagittarius, Pisces.

Energy keywords: Aspiration, benevolent, charitable, confident, dignity, expansion, extravagant, faithful, generous, growth, gullible, human, humorous, indulgence, kindness, merciful, optimistic, orthodox, philanthropic, poise, pompous, radiance, religious, reverent, understanding.

FRIDAY

Symbol: ♀

Planet: Venus.

Basic energy: Socialization.

Basic magick: Love, friendships.

Element: Air.

Color: Green.

Rules: Taurus, Libra.

Energy keywords: Affectionate, art, attractive, beauty, considerate, constructive, cooperative, courtesy, devotion, evasive, feminine, flirtatious, gentle, harmony, impressionable, indifferent, indolent, love, obstinate, original, refinement, responsive, sociable, vacillate.

SATURDAY

Symbol: ♄

Planet: Saturn.

Basic energy: Restriction, authority, crossroads.

Basic magick: Banishing, rewards.

Element: Earth.

Color: Black or midnight blue.

Rules: Capricorn.

Energy keywords: Authority, caution, defensive, diplomatic, fearful, humility, justice, law, old, patience, pessimism, respect, responsible, restrain, rigid, serious, severe, sincere, stern, thrifty, time.

There are a variety of ways that you'll learn to use magickal days, and their energies are very useful if you can't (for whatever reason) use the phases/quarters of the moon or the moon in the signs for timing a spell or other activity, or are just looking for a "good" day to do something.

Family members seem to learn the magickal days with more acceptance than any other technique because they are simple, and it doesn't take long for them to realize that they work! For example, if you need forceful energy to get your point across or need a little confidence, then choose a Tuesday—an action day. If you want to hand in extra-credit homework, work on a term paper, find research information, talk to a friend about something important, take a short trip, or must do several things at one time, Wednesday is the day. If you need to work for money (long-term cash, saving, and investing), then Thursday would be a good choice. Monday is for psychism, children, mothers, feminine interests, and working on your emotions in a positive way, as well as protection. Saturday is the day to throw things away, to banish bad habits, or to put limits

or structure to something, to work on manifesting rewards, and to talk to the dead. Friday is for love, parties, shopping, social activities, friendships, and working for fast cash. Sunday has always been the success day—a day of beginnings, joy, and harmony in respect to your will (what you want to do, as opposed to what you have to do). If you mention every Wednesday morning that Wednesdays are good days for communication, your family will eventually realize you are right. If you say often that "Tuesday is the war day," again your family members will (at some point) notice that people are a bit more active, maybe even more combative, on Tuesdays. After awhile, Mom might say, "I think I'll wait until Wednesday to talk to my boss about that research project. Didn't you say Wednesdays were good communication days?"

Seven-Day Spells

Many books on the Craft and magick talk about seven-day spells, where the magickal work is done on a particular day, and then repeated every day thereafter for seven days. These spells are constructed so that you can work with the planetary energies of each day, building to the ultimate completion of the spell that has all the powers of the seven classical planets. To help with visualization, candles are often used, though you can tailor any magickal operation to the seven-day cycle. Taper candles can be marked with seven notches, or you can use a "rainbow" candle, a pillar candle, a seven-day continuously burning glass-enclosed candle, or even an oil lamp with scented, colored oil that matches the overall goal. Some magickal people use seven small candles (votive or tea) rather than a single candle, and burn one of these smaller candles a day for seven days.

The most important choice in the seven-day spell rests on timing and the immediacy of your need. Can you wait for the right moon phase or not? Can you wait for the right flavor of the moon or not? Can you wait for the right day (Monday, Tuesday, etc.) or not? And, even if you can wait, will everything fit together? Maybe the moon phase and the flavor are right, but the day isn't what you'd normally choose. Perhaps you can't get the moon phase or the flavor, but you can hit the right day. There will be times that you wish you could just move things around to suit your magickal needs, but you know that you can't do that—or can you? Laurie Cabot, one of the most famous practicing Witches of our time, often added the following to her spells: "And may all astrological correspondences be correct for this working." That way, even if you can't physically work on the right day, or moon phase, or catch that unique flavor of the moon, you can touch the energies you need for that working. Cool, huh? It works. I've been doing it for years. However, the more correspondences that match in your magickal workings, such as astrological timing, the faster and more powerful your work will become.

Before we move on to the invocations for the seven-day cycle spells, we should talk about one more piece of timing—you. There will be occasions in your life when the moon isn't in the right place, the flavor is all off, and the day is the worst, but you will be all fired up to do magick. It just hits you with an exciting rush, and you think, "It's time to do magick." Maybe your fingers will tingle or your hands will grow warm. Perhaps there is a tightness in the muscles of your arms or a lightness around the solar plexus. Follow the signals that your body is sending you. Do the magick.

Classical Planetary Invocations

The following invocations are designed to invoke the energy of each of the classical planets separately, along with an invocation that ties them all together. If you begin your spellwork on a Sunday, then start with the Invocation of the Sun, followed the next day (which would be a Monday) with that of the moon, and so on. If you launch your spellwork on a Tuesday, then use the Invocation of Mars, followed by that of Mercury (on Wednesday), etc. Say each invocation three times: first, to declare and summon the spiritual assistance needed; second, to banish any unwanted energies; and third, to infuse the object or person with "the change" and to seal the spell (SEE PART IV, CHARMS).

Each day before repeating the invocation that matches the day, begin with the following:

1. Breathe deeply three times or more until you feel calm and relaxed.

2. Ground and center.

3. Cast the magick circle and call the quarters.

4. Repeat the following opening, which you can use for opening any spellwork:

Great Mother Goddess, allow me to reach into the vaulted heavens and bring that which is needed for this working into form. Purify all energies and fill them with harmony so that the Witch and the magick work in divine union and create the pattern that will crystallize into my desire here on Earth.

INVOCATION OF THE SUN (SUNDAY)

State the purpose of your working, then say:

O glorious sun, who lies at the center of our solar system, father of the skies who travels across the vault of Earth's starry heavens bringing golden light and love, infuse this working with power, generosity, and joy. Ruler of Leo, exalted in Aries, element of fire, bring to me my desire!

INVOCATION OF THE MOON
(MONDAY)

State the purpose of your working, then say:

*Moon's bright enchantment, Mother of the
Universe, she who rules the tides of the seas
of life, who grows from bright to dark,
and bright again, yet ever remains the silvery
queen of the night, bring to me the powers
of Witchery! Greatest Mother, whose throne
glitters in Cancer, who is exalted in Taurus,
and ruler of the mighty subconscious waters,
give life and love to this working.*

INVOCATION OF MARS
(TUESDAY)

State the purpose of your working, then say:

*Mighty Mars of iron will, ferocious force of action
and leader of passion, who empowers the Earth
with vitality and courage, who brings change in
movement, seed this working with your unending
strength and shield my enchantments from prying
eyes. Wolven howl of transformation, ruler of
Aries, exalted in Capricorn, element of fire,
energize this working!*

INVOCATION OF MERCURY
(WEDNESDAY)

State the purpose of your working, then say:

*Mercury, quicksilver messenger of the gods,
he who dances about the Earth carrying wisdom
and perception, whose versatility brings positive
change and creative thinking, I invoke thee and
call upon thee in my hour of need. Permeate this
work with celestial speed so that my desire may
manifest. Ruler of Virgo and Gemini, exalted in
Virgo, elements of air and earth, combine this
night in sacred birth!*

INVOCATION OF JUPITER
(THURSDAY)

State the purpose of your working, then say:

*Massive Jupiter, powerful ruler of gods and men,
he who brings loyalty, generosity, and faith from
the celestial powers, fill this working with your
generosity and good fortune and the freedom I
need to create the necessary change. Hurl your
thunderbolts in a positive way to create an opening so that my magicks may pass to the earthly
world. Ruler of Pisces and Sagittarius, exalted in
Cancer, elements of water and fire,
flow and force from the ultimate source!*

INVOCATION OF VENUS
(FRIDAY)

State the purpose of your working, then say:

*Queen of dawn's first blush and evening twilight,
she who orchestrates both love and war, whose
temples graced the ancient world, whose kisses
brought agreement and adoration, to you I now
implore—synchronize my work that force and
form work in harmony. Ruler of Taurus and
Libra, of strength and beauty, exalted in Pisces,
creatures of earth and air, daughter of
the moon and feminine embraces,
fill my work with love and care.*

INVOCATION OF SATURN
(SATURDAY)

State the purpose of your working, then say:

*Ancient Saturn, of bones and honored dead, he
who perseveres and guards the astral gates, who
leads the Lords of Karma and crystallizes that
which is needed and removes all negative blocks
from my path, grant me the authority required
over all legions to manifest my will. Ruler of
Capricorn, exalted in Libra, element of earth,
banish all evil energies that stand
in the way of my perfection.*

INVOCATION OF THE PLANETS

Seven planets light the heavens.

Seven metals rule the stars.

Seven angels stir the magick.

Seven spirits bring the charge.

Seven beasts and seven birds.

Seven drums beat out the word.

Seven chakras, seven days.

Seven pillars, seven rays.

Blend together into one.

As I will, it shall be done.

Seven powers, force and form.

Come to me, the change is born!

Repeat after each planetary invocation. Seal by making an equal-armed cross in the air over the spellworking.

Planetary Incenses

Use the following incense recipes for planetary spellwork. **Note:** Mix the dry ingredients first, then add the oil sparingly. This allows you to experiment with the consistency of the incense.

SUN

Mix equal parts of: Cinnamon, angelica, rosemary, sandalwood, and frankincense.

Oil: Cinnamon oil.

MOON

Mix equal parts of: Lemon balm, myrrh, and eucalyptus.

Oil: Myrrh oil.

MERCURY

Mix equal parts of: Lavender, marjoram, mint, and clover.

Oil: Lavender oil.

VENUS

Mix equal parts of: Lilac, rose, valerian, and vetivert.

Oil: Lilac oil.

MARS

Mix equal parts of: Allspice, basil, hops, and High John the Conqueror.

Oil: Allspice oil.

JUPITER

Mix equal parts of: Cinquefoil, clove, hyssop, nutmeg, and sage.

Oil: Nutmeg oil.

SATURN

Mix equal parts of: Comfrey, mullein, patchouli, and Solomon's seal.

Oil: Patchouli oil.

URANUS

Mix equal parts of: Cypress, mimosa, and slippery elm.

Oil: Cypress oil.

NEPTUNE

Mix equal parts of: Honeysuckle, linden, maple, and clove.

Oil: Sandalwood oil.

PLUTO

Mix equal parts of: Pine, wormwood, coriander, and ginger.

Oil: Pine oil.

COSMIC INCENSE

Mix equal parts of: Angelica, sandalwood, frankincense, myrrh, marjoram, valerian, hops, clove, patchouli, slippery elm, pine, orris root, and ginger.

Oil: Myrrh oil.

Astrological Conjuration While Mixing Incense

Begin with the planetary invocation, then repeat the following as you grind and mix the ingredients:

In thy name, Hecate,
Mistress of the Crossroads,
from the leaf and the resin
from the fire to the smoke
from a deed to a deed
may my desire be manifest.

Planetary Hours

Okay, I'm going to warn you right now, this is one of the more complicated areas of this book. Don't get excited if you don't understand it right away. I'm lousy at math, yet I was finally able to figure it out. If I could do it, so can you.

Astrologers and magickal people believe that timing greatly influences a spell, ritual, and planned events in daily life. Timing, in its own way, can allow us to look at the past as well as the future. By looking at where the planets were (or will be) on a certain day, we can see what planetary energies were (or will be) active at the time of an event. Where the planets are and the conversations they are having with each other can tell us how a situation might play out.

One timing method that Witches often use to choose the hour of the day that they might perform a spell involves consulting two tables called planetary hour tables. One is for sunrise and one is for sunset. Here's how this procedure works. These tables are pictured on page 197.

Each hour of the day is ruled by a planetary energy, and in that hour events and activities often coincide with the energy of that planet. There are seven classical planets, so there are seven types of energy available for spellcasting. Although we've covered the planets elsewhere in this book, let's look briefly at them again, just so

you completely understand where this section is going. For example, the hour of the sun would carry sun energy—*success* is a good keyword. The hour of the moon would relate to *magick* and *intuition*. The hour of Venus: *love*. The hour of Mercury: *communication*. The hour of Mars: *action*. The hour of Jupiter: *expansion*. The hour of Saturn: *constriction*. As the technique of the planetary hours was conceived hundreds of years ago, there are no correspondences for Uranus, Neptune, or Pluto—they hadn't yet been discovered when the table was invented.

To work with the planetary tables, you need two important pieces of information—the time the sun will rise and the time the sun will set on the day chosen for your magickal work. You can find this information by looking in your local newspaper under the weather section. Sometimes the local news channels on television also carry this information. Without knowing the exact time of the sunrise or sunset, you can't use the planetary hour tables. For convenience, you will also need a calculator. (Don't get excited, it's really not that bad.)

How to Calculate the Planetary Hour

Let's make believe that today is January 1, 1999 (okay, so we're going back in time, what the heck). It's a Friday. Tomorrow is Saturday. Everyone is going to be out of the house tomorrow, which gives you time to do some great magick without anyone disturbing you. They are planning to leave at 7:00 in the morning and will be back around 5:00 P.M., which means if you want to work magick, you will have to do it during the daylight hours. That's okay. You'd like to choose an hour that will vibrate especially well with what you want to do. Let's say you are working on better communication with your parents (they won't let you go to the movies tomorrow night because of a complete and total misunderstanding that you'd like to straighten out). Granted, this doesn't mean you'll get to go to the movies, but you don't like that negative energy hanging in the air. Tomorrow is already a good choice because it is a Saturday, and Saturday's energies lend well to banishing negativity. Still, you'd like to give that spell a little extra oomph, so you decide that you will calculate the planetary hours to find out which daylight hour tomorrow is ruled by Mercury (the planet of communication). In the spell, you will banish all communication blocks between yourself and your parents. Your first step is to get the local newspaper and find the weather section, which will list the time the sun rises tomorrow and the time the sun sets. You will also need a piece of paper to do your calculations, and a calculator.

STEP ONE: Find the sunrise and sunset times for your location for your chosen day from the local newspaper. Sunrise for January 2, 1999, occurs at 6:16 A.M. and sunset occurs at 5:49 P.M. Write those two times down. I know you're thinking that 6:16 A.M. does not fit in your magickal time window, but set that idea aside for now. To do our calculations, we have to have the exact time that the sun rises, regardless of when you are able to do the magick.

STEP TWO: To make our calculations easier, we are going to convert that P.M. time to military time. We won't need to touch the sunrise number because it is A.M., but we do need to take care of that P.M. number so that the calculations won't be too hard. Therefore, we will be converting 5:49 P.M. in this example. Here is a quick table to help you:

CLOCK TIME	MILITARY TIME
1:00 A.M.	1:00—01 hundred hours
2:00 A.M.	2:00—02 hundred hours
3:00 A.M.	3:00—03 hundred hours
4:00 A.M.	4:00—04 hundred hours
5:00 A.M.	5:00—05 hundred hours
6:00 A.M.	6:00—06 hundred hours
7:00 A.M.	7:00—07 hundred hours
8:00 A.M.	8:00—08 hundred hours
9:00 A.M.	9:00—09 hundred hours
10:00 A.M.	10:00—10 hundred hours
11:00 A.M.	11:00—11 hundred hours
12:00 Noon	12:00—12 hundred hours
1:00 P.M.	13:00—13 hundred hours
2:00 P.M.	14:00—14 hundred hours
3:00 P.M.	15:00—15 hundred hours
4:00 P.M.	16:00—16 hundred hours
5:00 P.M.	17:00—17 hundred hours
6:00 P.M.	18:00—18 hundred hours
7:00 P.M.	19:00—19 hundred hours
8:00 P.M.	20:00—20 hundred hours
9:00 P.M.	21:00—21 hundred hours
10:00 P.M.	22:00—22 hundred hours
11:00 P.M.	23:00—23 hundred hours
12 Midnight	24:00—24 hundred hours

In the example we are using, 5:49 P.M. would be 17 hundred hours and 49 minutes.

STEP THREE: To really make our calculations easier, we are going to convert all the hours to minutes. That way the math won't be so hard. First, we will work with converting the sunrise time of 6:16 to minutes. Do this by multiplying 6 times 60 (which gives you 360 minutes), then add those extra 16 minutes to 360. This gives you a total of 376 minutes. Therefore 6:16 A.M. equals 376. Now we are going to covert that military sunset time into minutes, too. We want to convert 17:49 (17 hours 49 minutes) to total minutes; 17 times 60 equals 1,020. Since our original time was 17 hours and 49 minutes, we now need to add the 49 minutes to that number to get the total number of minutes in the sunset time of 17:49. Therefore, we will add 1,020 and 49 together. When we do, we get the number 1,069—17 hours and 49 minutes converts to

1,069 minutes. (And you thought magick couldn't help you in math class—ha!) Okay, so far that wasn't too hard. We learned how to convert to military time, and then we learned how to convert hours to minutes. We're cooking! Trust me, this all has a purpose. Okay. We are now left with two numbers: 376 and 1069. Sunrise is 376 and sunset is 1069 (for January 2, 1999).

STEP FOUR: Now we want to know how many minutes there are between the number 376 and the number 1069. If it makes it easier, we want to figure out how many minutes there are between point A (376) and point B (1069). In other words, we want to know how much time (in minutes) it takes the sun to move from sunrise to sunset on January 2, 1999. This is super easy. We just subtract 376 from 1069. The answer is 693 minutes. On January 2, 1999, it will take 693 minutes for the sun to move from the point of sunrise to the point of sunset.

STEP FIVE: The planetary tables are divided by twelve, meaning there are twelve points of reference between sunrise and sunset, and there are twelve points of reference between sunset and sunrise. These points of reference are equal in length. Each point of reference stands for a planetary energy. Because each point is the same distance from the one before it, we need to find out what that equal number between them might be. To do this, we need to divide 693 (the total minutes between sunrise and sunset) by 12. The answer is 57.75. Since we don't use the decimal system in planetary hours, we are going to round that number to 58. Therefore, each daylight planetary hour on January 2, 1999, was approximately 58 minutes long. This length between points changes every single day during the daylight hours, and changes every single night during the nighttime hours. Therefore, if you wanted to work your magick in the evening on January 2, 1999, we would have to do an-

other set of calculations. We couldn't use the daylight hour points. Nighttime has its own.

STEP SIX: Now you know that each daylight planetary hour on January 2, 1999, is roughly 58 minutes long. You also know, from step one, that sunrise occurs at 6:16 A.M. To determine the starting time of each of those twelve points listed in step five (we know how long they are, now we want to know when they occur), we simply add 58 minutes to the sunrise time for the first planetary hour, and then we will keep adding 58 to find the successive number of hours. Therefore, our first hour was 6:16 A.M., right? We want to add 58 minutes to 6:16 A.M. to get the length of the first hour, which will also tell us when the second hour begins. We know the first hour begins at 6:16, but when does it finish? Fifty-eight minutes later. So we would add 58 minutes to 6:16 A.M., which gives us the time of 7:14 A.M. The first planetary hour on that day spans from 6:16 A.M. to 7:14 A.M. The second hour begins at 7:14 A.M. We know that the second hour is the same length as the first—58 minutes. When will the second hour end and the third hour begin? We will add 7:14 and :58 to get 8:12 A.M. Keep adding :58 to each hour to find the next hour, up to the twelfth hour. Here, the daylight planetary table calculations end, and the sunset calculations would begin. Because we rounded the number of minutes, that last hour won't exactly coincide with the sunset hour in the newspaper, but that's okay for what we are doing here.

To make it easier on yourself, you may want to list your calculations on a paper the way I have done here. On January 2, the division of time would occur this way:

Planetary Hour 1: 6:16 A.M. to 7:14 A.M.

P.H. 2: 7:14 A.M. to 8:12 A.M.

P.H. 3: 8:12 A.M. to 9:10 A.M.

P.H. 4: 9:10 A.M. to 10:08 A.M.

PLANETARY HOURS (SUNRISE)

Hour	Sunday	Monday	Tuesday	Wednesday	Thursday	Friday	Saturday
1	Sun	Moon	Mars	Mercury	Jupiter	Venus	Saturn
2	Venus	Saturn	Sun	Moon	Mars	Mercury	Jupiter
3	Mercury	Jupiter	Venus	Saturn	Sun	Moon	Mars
4	Moon	Mars	Mercury	Jupiter	Venus	Saturn	Sun
5	Saturn	Sun	Moon	Mars	Mercury	Jupiter	Venus
6	Jupiter	Venus	Saturn	Sun	Moon	Mars	Mercury
7	Mars	Mercury	Jupiter	Venus	Saturn	Sun	Moon
8	Sun	Moon	Mars	Mercury	Jupiter	Venus	Saturn
9	Venus	Saturn	Sun	Moon	Mars	Mercury	Jupiter
10	Mercury	Jupiter	Venus	Saturn	Sun	Moon	Mars
11	Moon	Mars	Mercury	Jupiter	Venus	Saturn	Sun
12	Saturn	Sun	Moon	Mars	Mercury	Jupiter	Venus

PLANETARY HOURS (SUNSET)

Hour	Sunday	Monday	Tuesday	Wednesday	Thursday	Friday	Saturday
1	Jupiter	Venus	Saturn	Sun	Moon	Mars	Mercury
2	Mars	Mercury	Jupiter	Venus	Saturn	Sun	Moon
3	Sun	Moon	Mars	Mercury	Jupiter	Venus	Saturn
4	Venus	Saturn	Sun	Moon	Mars	Mercury	Jupiter
5	Mercury	Jupiter	Venus	Saturn	Sun	Moon	Mars
6	Moon	Mars	Mercury	Jupiter	Venus	Saturn	Sun
7	Saturn	Sun	Moon	Mars	Mercury	Jupiter	Venus
8	Jupiter	Venus	Saturn	Sun	Moon	Mars	Mercury
9	Mars	Mercury	Jupiter	Venus	Saturn	Sun	Moon
10	Sun	Moon	Mars	Mercury	Jupiter	Venus	Saturn
11	Venus	Saturn	Sun	Moon	Mars	Mercury	Jupiter
12	Mercury	Jupiter	Venus	Saturn	Sun	Moon	Mars

Table 1. Planetary hours for sunrise and sunset.

P.H. 5: 10:08 A.M. to 11:06 A.M.

P.H. 6: 11:06 A.M. to 12:04 P.M.

P.H. 7: 12:04 P.M. to 1:02 P.M.

P.H. 8: 1:02 P.M. to 2:00 P.M.

P.H. 9: 2:00 P.M. to 2:58 P.M.

P.H. 10: 2:58 P.M. to 3:56 P.M.

P.H. 11: 3:56 P.M. to 4:54 P.M.

P.H. 12: 4:54 P.M. to 5: 52 P.M.

The newspaper said that sunset would be at 5:49 P.M., so we have a difference of five minutes by the end of the day. This only matters if, in magick, you are going to use planetary hour twelve—meaning you were going to do magick in that twelfth planetary hour, between 4:54 P.M. and 5:52 P.M. If this was the case, then you would make sure that you wouldn't start your magick in the last five minutes of that hour. You would begin earlier, to catch that hour's full energy.

STEP SEVEN: We're almost ready to use the planetary tables. To determine which planet rules which planetary hour on January 2, we have to know the weekday when we will do the magick. You decided that you will do the magick tomorrow, and tomorrow (as per the example) is Saturday. With that in mind, we can now look at the daylight planetary table (not the sunset one) above. Follow down the column for

Saturday. You will see on the table that the first hour is ruled by Saturn, the second by Jupiter, the third by Mars, and so on. You may want to write these planets beside your own calculations to keep things clear in your head.

Planetary Hour Tables

See tables on previous page. Here's an example for January 2, 1999:

P.H. 1: 6:16 A.M. to 7:14 A.M. Saturn

P.H. 2: 7:14 A.M. to 8:12 A.M. Jupiter

P.H. 3: 8:12 A.M. to 9:10 A.M. Mars

P.H. 4: 9:10 A.M. to 10:08 A.M. Sun

P.H. 5: 10:08 A.M. to 11:06 A.M. Venus

P.H. 6: 11:06 A.M. to 12:04 P.M. Mercury

P.H. 7: 12:04 P.M. to 1:02 P.M. Moon

P.H. 8: 1:02 P.M. to 2:00 P.M. Saturn

P.H. 9: 2:00 P.M. to 2:58 P.M. Jupiter

P.H. 10: 2:58 P.M. to 3:56 P.M. Mars

P.H. 11: 3:56 P.M. to 4:54 P.M. Sun

P.H. 12: 4:54 P.M. to 5:52 P.M. Venus

In our example, you decided that the Mercury hour would be best. On January 2, 1999, Mercury rules the sixth planetary hour (according to the table). Therefore, you will want to do your magick between 11:06 A.M. and 12:04 P.M.

What if the original planetary hour you chose did not fall within the window of time you had available? You could either choose another day, or you could look for a planetary energy that might also compliment your work that does fit into your time schedule, then word your spell accordingly. Some magickal people match the hour to the day; for example, if you chose a sun hour, then the magickal day would be Sunday; moon = Monday; Mars = Tuesday; Mercury = Wednesday; Jupiter = Thursday; Venus = Friday; and Saturn = Saturday.

The following table will help you to match your intention with the planetary hour.

Planetary Hour Operations[23]

SUN

Wealth, will, gain, prosperity, divination, find the favor of the rich or powerful (or whom you consider to hold power in a specific situation), dissolve painful or hostile emotions or reactions, make friends, find love, reveal kindness and compassion, make your presence psychologically invisible, focus your will.

MOON

Any issue having to do with water, travel over water, swimming, etc. Find lost objects, send emotional messages, speak with the deceased. Visionary work, divination. Prepare any magickal item that involves water or liquid, such as holy water or oil. Situations involve your mother, grandmother, or children.

MERCURY

Communications of all kinds with the living or the dead. Find eloquence in speech or writing (especially homework). Study science, divination. Mental games of all kinds. Work with computers and send messages via e-mail, video games.

VENUS

Love, fast cash, form friendships, find kindness, plan pleasant trips and parties, rid oneself of poison (mental or physical). Work with your hands or mind in any of the arts. Self-educate and work with the educational system. War.

MARS

Sports, winning, overcome enemies, overthrow enemies, call battle goddesses, resolve quarrels, gain courage, remove submissive behavior from oneself, take action in any given situation.

JUPITER

Expand any project, find and work with spirituality and faith, maintain good health. Long-term prosperity, plan ahead for important projects, make new friends, bring honor to your work. Draw love, kindness, and compassion to yourself.

SATURN

Bring good fortune and success to financial matters, buildings, towns, and group-oriented structures. Banish negativity, create chaos among evildoers. Overcome a quarrel, hatred, or discord. Banish illness, learn or establish new rules and financial goals. Garner rewards for work well done. Situations involving grandparents, fathers, the dominant parent or guardian, or those in authority.

Astrological Glyphs as Magickal Sigils

Astrological glyphs or sigils are symbols that represent the planets, signs, points, and dialog between them. Not only are they a great method of shorthand when analyzing any astrological chart, they are also extremely potent in magick (SEE SIGILS, SYMBOLS, AND MAGICKAL ALPHABETS IN PART IV for more information about working with sigils, patterns, and alphabets in general).

ARIES

Type: Zodiac sign.

Sigil: ♈

Basic energy pattern: Beginnings, action.

TAURUS

Type: Zodiac sign.

Sigil: ♉

Basic energy pattern: Manifestation, security.

GEMINI

Type: Zodiac sign.

Sigil: ♊

Basic energy pattern: Movement, mental energy.

CANCER

Type: Zodiac sign.

Sigil: ♋

Basic energy pattern: Emotions, home environment.

LEO

Type: Zodiac sign.

Sigil: ♌

Basic energy pattern: Success, courage.

VIRGO

Type: Zodiac sign.

Sigil: ♍

Basic energy pattern: Analysis, service.

LIBRA

Type: Zodiac sign.

Sigil: ♎

Basic energy pattern: Beauty, socialization.

SCORPIO

Type: Zodiac sign.

Sigil: ♏

Basic energy pattern: Regeneration, justice.

SAGITTARIUS

Type: Zodiac sign.

Sigil: ♐

Basic energy pattern: Idealization, study.

CAPRICORN

Type: Zodiac sign.

Sigil: ♑

Basic energy pattern: Building, business, and rewards.

AQUARIUS

Type: Zodiac sign.

Sigil: ♒

Basic energy pattern: Humanitarian and group work.

PISCES

Type: Zodiac sign.

Sigil: ♓

Basic energy pattern: Spiritual and visionary pursuits, transformation.

SUN

Type: Planet (in astrological terms).

Sigil: ☉

Basic energy pattern: Success.

MOON

Type: Planet (in astrological terms).

Sigil: ☽

Basic energy pattern: Emotions.

MERCURY

Type: Planet.

Sigil: ☿

Basic energy pattern: Communication.

VENUS

Type: Planet.

Sigil: ♀

Basic energy pattern: Socialization.

MARS

Type: Planet.

Sigil: ♂

Basic energy pattern: Action.

JUPITER

Type: Planet.

Sigil: ♃

Basic energy pattern: Expansion.

SATURN

Type: Planet.

Sigil: ♄

Basic energy pattern: Order.

URANUS

Type: Planet.

Sigil: ♅

Basic energy pattern: Experimentation.

NEPTUNE

Type: Planet.

Sigil: ♆

Basic energy pattern: Transformation.

PLUTO

Type: Planet.

Sigil: ♀

Basic energy pattern: Regeneration.

JUNO

Type: Asteroid.

Sigil: ⚵

Basic energy pattern: Marriage, partnerships.

VESTA

Type: Asteroid.

Sigil: ⚶

Basic energy pattern: Hearth and home.

PALLAS

Type: Asteroid.

Sigil: ⚴

Basic energy pattern: Wisdom.

CERES

Type: Asteroid.

Sigil: ⚳

Basic energy pattern: Creativity, regeneration.

CHIRON

Type: Comet.

Sigil: ⚷

Basic energy pattern: Healing.

DRAGON'S HEAD

Type: North moon node.

Sigil: ☊

Basic energy pattern: Expanding life path in a positive direction.

DRAGON'S TAIL

Type: South moon node.

Sigil: ☋

Basic energy pattern: Constricting a pathway.

CONJUNCTION

Type: Aspect.

Sigil: ☌

Basic energy pattern: Combining two forces.

OPPOSITION

Type: Aspect.

Sigil: ☍

Basic energy pattern: Mediating two forces.

SQUARE

Type: Aspect.

Sigil: ☐

Basic energy pattern: Creating challenge.

TRINE

Type: Aspect.

Sigil: △

Basic energy pattern: Harmony.

SEXTILE

Type: Aspect.

Sigil: ⚹

Basic energy pattern: Opportunity.

SEMI-SEXTILE

Type: Aspect.

Sigil: ⊻

Basic energy pattern: Mild support.

INCONJUNCT

Type: Aspect.

Sigil: ⊼

Basic energy pattern: Delays.

Retrogrades: Planets That Go Backward

A planet that appears to move backward in the heavens for a period of time is called a retrograde. You'll find retrograde planets uniquely useful when working magick and considering magickal timing. Retrogrades can help you catch a big wave of long-term energy and ride it through to completion.

The retrograde motion (going backward) is an illusion created by the orbit of our own Earth. Those planets never really go backward, it just looks like they do. Now, you would think that an illusion wouldn't affect reality, but it does. In fact, if you think about it, there are a lot of illusions that affect reality. For example, the idea that Witches are evil and worship Satan is an illusion created by false information—but for whatever reason, some stubborn people believe that silly rumor! Believing in that rumor affects the way they treat Witches (like trying to say we're not practicing a "real" religion). Not all illusions are negative. If we consider the human mind, we know that if you "believe" something, then you can create that something in reality (which is what magick is all about). Just like anything else in the world, there are good illusions and bad ones. We would like to believe that we have a choice.

All the planets in our solar system appear at one time or another to stop (the stopping part is called a "station") and then move backward. After a time they stop again (station) and appear to move forward (turn direct). Because some planets have faster orbits than others, the time they stop (station), turn retrograde, stop, and turn direct varies from planet to planet. The number of times that this happens in your lifetime also depends on the orbit of that planet.

Okay, so what does this really mean in magickal timing? When a planet turns retrograde, it is the universe's way of saying, "Hey! Hold up a minute! Time to take a breather. Sit back, relax, and just chill." Of course, we can't stop living just because a planet has decided to surf backward for a while, but in magickal timing there are ways to use these retrogrades to our advantage.

How do you know if a planet is retrograde, anyway? Look in your almanac. You will see the symbol for the planet and a little "Rx" beside it, along with the time it turns retrograde, and a "D" beside the planet when it goes forward again (turns direct). A retrograde planet acts a lot like a moon void (where the moon clams up and sashays along during her retrograde with an I'm-not-speaking-to-you expression on her face). You will notice that there are lots more moon voids in your almanac than planetary retrogrades. Moon voids are even listed differently—moon V/C, meaning moon void of course. (For more information on moon voids, SEE PAGE 299.)

Although every retrograde planet will behave according to its core nature, they all share some of the same phenomena when retrograde. A retrograde planet is very busy working on its own energy, therefore it pulls in this energy in a concentrated form. When another planet that is direct tries to speak to one that is retrograde, the energy exchange is either garbled or bounced back to the original planet. When the retrograde planet turns direct, the switch for exchanging information turns back on, and when that planet reaches the point where it first went retrograde in the heavens (the address where it turned on its heel and went backward), interesting and unexpected events take place in the areas that the previously retrograde planet rules.

To be honest, I love to watch how people act during planetary retrogrades. I can't help myself. It's sort of fun to sit there and watch everyone run around like crazy (especially during a Mercury retrograde) while you just relax next to that old tree and smile like a Cheshire cat because you and the universe are sharing an amusing secret and you, dear Dorothy, were prepared! Forget the red shoes, kid, you've got your almanac!

Magickal Tips for Retrogrades

FIRST TIP: The basic key for a retrograde is: "Don't start anything in the subject area that the retrograde planet corresponds to." You can finish things in that subject, research information, investigate, admire, learn, ponder, consider, experience, and enjoy . . . but if you start something that pertains to that planet's energy while that planet is furiously backpedaling in the universe, then what you have started will more than likely have to be done all over again when that planet turns direct.

SECOND TIP: Two days before that planet stations (stops), before it either goes backward (retrograde) or forward (direct), all heck is going to break loose involving the subjects that the planet corresponds to. Be prepared. The strength of the planet on those two days (what other planets it may be speaking to) determines the amount of upset you may experience.

THIRD TIP: The day a planet goes forward (after it's been going the other way), your magick in the area of that planet's rule will act like a slingshot. Although Witches and magickal people always try to be specific when working magick, be extra careful when a planet turns direct. Check and double-check what it is you truly want to accomplish. The old adage *Be careful what you wish for, you might get it* holds a great deal of meaning here.

The Retrograde Planets and Magick

To make retrograde planets a little easier for you to understand, I have listed them from the fastest moving (and most often retrograde) to the slowest moving (and the least often retrograde). Remember, too, that the faster the planet, the more often it turns retrograde and the least amount of time it spends peddling backward in the sky. Although all planetary retrogrades have a general meaning, each will be different in some way for every person because of:

1. Your personal astrological blueprint, your natal chart.

2. What house of life the retrograde planet is currently visiting.

These two factors can get fairly complicated, and if you haven't really gotten into astrology, they look like gibberish. You don't need to know these two factors to practice general magickal timing. Later, if you think you really like the topic of astrology, you can study these things on your own. Just as with the magickal days,

here we are more concerned with the essence of the energies available to you.

MERCURY

Basic energy: Communication.

Retrograde period: 3 times per year for a duration of 3 weeks each retrograde period.

What to expect/how people behave: Fights, arguments, communication snafus of all kinds. Travel delays, electronic and mechanical breakdowns, misplacing items. Computer viruses. Bad time to buy computer-related project or load software.

Magick to do: Think before you speak. Read, study, contemplate, work on old written projects you began earlier, do family genealogy research, tie up loose ends on old projects, do magick for investigative issues. Use the day Mercury stations direct to slingshot magicks involving vision, clarity, and communication.

VENUS

Basic energy: Socialization.

Retrograde period: Occurs every 18 months and lasts 40 days.

What to expect/how people behave: Affects relationships, dwindles ready cash, places blocks in the way of receiving small amounts of money; late payments or payments late; discussions on education always ensue but little is accomplished. People are attracted to the bizarre, unusual, or obscure. Not an ideal time to decorate your home or hire a decorator.

Magick to do: Evaluate your relationships and how you behave within the confines of those relationships. Research the whereabouts of estranged family members or lost items. Use the day that Venus stations direct to slingshot love magicks to give them extra oomph!

MARS

Basic energy: Action.

Retrograde period: Every 2 years and 2 months for ten weeks (70 days).

What to expect/how people behave: People are aggressive, won't take no for an answer, and refuse to look at the truth of the matter but plow on no matter how many individuals are hurt in the process. Brings confusion. Karmic matters. Old angers and resentments flair.

Magick to do: Review your actions within the last two years since the last retrograde. Pay back bills and work for closure on old, hurtful issues. Meditate on your mission in life. Exercise daily. Do physical work, such as cleaning out the garage, the basement, etc. Use the day Mars stations direct to slingshot a special project into action.

JUPITER

Basic energy: Expansion.

Retrograde period: Once a year for 120 days (approx. 4 months).

What to expect/how people behave: Energy is constricted, limited, held back. Finances go down the tubes if you have not prepared. People are less likely to be generous. If a Jupiter retrograde falls over a holiday buying season, people may overspend or not be able to purchase what they intended. Physical problems from overindulgence may manifest now.

Magick to do: Work on inner changes rather than outer manifestations. Work on manipulating energy with your hands for healing purposes, and practice circlecastings. Ex-

pand your horizons by studying psychology, the nature of dreams, and learn about other cultures. Window shop.

SATURN

Basic energy: Limits.

Retrograde period: Once a year for about 140 days (four and a half months).

What to expect/how people behave: Rules that previously worked well, fail. Political and hierarchal individuals are ousted. Group structures change, bend, or break. Those in authority turn a deaf ear. Rewards either do not manifest as you expected, are delayed, or don't come to fruition at all. Requires you to face reality. Issues of abuse are often discovered, whether in the home, at work, or in other types of group formations.

Magick to do: Banish unwanted influences in our lives—bad habits, negative associations, fears, friends, or organizations that are using us. Work on the structural change of ourselves. Restructure household chores, daily errands, etc., for more favorable use of time. Use the day Saturn stations direct as a slingshot for anything positive involving groups, organizations, student or national government, and personal maturation cycles.

URANUS

Basic energy: Destruction.

Retrograde period: Once a year for 148 days (about 5 months).

What to expect/how people behave: Freedoms are inhibited or threatened. Humanitarian issues stall and become lost either temporarily or permanently in proverbial red tape scenarios. Negativity of tribal behavior and gang activity increases. Slimeballs crawl out of the wall.

Magick to do: As Uranus is retrograde almost half the year, its influences are not easy to discern, and issues regarding this energy manifest slowly. Use the Uranus station to direct group change or to work on bringing the "real" you more in focus with the mask you normally wear.

NEPTUNE

Basic energy: Transformation.

Retrograde period: Once a year for 150 days (six months).

What to expect/how people behave: People tend to want to escape. Aggressive marketing techniques are bought easier by the public now as opposed to when Neptune is direct. Drug, alcohol, and fantasy indulgence appear to rise. Slanderous and libelous accusations with no foundation slither out from nowhere and are difficult to combat.

Magick to do: Like Uranus retrograde energy, Neptune retrogrades last a long time, therefore changes aren't always apparent. Great for group ritual where we seek to unify with our perception of Spirit. Good for vision questing, meditation, dream analysis, mysticism, writing poetry, practicing magickal dance, drumming, sitting under a full moon and asking the Mother to guide us in word and deed, and working on the personal unification of body, mind, and spirit. Talk to a butterfly, hug a tree, write your troubles on a piece of paper and give them to the Lady of the Lake. Use the Neptune station direct to slingshot you away from self-deceit or to help you learn to listen to the whispers of the universe.

PLUTO

Basic energy: Regeneration.

Retrograde period: Once a year for approximately 6 months.

What to expect/how people behave: On occasion, the shaking out of old stuff and turning sights to new ways for problem-solving makes the six o'clock news. People often choose a new religion or a new path within their religion right before or right after a Pluto retrograde.

Magick to do: Clean everything. Throw out all the old junk. Use photography in magick and ritual. Redesign rituals, redo your BOS, go back and study areas that you thought were too difficult to tackle before. Use the slingshot station direct for a total new you.

Retrograde Tips

MERCURY: If something is moving too fast and you want to slow it down (in the realm of communication), you can always place the Mercury retrograde symbol (☿℞) on a yellow candle, asking that, as the candle burns, the problem slows down until you have time to deal with that situation properly, or until you have the answer you need to proceed in a fair and honorable way. Petition the Greco-Roman god Mercury for assistance, or ask your guardian angel. The word *angel* means "messenger." (**Note:** The planet Mercury does not have to be physically retrograde in the heavens for you to cast this spell.)

VENUS: If you can't seem to hold on to your money, draw the Venus retrograde symbol (♀℞) on a white candle, and place that candle on top of the money you do have. Ask that you learn to slow down on your spending and hold on to your present savings. If you think that a love relationship is moving too fast, draw the Venus retrograde symbol on a blue candle. Place the candle over a picture of yourself. Ask that the relationship slow down until you can think clearly about who you want to associate with and why you are really interested in that person. Ask for clarity of thought. Venus will grant your desire. Venus is, after all, the Greco-Roman goddess of love, relationships, and passion. (*Note:* The planet Venus does not have to be physically retrograde in the heavens to work this simple spell.)

MARS: During a Mars retrograde, Spirit will show you who your friends are and who doesn't care a whit about you. Heads up.

JUPITER: Always have money in the bank before Jupiter goes retrograde, even if it is only a little bit. A Jupiter retrograde can expand on poverty as easily as it can expand your prosperity when it is direct. Be extra careful with your finances when Jupiter turns retrograde!

Retrograde Summary

As you can see, not all of the retrogrades may have a noticeable effect on your everyday magick. Those to look out for when planning most activities are Mercury retrogrades and Mars retrogrades, unless you want to work specifically with the retrograde energies (such as Pluto for self-transformation or Neptune for increasing your spirituality). If you don't want to work with retrogrades in spellcasting and ritual, then don't sweat it. The information I've given you is only a tool, sometimes to look at in passing and other times to use at your leisure. Often, retrogrades will give us a hint as to why something is happening within ourselves or around us. They are taps on the noggin to put you more in tune with the universal flow. Knowing the whys often helps us in dealing with different circumstances, so that we aren't blindly stumbling around in the dark of any situation. The study of retrograde planets does not stop here, as there is a great deal more information that can be gleaned from the illusionary backwards movements of the planets. This short dissertation is only the beginning.

Moon Aspects / Transits

Aspects are actually geometric angles that fold into a pattern and then unfold, releasing the energy back to the universe as the planets move through the heavens. If the snapshot is permanent (your natal chart, a point in time to review later), the dialog or the energy change between the planets is called an *aspect*. If we are looking ahead to future dialog that will occur between the position of natal planets, or discuss presently moving dialog (like what is happening in the heavens today), this movement and geometric pattern that unfolds (applying) and folds (separating) is called a *transit*. Yes, I know: confusing. This series of folding and unfolding translates into an energy exchange between two or more planets. It is this energy that astrologers and magickal people attempt (notice I say "attempt") to analyze and utilize in their magickal work (we don't get it right all the time). If you look in your planetary guide, you'll see that moon aspects don't last very long. Therefore, if you want to catch the wave (or miss it), you'll have to keep an eye on the clock, as the opportunity lasts approximately ten hours from the time it begins to the time of exactness (where the energy is strongest), growing steadily stronger each hour (depending upon the orb of influence you are using). Some magickal astrologers would cut this time in half, giving only a five-hour window for your magickal work, and others would give only an hour window in which you should do your work.

Traditional astrology commonly uses the Ptolemaic set of aspects, which places Earth at the center of the universe, to interpret the energy dialog between the ten planets. However, there can be hundreds of angles, depending on what astrological system you use. In magick, practitioners often employ the Ptolemaic aspects, adding a few others as the situation may require. Harmonics—patterns consisting of several geometric angles, such as the Seerer and the Skullcap—are not mentioned here, but are valuable if you wish to find the best times for divination and working with the dead, respectively.

The Ptolemaic aspects are:

Square: When two planets are 90 degrees apart. Squares usually represent challenges. There is a sharp difference between the two planetary energies and we are often required to make a choice. Squares are not "bad," they are dynamic.

Trine: When two planets are 120 degrees apart, they are considered to be in a harmonious energy pattern. This is a peaceful and often too-complacent aspect. The two planets are happily communicating with each other, like the soft drone of a conversation between two friends on a hot summer afternoon. If we take advantage of trine energy, we can get a lot accomplished—the problem is that during a trine transit we just may feel too complacent to do anything about it. If you have a bunch of trines and sextiles falling on the same day and no hard aspects in sight, this is a big "go" day to get as much done as you can. How will you know this? Either purchase your own astrological program that shows the transits to your natal chart, or obtain a free chart at one of the many websites listed at the end of this section.

Opposition: When two planets are exactly opposite each other, they are 180 degrees apart. An opposition requires us to balance the energies of both planets, hopefully finding a happy middle ground. Oppositions represent the need to compromise, mediate, and arbitrate (which isn't all that bad).

Sextile: Two planets that are 60 degrees apart and loving it. This is an opportunity for creative expression, if you grab the opportunity. If you don't, it will pass you by.

Semi-Sextile: When two planets are 30 degrees apart. Mildly supportive.

Conjunction: When two planets are within at least 10 degrees of each other (depending upon your astrological choice of study). Think of two partners dancing cheek to cheek; two energies that reinforce each other for either good or ill. Of all the Ptolemaic aspects, the conjunction is thought to carry the most energy, but it can also be a twitchy little bugger. For some, it will be incredibly dynamic; for others, you'll wish it never happened. The conjunction of the sun to any planet is also divided into parts, depending on how close each planet is to the sun at a given moment within that conjunction. These divisions are:

Under the Beams: When a planet is between 16 and 6 degrees from the sun. Here, the sun is beginning to outshine the energy of the other planet. Under the beams and combust are both situations where the sun is forcing a self-esteem problem on the other planet (figuratively, of course).

Combust: When a planet is between 6 degrees and 0 degrees, 17 minutes from the sun, and is a portion of the conjunction aspect. Many ancient astrologers felt that if a planet was combust, then its energies were weakened—meaning the sun finds it necessary to overcompensate for the other planet's presence. The moon is combust during a new moon. It is felt that a new moon is doubly powerful because the moon reflects whatever she touches. Therefore, if she is touching the sun, she is reflecting additional power to Earth.

Cazimi: When a planet lies between 0 degrees, 17 minutes and 0 degrees to the sun. Here, the sun has realized that the other planet really isn't any competition at all, and basks in the attention of that other planet's energies. The ancients felt that unlike the combust stage (which is 6 degrees to 0 degrees, 17-minute window), the cazimi stage adds more power to the conjunction. Therefore, if you were picking a time during a conjunction to do magick, and you wanted the best of both planetary energies (in this case, the sun and the planet of your choice), then you would trot out your ephemeris, astrological program, or planetary guide and determine when the conjunction is exact (when the planets are both located in the same degree and minute in the same sign). Once you've made this determination, plan your magickal working to begin approximately fifteen minutes before the exact conjunction. For example, you know that Mercury will conjunct the sun in Gemini tomorrow at 10:30 P.M. If you wanted to work magick for writing, studying, or assuring that your speech will go well at the Flower Club, begin your magick at 10:15 P.M. and work through the spell to its completion. (It's okay if the working goes past the 10:30 deadline, because you have already begun the work at the right time.) Just make sure that your statement of intent falls *before* 10:30 P.M. Some magickal practitioners (including me) like to raise power precisely at the moment of the exactness of the aspect.

Aspects of the Moon[24]

Below you will find a brief list based on the interpretations for magickal and event timing when translating the dialog between the moon and the other planets using the Ptolemaic aspects; the moon is the most useful planet when studying and predicting human behavior, psychology, and family dynamics, as it moves the fastest and stands for emotions. If you want to ask someone for something, check the aspects of the moon first. Remember that these energies don't *make* anything occur; rather, the geometric angles they create open a gateway that allows various experiences to manifest based on your previous behavior and your psychological makeup. Astrological magick allows you to use this crossroads opportunity (whether it be an easy or difficult one) in a positive way. Several moon aspects can occur each day, so keep an eye on the energy mixture at any given time for fine tuning. Remember, the flavor of the moon can give you additional ideas and add more detail not only in magick but in daily occurrences as well.

MERCURY

Conjunct the moon: Begin writings of all kinds, errands, make or attend appointments, send letters, e-mails, faxes, or messages. Make phone calls. Go over any type of written accounting. Work on your BOS, magickal alphabets, sigils, seals, numerology, and talismans.

- The moon will conjunct Mercury once a month.

Sextile the moon: Study, go over accounts, take on students, begin schooling and classes of all kinds, talk with individuals whom you feel are experts in your field. Research work for your BOS. Study the Tarot and the runes.

- The moon will sextile Mercury twice a month.

Square the moon: Refrain from arguments. Do magick for solutions to communication problems. Buying and selling may prove active.

- The moon will square Mercury twice a month.

Trine the moon: Perfect timing for getting your way with words or through communication of all kinds, studying, and making appointments involving learning. Working on inventions of all kinds, whether mental or physical.

- The moon will trine Mercury twice a month.

Opposite the moon: Workings of negotiation of all kinds, though you will be expected to give a little. Do ritual for rewards through writing and speech.

- The moon will be in opposition to Mercury once a month.

VENUS

Conjunct the moon: Considered a fortunate day—good for giving and receiving gifts. Magickal workings for love, harmony, and social success in business or pleasure. Workings for fast cash. Good time to phone or contact women. Beware of overspending. Healing and garden magicks.

- The moon will conjunct Venus once a month.

Sextile the moon: Work for love opportunities and chances to succeed in relationships. Good time to entertain. Beware of self-indulgence. Shop for gemstones and herbs, but watch the purse strings.

- The moon will sextile Venus twice a month.

Square the moon: Good day for analyzing people. The classicists claimed it was a time to hire or interview employees because they couldn't pull the wool over your eyes, yet you will be in a sympathetic mood. Beware of being overly possessive.

- The moon will square Venus twice a month.

Trine the moon: Work on self-love. A good day to throw a party. Buy new clothes and items for the home but beware of overspending. Do magick for love of all kinds, including pets. A good time for self-expression through the arts. Good time to phone or contact women. Beware overindulgence. Garden magicks.

- The moon will trine Venus twice a month.

Opposite the moon: Another good time, say the classicists, for hiring or interviewing employees. Beware of not making enough effort. Practice magick for discernment in relationships and reaping the rewards of positive past action with others.

- The moon will be in opposition to Venus once a month.

SUN

Conjunct the moon: Focus on personal life, domestic harmony, making positive changes in lifestyle. Work to bring secrets out in the open. Work on beginnings in spiritual matters, introspection, and harmony. Add candle magick to your sun/moon workings.

- The moon will conjunct the sun once a month on the new moon.

Sextile the moon: Fine-tuning aspects of your own personality. Work on the positive outcome of routine meetings and negotiations, harmony between people, bringing peace in the home, and drawing opportunities to yourself. A good time to ask for favors, especially from bosses and authority figures. Work on future goals.

- The moon will sextile the sun twice a month.

Square the moon: Brings tensions to the surface. Exercise; release stress and pressure through meditation and relaxation techniques. Use your skills to rise to the challenge. Think first, then act. Channel aggressive energy into charging candles and other items for protection.

- The moon will square the sun twice a month.

Trine the moon: Tailor workings to inner peace and balance. Correct any misunderstandings between yourself and others. Take advantage of and work for opportunities. Great time for working for anything you desire, as the sun connects to your will. To receive you must give—kindness, a helping hand, and presents are well received.

- The moon will trine the sun twice a month.

Opposite the moon: Work on coping with your problems through meditation and exercise. Do magick for personal balance between your will and emotions. Work on common lawsuits but not those that involve an opponent richer than you. Do magick for rewards through your skills.

- The moon will be in opposition to the sun once a month.

MARS

Conjunct the moon: All magicks for power and success. Channel excess energy into positive, active pursuits, including exercise, sports, and cleaning out your magickal cabinet. Good day to restock your supplies, re-empower objects where the energy may be waning, and physically clean tools and supplies. Practice dowsing, pendulum magick, and Tarot to teach yourself to focus when you are full of energy. (You may find this difficult but rewarding.) Go miniature

golfing and practice focusing on the sub-quantum level.

- The moon will conjunct Mars once a month.

Sextile the moon: Buy all manner of hunting, military, and sports gear. Work for winning in sports and championships. Good for all alchemical workings, and magicks for gaining respect. Take the initiative on opportunities to succeed. Be sincere.

- The moon will sextile Mars twice a month.

Square the moon: Keep your head low and your mouth shut—work magick instead. If you must speak of dissatisfaction, make sure your grievances are legitimate. Avoid making any new contacts. Exercise and meditate. Channel aggressive energy into charging items for protection and doing magicks for self-esteem.

- The moon will square Mars twice a month.

Trine the moon: Magicks for ease in overcoming any difficulties or challenges you are currently facing and for determining what is needed in any situation. Good for starting projects but since the influence is short be sure to follow up or your enthusiasm will wane.

- The moon will trine Mars twice a month.

Opposite the moon: Control your desire to behave in an irritated way. Seek to mediate with a fair and positive goal in mind. Work magicks for situations where you feel you have come to an impasse. Relations with the opposite sex may be difficult at this time, therefore magicks to resolve any issues can be done now. Channel excess energy through exercise and meditation.

- The moon is opposite Mars once a month.

JUPITER

Conjunct the moon: Time of good fortune. Work on expansions of all kinds. Excellent time for seeking counsel of attorneys and other legal employees, planning trips, and the additions to any business, and magickal workings for the same. A time to ask for favors, whether it be from the gods or human beings. Any type of magickal work for spirituality and understanding your place in the universe.

- The moon conjuncts Jupiter once a month.

Sextile the moon: Conversations about the law or with people in the religious or legal field. Work on opportunities for a bright future. Plan a vacation or business travel that will include some free time. Work on expanding your horizons through study and reading. Purchase metaphysical books and tools. Excellent time for group activities.

- The moon sextiles Jupiter twice a month.

Square the moon: Magicks for wisdom, social truth, philosophy, and overcoming dogma or fears negatively ingrained by any religious force. Beware of being self-righteous or arrogant.

- The moon squares Jupiter twice a month.

Trine the moon: Magicks for gaining friends, joining groups and organizations, learning new aspects of spirituality, asking for favors from others, contacting your guardian angel, working magickally with your pets, enjoying the out-of-doors, broadening your horizons, helping or receiving help from others, and experiencing metaphysical teachings on a physical level.

- The moon trines Jupiter twice a month.

Opposite the moon: Workings for personal freedom, initiative, and common sense. Expand spiritual pursuits and contemplate future desires. Come to grips with various dogmas.

- The moon is in opposition to Jupiter once a month.

SATURN

Conjunct the moon: Workings to expel loneliness and isolated feelings, jettison guilt, remove pessimism, combine your energies with appropriate structure, build on important life goals, overcome difficult relationships, study the Tree of Life or other structured magickal application, banish illness, work with the "no time" aspect of magick.

- The moon conjuncts Saturn once a month.

Sextile the moon: Magick for a good relationship with an older person; harmony with individuals in authority; learning and opportunities within a system that has a particular set of rules; meditation and reflection on life issues; emotional balance; ease in caring for sick and older people. Magicks for debt control, learning to save, and being generally thrifty.

- The moon sextiles Saturn twice a month.

Square the moon: Things usually look worse than they are under this aspect, so don't get too excited. Work in a positive way to overcome sickness and adversity. Meditate and evaluate personal development and where you would like to go from here without trashing your self-esteem. Watch for a tendency to fail in communicating with others. Keep your tone kind and gentle; a compliment helps. Seek calm solutions that will help to overcome angst shown by authority figures. Separation magicks.

- The moon squares Saturn twice a month.

Trine the moon: Seek counsel from older, wiser individuals. Work magick for rewards, self-esteem, and long-term goal planning. Learn timing; understand the significance of Karma. Study quantum physics, any system of government or set of rules, the Wiccan principles of belief, the Tree of Life, hermeticism, and history. Find new answers to old questions; repair anything; do magicks for building and a strong emotional foundation. Learn numerology.

- The moon trines Saturn twice a month.

Opposite the moon: This opposition triggers inner strength, which can be of great use in magickal applications where you must be focused and realistic. If you have worked very hard, this opposition can bring great rewards, therefore working to manifest such rewards is definitely in order. Magick for negotiations of contracts with bosses and figures in authority; practical and immediate solutions for all sorts of tasks, and common sense. Not a good time for hiring or interviews. Don't make or accept promises without some sort of written confirmation.

- The moon opposes Saturn once a month.

URANUS

Conjunct the moon: Tendency to be moody, impulsive, and impatient with others as well as yourself. Most moon/Uranus activity brings an emotional surprise or two, but they aren't necessarily head rippers. Go with the flow. Discipline usually goes out the window so magicks involving freedom

of expression and experimenting with the arts, music, and dance in your workings may be more fulfilling. Spontaneous ritual is a go. Beware the consequences of your actions.

- The moon conjuncts Uranus once a month.

Sextile the moon: Seek exciting and stimulating activities. Use your magick to change dull and boring situations or life patterns. Visit with friends. Enact ritual drama in a group setting. Work for unexpected opportunities through simple magicks (like affirmations or wish magick). Enjoy the outdoors. Play with faeries and devas. Go back to technical questions or projects that confused you before and read them again. Surf the Internet but keep your nose out of flame wars.

- The moon sextiles Uranus twice a month.

Square the moon: Above all, watch your reactions and don't act in haste. Wild things are okay as long as you don't go overboard. Try new techniques in ritual, work on writing ritual drama for the solitary or the group, write down the changes you would like to make in your life and review them when in a more emotionally balanced state. Keep an idea book for magick and ritual. Use Uranus energy to blow out cobwebby habits. Stay off the Internet.

- The moon squares Uranus once a month.

Trine the moon: Use this energy to work rituals of change. Sew outrageous ritual gear, design coven banners, crests, personal sigils, book covers, etc. Plan ahead for the best parties ever. Read cutting-edge material. Another excellent time for spontaneous ritual and ritual drama. Make whatever happens during this time period work for you, as bizarre as it may seem. Work for long-haul energy to deal with any current difficulties. Color magick.

- The moon trines Uranus twice a month.

Opposite the moon: Don't leap to the wrong conclusion—check it out first. Work to calm stormy relationships, find balance in a new and unusual way, and curb negative reactions through affirmations and meditation. Stay off the Internet and avoid weird strangers, especially if the planet opposite the moon is afflicted by squares and oppositions to other planets. Practice ritual breathing and magickal voice.

- The moon opposes Uranus once a month, and because Uranus is an outer planet and does not move quickly, you may experience the same type of situation when the moon is opposite Uranus for several months. As this experience may only last a few hours, keep a journal.

NEPTUNE

Conjunct the moon: Work for all types of psychism, spirituality, alternative realms, astral projection, aura training, visualization, chakra meditations, empathy, sensitivity, etc. Work magick to be a better listener. Communication with others is often difficult at this time—better to invest in solitary pursuits, reading poetry, listening to music, painting, or drumming. Sometimes this period of time makes you feel sleepy. Work on controlling your dreams and dream recall. Stay away from drugs and alcohol.

- The moon is conjunct Neptune once a month.

Sextile the moon: Sensitivity will be heightened, so stay away from negativity, drugs, alcohol, etc. Discuss occult, mystical, and spiritual ideas with friends who are open to such subjects. Writing fiction and creative articles are a good way to spend this time. Work magick for insights, the truth, creative ideas, and communicating with the dead. Guardian angel and totem magicks are especially successful during this time.

- The moon sextiles Neptune twice a month.

Square the moon: Beware of creating or taking part in gossip, slanderous and libelous campaigns, and any type of mass market hype. Use the alpha state of daydreams to visualize a positive future. Write down any mystical experiences, but interpret them later. Work on conquering your fears. Stay away from drugs and alcohol, and people who exude negative behavior. Read or study occult-related subjects. Don't take anything at face value.

- The moon squares Neptune twice a month.

Trine the moon: Excellent time for all spiritual work. As this is a very lazy transit, you may wish to daydream or sleep a great deal. Keep a dream journal and daydream actively to program yourself for future success. Quiet rituals centered on contemplation, understanding others, divination, and meditation suit this energy well. Charitable pursuits are also conducive to this energy. Practice telepathy and remote viewing with a friend. Celebrate ceremonies of remembrance and of honoring your ancestors.

- The moon trines Neptune twice a month.

Opposite the moon: There is a real danger in reacting not to reality but to illusion, often created by your own subconscious fears and previous patterning. Sometimes excellent opportunities are missed because our thoughts are in the way. Work on raising self-esteem, allowing creative opportunities to manifest, and a willingness to see clearly, both in our spiritual work and in daily life.

- The moon opposes Neptune once a month.

PLUTO

Conjunct the moon: Releases hidden energies for good or ill. If you have been working with mystery teachings or spiritual studies, the effects can be extremely fulfilling. Magicks for root spiritual change can put you miles forward in your studies, although you should avoid obsession. Excellent for reading and studying the occult, astrology, and other spiritual work. Use this energy to mundanely and magickally clean the house, make changes to your ritual area, and repair magickal tools. Use film and photography in magick.

- The moon conjuncts Pluto once a month.

Sextile the moon: Opportunity for deep-seated changes is knocking. Work magick for anything that requires intensity, or use those intense energies to satisfy a goal. Work on circlecastings, the cone of power, and raising energy in general. Good time to practice dowsing. Work on reorganizing or rebuilding your website. Excellent time for electronic art design.

- The moon sextiles Pluto twice a month.

Square the moon: Beware of compulsive behavior. Channel impulsive energy into magick and emotional self-assessment. Work on banishing guilt, jealousy, negativity, criminals, abuse, etc.

- The moon squares Pluto twice a month.

Trine the moon: Changes in religion or spirituality? Now's the time to enact them. Tear off the superficial and work on the inner you. Use your passion and feeling in your magickal work and tap into regenerative power. Work with the Witch's Pyramid; add intense energy to regeneration of important goals; mix herbs, incenses, and oils; practice energy ball exercises. Perform self-dedication and initiation ceremonies. Empower your altar and other magickal tools.

- The moon trines Pluto twice a month.

Opposite the moon: Work to resolve emotional conflicts in a way that builds toward the future. Jettison outmoded ways of behavior by working with the opposites within yourself. Work to clear away blockages in personal development. Curb anger and impulsive behavior with mental and physical exercises.

- The moon opposes Pluto once a month.

Planetary Dignities

According to ancient astrological practice, each planet operates most efficiently in two signs: the sign of its *rulership*, and the sign of its *exaltation*. Exalted planets are also called "in honor" or "exaltation." As there are twelve signs and only ten planets, not every sign in classical astrology has an exalted planet, and even in this respect astrologers differ. A planet in the sign of its exaltation is a very happy one indeed, and is considered to be in its most powerful position in the zodiac. The classification of a planet, such as "exalted," is a part of a planet's "dignity."

Just as there is an up, there is also a down—signs in which planets are either definitely not happy or are downright stubborn. Just as there are two signs where the planet is comfortable, there are two signs where each planet is uncomfortable. The prickly signs are when a planet is in its *fall*, which is opposite the sign of its exaltation, or in its *detriment*, which is the sign that opposes the sign that the planet rules. Although everyone is fairly firm on these positions for the classical planets, astrologers are still waffling on the dignities of the newer planets; therefore, I have not included them for the purposes of this book. I do encourage you to study outside of this material, run experiments, and make your own determinations. Notice Venus and Mercury rule two signs, therefore they are listed twice.

SUN

Rulership: Leo.

Detriment: Aquarius.

Exaltation: Aries.

Fall: Libra.

MOON

Rulership: Cancer.

Detriment: Capricorn.

Exaltation: Taurus.

Fall: Scorpio.

I: MERCURY

Rulership: Gemini.

Detriment: Sagittarius.

Exaltation: Aquarius.

Fall: Leo.

2: MERCURY

Rulership: Virgo.

Detriment: Pisces.

I: VENUS

Rulership: Taurus.

Detriment: Scorpio.

Exaltation: Pisces.

Fall: Virgo.

2: VENUS

Rulership: Libra.

Detriment: Aries.

MARS

Rulership: Aries.

Detriment: Libra.

Exaltation: Capricorn.

Fall: Cancer.

JUPITER

Rulership: Sagittarius.

Detriment: Gemini.

Exaltation: Cancer.

Fall: Capricorn.

SATURN

Rulership: Capricorn.

Detriment: Cancer.

Exaltation: Libra.

Fall: Aries.

Now that we have this information, what do we do with it? Planetary magicks done when the planet is in its own sign (rulership) and in its exaltation can carry an extra boost of energy, provided it isn't afflicted (having unpleasant conversations with other planets). You can go crazy with magickal timing in this way, however, especially when you are trying to gather the best energies of multiple planets. It's best to begin with one planet, choose the optimum time for that planet, and keep notes of your successes or failures. If you choose to expand your magickal expertise to event planning (electional astrology) and horary astrology (the birth of a question), you will learn to pay attention to the dignities and much, much more. The problem with planetary dignities is that they don't work the same for every individual. For example, although the moon is in its fall in Scorpio and

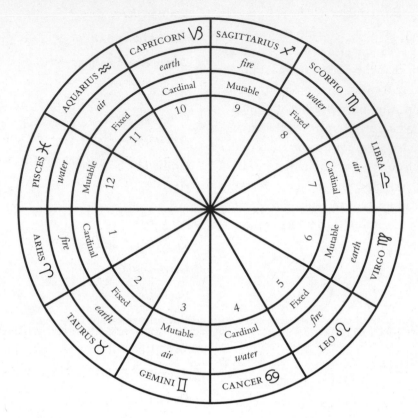

Astrological sign chart.

supposedly uncomfortable there, for me a Scorpio moon is fantastic because my natal chart supports the Scorpio moon energy. Magicks, for me, done under a Scorpio moon always pack the needed punch. Again, the best way to learn is to experiment and keep notes.

The Astrological Signs

The twelve signs of the zodiac lay down twelve different "paths" of life. . . . Every sign has its own manner of expression, birth in a higher and in a lower sense, and it depends on the person which options to take and how to use them.

—*Karen Hamaker-Zondag,*
author of Astro-Psychology

The planetary energies represent one-third of astrological study. The other two-thirds are the astrological signs and the system of houses one may choose as the backdrop for casting any type

of astrological chart. Above is a depiction of the signs as they fall in their *natural* houses (which most likely won't look like your natal chart).

ARIES

Sun visits this sign: March 21/22–April 19/20.

Ruling planet: Mars.

Exalted planet: Sun.

Sign keywords: Basic momentum: beginnings. Arrogant, brusque, competitive, courageous, domineering, dynamic, eager, executive, impulsive, independent, intolerant, lacks completion, lives in the present, me first, pioneering, quick-tempered, violent.

Quality: Cardinal fire.

TAURUS

Sun visits this sign: April 20/21–May 20/21.

Ruling planet: Venus.

Exalted planet: Moon.

Sign keywords: Basic momentum: manifestation. Artistic, comfort oriented, conservative, dependable, dogmatic, domestic, greedy, loyal, materialistic, patient, possessive, practical, self-indulgent, sensual, slow-moving, stable, stubborn, thorough.

Quality: Fixed earth.

GEMINI

Sun visits this sign: May 21/22–June 21/22.

Ruling planet: Mercury.

Exalted planet: None.

Sign keywords: Basic momentum: mental energy. Adaptable, changeable, clever, congenial, curious, dexterous, dual, expressive, inventive, lacking concentration, multitasking, quick-witted, restless, scatterbrained, scheming, talkative, ungrateful.

Quality: Mutable air.

CANCER

Sun visits this sign: June 22/23–July 23/24.

Ruling planet: Moon.

Exalted planet: Jupiter and Neptune.

Sign keywords: Basic momentum: emotional energy. Brooding, cautious, domestic, easily hurt, emotional, helpful, intuitive, lazy, manipulative, material, negative, self-pity, selfish, sensitive, sympathetic, tenacious, touchy, traditional.

Quality: Cardinal water.

LEO

Sun visits this sign: July 23/ 24–August 23/24.

Ruling planet: Sun.

Exalted planet: Pluto.

Sign keywords: Basic momentum: development. Ambitious, arts, autocratic, boastful, childish, creative, cruel, dignified, dramatic, generous, idealistic, leadership, music, optimistic, overbearing, pretentious, proud, romance, self-assured, status conscious, vain.

Quality: Fixed fire.

VIRGO

Sun visits this sign: August 23/24–September 22/23.

Ruling planet: Mercury.

Exalted planet: Mercury.

Sign keywords: Basic momentum: perfection. Clean, critical, discriminating, fact-finding, fears, humane, industrious, melancholy, methodical, pedantic, perfection, petty, picky, scientific, skeptical, sloppy, studious, worry.

Quality: Mutable earth.

LIBRA

Sun visits this sign: September 23/24–October 23/24.

Ruling planet: Venus.

Exalted planet: Saturn.

Sign keywords: Basic momentum: balance. Apathetic, artistic, companionable, cooperative, diplomatic, easily deterred, fickle, hypocritical, indecisive, judgmental, judicial, loves intrigue, peace at any price, peace-loving, persuasive, pouting, refined, sociable, suave.

Quality: Cardinal air.

SCORPIO

Sun visits this sign: October 24/25–November 21/22.

Ruling planet: Pluto (Mars).

Exalted planet: Uranus.

Sign keywords: Basic momentum: regeneration. Determined, executive, intolerant, investigative, jealous, motivated, overbearing, passionate, penetrating, private, probing, resourceful, sarcastic, scientific, secretive, suspicious, temperamental, vengeful, violent.

Quality: Fixed water.

SAGITTARIUS

Sun visits this sign: November 22/23–December 21/22.

Ruling planet: Jupiter.

Exalted planet: None.

Sign keywords: Basic momentum: idealization. Argumentative, athletic, blunt, broad-minded, enthusiastic, exaggerate, freedom-loving, gambling, generous, hot-headed, idealistic, impatient, just, missionary zeal, optimistic, philosophical, procrastinating, push, religious, scholarly, self-indulgent, straightforward, talkative.

Quality: Mutable fire.

CAPRICORN

Sun visits this sign: December 22/23–January 19/20.

Ruling planet: Saturn.

Exalted planet: Mars.

Sign keywords: Basic momentum: constructing reality. Brooding, Businesslike, cautious, cold, conventional, domineering, economical, fatalistic, hardworking, inhibited, judgmental, over-ambitious, perfectionist, practical, reliable, responsible, scrupulous, serious, status-seeking, stubborn, traditional, unforgiving.

Quality: Cardinal earth.

AQUARIUS

Sun visits this sign: January 20/21–February 18/19.

Ruling planet: Uranus (Saturn).

Exalted planet: None.

Sign keywords: Basic momentum: experimentation. Bored by detail, cold, eccentric, fixed, humane, impersonal, independent, individualistic, intellectual, inventive, logical, progressive, radical, rebellious, scientific, temperamental, tolerant, unique, unpredictable.

Quality: Fixed air.

PISCES

Sun visits this sign: February 19/20–March 20/21.

Ruling planet: Neptune (Jupiter).

Exalted planet: Venus.

Sign keywords: Basic momentum: spirituality. Charitable, compassionate, creative, dreamy, emotional, escapist, impractical, indolent, inhibited, introspective, intuitive, melancholy, musical, pessimistic, procrastinating, sacrificing, spacey, spiritual, sympathetic, talkative, timid, visionary.

Quality: Mutable water.

Aries Energy Spell

FAVORABLE TIMING: Tuesday, Mars hour, moon in Aries, or sun in Aries.

FOCUS: Aries gifts us with the power to overcome all obstacles, to forge ahead and rumble over roadblocks and anything else that might be foolish enough to stand in our way. Aries brings us courage in the face of defeat, and imbues us with the mastery of command. With Aries energy pulsing from our fingers, we are an indomitable force.

SPELL: On a piece of paper, draw what you envision as the obstacle you are facing. This can be a doodle, an accurate rendition, or simply a mass of colors that you feel represents what you desire to overcome. On the back of the paper, draw the desired outcome. On the bottom of the second drawing, write: *(Your name) using Mars energy (♂) focused through Aries energy (♈) overcomes the obstacle of (indicate difficulty).* At sunset (or using the favorable timing recommendations above), present your petition to Spirit, asking for assistance in your current dilemma. Outside, burn the drawing (fire magick) while watching the sun dip below the horizon, knowing that as the fire of the heavens is absorbed into the horizon of the Earth, the obstacle in your life will be absorbed by the universe and transmuted into positive energy. In the air, draw the sign of the equal-armed cross to seal the spell. Mix the ashes with the petals of a red rose. Scatter the mixture. Inside, light a white candle, asking Spirit to bring purification and cleansing into your life.

Taurus Energy Spell

FAVORABLE TIMING: Friday, Venus hour, sun in Taurus, or moon in Taurus.

FOCUS: Staying power is the glittering aspect of Taurus energy, with the ultimate target of peace and serenity. Taurus builds while erecting a formidable front. If you feel that change is not in your game plan, Taurus energy can stop any force that may desire to place you in a compromising posture. Finally, if persistence is necessary to get the job done, Taurus stamina can facilitate the process.

SPELL: Place the following in a deep-blue envelope: 7 dried daisy petals; a gold ribbon, 13 inches long, with a knot on each end, tied firmly around one iron nail; and one teaspoon of fertile earth. Seal the envelope with gold wax imprinted with your fingerprint. On the outside of the envelope, draw the astrological symbol of Venus (♀) and the symbol of Taurus (♉). Hold your hands over the envelope and ask Spirit to assist you in this situation. Be clear on your intentions and needs. Seal the spell by kissing the envelope. Bury the envelope in your back yard. If you live in an apartment or condominium, place the envelope at the bottom of a flower pot and cover with potting soil.

Gemini Energy Spell

FAVORABLE TIMING: Wednesday, Mercury hour, moon in Gemini, or sun in Gemini.

FOCUS: Lightning-quick and excellent in all manner of communication, Gemini energy surges forward, finding simple solutions to the most complicated problems. Gemini dynamism can also bring communication from the dead or add speed to any spell.

SPELL: *Silver's Mercury Powder.* You can use this magickal powder by itself, or add the powder to other forms of magick (for example, loading ⅛ teaspoon into the bottom of a candle). In a bowl, mix the following with a pestle: dried white rose petals, silver glitter, blue powder, dried vervain, ginger, and dried, crushed orris root. With your finger or a pencil, draw the symbol of Mercury (☿) and the symbol of Gemini (♊) in the powder. Hold your hands over the powder, asking that the mixture be instilled with the dynamic energies of Gemini. Store the powder in a plastic bag that contains a moonstone. For quick information, go outside, facing east. Place a teaspoon of the Mercury powder in the palm of your hand, then blow off your fingers, asking the element of air to speed your request and return the necessary details to you as quickly as possible.

Cancer Energy Spell

FAVORABLE TIMING: Monday, moon hour, sun in Cancer, moon in Cancer, full moon.

FOCUS: Home and hearth are the primary concentrations of Cancer energy. Fiercely protective, loyal, helpful, and creative, Cancer activity revolves around meeting one's needs. If something requires rebuilding, call on Cancer. If you are on a quest to amass resources, Cancer, the packrat of the universe, will do this nicely. Finally, if you are looking for privacy, use the Cancer vibrations as a protective device.

SPELL: One bowl of water; 3 jade stones, 13 new dimes. Empower the bowl of water under the full moon. If you can, capture the reflection of the moon in the water for at least thirty minutes. Slowly drop each dime in the water, making your intention clear. Wait until the water stills. Drop another dime. Complete the process until you use all the dimes. Hold your hands over the bowl and repeat your request. In the air over the bowl, draw the sigil for the moon (☽) and the sigil for Cancer (♋). Take the three stones and the thirteen dimes and place them in a green conjuring bag. Keep the bag with you until the request manifests. Sprinkle the water at the threshold of all doors leading to the outside, repeating your petition.

Leo Energy Spell

FAVORABLE TIMING: Sunday, sun hour, moon in Leo, sun in Leo, or Noon.

FOCUS: In astrology, to find the will of any individual we look to the house where the sun resides. The sun is like a giant battery in the sky, and anything this warm, heavenly body touches in your horoscope receives a giant boost of energy, sort of like feeding a barrel of soda pop to a bunch of kids at a birthday party—the zap quo-

tient will be way over the limit. Leo energy focuses on unconditional love, drama, creativity, and children. Having fun is also a Leo thing!

SPELL: Use the following Sunshine Spell to help with motivation, dancing with the muses, dealing with children, giving the gift of unconditional love, or just wanting to shine, shine, shine at your job. Find an old CD that you no longer wish to play. Place in the center of gold foil or old gold Christmas wrapping paper. Make sure CD rests on the back of the paper. Over the CD, sprinkle the following mixture: dried, crushed sunflower or marigold petals; yellow powder; gold glitter; dried orange peel; and the herb yellow dock. With your finger or a pencil, write the symbols of the sun (☉) and Leo (♌) in the mixture. Carry the foil, CD, and mixture carefully to where it will be covered in strong sunlight. Hold your hands over your supplies and state your petition clearly. Allow the sun to shine on your project for at least thirty minutes, then slowly fold the gold foil over the CD and magickal powder. Secure edges with tape. On a gold candle, mark your name and the sigils of the sun and Leo. Place the candle on the gold foil CD and allow candle to burn completely. Reaffirm your petition throughout the day as you gaze at the candle for a few moments. Put the CD in the area where you wish to shine, such as your office, work room, your vehicle, lunch bag, backpack, etc.

Virgo Energy Spell

FAVORABLE TIMING: Wednesday, Mercury hour, sun in Virgo, or moon in Virgo.

FOCUS: Virgo is the happy helper of the zodiac. The ultimate "fixer," Virgo uses the ability to discern and analyze any situation. "Let me make it better" is the Virgo anthem. If you need assistance in making a list, creating an agenda, or plotting out any project, Virgo energy, directed by its ruling planet of Mercury, is what you need to call.

SPELL: When the rest of the gods and goddesses hightailed it up to Mount Olympus, only one young heavenly beauty had the nuggets to stick around and help out humankind, thus earning her place in the zodiac ring of fame. When things get bogged down and you've lost your way, count on Virgo energy to save the day! Dig around in your desk drawers to find an unused check register. On the first page, list your ancestors. On the next page, write the current date in the "date" column. State your dilemma in the "description of transaction" line. Under the balance column write your hoped-for solution. There isn't much room, so you will have to be succinct. On the front of the transaction register, draw the symbol for Mercury (☿) and the symbol for Virgo (♍). Wrap a rubber band around the register and snap three times, while repeating affirmations you have written designed to bring your desire to you. Ask Spirit or your guardian angel for assistance. Each day, write down the mundane steps you have taken to solve the problem. In the balance column, repeat the same keyword you used for the solution. If you do additional magick, record that action as well, again using the same keyword under the balance section. Remember to wrap the rubber band around the register when you are finished, and snap the band three times, repeating your affirmations. When your desire has manifested, you have two choices: bury the register in your back yard, or turn to a new page and work a new spell, using the same method.

Libra Energy Spell

FAVORABLE TIMING: Friday, Venus hour, moon in Libra, or sun in Libra.

FOCUS: If you wish to restore balance, bring harmony into the home or workplace, or become charming in any social situation, turn your thoughts and energies into pulling Libra dynamics into your life. Well mannered, with a sense of fairness, wise use of personal integrity, and the ability to synthesize almost any situation or dilemma—all these characteristics are a part of Libra charm. Need to be persuasive? Turn on the Libra light.

SPELL: Canvas and paints, or paper and finger paints, or watercolor paper and watercolors are the focus of this spell. First, paint the symbol of Venus (♀) and Libra (♎) on the canvas or paper. These symbols can be the focal point, or used as a smaller part of your overall design. Play your favorite music, something that you think speaks to you about the situation at hand or the talent you wish to cultivate. Spend as much time working on the painting as you like. The idea is not to perfectly represent the desire, but to imbue the canvas with the emotions that you would like to create in your life. If you begin to worry or allow your mind to wander into a negative thought pattern, stop. Come back to the work when you have cleansed those impure emotions from your mind. Burning a pleasing incense while painting also helps to keep a positive, upbeat focus. Add spirals that begin from the outside, circling into the center of the canvas, while concentrating on pulling toward you the energies that you desire. When you are finished with the painting, hold your hands over the work and empower by sharing with Spirit, as clearly as possible, your need. Seal the painting by drawing an equal-armed cross in the air over the painting. Use the painting as an altar decoration while working other magicks for the same purpose.

Scorpio Energy Spell

FAVORABLE TIMING: Tuesday or Saturday, hour of Mars or Saturn, moon in Scorpio, dark of the moon, or sun in Scorpio.

FOCUS: Looking for strategic advancement or need to add that extra intensity punch? Scorpio energy will provide the depth of experience and bring the opportunities you desire. Scorpio energy brings power, influence, and long-term alliance. Above all other signs, Scorpio is the crisis breaker!

SPELL: Although Scorpio is a water sign, it carries the energy of the fire down below. Fill an old cooking pot with water (the bigger the problem, the more water). Add 3 pieces of jet; ½ teaspoon angelica; ½ teaspoon elder tree leaves; and one teaspoon lemon juice. On a piece of paper, outline the problem and the resolution needed. Draw the sigils for Pluto (♇) and Scorpio (♏) over the pot. Add to the top and bottom of your paper. Fold the paper into a small triangle. Bring mixture to a boil. Add paper triangle, visualizing a positive outcome. Boil dry. (Be careful, and watch the pot closely so you don't create an accident or hazard.) Turn off the burner. Allow pot to cool. Scrape contents into a bowl. Empty bowl at a crossroads at midnight.

Sagittarius Energy Spell

FAVORABLE TIMING: Thursday, hour of Jupiter, moon in Sagittarius, sun in Sagittarius, or new moon.

FOCUS: Expansion. Need a promotion, to learn more, or to take a cruise? Got a legal problem, desire assistance in those college exams, or wish to teach others something you know best? Enter Sagittarius! If you need to see the BIG picture, then this is the energy for you!

FOCUS: Pop one bag of unbuttered popcorn. As the kernels expand, think of the opportunities you wish to draw toward you. String popcorn and holly leaves on sturdy thread. The longer the garland, the better. As you string each piece, concentrate on your desire. Knot the thread to finish the garland, stating your intention aloud. Hold your hands over your project, again thinking of your intention. Make the sign of Jupiter (♃) and the sign of Sagittarius (♐) in the air over your work. Place the garland on your altar until your wish has been granted. Then burn the garland outside, thanking Spirit for the gifts you have received. *Note:* You can also hang the garland on your Yule tree, or over a doorway, for the holiday season.

Capricorn Energy Spell

FAVORABLE TIMING: Saturday, Saturn hour, sun in Capricorn, or moon in Capricorn.

FOCUS: The primary energy of Capricorn is that of building anything, and of doing the process extremely well. If boundaries need to be set, rules must be followed, or a concise plan of action laid as a sturdy foundation, invite the energy of Capricorn into your life.

SPELL: For this spell you will need an 8½ x 11 piece of graph paper and a pencil or pen. At the top of the paper (or on the back), write as specifically as you can what it is that you wish to build, the boundaries that must be set, or the foundation that you need. Follow by the symbols of Saturn (♄) and Capricorn (♑). On the back of the paper, write a list of your ancestors (because they are the foundation of you). Each day, fill in one line of boxes by coloring them in (with colored pencils if you like, or just the pencil). Burn your favorite incense while working. Repeat your intentions mentally or aloud as you work on the paper. After you complete each line, fold the paper into a square and place under a salt shaker (the foundation of life) that contains salt and dirt (preferably dirt from an ancestor's grave). When your desire manifests (even if you don't have all the lines filled in), bury the paper, the salt, and the dirt in your back yard.

Aquarius Energy Spell

FAVORABLE TIMING: Wednesday, hour of Mercury, sun in Aquarius, or moon in Aquarius.

FOCUS: Need to be wild, crazy, or avant-garde? Do you require commitment? Are you seeking freedom? Turn to Aquarius energy!

SPELL: You will need 13 ribbons (your choice of color); a bag of buttons; and a needle and thread. This spell takes some time to create, but the results are well worth the work. Set your intention clearly in your mind. Sew as many buttons as you can onto each piece of ribbon, saving about two inches at the top of each ribbon. As you sew each button, clearly state your intention. You may wish to put on your favorite inspirational music while you work. When you have finished with all the ribbons, tie them together at the top (or sew them firmly together). Hold your hands over your work, again stating your intention. Make the sign of Uranus (♅) and Aquarius (♒) in the air over the project. Take the ribbon spell outside and hang from a tree in your back yard, or from a porch railing, etc.— you choose the place. Again, state your intention aloud, and say:

> From heaven to Earth, from Earth to heaven,
> the winds circle about my desire, carrying my
> thoughts to the gods of the universe and returning
> with the gift of positive abundance. So mote it be.

Allow the project to hang outside until your wish has been granted. *Warning:* Uranus works with shocks, surprises, and sudden upsets. If you use this energy, be prepared for the unknown and be willing to accept positive change.

Pisces Energy Spell

FAVORABLE TIMING: Monday, hour of the moon, moon in Pisces, sun in Pisces, or full moon.

FOCUS: Passionate Pisces helps us to step out of the daily hum-drum and into a kaleidoscope of visions, dreams, and psychic pursuits.

SPELL: Place a dry sponge in a bowl. Mix patchouli oil and water in a separate, resealable container. Consider carefully how you want to use the energy of Pisces. Prophetic dreams? Visions in meditation? Learning to be compassionate to those less fortunate than yourself? Write one statement on a three-by-five-inch card that announces your intention. Place the card underneath the bowl. Slowly pour the patchouli water over the sponge, and say: "Like this sponge, I will soak up (state your intention)." Place a white rose on top of the sponge. Again, state your intention aloud. Hold your hands over the rose, breathing deeply, mentally touching the unconditional love of the universe. When you are finished, draw the sigil of Neptune (♆) and Pisces (♓) over the flower and bowl. After one week, wring out the sponge and offer the rose to free-flowing water. Repeat this spell once a week until you have reached your desire.

Purification Spell for Air Signs

If you need to get a message through to someone, move an issue that seems stuck, garner some added intelligence into decision making, or well-wish a friend health and happiness, air energy can push your spellwork to a speedy conclusion. You can use the following incantation for area purification, to cleanse and bless supplies, or to invoke air energy into your magick circle. For an extra bit of punch, carve the air signs of the zodiac (Gemini, Libra, and Aquarius) onto the candle color of your choice and burn during ritual or spellcasting, asking for assistance from the element of air.

> *Air flows pure, Spirit unbound.*
> *Inspiration! Sky to ground!*
> *Realize love with this sound.*

Ring bell seven times.

Purification Spell for Fire Signs

From inspiration to passion, fire energy can certainly excite your magickal work. After lighting any candle, needfire, balefire, bonfire, or hearth, you might try this easy incantation.

> *Fire makes the magick go.*
> *Inner peace begins to flow.*
> *Rise, O flame, and purify.*
> *Enchant this place, ground to sky.*

For added oomph to your magickal work, draw the sigils for Leo, Sagittarius, and Aries on pot, cauldron, or candle, or in the dirt at the south quarter of your circle. If you choose to boil a liquid in the pot, add the symbol for Scorpio (the "fire down below"). If you are really in an artsy mood, draw a salamander along with your other chosen sigils. Herbs and incenses placed on the prepared fire will add a puff of scent when lit, or you can wait and throw your herbal mixture into the fire at the peak of your spell or ritual. Vesta powder (be careful with this) will provide a mini explosion, colored flames, and interesting smoke effects when tossed onto a blazing fire (do not use on candles—I blew up my dining room table trying that one). Pumpkin spice will make the flames glitter and produce a pleasing aroma.

Purification Spell for Earth Signs

This little incantation has a variety of uses, especially for the magickal person who's constantly on the go. Repeat in the subway station (no kidding, it works), while relaxing in the park and feeding the squirrels, when walking down a dark street at night (remember next time to walk with a friend), when entering an unfamiliar place that makes you feel nervous, or to create sacred space for magickal work.

> *Earth to earth*
> *angels to ancestors*
> *riches to riches*
> *treasure to treasure*
> *hearth to hearth, bring blessings*
> *of the Mother upon me, Earth.*

Carve the zodiac symbols that relate to the Earth element (Taurus, Virgo, Capricorn) onto the candle color of your choice to add extra pizzazz to your magickal work, or mix up an earth powder that can include soil, salt, and a variety of herbs. Use in conjuring bags, as an outside purification powder at the entrance of your home or apartment, or load a small amount into your earth element candle.

Purification Spell for Water Signs

The incantation below is a purification protection spell that you can use as a part of a larger working, or alone when swimming, walking in the rain, boating, etc. It can also be used in preparing for the birth of a baby, or during the birthing process. If necessary, use the incantation as a drought buster.

> *Water protects the embryo*
> *ancestor love of long ago.*
> *Tides and rivers dance and flow*
> *enchant this place, let magick grow.*
> *Revive! Bring change! I make it so.*

For added water energy in a magickal working, carve the zodiac symbols of Cancer, Pisces, and Scorpio on the candle color of your choice. Stand candle in one-half inch of water for additional empowerment.

Astrological Sign Incenses

Use the following incense recipes for astrological sign spellwork, including the moon in the signs. *Note:* Mix the dry ingredients first, then add the oil sparingly. This allows you to experiment with the consistency of the incense.

ARIES

Mix equal parts of: Angelica, cedar, ginseng, basil, pine.

Oil: Cedar oil.

TAURUS

Mix equal parts of: Horehound, mugwort, oleander, vervain.

Oil: Vervain oil.

GEMINI

Mix equal parts of: Eyebright, hops, lemongrass, sage.

Oil: Rosemary oil.

CANCER

Mix equal parts of: Chamomile, feverfew, heather, myrrh.

Oil: Myrrh oil.

LEO

Mix equal parts of: Orange peel, galangal, rue, goldenseal.

Oil: Cinnamon oil.

VIRGO

Mix equal parts of: Bergamot, fennel, summer savory, mint.

Oil: Rose oil.

LIBRA

Mix equal parts of: Clover, benzoin, lavender, spearmint.

Oil: Lavender oil.

SCORPIO

Mix equal parts of: Sandalwood, boneset, coltsfoot, thyme.

Oil: Sandalwood oil.

SAGITTARIUS

Mix equal parts of: Cinquefoil, sage, nutmeg, betony wood.

Oil: Musk oil.

CAPRICORN

Mix equal parts of: Mullein, patchouli, comfrey, Solomon's seal.

Oil: Patchouli oil.

AQUARIUS

Mix equal parts of: Fenugreek, pine, broom, clover.

Oil: Pine oil.

PISCES

Mix equal parts of: Lemon balm, elder, lemon peel, orris root.

Oil: Lemon oil.

Decanates in Magick

Decans or decanates are another way to divide each zodiac sign. Each division in each sign consists of three parts. Each zodiac sign is thirty degrees, and each decan in that sign is ten degrees. The first ten degrees of any sign are said to carry the "nature" of that sign, and are the planetary ruler of the sign. For example, the first decanate in Aries behaves with Aries energy. The planet Mars is the planetary ruler of Aries, therefore Mars would be the ruler of the first decanate of

Aries. The next ten degrees (11 through 20) are said to have the nature of the next sign that shares the same element, which in this case would be Leo. The planetary ruler of that decanate (or decan) would be the sun. The last ten degrees, 21 through 30, are thought to carry the qualities of the last sign of the same element. The fire sign that falls before Aries is Sagittarius, and the planetary ruler would be Jupiter. The thing to remember with decanates is that they always represent only one element. As there are only three signs in each element, those three signs will always be used, though their location (decanate, in this case) will differ within the sign. Finally, although the rulers of the decanates are important, the second two—covering degrees 20 through 30—are thought to be "secondary" rulers, with the sign ruler always prominent. See chart, above right, which also includes the mansions of the moon.

There are various ways in which decanate divisions can be used in spellwork. For example, let's say the moon will be new in Aries in the second decanate. We know this because we've looked at our almanac and have checked the timing and position of the new moon. The primary planetary ruler of Aries is Mars. The second decanate is ruled by the sun; therefore, we can use both Mars and sun energies for that extra wallop of power. Even better, a new moon means that the sun and moon are dancing cheek to cheek, so this gives the sun an added extra energy bonus. You can choose the wording of chants and charms as well as the colors, herbs, incenses, and other correspondences to assist in melding sun, moon, Mars, and Aries energy in the way that you desire. Since the moon is categorized as falling in a water element (and we want to make her happy), it might be a good idea to check the lunar mansion in which she will fall at the moment of your working (SEE

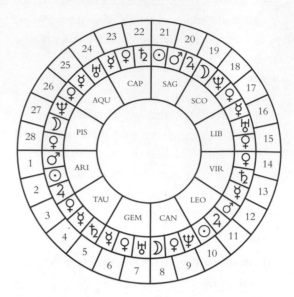

Zodiac signs, decanate rulers, lunar mansion number and placement.

LUNAR MANSIONS, PAGE 301). In this case it will be the second lunar mansion, Alka-tayn, who presides over finding hidden treasure, wheat production, strengthening prisons, removing anger, and capturing people or things. Here is where we use our creative inspiration. Which, if any, of these categories can be associated with our goal, and how will that association be made in our statement of intent? Granted, this is a little more work; however, once you get through the basics of spellcasting and ritual and begin to face boredom (it happens), techniques such as these can keep your practices in religion and magick fresh and active.

Basic Astrological Glossary

Below you will find a very basic astrological glossary, covering a variety of terms you may see in astrology and astrological magick. This dictionary is by no means complete and is provided only as a beginner's guideline.

Afflicted: When a planet sends or receives negative dialog from another planet. Typical afflictions include squares and oppositions.

Air Signs: Gemini, Libra, and Aquarius are the three signs of the zodiac attributed to the qualities of the element of air. Also known as the air triplicity.

Angles: The four angles of any astrological chart are the ascendant, the descendant, the midheaven, and the I.C. or *immum coeli*.

Angular Houses: The first, fourth, seventh, and tenth houses in a horoscope. When a planet passes over one of these mythical lines, stuff happens in your life that you didn't necessarily expect or were waiting for.

Applying and application: Used when describing aspects. An applying aspect is a window of time that begins when a planet reaches a certain distance from another planet, which will eventually (depending upon the speeds of the planets) create a geometric pattern, most commonly called an angle. This window lasts until the geometric pattern becomes mathematically "exact." Once the distance between the two planets is exact, the continued movement of the planets away from the geometric pattern (or angle) is called a separating aspect.

Arabic parts: Imaginary points on an astrological chart used during the Middle Ages by Arabic astrologers and calculated from the positions of the planets according to specific mathematical formulas. The Part of Fortune (PF) is the most common point seen in today's charts.

Aspect: When planets are at certain angles from each other, the planetary energies interact depending upon the nature of the planet, the angle, and the speed at which each planet is moving. These critical angles are called aspects. Each aspect has a name and common attributes. Traditional astrology commonly uses the Ptolemaic set of aspects; however, there can be hundreds of angles, depending on what astrological system you use.

Ascendant: First sign to rise on the left-hand side of a zodiac chart, usually associated with the first house; 180 degrees or opposite the descendant.

Asteroid: A heavenly body that is smaller than a planet and is encompassed in the sun's orbit. Usually found in bands and often consisting of rocks and frozen ice. The most common asteroids used in magick are Ceres, Juno, Pallas, and Vesta, and each is attributed to a particular goddess energy.

Juno: Roman wife of the God Jupiter associated with magick done for marriage, commitment, and relationships.

Ceres: Associated with the descent of the Goddess; caring, nurturing, maternal, and protective.

Pallas: From Pallas Athena, the goddess of wisdom, war, and accomplishment; creativity, using one's talents, studying, and so on.

Vesta: Roman goddess of hearth and home, and used in magick in relationship to these subjects as well as discipline and effort in completing tasks.

Astrology: "Speech of the stars," derived from the Greek word *astron*, meaning "star," and *logos*, which means "discourse" or "speech." The study of the energy influence of heavenly bodies on any behavior, activity, or condition on people, places, and things.

Birth chart: A figurative snapshot diagram of the heavens taken at the exact point in time when you were born. The diagram is usually circular (although the charts of the Middle Ages were shaped like boxes) and shows the position of the sun, moon, planets, zodiac signs, and other goodies (depending on the choices of the astrologer).

Burning Way: This is another old axiom, but I've found it incredibly useful in magick. Supposedly, if any planet falls between 15 degrees Libra and 15 degrees Scorpio, it has entered the Burning Way and trouble is afoot. However, I've discovered that if the planet in that position is in your favor, either natally or by a horary or electional chart, then you will be the winner against all odds. This is especially true with the planet Mars.

Cadent houses: The second, fifth, eighth, and eleventh houses.

Cardinal signs: Aries, Cancer, Libra, and Capricorn. These signs usher in the equinoxes and solstices, and are therefore seen as "starter" energies. All four elements are represented: Aries = fire; Cancer = water, Libra = air and Capricorn = earth.

Chaldean order: Ancient lineup of the planets, beginning with Saturn, Jupiter, Mars, sun, Venus, Mercury, and the moon. You will see this order when working with planetary hours.

Constellation: A group of stars located in the same section of the heavens. Usually associated with a mythical animal, person, or circumstance.

Culminating: An ancient term for reaching the midheaven in an astrological chart.

Cusp: The degree at the beginning of a house.

Day and night charts: The ancient astrologers concluded that the planets behaved differently depending on a day or night placement. It was believed that some powers of the planets were available only at certain times of the day or night.

Decan/decanate: The division of a zodiac sign into three parts. Each zodiac sign is 30 degrees, and each decan in that sign is 10 degrees. The first ten degrees of any sign are said to carry the nature of that sign. The thing to remember with decanates is that they always represent only one element. As there are only three signs in each element, those three signs will always be used, though their location (decanate, in this case), will differ within the sign.

Degree: A degree is $\frac{1}{360}$ of a circle. Each degree is divided into 60 minutes and each minute is divided into 60 seconds. The time it takes a planet to move from degree to degree around the circle is the main timing mechanism used in astrology and the magicks associated with it. Degrees are also used as addresses when locating where a planet is at any given time.

Descendant: Seventh sign from the first, located on the right of the zodiac chart, usually associated with the seventh house; 180 degrees, or opposite the ascendant.

Detriment: One of the planetary dignities. A planet is considered in its detriment when it is in the sign opposite the one that it rules. For example, the moon is in its detriment when in the sign of Leo; therefore, the moon in Leo is not as strong as you might first think. The best time to do planetary magick is when the planet is either in its ruling sign, or when it is in a sign where it is exalted. The moon, by the way, is exalted in Taurus (SEE TABLE ON PAGE 215).

Earth signs: Taurus, Virgo, and Capricorn are the signs associated with the element of earth, and are thought to have the qualities of that element. Also called the earth triplicity. (There are, by the way, day triplicities and night triplicities, but these are only used in classical astrology.)

Eclipse: The blocking of light from one heavenly body by another heavenly body. Eclipses of the sun and moon figure prominently in magickal applications. A lunar eclipse is said to affect situations for approximately six weeks, where an eclipse of the sun is said to last for six months.

Ecliptic: The yearly path of the sun in the heavens through the zodiac, divided into twelve equal divisions of 30 degrees, giving a grand total of 360 degrees.

Electional astrology: Studying various charts to determine the best day and time possible to enact an event, such as a wedding.

Ephemeris: A book of tables that shows the positions of the planets at any given time.

Essential dignity: There are five essential dignities. These dignities rely on the location of the planet in any given chart. The five dignities that are location dependent are rulership, exaltation, triplicity, term, and face. Although modern astrologers have thrown much of this out, magickal astrologers are learning that these old expressions of energy can be very helpful in predictive work. If you plan to study classical, horary, or event-driven (electional) astrology, you will learn to acknowledge the dignities.

Fire signs: Aries, Leo, and Sagittarius are the zodiac signs associated with the element of fire, and are thought to have the qualities of that element. Also called the fire triplicity.

Fixed signs: These are the stubborn ones: Taurus, Leo, and Aquarius. Magick done in a fixed sign, or using a planet that is currently in a fixed sign, will "set" the magick and give you long-term results.

Fixed star: A star that is so far away in the heavens that it appears to stand still and becomes a fixed position on any chart. Aspects to fixed stars tell you amazing nuances for magickal workings and even more so if you plan to go into predictive work. And don't let them fool you—conjunctions aren't just what it's all about. If you are really serious about the study, all the Ptolemaic aspects are important.

Geocentric: As viewed from the Earth's surface (or, to be precise, from the center of the Earth). Most astrologers use geocentric astrology, which is why astronomers think we're nuts.

Glyphs: Written symbols of the signs, planets, and aspects. (SEE TABLE ON PAGE 199.)

Horary astrology: The study of an astrological chart based on the time of a question. Horary has its own rules and relies on classical astrology, although modern interpretations are sometimes used.

House systems: There are a bunch of these and astrologers are always fussing over which is the right one to use. A house system primarily dithers over where the cusp lines fall—some are equal house systems (where the degrees always equal 30) and some are unequal. I'm not even going to venture to tell you which one to use.

I.C.: An abbreviation for the words *immum coeli*, a Latin term meaning "the lowest part of the heavens" (in this case it is the lowest point on any astrological house, and follows the fourth house cusp line).

Ingress: The entry of a planet into a sign or a house; therefore, you will see house ingresses and sign ingresses.

M.C. (midheaven): The highest point of the heavens, located at the top of any astrological chart and usually on or close to the tenth house cusp.

Mundane astrology: A branch of astrological study that interprets the charts of nations, eclipses, and solstices to monitor and analyze political events.

Mutable signs: Gemini, Virgo, and Sagittarius—these signs can move with the flow and interact with just about anyone on anything.

Nodes of the moon: There are two, the north node and the south node, sometimes called the Dragon's Head and Dragon's Tail, respectively. These are the points on the chart where the path of the moon crosses the ecliptic.

Orb/orb of influence: The range of degrees within which an aspect is considered to have an effect. Orbs differ by aspect and by the choice of the astrologer.

Stellium (satellitium): A grouping of three or more planets in a sign that are carrying on a conversation (meaning they are in aspect). Very useful for combining energies in magickal applications.

Succedent houses: Third, sixth, ninth, and twelfth.

Transits: The changing positions of the planets as they move through the signs of the zodiac. Transits influence planets and points in any type of chart and can trigger events. However, a single transit alone rarely triggers any situation. Conversely, single transits work quite well for planning magickal applications.

Zodiac: Means "little zoo," a small band of the sky about 8 degrees on either side of the ecliptic, which contains most of the motions of the planets.

Astrological Websites

Astrodienst Online (includes fixed stars): http://www.astro.ch/atlas

Astrolabe (free birth chart with small interpretation): http://www.alabe.com

Astrologer Alphee Lavoie: http://www.alphee.com

Astrology World (beginner and advanced material): http://www.astrology-world.com/ast_wrld.html

Astrology Zone (site of Susan Miller): http://www.astrologyzone.go.com

Astrology.com (at iVillage, geared for beginners): http://www.astrology.com

Astrology.net (free chart and brief explanation): http://www.astrology.net

Debbi Kempton-Smith, author: http://www.topquarkia.com

EasyScopes (lists all of the daily, weekly, monthly and yearly horoscopes on the web): http://www.easyscopes.com

http://www.astronet.com

http://www.pathfinder.com/twep/astrology

http://www.planetstarz.com

Night Light News (Tradition of Alice Bailey): http://www.nighlight.news

Planet Waves: http://www.PlanetWaves.net

Starcats: http://www.starcats.com

The Mountain Astrologer Magazine: http://www.MountainAstrologer.com

The Zodiac Master (hows and whys of astrology): http://www.thezodiac.com

University Centre for Astrological Research: http://cura.free.fr/

Zodiac Gazette (monthly magazine and news events): http://www.starflash.com/zodiac

Zodiacal Zephyr (lots of information and free chart generation): http://www.zodiacal.com/

Recommended Reading

A Star Gazer's Notebook by Debbi Kempton-Smith

A Time for Magick by Mara Kay Simms

Astrology for the Light Side of the Brain by Kim Rogers-Gallagher

Astrology for the Light Side of the Future by Kim Rogers-Gallagher

Easy Astrology Guide by Maritha Pottenger

KISS Guide to Astrology by Julia and Derek Parker

The Only Way to Learn Astrology (series of five books) by Marion D. March and Joan McEvers

The Witches' Circle by Maria Kay Simms

Please note that the moon in the signs and the elements are covered under their own sections in this book, in Part III and Part IV, respectively.

Aura

Scientists agree that every person has a rainbow-like energy field that pulses around his or her physical body, called an aura.[25] The aura is a measurable electromagnetic field close to your skin that can, depending upon your emotions and the state of your health, reach as far from the body as thirty feet.[26] The aura is made up of six layers, including the etheric body, astral body, lower mental body, higher mental body, spiritual body, and the casual body. In essence, you always wear a coat of many colors made of out light! Between the top of your head and the base of your spine, there is an electrical potential of around 400 volts, which is part of the body's electromagnetic field or aura.[27] However, when viewing auras, most people only see two levels, the etheric body and the astral body, which often blend together without a specific dividing line.

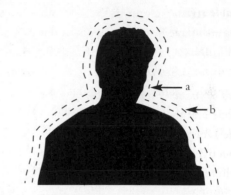

The etheric (a) and the astral (b) bodies.

Most pictures of the aura show an egg shape of light surrounding the human figure, though when you actually view someone's aura it might be lopsided or even be in a geometric shape. If you draw a stick figure on a piece of paper and encircle it with a big bubble, you've just drawn a simple representation of your aura. Your aura is linked to your physical self by the seven energy vortexes of the body, called chakras (SEE PAGE 239). Some people believe that the aura is a light manifestation of the soul. Always remember that the aura is considered an extension of the physical body, not something separate from your physical body, and that your energy field permeates your whole being. Body, mind, and spirit represent the "complete" you.

The layers of your aura send messages to your brain all the time. Have you ever stood close to a stranger and, even though he or she looks okay (doesn't growl or drool), you get a weird sensation—like something's not right? Your internal warning system is giving you a red alert, and the red alert comes from disturbances in your electromagnetic field. People call this feeling "instinct" or a "gut response." Sometimes our conscious mind overrides what we are feeling, and we sort of yell at ourselves for being stupid, then later we find that we should have listened to our internal warning system in the first place! How many times have you heard your mom or dad, or a friend, say, "I never liked that guy/girl anyway. I knew he/she was going to be trouble from the start!" They are saying this because they had that feeling, too, even if they didn't voice it out loud. If your aura is disturbed, and you are getting that funny feeling, pay attention! Your aura can combine with another person's (this is especially seen in couples who have been happily married for many years) or can repel each other (that feeling you get when you just don't like someone, but you don't know why).

It is important for the magickal student to understand the energy connections we have to other people. For example, if you have left a job through unfortunate circumstances, or a boyfriend or girlfriend has treated you badly and you walked away, you need to do a complete clearing on your own body, cutting away any tendrils of energy left attached to you by your length of association with that person. Some Craft groups do a monthly cleansing where the four elements are passed over the body, followed by a sword or athame to symbolically cut the negative attachments that others might have to you.

You will be surprised at how much information you can pick up about someone simply by being in their auric field (or they being in yours), especially as your skill in the Craft and spirituality grows. If someone says to you, "Oh, Sally's okay," and you're getting that "No, she's not" message in your head, listen to yourself. People also have what is called "charisma," which somehow makes them subconsciously glitter, yet charisma doesn't mean they are a good person, it means that they know how to manipulate situations (by accident or design) as well as people. Con artists have a lot of charisma, which is why they get away with so much. Through smiles, actions, and behavior, they try to override your internal warning system and confuse your conscious mind into thinking that you are just being silly. The longer you work with magick, energy, and ritual, the more you'll learn to trust your feelings on any person or issue.

The aura, energy work, meditation, breathing exercises, visualization, and the chakras all play an important part in magickal and spiritual studies. These categories were combined into the Mysteries, and with daily practice led the student to spiritual enlightenment and hopefully their version of the philosopher's stone (SEE PART IV, ALCHEMY). By practicing the mysteries every day, spirituality begins to flow through every part of your life in a happy, pleasing way. Things that would normally stress you out aren't such a big deal anymore. You are able to perform better in your schoolwork, as well as in athletic events, and things you like to do just for fun seem even better! The arts, such as music, painting, photography, and dance, seem to find new and exciting ways of expression in your hands.

I have only one gentle reminder. When we first begin using these spiritual techniques, they are lots of fun and we normally have fast results. The problem comes when we forget to do them because we are so busy with our lives. One day might move into the next, and then you find it has been six weeks or even six months since you've done any of your exercises (breathing, visualization, or other energy work). Maybe you do the occasional spell or ritual, but other than that there's exams, and dates, and work—you know how it is. Then one day we realize that we are really stressed out, majorly cranky, and things aren't going the way we want them to—that's when you go back to the exercises and you'll say to yourself, "Geez, I should have known better. No wonder things feel out of whack." Don't worry, we all do it; even people who think they are adepts at magickal work sometimes forget. If that happens, it's no big deal. Just bring the exercises back into your life.

Strengthening Your Auric Senses Exercise

Lie down and relax. Close your eyes. In your mind, imagine your aura moving all the way out to the edges of the room; now slowly bring it back. You can imagine the aura as light, or bands of color—it doesn't matter. Some people have a hard time imagining things, so if this is you, don't fret, work on "feeling" instead. Do this ten times. Now imagine that your aura only goes halfway across the room; bring it back. Repeat ten times. Finally, imagine that your aura is compacted to three inches from your skin, like a tight shield that nothing can ever get through (sort of like a force field). Pull it back. Practice this ten times. Do this every day for one month. Write down the changes in daily life that you experience as a result. For extra practice, do the exercise twice a day. If you are a person that can go the long haul, keep up the exercise for six months.

How to See Auras

You already naturally sense the energy fields of other people (plants and animals have them too). The next step is to try to see this field with your eyes. This isn't as hard as it sounds. In fact, you have probably already seen auras and thought that they were a trick of the light, or that your eyes weren't adjusting as quickly as they should to various types of lighting. When most people see auras, they view only two of the five listed, and these two seldom, if ever, are seen as separate bands around the body. Also, no two auras are ever alike—just as each person is an individual, so, too, each animal, plant, or human aura will be different.

In the following exercises, don't strain yourself to see auras. You really need to be relaxed and at ease. As I was writing this section, I had to take a break and visit my stockbroker—a very nice young fellow on the quiet side with penetrating blue eyes. As I sat across the desk I caught his aura out of my peripheral vision—it was blue and square (people that deal with numbers and like it often have this type of aura) and surrounded his head by at least eight inches. When he asked me what sort of books I wrote for a living, and I answered "On the occult—you name it, I study and write about it, fiction and nonfiction," his aura drastically reduced to a mere line around his head. The harder I tried to see his aura, the less I was able to see, and finally I gave up. My answer to his question definitely affected his internal response system, which in turn affected his aura. When I tried hard to see what was left, I lost the ability completely. The other problem with seeing auras occurs because you have to stare just above the person's head (or off to the side). This looks like you are staring at a giant bug that is about to descend on the subject's head, and they are going to wonder what the heck you are looking at. The longer I stared at my stockbroker, the more uncomfortable he became. Since it isn't nice to make people feel uncomfortable, I didn't look again.

Aura Exercise 1

Ask a friend to stand about eighteen inches to two feet in front of a white wall. Patterns or pictures on the wall will confuse your eyes, so make sure the surface is plain. If you don't have a white wall, you can paste a big piece of white paper behind your friend. The lighting in the room shouldn't be overly bright or pointed toward your companion. Although natural light is best, I've known quite a few people who have seen auras "by accident" while sitting in crowded conference rooms with fluorescent lighting.

Stand back about ten feet, directly in front of your friend. Tell them to relax and breathe normally, and ask that they move slowly from side to side (this will ensure that you're not just having "eye burn").[28] Now, look past the person's head and shoulders. Focus on the wall in back of them. As you stare at the wall, you will begin to notice a fuzzy outline around your friend. Sometimes it is white, or gray-silver, sort of like a bubble around the top of their head, sometimes around their entire head and shoulders. It looks sort of like a halo you see on religious paintings, except it has no firm outline and fluctuates. See, I told you that you've seen this before! Who hasn't stared at a teacher in class out of sheer boredom and seen the aura? This light almost looks like it is behind your friend. And, as fast as you saw it, it may disappear. That's because your eyes try to naturally focus on the person, rather than on the aura. As soon as you go back to looking at the wall, the aura will pop back into your field of vision. The hardest thing is to keep your eyes from trying to refocus. It may take a couple of times, or maybe several, until you can see that envelope of light for any length of time.

By now your friend has probably started to giggle, and his or her breathing speeds up; when this happens, the aura appears to shrink, which is why they need to stand still and breath normally, even deeply, while you practice looking at their aura. Now let them try!

Aura Exercise 2

This one is tougher and it may take you several days or weeks to actually see the colors. A few people never see them (but don't give up too soon) because they feel the colors rather than actually see them. Most people, however, can see auric colors if they practice long enough. Experts say that yellow or pink is usually the first color the student sees, and with continued practice, more colors become evident. For colors, natural lighting is the best, and fluorescent light is said to be the worst. Direct sunlight isn't very good, either, but candlelight, as long as you don't get confused by the shadows, can give excellent results.

For this exercise, set your friend by the wall the same way you did in exercise one. Concentrate on seeing the white/silvery outline first, then allow yourself to feel the color (sometimes this helps to see it). Have your friend rock from side to side, breathing deeply. Their aura will naturally move with them. Sometimes you'll see a ball of a particular color or even a line of light. Try not to will the colors into being. Take your time, breathe deeply, and eventually the colors will come.

Auric Exercise 3

Time to look at the auras of plants and animals. Most animals will not stay still unless they are sleeping, but plants will happily sit against the wall. Write down what you see and compare your notes with a friend. Some people find it easier to learn to see auras around plants and inanimate objects (yes, they have an aura, too) than people.

Auric Exercise 4

Practice seeing your own aura in a mirror or, even better, while you are sitting in a pleasantly scented bath. Rest your feet on the rim of the tub and gaze at them. The first sign of your aura might be a shimmering outline around your feet, sort of like rippling light. As you relax and watch your feet, you'll see the light begin to shimmer in various colors.

Sitting in a classroom situation, I've found, is the easiest way to practice seeing auras, especially if you are relaxed, as it's easier to get into the alpha state.

What the Colors Mean

If the aura is clear and strong, the person is healthy and happy. If the light is murky, then they are either not feeling well or may be having a bad time in life. Although I've provided the color chart below, please use it only as a general guideline. You'll learn what the colors you see mean to you after you practice.

Purple: Spiritual attainment, responsibility for others

Indigo: Wisdom, artistic talents

Blue: Intelligent, logical (too dark: suspicious)

Green: Balance, harmony; adaptable if clear and bright, but pea green indicates possible sickness and jealousy if a person is not well

Yellow: Love and kindness, creativity

Orange: Physical vitality, harmony, possibly too much pride (too dark: not extremely intelligent)

Red: Vitality, ambition, sexual power, leadership, the need to be in charge (too dark: anger, materialistic)

Pink: Selfless love, financial success, possibly stubborn

Brown: Selfish

Gold: Harmony, talent, unlimited potential

Silver: High energy, able to adapt easily, idealistic

Bronze: Humanitarian, generous

Gray: Unhappiness and low energy

Black: Evil

White: Illumination and inspiration

Most often, auras have a base color that is close to the body and radiates no more than one to three inches from the head and shoulder area. Although your aura encompasses your body, it is easiest to see around the head and shoulders. The base color might be mixed with another color, usually the next higher or lower color on the spectrum of light. When it comes to colors, there isn't a right or wrong one; brightness and clarity tell us how happy, peaceful, or healthy that person might be. The aura is by no means stable, and it changes all the time. Your aura can be affected by what you think, what you eat, and what you wear, as well as things outside of yourself, such as other people and animals.[29] The speed that a person's aura vibrates determines the color that we see. Purple, blue, and gold are the hardest colors to see because they vibrate faster than the others. Some people even see shapes in auras. With practice you will be able to see a variety of auras, colors, and geometric patterns.

Imprint Your Aura for Success

Let's face it, even though you studied your heart out this whole week, you just know you're going to fail that math test or history exam. And finals? Oh, please! How do they expect you to remember all that stuff? Many people do not fit into the test-taking mold. They freeze up, get nervous, maybe even have an upset stomach. I would study so hard that I could see the page the answer was on in my mind (including the pictures and the page number), but for the life of me I could not remember the answers to the questions. If you've studied, but have trouble taking tests, try this great exercise. Once you practice, and you've done the groundwork of studying the material (history, geography, finals, or college boards), you should never have trouble with a test again.

SUPPLIES: Your study materials and something you will be allowed to have with you (a crystal in your pocket, a favorite pencil, or a lucky shirt you can wear). Place the study material on the bed with you or under your chair.

ATMOSPHERE: Should be undisturbed (no siblings running in and out). Soft music is okay, but nothing that will draw your attention away from concentrating on the exercise. Some students prefer drumming tapes.

INSTRUCTIONS: Find a comfortable position. Hold your lucky item in your hand (although we know this exercise has nothing to do with luck and everything to do with training your mind). Close your eyes. Take three to five deep, even breaths (in through the nose, out through the mouth). As you inhale, think of pure white light entering your body. As you exhale, allow your worries and troubles to slip away from you. Count backward from ten to one. Now see yourself on the day of the test entering the examination room. If you can't see pictures in your mind, think of feeling relaxed and composed as you walk through the door and find your seat. See yourself taking the test, calm and relaxed, feeling happy that you know every answer. In your mind connect the lucky item with a 100 percent grade on that test. Move forward in time to the day when the teacher hands back the papers. See yourself smiling as you look at that fantastic grade. If you can visualize well, see the grade (100 percent or A+) and even a comment

written on the paper, like "Great job!" or "Excellent work!" Take another deep breath and open your eyes. Continue to study. On the day of the test, be sure to take your lucky item with you. If you start to panic during the test, or feel unsure of yourself, touch the lucky item, take a deep breath, and then continue. If you practice this exercise every time you study, you will be amazed at how much your grades will improve. What happens if you don't do so hot the first time? As much as you may groan (though this stuff is actually fun when you realize how much you can accomplish), practice makes perfect. The more you practice auric imprinting, the better you will get at it. You can also use this technique for just about anything you need, from healing to saving enough money to buy your favorite CD, your first car, or planning ahead for your career. Share this one with your parents, once they practice, too, they will be amazed at the difference in their lives.

Recommended Reading

Aura Reading for Beginners: Develop your Psychic Awareness for Health and Success by Richard Webster

Auras: See Them in Only 60 Seconds! by Mark Smith

Aura Energy for Health, Healing and Balance by Joe H. Slate, Ph.D.

Breathing

Stress will muck up magick faster than anything. If you are breathing under tension, your whole body resists the melding of mind, body, and spirit, and this can actually change the chemistry of your body. Likewise, tight clothing can restrict normal breathing patterns. If your belt cuts into your waist, you may breathe only from the upper area of your lungs. If your shirt confines your chest in an uncomfortable way, you may be forced to breathe from the middle part of your lungs. A robe, such as those used in magickal ceremonies, actually frees your body from breathing restrictions, which in turn might hamper ritual or other magickal applications, depending upon the theme.

Proper breathing brings oxygen to all areas of the body and ignites the energy centers, or chakras, with positive energy, which helps to reduce your level of stress. In occult philosophy, the breath is also associated with the Spirit of god/dess and is believed to be charged by the Earth's magnetic field. Therefore, when you breathe in and out, you are becoming one with the universe, not only physically but mentally and spiritually as well. Indian philosophy speaks of *prana* and the Chinese relate sacred breath to *chi*. Free-flowing prana or chi in and around the body lessens stress and increases the body's defenses against disease.

Many magickal systems include holy breath. For example, in Pow Wow (German magickal techniques for healing and magick), the practitioner always breathes in and out three times before beginning any technique, and then blows three times on the object or person at the conclusion of the work. At the same time, the practitioner envisions pure white light surrounding the object or person, followed by making an equal-armed cross in the air. This isn't just a bunch of motions without meaning. While breathing three times on the object or individual, the Pow Wow is connecting with Spirit, reaching up to bring the holy breath of the divine into his or her own body and out his or her mouth to infuse the magick. The white light is that of purity and divinity, and those who practice repeated visualizations find that if they add

lots of light to their mental picture, the thing they desire will manifest faster. The equal-armed cross helps the mind to visualize a closure to the work and keep the magick (or energy) from escaping.

When working in a magick circle with others, the first step is often to breath in unison with the people in the group, not as an effort but as a natural rhythm. Sometimes this can take several minutes until everyone catches the wave. This is the beginning of what is called a temporary group mind.

Sacred Breathing Exercise 1

Choose a time when you won't be disturbed. While standing, do three toe-touches or other stretch-type exercise. Sit comfortably in a chair with a straight back. Rest your hands on your thighs, palms up. Make sure your feet are placed firmly on the floor.

Close your eyes and relax. Breathe in through your nose and out through your mouth as slowly and evenly as possible (this gets easier as you continue). Try to take the same amount of time breathing in as breathing out. If it helps, trying breathing in to the count of four, and then breathing out to the count of four. This is called the rhythm of sacred breath. Practice breathing in and out, letting yourself relax. Envision yourself surrounded by a pure, white light. Try this every day for a week, more if you are upset or working hard. Teach parents, spouses, and kids this exercise so they can do it with you. Most magickal people practice rhythmic breathing, meditation, and visualization every day of their lives.

Sacred Breathing Exercise 2

Follow the same instructions as in number one but, before you open your eyes, imagine every time you are breathing in that you are drawing a beautiful, white, healing light into your body. Every time you breathe out, imagine all the negativity of the day leaving your body. After a while you might feel a "floaty" feeling: that's cool, you are now relaxed and moving into a deeper alpha state. It is from this feeling that meditation and visualization, two of those esoteric mystery teachings I was telling you about earlier, take place. You will know that you have reached your objective when suddenly you feel at one with the universe. This incredibly pleasant feeling will wash over your body and you will feel love all around you. When you are ready, count from one to five, open your eyes, and shake your hands. If you can, do this exercise twice a day for a month.

Grounding and Centering

Magickal breath is incorporated in the two Craft-related techniques called grounding and centering, which help to put you in the right frame of mind before (or after) a magickal working. Grounding means to feel secure, to root yourself to planet Earth, to bring nature into yourself, and yourself into nature. Centering means to find the ultimate, peaceful calm at the center of your being, stretching out to the center of where you are standing, out to the center of the planet, into the center of the universe. It is the still point—the absolute moment of calm when you feel like you are one with the universe.

The practice of grounding and centering comes in handy for a variety of circumstances, including relaxation, preparation for magick or ritual, and removing stress and negativity from the body. Some Wiccan teachers require that the student ground and center before and after any magickal or ritual practice, where others require grounding and centering only after the work. I suggest using the exercise before and after any magickal application while you are learning.

There are several techniques for grounding and centering, including meditations that can encompass the four elements, the planetary energies, and archetypes (gods and goddesses). The act of grounding and centering itself can take only a few moments or blossom into a full meditation. These practices become easier each time you use them, and will enhance and strengthen your psychic and magickal abilities. There is an added benefit to learning grounding and centering—anytime anyone treats you unfairly, or you lose your cool, or you feel that you are disconnected and lost, floating in this big universe all by yourself, practice the technique.

Use grounding and centering techniques:

- Before and after meditation.

- Before and after any spellcasting procedure.

- Before and after ritual.

- When you are angry, upset, or sick.

- Each morning as part of your daily devotions. Some Witches perform grounding and centering at the four sacred hours (dawn, noon, dusk, and midnight).

Grounding and centering can be done while standing or sitting, and doesn't take very long to do. The more you practice, the faster you will be able to ground and prepare for magick by centering yourself—sort of like a diver preparing to make the jump of his or her career into the magickal waters below. It is easier to learn grounding and centering by going outside the first few times.

TO GROUND: Take three deep breaths in through the nose and out through the mouth. Close your eyes. Imagine that you are a tree and that your feet (your roots) grow deep into Mother Earth. Feel the stable, secure energy of the planet.

TO CENTER: Imagine that your energy is merging with that of the universe. Allow the sounds and smells of the world around you to pass through you, like you are floating in a magickal pool. Let your concentration center on your solar plexus area. Imagine there is a beautiful sun burning there (some prefer to visualize a ball of light). Slowly, allow yourself to become one with the universe. This is the still point. Now you are ready for magick and ritual!

Chakras

The word *chakra* comes from the ancient Sanskrit, meaning "wheel of light."[30] According to esoteric teachings, the body has seven major and twenty-one minor chakra points, each representing a vortex of energy that appears to spin like a wheel. The chakras and your aura are connected and are part of your energy body. Together with the life force known as *chi* (cosmic energy), they work to maintain your balance and good health. They are like gas stations on your personal energy highway, creating a network (meridians) that feeds energy to your entire body. Each chakra supports a different area of the body. Any blockages along the network can create illness. Therefore, when we visualize healing for ourselves and others, our primary picture should be a free-flowing network of energy within the body. This is also true for any living thing, so don't forget that your pet also has a chakra system. Where our system runs along a vertical plane, theirs runs horizontal. The Earth also has an energy highway, called ley lines.

Chi has many names, including god/dess force, life force, prana, Spirit, or primordial glue. Some people believe that chi might be the basis for electromagnetic energy. All life taps into this cosmic energy![31] Eastern philosophers believe that chi enters the body from the top of the head and, as it flows downward, it activates the

seven primary chakras, which in turn activate other energy vortexes in the body. When we are at the peak of health, all chakras spin or vibrate at an incredible speed. When all things in the body are working well and balance occurs, the chakras open like beautiful flowers. The rainbow is the universal symbol of the chakras, and each vortex is normally assigned a particular color that helps us visualize them in meditation. The chakras can be nourished by breathing exercises, chi, meditation, taking care of your body, and eating right.

The study of quantum physics tells us that there is a mathematical way to convert any pattern, no matter how complex, into the language of light waves. Each wave carries a vibration. Different areas in our brains process this vibrational data. For example, our sense of smell is based on cosmic frequencies.[32] Not only do we interpret this data, we also create our own, shifting stored information and reworking that information and energy to manifest our mental, physical, and spiritual health. According to some quantum theorists, objective reality is nothing more than a resonating symphony of wave forms that is transferred into the world as we know it only after it has entered our senses. This means that everything, within and without our bodies, is affected, created, or destroyed by our thoughts and actions. We can literally make non-things become things by rearranging patterns of energy. We can and do affect things by mental and physical vibrations. Some call this the "cosmic light force."

The four lower chakras—heart, solar plexus, sacral, and base—work with the elements. Earth = base; water = sacral; fire = solar plexus; and air = heart. The other chakras—throat, brow, and crown—work with the more spiritual realms. As Witchcraft manipulates energy in all forms, it is necessary for us to learn the chakra system, what each vortex stands for, and how to keep our system in balance. When we raise energy in meditation, spellwork, magick, and ritual, we are tapping into the cosmic life force. Therefore, if a person continually worked negative magick (which we do not), their energy body would eventually sicken and die. This sickness may affect the mind, or the body, or both. The Wiccan Rule of Three—*What ye give out comes back to thee, three times three*—is in direct relation to how you handle the force of life (chi), as well as a warning that if you use this energy improperly, you will pay the price.

Most modern Wicca studies include basic chakra work to teach the student about his or her energy body, because all magick and healing work relies on how well you learn to use the life force that feeds the universe. You'll discover that a color isn't just a color but an energy vibration that can jumpstart and continue to feed a spell, a ritual, or even a meditation. When a spell recommends a particular candle color, gemstone, or herb, it is the energy of that item that's important. When we speak of things being "in sympathy," we are talking about the energy of that item and how it relates to, or affects, something else. For example, if a person is having trouble with his eyesight or sinuses, you might burn a blue candle (representing the brow chakra, which controls the energy flow of the face as well as the more spiritual energy of intuition and insight). You might also make a small blue bag out of felt and add natural blue stones and petals from blue flowers. This little package is a conjuring or gris-gris bag. Items like the conjuring bag and candles have two distinct purposes: their vibrational qualities and their ability to help you focus on a person, place, or thing. Most magickal books call the relationship between things and colors *correspondences*. The use of items like the magick wand, staff, or rod (three different items) are linked to the manipulation of cosmic forces or chi.

Sound is also an important aspect of energy manipulation. A loud, unpleasant sound affects the body in a negative way, where a pleasing, soothing sound creates harmony within and around the body. This is why some magickal books recommend specific types of music for various workings, and why Witches use chanting, song, bells, singing bowls, rattles, and drums in ritual and magickal work.

The following list will help you to match the colors of the seven major chakra vortexes to different areas of the body. You may find this information helpful in planning your healing work.

CROWN

Color: White.

Association: Universal consciousness, wisdom, transformation in a spiritual way.

Body areas: Brain and pineal gland.

Emotional: Peace, purity, cuts through mental confusion, encourages the growth of new ideas. Helps shy people open up.

BROW (THIRD EYE)

Color: Violet.

Association: Intuition, insight, paranormal abilities, connecting with the group mind and universal consciousness.

Body areas: Face, nose, sinuses, ears, eyes. Brain functions that include the pituitary gland, cerebellum, and central nervous system.

Emotional: All knowledge, spiritual advancement, cleansing for emotional addictions, release of painful memories, heals the emotionally shattered. Brings the sleep cycle into balance.

Chakras, from top to bottom: Crown, Brow/Third Eye, Throat, Heart, Solar Plexus, Sacral, and Base.

THROAT

Color: Blue.

Association: Creativity, self-expression, and communication. Changing the vibrations around you through sound.

Body areas: Throat, neck, thyroid, ears, windpipe, and upper part of lungs.

Emotional: Peace, calm, serenity. Looking back on the past to learn and grow, frees the power of the spoken word, releases mental confusion.

HEART

Color: Green.

Association: Unconditional love, compassion, healing, learning to live in balance, bridge from physical to spiritual.

Body areas: Heart, upper back, breasts, general function of the lungs, blood and air circulation. There is a secondary chakra close to the heart chakra called the thymus, which controls lymphatic systems.

Emotional: Emotional clearing and insight, clarity, stability. Healing for both body and mind as one complete package. Brings balance, focus. Green/gold works on nervous tics and stammering.

SOLAR PLEXUS

Color: Yellow.

Association: The storehouse of spiritual and physical energy; keeps the other chakras healthy. When we ground and center in magick, we are concentrating on the solar plexus chakra.

Body areas: Lower back, digestive system, liver, spleen, gall bladder, pancreas, and the production of insulin.

Emotional: Forgiveness, removes depression, negative thinking, boosts self-esteem, helps to release fear and phobias, and adds the energy of joy and laughter. Emotional success, abundance, and vitality. Gold helps to relieve suicidal tendencies.

SACRAL

Color: Orange.

Association: Purification, joy, receptivity to nature, feminine energy, immunity from disease. Located around the pelvis.

Body areas: Pelvis, kidneys, production of adrenaline, womb, bladder, and the liquids of the body—blood, lymph, gastric juices, and sperm.

Emotional: Breaks down barriers, helps in cases of mental breakdown, depression, rape, divorce, and accidents. Best color for dealing with grief, loss, or shock. Helps to eliminate fear.

BASE

Color: Red.

Association: Root of the collective unconscious, vitality, stability, and survival.

Body areas: Bones, teeth, nails, rectum, colon, prostate gland, blood and blood cells.

Emotional: Renews enthusiasm, strength to carry on, power to do something you dread. Courage, support, and willpower. Removes sluggishness.

Basic Chakra Meditation

Find a place where you will not be disturbed for about a half hour (though your first meditation experiences will probably be much less than that). Sit comfortably in a chair. You can lie down, but sometimes when we do that if we are very tired, we'll fall asleep. Close your eyes and take three deep breaths. Imagine that your entire body is surrounded by white light. Take a minute or two to think about the white light. Don't worry if you can't visualize right away. You'll get better at it as you go along. Take a deep breath and relax.

Now, imagine the white light of the Goddess (chi) coming down into the top of your head and slowly moving down your entire body, into your neck, shoulders, chest, arms, fingers, pelvis, legs, and down into your feet. Allow any negative energy collected in your body to flow out of the bottom of your feet. Take a deep breath and relax.

Follow the same visualization again, using the visualization of God energy (chi) doing the same thing, all the way down to your feet. Take a deep breath and relax.

Imagine the base chakra glowing red; you can think of it opening like a flower or spinning like a ball of light. Sometimes I see the chakras as colored flames. Like a flower turning toward the sun, imagine your inner self turning toward Spirit and receiving the right amount of cosmic energy that is right for you. Move up to the next chakra (sacral), and visualize orange. Work through all the chakras in this way, matching the color to the point on the body. When you finish with the crown chakra, take a deep breath and relax, imagining the chakras closing one by one, from the crown down to the base. Take another deep breath and open your eyes. Shake your hands lightly. The meditation is finished. Try practicing this meditation every day for at least a month. Most magickal people meditate every day for their entire lives.

Divination

We are all psychic, whether we like it or not.
Our brains operate more like time machines,
and information from the future must influence
choices made in the past. This is
an evolutionary transformation.
—*Dr. Fred Alan Wolf* [33]

What Dr. Wolf is actually saying is that time is not linear—it does not travel in a straight line. He is also suggesting that we are quite capable of not only looking into the future, but of changing our choices of behavior on the basis of what we see—meaning that each person has several futures available to him or her. Life is not fixed or fated.

A reading is not a parlor game, and at some point in time you may be trying to explain Dr. Wolf's philosophy to the individual whom you are reading for. People with closed minds have difficulty understanding that the world is a vast universe of choices. The divination tool allows you to review these choices and then find the best solution or path of movement that would be best for you.

Most Witches choose at least one divination tool to support their spiritual needs. The problem with divination tools is that everyone tries to make them complicated, when, honestly, the message is the message is the message. Any Witch, once they have learned the basics of divination, should be able to pick up any divination tool and use it immediately, even if they have never seen it before (and yes, you can have a cheat sheet). What I'm trying to say is, although the tools are different, the mental process is always the same.

Divination is not the work of some strange devil. All you are doing is scientifically "viewing" that future light path or cone that, given the current actions of yourself or your client, will most likely unfold.

Why Use Divination?

Divinatory tools (Tarot, I Ching, runes, yes/no stones, playing cards, lots, shells, cartouche, scrying, and predictive astrology, to name a few) are keys to unlock your subconscious mind. By themselves, these tools of divination mean nothing. They will not work alone. They need your higher mind to perform. Witches use divination (the art of telling the future, past, or present) to aid us in our magickal applications as well as everyday life; however, we must always be reminded that we cannot rely on divination alone to assert ourselves and our ideas into the physical world, and they cannot take the place of calm, rational thought or the mental process of decision making that we, as humans, must endeavor to perform on a daily basis.

The Truth About Divination

When a client sits down, ready to have a reading with me, I give them the following speech. I know it so well that I rattle it off like a freight train clanking full throttle down a brand-new track:

"The Tarot is a tool, nothing more, nothing less. A reading is like a road map, and provides you with information so that you may make wise choices, just like when traveling on a road you can use a detour, or you can go under the speed limit through highway construction. A Tarot reading merely represents signposts on your highway of life. Your future is not fixed or fated. It is a subtle fabric that billows and folds with your experiences and your choices in life. I will not read beyond six months, as there are too many choices that you could make between then and now to make the reading an accurate one. A card reading tells you what will most likely happen should you stay on the path you are presently traveling. There is no boogyman standing over my shoulder telling me your future: not a ghost, an angel, or a demon. The cards are merely a psychological tool that we will use to try to make your future a better one. Within the next fifteen minutes, consider me your best friend. I have no judgments on your life choices. Do you understand?"

Whether they have understood my speech or not is evident at the end of the reading. If they ask me questions like "Will I ever get married? Will I lose weight? Will I find my soulmate? Will I get pregnant?" I know they haven't listened to a word I've said. My answers to these questions are:

1. Do you want to get married?

2. Do you want to lose weight?

3. I don't believe in soulmates.

4. I have a ritual for you if you want to get pregnant.

To me, if you want to get married in the future, or if you truly want to lose weight, you'll do it. If you want to be a famous writer, you'll do it. If you want to find the cure for cancer, you'll do it. Desire has incredible influence on what you accomplish in life, and what you don't. Like I said in the speech, nothing is fixed or fated. Now, if the client said, "I'm trying to get pregnant, do you have any advice for me?" then that's a whole different ball game and we could certainly read the cards on that. If they said, "I'm working on a weight-loss program, can we see if I'm making wise choices?"—there again, we could read on that. The decision in both cases has already been made, and we'll look ahead to see the result of those decisions. The cards cannot decide for you. You must make the choice.

The hardest question to answer, but the one most frequently posed by the more spiritual clients, is "What is my mission in life?" My answer is always "That which you most enjoy doing."

What Can We Use a Divination Tool For?

Keeping in mind that any divination tool is only an aid used by the higher mind, the tool can serve a variety of purposes:

- We can use the symbolism of any card or lot (runes) as a catalyst in magick: a visual (or tactile) trigger.

- We can determine which way is best when confronted by two options.

- We can determine *what is most likely to happen*, should we stay on the path we are currently traveling.

- We can attempt to counsel others (notice I say *attempt*!) through the use of the cards. However, a divination tool should never be used in place of qualified medical expertise. Meaning, if you feel sick or if you are having a rough time getting over the death of a friend, you should seek appropriate help. Divination never precludes qualified legal or medical services.

- We can use the tool to decide if we should do a particular ritual, if a magickal plan of action is in our best interest, or in choosing the right spell to fit the circumstances.

- We can use our divination tool for meditation, vision questing, or dream catalyst or analysis purposes. This is extremely useful when first learning the tool.

- You can use the divination tool to determine the past, the present, or the future about a subject or individual by following the path of his or her decisions. However, there are ethics to this. I don't know how you will eventually use your divination vehicle, but I never pry into another person's affairs unless their choice in some way has or will directly affect my life. The only time

I sway from my personal code is if I am working on a criminal case.

- Some divinatory procedures are used to train the magickal student in areas of energy work. For example, many Witches are taught dowsing and psychometry primarily for the experience of sensing and manipulating energy rather than strictly for the idea of pure divination.

The tool you use is as flexible as you choose. Its primary use is up to you. All divinatory tools require years of study to acquire expertise, but this doesn't mean you cannot use the vehicle you have chosen immediately, nor does this mean your readings will be lousy for the next ten years. Time, and patience, are required.

Divination Tips

My best advice in studying any divinatory tool is to use the following framework.

- Acquaint yourself with the tool through a hands-on approach. Look at all the cards, or symbols, or whatever. Use your hands, your imagination, and your logical thought process equally. If you are using cards or a tool that is highly colorful with many pictures, talk to the characters on the cards. Keep a running dialog. You will be surprised how much you'll learn. Place one unit (one card, one rune, etc.) under your pillow each night when you go to sleep.

- Take your time. Do not expect things from yourself that you are simply not ready to produce. Keep notes of sequences that keep popping up.

- Lose your fear of being "wrong." The tool is never wrong, but sometimes you won't interpret the tool correctly. For now, at the beginning, don't force yourself, and don't give up. Take little steps and build slowly.

You will benefit. Know that, at some point, you will be wrong. In fact, sometimes you are *supposed* to be wrong.

- Remember to take a break while learning, even if it is a few weeks or so. Sometimes, we need to grow within to reach the higher aspects of the tool we are using. That means we must be patient. We must allow ourselves to assimilate the information so that we may use it to our advantage later.

- Keep a record, at least when you begin, of your readings. This is vital. It allows you to see where you were correct in your interpretations, and where you were in error.

- Compile a separate notebook of your personal study. Remember to annotate where you got what information for later use. You may need, at some time, to teach this same material, and you will want to know where you got your information. Even if you don't want to know, the student will inevitably ask you, "Where did you get this?" Although you would like to tell them "It's a secret," since you have no clue where you dug up the information, that would be unfair. Best to keep accurate records.

- Use as many resources as you can when studying any divinatory tool. Books, tapes, interviews with readers, discussions with others. The more resources you use, the broader your knowledge.

- Have divination parties with your friends. The premise contains ten prewritten questions that everyone reads for. At least one question should be a local (or national) unsolved crime. One member of the group should keep track of the case until (if ever) its completion, along with what each individual claimed in his or her reading. This type of gathering is better in person, where the divination vehicle can be laid out on a large table and all can view it.

- For the first month, don't use any resource material. Just read from the gut. Your work will be better for it.

One thing I can tell you for sure: you will never stop learning the tool you choose. Even after twenty-five years of reading the Tarot, I am still learning new things about the system. Gut feelings are the basis of psychism. I call them "red flags"—kind of like little men down in the basement of your mind who jump up and down, screaming and waving crimson pennants, trying to get your logical mind to listen. Learning to listen to these feelings takes patience and the willingness to make mistakes. Sometimes our logical mind tries to fake being a little man in the basement. The logical mind whispers stuff to you, and then you get royally confused. *Was that a gut thing? Or was that my brain trying to logically sort things out?*

You will have to be patient and be willing to spend LOTS of time learning the difference between those two voices. No one can do this for you but yourself. Diligent practice of meditation, visionquesting, and dream analysis can help you speed this process along, but it will still take time. Patience, again, is the key.

I am sure that you have seen unusual practices that different readers incorporate in an effort to perform. You will develop some odd traits, too; however, keep in mind that this is unnecessary behavior and what may work for one reader will not serve another well. From covering your divination tool with a black cloth to keeping a moonstone with your cards, these are all personal foibles, and are only as important as you allow them to be.

Here are some common practices:

- Cleanse your divination tool under the full moon or the noonday sun.

- Between readings, use a rattle to break up negative energy over the tool.

- Rub your hands with a "vision oil" before readings and after an especially difficult reading.

- Pass the tool over sacred flame.

- Utter a favorite prayer before the divination process.

- Use a special colored candle to reflect the type of divination you wish to perform.

- Sprinkle holy water over the tool after a particularly difficult reading.

- Use a special cloth on which to lay your divination tool.

- Entreat the assistance of a dead loved one.

- Knock on the deck three times after it has been shuffled to set the energies for that reading.

- Cut the cards in a specific way.

- Place a statue, crystal, or other protective device on the reading table. (This is very important if you will be reading in public like a tea house, psychic fair, or other areas with large numbers of people.)

- Learning to trust your intuition is by far the most difficult thing to do when using a divination tool. Many experienced readers, including myself, claim that when the juices are really going, the reader will not recall what he or she said to the client. This is because your higher mind has taken over, and you are in the alpha level of mind when you are speaking to the client. The very best thing to do is just open your mouth and let 'er rip. This takes practice because your logical mind is throwing a tantrum, saying, "No, no, no! That can't possibly be right!" My advice? Do not read your suspicions, read *what is there*.

Know this:

- The tool will often give the information that the client (or you) most needs to know, not necessarily what you *want* to know.

- Each reader will develop a specialty, meaning that they are very good at certain types of questions and abysmal at others.

- Most people lie to themselves. They will also lie to you, consciously or unconsciously.

- Most people will not hear the entire reading. The mind is a very selective grandma. They may block out statements that apply to what they already know (especially true in individuals who are also psychic and who are readers themselves). Other people will tune out things that they don't want to hear about and will purposefully avoid that subject, or walk away from the table blocking what you may have said in their own best interests. Other individuals will be so inundated with information that they will pull out the best parts of the reading, or those things that relate to what they really wanted to know, and miss several other issues.

Pitfalls in Divination

Although there are a few I can think of when dealing with clients, the worst pitfall will be the hole your logical mind will dig for you. I can remember one reading where I did not listen to my intuition, and I did not read the cards as they stood. My logical mind told me that my friend could not be pregnant because my misguided memory told me that she had gone through

surgery in the past and wasn't capable of it. Therefore, I read the cards in another way. I was wrong.

You will also discover that there are certain people that you can't read for, or something will happen between you and a client that will forever change your capabilities of reading for them: meaning you have to quit. They, or you, may be subconsciously twisting the reading. It can happen. Acknowledge it, and deal with it.

Know, and understand, that sometimes you will be wrong. Just flat-out inaccurate. Factors here may include:

- You are tired, sick, overworked, or mentally dealing with an issue of your own that clouds your judgment. You must learn how to say no to people when you are in this position.

- The universe thinks it is a *very* bad idea that this person is seeking a reading at this time. They must make decisions without the help of an intuitive tool. This could be karmically based, or simply a need for this person to stand on his or her own two feet.

- Not wording your question correctly. This is a big, fat hole that you can fall into before you realize you're at the bottom. This especially happens when you are experienced at reading, think of the question quick, then throw the cards (or whatever). Halfway through the reading you realize you forgot the question. Absolutely infuriating.

- Asking too many questions at one time that deal with different issues. I really hate it when a client sits down and says, "I want to know about this, or maybe that, or how about . . ." while he or she is shuffling the cards, or they are gossiping about someone else. A bad reading can also result if they aren't into the reading, or they are not paying attention to the business at hand and are chatting about something else. You must be firm and stop them, have them concentrate, and then reshuffle the cards or shake the bag, or whatever it is you are doing.

- Rule of thumb: If by the third sentence into their reading the client looks confused or claims this isn't right, just smile and say, "Then let's reshuffle." If they ask why (some of them will), simply say they need to concentrate on what they most want to know so that you can give them the best, most accurate reading.

- Readings for yourself can get tricky. Once you know your divination tool inside out and upside down, you also will have the ability to influence that tool. Now, in a way, that's okay, because you can influence the outcome of the event as well by hard concentration; however, there are certain people who have a habit of negative concentration and they inevitably receive the negative cards or lots that they were thinking about. When this happens, it is time to use a different tool for yourself.

- Being "too positive" or "too negative." If you are too negative, you've got a problem: Stop reading for awhile until you pull yourself out of whatever funk you are in. Too positive can be a blessing if you are reading for a living, but fooling yourself is the trap you can snap on your own life if you are not careful. If the situation is bad, and you know it, and if the reading does not show light where you need it, do magick.

- You can't turn psychism on and off like a light bulb. Sometimes you will be really in the flow, and other times, nothing. This is especially true with the more mind-altering types of divination, like scrying and psychometry.

- A disbelieving audience can diminish or destroy your concentration. Don't be a show-off. If a friend makes fun of you, but they want a reading anyway, tell them to forget it. A divinatory tool is not a Victorian parlor game and you don't need to be the brunt of their angst.

Reading for Others

Once you are comfortable with your divination tool, you will most likely want to read for other people. When you are first learning, be sure to tell those whom you read for that this is new for you. Make sure you give ground rules on the types of questions they may ask or how much time you plan to devote to these trial-and-error readings. In the beginning you will enjoy reading for others and will openly look for opportunities to use your new skill, but there will come a point (and it never fails) that people will begin to abuse you for your skill. They don't do it on purpose (okay, some will).

At first, my teenage daughter adored reading the cards for her friends and their mothers, but after awhile, they only wanted to call her, see her, or have her visit because she could read, and then they would ply her for hours with questions. Not only is this tedious, but it is also very tiring. Finally, my daughter came to me, asking what to do. Here were my suggestions:

- Don't carry your divination tool with you anymore. Leave it at home, especially when you go to a party (unless you think the party will be dull, or you want to be the center of attention).

- Impress upon your friends and family that the divination vehicle is a tool, not a toy, and should be treated with respect. You can't just ask "any little old question" and expect to get a reasonable answer. They are for goal planning and conflict resolution.

- From the beginning, don't read for friends or family who are psychologically unsound. Becoming dependent on you, or the cards, is not how to deal with life.

- Learn to say no politely and stick to your guns.

- Bluntly tell people you won't read over the phone anymore.

- Limit the questions or the time.

To the Witch, the divination tool is not merely a window to the future or a peep into the past. It is a vehicle from which we can build better lives for ourselves and assist others too. The divination tool should be a part of your spiritual plan, not the overall plan itself.

Meditation and Your Divinatory Tool

A very simple technique of meditating on your chosen divinatory tool is to work with one card (or unit) at a time. Just relax and look at the card. Try not to have a running dialog in your brain. When you mind wanders, gently bring it back. Start easy: one minute, tops. Then go to two, and finally to three. A kitchen timer works well for those of you who are worried about seconds. This type of meditation is classified as passive, where you don't let your mind wander or allow yourself to visualize anything but the card. Once you have practiced passive meditation with your divinatory tool, you can move on to active meditation, where you incorporate your choice of visualization to link with the card or symbol, link thoughts through word association and write them down, or hold an internal conversation with the pictures on the card. For example, if you want to be successful at something, you may pull out the Sun card in the Tarot deck and form a picture of success in your mind while holding the card. This simple type of active meditation done every night for thirty days can help push you forward into the success that you desire. It sounds so simple, but it works.

Meditation for the Dawn

There is nothing more awe inspiring than working magick as the sun sprays golden light across the heavens when the dawn graces us with the beginning of a new day. Although most people equate Witches with the night, we are just as powerful during the daytime as well!

SUPPLIES: Proper dress for the climate; one white seven-day candle; lighter; your divination tool.

INSTRUCTIONS: Carefully select special card, lot (if you are using runes), or symbol from your divination tool that best describes something that you would like to accomplish in the future. Check the newspaper or almanac to determine when the sun will rise on the day you choose to do this magick meditation. On the chosen day, sit outside facing east with the unlit candle before you.

Take several deep breaths and relax. Ground and center. Close your eyes and connect with the nature around you: the trees, grass, perhaps ocean and sand. If you live in the city, don't despair: the earth is under you, there are birds and squirrels, maybe a windowbox or even a coffee can with flowers, and the sky above. Nature is there, even if she is hidden by concrete, macadam, and stone. Slowly, you will feel the nature spirits around you, which will fill you with a pleasing, peaceful sensation.

As the sun begins to peek over the horizon, hold your candle up to the light so that the ball of the sun (in your view) sits on the unlit wick. Blow one soft, deep breath onto the candle. Close your eyes and ask for the blessings of Spirit on this new day, on your life in general, and on your specific request. Lower the candle and light the wick. Set the burning candle in front of you, on top of or near the divinatory representation you brought with you.

Close your eyes and connect with your Spirit helpers. This could be the angels, a totem animal, or your support group on the other side of the veil (yes, we all have one). Suddenly, where you are sitting will feel crowded, and that's perfect. You'll feel love all around you. You may also plug into other souls who are doing the exact same thing that you are: communing with Spirit and the sunrise. You may see (in your mind) someone sitting on a hill in an unpopulated area, or perhaps you will connect with someone standing on top of a tenement building. The name or the face doesn't matter; the communion with the divine does.

When you are finished, take the candle inside and allow it to burn continuously in a safe place. If you aren't allowed to have candles, you can still do this meditation and use your divinatory tool. Simply hold the tool toward the sun as you would the candle. You may like this meditation so much that you practice it at sunrise on a regular basis.

Dowsing

For the magickal person, dowsing is an excellent way to learn to sense energy fields. Those involved in the study of psychic phenomenon believe that dowsing (for water) predates the art of writing, claiming that cave paintings in the Atlas Mountains of Algeria and depictions of Egyptian art show the inhabitants of both cultures practic-

ing the art of dowsing. The divining rod, cut and used in a highly ritual manner to find ore, came from Germany in the mid-sixteenth century, gaining popularity a hundred years or more later.[34] During the Vietnam War, US Marines acting without official sanction dowsed for boobytraps, mines, and enemy fox holes.[35] As you can see, whether you are seeking water, energy, or objects of war, the art of dowsing is far from defunct. Although dowsing is often done with a forked stick (which bends downward when the object is found) or metal rods (one rod held in each hand; metal hangers with the hooks cut off work well) that swing from an outward position inward when the object is found, the crystal or metal pendulum that dangles from a string or cord is considered a form of dowsing as well. This type of dowsing has been used by some psychics to find missing persons or objects when the pendulum is held over a map or self-made diagram.

As with psychometry, Wicca 101 students often enjoy at least one group lesson that revolves around the various types of dowsing. The practice is as follows:

1. Determine what you will be dowsing for: water, energy, or an object in the ground.

2. Firmly state in your mind the name of the person or thing.

3. Follow the directions that come with the tool. Rods and some pendulums can be purchased in kit form.

4. Keep accurate records.

If you can't afford a pendulum kit, you can tie a twenty-four-inch string to an inch-long crystal that has been cleansed under running water. Keep your fingers together and loop the other end of the string over your first two fingers. Hold the pendulum so that the crystal dangles straight down. Before you begin, you need to determine which movement means what. For example, first you would say, "Show me *Yes*." Try to keep your hand still and not move the pendulum by physical reaction. After a while, the pendulum will begin to swing. It may go back and forth or in a circle. Stop the pendulum, and say, "Show me *No*," and again watch the movement and make note of it. Stop the pendulum. Finally, say, "Show me *I Don't Know*" and write down how the pendulum moves. You are now ready to ask your first question.

Some individuals have great success with the pendulum and others find it unreliable. There are a few rules for pendulum dowsing:

- Formulate your questions before you pick up the pendulum.

- Breathe easy and view the process as something relaxing, rather than tensing all your muscles in anticipation of an answer.

- Try to keep your hand still so that the pendulum does its own work.

In a group training format, the rods are used to measure how well a student is raising energy, and can detect the energy of a cast circle. Actually seeing the movement of the rods during energy work is a great way to understand the dynamics of energy movement.

Dowsing Experiment 1: Checking Your Circle

You will need two metal coat hangers. Cut off the hooks, but leave the hangers in their triangular shape. Hold the hangers by the long straight ends, one in each hand. The twisted area of the hanger becomes the "pointer." Don't hold them so loose that they swing as you walk, yet don't grip them so tight that they cannot move. When you begin, the pointers should be out to the left (of the left hand) and out to the right (of the right hand). Once you've practiced this, put them down and cast a magick circle. Cut a door.

Walk outside of the circle. Close the door. With the hangers, walk several feet away. In your mind, think about divining for circle energy. Adjust the hangers in your hands and then walk forward. What happens to the hangers? The closer you get to the circle, they should swing and point toward the circle. How close did you get? Now try this inside the circle. What happens? Check the door you cut. What happens there? If energy is seeping out, you need to work on your visualization. Take the circle down. Try again. What happens? If you didn't get it down (which sometimes new students have difficulty doing), then you need to work on that visualization technique as well.

In experiments with first-year students, I've learned that most will cast a circle approximately three feet from all sides of the body, where the more experienced students are able to cast approximately twelve feet from the body in all directions. Even the first-time student can usually get the circle up without difficulty, though taking it down is another matter entirely. My best advice is to take your time. Too often new students are patient in casting the circle (especially if they are walking the circle three times), but spend little time in taking it down (going just once around in a counterclockwise direction) and are looking ahead to what they will do next (running an errand, calling a friend, etc.). In your experiments with the rods, as the circle comes down, the rods will swing open.

I have also discovered that if you walk through a circle without taking it down, the energy fizzes in all directions and the time spent casting the circle, calling the quarters, etc., was spent in vain. Cutting the door is another problem. The circle of a beginning student begins to disintegrate in approximately twenty seconds if the door is left wide open. If the student does not take his or her time in closing the portal, or does not visualize the closure, the energy will seep away and the circle will come down. A flick of the wrist and telling the others in the circle that the door is closed is not enough. In your experiments, the rods should swing open as the door is cut, and swing closed as the door is shut.

Dowsing Experiment 2:
Magickal Hide and Seek

This works just like the children's game Hide and Seek, though this time only one friend will hide and you will dowse with the rods for that person. You can also dowse for your pet. Just remember to formulate in your mind "what" or "whom" you are dowsing for. Once you have this technique down, your mother will never again lose her car keys. You can dowse for them!

Dowsing Experiment 3:
Chakra Exercise

This exercise requires a partner and is used to check the ability of an individual to open and close the various chakra points on the body. When the participant mentally opens a chakra point, the rods should swing closed toward the chakra point. When the individual mentally closes the chakra vortex, then the rods should swing open over that part of the body. How quickly they open and close gives you an idea of the meditational focus the individual has. Although we've tried several ways to do this exercise, it appears it is best done if the individual lays faceup on a table. He or she should close the eyes, then ground and center. The standing partner now gives the command, "Open the crown chakra." When the rods have swung to a point over the chakra, the standing partner should say, "It's completely open. Now, close the chakra." If the rods do not open or close right away, the standing partner should inform the meditating one, and give encouragement, perhaps helping with the visualization process. Practice monitor-

ing all the chakra points, as well as extending and compressing your energy field. Once the exercise is completed, switch places.

Dowsing Experiment 4:
Checking Energy Levels

Use to check energy levels of magickal tools, your altar, or other empowered items. Ground and center. Stand six feet from the item, with rods pointing outward. As you walk toward the item make note of where the rods begin to swing shut, then at what point the rods swing to completely touch each other. When you finish any working, you can always double-check the amount of energy contained in an object in this way. If you work with your altar daily, the rods should swing shut (and touch each other) approximately three feet from the altar surface. If the altar surface remains dormant for any period of time, the rods will probably not touch until you are directly over the surface. During a ritual, an activated altar could throw energy as far as six feet from the edge of the altar.

Dowsing Experiment 5:
Drawing Down

This exercise requires two individuals. Following the instructions on page 298, one partner performs the DDM (Drawing Down the Moon) while the other partner monitors the energy fluctuations with the rod. Switch places. Record your results.

Dreams and Visions

Dreams used as visions and prophecy were common in the ancient world. Indeed, no matter where you might journey, you were likely to fall over a prophet or two, religious and otherwise. In the Middle Ages, flying dreams were associated with Diana, the Roman goddess of the moon.[36] The Night Battles discussed by Ginzburg[37] in his treatise on the *benandanti* (well-farers) of the same time period could have been the product of dream sequences, or they could have been ritual drama practiced as part of the culture of the day. In most historical cases, however, dreams fell into a category of heavenly magic toward which the church authorities felt able to be relatively relaxed. Indeed, there were worse forces abroad of which the clergy must contend.[38] Religion thus reinforced the ancient belief in the divinatory power of dreams, though it was felt that divine dreams were unlikely, yet possible. Manuscript guides to dream interpretation dating to the early medieval period were continuously replaced and updated and circulated through the 1800s.[39]

If you really think about it, humans experience several types of dream states—night dreams, daydreams, visualization, pathworking, and some meditation sequences. Our conscious mind works to perceive and analyze reality. The unconscious mind runs our automatic functions and communicates through our senses, thoughts, and feelings. Its language is that of pure symbolism. Our higher self is our connection to Spirit and can provide a moment of inspiration, fuel our creativity, and help us experience that feeling of oneness with the universe. When we work to balance the conscious mind, unconscious mind, and the higher mind, we can achieve miracles. Many times this achievement is a direct product of our dreams, meditations, and pathworking experiences.

Today, health care providers tell us that one of the biggest areas of concern in teen and workaholic adult wellness issues stems from sleep deprivation. Your schedule is so full that there just doesn't seem to be time for sleep, but a teen actually needs up to ten hours (sometimes more)

to stay healthy and unstressed. During the teen years, the pituitary gland (located in your brain) releases large amounts of growth hormones. If you want to grow at the highest rate possible for your body type, you need to make an effort to get plenty of sleep. When we sleep, we also dream. Cutting out the sleeping also cuts out the dreaming, which relates to our psychological health.

Most researchers agree that humans have four or five dream periods per night. Within each dream period there can be any number of dreams. Every once in a while you may wake up remembering a succession of dreams—scenes that blended from one to the other. When this happens you are remembering part or all of a dream segment. Dreams usually occur during REM (rapid eye movement) sleep, first observed by Eugene Aserinsky in 1953 at the University of Chicago.[40] Later scientists discovered that daily rest cycles and sleep cycles were the same, and they also discovered that REM cycles occur on a subtle level during the day while we are awake. Now, what does all this mean to us, as magickal people? Basically that all levels of the mind, body, and spirit function as one, even though we don't have the slightest idea that all this activity is going on in our bodies. When something is out of whack with any of these cycles, we get sick or depressed. By using tools like meditation, self-hypnosis, daydreams, and night dreams, we can guide our lives to ultimate success. And you thought Witches only cast spells!

When we lie down to go to sleep, our bodies begin to relax. The same occurs when we begin a meditation sequence. Our brain waves slow down from beta (the waking state) to alpha (a light trance state with several levels). As we relax we have those familiar flashes where our minds wander. These snatches are called "dreamlets," or stream of conscious energy.

Sometimes our bodies jerk as our system shuts down for relaxation. This is normal and appears to be linked with how busy or stressed out we were that day. Sensations of falling come from this powering down of the body's various systems. As we wake up and our body starts to throw those switches to meet a new day, these dreamlets occur again and are often those we remember the best. It is during these dreamlets when falling asleep or from slight arousal to full awakening that our minds are the most creative and fertile. It's here that we can program ourselves with positive suggestions and affirmations. Why not write down your favorite affirmation (or take the time to compose one) that you will use next time you experience dreamlets? Try to remember to insert this affirmation every night (or morning) for the next month. What happens?

From the dreamlet stage when we are falling asleep, our bodies and minds move into four successive states that equal one sleep cycle. As I mentioned earlier, we will have four to five sleep cycles per night. The time we spend in each stage depends upon the person. For most people, their heaviest sleep of the night falls within the first three hours. During sleep, we move from alpha to theta, and finally to delta before we ascend again to begin a new cycle. In the first cycle of the night, dreaming only occurs for ten minutes toward the very end of the cycle.[41] As we continue to sleep, the REM lasts longer, until finally about 90 percent of the last sleep cycle is filled with dreams. These are the images most individuals use for dream recall. Still, no one really knows why we dream! While you dream, your higher conscious sends you messages that are encoded by your unconscious mind. Your conscious mind must meet the challenge of decoding the message, but first we have to teach ourselves to remember our dreams.

Everyone dreams (even though they say they don't). The trick is remembering them. If you practice telling yourself each night that you will remember the dreams that carry the most important information, you will begin to have better recall. Keep a pen and pad by the bed to jot down dreams or even phrases you might hear in your mind. Don't worry about decoding them in the night. It's better to let your conscious mind haggle over it the next day. If you keep up this practice, you will soon have a journal full of dreams. You might try the following spell before falling asleep to help with better dream recall.

Dream Recall Spell

SUPPLIES: One cup of hot, brewed chamomile tea; dried, crushed lavender; a white hankie.

INSTRUCTIONS: Place the lavender inside the hankie. Fold neatly. Place between the pillow and pillowcase. Drink the tea. Recite the following incantation three times:

From my higher self I bid thee come from the deep rushing river of my dreams—great winged thoughts of inspiration, knowledge, growth, and learning. I welcome with joy the symbols and vivid colors brought forth, up through the depths of my mind, and I will remember only those dreams that are significant. I will decode these with little difficulty upon waking by using the keyword (insert a special word of choice here). *So mote it be.*

Ground and center. Turn out the light and close your eyes.

It may take several weeks before you are able to recall significant parts of the dream segments, but don't give up. How we wake up also has a lot to do with what we recall. If you are overly tired and then roused by an alarm or a screaming sibling, it's highly possible you won't remember a darned thing. Sit quietly in bed and say your keyword aloud. If that doesn't work, there's always tomorrow.

Most of us don't have time to decode our dreams right away. This is especially so if you have to get ready for school or you have some other commitment. When you do have the time, my best advice is to use word association rather than a dream dictionary. Yes, some symbols might be universal, but these are *your* dreams and *your* private code from *your* unconscious mind. Only you hold the complete dictionary.

Go through your notes and pull out the most colorful symbolism. I had a dream once where a giant wave of water rose up over the whole town and threatened to wash us all away. In the dream, the wave was the most prominent symbol, both by its size and the vivid color of the water. So I wrote down "big wave" and then did word association by writing down the first ten words that came into my head. I repeated the symbol aloud—big wave—then wrote down "Fear, Overcome, Drown, Loss, Float, Flow, etc." The dream meant that I felt I was being overcome by something much bigger than myself, and that in this mental helplessness I was afraid that I would lose something precious to me. As I continued to think about this, I realized that FEAR means "False Evidence Appearing Real," and that the big wave was actually a representation of my worry. My mind was telling me that I was drowning in my own fear and worry, and that I was supposed to "go with the flow."

Granted, some dreams have so much symbolism that it takes awhile to decipher them, and on occasion they will appear so cryptic that you toss your pencil across the room in frustration. If this happens to you, let the dream sit for a few days (even a few weeks) and then go back to it. By then you'll probably look at the dream and smack yourself on the forehead, saying, "Duh!" because the answer will come to you immediately. That's because even though you haven't worked on the dream in a few days (or weeks), your subconscious mind continued to shoot additional clues to your conscious mind.

Using Your Divination Tool to Decipher Your Dreams

If you have been working with a favorite divination tool for any length of time, you have gained experience in decoding symbols, moving from your intuition to your conscious mind and sometimes back again. If a dream is particularly puzzling, take a deep breath and relax, then shuffle the cards (or whatever your tool requires) as you re-read the dream. Your final question should be, "What important message or messages are contained within this dream, and how can I use this message to become a better person?"

Let's use the example of the Big Wave dream and a deck of Tarot cards. You can use your favorite card spread, or you can simply draw two cards—the first for the message of the dream and the second for how you can use the message. I drew the Six of Wands, meaning that all obstacles are surmountable, and the Three of Wands, meaning I should welcome change (and not be afraid of it) and continue to assert my efforts in positive ways. The suit of Wands also tells me that my worries were about communication and my inner resources. True enough.

If you are into astrology, you can cast a chart for the moment you woke up and wrote down your dream. Not only is this a cool way to learn astrology, you'll also get some major insights on what's going on inside your brain!

Dreams of Prophecy

As dreams are so incredibly personal, it is difficult to discern what may be an outlet of our fears and what may, indeed, be an indication of what is to come. Unfortunately, every segment of history has had its prophets of gloom and doom. Most were wrong, a handful managed to get it right, but in the meantime, thousands of people have been frightened or even lost their lives over false prophecies. When the attack on America occurred on September 11, 2001, some of the members of the magickal community indicated their angst that the "leaders" of our community hadn't found a way to warn the victims of this disaster. Why didn't they know?

Prophetic dreams are funny animals, as I have come to discover. I can only tell you my experience, and you can draw your conclusions wherever you like. On August 11, 2001, I awoke from a very vivid dream. In the dream I was on a white road. There was sand all about. In the distance I could see a man walking toward me dressed in Arab garb leading a camel. He walked up to me and smiled, but a loud voice in my mind said, "This is a very bad man. He carries the evil eye." The man reached his hand out to me and between this thumb and index finger was a real eye. I looked up and saw a snow-white obelisk behind him. Instantly it was covered with what looked like red Arabic writing. The writing began to drip like blood. When I woke from the dream I immediately wrote it down because it was so strange and so very vivid. I tried my usual dream-recall sequence but could not find an adequate association to the dream. I checked the news—papers, Internet, television—nothing stood out. Days passed, then weeks, and I forgot about the vision. Throughout the first week in September I received several e-mails from community members speaking of disaster dreams (many of them teens, by the way), however no one could come up with a place, a time, or a day. Such is the rub, for most of us, of prophetic dreams. On September 10, as I lay down to sleep for the night, I went through my normal meditation sequence when suddenly everything tunneled and I found myself in a black tunnel, looking out a hole shaped like a round doorway. The world outside of the tunnel was deep twilight—an eerie blue-purple mix. As I sat protected in the tunnel, hundreds of silhouettes of people silently marched by. I have no idea how long I watched the people silently shuffle along, I only know that there were no silhouettes of children in the line. Disturbed, I stayed up all night trying to understand what I had seen. Was it a product of my own imagination? Was it real? If so, what was I seeing? Finally, toward dawn I gave up my pondering and went back to work on this book. My husband was watching the stock channel when the first plane hit. I saw the second plane hit myself. The rest is history.

There was once a famous mystery writer who always added the sentence, "Had I but known . . ." in just about every novel she wrote. Even if I had known the dream and the vision were true prophecy, there was no additional signage or blinking lights telling me when, where, why, or what time. All I got was a "who," and even then I didn't get a name—just a face, and at that time, it was a face among millions. Yes, there were hints in the dream and the vision, but hindsight is 20/20 and we can always draw correlations where we wouldn't have possibly seen things before.

How many of us were warned by visions and prophecy? Probably quite a few. I'm sure I'm not the only person who couldn't sleep the night of September 10. However, I'm also sure that hundreds, maybe thousands like me received only pieces of the oncoming nemesis that was about to hit. Future shock waves? Something like a collective unconscious tuning fork? Psychiatrist Montague Ullman, the founder of the Dream Laboratory at the Maimonides Medical Center in Brooklyn, New York, believes that nature is concerned with the survival of the species and in that concern provides dreams to counteract our seemingly unending compulsion to fragment the world. Dreams reflect our individual experience because there is a greater underlying need to preserve the species, to maintain an interconnectedness with all humans.[42] If this is so, perhaps, as Ullman postulates, dreams are a bridge between the perceptual and nonmanifest orders and can warn us of an upcoming transformation that will affect large numbers of people. Until we are able to scientifically measure prophetic dreams, we can only gather data and wait, and since many people fear drawing attention to themselves or have a legitimate desire not to frighten people unnecessarily, we can't retrieve most of the prophetic data floating around out·there in every social structure. One thing is certain; we must never, ever be afraid.

Health and Healing

During the Middle Ages, herbs and ointments were often mixed with holy water or oil. Popular manuals for healing (called "leech books" or "doctor books") encouraged their readers to say prayers over a compendium of recipes specifically designed for the treatment of various maladies. In fact, it is through these books (and others like them) that we can follow the pre-Christian culture of northern Europe and its folk magick practices as the area and its people were slowly overtaken by the domination of the Christian political machine.

By the tenth century, folk charms and spells, classical correspondences (from the Greeks and Romans) mixed with local herbal lore, and astrology (from Greek, Roman, and Arabic) and prayers (often rehashed versions of the original magickal incantations) were bound together in these books in an effort to promote health and healing for everyone in the community. The clergy, royalty, and even some regular people like you and I had these doctor books that listed formal prescriptions mixed with magick.

For example, if you wanted to cure a skin disease, you might mix the specific parts of four herbs together, then squeeze the juice into a bowl, to which a small amount of soap would be added. This was the medical part. Yet, the prescription goes on to instruct the healer to take a small amount of blood from the patient at sunset and pour it into running water. The healer is then to spit three times, and say, "Take this disease and depart with it." The healer is also instructed to walk back to the house by an open road, and to walk each way in silence. The timing and the procedure for transferring illness to running water, spitting, uttering words of banishment, and walking to and from the water in silence (its attendant rituals and taboos) is clearly magickal.[43]

Even then it appears that people somehow knew that, no matter what dread disease a person might have, no matter how bad it looked, that 90 percent of the human body is water. Not cancer, not AIDS, not infection: It is water. That means that 90 percent of the physical body is already healthy, we then only have to work with the 10 percent of that body that is not at ease, or rather is dis-eased. Looking at it in that way makes the task a little less daunting and helps you believe that you can really make a difference. In healing, the boundaries between acceptable magickal practices and those techniques that were considered inherently evil by the church were blurred simply due to the lack of knowledge on health care issues; meaning if there was no tried and true cure (no distinctive method to relieve suffering), then magick was an okay thing (within limits, of course). Thus such remedies as that listed above—the conjuring of herbs, adding holy water or holy oil and the utterance of magickal prayers—was acceptable. There was, however, a limit to the patience of the church, and in its anxiety to repress popular magick the early sixteenth-century church took control of the licensing of doctors and midwives during the reign of Henry VIII.[44]

At this point you're probably saying, "Thank goodness for modern medicine! Weren't those people stupid? Everyone knows that disease is caused by germs!"

Um . . . not so fast.

Anthropologists believe that magick is dominant in a society when the control of the environment of that society is weak. In healing matters in the ancient world, in the Middle Ages, and even today, sickness is often beyond the realm of our control; therefore, mixing medicine with magick was not and is not an illogical outpouring of our behavior. Although these same anthropologists believe that the magickal rites themselves are illusionary, that the charms cannot make crops grow or wounds heal, the magick itself is not in vain, and this has everything to do with the side effects—that of human psychology. As Keith Thomas postulates,

> *The act of ritual lessens anxiety, relieves pent-up frustration, and makes the practitioner feel that he or she is doing something positive toward the solution to his or her problem. By its practice, the person is converted from a helpless bystander into an active agent.*[45]

The magick, therefore, is in the science of the mind, for which we still do not have all the answers. And whether it is the power of the mind, the power of Spirit, or both, there's one thing I have learned: Healing magick works!

Before we go any further, let me be the first to say that magickal remedies should never be used in place of modern medicine. If you had five dollars, would you throw away the other four because you already had one? No, you wouldn't. When it comes to healing, we can use all the information we can get! When you are sick, you should immediately go to a doctor. This said, let's talk about healing magick in the life of the modern Witch.

Most Witches today practice two separate types of activities when dealing with health and healing, preventative care and active care. Preventative care of body, mind, and spirit includes regular check-ups with the doctor and dentist; checking for symptoms of disease; practicing meditation and self-talk techniques to relieve stress and maintain a daily, positive frame of mind; and practicing spells, prayers, and rituals during seasonal celebrations (and other times) to welcome good health and positive abundance into their lives. Active care, on the other magickal hand, begins as soon as a symptom rears its ugly head. First, a trip to the doctor for adequate diagnosis (as your magick works better if you know what the heck you're dealing with, though don't allow any finite, scary, medical mumbo-jumbo to take all the oomph out of your magick—after all, physicians don't know everything. If they did, we'd never get sick). Even though you may be only sixteen, you're certainly smart enough to be an informed patient. If the problem is small, no biggie—but if it is something else, start researching. Many times those Witches who become immersed in the healing arts later in life began at a young age because they were forced to study a particular malady. Perhaps Grandpa has shingles, or Grandma has a heart condition. Maybe your brother has seizures. You would be surprised how much good you can do just by "being informed" and studying everything you can get your little magickal hands on. Just because you're a teen does not mean you don't have a brain. Once you have the diagnosis and the suggested medical treatment, you're ready to go on the magickal end, and there are a compendium of chants, spells, and rituals that can be done from the time you know you are sick on through the healing process. Just remember this: You didn't get sick in a day, and you won't get well in a day. Healing magick, above all other magickal applications, requires patience and faith.

So what is disease other than a bunch of nasty germs? People in the holistic end of medicine and modern alternative medical practices say that *disease* means *dis-ease* of the body. Stress seems to be a prime flag waver for the sick-bug to come a runnin' in your (or anyone's) direction. They also believe that you can think yourself sick when you engage in negative self-talk. There are thousands of cases that prove a qualified hypnotherapist can help a patient get well by helping the people to use their minds (along with standard medical treatment) to get better. We also know that prayer has brought miracles. The realm of medical astrology can actually help us pinpoint hot spots in our natal charts wherein during those cycles, we can practice good health care to prevent major difficulties. All this information tells us that if we use proper medical treatment, our minds, our belief, and our magick, amazing things in the realm of health and healing can occur.

Okay, so what's the first magickal step? Always a banishment of some kind. In medieval times, this was called an adjuration or an exorcism. This is you telling negative energy that you mean business and you won't take no for an answer. I was taught that "a Witch who cannot hex cannot heal." One meaning for this statement is obvious. If you can't banish the boogyman, then you haven't opened a pathway for positive energy to move and do its job. In fact, if you throw lots of positive energy at some diseases (like cancer) without first doing the banishment, they will grow! The banishment is followed by the spell you've selected for healing and an act of blessing for the afflicted person. If you are the one who is ill, positive self-talk throughout your illness is also very important. Many healing spells combine the adjuration, the magick, and the blessing all in one activity, which works well for smaller ills; however, if you are squaring your shoulders and facing something bigger, I've found that separating the three (working three distinct rituals or spells) seems to work better.

Once you have practiced a number of healing techniques, you will begin to select which spells, charms, rituals, and practices seem to work better for you than others. You'll also find that the more you work healing magick, the better and more confident you will become. Another interesting side-effect is the energy that gathers in your hands, especially if you use Reiki (SEE PAGE 320), Pow Wow (SEE PAGE 311), or touch healing. Like a muscle, the more you practice healing magicks, the better you get.

As with all things in life, you will, at some point in time, fail. Is it your fault?

If you tried the best you could, then the answer is no. By trying, you have fulfilled your duty. There are any number of factors in a healing that are beyond your control. If Spirit says that it is time for Aunt Jane to go to the Summerland, then you aren't going to be able to stop it, though you can make her passing easier because you have worked the healing magick. Just because it didn't work on her physical body does not mean that it failed in regard to her spiritual self. Another problem you'll find in healing magick is the cantankerousness of the patient. Some people like to be sick. For them, illness is a crutch, a way to not deal with the daily problems of life—they can mentally check out (hopefully only for awhile) while their difficulties supposedly slip away. Their problems, they will discover somewhere down the road, do not go away. Indeed, now they have *more* troubles because they are sick. Finally, some people like to be sick because they enjoy the attention they receive. In these cases, unlike magick that you do for yourself, you are not totally in control of the situation. This lack of control (for good or ill) is a magickal wild card. Once you understand this particular kink in the world of healing, the better prepared you will be should you appear to have been defeated.

There is one more thing I would like to add on this subject. There will come a time when you fully realize that you are too late to do any good (this will come through a personal analysis of your skills and what is going on around the patient). Should you throw up your hands and back away? No. In this case, god/dess is telling you to concentrate on the spiritual side of the person. It is never too late to banish negativity or bestow a blessing. Never.

So what about permission? Ah! A sticky subject in the occult world, so sayeth the experts. They claim that you must ask the sick person if it is okay to do magick for them, and if they refuse, your magickal hands are tied. How convenient. You cannot impose on another's free will, they chant. You cannot interfere with their spiritual plan, they rave. Send loving energy, some say, and be done with it—where others forbid even that modicum of thought. In my early years in the Craft, I listened to this blather. I even recommended to my students that they could re-word their request in a way that would be pleasing to the recipient. Not anymore.

Sigh. Why do people have to make the world such a complicated place?

If Uncle George is sick, and you know that he would never ask anyone for help (let alone you), are you going to let him lie there and rot? I heard that. So, you've forgotten your oath of service already, have you? For shame. When you said you were going to be a Witch, you indicated somewhere along that path that you would be of service to others (which is what being a Witch is all about). If you doubt this, you might be in the wrong religion.

In most cases I do ask the individual if they would like to have my assistance (or that of the Black Forest, my clan). On occasion, however, circumstances will prevent you from taking the easy way out, so you have to be creative instead. Do the magick anyway, and give it up to Spirit. Let Spirit (god/dess) decide who is to be healed and who is not. Ask also that, should the healing energy not be accepted for this person, it goes to someone who does need it. In this way, you have not made excuses and turned away from someone in need through conscious choice.

By choice, by design of Spirit's mind
I render this healing unto (person's name).
And should my spell be unwelcome there,
Spirit take it, work it, make it, give it
to the soul that is worthy to keep it.

How Disease Occurs

When working to banish any disease, from a minor cold to something more serious, the very first step is to consider the surrounding circumstances in that individual's life. A cold isn't just a cold—it is the end process of disharmony. Therefore, we have to figure out what the stressors are or were around the individual before we can work for total healing. If you practice a great deal of healing magicks, you will soon see patterns—stresses that are related to specific illnesses. For example, people who have suffered any type of back injury usually indicate that they have felt like they were carrying the world on their shoulders right before the injury occurred. In many cases, this person was the sole bread-winner for the family and experienced one of the following life events right before the injury:

- The threat of job loss or downsizing in their company.

- Actual loss of their job.

- Loss of additional income coming into the home (part-time job went down the drain, wife or husband lost a job, etc.).

- An additional expense in the home (such as a new baby, problems with taxes, a relative coming to live with them).

Women who suffer from breast cancer have often experienced a life-threatening circumstance (or major stress) involving a relationship with the opposite sex. People prone to colds have difficulty communicating with others—they may feel that others on the job or in the home are not listening to them, and they also appear to have been inundated by mental work (such as a big project that requires a lot of thinking or writing that may not be going smoothly) and the fear of failure. In all cases, the body is telling the mind that it is time to take a breather, to relax, step back, and review the current life situation. All this information leads us to the conclusion that when we work healing for another person (or ourselves), we need to investigate the surrounding life circumstances so that we can heal the whole person, not just target the symptom.

As an example, let's say that Jennifer, who is a senior in high school, has come down with a nasty cold right after New Year's. Granted, just about everyone in the school has been hit by such cold/flu symptoms, and we've taken that into account. Regardless, we want to review

Jennifer's life to see what may be going on (stress-wise) that can be alleviated.

The first pattern we noticed is that Jennifer isn't the only person who is ill. Half the school is down with the flu. Scientifically we know how the germs were spread and why so many are sick, but should we look for something else—something not on the surface? We know that there are individual stressors, but what about stressors to the group mind? If we look hard enough, we'll probably find them. In Jennifer's case there is a major battle going on between the administrator and the teaching staff. Although there hasn't been much said about it in the newspapers, these stressors are bleeding into the group mind of the student body. We also know that the school has decided to change some of its policies, both learning curriculum and disciplinary. To double-check just how messed up the group mind might be, we would ask Jennifer a few questions and check our divination tool. Whether school, work, coven, or family environment, mass sickness is usually a red flag that there is disharmony in the group mind.

Next we ask Jennifer about how things are going for her in her personal life. If Jennifer says, "Just like usual," don't take that answer. Dig deeper. We already know that Jennifer is a senior—that alone tells us that there are stressors present, those that revolve around the upcoming major change in her lifestyle from the environment of a high school to that of full-time work or college. We also discover that she is worried about some of the disciplinary changes incorporated by the school, and how some teachers seem to be using these new policies in an abusive way. Although Jennifer has not gone through these disciplinary measures, she sees what is happening to others and she subconsciously (or consciously) fears for herself. Jennifer has been looking at pre-admission for college and one wrong move, she believes, will ruin her chances of a good future. There are also minor problems at home. Her mother is working two jobs to cover the expense of roof damage after a nasty storm, and has asked Jennifer to care for her two younger siblings between three and six in the afternoon for the next month. Although Jennifer is a loving person and the care of her brother and sister is only temporary, deep down she feels that her siblings are her mother's responsibility and that she should not be made to care for them, especially right now—her senior year! On top of this, she has a major term paper due that encompasses three of her classes and the librarian is being a total jerk on helping her find the information she needs. She is sure she will fail. Now, on top of everything, she's sick. From all this we know that Jennifer is battling with three major stressors: fear, change, and anger. Therefore, when we work a healing spell for her, we need to help her find a positive way to reduce those stressors. Just getting Jennifer to calmly talk about how she feels is the first step to recovery.

Blessing Medicine

Before you take any medicine, check with your pharmacist about the effects of that drug and how it may interact with drugs you are already taking. Because there are so many specialists today who may prescribe various drugs, it is your job to make sure that what goes into your body is the right medicine for you. Once they bring the medicine home (and have double-checked with the pharmacist), many Witches bless the drugs as a further precaution. To do this, cast a magick circle. Cleanse the bottle with the four elements. Hold your hands over the bottle, and say:

> *Gracious Lord and Lady, You who were at the beginning of the world, You who command the energies of love, peace, and healing, please bless and consecrate, in your names, this medicine, given to me to bring good health and heal my body. I believe that I deserve the health, happiness, and joy that You can bestow upon me. May this medicine work for me the way it was intended and may it work with my body in a healthy way. So mote it be!*

Release the circle.

Banishing Illness

Magickal banishments of illness should include:

- Seeking expert medical care.

- Discussing stressors/events that took place at the inception of the illness.

- Encouraging the patient to make lifestyle changes, including more rest, exercise, letting go of projects or situations that are no longer serving them well, and helping them find solutions to problems that might be worrying them.

- Thoroughly cleansing the area with burning sage, bells, musical bowls, rattles, or incense and holy water on a repeated basis until the sickness is gone.

- Encouraging the patient to take a spiritual bath or daily spiritual shower.

- Writing a daily devotion or prayer that concentrates on wellness, for the patient to use each morning and evening.

- Banishing negativity and sickness in spellwork and ritual.

- Working for continued healing in spellwork and ritual once the banishment is done.

At this point some of you will be saying, "Gee, is that all there is to healing magicks?" and others will be exclaiming, "This is too much work, isn't there something simpler?" In all honesty, magick in general, and specifically healing magick, is a lot of hard work. The Witch must combine knowledge, magick, patience, faith, and general activity on a consistent basis to receive results. What often overrides one's worry about the effort is one's love and compassion for another person or animal. If your grandmother is sick, you'd probably move mountains to help her get better. That love thing is a mighty motivator. I watched my son chant his heart out over a dying rat. It lived.

When a Witch works healing magick for people, you will hear the following exclamations from doctors, which come back to you through the patient, who is normally grinning with glee. Doctors have said, "I don't know what you're doing, but something is working. You are healing much faster than expected!" or "I can't believe the progress you've made in such a short time!" Even better: "We've made a mistake. That's not a tumor," or "That's not cancer, it's a shadow on the X-ray. I don't know how we could have made that kind of error. The second set of X-rays we took yesterday shows no anomaly. I don't know how this could have happened."

Oh, yeah?

We know how.

And know this: When magick is afoot, a terminal illness is not always terminal.

Banishment Chants[46]

NINE SISTERS CHANT

To be recited nine times over a wound, tumor, or infection three times a day for twenty-one days (or less, should the wound close quickly). This Anglo-Saxon leechbook chant can also be used repetitively to remove evil from the home as the household is sprinkled with holy water and censed with a burning banishment herb, such as sage.

Nine were Noththe's sisters.
Then the nine became eight
and the eight became seven
and the seven became six
and the six became five
and the five became four
and the four became three
and the three became two
and the two became one
and the one became none.

Follow by drawing the equal-armed cross in the air and saying "It is so."

ALL-PURPOSE CALL TO THE EARTH GODDESS

To be sung over any wound or malady. Works especially well in an emergency situation where you must deal with several stressors at once.

May the Earth destroy you
with all her might and main.

Follow by drawing the equal-armed cross in the air and saying "It is so."

THE SPIDER HEALING CHANT

For fevers, colds, flus, and other assorted nasties. In this chant, the spider is a benevolent spirit that is called by you to assist the patient. Her job is to drive out the sickness by using her web to entangle the spirit of the illness. In the chant, the diseased spirit is told that it will be used as the spider's steed, and therefore will be harnessed and eventually driven out of the body. The "sister" is another spider who comes to aid the first and finishes out the cure.

The explanations in parentheses should not be spoken aloud. The chant should be said three times every half hour until the fever breaks, and then thrice a day for nine days, or longer should the disease be a more difficult one. You may also wish to hang a rubber or stuffed spider in the sick room until the patient recovers, empowered to "take off" the illness from the individual. If cleansed properly, the spider can be used on a repetitive basis.

In the eleventh century, the magickal person sang the chant/charm first in the patient's right ear, then in the left, and then over the crown of the head. Names of divinity or of famous personages like Maximianus, Malchus, Johannes, Martimianus, Dionisius, Constantinus, and Serafion were written on small wafers, which were strung on a red thread and hung about the patient's neck until the illness totally left the body.

Here a spider-wight (spirit) *came in.*
She had her web (to trap you) *in her hand.*
She said that you were her steed,
she laid her cords on your neck.
They began to set off from the land
(leave the body).
As soon as they came from the land,
then they began to cool (fever reduction).
Then the sister of the beast came in.
She put an end to it (sealed the healing so
that disease could not return)
and she swore oaths
(created a warding effect)
that this should never hurt the sick person
nor him or her who could obtain this charm
or knew how to sing this charm.
So mote it be.

Follow by drawing the equal-armed cross in the air and saying "It is so."

Healing Animals

Animals, like people, respond well to your healing efforts, and even though they may not understand your spoken word, they do respond to your feelings and emotions. They can sense your intentions, and they especially feel your love.

Animals are always in the alpha state, a brain-wave pattern that allows them to connect to you (and each other) without the necessity for speech. This is why pets of magickal people are often more alert and healthier than those of individuals who are not working on their spirituality in the home environment. Pets like the energy created by magick, meditation, and energy work. Magickal people have discovered that their pets gravitate to their altars, shrines, and magick circles like dust to a television screen (which is not always safe for the animal if you have burning candles or oil lamps). Pets love to soak up the harmonious energy you raise!

All of the healing techniques given in this book in relation to people will work for animals too, though there are a few special guidelines for animals that you might wish to use.

• Just like people, each animal is different, and just like people, remember to concentrate on *all* of the animal—body, mind, and spirit.

• Don't rush an animal into a healing. Let them know by speaking aloud and thinking about your healing intent while you hold them (or are near them, in the case of wild animals).

• If you are working with your hands, allow the animal to determine when he or she has had enough. In most cases, your pet will get up and walk away. Let them go.

• Cast a magick circle around the animal and yourself before you work any hands-on healing.

• If the animal does not want to be touched, you can place your hands a short distance away.

• Never touch a strange animal unless the owner is holding that animal. Never touch a wild animal.

- When using color in healing, work with orange for general healing and shock, indigo for tumors, blue for fevers and stress, and red for malaise.[47]

- My family has discovered that giving your pet bottled spring water charged with a clear, quartz crystal rather than water from the tap helps to promote healing. To charge, hold the crystal over the water bowl for about thirty seconds.

- Remember to call the totem spirit of your pet and ask that energy to aid in the healing process. You can also put a statue of the totem on your altar, on top of a picture of your ailing pet, to add extra healing energy.

Note: Some animals (like dogs and rats) can get people diseases like strep throat (dogs) and colds (rats). If your family seems to be going bout after bout with a particular medical problem, make sure that your pet visits a vet for a wellness check-up too.

Healing Blessing for Animals

SUPPLIES: Find a photo of your animal taken when you know for certain that the animal was healthy. One candle matching the curative properties for the dysfunction (optional; see pages 137–138 for candles and purposes).

TECHNIQUE: Hold the photo in your hand. Sit quietly and try for no interruptions, if possible. Close your eyes and ground and center. At this point you can hold the animal while saying or singing the chant, or if the animal isn't of the cuddly type, repeat the words from afar holding the picture. If you are holding the animal, place the picture under a cleansed, consecrated, and empowered candle. As you hold the animal or picture, try to reach that still point where you feel connected with all things. Remember deep breathing and calming techniques and use them if necessary. In your mind, reach out and encompass your pet in white light. Allow the light to grow until it feels strong and pure. Begin chanting "I am," finding your magickal voice (SEE PAGE 312) and allowing the sound to resonate throughout your entire body. Practice three times daily until your pet is healed.

Doing Your Part for World Health

It is my firm belief that for every illness on this planet there is a cure, we just have to get our heads out of the sand and find it. If we all work together, we can open the pathways to discover those cures. Sure, it may take awhile, but every bit of magickal energy we expend toward helping physicians and scientists ascertain and implement these desperately needed cures, the faster they will be found. At every healing circle I conduct when I'm on the road, I ask the participants to send positive energy toward finding and implementing the right cure for AIDS. Maybe you'd like to work toward that goal, or perhaps work on a malady that has afflicted your family. Here is a prayer you can say at every full moon (or even each day, should you be inclined to do so). Although you may think that the first four lines belong to the Christian church, they indeed do not. They were sung over 4,000 years ago in celebration of the Sumerian goddess Ishtar.[48]

Hail, Queen of Heaven.
Hail, Lady of the Angels.
Salutation to thee, root and portal
whence the light of the world has arisen.
I ask for thy blessings in the form
of healing for the world.
Please heal the sick and the wounded
and may the passing of the dying
be eased in your loving arms.

Call forth the power of curative forces
that they be discovered and implemented,
specifically in the realm of
(name the disease).
I affirm your love.
Blessings upon you.
So mote it be.

Medicine and Moon Magick

In magick and astrology all parts of the body have been assigned a sign of the zodiac, and if we dip into history we discover that medical diagnosis and treatment, magick, and astrology have been linked together for a very long time. Sybil Leek, famous Witch and astrologer, taught her students that "one of the effects of the moon is in the realm of health, and it is never wise to have surgery when the moon is transiting in the sign known to affect that specific part of the body."[49] Socrates left us an important rule that has been forgotten over the lost centuries. He said, "Do not let iron touch the part of the body ruled by the present moon sign."[50] What he meant was don't undergo surgery if the moon rules the part of the body that's going under the knife. The following list indicates what part of the body is associated with each sign of the zodiac. If the moon is in Aries, for example, moon lore has it that you should not schedule surgery for the head, face (except nose), brain, or eyes. You should choose a day when the moon is not in Aries for those related body parts, and some astrologers feel that you should also avoid surgery when the sun is in the same sign as the ailment that sign rules. You will find this same information in many astrology books, including William Lilly's *Christian Astrology,* written in the 1600s. Another example would be to avoid having your ears pierced when the moon is in Taurus. Medical astrologers believe that if you don't follow this rule, complications can arise, such as

infections, slow healing, increased pain, mistakes in anesthesia, as well as limited healing or more serious difficulties. They also believe that surgeries performed at the exact changing point from one quarter to another, especially when the moon moves from the second quarter (full moon) to the third (waning moon), are rarely successful. Use an almanac to avoid these times.

In magick it is okay to work when the moon is in the ruling sign of the ailment, as you are working to promote healing rather than disturbing the physical body with invasive surgery, which is always a shock to the system. Likewise, working to promote preventative health care can also be done when the moon is in the ruling sign.

ARIES

Rules: Head, face (except nose), brain, and eyes.[51]

TAURUS

Rules: Neck, throat, tonsils, ears, teeth, and jaw.

GEMINI

Rules: Shoulders, arms, fingers, lungs, thymus gland, upper ribs.

CANCER

Rules: Stomach, diaphragm, chest, lymph system, liver, and gall bladder.

LEO

Rules: Heart, aorta, back, and spine.

VIRGO

Rules: Colon, small intestine, pancreas, nerves, spleen.

LIBRA

Rules: Kidneys, bladder, inner ear, and skin.

SCORPIO

Rules: Nose, genitals, rectum, colon, blood, urethra, and, on occasion, the back.

SAGITTARIUS

Rules: Hips, thighs, liver, and veins.

CAPRICORN

Rules: Teeth, bones, joints, and skin.

AQUARIUS

Rules: Calves, ankles, varicose veins, and circulatory system.

PISCES

Rules: Feet, toes, lungs, and bodily fluids.

Other Bits of Magickal Medical Knowledge

Medical astrologers have found that they can follow the progression of a disease by the lunar phases, and can predict which days will be critical. These are the days in which to work magick to help the patient over the medical crises. Critical days are multiples of seven (7, 14, 21, and 28), calculated from the first day of the onset of the disease.[52] In critical illnesses, such as a stroke or heart attack, if the patient survives until the moon returns to its beginning phase (the same day 28 days after the onset of the disease), he or she will most likely overcome the onslaught of the illness. The fourteenth day is usually seen as the most critical of all. Therefore, in magick done for healing purposes, always ask for the date that the patient recognized there was a problem. If that is not available or if they can't remember, ask for the date that they first visited their physician for their ailment and received a diagnosis. When and if you study astrology, you will be able to tailor your magick to combat the disease more effectively and look ahead to see if there are any possible problems looming by

checking not only the transits to an individual's natal chart, but also the celestial activities for the date and time they first felt ill. For now, with the knowledge of the date, you can work magick in multiples of seven, giving extra energy on those critical days. Use the symbols for the moon, conjunction, and Mars ($\mathrm{D\ \sigma\ \sigma^{?}}$) on candles burned for the sick, as when the moon is conjunct Mars, the healer has a better chance of success.

Dental work also has its own lunar associations. Fillings seem to last longer if the waning moon is in Leo, Scorpio, and Aquarius (three of the four fixed signs), and procedures that cause a great deal of bleeding, such as periodontal treatment or pulling wisdom teeth, should always be performed during a waning moon, and definitely not in the sign of Taurus.[53] Sybil Leek felt that one should also avoid the Aries moon for dental surgery because your fleeting bit of bravery may totally escape by the time you get into the dental chair.[54]

We've only skimmed the surface in discussing healing techniques, and you will find other spells, information, and recommendations for health and healing throughout this book, but don't stop there. Widen your healing horizons with research, study, and additional practice. In doing this, not only will you learn to help yourself, but you will be of invaluable service to others. You can find more information on magickal healing in my book *American Magick.*

When You Are Ill

There is nothing more irritating than being a sick Witch. Here you are, lying on the sofa, snotty tissues at hand, half-eaten chicken soup congealing in the bowl on the coffee table, coughing and hacking right at the good parts of *Buffy.* The last thing on your mind is doing magick, and the idea of dragging your sorry Witch carcass around to do a full ritual carries more laughs than the Comedy Channel. Or maybe you've had dental surgery—that always puts the body in a go-getting mood. *Not.*

Here is where the mental magicks and meditation you've been doing come in really handy. Even though it takes a little effort, try to get through at least one meditation sequence or visualization exercise that surrounds your body with white, healing light. I've been so sick that I've drawn magickal symbols on my body with makeup because I knew there was no way I could get up and do a full healing ritual. My family thought I was nuts, but I did get better faster than anticipated. I've also learned to make gris-gris bags and empower candles when I'm well, then store them in my magickal cabinet for those few sick days. The key is to put the whole ritual into the candle or bag, then activate it by words of power or touch. Here is a checklist to cover when you are ill:

1. See a physician.

2. Get plenty of rest and follow the doctor's orders. Don't fudge on the recuperation time, that's how people dropped dead from the influenza epidemics in the early 1900s. Just because you are starting to feel better doesn't mean you're ready for the New York Marathon.

3. Cleanse. Cleanse. Cleanse. Use spiritual baths or showers, sage the house (especially the sick bed area), use bells to break up pockets of negativity, etc.

4. Do mental cleansings through meditation and visualization.

5. Activate any simple magicks you've stored for sick times.

6. If you are lucky enough to have a magickal friend, ask them to work a healing spell for you. This does not leave you off the hook on items one through five, but a little extra help is always welcome.

7. Use this downtime to your best advantage. Yes, I know that sounds stupid—you should be concentrating on getting well and all that; however, when we are off our feet and not out cold, there are a variety of things that we can do, like consider what stressors may have led to the sickness in the first place, and think of solutions on how to best handle or remove those issues from our lives.

Apples and Oranges Healing Garland Spell

INGREDIENTS: Five apples; lemon juice (enough to cover the apples); 2 teaspoons salt; 6 teaspoons cinnamon; 2 teaspoons allspice; 2 teaspoons cloves; 2 teaspoons arrowroot powder; one teaspoon nutmeg; 5 oranges. **Note:** You can also use cookie cutters for interesting apple and orange shapes that may apply to your spellwork, such as stars and moons.

INSTRUCTIONS: Hold your hands over all ingredients. Cleanse, consecrate, and empower for healing. Core and slice apples about ¼-inch thick. Soak slices in lemon juice for 5 minutes. Pat dry with paper towel. Mix remaining ingredients in a large plastic bag. Add apples and shake to coat. Slice oranges ¼-inch thick. Heat oven no hotter than 160 degrees. Lay apples and oranges flat on cookie sheet. Bake oranges for 4 hours, apples for 6 hours. Lay slices on wax paper to dry.

SUPPLIES FOR GARLAND: Cord or yarn; silver bells (optional); dried orange and apple slices.

INSTRUCTIONS FOR GARLAND: Braid or tie bells with apples and oranges onto cord or yarn. Empower completed project for healing.

SUPPLIES FOR RITUAL: One green taper candle; a small amount of tinfoil; one apple that sets well on a flat surface; the garland; a picture of your sick friend or family member. (If you can't get a picture, write their name on a piece of paper instead.) Choose a ritual format.

INSTRUCTIONS FOR RITUAL: Core apple and fill with tinfoil to support the green taper candle. Follow ritual format. Place all supplies on your altar. Put the picture of the sick person under the apple. Encircle the apple candle holder with the garland. Light the candle and repeat the Thirteen Powers verse on page 4. Finish with:

> *May all astrological correspondences be correct*
> *for this working and may this spell not reverse*
> *or place upon me any curse. I know you will*
> *do this for me. So mote it be!*

Finish the ritual. Allow the candle to completely burn. Dispose of candle end and apple off of your property, saying: "As this apple rots, so will sickness be taken from (say the person's name)." Place the garland and the picture (or name) in a safe place until the person has been completely healed. Use the garland again for the same person if this is a long-term illness that requires repeated work. Dispose of garland when the individual is well or has reached the level of healing asked for.

Herbs

Learn and learn, ask and ask,
do not be ashamed.
—*Paracelsus*

Modern Witches may use herbs in two ways: through homeopathy and natural medicine, and in magickal applications for health and healing as well as success, prosperity, harmony, etc. The magickal intent of the herb always matches its medical intent, which is good—there's less to confuse the mind. Therefore, if you don't know what an herb can do on the magickal realm, and you can't find it anywhere in books on magick, you can always read about its medicinal properties and match the energy of the plant to a specific magickal working. That means if Grandma is suffering from a cold, and we know that certain herbs mixed together in the right way to make a tea for her to drink can ease her symptoms, then we can also mix those same plants together and put them in an incense to smudge her room, in a sachet to put under her pillow, or in a magickal garland to hang over her bed. The nice thing about herbs in magick is that we don't have to worry about dosage (how much Grandma should take that is safe), because Grandma is not eating or drinking your magickal project. The magick you do is a companion to what the medicine does; however, the magick should never take the place of the medicine. The magick is a healing helper, and sometimes, especially in emergencies, it is a healing starter.

At this point you might be saying, "Okay, but what if Grandma isn't into herbs or natural medicine, and she hates tea? She's taking something else. Will the magick still work?" Yes, because you have matched the healing properties of the herb to her illness. She can be taking prescription drugs from her doctor and you can be working healing magick with herbs, and they will still work together even though Grandma isn't ingesting those herbs.

How can this be so? So far in this book we have talked about the unity of all things and how energy moves easily and in a natural way. We've also discussed the power of your mind and how it can be harnessed to work for the good of all, and how thoughts are things or energy that we can use in a positive way. In the correspondences section I've explained how the individual energy of a person, place, or thing can match, or be in sympathy, with a stone, plant, animal, or planet. If we put all these ideas together in one spell (which is what a spell is actually made of, these different ideas layered into one), then we can reach success without having Grandma drink something she thinks tastes nasty. Granted, Grandma will get better faster if she takes good care of herself, gets lots of sleep, eats right, reduces stress, visits the doctor, and keeps a positive mental attitude. As you can see, Grandma's healing depends a lot on Grandma's actions. That's why, in any kind of healing, you can only say, "I will try."

How do we know that using herbs in magick works? We've talked about healing, but what about success, getting a job, making more money, or passing that blasted chemistry exam? As with all magick, it begins with the certainty that what we want will come about, and the belief that what we are doing can work. This belief grows stronger with every magickal application we do. Once one spell works, then your confidence builds. This is why experimentation and practice on your part is so important to your ultimate success. To win, you have to try.

The History of Herbal Magick

Up until the seventeenth century, the sciences (magick, astrology, astronomy, philosophy, chemistry, and medicine, to name a few) were all lumped together. If you studied one, you studied them all. As a magickal person it is important that you know this because today, you are like those famous men and women of the Renaissance period who turned their eyes to the betterment of humankind. Many of them began studying at your age or even earlier. That's why I laugh when some people say that teenagers can't study magick. Some of the greatest medical and magickal works in history began germinating in the teen brain, except they weren't considered teens then, they were considered adults. Only in this century are you given such a long life-span. Before, if you hit thirty, you were lucky. Plague, war, famine, and acts of political stupidity took you out at an early age.

Your historical company includes Michelangelo, Leonardo da Vinci, Kepler, Copernicus, and others. You laugh? Where are you right now? Are you out with the "common" teen, drinking in the parking lot? No, you are here with me, trying to figure out what makes the universe tick, and in that discovery working to make your life, and the lives of others, better—teen or otherwise.

In your studies of the Craft and magick, you will eventually have a more complete library than most people. It just happens. The more we seek, the bigger our library grows. In these books you will find tables of correspondences handed down from centuries past. Where did these tables come from and who put them together in the first place? Are these tables reliable? Just because it is in a book doesn't make it so. We know that lots of errors have occurred in the past, especially where magickal work is concerned, due to the fact that it had to go underground. To answer some of these questions, we need to ride in the time machine of your mind and go back into history. Oh, don't groan. When you go to your first Pagan festival, you can wow them with your astute grasp of the occult.

While the study of herbs can be traced to the early Greeks, one of the first writers to address the field of plants and medicine and their association to astrology and the magick of the times was Dioscorides. He was a Roman and his book was called *De Materia Medica*, published around A.D. 77. That's about 2,000 years ago. While Dioscorides studied plants, his followers studied him! This means that for quite some time, future writers on the subject did not work with the plants themselves, but tried to match Dioscorides' ideas to the vegetation in their own areas (which didn't always match). This actually happens a lot in history, where information is handed from generation to generation, and in the process things get mixed up. If you consider your own classes at school, you'll see what I mean. Think about the classes where you actively experiment with what you learn and compare them with the classes where you only study a book and don't put what you've learned to the test of daily living. The hands-on stuff is fun and, because you did it yourself, you remember more. The book stuff is boring and you forget it faster. When you try to remember what you read you might get it wrong because you didn't do any experiments to see if what you were reading was or is true.

By the 1500s, the European printing press was going full blast and even though the church condemned and murdered at will, brave thinkers like Agrippa von Nettesheim (1486–1535); Trithmius (1462–1516), and Philippus Aureolus Paracelsus (1493–1541) were pushing the envelope. Rather than just reading about stuff, they did experiments on what they wanted to learn, and the subjects of their study included alchemy, medicine, herbs, astrology, theology, and more.[54] These guys were the scholars of their time, so you see you are in good company. What's even better, they published their work (or at least took great lengths to preserve it) so that every-

one could see it. Such people reexamined the classical works (Greek and Roman), and made revisions based on their own experiments. For plant lore this meant traveling to other areas, talking to all sorts of healers, and then bringing the information back to test. When the "doctors" of their time cut and ran because of the plague, these guys stuck around and tried to do the best they could. And you can probably guess that because of their individual courage they were hated by those guys that bailed out.

These men (Agrippa, Trithmius, and Paracelsus) and many of their contemporaries were certain that a world-soul existed—that we are all linked together in some way—and it is from this idea that correspondences involving herbals and astrology and magick were researched, developed, studied, and, most importantly, written down. It was Paracelsus who said the body was not a separate thing, but a house for the soul, and the physician should therefore treat both body and soul to turn the sick person into a well one. And you thought the idea was a New Age thing!

Just how famous were these guys? As an example, the Swiss Paracelsus is considered the father of pharmaceutical chemistry, modern wound surgery, and homeopathy—not bad. What interests us, however, is that he was also a magician who used folk remedies, amulets, talismans, and a variety of studies to heal his patients, which really made his Renaissance contemporaries angry and put church leaders in orbit. Paracelsus traveled all over Europe, talking to doctors, barbers (who often seconded as physicians), wisewomen, sorcerers, alchemists, nuns, bath attendants, magicians, knights, princes, kings, gypsies, and monks[56]—from the low ranks and from those of nobility, from the intelligent and the simple-minded—to collect as much information as he could for the purposes of healing. The fear of disease, he said, is more dangerous than disease itself.[57] And just how many times have you heard that statement? If you've been involved in magick or healing for any length of time, probably once a day.

It is within the spirit of Paracelsus that we should view herbals and their vast healing properties, both medicinal and magickal. His Doctrine of Signatures stated that all plants were stamped with some physical sign of their qualities for healing as well as their qualities for things like success, protection, banishing, harmony, and so on. Over time, modern doctors threw this idea out because they had no knowledge of the occult. The idea that things might be "in sympathy" was considered stupid and childish, and they sought to disprove this theory. Because writers after Paracelsus fiddled with the original product and because the theory of the times was mixed with superstition (meaning things yet unproved), errors in the Doctrine of Signatures multiplied; however, Paracelsus wasn't talking just about internal consumption, he was also talking about magick.

In the Doctrine of Signatures, Paracelsus and other scholars of his time looked at a plant's family, the conditions in which it grew naturally, and the illness it supposedly cured when assigning a planetary association for healing and for magick. Granted, not every assumption made was accurate, and superstition (as mentioned earlier) still ran rampant in the fifteen and sixteen hundreds. Some people actually believed that bugs were created by rotting matter and that a crystal gemstone was petrified ice (both at which Paracelsus scoffed, by the way).

As the centuries progressed, the sciences split—chemistry moved into its own realm, medicine another, astronomy to yet a different area, magick went underground, and astrology drifted in and out of favor. As in Paracelsus' time, the mood has shifted again, and we are back looking at the world-soul; the links between mind, body, and spirit; and the quest for magickal applications as we once again seek the understanding of how the human fits into the scheme of the universe.

Herbs and Astrology

Unlike other individuals who use herbs in the healing practice, the Witch pays attention to two distinct sciences: homeopathy and astrology. Homeopathy tells us the most modern information about the medical uses of the plant, and astrology gives us information on timing and sympathetic associations (the matching of energy patterns) between the plant itself and the purpose of the magick.

On the surface, the medical healer may pooh-pooh the idea of astrology mixed with medicine and personal well-being, and to be fair, we really can't blame them. When the sciences split, people tended to focus on their chosen study to the exclusion of all else. If, then, they were only into the healing properties of plants, and spent years in experimentation, they would most likely not be wasting time looking at a science that they (on the surface) believed to be dissimilar. If, in the meantime, this dissimilar science fell out of favor, its information moving underground, the scientist would not be particularly joyful when it tried to reassert itself in society. This is exactly what happened between the medical community and the magickal one, and although the magickal community did not drop its understanding and search for real science, real science lost all concept of the occult teachings.

When dealing with herbs and magick in the modern Craft community, you will run across a book called *Culpeper's Herbal*, which was first printed in 1652 in London under the title of *The English Physician*. Nickolas Culpeper became famous because he took the trouble to translate herbals into wording that common people could understand, and threw out exotic ingredients that could not be obtained by the butcher, baker, farmer, or candlestick maker. Notice, if you will, that this is one hundred years after Paracelsus was born. Culpeper stuck only to the healing properties of the herbs and threw out the magickal stuff, yet retained the astrological associations. With the magick gone, future readers and scholars of botany assumed that Culpeper did not follow the Doctrine of Signatures, not understanding that he did indeed include it, because he always added the planetary influence under each entry. Culpeper's herbal is important because (*a*) it is still quite popular (new editions give modern healing information as well as Culpeper's original prose), and (*b*) it is one of the few books that managed to stay in print from the 1600s until now that hints at the magickal associations of plants (through the planetary associations listed). If you ever wonder what magickal folks in the 1900s were using for magickal research involving plants, you need only look at Culpeper's herbal to get a general idea, because by then, little was available on the open market for magickal research purposes. Today, we are one up on Culpeper. Thanks to the late Scott Cunningham and his *Cunningham's Encyclopedia of Magickal Herbs* and Paul Beyerl's *A Compendium of Herbal Magick* you have a broad range of information that joins magick and herbalism together. In all honesty, we've only scratched the magickal surface when it comes to the realm of astrology, botany, and magick, but the information in this section will be enough to get you started. Where you take it from there is entirely up to you.

Supplies for Herbal Magick

Modern practitioners of magick believe that you can add an herb to any enchantment based on its inherent power (life force) and its associations, otherwise known as correspondences. General supplies for working with herbs include a mortar and pestle (preferably ceramic); a glass jar; a special knife that has been specifically cleansed, consecrated, and empowered for harvesting herbs and flowers; a small, wooden cutting board; and a strainer or cheesecloth. Other supplies might include small vials for elixirs, perfumes, oils, tinctures, and fluid condensers; cloth pouches for conjuring bags and sachets; needle and thread for stringing dried blossoms and herbs; cord (for hanging herbs upside down to dry); and small resealable plastic bags for storing powders, incense, and raw herbs. The most expensive item on this list is the mortar and pestle. You will also, at some point in time, need a large box or cabinet in which to keep these supplies.

Many modern practitioners also use spice grinders and food processors to grind difficult powders, nuts, fillers (such as rice), and cantankerous pieces of small bark. Read the machine's instructions carefully, as most will not be adequate for your use and the equipment that can handle your heavy-duty work may be a bit pricey. This does not mean, however, that the mortar and pestle is abandoned. The mixture (when created in such a machine) is additionally hand ground in a magick circle with mortar and pestle, and often empowered at the same time through the clockwise grinding motion.

Herbal Doctrines and Signatures for Basic Empowerment

When studying history we learned that just about everything, at one time or another, was associated with the elements, planetary influences, and astrological signs. Many magickal people study this lore to determine when they can get the most out of what. The only problem is that there are lots and lots of tables, lists, and books that describe the virtues (magickal correspondences) of any given object. As much of this information has been changed over time, how do you know what is "right" and what isn't? The best way to handle this is to follow the idea that these tables (such as the ones provided in this book) are good for giving you a place to start, and then, as you learn more about magick and can draw from personal experience, follow up with your own ideas. Please remember that any herb can be empowered at any time, especially if the need is great.

The following list is provided for those who wish to plan a magickal application that takes advantage of the astrological and elemental energies associated with each section of a plant. A spell is offered afterward to show how you might use this information.

General Herbal Empowerments

ROOTS

Type of elemental magick to use: Earth/air.

Associated planet: Saturn.

Empower when the moon is in: Capricorn or Aquarius.

SAP

Type of elemental magick to use: Fire.

Associated planet: Sun.

Empower when the moon is in: Aries or Leo; or when the moon is in your sun sign.

BARK

Type of elemental magick to use: Air/earth.

Associated planet: Mercury.

Empower when the moon is in: Gemini or Virgo.

LEAVES

Type of elemental magick to use: Water.

Associated planet: Moon.

Empower when the moon is in: Cancer or when the moon is in your natal moon sign.

FLOWERS

Type of elemental magick to use: Air/earth.

Associated planet: Venus.

Empower when the moon is in: Taurus or Libra.

FRUIT

Type of elemental magick to use: Fire/water.

Associated planet: Jupiter.

Empower when the moon is in: Sagittarius or Pisces.

SEEDS AND PEELS

Type of elemental magick to use: Air/earth.

Associated planet: Mercury.

Empower when the moon is in: Gemini or Virgo.

Let's say you would like to do a flower spell for love. You might go to the store and choose specific flowers, or you might want to work with the ones in the back yard if you are short on cash. Let's also say that you have gone through one of the herbal books I mentioned above or checked out the flower table on page 280 and noticed that the flowers you have chosen are assigned planets or elements that do not match each other, or perhaps there is no mention of the planetary or elemental association at all. What should you choose? This is where the above list comes in handy.

In our list, flowers are ruled by the elements air and earth, and specifically ruled by the planet Venus. As Venus (in goddess form) is the energy of love, she's the deity figure we'll use in this spell. According to our chart, we can choose either air magick or earth magick (or both). For this spell we will whisper a chant, which matches the air element. As Libra is the air sign associated with flowers, we'll choose a time when the moon is in Libra. Now, that does mean that we'll have to wait until the moon slides into Libra. What if we look in our almanac and see that when the moon is in Libra, it's in the wrong quarter to pull something toward you? Now what do you do? First, look to see if the moon in Taurus falls at a better time (which it probably does). In that case, choose the moon in Taurus. This is okay because the planet Venus also rules Taurus. Yes, you could change the type of magick to earth magick and get the same results to better match the Taurus energy, but I'm being difficult on purpose so that you can see how this works.

Now it's time to choose other ingredients for this love spell. How about a pink candle, your favorite perfume, a pencil, gold thread, and a needle (as well as the flowers you have selected).

On the night you chose in advance (from looking at the table above and your almanac), place all your supplies on the altar. Cast a magick circle and call the quarters. Cleanse, consecrate, and empower the supplies with the four elements and the appropriate words of power. With a pencil, draw the symbol of the planet Venus (♀) on the candle. Dress the candle with your favorite perfume. Hold the candle in your hands, thinking about the type of love you would like to draw toward yourself (don't think of a specific person, as that would be inhibiting his or her free will). Connect with the Lady Venus. Visualize what you think she looks like. Now ask her to bring love into your life. Know that love belongs to you and believe that you can have love. Accept this love. Light the candle.

Thread the needle and tie a knot at one end. Carefully string the flowers along the thread. Your flower garland will be as long as the thread you've cut, so be sure to have enough flowers and keep at least four inches of thread on either side of the flowers. As you string the flowers, keep repeating:

I walk in beauty, like the night
of cloudless climes and starry skies;
and all that's best of dark and bright
meet in my aspect and my eyes.[58]

When the garland is finished, hold your hands over the flowers and say:

Lady Venus, my path has led me
to new realms of spirituality.
I seek relationships that will
show me the fulfillment of life,
that can allow me to exercise true harmony
on my spiritual path, and bring toward me
eloquence of thought and deed.
So mote it be.[59]

Thank divinity, release the quarters, and release the circle. Hang the garland outside your bedroom window, saying:

Spirits of air and spirits of earth
(if you chose the moon in Taurus),
guide my desire to its fruition.

Herbal Magickal Applications

Like gems and stones, herbs can be carried in a pocket or purse and used as amulets and talismans. These herbs are usually cleansed, consecrated, and empowered by the Witch in a magick circle. Roots and seeds work particularly well as an amulet or talisman as you don't need to put them in a cloth bag (though you can to protect their energy). The following list gives you the herb, purpose, planetary influence, the best day, and the preferred quarter of the moon on which to empower the herb.

Herbal Amulets and Talismans

Please note that none of the following are meant to be eaten.

ACORN (FROM OAK)

Purpose: Health, money, healing, protection, and luck.

Planetary influence: Sun.

Day to empower: Sunday.

Quarter to empower: First and second or when the moon is in your sun sign.

ALMOND

Purpose: Prosperity, money, and wisdom.

Planetary influence: Mercury.

Day to empower: Wednesday.

Quarter to empower: First and second.

APRICOT PIT

Purpose: Love.

Planetary influence: Venus.

Day to empower: Friday.

Quarter to empower: First and second.

AVOCADO PIT

Purpose: Beauty.

Planetary influence: Venus.

Day to empower: Friday.

Quarter to empower: First and second.

BAMBOO

Purpose: Protection, luck, repelling negative energy, wishes.

Planetary influence 1: Sun—luck, wishes, and protection.

   Day to empower: Sunday.

   Quarter to empower: First and second.

Planetary influence 2: Saturn—banish negative energy.

Day to empower: Saturday.

Quarter to empower: Third or fourth.

BRAZIL NUT

Purpose: Love.

Planetary influence: Venus.

Day to empower: Friday.

Quarter to empower: First and second.

CASHEW

Purpose: Money.

Planetary influence: Sun.

Day to empower: Sunday or Thursday.

Quarter to empower: First and second or when the moon is in your sun sign.

CEDAR

Purpose: Healing, money and protection.

Planetary influence: Sun.

Day to empower: Healing—Sunday; money— Thursday; protection—Saturday.

Quarter to empower: First and second or when the moon is in your sun sign.

CHESTNUT

Purpose: Love, money.

Planetary influence: Jupiter.

Day to empower: Love—Friday; money— Thursday.

Quarter to empower: First and second.

CINNAMON STICK

Purpose: Spirituality, success, healing, psychic powers, protection, love and money.

Planetary influence: Sun.

Day to empower: Sunday.

Quarter to empower: First and second or when the moon is in your sun sign.

CLOVES

Purpose: Protection, exorcism, love, money.

Planetary influence: Jupiter.

Day to empower: Protection—Monday (*Quarter to empower:* First and second); Love—Friday; Money—Thursday; Exorcism—Saturday (*Quarter to empower:* Third or fourth).

COTTON

Purpose: Luck, healing, protection, rain.

Planetary influence: Moon.

Day to empower: Monday.

Quarter to empower: First and second.

FIG

Purpose: Divination, love.

Planetary influence: Jupiter.

Day to empower: Thursday.

Quarter to empower: First and second.

GINGER ROOT

Purpose: Love, money, success, power.

Planetary influence: Mars.

Day to empower: Tuesday.

Quarter to empower: First and second.

GINSENG

Purpose: Love, wishes, healing, beauty, protection and lust.

Planetary influence: Sun.

Day to empower: Sunday.

Quarter to empower: First and second or when the moon is in your sun sign.

HIGH JOHN THE CONQUEROR ROOT

Purpose: Money, love, success, happiness.

Planetary influence: Mars.

Day to empower: Tuesday.

Quarter to empower: First and second.

HOLLY LEAF

Purpose: Protection, luck, dream magick.

Planetary influence: Mars.

Day to empower: Tuesday.

Quarter to empower: First and second.

HORSE CHESTNUT

Purpose: Money and healing.

Planetary influence: Jupiter.

Day to empower: Thursday.

Quarter to empower: First and second.

MINT SPRIG

Purpose: Money, healing, travel, protection, banishing.

Planetary influence: Mercury.

Day to empower: Wednesday; Saturday (banishing).

Quarter to empower: First and second except banishing, which is third or fourth.

MOSS

Purpose: Luck and money.

Planetary influence: Moon.

Day to empower: Monday.

Quarter to empower: First and second.

MUSTARD SEED

Purpose: Protection, mental powers, faith.

Planetary influence: Mars.

Day to empower: Tuesday.

Quarter to empower: First and second.

PEACH PIT

Purpose: Love, longevity, wishes, banishing.

Planetary influence: Venus.

Day to empower: Friday; Saturday (banishing).

Quarter to empower: First and second for all except banishing, which is third and fourth.

PINE CONE

Purpose: Healing, protection, money, banishing.

Planetary influence: Mars.

Day to empower: Tuesday.

Quarter to empower: First and second for all except banishing, which is third and fourth.

PISTACHIO NUT

Purpose: Break a love spell (in case you made a boo-boo).

Planetary influence: Mercury.

Day to empower: Wednesday.

Quarter to empower: Third and fourth quarter.

RADISH

Purpose: Protection.

Planetary influence: Mars.

Day to empower: Tuesday.

Quarter to empower: First and second.

SUNFLOWER SEEDS

Purpose: Wishes, health, wisdom.

Planetary influence: Sun.

Day to empower: Sunday.

Quarter to empower: First and second or when the moon is in your sun sign.

VANILLA BEANS

Purpose: Love and mental powers.

Planetary influence: Venus.

Day to empower: Friday.

Quarter to empower: First and second.

WALNUT

Purpose: Health, mental powers, wishes.

Planetary influence: Sun.

Day to empower: Sunday.

Quarter to empower: First and second or when the moon is in your sun sign.

Asperging

Asperge means to sprinkle sacred water around an area in a ritual way. This is often done by bunching fresh herbs together, empowering them for purification, then dipping them in a chalice or cup of holy water and allowing the water to lightly drip off the herbs as you walk clockwise around the ritual space. You can use specific colored ribbon or plain cord to bundle the herbs. Although fresh is best, you can dry bunches of herbs to use in asperging at a later date (SEE PAGE 283).

The following list represents the most common herbs and flowers used for asperging. Although you can conjure an herb to work at any time, they may work better for you when the moon is in the associated astrological sign. ***Note:*** For those of you who are using Culpeper, Cunningham, or Beryl's herbal guides, you will notice that the elements listed here do not match the elements in these books. Those listed here are taken from what is called classical astrology, and elements match the originally assigned planetary rulers of material written in the 1600s.

AFRICAN VIOLET

Ritual purpose: Spirituality and protection.

Planetary/elemental influence: Venus/air, earth.

Use when moon is in: Libra or Taurus.

ALOE

Ritual purpose: Love and spirituality.

Planetary/elemental influence: Moon/water.

Use when moon is in: Cancer or when the moon is in your moon sign.

ANGELICA

Ritual purpose: Banishing, protection, healing, visions.

Planetary/elemental influence: Sun/fire.

Use when moon is in: Leo or when the moon is in your sun sign.

BASIL

Ritual purpose: Astral travel, love, banishing, wealth, protection.

Planetary/elemental influence: Mars/fire, water.

Use when moon is in: Aries or Scorpio.

BIRCH

Ritual purpose: Protection, banishing, purification.

Planetary/elemental influence: Venus/air, earth.

Use when moon is in: Libra or Taurus.

HOLLY

Ritual purpose: Protection, luck, and dream magick.

Planetary/elemental influence: Mars/fire, water.

Use when moon is in: Aries or Scorpio.

HONEYSUCKLE

Ritual purpose: Money, psychic powers, and protection.

Planetary/elemental influence: Jupiter/fire, water.

Use when moon is in: Sagittarius or Pisces.

IVY

Ritual purpose: Protection and healing.

Planetary/elemental influence: Saturn/earth, air.

Use when moon is in: Capricorn or Aquarius.

LAVENDER

Ritual purpose: Love, protection, sleep, longevity, purification, happiness.

Planetary/elemental influence: Mercury/earth, air.

Use when moon is in: Virgo or Gemini.

LETTUCE

Ritual purpose: Protection, love divination, sleep.

Planetary/elemental influence: Moon/water.

Use when moon is in: Cancer or when the moon is in your natal moon sign.

LILAC

Ritual purpose: Banishing and protection.

Planetary/elemental influence: Venus/earth, air.

Use when moon is in: Taurus or Libra.

MIMOSA

Ritual purpose: Protection, love, prophetic dreams, and purification.

Planetary/elemental influence: Saturn/earth, air.

Use when moon is in: Capricorn or Aquarius.

MINT

Ritual purpose: Money, healing, travel, banishing, and protection.

Planetary/elemental influence: Mercury/air, earth.

Use when moon is in: Gemini or Virgo.

OAK

Ritual purpose: Protection, health, money, healing, fertility and luck.

Planetary/elemental influence: Sun/fire.

Use when moon is in: Leo or when the moon is in your sun sign.

PARSLEY

Ritual purpose: Protection and purification.

Planetary/elemental influence: Mercury/air, earth.

Use when moon is in: Gemini or Virgo.

PINE

Ritual purpose: Healing, protection, banishing, and money.

Planetary/elemental influence: Mars/fire, water.

Use when moon is in: Aries or Scorpio.

SNAPDRAGON

Ritual purpose: Protection and purification.

Planetary/elemental influence: Mars/fire, water.

Use when moon is in: Aries or Scorpio.

SPANISH MOSS

Ritual purpose: Protection and purification.

Planetary/elemental influence: Mercury/air, earth.

Use when moon is in: Gemini or Virgo.

TULIP

Ritual purpose: Prosperity, love, and protection.

Planetary/elemental influence: Venus/earth, air.

Use when moon is in: Taurus or Libra.

WILLOW

Ritual purpose: Love, divination, protection, and healing.

Planetary/elemental influence: Moon/water.

Use when moon is in: Cancer or when the moon is in your natal moon sign.

Herbs are also used in holy water, as adornment for the body, the altar, and for sacred space, in spiritual baths, food preparation, floor washes, magickal powders, incense, pillows, sachets, and poppets. They can be strewn about a ritual space, pressed and placed under a candle in candle magick spells, or strung on string as garlands. They are sometimes used as the sole focus of a spell and at other times as useful additions to the magickal working.

The Magick in Flowers

In the discreet courting process of the Victorian era, a bouquet of flowers came to serve a specific purpose as a secret code, which added to their magickal lore. The number of leaves on a decorative branch might indicate the date and time of a secret rendezvous, and the blooms meant the emotional intent of the exchange. First circulated in lists, and then in published books, coded bouquets were, for a while, extremely popular.[60]

Flowers for Magickal Sachets, Dream Pillows, and Poppets

ASTER

Magickal purpose: Love.

Herbal code: Beginnings.

Planetary influence: Venus.

Best day to empower: Friday.

BACHELOR'S BUTTON

Magickal purpose: Love.

Herbal code: Hope and solitude.

Planetary influence: Jupiter.

Best day to empower: Thursday.

BIRD OF PARADISE

Magickal purpose: Love.

Herbal code: Strange and wonderful event.

Planetary influence: Mars.

Best day to empower: Tuesday.

BUTTERCUP

Magickal purpose: Love and healing.

Herbal code: Childlike.

Planetary influence: Moon.

Best day to empower: Monday.

CHRYSANTHEMUM

Magickal purpose: Protection.

Herbal code: Truth (white); slighted love (yellow).

Planetary influence: Sun.

Best day to empower: Sunday.

CROCUS

Magickal purpose: Love and visions.

Herbal code: Do not abuse.

Planetary influence: Venus.

Best day to empower: Friday.

DAFFODIL

Magickal purpose: Love and luck.

Herbal code: Chivalry.

Planetary influence: Venus.

Best day to empower: Friday.

DAISY

Magickal purpose: Love.

Herbal code: Innocence.

Planetary influence: Venus.

Best day to empower: Friday.

DOGWOOD

Magickal purpose: Protection and wishes.

Herbal code: Endurance.

Planetary influence: Moon.

Best day to empower: Monday.

FORGET-ME-NOT

Magickal purpose: Love and memory.

Herbal code: Remembrance.

Planetary influence: Mercury.

Best day to empower: Wednesday.

GARDENIA

Magickal purpose: Love, peace, healing, and spirituality.

Herbal code: Grace.

Planetary influence: Moon.

Best day to empower: Monday.

HEATHER

Magickal purpose: Love, protection, rainmaking, and luck.

Herbal code: Passion (red); protection from passionate acts (white).

Planetary influence: Venus.

Best day to empower: Friday.

HONEYSUCKLE

Magickal purpose: Love, money, psychic powers, and protection.

Herbal code: Captivating love.

Planetary influence: Jupiter.

Best day to empower: Thursday.

HYACINTH

Magickal purpose: Love, protection, and happiness.

Herbal code: Flirting.

Planetary influence: Venus.

Best day to empower: Friday.

IRIS

Magickal purpose: Purification and wisdom.

Herbal code: Messages.

Planetary influence: Mercury.

Best day to empower: Wednesday.

JASMINE

Magickal purpose: Love, money, prophetic dreams.

Herbal code: Good luck.

Planetary influence: Moon.

Best day to empower: Monday.

LAVENDER

Magickal purpose: Love, protection, sleep, longevity, purification, happiness, and peace.

Herbal code: I don't trust you.

Planetary influence: Mercury.

Best day to empower: Wednesday.

LILAC

Magickal purpose: Banishing and protection.[61]

Herbal code: Love's first crush.

Planetary influence: Venus.

Best day to empower: Friday but use on a Saturday for banishing.

LILY

Magickal purpose: Protection, breaking love spells.[62]

Herbal code: Innocence and purity.

Planetary influence: Moon.

Best day to empower: Monday but use on a Saturday for banishing.

MAGNOLIA

Magickal purpose: Love and fidelity.

Herbal code: Dignity.

Planetary influence: Venus.

Best day to empower: Friday.

MARIGOLD

Magickal purpose: Protection, dreams, legal matters, and psychic powers.

Herbal code: Success.

Planetary influence: Sun.

Best day to empower: Sunday.

ORCHID[63]

Magickal purpose: Love.

Herbal code: Ecstasy.

Planetary influence: Venus.

Best day to empower: Friday.

PEONY

Magickal purpose: Protection and banishing.

Herbal code: Secrets, shyness, and prosperous.

Planetary influence: Sun.

Best day to empower: Sunday but use on a Saturday for banishing.

ROSE

Magickal purpose: Love, psychic powers, healing, love divination, luck, and protection.

Herbal code: Jealousy (yellow); love (red); white (silence).

Planetary influence: Venus.

Best day to empower: Friday.

ROSEMARY

Magickal purpose: Love, protection, mental powers, banishing, purification, healing, sleep, youth.

Herbal code: Remembrance.

Planetary influence: Sun.

Best day to empower: Sunday, but use on Saturday if you are banishing.

SUNFLOWER

Magickal purpose: Wishes, health, wisdom, money magicks.

Herbal code: Power.

Planetary influence: Sun.

Best day to empower: Sunday.

SWEET PEA

Magickal purpose: Friendship, courage, and strength.

Herbal code: Impetuous.

Planetary influence: Venus.

Best day to empower: Friday.

TULIP

Magickal purpose: Love, prosperity, and protection.

Herbal code: Declaration of love.

Planetary influence: Venus.

Best day to empower: Friday.

VIOLET

Magickal purpose: Love, luck, wishes, peace, healing, and protection.

Herbal code: Faithfulness.

Planetary influence: Venus.

Best day to empower: Friday.

WISTERIA

Magickal purpose: Mental clarity.

Herbal code: I cling to thee.

Planetary influence: Mercury.

Best day to empower: Wednesday.

Drying Herbs and Flowers for Magickal Use

Although you can buy prepackaged herbs and dried flowers, you may wish to dry your own to ensure that they have been harvested at the right time. You can hang bundled herbs with long stems from the rafters of your attic or garage, or you can screw cup holders into the wall, balance a dowel between them, and hang the herb bunches from the dowel. Another method is to hang the bunches from coat hangers. Choose a place without direct sun, as sunlight will darken the leaves and evaporate essential oils. Dry herbs also need air circulation to prevent molding. Scatter those herbs that are too small to be tied into bundles on clean stainless-steel window screening. Screens can be stacked using wooden blocks or bricks that leave a six-inch space between the screens. For magickal purposes, it is unnecessary to separate stems from leaves (though some magickal people prefer to separate them), but you do want to remove discolored or molded leaves, and store the leaves whole. The less you handle them, the better. Store in airtight plastic bags, plastic containers, or glass jars. Flowers and leaves maintain their magickal properties for one year; roots and bark for two. Remember to label all herbs with their names, harvest dates, and magickal properties.

Healing Herbs for Magickal Purposes

The following list details the most common ailments and the healing herbs associated with them using homeopathic rules (hence some of the duplications); however, the table is for magickal purposes only and does not represent anything to be eaten. It is also understood that if you or a family member suffers from these conditions, you have consulted a qualified physician for assistance. Another note of caution: When you handle herbs for magickal purposes, you should wash your hands before and after working with them. Never put your fingers in your mouth while mixing herbs. If you burn any of the herbs, do so in a well-ventilated area, and do not put your face directly over the smoke of any herb that you haven't first researched.

Use one or all listed in each category below in an herbal sachet or poppet, or scatter at the base of a candle. These are not to be eaten. The curative herbal association mixtures are for magickal purposes only. *Note:* Only classical planetary rulerships are used in this listing.

ABSCESS

Herbal mixture (planetary influence, associated element): Dandelion (Jupiter, fire). Echinacea (Jupiter, fire). Yellow dock (Jupiter, fire).

Empower when the moon is in: Sagittarius.

ANEMIA

Herbal mixture (planetary influence, associated element): Dandelion (Jupiter, fire). Nettle (Mars, fire). Yellow dock (Jupiter, fire).

Empower when the moon is in: Sagittarius or Aries.

ANGINA

Herbal mixture (planetary influence, associated element): Garlic (Mars, fire/water). Ginger (Mars, fire/water). Hawthorn (Mars, fire/water).

Empower when the moon is in: Scorpio.

ANXIETY (1)

Herbal mixture (planetary influence, associated element): Hops (Mars, fire). Rue (Mars, fire). St. John's Wort (sun, fire).

Empower when the moon is in: Aries or Leo, or when the moon is in your sun sign.

ANXIETY (2)

Herbal mixture (planetary influence, associated element): Oats (Venus, air). Passionflower (Venus, air). Skullcap (Saturn, air). Valerian (Venus, air). Vervain (Venus, air).

Empower when the moon is in: Libra.

ARTHRITIS (1)

Herbal mixture (planetary influence, associated element): Burdock (Venus, air). Celery seed (Mercury, air). Evening primrose (Venus, air). Feverfew (Venus, air). Turmeric (Mercury, air). Willow (moon, water).

Empower when the moon is in: Libra or Gemini.

ARTHRITIS (2)

Herbal mixture (planetary influence, associated element): Cayenne pepper (Mars, fire). Ginger (Mars, fire). Nettles (Mars, fire). Pineapple (sun, fire).

Empower when the moon is in: Aries or the sun, or when the moon is in your sun sign.

ASTHMA

Herbal mixture (planetary influence, associated element): Coffee (Mars, fire). Garlic (Mars, fire). Rosemary (sun, fire). Tea (sun, fire).

Empower when the moon is in: Aries or the sun, or when the moon is in your sun sign.

BACK PAIN

Herbal mixture (planetary influence, associated element): Cayenne pepper (Mars, fire). Chamomile (sun, fire). Cinnamon (sun, fire). Ginger (Mars, fire). Rosemary (sun, fire). St. John's Wort (sun, fire).

Empower when the moon is in: Aries or the sun, or when the moon is in your sun sign.

BLADDER INFECTION

Herbal mixture (planetary influence, associated element): Corn silk (Venus, air). Cranberry (Jupiter, water). Dandelion (Jupiter, water). Echinacea (Jupiter, water). Goldenrod (Venus, air). Uva ursi (Jupiter, water).

Empower when the moon is in: Libra or Pisces.

BURNS

Herbal mixture (planetary influence, associated element): Comfrey (Saturn, earth). Lavender (Mercury, earth).

Empower when the moon is in: Capricorn or Virgo.

CHOLESTEROL (HIGH)

Herbal mixture (planetary influence, associated element): Fenugreek (Mercury, air). Garlic (Mars, fire). Ginger (Mars, fire).

Empower when the moon is in: Mars or Gemini.

COLD OR BRONCHITIS

Herbal mixture (planetary influence, associated element): Cayenne pepper (Mars, fire). Echinacea (Jupiter, fire). Eyebright (sun, fire). Garlic (Mars, fire). Horehound (Mercury, air). Hyssop (Jupiter, fire). Peppermint (Mercury, air). Thyme (Venus, air). Yarrow (Venus, air).

Empower when the moon is in: Aries, Leo, Sagittarius, Gemini, or Libra.

DEPRESSION

Herbal mixture, planetary influence, and associated element: Ginseng (sun, fire). Lavender (Mercury, air). Oats (Venus, air). St. John's Wort (sun, fire). Vervain (Venus, air).

Empower when the moon is in: Leo, Gemini, or Libra, or when the moon is in your sun sign.

GALLSTONES

Herbal mixture (planetary influence, associated element): Dandelion (Jupiter, water). Milk thistle (moon, water). Peppermint (Mercury, air). Turmeric (Mercury, air).

Empower when the moon is in: Cancer or Gemini.

HEARTBURN

Herbal mixture, planetary influence, and associated element: Aloe (moon, water). Cabbage (moon, water). Peppermint (Mercury, air).

Empower when the moon is in: Cancer or Gemini.

HIGH BLOOD PRESSURE

Herbal mixture (planetary influence, associated element): Dandelion (Jupiter, fire). Garlic (Mars, fire). Hawthorn (Mars, fire).

Empower when the moon is in: Pisces or Scorpio.

INFECTION, GENERAL

Herbal mixture (planetary influence, associated element): Garlic (Mars, fire). Ginger (Mars, fire). Lemon balm (moon, moon). Orange peel (sun, fire). Olive (sun, fire).

Empower when the moon is in: Cancer, Scorpio, or Leo.

INSOMNIA

Herbal mixture (planetary influence, associated element): Catnip (Venus, air). Chamomile (sun, fire). Lavender (Mercury, air). Lemon balm (moon, water). Skullcap (Saturn, air). Valerian (Venus, air).

Empower when the moon is in: Libra, Gemini, or Cancer.

MULTIPLE SCLEROSIS

Herbal mixture (planetary influence, associated element): Evening primrose (Venus, air). Purslane (moon, water).

Empower when the moon is in: Libra.

PNEUMONIA

Herbal mixture (planetary influence, associated element): Echinacea (Jupiter, fire). Goldenseal (sun, fire). Licorice (Venus, air).

Empower when the moon is in: Leo, Sagittarius, or Libra.

OSTEOPOROSIS

Herbal mixture (planetary influence, associated element): Alfalfa (Venus, air). Horsetail (Saturn, air). Red clover (Mercury, air).

Empower when the moon is in: Libra or Aquarius.

SPRAIN

Herbal mixture (planetary influence, associated element): Chestnuts (Jupiter, fire). St. John's Wort (sun, fire). Witch hazel (sun, fire).

Empower when the moon is in: Leo.

STRESS

Herbal mixture (planetary influence, associated element): Chamomile (sun, fire). Hops (Mars, fire). Linden (Jupiter, fire). Passionflower (Venus, air). Valerian (Venus, air).

Empower when the moon is in: Sagittarius, Leo, or Libra.

STROKE

Herbal mixture, planetary influence, and associated element: Alfalfa (Venus, air). Garlic (Mars, fire). Ginger (Mars, fire). Hawthorn (Mars, fire).

Empower when the moon is in: Aries.

WARTS

Herbal mixture (planetary influence, associated element): Banana peel (Venus, air). Bloodroot (Mars, fire). Cedar (sun, fire). Dandelion (Jupiter, fire). Pineapple (sun, fire).

Empower when the moon is in: Libra or Leo.

Herbal Sachets for Healing

Herbal sachets are easy to make. All you need is a white handkerchief, a ribbon, and herbs. A small picture of the sick person can be placed inside the bundle, or you can put the bundle on top of the picture. Grind the herbs with mortar and pestle. Place in the center of a new, clean, white handkerchief. Empower the herbs in the magick circle, using your favorite ritual format. You can also add small gemstones or other natural objects to the bundle. Close the bundle by pulling up each corner, one at a time, saying:

From the east—healing and happiness
for (say the person's name).
From the south—healing and happiness
for (repeat name).
From the west—healing and happiness
for (repeat name).
From the north—healing and happiness
for (repeat name).
From the four corners of the universe,
I call for healing for (repeat name).
In the name of (name your personal deity,
or a healing deity here),
the healing has begun!

Tie the bundle shut, chanting: "The healing has won, the sickness is done!" When you are finished, say: "So mote it be!" (And mean it.)

Give to the sick person as a healing charm, or if you think they would not accept it, place the bundle on your altar. Burn a white candle to boost the spell. You may wish to select three or more herbs from the general healing list below. Remember fire and air work best together, and earth and water work best together. Because certain planets rule more than one sign, or share signs, you may have a choice in element due to the classical associations. For example, in the classical system, Mars rules Aries, a fire sign, and Scorpio, a water sign.

ASH

Ruling planet: Sun.

Element: Fire.

CARAWAY

Ruling planet: Mercury.

Element: Air/earth.

CORIANDER

Ruling planet: Mars.

Element: Fire/water.

FERN

Ruling planet: Mercury.

Element: Air/earth.

GERANIUM

Ruling planet: Venus.

Element: Air/earth.

JUNIPER

Ruling planet: Sun.

Element: Fire.

MARJORAM

Ruling planet: Mercury.

Element: Air/earth.

NUTMEG

Ruling planet: Jupiter.

Element: Fire/air.

OAK

Ruling planet: Sun.

Element: Fire.

RUE

Ruling planet: Mars.

Element: Fire/water.

ST. JOHN'S WORT

Ruling planet: Sun.

Element: Fire.

SASSAFRAS

Ruling planet: Jupiter.

Element: Air/fire.

TANSY

Ruling planet: Venus.

Element: Air/earth.

THYME

Ruling planet: Venus.

Element: Air/earth.

WALNUT

Ruling planet: Sun.

Element: Fire.

The Herbal Code

In old magickal recipes and spells, strange ingredients are often called for that cannot always be taken literally. In one ancient Greco-Egyptian spell, the recipe called for "the navel of a male crocodile," which really meant pondweed; "the heart of a baboon" meant oil of lily.[64] Here's what those unusual nouns really meant! (Examples taken primarily from Raven Grimassi's *Encyclopedia of Wicca and Witchcraft*, pages 180 and 181.) The "sacrifice" in folklore was usually an egg buried in the ground.

Dead man: Ash or mandrake root carved in a crude human shape or poppet

Adder's tongue: Plantain

Bat's wing: Holly leaf

Bat's wool: Moss

Blood: Elder sap

Bloody fingers: Foxglove

Bodily fluids: Houseleek

Brains: Congealed gum from a cherry tree

Bull's blood: Horehound

Corpse candles: Mullein

Crocodile dung: Black earth

Dragon's scales: Bistort leaves

Ear of an ass: Comfrey

Ear of a goat: St. John's Wort

Eyes: Eyebright

Fingers: Cinquefoil

Hair: Maidenhair fern

Hand: The expanded frond from a male fern used to make the true hand of glory, which is nothing more than a candle made of wax mixed with fern

Heart: Walnut

Lion's tooth: Dandelion

Skin of a man: Fern

Skull: Skullcap

Snake: Bistort

Snake's blood: Hematite stone

Tongue of dog: Hound's tongue

Tooth or teeth: Pinecones

Unicorn horn: True unicorn root

Worms: Gnarled, thin roots of a local tree

Herbal/Animal Associations

Blue jay: Bay laurel

Cat: Catnip

Cuckoo: Orchids or plantain

Dog: Crouchgrass

Frog: Cinquefoil

Hawk: Hawkweed

Lamb: Lamb's lettuce

Linnets: Eyebright

Lizard: Calamint

Nightingale: Hops

Rat: Valerian

Sheep: Dandelion

Snake: Fennel or bistort

Toad: Sage

Weasel: Rue

Woodpeckers: Peony

Herbal Glossary

The following is a limited glossary of magickal herbal terms.

Attunement/Enchantment: Psychically infusing the herbal mixture with a mental picture of your need.

Bath (spiritual/herbal): Used to cleanse body, mind, and spirit by empowering the properties of the herbs and placing in bath water through means of a sachet or infusion.

Blessing: Connecting the power of the herb to the power of deity.

Chaplet: Flowers and leaves woven to create a crown for handfastings and High Holy Days.

Conjuration: Cleansing and consecration that involves removing all negativity from the herb, and then attuning that herb to the service of the divine.

Decoction: Much like an infusion except that it is made from roots and barks. Boil for up to twenty minutes to activate the chemical, rather than steep.

Incense: A combination of plant materials (and sometimes essential oils) and a base material that is mixed, then burned or smoldered on a charcoal briquette designed specifically for incense.

Infusion: The process of soaking herbs in hot water. Use one teaspoon dried herb to every cup of water. Heat water until just boiling. Pour over herb. Cover. Steep ten to twenty minutes. Strain and cool before

using. Infusions, considered the original Witch's potion, are drunk as teas, added to baths, rubbed into furniture and floors, or used to anoint the body. *Warning*: Short shelf life.

Ointment: Herbs mixed with a lard or beeswax base. More modern practitioners use one teaspoon of an herbal tincture with one ounce of commercial skin lotion.

Powders: Herbs ground to a fine powder and added to colored talc or fine-colored sand. Used to place under carpets, around doorsteps, in gris-gris bags, stuffed in poppets, loaded in candles, etc.

Sachet: Attuned herbs placed in a small bag or piece of cloth that is tied or sewn shut. Sachets can be worn or placed under pillows or other areas of the house for all manner of magickal workings. Sometimes called mojo bags, charm bags, or gris-gris bags.

Tincture: Extract made with alcohol rather than a water base. More concentrated in form and a longer shelf life. Standard formula for a tincture is five ounces of vodka, brandy, or apple cider vinegar and one ounce of the herb left to sit for six weeks in a sealable container. Shake the mixture every few days and, as with all herbals, keep out of direct sunlight. For purposes of this book, tinctures are not to be taken internally.

Hoodoo

When you begin to delve deeply into herbal and folk magicks in an effort to further your personal magickal education, you will invariably run across Hoodoo (and Pow Wow). They are an intricate part of historical America, where these two systems have flourished for hundreds of years, and have affected (to some degree, depending upon your personal opinion) the current religion of Witchcraft. In an effort to give you basic information, Ray Malbrough has written a section for you on Hoodoo, and I have provided a section on Pow Wow further on in Part III. Once you learn the patterning of these two systems, you will discover that several of the older American Craft grimoires contain mixed elements of these practices.

Hoodoo Magick
by Ray Malbrough

Hoodoo has become an Americanized adaptation of the indigenous African religion relating to the Fon people of Benin and Togo, found on the western coast of the African continent (also referred to as the Ivory Coast). Hoodoo thrives within the indigenous magickal tradition of people living in Louisiana, and deals much with the working of herbs and roots to make charm bags, called gris-gris bags. The gris-gris bags are very similar to an American Indian medicine bag. Hoodoo also uses packets that are carried in a person's shoes. Hoodoo's magickal teaching is carried down from male to male and female to female. The only exception to any magickal knowledge being carried over from male to female or female to male was to keep the practice within the family bloodline.

The Hoodoo practitioner is also taught how to prepare the magickal and spiritual baths that are also an integral part of Voodoo as practiced in Haiti today. The practitioners are also skilled in making and using magickal powders, used to influence people when worn or in contact with a person's body. For example, when a man or woman desired to attract a certain person to be their lover, a powder would be worn after bathing to help draw the forces of love into their own life. Or the powder would be sprinkled about a place where the beloved was sure to walk or sit. The charge that is put into the powder would begin to have an effect on the other person. These magickal powders are also sprinkled onto candles to give extra power to the candle as it burns. Practitioners of Hoodoo or Voodoo don't believe that magick is black or white. It just simply is, neutrally.

The main difference between a practitioner of Hoodoo and a priest or priestess of Voodoo (also spelled Voudu) is that Hoodoo invokes the aid of the Catholic saints. The Voodoo practice makes use of the vèvès in order to invoke the aid of the African spirits when petitioning for help in solving the problems in life. One thing that is common to both, besides the practice of magick, is a reverence for the dead and communication with the dead and the ancestors that have gone to the other side. Death is not viewed as an end to the relationship, but as a beginning to the relationship on a spiritual level. The dead continue to show interest in the lives of their descendants on Earth. Offerings are made to the dead, and they are petitioned for help as well.

Some of the main African spirits (or *loa*, as they are called) have been equated with a Catholic saint.

Damballah: St. Patrick

Erzulie-Fréda Dahomey: The Sacred Heart of Mary

Papa Legba: St. Anthony of Padua

Baron Samedi: St. Gerard Majella

Erzulie Dantor: Our Lady of the Seven Sorrows

The Marassa: Sts. Cosmas and Damian

The African spirits mentioned are thought of more as planetary spirits and not as gods. In Fon mythology, God the creator is viewed as Mawe-Lisa, a creator being who is both male and female. Each loa or spirit has his or her own type of offerings that are given, as well as colors and symbols. The African spirits eat and are given food and blood offerings. The Catholic saints accept the offering of candles and magickally prepared oil lamps, but do not require a food or blood offering as the African spirit does. It is this change that has helped the indigenous African culture of the Fon people to flourish and survive on the shores of America, becoming an accepted practice with the European descendants of Louisiana. However, there is one important rule in Hoodoo: All magickal practice is kept in secret.

Love-Drawing Powder

Take 1 tablespoon rose petals, 1 tablespoon orris root, ¼ teaspoon cinnamon bark, and ¼ teaspoon cloves. In a mortar and pestle, grind them down to a fine powder. As you do so, pray over the herbs so that they will help to draw love into the life of the person who will wear them on their body. When finished, the powdered mixture is then added to one cup of talc and blended well. This herb-talc mixture is then put on your altar, and a red candle is lit next to it. You will dedicate the love-drawing powder to the Sacred Heart of Mary, asking her to bless the powder so that it will bring love to the person who will wear it. This is done for nine days, lighting a new candle each day. When all the candles are burnt out, the powder is ready to wear. *Caution:* Do not leave an open candle flame unattended. We do not need to burn the house down.

Overcoming Obstacles: A Gris-Gris Bag

First, find an old skeleton key. You will take the skeleton key and go to seven different places and touch the door of each place with the key.

1. A store
2. A bank

3. Supermarket
4. Place of business
5. Hospital
6. Jail
7. Lastly, the cemetery gate.

The key is then anointed with High John the Conqueror oil and placed in a red flannel or chamois bag with the following: a small adventurine stone, a piece of John the Conqueror root, 3 bay laurel leaves, a pinch of five-finger grass (cinquefoil), and 2 lodestones. When finished with the bag, place it next to a statue of St. Anthony of Padua and light a white candle, asking that he always intercede on your behalf to remove the obstacles that you encounter in your journey in life. Each day for thirteen days, light a new candle, praying that St. Anthony will bless the gris-gris to work for you in removing obstacles. After all the candles have burnt themselves out, you can wear the charm bag next to your skin, under your clothing so that no one will see it.

A Spiritual Bath to Remove Negative Vibrations

To a half gallon of water, add the following: ¼ cup holy water, 3 tablespoons Florida Water cologne, and 1 cup of tea made from the herb basil. Strain the basil from the water of the tea and discard the herb. You will use only the tea, not the herb. Bring this to your altar and light three white candles in the form of a triangle, with the container with the spiritual bath in the center of the three candles. Dedicate this spiritual bath to your holy guardian angel, asking him or her to bless the bath so that its influence will remove all negative vibrations you may feel around you. When the candles have burnt themselves out, the bath is ready to use. You will take one third of the spiritual bath and add it to one-half tub of clear bath water. Take your soap bath first. You will soak in the tub with the spiritual bath for about ten minutes, pouring the water over yourself as you pray that the negative influences are removed. Allow the water to air dry on your skin. Take this bath for three days.

Meditation

Everything you do begins with your mind power. Finding a balance between body, mind, and Spirit is up to you—it is a choice. Confucius was a Chinese philosopher who believed that goodness and benevolence were fundamental for living a harmonious life. He said that if the individual was balanced, then that balance would expand. He also felt that the health of the world depended on the balance of each and every person living in that world. Wiccans believe this too. One of the old rules for training insisted that you must have "your own house in order" (meaning yourself) before you could attempt to help other people through magickal means or hope to reach the heights in spirituality and the magickal arts. If you were unbalanced, then that disharmony would be transferred to your students, and consequently to the world around you. Wiccans also believe that, as you spiritually progress, your home and work life will improve. You become the center of a chain reaction for good, and therefore negativity will be forced either to transform into something harmonious or leave. The Hindu culture also mixes spiritual ideas of balance and wisdom with the everyday concerns of health and prosperity. The cultures of China and India employ meditation to further one's spiritual self in a practical world.

We can probably thank Madame Blavatsky for driving Europe and the Americas headlong into Eastern practices. While others of her time were mulling over the Egyptian mysteries tinged with Aramaic studies, Blavatsky and her entourage were pulling practices from Ceylon, India, and Tibet into the parlors of the European and American elite, as well as stoking the creativity of some of the most famous writers and artists of the times. Rich society men and women with nothing better to do than campaign for whatever cause pleased their fancy also looked for the exotic in spirituality—meditation, breathing exercises, and other Eastern practices were just unusual enough to spark their interests. As these society-elite railed against the confines of Christianity, they found new outlets as they pursued the meaning of life. Their behavior affected the creative class—those men and women dedicated to dance, music, painting, theater, and storytelling, who reinforced their desires for material with that striking twist. The New Age information we see today is not so new after all—it's just (once again) been wrapped up in a different package.

Regardless of how meditation practices landed in Europe and the New World, it hasn't passed out of favor in over a hundred years (not to mention the thousands of years in India, Tibet, and China) because it works. Ivan Pavlov, a Russian scientist, proved the power of the mind in his studies on conditioning, and gave us the understanding that what we think, we create.[65] One way to create positive change in our lives is through the practice of meditation. Meditation and affirmations are a healthy way to condition our minds and create balance and a better way of living. Magickal people have also discovered that using daily meditations can enhance their personal power in all areas of magick and ritual. Scientists have also discovered that the happier we are, the greater access we have to the sixth sense, the intuitive part of our mind that shapes our lives.[66] Meditation is an excellent vehicle that can help us to remove stress, focus on our mental and physical behavior to make positive change, and assist us in planning for a brighter future, so the happiness that these practices bring can strengthen our psychic abilities as well.

Basic Meditation Guidelines

When we meditate, we make a conscious decision to sit quietly and relax body and mind. You can meditate for five minutes a day, or half an hour or more. How long you meditate is up to you and should fit your current lifestyle. Meditation is often linked to deep breathing exercises, which help to relieve daily stress. If you learn to meditate on a consistent basis, you can expect your grades, sports activities, and daily life to improve, but like all things hard-won, it takes time for you to visibly see the positive results of meditation. Your motto when learning to meditate should be "Don't give up." Here are a few tips to help you during meditation.

- Always try to meditate in a quiet, peaceful place. You can't focus your mind inward if there is commotion around you. Try to choose a time and place where you will not be interrupted, as breaks in meditation can cause emotional stress because you become irritated at the intrusion.

- Soft, peaceful music and low lighting can help.

- Practice deep breathing exercises with your meditation. Breathe in to the count of ten, and breathe out to the count of ten at least three or more times before beginning a meditation sequence. Follow the grounding and centering instructions on page 238.

- Slowly count down from fifteen to one in your mind after the breathing exercises. This helps to keep the conscious mind busy and signals your body, mind, and spirit that you are preparing to meditate.

Body of Light Meditation

This meditation works well for:

- General grounding and centering.

- Removing daily stress.

- Removing sickness from the body.

- Finding answers to important questions.

Find a place where you won't be disturbed. Sit in a comfortable chair. Close your eyes. Take three deep breaths and relax. Count down slowly from ten to one. Imagine that there is a pinprick of light inside your body, hovering around your naval. Slowly encourage this light to grow, moving into the trunk of your body, into your legs, then into your shoulders, arms, and neck, moving into your feet, and spreading out to the top of your head and the tips of your toes.

Take a deep breath and relax.

Now envision this light sparkling right underneath every inch of your skin. Allow the light to move through the skin and form a dancing white aura around your body, and remember that this light is still coming from the inside of your body. Allow yourself to feel that you are one with the universe. There is no care or worry, no pain or unhappiness. Ask yourself, "What do I need?" and allow a picture to come forward in your mind. It doesn't matter how stupid or silly the image. Just let one come.

Take another deep breath and relax. Let the light continue to swirl around you. Let go of the image, if you haven't already. Allow the light to retract inside your body. Count from one to five and open your eyes, telling yourself that you feel refreshed and filled with harmony.

Write down the image you saw. Think about what it may mean to you. If you don't understand the image, that's okay. You made a record of it, and perhaps later it may make sense. The mind is funny that way sometimes, and needs a day or two to consciously mull over those gifts from the subconscious.

Meditation and Prayer

Prayer allows us to attune our mind, body, and spirit to that-which-controls-the-universe. Call it God, Goddess, the collective unconscious, Allah, or whatever—it doesn't matter. What matters is what you believe exists. In reality, all spellcasting, conjuring, and the use of charms and incantations are acts of focused prayer. If we combine meditation techniques with focused prayer, we get quite a wallop for our efforts because we are combining the work within with the work without. The following prayer can be used during any meditation, before spellwork or ritual, or before using your divination tool. If the Wiccan prayer of alchemy doesn't suit you, you might try writing your own prayer to fulfill your needs. Prayers you write yourself are exceptionally powerful.

Wiccan Prayer of Alchemy

The stillness touches deep inside
in silent darkness Mother sighs.
I reach within with breath and light
and conjure Spirit, warm and bright.
The primal matter, the fire of mind
vibrational waves to particles kind
I am the flask, the Witch who brings
the change desired, that curious ring
of power and magick that others don't see
and yet I know it lies in me.
From black to red, then white to gold
as above and so below
one to two, and two to three,
the fourth is One.
So shall it be!

Moon

Pray to the moon when she is round,
Luck with you will then abound.
What you seek for shall be found,
On the sea or solid ground.[67]

Moon Goddesses

Chinese: Yin

Egyptian: Isis, Hathor, Neith, Ma'at

German: Holda

Greek: Demeter, Hera, Artemis, Aphrodite, Selene, Persephone, Hecate, Europa, Pallas Athena

Indian: Kali, Aditi, Durga

Japanese: Kannon

Middle Eastern: Inanna, Tiamat, Ishtar, Astarte, Lillith

Norse: Freya

Roman: Juno, Diana, Luna, Titania

Tibetan: Tara

The moon is the closest celestial body to the Earth—about 221,000 miles when it is nearest and approximately 252,000 miles at its farthest orbit. The moon circles the Earth approximately once every 27 days, 7 hours, and 43 minutes, to be exact. Together, the Earth and the moon, like the other seven planets and their moons, circle the sun. Whether we are talking about the moon in ancient cultures, in astrology, or even in alchemy, we find the basic meaning much the same: reflective, passive (as opposed to active), and feminine in magickal nature (although in some cultures the roll of sun/male and moon/female were reversed). In Wicca, the moon represents the divine Goddess, where the sun normally represents the power and force of the God. The idea of gender associated with the planets is an ancient one, dating back to about

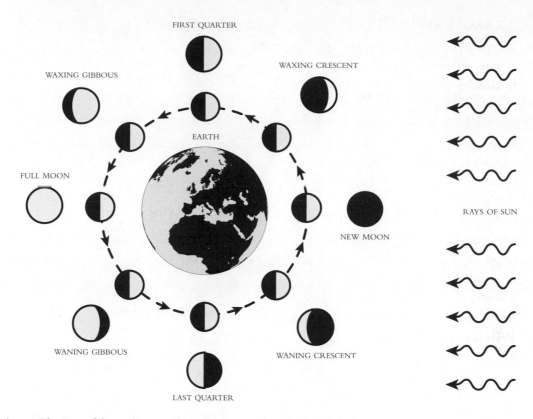

FIRST QUARTER

WAXING GIBBOUS

WAXING CRESCENT

EARTH

FULL MOON

NEW MOON

RAYS OF SUN

WANING GIBBOUS

WANING CRESCENT

LAST QUARTER

An outside view of the sun's rays striking the moon as it orbits the Earth.

500 B.C. and the Greek mathematician Pythago-ras, and may be older still, stretching into the 4,000-year-old Chinese concept of yin and yang, the primal elements of the universe, where yin symbolizes the feminine, dark, closed, wet, and cold, and yang the masculine, light, open, dry, and hot.[68]

Wiccan celebrations are patterned after the celestial energies of the moon and the sun. Es-bats are evenings designed to work with the phases of the moon, and sabbats are ceremonies dedicated to the seasonal changes governed by the Earth's movement around the sun. Most Witches these days refer to esbats as circle nights. In astrology and Wicca, both the sun and moon are honorary planets, enjoying the same status as the other eight, and are considered two of the "big three" when choosing dates and times for magick and daily living. Throughout this book you've seen the importance of the moon in magick and timing under various subject head-ings, and I've given you quite a few tables to use in your magickal practices that involve lunar en-ergy and timing. By this time you've probably come to the conclusion that moon lore is so vast and so intrinsic to our practices that it touches almost every subject in Witchcraft, from healing to gardening to happiness and success.

Phases of the Moon

Throughout this book I've used moon quarters rather than moon phases so that you can work magick by looking at the almanac in the daily newspaper, or using the magickal almanacs cur-rently on the market. Many Wiccans also use moon phases to calculate the timing of their spells and rituals. Although quarters and phases are essentially the same, the quarter is a division by four and the phase a division by eight.

NEW MOON

- Moon is 0–45 degrees directly ahead of the sun.
- Moon rises at dawn, sets at sunset.
- Moon is from exact new moon to 3.5 days after.

  Purpose: Beginnings and impulses.

CRESCENT

- Moon is 45–90 degrees ahead of the sun.
- Moon rises at midmorning, sets after sunset.
- Moon is 3.5 to 7 days after the new moon.

  Purpose: Movement and action.

FIRST QUARTER

(Not to be confused with almanac's first quarter—SEE ALMANACS, PAGE 163).

- Moon is 90–135 degrees ahead of the sun.
- Moon rises at noon, sets at midnight.
- Moon is 7 to 10.5 days after the new moon.

  Purpose: Shaping energies and building.

GIBBOUS

- Moon is 135–180 degrees ahead of the sun.
- Moon rises in midafternoon, sets around 3 A.M.
- Moon is between 10.5 to 14 days after the new moon.

  Purpose: Detail work and personal growth.

FULL MOON

- Moon is 180–225 degrees ahead of the sun.
- Moon rises at sunset, sets at dawn.
- Moon is from 14 to 17.5 days after the new moon.

  Purpose: Completion and harvest.

DISSEMINATING

- Moon is 225–270 degrees ahead of the sun.
- Moon rises at midevening, sets at midmorning.
- Moon is 3.5 to 7 days after the full moon.

  Purpose: Initial banishing and putting what you have learned before the full moon to good use.

LAST QUARTER

- Moon is 270–315 degrees ahead of the sun.
- Moon rises at midnight and sets at noon.
- Moon is 7 to 10.5 days after the full moon.

  Purpose: Destruction.

BALSAMIC (DARK MOON)

- Moon is 315–360 degrees ahead of the sun.
- Moon rises at 3 A.M., sets midafternoon.
- Moon is 10.5 to 14 days after the full moon.

  Purpose: Rest.

Drawing Down the Moon

In the religion of Witchcraft, the full moon stands for the power of the God and Goddess combined, though many see the moon itself simply as a representation of the Goddess. Religiously, a full moon is a celebration of the sun, the moon, and the Earth—a sacred triad of energies. In astrology, the moon and the sun are considered planets, even though astronomically they are not considered planets. The sun is a star and the moon is a satellite of the Earth. Scientifically, a full moon occurs when the moon is directly opposite the sun. The sun's light bounces off the surface of the moon (which is why it seems to glow). The moon in turn reflects that light to the Earth.

If we look at this process in a spiritual sense, then the power of the sun (the God) is given into the arms of the moon, who (as the Goddess) sends that power to us for our use. This is the most basic definition. What makes moon magick so interesting is the zodiac sign that the moon is visiting when the process occurs. Therefore, if you plan your esbats over the thirteen full moons throughout the year, each moon celebration will be different, so each esbat we get a special "flavor" of power. (SEE PART I, ESBATS.)

Some of the European Renaissance grimoires taught their students not to use the full moon. That's because they were going from an astrological point of view, wherein an opposition (any planet opposite another) says that there will be a push me/pull me effect, and the energies of each planet involved in the opposition will be at war with one another. Only a compromise will win the day. Although Witches acknowledge the opposition energy, they've learned how to work the will (the sun) with the emotions (the moon), thereby making the compromise within themselves (by Drawing Down the Moon), then turning around and focusing that energy into a magickal project, meditation, or other Witchy endeavor. Sounds complicated, but it isn't. You'll be a natural at it. All you have to do is look at the moon and allow your feelings to flow to that "feeling of perfection" I talked about under the topic of Elemental Planes. In this way, Witches harness the power of both the sun and the moon and put them to good use.

The rite of Drawing Down the Moon is deceptively simple. A rite is a portion of a ritual; therefore, if you plan to use the next esbat just for doing the DDM (Drawing Down the Moon), you'll need to follow those thirteen ritual steps I gave you on page 23, under the Esbat section of this book.

At no other time does the moon more represent the raw material of the universe than at the new moon, which astrologers tell us is the prime time for working magick to begin any project. The full moon, especially when it appears golden, is the epitome of the manifestation energy of the divine, and therefore represents the harvest or completion of any magickal operation. This is a moon filled with spiritual power. When a Witch Draws Down the Moon, he or she is mentally allowing his or her mind to be filled with the receptive, passive, reflective energy of the moon. This is the time to touch the primordial energy (new moon) or power (full moon) and draw this energy into oneself for furthering our greatest desires. Wishes spoken to the full moon in seriousness and truth are usually granted, unless your spiritual plan dictates otherwise.

But where did the idea of Drawing Down the Moon come from? We find a hint from Ovid's *Metamorphoses*, in Medea's speech, which is a great pick-me-up if you are feeling a little down about your magickal abilities:

> *O Night, most faithful to these my mysteries, and ye golden Stars, who with the Moon, succeed the fires of the day, and thou, three-faced Hecate, who comest conscious of my design, and ye charms and arts of enchanters, and thou, too, Earth, that does furnish the enchanters with powerful herbs; ye breezes, too, and winds, mountains, rivers, and lakes, and all ye Deities of the groves, and all ye Gods of night, attend here; through whose aid, whenever I will, the rivers run back from their astonished banks to their sources, and by my charms I calm the troubled sea, and rouse it when calm; I disperse the clouds, and I bring clouds upon the Earth; I both allay the winds, and I raise them; and I break the jaws of serpents with my words and my spells; I move, too, the solid rocks, and the oaks torn up with their own native Earth, and the forests as well; I command the mountains, too, to quake, and the Earth to groan, and the*

*ghosts to come forth from their tombs. **Thee, too, O Moon, do I draw down!**[69]*

Ronald Hutton, the eminent Bristol University historian, adds his thoughts to the practice of Drawing Down the Moon (from private correspondence dated 9 August 2002):

It is certainly in Ovid, but also in other Roman authors of his time, such as Lucan, and I can trace it right back to the Greek playwright Aristophanes in the fifth century B.C. *It refers to a trick first especially associated with the witches of Thessaly, later (in the Common Era) with all witches, of plucking the moon out of the sky and making it lie on the earth. Confusion with another ancient tradition, at first specifically Egyptian, of invoking deities into statues, and later into human beings, was not made until Gardner's time.*

Drawing Down the Moon should be done in private unless you are working within a magickal group where all gathered understand the seriousness of this rite. Most Witches cast a magick circle and then call the quarters, followed by a statement of intent for that night's working. Turn to the moon and allow your gaze to rest there for a few moments as you ground and center. Synchronized breathing in a group format helps to stabilize the rite and put everyone in tune with the work to be done. If you are alone, breathe deeply and slowly until you feel at one with the universe. Drawing Down the Moon is a part of the alchemical Great Work. You are illuminating yourself with the divine spirit on the inside to further the welfare of yourself or others on the outside. If you are working magick, again state your purpose, then slowly raise your hands toward the moon. Your palms or fingers may tingle or grow warm—that's okay. Allow the energy of the moon, as representative of the divine and sacred Goddess, to fill your body with white light. Imagine the

light coming in through your fingertips and flowing into your body, filling every fiber of your being with divine energy. Let your mind touch the primordial matter (new moon) or golden power (full moon) and silently make your request again. Once you have a strong grip on the feeling, you can begin to chant or sing. When you are finished, slowly lower your arms. By raising your arms and then lowering them, you are physically acting out part of the alchemical process—*As above, so below.* As your arms lower, you are bringing your request into existence on Earth. The alchemical process has begun! Ground and center. Release the quarters and the circle.

This is only one way to Draw Down the Moon. Various Wiccan traditions or groups may practice this rite in a different way, perhaps intoning special words that mean something to them or using particular body or hand movements. Some Witches Draw Down the Moon by pointing their wand, staff, or rod at the moon. I've also used long-stemmed roses, mirrors, and crystals for special workings of love, protection, or healing. There is no end to your creativity. Here is a numbered review to help you Draw Down the Moon.

Step One: Take several deep breaths.

Step Two: Ground and center.

Step Three: Cast a magick circle.

Step Four: Look at the full moon. Take your time. In your mind, connect the full moon with the power of the God and the reflective energy of the Goddess.

Step Five: Hold your arms up and link your hands loosely together so that your palms face the moon, and you can see the moon in a triangle made by your index fingers linked and your thumbs touching one another.

Step Six: As you watch the moon, think of your will and your emotions working together.

Step Seven: In your mind, go to that perfect feeling. Close your eyes. Let the feeling well up inside of you. Hold on to this feeling as long as you can.

Step Eight: Open your eyes and make a wish while you look at the moon. Nothing silly. Something seriously spiritual is best.

Step Nine: Thank deity.

Step Ten: Put your arms down, and breathe deeply.

Step Eleven: Ground and center.

Moon Void of Course

Throughout this book we've discussed different methods of timing a spell or ritual for the best results. From moon signs to phases, to days of the week and planetary hours, the Witch has several methods to help him or her in magickal timing. No matter the technique you choose, one constant remains the same: Always check to see if the moon is void, because the moon can make or break your spell. To determine if the moon is void on any given day (and the moon voids about twelve times a month, sometimes for minutes and sometimes for days), you will need an almanac (SEE ALMANACS). Don't worry, I'll explain it—keep reading.

In this book you have learned that the moon visits each sign of the zodiac once a month. If it makes it easier, let's think of the moon as a substitute teacher who visits different schools. There are twelve schools in the school system that she works for. Each school in the system has its own name (just like in your school system). Their names are Aries, Taurus, Gemini, Cancer, Leo, Virgo, Libra, Scorpio, Sagittarius, Capricorn, Aquarius, and Pisces. According to the moon's

job description, she's only allowed to stay at each school for 2 to 2½ days, and no more. Then she must move on to the next school.

The moon has nine close friends who are also substitute teachers who travel from school to school just like she does. Their length of stay is different than hers, but we don't need to get into that right now. What is important is that all of these teachers (the moon, sun, Mercury, Venus, Mars, Jupiter, Saturn, Neptune, Uranus, and Pluto) carry cell phones with them so that they can talk to each other whenever they want to. Just like friends, sometimes their conversations are nice and sometimes they are not so nice. In astrology, these conversations are called aspects.

When the moon is packing up her stuff to go to the next school, and while she is en route to the next school on her list, she has to turn her cell phone off. It's one of the rules of her job. Her employer believes that she must have some downtime—some time to relax and gather her thoughts together. The moon is special. She's the only one that gets this type of downtime. All the other planets (except the sun) do get to rest, but their down time is called a retrograde (SEE RET-ROGRADES, PAGE 201). Again, we don't need to get into that right now, but it's good for you to at least see the word.

During the moon's down time, none of the other planets can reach her while she is on the road. Basically, the roving capabilities of her universal cell service stink, but that's how it works. This period of silence (sort of like dead air on the radio) is when the moon is said to be *void of course*. She can't take any calls.

Just like in your school system, the various schools may be close together or far apart. The amount of time her cell phone doesn't work depends on the amount of time it takes her to drive to the next school, or astrological sign. This period of being void can be as long as a day, or as short as twenty minutes. The nice thing about the moon and the other planets is that they always follow a schedule, they are always on time and, unlike real people, they are never late and they will never disappear. You will find all of their schedules in the almanac.

To find out when the moon is void, we need to take a look at her schedule. Her time table is listed in the almanac, but reading the schedule is a bit confusing at first. When the moon is void, her schedule will look like this:

7:08 A.M. ☽ v/c

Meaning the moon stopped talking to everybody at 7:08 A.M.

Now that's she's turned her cell phone off, when will she turn it back on? We need to look at her schedule again to find out. Somewhere under the same date in the almanac (or the next day), you'll see something like this:

☽ enters 6:09 P.M.

This means that she turned her cell phone back on at 6:09 P.M. and she can now take calls from the other planets. The only thing you have to be very, very careful about when checking her schedule is the time zone, and in some almanacs there are two pitfalls where you can easily make a mistake. First, let's look at that first listing again, adding exactly what you will see in the almanac.

7:08 A.M. 4:08 A.M. ☽ v/c

Here is where you might make your first mistake. Which time do you choose? In the almanac I'm using it says at the bottom of the page that Eastern Standard Time is in medium type and Pacific Standard Time is in bold type. As I live in the Eastern Standard Time Zone, then the first time applies to me and my magickal work—7:08 A.M. The second time does not apply to me or my work. If I lived in the Pacific Standard Time Zone, then the 4:08 A.M.

time would be the one meant for me. What if I live in a time zone that isn't listed in the almanac? Every almanac has a page dedicated to time zone conversions—don't worry, it's not hard to use the table. Okay, so that's where we might make our first mistake on timing—picking a time that doesn't match the time zone we live in. What's the second mistake?

One I've made quite often, in fact, because I've been in a hurry. Many almanacs do not take Daylight Saving Time into consideration, which is a major pain. Let's say that today is June 1. The time we use in the states in the summer is called Daylight Saving Time. The almanac says:

7:08 A.M. 4:08 A.M. ☽ v/c

—but that's for Standard Time. Therefore, the calculation we are reading is off by one hour. How do we know how to fix it? Always remember the old adage: *Spring forward, fall back.* Daylight Saving Time always adds one extra hour to the time. When we revert back to Standard Time (around October 31 in the States), the above entry would be correct. So, if today is June 1, then the moon would be void at 8:08 A.M. (adding one hour) for those in the Eastern Standard Time Zone, and it would be 5:08 A.M. for those living in the Pacific Standard Time Zone. To make sure you are clear about this, if today was November 14 (when Daylight Saving Time is not in effect), the above entry (7:08 A.M. **4:08** A.M. ☽ v/c) would be correct.

Why should we give two rats and a basketball about when the moon can and cannot talk to the other planets? Who cares? Isn't this complicated? At first, yes, it takes some time getting used to; however, this is such a major magickal tool that we don't want to overlook it.

The moon void is very important in magickal timing because when she is void (or has her cell phone turned off), she's not taking any calls—not even yours. Whether we're talking about magick or daily life, things started during a void moon do one of the following:

- Never come to fruition. Plans just fall apart.

- Don't work out the way you planned.

- The plans were never heard at all—no kidding.

Let's take three short examples. Let's say Sara calls you and asks you if you want to go shopping on Saturday because there's a big sale. You tell her that's wonderful and you make the plans. Come Saturday, however (example one), your mother tells you that you have to go take your SAT tests instead; or (example two) you get to the mall but there's no sale; or (example three) you totally forgot your promise to Sara and make a date with Ted instead. When Sara confronts you, you honestly (quite possibly) tell her that you didn't remember making the plans with her. The exact same reasoning applies to magickal work as well, which is why most Witches at least check to see when the moon is void before they cast a spell.

The moon void has a flip side. It can be useful. If you don't want someone to listen to you, then plan to talk to them during a void moon. If the subject is controversial, and you want to "avoid" the issue, yet you are forced to discuss it, do it during a void moon. They'll never hear ya. The moon void is like an astrological nonstick surface. The only problem with this is eventually the situation will come back to haunt you (just like incidents that keep reappearing during retrogrades) until you darned well deal with it. voids are great for taking a break, doing meditation, and assessing where you've been and where you are going: sort of a cosmic time-out deal. Once you learn to flow with voids, then retrogrades (those time-outs that the other planets take) are much easier (and more fun) to play with.

Lunar Mansions

And seeing the moon measures the whole space of the zodiac in the time of twenty-eight days, hence it is that the wise men of the Indians, and most of the ancient astrologers have granted twenty-eight mansions to the moon. And in these twenty-eight mansions lie hid many secrets of the wisdom of the ancients, by which they wrought wonders on all things which are under the circle of the moon; and they attributed to every mansion his resemblances, images, and seals, and his president intelligences, and worked by the virtue of them after different manners.
—*Francis Barrett, 1801* [70]

Lunar mansions come to us through classical astrology. They are yet another way to divide each sign into three parts, except with the lunar mansions, the segments overlap from sign to sign. In the end you still get the 360-degree circle, but these divisions are in segments of 12 degrees, 51 minutes, and 26 seconds.

According to Donald Tyson, in his annotated version of *The Three Books of Occult Philosophy* by Henry Cornelius Agrippa, "the mansions of the moon are derived from the Arabic *Al Manavil al Kamr* (resting places of the moon) signifying the noonday rest of a camel rider in the desert." Tyson feels that they are perhaps the most ancient divisions of the heavens, older even than the zodiac. They are found in India, China, Arabia, Babylonia, Egypt, Persia, and other sites of early civilization. Vedic astrology (of Hindu derivation) has twenty-seven mansions, where the Arabic has twenty-eight. The difference in the two systems lies in the revolution of the moon. "Up until the time of Christ the list of mansions began with the Pleiades at the beginning of Taurus, but after this time it was shifted to the stars in the beginning of Aries due to the precession of the equinoxes."[71]

Like planetary hours, checking the lunar mansion in which the moon or any planet falls can give you some information on an event that has occurred or one you have planned. They can also be used as a timing mechanism for a particular spell. For example, if you wanted to do a spell for safe travel, then you might perform that spell when the moon is between 0° Aries and 12° 51' 26" (12 degrees, 51 minutes, 26 seconds) Aries, during the first and second quarters of the moon (taking care that the moon is not afflicted—meaning she has a very nice conversation with the planets and she's not void). Granted, the moon won't always be where you want it for this type of timing mechanism, but you can use it for the location of other planets too, keeping in mind their initial energy structure. Classical magickal astrologers try to match the rising sign, the planetary hour, and the lunar mansion—however, this means you have to wait until the right circumstances occur and take advantage of them, therefore magickal timing in this way is normally a long-term planning mechanism.

1, ALVACH[72]

Degree span: 0° Aries to 12° 51' 26" Aries. Horns of Aries.

Lord of mansion: Geriz.

Magick first and second quarter: Safe travel and building energy. Excellent for spellwork involving people.

Magick third and fourth quarter: Causes fights between friends. Excellent for spellwork involving people.

2, ALKATAYN

Degree span: 12° 51' 26" Aries to 21° 42' 12" Aries. Belly of Aries.

Lord of mansion: Enedil.

Magick first and second quarter: Find hidden treasure; wheat production; strengthen prisons; anger removal; capturing people or things. Reach for opportunities. Fashion pentacles for magickal applications. Work on self-expression and creativity.

Magick third and fourth quarter: Destroy a building before it is complete; cause arguments between people.

3, ACORAXA

Degree span: 21° 42' 12" Aries to 8° 3' 2" Taurus. Showering or Pleiades.

Lord of mansion: Annuncia.

Magick first and second quarter: Salvation of sailors and their safe return; strengthening imprisonment of captives; works of alchemy; all work done with fire; hunts in the country and the creation of love between a man and a woman; acquisition of all good things.

Magick third and fourth quarter: Work to curb overindulgence.

4, ALDEBARAN

Degree span: 8° 3' 2" of Taurus to 21° 25' 20" Taurus. Eye of Taurus.

Lord of mansion: Assarez.

Magick first and second quarter: Find hidden treasure. Orchestrate an influential meeting in your favor. Magickal work for big-ticket items.

Magick third and fourth quarter: Destruction of a city or building; cause arguments between a coworker and the boss; creation of discord between man and wife; destruction of fountains and rivers; destroy and bind all reptiles and venomous animals; fumigation.

5, ALMITES

Degree span: 21° 25' 20" Taurus to 4° 17' 20" Gemini.

Lord of mansion: Cabil.

Magick first and second quarter: Mystical teachings; safety of travelers through other countries; swift return from traveling; safe travel on water; strengthening buildings;

create good will between two people; receiving good things from kings and officials; to see anything in your dreams. Creates good health. Communicate in a practical way. Good for spells involving schooling and learning of all kinds.

Magick third and fourth quarter: Destroying alliances and friendships.

6, ATHAYA

Degree span: 4° 17' 20" Gemini to 17° 8' 36" Gemini. Little Star of Great Light.

Lord of mansion: Nedeyrahe.

Magick first and second quarter: Bringing friendship between two allies; good hunting; love between two people. Building links of all kinds. Make peace between enemies.

Magick third and fourth quarter: Destroy cities, castles, and business empires, and for besieging them, for revenge against enemies and kings; destruction of crops and trees; destruction of medicines so that it cannot be dispensed.

7, ALDIRAH

Degree span: 17° 8' 32" Gemini to 0° Cancer. Arm of Gemini.

Lord of mansion: Selehe.

Magick first and second quarter: Increase in trade and its money; for good travel, to cause friendship between enemies and allies, good for approaching the presence of the king (boss) or any other person; inclining benevolence from whatever person; acquisition of all things. Work to influence a situation in your favor. Strengthening social contacts.

Magick third and fourth quarter: Drive away flies and prevent them from coming in; destruction of high offices.

8, NATHRA

Degree span: 0° 51' 26" Cancer to 12° 50' 26" Cancer. Misty or Cloudy.

Lord of mansion: Annediex.

Magick first and second quarter: Love and friendship; travel roads safely; creation of friendship between allies; imprisonment of captives may be strengthened and fortified; victory. Orchestrating unexpected events. Family magicks of all kinds.

Magick third and fourth quarter: Destruction and prostration of captives, drive mice out of the establishment. Mother magick and defense.

9, ATRAF

Degree span: 12° 50' 26" Cancer to 25° 42' 51" Cancer. The eye of the lion.

Lord of mansion: Raubel.

Magick first and second quarter: Defend yourself against others. Help others. Work to acquire empathy or strengthen empathic abilities.

Magick third and fourth quarter: Destruction of harvest; unfortunate travel, do evil to all men, cause disputes between allies; for creating weakness and infirmities.

10, ALGEBHAL

Degree span: 25° 42' 51" Cancer to 8° 26' 18" of Leo. Neck or forehead of Leo.

Lord of mansion: Aredafir.

Magick first and second quarter: Create love between man and a woman; goodwill of allies; assistance of allies; healing of illness and ease of childbirth. Using your imagination. Strengthen anything from buildings to personal characteristics.

Magick third and fourth quarter: Destruction of enemies.

II, AZOBRA

Degree span: 8° 26' 18" Leo to 25° 2' 44" Leo. Hair on the Lion's Head.

Lord of mansion: Necol.

Magick first and second quarter: Release of captives; strengthening of buildings; enlarge the wealth of allies, retaining respect and good things; have someone fear you; obtain honors. Magick and activity for all manner of good fortune. Expanding one's luck.

Magick third and fourth quarter: Setting armies to cities and castles.

I2, ACARFA

Degree span: 25° 2' 44" Leo to 4° 17' 6" of Virgo. Tail of the Lion.

Lord of mansion: Abdizu.

Magick first and second quarter: Increase of harvest and plants; increase of destruction; for the betterment of learned men and allies; and to make captives and servants give good service. Starting fresh. Receiving what you want in all contracts involving your labors or the labors of others.

Magick third and fourth quarter: Destruction of ships; separation of lovers. Banishing bad habits and old things that no longer serve you well.

I3, ALAHUE

Degree span: 4° 17' 6" Virgo to 17° 8' 36" Virgo. Dog Stars or the Wings of Virgo.

Lord of mansion: Azerut.

Magick first and second quarter: Increasing trade and your money, increase harvests, that buildings may be completed, and the liberation of captives. Working within convention to achieve your desires. Prosperity magicks and cleverness in financial dealings.

Magick third and fourth quarter: Maintaining the status quo.

I4, ALCIMECH

Degree span: 17° 8' 36" Virgo to 0° Libra. Spike of Virgo or Flying Spike.

Lord of mansion: Erdegel.

Magick first and second quarter: Love of men and women, curing for the infirm; sailors have good conditions; love of allies; curing impotence or bringing a man or woman together who otherwise it is seen they cannot meet. Strengthening divinatory studies. Working for material gain.

Magick third and fourth quarter: Destruction of harvests and plants, destruction of desire. Letting go of rigidity.

I5, ALGAFRA

Degree span: 0° Libra to 12° 51' 26" of Libra. Covered or covered flying.

Lord of mansion: Achalich.

Magick first and second quarter: Locating treasure and taking advantage or promoting new opportunities.

Magick third and fourth quarter: Impeding travelers to keep them from going on trips; separation of a married man from his wife forever; creation of discord between friends and allies; destructions of houses and enemies.

I6, ACUBENE

Degree span: 12° 51' 26" Libra to 25° 42' 52" Libra. Horns of Scorpio.

Lord of mansion: Azeruch.

Magick first and second quarter: Liberation of captives from prison; obtaining friendship and all good things including selling and earning. Working for opportunities.

Magick third and fourth quarter: Destruction of wages, crops, plants, creating discord between man and woman.

17, ALICHIL

Degree span: 25° 42' 52" Libra to 8° 36' 2" of Scorpio. Crown of Scorpio.

Lord of mansion: Adrieb.

Magick first and second quarter: Placement of armies; making buildings strong and stable; and safety of sailors. Love magick with ordinary durability.

Magick third and fourth quarter: Drive away thieves and others who would break into your home or place of work. Workings of justice.

18, ALCAKL

Degree span: 8° 36' 2" of Scorpio to 21° 25' 44" Scorpio. Heart of Scorpio.

Lord of mansion: Egrebel.

Magick first and second quarter: Victory over the enemy; strengthen buildings; healing of fevers and other infirmities of the belly. Strengthening integrity. A sacrifice of outmoded behavior may be needed to complete your working.

Magick third and fourth quarter: Destroy friendships.

19, EXAULA

Degree span: 21° 25' 44" Scorpio to 4° 27' 10" Sagittarius. Tail of Scorpio.

Lord of mansion: Annucel.

Magick first and second quarter: Place armies outside cities and advance upon them; increase of crops, for capturing of fugitives; hurrying the menses of women. Developing ideas. Poor time to begin a business. Making decisions.

Magick third and fourth quarter: Destruction of ships.

20, NAHAYM

Degree span: 4° 27' 10" Sagittarius to 17° 8' 26" Sagittarius. Beam.

Lord of mansion: Queyhue.

Magick first and second quarter: For animals wild and domesticated; hunting in the fields. Draw an individual to a specific place at a specific time.

Magick third and fourth quarter: The destruction of a disagreement between friends.

21, ELBELDA

Degree span: 17° 8' 26" Sagittarius to 0° Capricorn. Defeat.

Lord of mansion: Bectue.

Magick first and second quarter: Strengthen buildings; good for harvests. Workings for sexual prowess.

Magick third and fourth quarter: Separate women from their proper husbands.

22, ACADALDEBA

Degree span: 0° Capricorn to 12° 51' 26" Capricorn. Pastor.

Lord of mansion: (unknown)

Magick first and second quarter: For the safety of those who are ill. Doing the right thing within the confines of society.

Magick third and fourth quarter: Create discord between two people.

23, CACIDDEBOLAH

Degree span: 12° 51' 26 Capricorn to 25° 42' 52" Capricorn. Swallowing.

Lord of mansion: Zequebin.

Magick first and second quarter: Cure the sick; marriage. Revealing secrets and seeking advice.

Magick third and fourth quarter: Destruction.

24, CAADACHAHOT

Degree span: 5° 42' 52" Capricorn to 8° 34' 28" Aquarius. Star of Fortune.

Lord of mansion: Abrine.

Magick first and second quarter: Good will between mean and women; the increase of trade; increase of herds.

Magick third and fourth quarter: Gain power over enemies and unveiling liars.

25, CAADALADBIA

Degree span: 8° 34' 28" Aquarius to 21° 25' 17" Aquarius. Butterfly or spreading forth.

Lord of mansion: Aziel.

Magick first and second quarter: Repairing buildings, protection of orchards and crops. Seeking new solutions for old problems. Finding courage.

Magick third and fourth quarter: Separate women from their men.

26, ALMISDAM

Degree span: 21° 25' 17" Aquarius to 4° 17' 10" Pisces. First drawing.

Lord of mansion: Tagriel.

Magick first and second quarter: Goodwill of men and the creation of love.

Magick third and fourth quarter: Breaking barriers when people will not listen to you.

27, ALGAAFALMUEHAR

Degree span: 4° 17' 10" Pisces to 17° 8' 36" Pisces. Second drawing.

Lord of mansion: Abliemel.

Magick first and second quarter: Increasing trade; clairvoyance; psychic pursuits and enhancing spirituality.

Magick third and fourth quarter: Obstruct the construction of buildings; endangering sailors; destruction of springs and wells.

28, ARCEXE

Degree span: 17° 8 ' 36" Pisces to 0° Aries. Belly of the fish.

Lord of mansion: Anuxi.

Magick first and second quarter: Increase trade; creation of peace and agreement between man and wife; strengthen the imprisonment of captives, bring fish together in one place; group work that causes favor and love. Inner tranquility. Visualize the future.

Palmistry

by Richard Webster[73]

Palmistry is one of the oldest of the occult sciences, and scientists have recently confirmed many things that palmists have known for thousands of years. For instance, scientists have proved that our palms reveal potential illnesses well before they occur. Just recently, scientists at Barcelona University discovered that people's intelligence can be determined by looking at their palms.

It takes a great deal of practice to become a good palm reader, but fortunately, virtually everyone has a hand and most people are only too pleased to let you examine it. Be careful, though: I read the palm of a young woman many years ago, and four years later, I married her.

The first thing to look for is the shape of the palm. Mentally remove the thumb and the fingers and see if the shape that is left is square or oblong in shape. If it is square, the person is down-to-earth, capable and practical. The more oblong it is, the more of a dreamer the person will be.

Now look at the fingers and see how long they are. People with long fingers enjoy details. They often end up in careers involving facts or figures. People with short fingers prefer to skim over the surface of things and do not enjoy details. They are quick thinkers who are often better at starting than they are at finishing.

This gives us four possibilities: Square palms with short fingers are known as earth hands; square palms with long fingers are known as air hands; oblong palms with short fingers are known as fire hands; and oblong hands with long fingers are known as water hands.

People with earth hands are reliable, practical, and enjoy physical work. They generally have good senses of humor, and are tireless when they are doing something they enjoy. They like challenges.

People with air hands have practical minds. They come up with good ideas and then like to make them happen. They love communicating their ideas and express themselves clearly. They are logical, and tend to distrust their emotions.

People with fire hands are great fun to be with as they are constantly full of ideas. They are better at starting projects than they are at finishing them. They are enthusiastic and intuitive.

People with water hands are dreamy, impractical people who envisage a perfect world where everyone gets along with everyone else. They are loving, caring people, but often need someone else to lean on for help and support. They are emotional and highly intuitive.

Once you've done this, you can look at the major lines on the palm. The first of these is the heart line, which is a clearly marked line close to the fingers. It runs from the little finger side of the palm and ends somewhere between the first and second fingers. If it curves and ends between these fingers it is called a physical heart line. People with this can express their feelings easily.

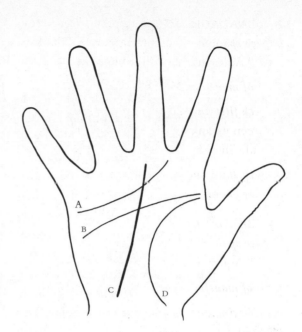

The heart (A), head (B), destiny (C), and life (D) lines.

If the heart line does not curve toward the fingers at the end it is called a mental heart line. People with this need to be reassured that they are loved and cared for. They find it hard to express their innermost feelings. The heart line represents the emotional side of life. Consequently, most people have small islands, like braiding, inside this line, indicating times when their emotional life was not going well. Ideally, this line should be as smooth as possible.

The head line represents the person's intellect. It runs roughly parallel to the heart line for most of its length. It starts joined or close to the life line (the line that curves around the thumb), and either runs in a straight line across the palm, or else curves up toward the wrist. If it is joined to the life line, it means the person is cautious and thinks first. The bigger the gap between the head and life lines, the more independent and impulsive the person will be. If the head line is an almost straight line, the person is down-to-earth and lives in the real world. The more it curves toward the wrist, the greater the imagination. People with long head lines are detailed thinkers, while people with short head lines like to get in and get the job done as quickly as possible.

The life line is the one line that most people know. Unfortunately, they tend to think it relates to length of life, which is not correct. It starts on the side of the hand, between the thumb and first finger, and swings around the thumb, usually ending close to the wrist. The size of the mound of flesh it encircles shows the degree of vitality the person has. Someone with a large mound here will have much more energy than someone with a small mound encircled by a life line that hugs the thumb. Breaks in the life line indicate periods of uncertainty in the person's life. This may, or may not, have anything to do with health. Often, these breaks are protected with an overlapping line, known as a "sister" line.

The other major line is called the destiny line. Some people call it the fate line, but I do not like this name, as it makes it sound as if our lives are all predestined. We have control over our own lives and are able to change our destinies, if we wish. Not everyone has a destiny line. People without one jump from one thing to another, and do not follow a normal type of career. The destiny line starts near the wrist and heads toward the fingers, usually ending beneath the second finger. It is not as clearly marked as the other three major lines. If it starts close to, touching, or inside the life line, it means there was a strong influence on the person while he or she was growing up. This is usually a family influence. The farther away from the life line the destiny line starts, the more independent the person saw him- or herself in the growing-up years.

Ideally, this line should be straight, long, and well marked, showing the person follows a career all the way through life. Many people have changes in their careers, and these are shown by changes of direction and breaks in the line. The destiny line crosses the head line at the age of 35, and the heart line at 49, showing that most people are established on their path through life by the time they reach 35.

As you can see, even a quick look at the shape of the hand and the four major lines is extremely revealing. The best way to learn is to look at as many hands as possible. Read as much as you can, and then check what you have learned with people's hands. Every hand is different. Even your left and right hands will have a number of differences. Being able to read palms will help you empathize and understand people, and, with practice, you will be able to help many people with your skills at palmistry.

Pentagram/Pentacle

The symbol that is, perhaps, the most recognizable in the Craft is the five-pointed star, better known as the pentacle or pentagram, sometimes called the Star of the Microcosm (because the upright star can be seen to represent a human being with arms and legs outstretched), Eastern Star, the Morning Star, the Evening Star, Endless Knot (because it can be drawn without lifting the pen or pencil from the paper), the Druid's Foot, the Witch's Foot, and the Goblin's Cross (here, "Goblin" refers to the King of the Earth Elementals, called "Ghob," who presided over

earthly power and riches in medieval terminology). Technically, the star without the circle is called a pentagram, and the star with the circle is the pentacle. Not only have modern Witches adopted both symbols, but the design of the pentacle is also the herald of the feminine counterpart of the Masonic Lodges, called the Order of the Eastern Star, and figures in various American law enforcement and military symbology. The pentagram/pentacle is a linear symbol in that you don't have to raise your pencil from the paper to draw the entire symbol, which means that the line is unbroken and the power of the design remains intact.

The five-pointed star is most likely the result of astrological/astronomical research done in the Euphrates-Tigris region (modern-day Iraq and Iran) about 6,000 years ago,[74] which already tells us it has nothing to do with the devil, Christianity, Satanism, or the medieval madness of the Inquisitions—all that nonsense came thousands of years later. Archeologists have found pot shards in Palestine at the 4000 B.C. level inscribed with the pentagram, and there is evidence that the design was commonly used by Sumerians around 2700 B.C.[75] From other research found in this book we know that the Babylonian/Sumer cultures were the first of the stylized "Ancient Civilizations," so this tells us that the pentagram is one of the oldest signs used by humankind. In 4000 B.C., if you signed your letter with a pentacle, you were offering good luck and good health to the recipient. The pentagram appears in Italy around 700 B.C. and later, in the sixth century B.C., the pentacle (star with circle) was used in Pythagorean mysticism, where it was said to symbolize the human being, with the five points representing the head, arms, and legs of a person, and the circle added for the unity of humanity to Spirit and the idea of the cosmic egg (uroborus). This is the definition supported by modern Witches today, and is the explanation

they will give you on the meaning of the pentacle they wear around their necks.[76] The pentacle played an important role as a sign on the official seal of the city of Jerusalem during the period 300–150 B.C.,[77] and has been called Solomon's Seal or Solomon's Shield in medieval Jewish mysticism. The Six-Pointed Star is also called the Seal of Solomon, which is a double triangle and a symbol of *As above, so below,* and is used in Kabbalah and Jewish mysticism. Legend has it that King Solomon wore the pentacle on his left pinky finger.

The pentagram, however, has an even more dynamic mystery than all of the above combined because astronomers have found that the pentagram is actually the geometric design depicting how the planet Venus moves in the heavens, and it is from this design that they believe the peoples of the Euphrates-Tigris region drew the first pentagram eight thousand years ago. The pentacle is reflective of Venus' pattern in the sky from our point of view and the circular motion of Venus around the sun. This explains why the pentagram is sometimes called the Morning Star and the Evening Star, and why in the Sumer culture the symbol was related to Innana, Ishtar/Astarte (a powerful goddess of love and war whose ruling planet was Venus, though of course under a different name) and, later on, Venus/Aphrodite herself (Morning and Evening Stars—which are the same planet) in the Greco-Roman cultures. "If we chart Venus synodic orbital time in the zodiac, we find she moves through five positions as the Morning Star, which takes exactly eight years plus one day . . . and forms the design of the pentacle in the vault of the heavens."[78] In the occult, the number eight stands for mastery and is the symbol for infinity (or the uroborus), and in the Craft, the eight cycle stands for the eight paths of power and the eight phases of the moon.

But there's more.

If we look at the study of alchemy (yes, we're going to touch on that again), each point stands for an element (earth, air, fire, water) and the quintessence (remember that word?), which means Spirit—the fifth element. Surrounded, then, by the circle, we have divine transformation, the idea of the philosopher's stone, and the total purification of body, mind, and Spirit—far from the ridiculous notion of evil presented by Hollywood horror films!

As we discussed under Elements, in some Craft traditions (usually those that lean more toward ceremonial practices) the pentacle is drawn in different ways to invoke and dismiss the various elemental energies. It is also used by some groups as a centerpiece for their altars or is drawn on the floor, which combines the two energies of circlecasting and the invocation of the Goddess (as the pentacle is normally associated with the divine feminine) in one ritual act. This process also symbolizes the ascent of the human spirit. If you draw the design from the top down, you are saying that Spirit comes down to matter, and if you draw from the bottom to the top, you are symbolizing matter in its highest form. The horizontal line across represents our development of intellect and the connection of force and form. Using the pentacle in this way has been associated with the ceremonial Great Star of Light or Flaming Pentagram in affirmation of the divine forces found within the symbol.[79]

In modern-day magick, the pentacle is worn for a variety of reasons that are associated with its history:

• As a protective device.

• As a symbol to promote personal power.

• As a representation of the Wiccan religion.

• As a magickal device, whether invoking or banishing.

The pentacle, like any other symbol, can be worn by anyone, including people who don't follow the Wiccan Principles of Belief, nor do they have any idea of the vast history tied to that cool-looking star. It might also be worn by "dabblers"—those individuals who use bits and pieces of magick from various systems, yet study none thoroughly and do not ascribe to the Wiccan religion. This is why many modern Witches wear their pentacles under their shirts if not among friends or family, seeing it as a personal, private, religious symbol that is useful and meaningful as opposed to being simply decorative. Another difficulty in the use of the pentacle is the association of the inverted (upside-down) pentacle in horror flicks and other unfortunate acts associated with the criminal element of our society. However, when traditional Witches go through their second-degree training and experience the Descent of the Goddess in ritual (where one casts off all evil and negativity and confronts the shadow side of the persona), the inverted pentacle is used as a representation of that descent and of the power you have to control the dark side of your own personality (as opposed to letting your negative feelings run rampant all the time). In a few traditions, these students are required to wear the inverted pentacle out of sight until they reach third degree (the clergy level), where the symbol is again righted, showing their movement from inner contemplation to the outer work of the third degree. You will find this same association with the Hermit card of the Tarot deck, where the spiritual student is required to work on balancing the personality before he or she is ready to illuminate the world with his or her discoveries. In this inverted use, the upside-down pentacle represents the light of Spirit hidden by matter.[80]

It appears that the pentagram was first brought into ceremonial magickal circles by Eliphas Zahed Levi (SEE PART I, RITUAL), who invented the invoking and banishing pentagrams used in ceremonial Witchcraft today. He recommended drawing the sign in the air according to a particular pattern above each quarter to call up the elementals, and drawing it in the opposite direction to banish them at the end of the ritual.[81] Empower the pentacle for the following:

- Bothered by unwanted calls? Cut a star out of tinfoil. Empower for protection. Place the shiny side faceup under the phone. Replace every thirty days.

- Draw on notebooks to protect them against theft and prying eyes.

- Draw on your hands and forehead with holy oil or skin-safe anointing oil before ritual, magick, or meditation to banish unwanted energies and enhance your psychic powers.

- Disturbed by bad dreams? Draw the pentacle on a piece of paper, sprinkle with lavender, and place under your bed. Renew once a week.

- Carve on candles to banish negativity and empower with the energies of the five elements (earth, air, fire, water, Spirit).

- Spending too much? Carefully draw a pentacle on garlic skin, then burn to keep money in the home.

- Banish sickness by making small clay pentacles. String them together with red yarn and place in a red conjuring bag along with the name of the person who is ill.

- Add to bind runes.

All-Purpose Pentacle Spell

SUPPLIES: A piece of construction paper (you choose the color to match your working); a pen; incense to match your intent; scissors; cellophane tape; a bowl of water.

INSTRUCTIONS: Draw a large star on the construction paper. Cut out. Write your desire in the center of the star. In a magick circle (in the appropriate moon quarter), begin with your hand in the air over your head, as if you are reaching up to grab something. Then, as you recite the charm, lower your arm and touch the points of the star in a clockwise direction (to draw something toward you) or counterclockwise direction (to push something away from you). Repeat the following charm three times:

*From the heavens to the ground
stars above send energy down.
Earth and air, fire and water
soul of man, son and daughter.
Circle round without an end
evil flees and time will bend.
Star of power, points aflame
unify in Goddess' name!*

Beginning with the top point, fold each point clockwise toward the center of the star. Tape to secure. Carry in pocket or purse until your desire has manifested. Be sure to say thank you and burn, scattering the cool ashes in the wind.

Pow Wow

Pow Wow is approximately 300 years old and is an indigenous magickal system used by the German-American population that consists of three elements:

1. German folk magicks

2. High German ceremonial magicks, including alchemy

3. Native American herbal lore

Although most prominent in the Pennsylvania German-American communities, strands of Pow Wow drifted up and down the eastern seaboard, and then westward into West Virginia and Ohio. The words "Pow Wow" are of Native American derivation, meaning "he who dreams." The root word "powwow" stems from an Algonquin Indian word, first recorded in English in New England in the 1640s. Its basic concept is healing through magickal voice, herbals, rhythmic charms, and physical triggers such as hand motions. As Pow Wow was a system and not a religion, the ethics of the practices varied from person to person, depending on their environment, family history, and personality. Like most systems, it also carried its own unique set of taboos, but these, too, depended upon the practitioner as well as the teacher from whom he or she received "the power."

Studying Pow Wow and its history allows us to understand what type of magicks were used by the everyday person in America 300 years ago as well as in subsequent centuries, and gives us an idea of what other social-magickal models might have been like in the ancient world, where magick was as prevalent then as the use of the automobile is for us today. It shows us how people like you and me mixed magick, religion, and daily life together. Most Pow Wow magick is highly practical, dealing with animal husbandry, farming, community welfare, protection, and general success. With its hands-on healing techniques, it is the American version of Reiki (SEE PAGE 320). The system also uses objects from daily life—needle, thread, scissors, yarn, ribbons, vegetables, creek stones, nails, dinner plates,

taglocks, etc.—rather than tools, which at first glance scream magick. All these everyday items are considered part of folk magick (sometimes called low magick). Yet Pow Wow also has its ceremonial (high magickal) components—astrology, magickal voice, and numerous sigils borrowed from European and Arabic systems that used a more scholarly approach. In the system of Pow Wow, as in the religion of Wicca, magicks were a fine mix of new world and old world, practical knowledge and academia. Most of the spells in this book are of Pow Wow origin, unless otherwise indicated, fashioned to fit within the ethical construction of the Wiccan religion.

Magickal Voice

Pow Wows were well-known for using magickal voice, either speaking aloud or, in many cases, whispering. Everyone has a magickal voice. It is the tone that you utter that vibrates your body, and is unique to each individual. Your voice can synchronize the entire body's energy system, which, in turn, brings body, mind, and spirit into harmony. For some people, the sound formats the word into a sing-song; for others, it may be an individualistic drone. The magickal voice is different for everyone.

To practice your magickal voice, be sure to choose a place and time where you won't be disturbed or overheard. Many new students are shy about practicing, focusing on old beliefs and behaviors where using such a voice is considered silly; yet, think back to when you were small, when you listened to the sound of your own voice and played with the various notes that you could make. In a sense, you were instinctively seeking your own magickal voice all those years ago.

Sit or stand in a comfortable position, but don't slouch. Close your eyes. Take several deep breaths where you inhale through the nose and exhale through the mouth. Begin with the lowest note for which you are capable and intone that note for at least a minute. Work up through the scale. It's okay if you can't sing or are tone deaf—you are searching for the note that vibrates your entire body. Once you've found that note, you'll know it because you will feel the tingling sensation in your body and, if you keep it up, you will begin to feel your energy "click" softly and notice a sensation of gentle harmony all around you. This is the tone of your magickal voice.

Take several more deep breaths, then repeat the tone, this time concentrating on being one with the universe, as I taught you earlier. Find that still point and merge the sound coming from yourself with that meditative state. Continue practicing this exercise for several minutes, but don't push yourself. When you get tired, or can't seem to keep it together anymore, stop. This is natural.

As you practice over the next few days, you'll find that your magickal voice changes a bit. It may be higher or lower than on that first day. This is also normal and a signal that total self-harmony has begun. After several days, the tone will seem like a natural part of you (which it is) and you can begin practicing different words, chants, and invocations in that tone. Continued practice melds this voice with daily habits, and you'll soon discover that magickal voice emerges on its own when you need it without pressure or consciously thinking about it. It will even, as in the practice of the Pow Wow artist, materialize as a magickal whisper.

Banishing Negativity Using Magickal Voice

To quickly cleanse yourself and the area in which you stand of negativity, turn and face the west. Stand with your heels touching and toes pointed slightly outward. Make a diamond with your hands by touching the tips of your fingers together. The opening between your index fingers (that are touching) and your thumbs (that are touching each other) looks like a diamond or a candle flame. Ground and center. Take three deep breaths: the first to cleanse the body, the second to cleanse the mind, and the third to cleanse the soul. Take a nice deep breath and begin vibrating your magickal voice, saying the sound "keeeeee" (the sound of banishment) as you let the air slowly out of your lungs. Repeat this procedure at least three times, seven if you are highly upset, frightened, or worried. Rather than concentrating too hard on what to think, release your mind and simply let the sound carry through the room. You may feel a lightness around your shoulders, as if a burden has been released from your body. When you are finished, take another three deep breaths: the first to cleanse the body, the second to cleanse the mind, and the third to remove any roadblocks standing in your way. Ground and center. Open your eyes.

Pow Wow Spell for Prosperity

SUPPLIES: Lemon oil; yellow candle; 5 gold-colored coins; black or white paper; gold or green pen; the sigil below; holy water; a small, red cloth bag. *Note:* If you cannot find gold coins, you can use 5 gold-painted pebbles.

INSTRUCTIONS: Draw the alchemical symbol shown on the next page on a piece of black paper with a gold pen, or on a piece of white paper with a green pen.

The drawing on the following page is the alchemical symbol for manifestation. It begins with the black circle (the void), with the manifesting spiral in the center, and is surrounded by the four elements, earth at the top, air to the right, water at the bottom, and fire to the left.

Crowning the symbol are the ideograms for "Spirit," and then "mixing" (called amalgamation). The base symbol (connected to fire and below) is the symbol for gold (successful completion). You can also draw this symbol on the yellow or gold candle with a pin, nail, or carving tool of your choice. If you want to take your time, you can draw the symbol with corn meal onto a flat board surface, then place the candle on top.

Ground and center. Cast a magick circle and call the quarters. Place the symbol of manifestation on the center of your altar. Cleanse, consecrate, and empower all supplies you will be using. Rub the candle with lemon oil, focusing on prosperity or on a particular amount of money that you may currently need. Present the candle to the four quarters, beginning with the north and moving in a clockwise direction. Place the candle on the alchemical symbol at the center of the altar. Gather the five coins (or gold stones) and sprinkle with holy water. Using the sound of your magickal voice, running through the vowels a-e-i-o-u, allow the vibrations to enter the stones as you lightly shake them. Think of the color

"gold" as it is associated with prosperity. Now take the stones to the four quarters, beginning with the north, and ask for the blessings of each quarter in the manifestation of prosperity for yourself (or for another if you are asking for someone else).

Return to the altar and place the five coins (stones) around the base of the candle. Hold your hands over the altar. Take three deep breaths and relax. Light the candle. Focus on the flame. Picture what you need at the core of the flame, and repeat the following charm nine times:

> *Forever the silver cord brings*
> *spiritual enlightenment,*
> *the golden bowl be filled with harmony,*
> *the pitcher be empowered and overflow*
> *like the fountain,*
> *and the wheel of life be filled with success.*

After the ninefold repetition, say:

> *This I know you will do for me.*
> *As I will, so mote it be.*

Draw an equal-armed cross in the air over the candle flame. Allow the candle to burn completely. When the candle has extinguished, place the five stones or coins, some of the wax from the candle, and the alchemical symbol in the red bag, and carry on your person. Every time doubt enters your mind that you will not receive your desire, hold the bag in your hands and repeat the above verse three times, followed by the closure (*This I know you will do for me . . .*, etc.).

When you have received your desire, place the red bag on the altar and remove all items. Burn the manifestation symbol and thank deity for your gifts. Scatter ashes to the wind. Bury the candle pieces. Wash the coins or pebbles with holy water and place in the sun for one day. Store coins/pebbles and bag to use again.

Recommended Reading

American Folk Magick by Silver RavenWolf

Amish Folk Medicine: Simple Secrets to a Healthier Body, Mind, and Soul by Don Yoder, Ph.D. and Barbara Duncan, Ph.D.

Psychism and the Paranormal

A 1997 newspaper poll in Great Britain showed more than 90 percent of adults admitted to believing in the paranormal. But because this phenomena is elusive, preferring to lurk on the fringes of real life and almost never turning up for appointments in laboratories, the paranormal has been denied for decades.
—*Uri Geller* [82]

These same paranormal forces that have powered religion and society since the beginning of ancient history do not officially exist for those who desire to control the minds of others, whether that control be for money, power, or simply by fearing that if others don't believe as they do, their stability is lost.

Many new students mistakenly believe that psychic phenomena is the pathway leading to Wicca. Although studying the occult sciences and practicing the religion of Wicca can open psychic channels and enhance paranormal experience, the varied practices and results (scrying, dowsing, telekinesis, telepathy, remote viewing, reading a divination tool, clairvoyance, clairaudience, etc.) are not representations of the religion of Wicca. They are each a science and practice unto themselves, and do not require a Wiccan structure to be experienced. It is true that Wicca is one of the few religions that encourages the student to have an open mind on these topics, and it is also true that Wiccans who have practiced for many years develop senses other than

sight, smell, hearing, taste, and touch due to the various mental exercises they practice on a daily basis.

Some Wiccans have learned that by meditating and practicing the mental arts, psychic centers naturally open at the speed that is right for you. This is a lot of hard work and requires patience as well as daily practice. You can't force psychic abilities, and you can't turn them on and off like a light bulb; rather, they unfold within each person in a way that is right for the individual. If your intent is to reach a harmonious balance and work on self-perfection in a spiritual sense, then psychic skills can develop at a faster rate, yet the progress is still governed by your individual path.

For some, the Wiccan religion releases buried or ignored psychic skills that they had as children; for others, they are a new experience that must be developed if the person desires to use them. Regardless, most Wiccans believe that all humans and animals have psychic abilities, and that anyone can unlock these hidden talents. The first step is the acknowledgement that such abilities exist. The second, and much more difficult leap, is to practice the mental exercises necessary on a repetitive basis to encourage one's own development.

Paranormal Glossary

These are terms you will often see in reference to paranormal and psychic studies.

Akashic records: Records of the Spirit. The universal library that records every thought, word, and deed of each individual, which can only be accessed through meditation. This library does not exist in three-dimensional form. Sometimes called the Hall of All Knowledge or Hall of Records. Discussed often by Edgar Cayce (deceased).

Altered state of consciousness: Accidental or planned process in which the brain accesses information that is otherwise unavailable. An altered state of consciousness can be reached through meditation, ritual, self-hypnosis, etc.

Anthroposomancy: Reading a person's character by studying his or her face, expressions, and body movement.

Astral body: The energy of a soul or person.

Bilocation: Being seen in two places at one time, or being able to visit a place with your mind while your body remains in a different place.

Chi: Life energy.

Clairvoyance: Seeing objects, people, or situations as they occur without conventional vision.

Divination: Using a tool, such as Tarot cards, a crystal ball, coins, etc., to examine the past and view possible future events.

Dowsing: Sensing the hidden presence of water, minerals, people, animals, objects, or energy.

Extrasensory perception (ESP): Telepathy, precognition, clairvoyance, and psychokinesis.

Graphology: Examining a person's character by studying their handwriting.

Kundalini: The free-flowing energy of consciousness.

Ley lines: Paths of energy that travel the surface of the Earth.

Lucid dreaming: Vivid dreams that are totally under the dreamer's control.

Meditation: The focus of the mind.

Medium: A psychic individual who can speak with the deceased.

Mindpower: The energy of human intelligence.

Near death experience (NDE): An out-of-body experience at the moment of death, followed by physical recovery.

Numerology: The practice of using numbers as a divination tool.

Out-of-body experience (OBE): Voyages of the human spirit experienced in astral travel.

Palmistry: Learning the character of an individual by studying the size and shape of hands and fingers, and reviewing the lines in his or her hand.

Parapsychology: The study of extrasensory perception in humans and other natural phenomenon that appears to be supernatural.

Poltergeists: Noisy, sometimes violent physical phenomena that is usually caused by hormonal imbalance or regressed anger.

Precognition: Knowing the future.

Premonition: A forewarning of events to come.

Psychokinesis: (parakinesis/telekinesis) Moving physical objects with the mind.

Psychometry: Sensing a person's or item's past by holding an object.

Remote viewing: Seeing an accurate version of a distant site or person.

Scrying: Seeing the past, present, or future in a shining surface such as black glass, a crystal ball, or a bowl of water.

Synchronicity: What appears to be a coincidence that actually happens for a reason, and therefore is not a coincidence.

Telepathy: Sending thoughts to others, and reading others' thoughts.

Transcendence: Experiencing the "oneness" of the universe.

Recommended Reading

ParaScience Pack by Uri Geller

Association for the Study of Anomalous Phenomena:
    http://www.parapsychology.org

Uri Geller's website:
    http://www.uri-geller.com

Debunking rumors on all subjects, including parapsychology:
    http://www.urbanlegends.com
    http://www.snopes.com

Active Meditation to Increase Spirituality and Psychism

Spirituality in any religion isn't something you learn, it is a way of becoming. Learning to focus, however, can help to open the door to your self-confidence in magick, ritual, and spirituality in general, and allows psychism to peek through normal conscious thought. Try the basic exercise at least once a day for two weeks, then go on to the intermediate exercise, and then the advanced exercise, which you will practice at least once a week for three months using different clay shapes. Please do not skip the beginner's exercise. Even if you are a pro, you could still use the practice at control.

SUPPLIES FOR BEGINNER AND ADVANCED EXERCISE: None. *Optional:* Incense and candlelight for exercise 1.

SUPPLIES FOR ADVANCED EXERCISE: Modeling clay of any kind (Crayola makes great single pack colors.) *Optional:* Incense and candlelight.

BASIC EXERCISE: Close your eyes. Take three deep breaths. Ground and center. Visualize yourself sitting in the center of protective, white light. Count down slowly from 25 to 1. Imagine that there is a third eye at the center of your forehead that is currently closed. If you are good at visualization, you can get a bit fancy here. (Because I'm a girl, mine has cool eye shadow, some sparkles, and an interesting tattoo at the corner.) Take a deep breath and concentrate on that eye. It is not bad or evil, it is simply another sense—the sixth sense that you've read so much about. Normal. Natural. It can "see" things that your other senses may subconsciously pick up (and they do), but they aren't strong enough to bring the information to your conscious mind—you need this eye (for the moment) to do that. Take your time visualizing with and connecting to the idea that you do, indeed, have this psychic gift. As we already know that everyone has this ability and that you simply have to work with it to succeed (like you are doing now), this won't be too hard. If you have any trouble thinking you are psychic, look back into your childhood when all things seemed magickal. It won't take long to capture that feeling again.

For the first two weeks, concentrate simply on opening this eye. What does it feel like as this eye slowly awakens? Do you feel hot? Cold? Is there a pleasant tingling sensation? Each person will experience different phenomena. Fear is not an option. If you are afraid, go no further. You are not ready to awaken your gifts, and don't get all excited about it. Perhaps you need to study more, or overcome something more important in your life right now. Anger management might be an issue. If you are not afraid, move the eye around with your mind. (Remember, your other two eyes are closed.) Check out the room. What do you see? If it isn't clear, don't panic. You are exercising a talent that has been dormant for a long time. Don't strain. When you feel you've had enough, concentrate on closing the eye. Ground and center again, then count from 1 to 5. Open your eyes and take a deep breath. If you had any psychic flashes at all (which for most won't occur in the beginning), write them down in a notebook.

INTERMEDIATE EXERCISE: The intermediate exercise is not done in your home or apartment, but during moments of active life. Carry a small notepad with you to take notes, if necessary. The key to this exercise is to follow the directions without skipping anything. No matter when you open the third eye, you must always remember to consciously conjure that protective white light around you to avoid the emotional connection.

Step One: Ground and center.

Step Two: Visualize white light all around you.

Step Three: While your eyes are open, look at a particular person, where their third eye is located.

Step Four: In your mind, open your own third eye.

Step Five: Without emotion, catalog the impressions you receive, if any. Do not be intrusive or try to probe someone's mind. That's not what this exercise is all about. (It's also rude and eventually you'll be caught. The backlash you receive won't be pleasant.)

Step Six: Mentally close your third eye.

Step Seven: Take a deep breath, pushing all negativity away from you as you exhale. Later, record your impressions without allowing your emotions or personal judgments to interfere (which is also an exercise well worth learning to control).

How do you know when this exercise has been successful? First, if you begin seeing the "spirit body" of the person when you look at them, then you are on the right track. When looking at a spirit body, all emotion you attach to that person drains away. You are seeing them for what they really are—normally glowing light (the wattage depends on a number of factors, including their health and state of mind). Second, if the information you receive later proves to be true, then you know that your sensing capabilities were accurate. One note of caution: Sometimes you will have off days, or your own state of mind won't be the best, or perhaps you're not physically feeling well yourself—in those instances, the information you receive may not be accurate, which is why we must always stay away from snap judgments and be patient when it comes to dealing with psychism and information gained in this way.

ADVANCED EXERCISE: I have nine different objects that you can make and the intent statements that go with them listed below. In a magick circle, cleanse and consecrate the clay, then make the object with your hands, considering the intent. Allow to dry.

When you are ready, situate yourself comfortably for meditation, holding the object in both hands in your lap. Think about the statement of intent associated with the object. Close your eyes. Take three deep breaths. Ground and center. Visualize yourself sitting in the center of protective, white light. Count down slowly from 25 to 1. Imagine that there is a third eye at the center of your forehead that is currently closed. Take another deep breath and concentrate on that eye. Take your time visualizing with and connecting to the idea that you do, indeed, have this psychic gift, and that such a gift enables you to reach the intent represented by the object held in your hands. Slowly open your inner eye. Connect your psychic vision with the intent of the object in your hands. Relax and let the images come.

What do you see? If it isn't clear, don't panic. Don't strain. If nothing happens, don't worry about it. Work with the object for one week. If you still get nothing, move to a different object the following week. Later, once you have worked with all the objects, you can use them again for purposes designed for yourself.

When you feel you've had enough, concentrate on closing the eye. Ground and center again, then count from 1 to 5. Open your eyes and take a deep breath. If you had any psychic flashes at all (which for most won't occur in the beginning), write them down in a notebook.

Week 1—The Goddess. Intent: Connecting with Goddess energy.

Week 2—The God. Intent: Connecting with God energy.

Week 3—Your Favorite Totem Animal. Intent: Connecting with the animal kingdom.

Week 4—A Mountain. Intent: Connecting with Earth energy.

Week 5—A Cloud. Intent: Connecting with air energy.

Week 6—A Flame. Intent: Connecting with Fire energy.

Week 7—A Waterfall. Intent: Connecting with Water energy.

Week 8—An Angel. Intent: Connecting with angelic energy.

Week 9—A Wheel. Intent: Connecting with the tide of the seasons and the tides of life.

Week 10—A Circle. Intent: Connecting with all positive religions on the planet. Learning to feel oneness with the universe.

Week 11—A Pentacle. Intent: Connecting mind, body, and spirit to work as one.

Week 12—A Skull. Intent: Connecting with your ancestors in a positive way.

Psychometry

The word *psychometry*, meaning "soul measurement," was coined by American physiology professor Joseph R. Buchanan in 1840. It is believed that objects collect energy (positive and negative) from people and animals who have touched them, making the skilled psychometrist somewhat of a psychic bloodhound, which isn't far off. In modern history, Uri Geller used psychometry to give police the vital clue they needed to catch the nefarious Son of Sam.[83]

The degree of the energy encoded by frequent handling into an object depends on:

- The material of the object (cloth, metal, etc.).

- The nature of the person or the nature of the animal.

- The energy of the environment in which the object was placed.

- How many people have touched the object since its original ownership.

Practicing psychometry teaches the student why Witches cleanse, consecrate, and empower those things we own or use in a ritual environment. A night of developing psychometric skills in a group format will impress you with just how much energy an item can store!

The best way to perform psychometry is to practice and keep a record of your impressions. Photographs are the easiest way to start because you can mix what you are seeing with what your mind is sensing, then close your eyes and continue. Most Wicca 101 courses contain some type of psychometry lesson to teach you to move beyond the five senses. Some people will receive only "feelings" about the object, where others might see brief mental flashes or just "know" information without seeing or feeling a thing. The major stumbling block in psychometry is when you are pressed for information, so your logic tries to fill in the gaps.

Here are the rules of psychometry:

- Always say the first thing that comes to mind, no matter how dumb, how unrelated, or how stupid it may sound.

- Close your eyes to shut down visual impressions, cutting off part of your current beta experience (waking mind brain waves) and allowing your mind to move directly into alpha.

- Don't get excited if someone tells you "That's not right." Here's why:

  (a) They may not know all the places an object has been, and you may be picking up an energy nuance that they are unaware of.

  (b) Different people perceive the world in various ways. You may be right on with your conclusion.

  (c) They may be lying to you on purpose, or in error. A bad experience can be blocked by the best of people.

Please note that there will be times when you will get nothing. Zip. Nada. Blank. That's life. When friends know that you have even a modicum amount of psychometric ability, they may press you to show them. Don't do it. The most frustrating experience is to sit in a room full of people with everyone trying to give you something to hold. Unless you have an incredible talent for it while you are learning, keep the demonstrations to a minimum. Also, one last warning, but please take it to heart: If there is someone around you that you know is involved in illegal activities, or it's a friend of a friend that just gives you the creeps, keep your head down and your mouth shut as far as your divination abilities are concerned. Once you be-

come adept at your form of chosen divination, there is little information that will escape your knowledge. Granted, as with all things, you won't always be right—but other people don't know that, especially if they have seen evidence of your skill. Divination is not meant to be used in illegal activities, nor should you make yourself a target because of knowledge someone *thinks* you might have.

Reiki

by Autumn Ayla Craig[84]

Reiki is a channeled form of energy healing that originated in Japan. The word comes from Japanese picture writing, known as kanji, in which *Rei* means "spiritually guided" and *ki* refers to life-force energy. Reiki was rediscovered by Mr. Mikao Usui of Kyoto, Japan, toward the end of the nineteenth century. He believed it to be the ancient healing method of all the world's great healers, including Jesus and Buddha. He was a monk and after years of study, research, and travel, his discovery came as part of a vision following twenty-one days of fasting and meditation at the top of a sacred mountain in Japan. After his vision he decided to use Reiki to heal beggars and help them to establish a better way of life. However, he found after years of this service that he had not taught them gratitude, and unfortunately many didn't appreciate the gift of healing. Wanting to pass his knowledge on, he decided to go out to find some true seekers, and subsequently developed a large following of students, including Dr. Chujiro Hayashi, a reserve naval officer. After Mikao Usui's death, Dr. Hayashi opened a Reiki clinic and trained a staff of practitioners. Most of his clients were titled or wealthy individuals. It was believed that only if one paid a great deal could they appreciate the gift of healing, and that giving it away for free did not establish it as being something of value.

Along with the training, Dr. Usui passed on the Reiki Ideals, which are just as valid today as they were then. "Just for today, do not worry. Just for today, do not anger. Honor your teachers, your parents, your neighbors, your friends. Give thanks for all living things. Earn your living honestly."

Hawayo Takata was of Japanese descent but born in Hawaii. She traveled to Japan to visit her family and became very ill while she was there. When she asked if there were alternative treatments for her condition, her doctor referred her to the Reiki clinic. After regaining her health, she was determined to keep it, but to do so she would need to learn Reiki herself. After making many requests, her doctor appealed to Dr. Hayashi, and she was admitted into the vigorous training and required service in the clinic, eventually returning to her home in Kauai in 1937. During her lifetime she trained twenty-two Reiki masters.

Each Reiki practitioner or master maintains their Reiki lineage, and all of us who practice Reiki today can trace our lineage back through our instructor through to one of these twenty-two masters, to Mrs. Takata, Dr. Hayashi, and finally to Dr. Usui, in an unbroken line.

Reiki is not learned like other methods of healing. In order to perform Reiki on yourself and others, you need to have your energy "tuned in" to channel it. This energy transference that occurs between the master and the student is called an attunement. During the attunement, sacred symbols are sealed into your energy field and your crown, heart and palm chakras are opened to accept the energy. Once you have your attunement, you are able to do Reiki immediately, and it will be there for your entire life whether you choose to use it or not.

The practitioner draws upon the unlimited supply of universal life energy and pulls it in through the crown chakra and out through the hands. The energy is then transmitted to the receiver by placing the hands on the individual or in their energy field (aura). This is done through a series of standard hand positions, which cover all the vital areas in the body. Unlike other forms of energy healing, Reiki never uses the practitioner's personal life force energy. As they channel the energy through themselves, they are also getting the benefit of the energy, and treatments can be done on yourself as well as other people, animals, or plants. After additional training, Reiki can be sent to distant places to heal at a distance, or even along with past or present situations in your life. It is a very useful tool and can be though of as carrying your own personal first aid kit inside you at all times.

Recommended Reading

Diane Stein, *Essential Reiki*

Runes

The runes are a system of magick and divination that we have inherited from the Teutonic peoples of the ancient north. As early as 3,500 years ago, the many tribes of these ancient folk developed a unique and complex material and spiritual civilization across northern Europe. From the solar culture of the Nordic Bronze Age to the period of the folk migrations in the latter part of the Iron Age, the Teutonic world had considerable influence and prominence in Europe after the collapse of the Roman Empire. Teutonic paganism thrived in early medieval times in Viking

Scandinavia, Iceland, and Germany. The British Isles were the focus of waves of raiding and settlement by both Saxon conquerors and Norse seafarers, who laid the foundation of our English language, law, and traditions.

We know that the earliest runic forms were rock-art symbols that represented the cosmic insights of Bronze Age shamans. These holy glyphs were designed from the visions and realizations gained in trance states, when the shaman's soul communed with the spirit worlds and interacted with the beings who inhabited those worlds. It is thought that around 500 to 400 B.C.E., the tribe of the Eruli developed a sacred code of these magick signs, and connected them with the sound values of the North Italic (Nordic) letters, the runic system we know today. The runes became widely used for wizardry, communication, oracles, and inscriptions among practically all the Teutonic peoples. The Germans, Goths, Old English, and Vikings each evolved their own distinct forms of the runes, which is why in the magickal community today, you will find various rune sets with sometimes differing meanings.[85] There are also Witches' runes, which are relatively modern and not to be mistaken with the original Teutonic divinatory tool, of which I have seen several sets from various authors.

Today runes take two forms: runic cards (much like a deck of Tarot cards) and runic stones (small stones, each inscribed with a particular rune). Both sets are used as divinatory vehicles as well as tools for magick. Runes are not normally used as a magickal alphabet because most rune masters agree that forming words with runes (which can be done) creates a magickal vortex that you did not intend—meaning that the magick created does not match the English translation of the word (or Spanish, or French, or whatever).

Although there are many ways to read the runes, the most powerful spread is tossing the lot of them on a mat. Those in the center define the significant energies of the reading, where those farther away are considered supporting information. Those stones that fall faceup (where you can see the design) contain information that is evident, and those that fall facedown (where you cannot see the glyph) indicate information that is hidden.

Runes are popular in today's magickal communities because they are a quick and easy way to read the energies of a situation, there are only twenty-four of them to memorize, you can make them yourself with clay or wood, and each glyph (alone or combined with others) creates powerful energies when invoked properly. Like other tools, intensive study is required; however, the runes are very user-friendly, and will work for the student in their capacity to understand them—meaning that as your knowledge grows, so does your expertise with the tool. Below is a list that you may find helpful in learning the runes; however, it is only a basic outline. If you wish to study the runes, please see the recommended reading list that follows.

 FEOH

Basic meaning: Money, wealth, sense of worth, ego, karma.

Magickal application: Advance projects, used to "send" the energy of other runes, temporary changes.

Deity associations: Freyja, Audhumla, Surt, Niord, Frey.

 UR

Basic meaning: Strength, healing, mental powers, internal transition, spiritual strength.

Magickal application: Enhances strength, "sends" courage.

Deity associations: Firogynn, Thor.

THORN

Basic meaning: Protection, unfortunate event, self-discipline, organization, purification, meditation.

Magickal application: Breakthroughs, defense, change.

Deity associations: Thor.

 ASA

Basic meaning: Promotion, leadership, information through the spoken or written word, planning carefully, divine wisdom.

Magickal application: Wisdom, eloquence, inspiration, sending information.

Deity associations: Odin, Huginn, Muninn.

 RAD

Basic meaning: Traveling, short errands, moving ahead, transportation, change in thought patterns, a new spiritual path.

Magickal application: Protection in astral or physical travel, getting something to move ahead.

Deity associations: Regin.

 CEN

Basic meaning: Documents, letters, books or other recorded information, insight, ideas, solutions, success, creativity, enlightenment, finding an opening.

Magickal application: Creating an opening, banishment, illumination, fire magicks of all kinds.

Deity associations: Freyja.

 GYFU

Basic meaning: Partnership that you enjoy, material gift, generosity, one's oath, divine gift or skill (such as artistic or musical).

Magickal application: Creating balance, healing, bonding energies, air magicks of all kinds.

Deity associations: Idunna, Gefion.

 WYN

Basic meaning: The group mind, whether it is family, clan, group, or coven. Celebrations, holiday activities, success, fulfillment, harmony.

Magickal application: Wish rune, success, "sends" projections of authority, binds group energies in a positive way.

Deity associations: Alfs.

 HAEGL

Basic meaning: Disruptive physical event, disillusionment, spiritual struggle, protection against enemies.

Magickal application: Overcoming obstacles, banishing, blessing, defense activities.

Deity associations: Mother Holda, Gandreid.

NYD

Basic meaning: Material, emotional, or spiritual need.

Magickal application: Seeking freedom, finding liberation, turning a bad situation to a good one, turning away enemies.

Deity associations: Nott, Dark Elves.

ISA

Basic meaning: Material, mental, or spiritual inactivity.

Magickal application: Blocking negative energy, freezing a situation, finding clarity, binding negative energies.

Deity associations: Frost Giants, Skadi.

JERA

Basic meaning: Improvement of physical circumstances, new home, renovations, new job, new relationship, improvement on mental outlook, drawing closer to spiritual attainment.

Magickal application: Gentle change, harvesting what you have done, bringing rewards to you that you have earned, improving on a situation, building.

Deity associations: Frey, Scyld, Sif.

 EOH

Basic meaning: Sudden but beneficial change in physical location, return of an old friend or enemy, death, confronting our shadows, the process of spiritual initiation.

Magickal application: Attuning energies, hunter rune, achieving true aims, finishing projects, laying fears to rest, closure.

Deity associations: Uller, Frigg, Dises.

 PEORTH

Basic meaning: Magick, the results of one's magickal applications, secrets revealed, interest in the occult, divine intervention.

Magickal application: Understanding the underlying energies of a situation, initiation, secrets, visionquesting, shamanistic work, fate.

Deity associations: Wyrd Sisters, Mothers, Norns.

 ALGIZ

Basic meaning: Help and assistance from the outside, ethics and values, protection, divinity, the path of enlightenment, intuition, information from a divine source.

Magickal application: Protection, luck, defense, opening one's psychic abilities with divine guidance.

Deity associations: Valkyries, Heimdall.

 SOL

Basic meaning: Success, healing, achievement, combining one's energy with divinity, finding the right path, knowing your true will.

Magickal application: Bringing about victory, success, or healing; making wise choices for advancement.

Deity associations: Sunna, Baldur.

 TYR

Basic meaning: Justice, winning battles, finding mental and emotional order, building one's faith.

Magickal application: Justice, honor, victory, faith, order, personal security, defensive movements, courage.

Deity associations: Tyr, Saxnot.

 BEORC

Basic meaning: Birth, conception of a child, a new job, a relationship, emotional well-being, feminine mysteries, protection for women.

Magickal application: Starting a new project, spells for birth, purification, motherhood, reincarnation and protection specifically for women and children.

Deity associations: Berchtholda, Berchta.

EH

Basic meaning: Movement and the vehicles of movement, cooperation between two parties, negotiations, meeting of the minds, drawing in divine and psychic power.

Magickal application: Making something move, creating a partnership between yourself and another, overcoming obstacles through group work, psychic abilities in connection with other people.

Deity associations: Sleipnir, Divine Twin.

 MAN

Basic meaning: Issues concerning career, groups of people, and organizations such as a club. Friendships. Connecting with divinity in group work.

Magickal application: Creating singular thoughts and sending them, intelligence, advancing career and school work, arbitration wherein you will be treated fairly.

Deity associations: Mannus, Ask, Embla.

 LAGUS

Basic meaning: Heightened sensitivity, unconscious activity, dreams, universal love, collective unconscious, psychism.

Magickal application: Strengthening occult work, interpreting dreams and other psychic phenomena, fascinations, glamouries.

Deity associations: Mani, Bil, Hjuki.

 ING

Basic meaning: Nature and the world around us, passion, balance, conclusion to something that has bothered you, finding harmony in all things, including the world of nature.

Magickal application: Learning to focus, grounding and centering work, finding opportunities, overcoming mental illness, calming domestic issues.

Deity associations: Light Elves, Elf Lights.

 ODAL

Basic meaning: Structure such as a building or house, one's emotional structure, lineage, protection of one's property.

Magickal application: Bringing prosperity into the home, finding fortunate influences to affect home or property, one's inheritance.

Deity associations: Hlodyn, Odin.

 DAG

Basic meaning: Satisfaction with any situation, having a positive outlook (or one is required), finding balance and harmony in one's spiritual views, transformation to a new way of living.

Magickal application: Finding and promoting spiritual enlightenment, making choices that affect your spirituality, changing your outlook from negative to positive, increasing happiness and wealth, finding good luck.

Deity associations: Baldur the Beautiful.

BLANK

Basic meaning: Information is not available at this time—or, the future is what you make it.

Magickal application: None.

Deity associations: None.

Bind Runes

Unique to the runic system is the use of bind runes, where two or more runes are drawn together to enhance their power. Then, in ritual, this combined force is directed within the magickal working. The Aegishjalm (meaning the Helm of Awe), on page 326, is a bind rune used for protection, purification, and runic power. How many runes can you find in the Aegishjalm?

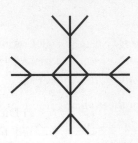

The Aegishjalm, or Helm of Awe, bind rune.

Here are examples of other bind runes that you can use in your magickal work.

 To assist those who are unhappy, depressed, or in sorrow, use Fehu, Ing, and Lagus.

 For healing, combine Ur, Jera, and Sol.

 For binding foes, use Thorn, Isa, and Nyd.

 To release yourself from a constraining situation, use Asa, Fehu, and Ing.

 To return negativity to its sender, use Hagel, Jera, and Rad.

 To slow a situation down, use Isa, Lagus, and Nyd.

 To bring about a reconciliation, use Gyfu, Man, and Wyn.

 To control adverse weather, use Gyfu, Asa, and Rad.

 To stop an astral attack, combine Dag, Eh, and Lagus.

 For general protection, combine Sol, Algiz, and Asa.

 For communicating with the dead, combine Hagel, Nyd, and Tyr.

 For mystical knowledge, combine Eh, Man, and Asa.

 To set things in motion, use Sol, Rad, and Cen.

 For attracting a boy- or girlfriend, use Cen, Jera, and Ing.

 To work with the elements, use Eh, Lagus, and Rad.

 To win an argument, combine Asa, Tyr, Wyn, and Rad.

 For victory, use Tyr, Wyn, and Odal.

 To protect your privacy, use Asa, Lagus, and Ur.

 For monetary growth and success, use Feoh, Birca, and Sol.

How to Empower Bind Runes

Draw the chosen bind runes on clean white paper (or parchment, if you can obtain it). Write the individual's name whom the rune is for on the back of the paper. Ground and center. Cast a magick circle and call the quarters. Draw the

Helm of Awe on your forehead with holy water. In this spell, when invoking Spirit, use only Germanic deities, the Lord and the Lady, or the word "Spirit" in general. Runes do not react well to pantheons other than their own.

Pass the paper through your favorite incense. Place a clean dish on the altar. Put an ice cube on the dish. Place a tea candle on top of the ice cube. Hold your hands over the dish, and say: "I invoke the powers of frost and fire, work my will as I desire!" Light the tea candle.

Hold your hands over the paper, and say:

Ye hallowed powers of fire and frost
of ancient worlds and memories lost
from Asgard to Hel attend to me
from roots to crown of the blessed tree
invoke the powers of this sacred rune
and bring to me your special boon!
Weave your web, sweet sisters three
as I will, so mote it be!

Pass the paper over the candle flame three times. Breathe on the paper three times, then seal with a kiss. The bind rune is now empowered to add to other spell or ritual work, or you can let it work on its own. Thank deity, close the quarters, and release the circle. Allow the tea candle to burn completely. Pour the water from the ice cube outside, saying: "To the gods!"

Note: You can also carve bind runes onto candles and paint them on backpacks, skateboards, and purses. Just as the ancient Egyptians inscribed hieroglyphics directly on the skin to promote healing and well-being, the runes can be used in the same manner. Remember to use skin-safe body art materials.

Recommended Reading

Leaves of Yggdrasil by Freya Aswynn

Rune Magic by Donald Tyson

Witches' Runes (book and card deck) by Nigel Jackson and Silver RavenWolf

Scrying

By viewing the patterns that are forming in the astral material, one can project the likely outcome in the material world.
—*Raven Grimassi*[86]

According to the Oxford English Dictionary, the word *scry* is actually a truncated form of the French derivation *descry*, of the Latin *describe*, which is linked to three meanings: "to call out," "to catch sight of from a distance," and "to discover by observation." The word *descry* was linked to astronomical texts and the magickal arts in the 1300s.[87] Although noted in French and English history, scrying can be traced to ancient Egypt, where the magician would take a bronze bowl engraved with a figure of Anubis, fill it with water, and cover the water with a thin film of oil. The medium chosen (not necessarily the magician) would gaze into the still surface of the liquid and prophesize what he or she saw there.[88] Scrying, then, is a means of foretelling the future, or reviewing the present or past, by gazing into a smooth, still surface—often a dark surface, though not always. The famous Irish Witch Biddy Early used a blue glass bottle filled with water as a convenient and unobtrusive scrying tool.[89]

The tool most associated with scrying in medieval literature is the speculum, of which there were two kinds, one used for surgery, and another—a mirror or reflective device made of highly polished metal or glass and sometimes containing a lens—was used in scientific study and astronomy. It is this second tool from which scrying tools, no matter the shape, size, or content, got the name *speculum* (such as Biddy's blue glass bottle).

Whether you are using a black bowl filled with water, a piece of glass with one side painted black, a colored bottle, a crystal ball, or other object that suits your fancy, most magickal practitioners agree that the best time to make your speculum is a waxing moon, and that it should be empowered with moonlight (sunlight is considered too strong a natural force). Astrologically the two prime dates would be when the moon or the sun is in Scorpio. It is also believed that the best time to use your speculum is during a full moon. Although scrying methods are often related to liquid or earth, fire gazing by looking into a candle flame or hearth fire is also popular.

How to Scry Using a Colored Glass Bottle

SELECTING THE BOTTLE: Choose a tall bottle with as few raised letters or indentations as possible. The darker the color, the better the results, though I've used a turquoise bottle with great success.

INSTRUCTIONS FOR PREPARATION: First cleanse, consecrate, and empower the speculum in a magick circle while the moon is waxing. You may wish to dedicate the tool to your favorite god or goddess, or simply use the words "Spirit" or "Lord and Lady" for the consecration. On the full moon, fill the bottle with holy water, or a mixture of holy water and a favorite scented, blessed oil. Cap it. Take the bottle outside to charge it. If you can't go outside, be sure you are in front of a window where you can see the full moon. Turn the bottle so that the surface catches the moon's reflection. Leave the bottle in the moonlight for least one hour.

INSTRUCTIONS FOR SCRYING: (These instructions will also work for other speculums, such as crystals or magick mirrors.)

> **Step One:** Remove all fingerprints from the surface of the bottle. Cast a magick circle and call the quarters. Sit comfortably in the center of the circle with the bottle. Most scrying is done by candlelight or in very low light, as bright lights reflecting off the surface of the scrying tool inhibit the process. The light should be behind you and should not shine directly onto the bottle. You can play soft music or light fragrant incense if you like.

> **Step Two:** Ground and center. Take three deep breaths, inhaling and exhaling slowly. Close your eyes and count down from ten to one. Allow your body to relax, and envision any negativity you have been feeling drain away. See yourself surrounded by pure white light.

> **Step Three:** Hold the bottle comfortably in your lap. Once again make sure the surface area of the bottle that you will view is clear of fingerprints. Later you may prefer to set the bottle on a raised flat surface, but for now, while you are learning, hold the bottle tilted gently in your hands so that you can view the smooth surface comfortably. Stare at the surface of the bottle, but don't strain. If you tense up, you won't be able to easily enter the altered state of consciousness so easily. If you have been meditating for a while, the transition from waking state to the alpha state will happen faster. Regardless, you will not really notice the transition, as the alpha state also occurs when you are watching television, daydreaming, or eating.

> **Step Four:** The edges of the bottle will slowly grow blurry, or you may see silver clouds on the surface of the bottle, a fine mist, or even bits of light here and there. This is normal and is the first stage of scrying. Rather than tensing when you see these things, allow your body to relax. If you are the least bit nervous, close your eyes and re-create the white light around you, then

open your eyes and allow this "misting" to continue.

Step Five: The clouds will gradually change into a soft, inky blackness (sometimes dark blue)—almost like you are looking at liquid velvet. Then, the blackness will begin to break or slip away, revealing the third stage of scrying—the vision itself. This vision may be in your mind's eye, or you may see something tangible. Depending on your personality, the visions may be literal, symbolic, or much like visions in a dream state that must be interpreted later.

Step Six: When you are finished, set the bottle down and close your eyes. Ground and center, keeping your eyes closed. Breathe deeply three times, inhaling and exhaling slowly. Count from one to ten and then open your eyes. Take another deep breath. Write down your impressions in a notebook and keep for later reference. Close the quarters and release the circle. Store the bottle in a safe place out of direct sunlight. You can continue to use this same bottle throughout the month. At the next full moon, empty out the water, rinse thoroughly, and fill with holy water again. Empower in the moonlight for at least one hour.

As with all psychic endeavors, successful scrying takes committed practice. Many experts recommend practicing daily, for fifteen to twenty minutes each day, until you feel competent, which could be anywhere from one month to an entire year.

Spells

I wish I had a nickel for every time a reporter or radio talk show host asked me the following: "Do spells really work?"

Yes. Of course they work!

A spell is nothing more than linking physical actions with focused prayer. That's it. No mist rising from the graveyard required. No discarnate spirits hovering over your shoulder a necessity. No ghost riders waiting outside to carry you off to a moldy, evil castle of doom and gloom. Words. Actions. Stuff. That's about the long and the short of it.

Whether we are talking about spells performed in ancient civilizations or modern times, most spells have the following in common:

- They are like recipes that call for different ingredients, and these ingredients are chosen by correspondences (SEE PART IV, CORRESPONDENCES).

- They have some sort of timing mechanism attached to them—day of the week, moon quarter or phase, planetary alignment, planetary hour, season, or other significant association with a heavenly body action such as a comet, eclipse, blue moon (the second of two full moons that occur in a calendar month), etc.

- They are done in a magick circle, and often in a ritual within that circle.[90]

- They work best if tailored to a specific religion that encourages ethical and moral behavior.

- They link to a deity of some sort, whether that deity is from a particular pantheon or is viewed as all-encompassing Spirit. Higher powers can also be included, such as angelic/planetary energies that represent the pure essence of deity. The idea of handing a problem over to god/dess is not a Christian fabrication. You've heard some Christian sects say "Give your problems to Jesus," or "Give your problems to God." The idea of handing troubles over to deity and higher powers was common among people as far back as 400 B.C.,[91] long before Christianity came into being.

- They are accompanied by spoken or written formulas that may include prayers, invocations, or charms.

- Many include the use of symbolism, from the colors chosen to the design of sigils.

- Most employ some type of repetitive form (words or symbols) that may also use analogies, metaphors, similes, or rhythmic phrases.

    Analogy: Showing the similarities between two different things—"As the moon's light grows so shall my own power increase." The similarity here is that both humans and the moon have power that can be increased.

    Metaphor: Descriptive phrase in which one kind of object or idea is used in place of another to suggest a likeness between them—"May all negativity be cut from me as the ship plows the sea."

    Simile: A figure of speech comparing two unlike things that is often introduced with the words "like" or "as"—"May the disease rot as this potato rots in the ground." "May she be as gifted as an angel with a lyre."

- Fully state the intent of the practitioner and of the work, including the name of the practitioner and the name of the individual for whom the working is designed. If a full name could not be found, then a descrip-

tion of the person or his or her family lineage was also used.

- Most spells have some type of sealing device, from hand motions in the air, sealing with wax, tying with string or thread, or using another object. Ancient spells often used nails, not with the intention to harm, but with the analogy that if a nail holds a board into place, it will hold a spell into place too.

If we divided the process of spellcasting in half, there are two main portions: the spell itself and the accompanying rite (set of actions); and both are normally done within the confines of the magick circle. In spellcasting, practice makes perfect and the more you learn, the better you become at casting spells. You can't read a book, do one spell, fail, and think that's all there is to it. It's more complicated than that; practice is the key to success. This doesn't mean that your first spells will automatically fail (indeed, your success will probably amaze you), but magick is hard work, after all, and, like some recipes, not every spell works well for every person.

Spellcasting is certainly not new, and we can find references to spells in all the ancient cultures and several modern ones as well. It is important to remember that the casting of spells was not relegated to priests and priestesses (or clergy) of the ancient religions. Both aristocrats and peasants firmly believed and used either the services of one who knew how to cast spells, or practiced whipping them up themselves. Greek, Roman, Celt, Jew, Druid, Egyptian, Islamic, Persian, Sumerian, Norse, Christian, and German (yes, I know I'm mixing religions, cultures, and countries, that's the point)—all incorporated the belief of spellcasting in their daily lives,[92] and no amount of convincing—from Roman law to Saint Patrick to the pope to Martin Luther to the Puritans and finally the fundamentalists of later years—has ever been able to fully eradicate the practice.

Why?

Because spells work.

There will always be a debate, however, about *why* they work, and for that we have to look into the mind of the practitioner. When a person begins to practice magick or study the Craft, he or she is moving from a passive attitude about life and stepping forward into an active, participatory one. He or she is no longer the victim of circumstances, but agrees that by using his or her willpower and level of belief, he or she can accomplish anything. And that's precisely what they do—they succeed. Witches believe that all acts of magick and ritual will change the practitioner's perception on any given issue. If you work for harmony (which is the best idea), then you are raising your energy vibration to accept and welcome that harmony—all negativity then naturally fades away. The length of time for the spell to work depends largely on the amount of imbalance in the situation. In spellwork you are conquering your own fear, negative thoughts, and doubts by finding the courage to go beyond issues, self-defeating conditioning, and people that try to hold you back. Other Witches have different ideas on why spellcasting works; however, if you want to dissect why spells work, that's fine and you'll find a great deal of musing in both scholarly texts and magickal ones. What is most important is that you don't have to analyze a spell in order for it to succeed.

You need only believe.

For further discussion on why spells work, please refer to PART IV, MAGICK.

Super Simple Spellcasting

Let's say you found a cool spell in a book and you want to try it, and let's also say that this particular spellbook isn't big in the instructions department (many aren't). That's because they assume that you already know how to cast a spell, so in their minds you really just need the ingredients. For the sake of argument, let's include that you know how to do ritual, that you have a basic understanding of magickal timing (particularly the moon in the phases), and that you've read through most of this book, therefore you already understand why the magick circle is important, why the quarters are important, etc., etc. All you really need is a basic spellcasting ritual that you can do from memory and plug in the spell you've chosen. The fact that you will do this same simple ritual for your spells on a repeated basis helps to ensure a successful working (the beauty of repetition). Although I provided you with a basic ritual (SEE PAGE 23), this one is designed only for spellwork. First, let's work through an example of super simple spellcasting, and then I'll give you some spells in the form of recipes that you can plug in. Remember, the key is memorizing the format so that eventually you can do it by heart without having to look at a book. To make this procedure interesting and unusual, I've added a spell rod. (SEE PART II, WAND, ROD, STANG, AND STAFF.)

Silver's Spellcasting Ritual

SUPPLIES: You will need a spell rod, which is nothing more than a dowel ¾ to 1 inch in diameter and 3 feet long. Paint half the rod black. Allow to dry. Paint the next four inches red. Allow to dry. Paint the next four inches white. Allow to dry. Paint the remaining end of the rod gold. Cover a small portion of the black end with soft red leather or red cloth for a hand grip. Glue in place. Tie three bells with black ribbon at the bottom of the hand grip. These colors— black to red, red to white, and white to gold— are the original alchemical colors (SEE PAGE 360).

The spell rod is used only for spells, nothing else, which is why I haven't suggested using your wand or athame, though you certainly could if you like. By keeping the spell rod separate from your other workings it retains only that energy used for spellwork. Cleanse, consecrate, and empower the spell rod when it is completely dry; this is best done during a full moon. Allow the rod to sit in the light of the moon for at least one hour. Also, I always burn a white candle and set out a white bowl of water, no matter what ingredients are called for in the spell.

STEP ONE: Gather all the supplies necessary for the spell, as well as any written information needed to cast the spell, and place everything on your altar or working surface. Light any illuminator candles that you feel you may need. For advanced students, you may also wish to devote the altar at this time. Ground and center.

STEP TWO: Cast the magick circle in the following manner: Beginning at the north, walk clockwise once around the room, with the gold end of the stick pointing out and down to start and slowly raising the rod as you intone the circlecasting. When you reach the north quarter the third time, the spell rod should be raised directly vertical toward the sky. I have added the reasoning for each line in parentheses so that you can better understand what will manifest as you cast this circle. This will also help you choose other suitable circlecastings for your work in years to come.

Black and red, white and gold
(invoking the alchemical energies from
void to perfection)
rising circle taking hold.
(bidding the circle energy to coalesce)
New moon's blessing bright and clean
(asking for cleansing and consecration)

full moon's magick sight unseen.
(asking for protection)

You should have made one pass around the circle. Now walk the circle again, reciting the next four lines and stopping briefly at the quarters.

North is earth and east is air
(invoking the elements)
mighty ones, attend me here.
(invoking the angels or guardian protectors)
South is fire, and west the sea
(invoking the elements)
ancient ones, please be with me.
(invoking the ancestral dead)

You should have made the second pass around the circle. Now walk the circle one last time, reciting the final four lines.

Rise, O circle, Queen's great cloak
(building the circle energy and
calling on the Goddess)
hunter's might and Witch's oath
(calling on the God and invoking
one's oath of service)
planets spin and kiss the stars
(calling the correct astrological energies)
hearken to the Witch's charge!
(awakening planetary energies)
Make the magick make the change
(calling for the energy needed to
complete the tasks this night)
nothing is beyond my range.
(declaring one's power—and believing it)
Between the worlds this circle sealed—
(sealing the circle)

Tap the rod on the ground once.

And naught within shall be revealed.
(secrecy while circle is cast).
As above and so below
(alchemical invocation)
as I say, it shall be so!
(declaration of belief)

STEP THREE: As this particular ritual is designed for speed, the quarter call will be a bit different than shown in either the basic ritual or the esbat rituals. Stand in the center of the circle and face north. As you intone the quarter call, point the rod in the air toward the intended quarter with arm extended at forehead level. As you say each element, visualize that element. This is extremely important with this particular quarter-calling procedure. If you say *earth*, then think about the rich, loamy soil. When you say *air*, think of the breezes, the winds, the joy of breathing. *Fire* should have a strong brazier of flame, and *water* could be a waterfall, the sea, or a flowing river. You already knocked on their door in the circlecasting, but now you are required to open that door.

Ye elemental gates open here
(statement of intent)
bring your special powers near.
(asking for assistance)
Earth! (opening the north quarter)
Air! (turn east, opening the east quarter)
Fire! (turn south, opening the south quarter)
Water! (turn west, opening the west quarter)

No other associated powers are called because each spell is different, and some spells may make specific mention of what should be invited into the circle along with the element (angels, totems, ancestors, etc.). If your spell calls for any of these, or has its own quarter call, insert that information here.

STEP FOUR: Identify yourself, invoke deity, and indicate your intent. Check the spell. If deity is not mentioned, you should insert your own spiritual power and call upon that deity. If you are worried that the deity you chose will not fit with the essence of the spellwork, simply say Spirit. Again, this spellworking format is designed for speed. That doesn't mean you should rush through the spell, speak quickly, or hurry any of the parts, but it does keep the working smooth and simple. As you state the words of intent, hold your dominant hand above your head (if you are right-handed, it would be your right hand—left-handed, your left hand) or, with your dominant hand, point the gold end of the rod to the heavens.

Below is an example statement for you to use. When writing your own portion of this ritual, be sure to keep your statement of intent clear. You've already seen a statement somewhat like this in Part I (SEE QUARTER CALLS), so it should be somewhat familiar to you.

Hail, Mistress of the Universe!
I, (say your name), *your son/daughter of the Craft of the Wise, do call thee forth and beseech you in the name of your earthly child,* (name the person or animal you are working for. If it is yourself, then reword this section), *who is in need of your assistance. Great Mother, lend me your ear in this situation.*

Now describe the situation in specific terms and indicate what you are requesting. For example, "That Jane Doe finds solace and comfort in her hour of need," or "That John Doe finds a new job that brings him the income he needs as well as personal satisfaction and a good working environment without having to drive too far," etc. Continue by saying, "I know that you will do this. So mote it be!"

To let you see what it looks like all together, here is a quick example:

> *Hail, Mistress of the Universe! I, (say your name), your son/daughter of the Craft of the Wise, do call thee forth and beseech you in the name of your earthly child, Tiffany Doe, who is in need of your assistance. Great Mother, lend me your ear in this situation and provide protection for Tiffany as she travels from her home to visit her grandmother in Portland, Maine. Please protect her until she safely returns home again. I know that you will do this. So mote it be!*

STEP FIVE: Cleanse, consecrate, and empower all supplies, regardless if the spells says you should nor not.

STEP SIX: Insert the spell, which will probably in some way repeat your original statement of intent. Repetition in magick is not only expected, but helps to focus the work. Perform all aspects of the spellwork, which includes raising energy. If the spell does not say to raise energy, it is assumed you will do it anyway. Sometimes this is done by repetition of a chant or drumming, but some spells tell you to mix something and light a candle without additional information. If this is the case, take the time to raise the energy. The easiest way is to stand with feet apart and slowly raise your arms, focusing on your intent. You will feel the energy move through your body and out through your upraised hands. As you become more experienced in raising energy, you will feel a very cool rush as you lift the energy up and out. I would also like to remind you here that you are not raising your own energy (which would make you feel tired) but gathering the energies you have called (deity, quarters, etc.) to do the job for you. If you feel tired after a ritual, then you have expended too much personal energy. You should feel energized and wide awake! Remember to seal the spell by blowing on the material three times or drawing an equal-armed cross in the air over the project. Many spell books don't include this information.

STEP SEVEN: Thank deity.

STEP EIGHT: Close the quarters by facing west, and saying:

> *Ye elemental gates begin to close your gifts were welcome, your energy goes.*

Point the rod to the west, and say "Hail and farewell." Turn to the south and repeat "Hail and farewell." Then to the east, repeating the closure, and finally to the north, saying, "Hail and farewell. Everything comes from the north!"

STEP NINE: Beginning at the north quarter, point the rod away from your body and toward the ground. Slowly move in a clockwise direction, envisioning the circle lifting and pouring into the rod as if the rod is a type of magick vacuum cleaner. Continue moving counterclockwise until you reach the north quarter again. Tap the rod once on the ground, and say: "This circle is open but never broken. So mote it be."

STEP TEN: Ground and center. Clean up the area and put all supplies away.

Spells to Try

Here are spells that you can try using the simple procedure we just learned. Remember to write out your statement of intent before you begin. These spells appear here just like you might find them in a spell book, which means that you may have to add things (like incense or other favorite supplies) on your own. You'll also have to think about timing. Don't forget the basics like grounding and centering, raising energy, and remembering to seal the spell with sacred breath or the equal-armed cross. If you follow the previously given spellcasting ritual, these conjurations should work well for you.

Money and Prosperity Spell

Fill a small, black purse with silver coins. Add three mint leaves (to draw money), four garlic peels (to keep money once you have it), one silver pentacle (or draw the pentacle on a piece of yellow paper), some silver glitter, three silver bells (to dispel negative energy around your finances), a spring of rue, and a piece of pepper plant. On a slip of paper, write your name and the amount of money needed, then add the words "and a little extra." Place paper inside the purse. Close the purse. Say the following chant nine times while shaking the purse:

> *Money, money, come to me.*
> *Bring to me prosperity.*
> *Silver coins and silver bells,*
> *silver star the money swells!*

Begin saying softly, then increase volume of voice as you raise energy. Leave the purse on your altar or carry with you until you receive the money. To keep money flowing toward you, remember to give some of what you have received to charity or a friend in need. Save the money bag until you need it again. Add fresh herbs and three more coins to reactivate the energy.

To Banish Someone's Influence from Your Life

Write the person's name who is giving you problems in big letters on a large piece of paper. With mortar and pestle, mix salt, black pepper, and red pepper together. Trace the letters on the paper with glue. While still wet, sprinkle the glue with the banishing mixture. As the glue dries, repeat the following chant:

> *Goddess made thee man/woman (boy/girl)*
> *and dog, nose to the ground and let me be,*
> *run—not walk—away from me.*

When completely dry, burn the paper and place the ashes near the person who is bothering you.

To Find Love

Take the Ace of Hearts from a card deck and place faceup on your altar. Sprinkle with a bit of brown sugar. Place three pink rose petals on top. Burn a pink candle with your name on it. Hold your hands over the Ace and say twenty-one times:

> *Aces are winners and I'll win in love,*
> *kisses and hugs from heaven above,*
> *bring me affection that I'm thinking of.*

Place the Ace, sugar, and rose petals in a pink conjuring bag. Carry with you until your desire is granted. Keep until you wish the relationship to end, then open the bag and scatter to the winds, saying five times:

> *Aces are winners and I've had my fill,*
> *leave now with happiness, and leave me no ill.*

To Gain Entrance into a Group or Club

Mix dried clover, white sugar, and ground orange peel together with mortar and pestle. Draw or find a picture of the group's insignia. Draw the bind rune below over the insignia.

Write your name over the bind rune. Write the club's name on the back of the paper. Activate the rune as explained on page 326. Sprinkle the herbal mixture onto the front of the paper (the side containing the bind rune). Fold the four corners of the paper over to completely cover the herbal mixture. Securely tape. Seal with red wax. Place in a small, red felt bag. Carry with you until entrance is obtained. If for some reason you decide to leave the group, take the spellwork apart in ritual and burn everything in a fire-safe bowl.

To Activate Group Effort

Many times a teacher or professor will insist that you work with others on a class project. Although this is meant to encourage group participation, invariably one person is stuck with most of the work (that one person is probably you). To ensure that everyone does their fair share, try this spell.

Write the names of those people involved in your project on the inside bottom of a white paper bowl without spaces between the names (so it looks like you have one big, huge, crazy word). Write the name of the project underneath. Place a magnet in the bowl. Place a handful of sunflower seeds (for success) on top of the magnet. With a clean wooden spoon, stir the seeds twenty-one times, visualizing everyone working together and having a fun time. As you stir, say: "Become one, be one." You'll notice that you'll sometimes confuse "become one" and "be one"—that's okay. Keep going. That means the spell is working. If, over time, the group starts to pull apart, or someone is not doing what they are supposed to, repeat the stirring process along with the chant. Don't forget to do your fair share. When the project is finished, scatter the sunflower seeds outdoors, burn the bowl, and cleanse the magnet in holy water or moonlight.

To Gain Understanding of Literature or Other Material

First, you must study! Make a bookmark out of yellow construction paper. (If you are having trouble with more than one subject, make a separate bookmark for each subject.) Punch a hole ¾-inch from the top. Loop a gold cord through the hole. Tie carefully. Tie a white feather to each loose end of the gold cord. Draw the following bind rune at the top of the bookmark, about ½-inch below the hole.

Activate the bind rune following the instructions in page 326. Rub the bookmark with dried, crushed peppermint. Put the peppermint (herb) in a baggie, as you will use it again later. Hold the bookmark over the book you are currently studying, and say: "I empower this bind rune to open the way for me to understand this material." Pass the bookmark around the book three times clockwise. Open the book and riffle the pages with your left hand so that the air from the moving pages flutters the bookmark that you are dangling from your right hand. Do this three times. Now find the chapter you are to study and begin to do so. Keep the rune visible on the desk at all times. If you come to a particularly difficult passage, close your eyes and tap the rune three times. Take a deep breath, then open your eyes. Continue to study. If you are still having difficulty, take a five-minute break, then return to the passage. When you are finished studying for the day (or for a longer break), place the bookmark in the book at the page where you stopped working. Keep the bookmark in the book until you have finished that book or project. To reactivate the bookmark, place it in the baggie with the crushed peppermint and sit the bag outside in the sunlight or moonlight for at least one hour. Renew the peppermint every thirty days. When you are finished with the book or project, burn the bookmark and scatter the ashes to the wind, thanking deity for the assistance you received. *Note:* This spell does not relieve you of the responsibility of studying. It is merely a helpful tool.

To Cleanse an Area Before and After a Party

You will need one new salt or pepper shaker with large holes, and one with normal holes. If the holes are not large enough and the cap is metal, very carefully widen the hole with a nail by tapping lightly with a hammer. Turn both shakers upside down and paint a black pentacle on the bottom of each. Allow to dry. Drop one large jingle bell into each shaker. Mix sea salt, basil, powdered clove, and ground lemon peel in a bowl. Transfer to mortar and pestle. Grind to a fine powder. Cleanse, consecrate, and empower mixture using the herbal charm on page 381. Fill the shaker with the larger holes. Test shaker. If the mixture pours out too rapidly, the holes are too big. Cap tightly. Fill a second shaker with holy water. Before the party, begin at the center of the room and walk clockwise around the room, sprinkling the holy water and herbal mixture, saying: "Clearing, cleansing, sparkling clean. Banish evil sight unseen." Vacuum. After the party, begin at the center of the room and walk counterclockwise around the room, sprinkling

the holy water and the herbal mixture, repeating the chant. Vacuum the area thoroughly.

Money Wheel

You will need clay (such as Crayola Model Magic), twelve large paper clips, twelve new one-dollar bills, and one magnet. Shape clay into a smooth ball. Flatten. Draw a pentacle in the center with pencil or nail. Write your initials in the center of the pentacle. Embed the paper clips on end around the pentacle, like the spokes of a wheel. The paper clips should be positioned so that they can hold a folded dollar bill or a small piece of paper. Allow to dry. Write the following on each dollar bill: *Money must come to me.* If you don't want to write directly on the money, you can write the words on a removable label or cello tape, and tape on the bill. Rub each dollar with a mixture of ground cinnamon and clove, repeating the statement seven times for each dollar. Neatly fold the dollars. Place one dollar on each paper clip, repeating: "Money must come to me." Place the magnet in the center of the pentacle. Set your project on your altar. Each day for seven days turn the wheel seven times, repeating: "Money must come to me." If you have a specific amount of money you need, then place the dollar amount on a piece of paper with the words "and a little extra." Fold the paper and put under the magnet. You may also wish to burn one green votive candle inscribed with the Feoh rune (SEE PAGE 322) each night to add strength to the spell. This spell works extremely well in a Taurus moon.

Success in Sports

You will need a sport headband or wristband that you have worn. On a small piece of paper write the name of your team, the position you play, and your name. Cover with the Victory rune from page 326 or choose your favorite symbol of victory and self-empowerment. Activate the symbol. Most headbands and wristbands are double-ply, meaning you can carefully cut a small slit on the underside of the band. Slip the paper into the hole. Sew shut. Wear or carry with you throughout the season. If you will play again next year, you can save the band as a lucky talisman and re-empower it at the start of the new season, or you can burn this one, scattering the ashes to the winds, and make a new one next year.

To Relieve the Pressure of an Unfair Professor

Let's face it, not all teachers and professors are kind, gentle, loving people, and even some of the good ones have very bad times in their lives—they are only human, after all. This spell has two purposes: to help you become more understanding and see what may be possibly causing the root of the difficulty you are experiencing, and with that information to use it wisely to sweeten your position. You will need a large potato, white sugar, brown sugar, vanilla, basil, and an indelible marker. Write your name on one side of the potato and the professor's (teacher's) name underneath. Beside each name draw the symbol for Mercury (☿) to enhance the flow of information and communication. Turn the potato over. Carefully scoop out at least one inch of potato with spoon or knife. In a bowl, mix a small amount of the sugars (to sweeten the situation) and basil (to bring understanding) together. Empower for information, wisdom, and understanding. Sprinkle into the opening of the potato. Add three drops of vanilla. Empower for stated purpose. Place one nail in the potato to seal the spell. Set outside in the sun. As the potato rots, the evil will break down and understanding will come. If you are doing this during the cold months of the year, when it won't be possible for the vegetable to rot, use a sweet potato instead and bake in your oven until soft. At a place with moving water (stream, ocean, etc.), remove the nail and throw the potato into the water. Dispose of the nail in a dumpster off your property.

Giving a Problem Over to Deity

In this section we discussed how the practice of giving our problems over to deity is an ancient application. This doesn't mean that you can act like a jerk and then expect Spirit to fix it. It does mean, however, that you always have a spiritual support system, especially when you are so confused that you have no idea where to begin. We've all had situations where we feel that a tidal wave has hit us and we are being carried along, helpless and alone. If this is how you feel, try this spell.

SUPPLIES: Any and all items that are associated with the problem, as well as a complete written page (or more) of what that problem entails. On the paper around your account of the events, draw your favorite magickal symbols or sigils, asking for empowerment and harmony. You may have to do a little research to determine which symbols fit the issue—that's okay. The more you learn, the wiser you become. The supplies used could be pictures, jewelry, etc. A piece of black cloth—the size depends on how much junk you have collected. A bottle of holy water made at the full moon.

INSTRUCTIONS: Place all items collected in the center of the black cloth. Douse with holy water, asking Spirit for a thorough cleansing of the issue. Tie the four corners of the cloth together, making a bundle out of your junk. Spit on the bundle three times, then seal by making the sign of the equal-armed cross in the air. Throw the bundle into a dumpster off your property, saying:

Great Mother (or deity of your choice), *I have bound this issue into this bundle and I am giving it over to you. Please take this negativity away from me and in its place bring love and harmony. I know you will do this for me. So mote it be.*

Reversing Your Own Spellwork

Granted, all spellwork should be composed for balance, and sometimes moving toward that harmony isn't particularly pleasant. In that case we have to wait and be patient. Every now and then, however, we realize that our spellwork is not going where we wanted it to, or perhaps we have changed our minds and decided that what we asked for is not what we really wanted after all. If either of these two situations are the case, use the following conjuration to break and de-magick the original work.

INSTRUCTIONS: Go back over your notes and read over exactly what you did in the original spellcasting procedure (this is another reason why you should keep some sort of magickal record—just in case you think you've done a flubbo). Use the same ritual that you used before until you come to the point where you cast the original spell. Hold your hands over any of the physical components of the spell (such as a Witch's bottle, a cord with knots, etc.) This is another reason why most spells have something physical attached to them, just in case you want to change your mind. In spellwork, this is called an "out." Say:

> *Backward, oh backward, O time in its flight*
> *unfetter the binding of magick and might.*
> *Reverse the intent with love and with grace*
> *disperse and return to your original state.*

State loudly and firmly exactly what you are trying to undo, then sprinkle the project with holy water. Break the project into pieces, then dispose in the garbage or burn as much of the project as possible, saying: "The spell is reversed without hatred or curse. So mote it be!" Finish the ritual as originally done.

Note: For whatever reason, if you no longer have the object, simply place your palms on the altar and visualize the act of removing the magick and taking apart the project you made. Finish by sprinkling your hands and the altar with holy water.

Reversing the Spellwork of Another

A note of caution here—the ups and downs of life do not automatically indicate that someone has put a curse on you or sent negative magick your way. More often than not, we are experiencing unfortunate circumstances because we did something stupid, or because the lesson is in your life plan. Blaming a curse or other magickal vehicle is buying into superstition, and we really don't want to go there. In fact, it takes a lot of effort to throw a curse, and even when that is done the rule of three always applies, hence most magickal people don't mess with curses because there are several ways to handle the issues of life without bringing negative magick into the mix. I say "*most* magickal people" because there is always that particular soul that feels he or she knows best and thinks there is more power in negative magick. Wrong. These people are not real Witches, they are dabblers with a major self-esteem problem. Trust me on this one—I've watched a few people crash and burn through sheer stupidity of this kind. I've had letters from a few teens that tell me their friends have "cursed" them openly, and to be quite frank with you this has nothing to do with modern Witchcraft and everything to do with psychological terrorism, meaning that you have to believe they can hurt you for the curse to work, as it is your own mind that fulfills their prophecy.

If you realize that they are truly powerless, then you will be just fine.

This is not to say that evil does not exist in the world. We know that it does. Therefore, regardless of how the negativity got to you in the first place, the following spell, taken and rewritten to match the times from ancient texts, should do the trick. Use the spellworking formula given in this section and plug in where needed.

Bowl Reversal Spell

SUPPLIES: One large paper bowl; one black marker; 3 candles—red, white, and black.

INSTRUCTIONS: In a magick circle, write the incantation below on the inside of a paper bowl, starting with a circle in the middle and then spiraling out. Place on the altar. Light the black candle first, followed by the red, then by the white. Say: "The void, the action, the spirit of harmony, I invoke thee now!"

Now read the incantation:

Overturned, overturned, overturned, overturned, overturned is the Earth and the heaven, overturned are the stars and the planets, overturned is the gossip of the people, overturned is the curse of he or she who stands in the open field and in the town, and on the mountain and in the churches, and in the city and in the suburbs, in the home and in the place of business. In the name of Hecate, Dark Queen of the Witches, whomever transgresses against me shall be bound by their own negativity and banished as the rays of the sun banish the mists in the valley. All that is of the Earth calls and all that is of the heavens obeys! I implore our Lady, who is the voice of all the heavens and of all the Earth, of all the stars and the heavenly bodies, and who receives all

souls from this world. Should I have brought this upon myself with my own fear, overturn this negative energy and replace it with harmony. I know you will do this for me. So mote it be.[93]

Carefully, so as not to start a fire, drip the black wax over the incantation and say: "All negative energies that oppose or surround me are banished back to the void." Drip the red wax, saying: "By the action of my words." Drip the white wax on the red, saying: "By the hand of Spirit, this spell is sealed. So mote it be."

Bury the bowl off of your property and seal with an equal-armed cross in the dirt.

Tarot

Although the Tarot cards are not a prerequisite in learning the mechanics of Witchcraft, it does seem to be one of the most popular divination tools used among modern-day Crafters. With the variety of decks currently available, take your time in choosing the deck that resonates with you. When I teach the Tarot I don't allow my students to read any books on the subject for the first three weeks of training. Instead, I encourage them to work with the cards and gather intuitively what they may mean. Interestingly enough, even though their initial meanings for the cards don't "go by the book," what they intuitively gather often matches the circumstances perfectly. This "no book" technique, coupled with daily meditations on the cards, encourages students to allow their psychic senses to open in a comfortable way. Below you will find a keyword table of standard meanings of the cards, though I do encourage you to meditate and work with the cards each day, and to read books dedicated solely to the subject.

The Tarot may have appeared in Europe as early as the twelfth century and hasn't changed that much over the successive years. There are seventy-eight cards divided into two distinct sets: The Major Arcana, consisting of twenty-two major trumps, and the Minor Arcana, made up of four suits of fourteen, totaling fifty-six individual cards. I have been reading cards since I was thirteen years old—meaning I've been reading the Tarot for the last thirty-three years. Below you will find my personal interpretations for the cards; however, feel free to use your own research and intuition.

Major Arcana

0, THE FOOL

Potential; starting something new; childlike innocence; learning by experience; taking risks.
Astrological association: Uranus.

1, THE MAGICIAN

Having the power to change thought into form; creative control and mastery; time to take action and seize opportunities; skill and initiative.
Astrological association: Mercury.

2, THE HIGH PRIESTESS

Mysteries revealed; occult teachings and study; often shows up right before an epiphany or initiatory experience; secrets; intuition; the subconscious; wisdom; the symbol for alchemy and the goddess Sophia.
Astrological association: Moon.

3, THE EMPRESS

Heralds pregnancy in body, mind, or spirit; abundance; fertility; motherhood; nurturing experience; gardening; female entrepreneurship; Gaia; domination over the Earth.
Astrological association: Venus.

4, THE EMPEROR

Leadership capabilities; business pursuits; male entrepreneurship; authority; CEOs, bosses; responsibility; fatherhood; power.
Astrological association: Aries.

5, THE HIEROPHANT

Tradition; need for approval of others; stuck in dogma; conformity; spiritual guidance; search for enlightenment.
Astrological association: Taurus.

6, THE LOVERS

A choice; a contract; love and desire; temptation; struggle between love and infatuation; working toward harmony.
Astrological association: Gemini.

7, THE CHARIOT

Balance; victory after a struggle; possible purchase of a new vehicle or a vehicle requiring repairs; achievement; success; control; self-discipline; greatness; movement in life/career; travel.
Astrological association: Cancer.

8, STRENGTH

Speech or the written word over forceful actions; inner strength; quiet determination; using your talents to your best advantage; integrity; courage.
Astrological association: Leo.

9, THE HERMIT

Self-analysis; solitary search for the truth; philosophical pursuits; self-reflection; solitude; meditation.
Astrological association: Virgo.

10, THE WHEEL OF FORTUNE

Unexpected change in fortune or luck; a new chapter in an old project; new choices; new circumstances; learning to flow with circumstances without being a victim.
Astrological association: Jupiter.

II, JUSTICE

Justice; equality; being fair; court cases or legal proceedings; finding reasonable solutions to difficulties; impartial judgment.
Astrological association: Libra.

12, THE HANGED MAN

Sudden reversal in thought; surprising others with your actions; postponement of plans; letting go of people, places, or things that no longer serve you well; suspending issues.
Astrological association: Neptune.

13, DEATH

Change; transformation; communicating with the dead; abrupt ending; release of outmoded life patterns followed by new growth; new ideas and opportunities.
Astrological association: Scorpio.

14, TEMPERANCE

Your guardian angel watches over you; learning to be patient; self-control; making sound decisions; working with groups of people; compromise; happy partnerships.
Astrological association: Sagittarius.

15, THE DEVIL

Constricted; bound to something for good or ill; drug/alcohol addiction; personality disorders of all kinds; unethical behavior; abuse of power; avoiding responsibility; temptation; denial.
Astrological association: Capricorn.

16, THE TOWER

Feelings of guilt; being in the wrong place at the wrong time; disaster that brings enlightenment; overthrow of plans; shattered illusions; learning humility; breaking down of an existing structure to rebuild.
Astrological association: Mars.

17, THE STAR

Hopes, dreams, and wishes; the interest in astrology; understanding; clarity of thought; renewal of faith; insight; harmony; optimism; success ahead; positive guidance; promise given.
Astrological association: Aquarius.

18, THE MOON

Intuition; deception; night work; hidden dangers; instinct; struggle for sanity; change; possible confusion; magick; gossip; stuck between a rock and a hard place; self-esteem issues; empathic.
Astrological association: Pisces.

19, THE SUN

Success; the will; happiness; pleasure; good partnership or marriage; positive attitude; creativity; action oriented.
Astrological association: Sun.

20, JUDGMENT

Things coming back to haunt you; revisiting and taking responsibility for one's actions (past or present); spiritual awakening; forgiveness; facing consequences; learning from experience; reaping what you have sown.
Astrological association: Pluto.

21, THE WORLD

Conclusion of a cycle; success and fulfillment in any project; completing anything; alchemy; spiritual understanding; movement and travel; searching for the philosopher's stone; the study of science and quantum physics.
Astrological association: Saturn.

Pentacles

Money, property, and things you value
Astrological association: Earth
Season for timing: Winter

ACE OF PENTACLES

Abundance; wealth, a monetary contract; accomplishment; good news; a new start, especially in financial and property matters; gifts; positive material gain; new business proposition.

TWO OF PENTACLES

Juggling money; robbing Peter to pay Paul; balancing situations that often involve money or property or something that you value; competition; conflict of interest; a little money coming; learning to be flexible in financial and business affairs; possible monetary partnership that requires added responsibility but may not be financially lucrative.

THREE OF PENTACLES

Going to school, especially college or work-related courses; specializing in something that will bring monetary success in the future; skill; artistic achievement; initial stages of a project have successfully begun; approval or recognition for hard work that could involve a raise, a certificate of achievement, or other financial perks.

FOUR OF PENTACLES

Beginning a garden; adding on to a building; purchasing property; home and property renovations; setting down roots of a project; prosperity; stability; working toward ambitions.

FIVE OF PENTACLES

Unexpected financial difficulties or problems with something that you value; feeling emotionally out in the cold; setbacks; distress; disappointments; solving problems brought on by divorce or death in the family; probate difficulties; legacy problems; financial loss; lack of detail in finances.

SIX OF PENTACLES

Generosity of yourself and others; prosperity; kindness; deserved reward; acquiring a benefactor; gifts of all kinds.

SEVEN OF PENTACLES

Investing to reap later; progress and gain. A change in luck based on your performance. Success revolving around something you value. Career changes coming that will positively affect you if you have worked hard. Change in direction that involves financial planning or projects having to do with finances. Decisions now will have far-reaching impact on your financial standing.

EIGHT OF PENTACLES

Mastery of a skill; pleasure in your work; handicrafts and the arts; reaping what you sow; completing a cycle in finances or business; apprenticeship; new directions in career planning possible; taking a more profitable road without hesitation.

NINE OF PENTACLES

Obtaining wisdom; being happy and worthy; an appreciation of what you have; material and financial security; building a legacy for your children or loved one; monetary gratification.

TEN OF PENTACLES

Material fulfillment; efforts rewarded; completion of a particular job, project, or settlement on a home or property; a happy conclusion; security assured. Solid foundation.

PAGE OF PENTACLES

Harbinger of good news involving money, property, or rewards. A young person with new, creative ideas.

KNIGHT OF PENTACLES

The coming or going of any matter relating to money or property. Endurance and patience. Dedication to a particular cause.

QUEEN OF PENTACLES

A down-to-earth woman known for her financial acuity; nurturing; one who enjoys the out-of-doors and gardening; one who saves; financial fertility; putting practical ideas to good use.

KING OF PENTACLES

Experienced, successful businessman or leader. One who saves and is reliable, steadfast, and often resourceful. Good planner. Down-to-earth personality.

Staves / Wands

Communications, thoughts, and ideas
Astrological association: Fire
Season for timing: Spring

ACE OF WANDS

New venture, idea, project or trip. Translating ideas into action. Using one's imagination. Creativity. Aces always stand for beginnings.

TWO OF WANDS

A new partnership; using leadership to solve communication difficulties; meetings; resolving conflicts; appropriate mitigation of circumstances; business merger; success; using one's initiative to overcome obstacles.

THREE OF WANDS

Possible travel over water, such as a vacation or traveling sales, or a career that involves travel; international trading; business savvy; the initial completion of a project; looking at overseas investments or travel; working with others in a leadership position. The "idea person" of a group. Conferences, symposiums, and trade shows.

FOUR OF WANDS

Setting prosperity; peace; joy; setting down creative roots; attending or participating in a marriage ceremony; festivals; picnics; holiday fun; celebrations of all kinds including birthdays, anniversaries, retirements, and accomplishments. Building a gazebo and buying outdoor or patio furniture or accouterments; romance, but look at the other cards surrounding this one.

FIVE OF WANDS

A meeting of the minds through conflicts; debate; verbal conflicts that result in new ideas; competition; mental struggle; rebellion (check the surrounding cards); delays and frustrations; difficulty deciding between will and desire.

SIX OF WANDS

Victory and success; feelings of triumph; receiving public or outward recognition for your hard work; overcoming all obstacles; winning; promise of fulfillment is genuine.

SEVEN OF WANDS

Going where angels fear to tread; fulfillment through courageous action; challenges but they can be overcome; uncertainty and risk; success after extreme difficulties.

EIGHT OF WANDS

Messages; communications; Internet surfing and business; e-mails; phone calls; faxes; long-distance travel; hasty action; letters of love and passion; action and excitement; forward pursuit of one's goals; much can be accomplished if you think before you act.

NINE OF WANDS

Taking the bull by the horns and moving forward; action; the ability to inspire others in a positive way; liberation in thinking; acquiring a position with leadership; determination in the face of opposition; travels, journeys, and moves.

TEN OF WANDS

Overworked; carrying too many burdens; too many family or work responsibilities; feeling like a project will never end, but you are advised not to give up—the end is closer than you believe. Trying to hold on to outdated or outmoded situations. Trying to accumulate too much too fast.

PAGE OF WANDS

Messages having to do with information, career, or creative ideas. A young person who is impulsive and enthusiastic.

KNIGHT OF WANDS

Coming and going of issues involving your career, projects, or ideas that you may have. Well-intentioned though often unreliable young man.

QUEEN OF WANDS

Success in family, career, and outdoor recreational pursuits; love of beauty; intelligent, quick-thinking woman.

KING OF WANDS

Creative individual with an eye for beauty; oft times impulsive but friendly. Helpful in business or communicative pursuits.

Cups

Emotions

Astrological association: Water
Season for timing: Summer

ACE OF CUPS

Beginning of a romance or something that you love; overflowing with happiness; productivity caused by emotional pleasure; a gift of beauty; a new project full of potential that pleases you. Landing a project or situation that you feel will be emotionally fulfilling.

TWO OF CUPS

Partnership based on positive emotions; new friendship; an affair; harmony and balance.

THREE OF CUPS

Joining a group of like-minded individuals; emotional celebrations of all kinds; positive group mind; comfort; a happy outcome of an emotional situation; good luck; emotional fulfillment of something long awaited.

FOUR OF CUPS

Too much of a good thing; emotional indecision; apathy; making the wrong choice due to emotional dissatisfaction or emotional baggage; weariness; histrionics (making a mountain out of a molehill); boredom; refusing to see the good in a situation and concentrating on the negative.

FIVE OF CUPS

Emotionally hurtful conflict; a change brought on by loss or regret; pay attention to the positive things that you have left; emotional disappointment; loss of a friend; foolish regret.

SIX OF CUPS

Living in the past; not willing to let the past go; the study of history or genealogy; a discovery about the past; meeting someone from your past; learning about a legacy; a gift from an admirer (usually supported by other cards); nostalgia; the possibility of a lover returning (again, look at surrounding cards). Actions of the past bear emotional fruit in the present; sentimental journey.

SEVEN OF CUPS

All that glitters isn't gold; read the fine print; concentrating on illusion—whatever that may be; illusionary magick; imagined success; self-deception; possible personality disorder; denial; wearing many faces but not allowing yourself to be the "real you." The warning with this card is: "To your own self be true. Look at the writing on the wall and read it." Possible poison in your choices—beware, someone is trying to trick you.

EIGHT OF CUPS

Walking away from people, places, or things that no longer spiritually serve you. Taking a fresh look at yourself and moving on to brighter horizons. Disappointments in love. Moving to a higher level of spirituality. Time to do emotional housecleaning; purposefully changing one's lifestyle to create spiritual harmony; death of unwanted or unneeded emotional tags.

NINE OF CUPS

All your wishes will be granted. One of the best cards in the deck. Prosperity, oodles of love, and emotional satisfaction. Just be careful what you wish for. Success in magickal endeavors.

TEN OF CUPS

Success; lasting happiness; a happy home environment; loving friends and partners; excellent friendships and great love; contentment and emotional reward.

PAGE OF CUPS

Message of an emotional nature. An artistic, imaginative student. An emotionally expressive and creative child.

KNIGHT OF CUPS

The coming or going of any emotional matter. Possible message or invitation. Fickle young male. Young person emotionally striking out on their own.

QUEEN OF CUPS

Secretive, creative woman. Oft times "the other woman" in an illicit affair. Gossipy and vindictive. Emotional.

KING OF CUPS

Emotional, self-possessed individual. Creative. Emotional. Not particularly stable. Ill-tempered. Wears many faces but owns none. Possible cheater and trickster.

Swords

Intellect, health issues
 Astrological association: Air
 Season for timing: Fall

ACE OF SWORDS

A striking new idea; using your intelligence to attack a problem in a new way; a personal victory.

TWO OF SWORDS

Can't see forward and can't see backward; stuck between two opposites; coming to grips with the duality of a situation; dealing with gossip; indecision; a search for balance.

THREE OF SWORDS

Grief and pain. Querent has definitely experienced some sort of loss in the recent past (although sometimes they are in denial about this, though this is rare). Emotional agony, disappointment, betrayal; quarrels and separations.

FOUR OF SWORDS

The need for rest and relaxation; the need for a stress-free environment; time to take a vacation, preferably around nature; a welcome release or a change for the better.

FIVE OF SWORDS

Theft by a friend; loss or defeat; humiliation; the inability to defend oneself; unfairness; understanding one's limits before success can be achieved; up against a bully.

SIX OF SWORDS

Moving away from illness, pain, or sorrow; recovery; taking action to overcome one's problems; better times ahead so keep going; a journey often planned due to unhappy circumstances; the need to "get away."

SEVEN OF SWORDS

Theft by a stranger; possible move of house; a setback; a cycle of bad luck; tact is necessary in any situation; partial success that will not justify the risks involved.

EIGHT OF SWORDS

Bound by the garbage everyone is feeding you; low self-esteem caused by the negative comments of others; crisis point; imprisonment with eventual release; restrictive surroundings; learn to think for yourself.

NINE OF SWORDS

Nightmare; bound by your own fears; difficulty sleeping at night; personally imposed misery or disappointment; worrying needlessly; being disappointed in someone; possible danger—check surrounding cards.

TEN OF SWORDS

The desire to escape from pain and unhappiness; it's always darkest before the dawn—this situation will change; feeling like you've been stabbed in the back; mental anguish; emotional detachment to protect the self.

PAGE OF SWORDS

Messages of a fact-finding nature. Young, intelligent individual. A flair for secrets and spying. Individual with an impressive network that can relay information.

KNIGHT OF SWORDS

The swift coming and going of any matter. Fearless defender of justice.

QUEEN OF SWORDS

Loyal, decisive, business-minded woman. No funny business. Logical. Smart and intense. Sometimes lives alone, but not always. Aggressive, occasionally emotionally detached; sees through plots, cons, and other nefarious dealings. An excellent friend and unbeatable foe.

KING OF SWORDS

Strong, powerful authority figure. Loyal, intelligent, often involved with law, the courts, the military service, or dangerous occupations such as police officer or EMT personnel. Good doctors and surgeons. An excellent friend and unbeatable foe.

Reading the Cards

Cleanse the cards with a bell, holy water, or other magickal device before, after, and between readings. Shuffle the cards (here Tarot cards readers are at odds, some say to have the querent, or person asking the question, to shuffle the cards, others say not to allow anyone to touch the cards but the reader. As I usually do multiple readings in one day, I prefer to shuffle the cards myself.). The number of times the cards are shuffled also varies. Most just shuffle the cards until they think they should stop or until it feels right. Asking the querent to concentrate on the question being asked while you shuffle is appropriate. If they are busy blabbing, all sorts of strange stuff can enter the reading.

Next, the cards are cut into three separate piles. Some readers will turn over each stack and read the three cards. This is called reading the cut. Others simply place the stacked cards backed together—right stack on top of left stack on top of the center stack. The cards are then laid out in the spread the reader chooses to use. (SEE PART III FOR A DISCUSSION ON DIVINATION TECHNIQUES AND READING FOR CLIENTS.) Since the Celtic Cross Spread is most often used in reading Tarot cards, I have given it as follows:

The Celtic Cross Spread

Choose one card from the deck before it is shuffled that most represents the person for whom you are doing the reading. For example, I am always represented as the Queen of Swords, and my husband always comes up in a variety of readings as the King of Swords, therefore, we use those cards to represent ourselves. If you are unsure, close your eyes and think of the individual's face and personality, then allow your mind to do a bit of free association. The card chosen is usually a court or major arcana card.

You can also choose a card that matches the situation. For example, if you know that your friend has an abusive husband and she wants to know the outcome of the current events, you could begin with the Devil card and move from there, though I don't advise this practice until you feel very comfortable with your skill level.

Card 1 (significator) is placed vertically on top of the querent's representative card. This will represent the influence that covers the querent's life at the present moment.

Card 2 (card that crosses) is placed horizontally on top of the first card. This will represent the influences that cross or oppose the querent at present.

Card 3 (conscious mind) is placed vertically beneath the first two cards. This represents a past influence beneath the querent that caused the current situation in the querent's life.

Card 4 (subconscious) is placed to the right of the first and second cards. This will represent an influence that has just recently passed or is on the way out of the querent's life.

Card 5 (past) is then placed above the first and second cards. This card indicates the influence that is coming into being in the querent's life, as this is what "crowns" the querent.

Card 6 (immediate future, 1–2 weeks) is placed to the left of the first and second cards. This card shows the future influence that will act upon the querent's life.

Cards 7, 8, 9, and 10 are then laid out in a vertical line going from the bottom to the top.

The seventh card (future 4–6 weeks) represents the querent's fears on the situation.

The eighth card (what others think of you, not necessarily what you know of yourself) represents the friends, family, and environment in the querent's life that will have an influence on the outcome of the situation.

The ninth card (fears and wishes) represents the querent's hopes within the present situation.

The tenth card (outcome, six months) is the final outcome for good or bad that the querent will experience in the situation.

Cards 11, 12, 13, 14, and 15:

The eleventh card represents action to take using earth energy.

The twelfth card represents action to take using air energy.

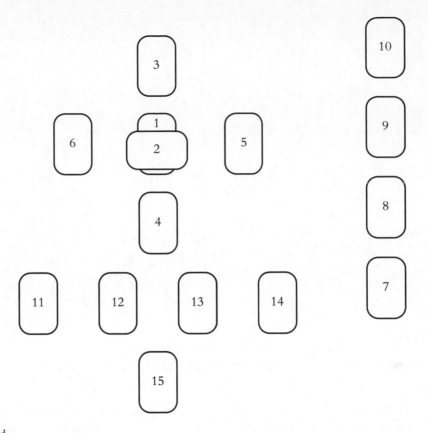

Celtic cross spread.

The thirteenth card represents action to take using fire energy.

The fourteenth card represents action to take using water energy.

The fifteenth card represents action to take to encourage spiritual transformation.

Note: It is important to remember that the meaning of each card is interpreted in relationship to the position it falls within in the spread. Try to make the reading an interesting story in the querent's life but read all events as pertaining to the querent. Remember that there are several interpretations of the positions in the Celtic Cross. This example is merely one of them.

Tarot and Astrology

There are two types of spreads that lend themselves well to the Tarot: the Planetary Spread and the Astrological House Spread (SEE DIAGRAM ON PAGE 216).

The Planetary Spread

The Planetary Spread works particularly well if you want to focus on a specific person and understand what energies, emotions, and circumstances they are currently dealing with in respect to recent life choices.

Shuffle the deck. To begin, lay out two cards in the nine positions, facedown in a fan pattern, as shown. When reading, the first card in each pile tells the past/present, where the second card may tell the future.

Position 1 is the sun. It shows where the individual is focusing most of his or her

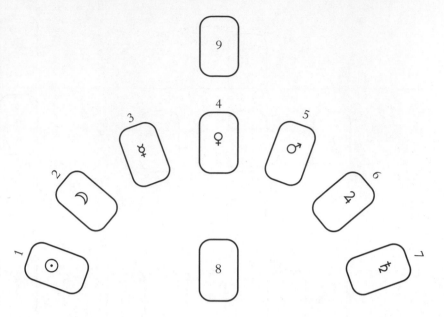

Planetary spread. Card 1: Sun, 2: Moon, 3: Mercury, 4: Venus, 5: Mars, 6: Jupiter, and 7: Saturn.

thoughts, feelings, actions, and recent choices—where he or she is placing his or her "will" at the moment.

Position 2 is the moon. This position lets you know how the person is currently dealing with the emotional ups and downs of life. It is highly possible that when reading this position, the person will say, "No, that's not how I feel," because you are reading the subconscious (that which is hidden), and we don't always acknowledge what is deeply buried within us.

Position 3 is Mercury. This is how the person is communicating, and what type of verbal interplay he or she is involved in at the moment. Cards, letters, e-mails, and faxes are also included in this category, as well as travel plans.

Position 4 is Venus. This tells you about the person's love life and social skills. It can also hint at educational pursuits.

Position 5 is Mars. Here we see the type of energy the person is actively using. He or she may be aggressive or complacent; recent events they have had to deal with often pop up here.

Position 6 is Jupiter. This position tells you where the person is expanding in his or her life at the moment. Sometimes it speaks of hopes and dreams that they are working on, or added responsibilities that they feel are fulfilling. If these responsibilities are stifling, then they will appear under the Saturn category. You can also tell if a person's faith in something is right on target or misplaced.

Position 7 is Saturn. This is a category of endings, rules, restrictions, limitations, structure, parental influence, and sometimes honor (especially if the sun card falls here). It can also focus on sickness and recovery.

Position 8, at the bottom of the fan, tells you what is the next best move in relation to all the other cards.

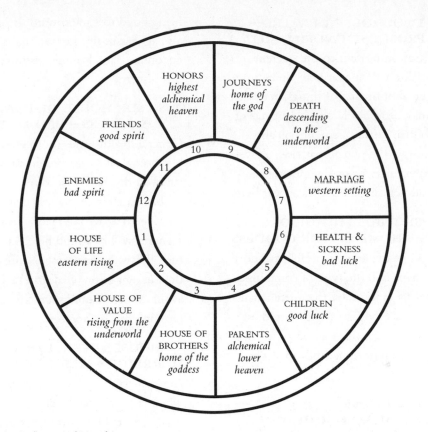

Roman antiquity house relationships.

Position 9, at the top of the fan, tells you where your focus should be for the next six months in regard to your spiritual path.

Note: If you want to spend more time with this type of reading, you can lay out positions for Uranus, Neptune, and Pluto (the outer planets). Uranus says where you should focus your humanitarian contributions. Neptune is the type of overall vision you need to accomplish your goals. Pluto discusses both power and regeneration. The three outer planets often cover what is happening in your environment (school, town, community, country) and your place within those changes. Use these three cards for meditation purposes.

The Astrological House Spread

You can use the diagram on page 216, or you can use the classical interpretation shown above, employed by Roman astrologers in the fourth century A.D.

HOUSE ONE: HOUSE OF LIFE— EASTERN RISING

Here is the vital spirit of the querent, how he or she thinks about themselves and what is "rising" in his or her life. Future trends and ways of new thinking will fall here. The basic character of the person at this point in time will be revealed. Normally the first house connects with all the others and will show a theme throughout the reading.

HOUSE TWO: HOUSE OF VALUE— RISING FROM THE UNDERWORLD

What is most important to the querent in terms of value will appear here. Sometimes this will be about material things, but other times it may be about intangible aspects of the individual. This placement will also show you how the person has risen above recent experiences or overcome events. Personal addictions sometimes appear here.

HOUSE THREE: HOUSE OF BROTHERS—HOME OF THE GODDESS

The impact of the actions of siblings, short-distance travel, and the type of communication currently enjoyed by the querent will be found here. Goddess-centered studies, magicks, and rituals that can be performed to help the querent sometimes appear in this position.

HOUSE FOUR: HOUSE OF PARENTS— ALCHEMICAL LOWER HEAVEN

The current relationship with parents and family might be clarified by the cards in this house. Depending on how this chart is read, the dominant parent would be in the tenth house and the more submissive or supportive parent in the fourth. This is also the house of endings, therefore after the entire spread is read, any cards in this placement can give you a specific end to the matter. The Alchemical Lower Heaven shows what efforts the querent is making to build toward a better future in the realm of "home base," and relates to bringing thought into form.

HOUSE FIVE: HOUSE OF CHILDREN— GOOD LUCK

If the individual has children, the impact of their actions fall here. If one has a pet that is considered a family member, you'll find this friend in the fifth house too. Opportunities of future good luck and people who bring good fortune toward the client will also appear in this house. Affairs or chance encounters and hobbies also show up in this placement.

HOUSE SIX: HOUSE OF HEALTH AND SICKNESS—BAD LUCK

General health issues (both good and bad), psychological recovery, and daily tasks are ruled by the cards placed here. Any recent unfortunate circumstances that would be considered a "wrong place, wrong time" scenario will be found here. As to the future, this is the house of warning, letting the querent know what can be changed to avoid disaster should such circumstances be looming on the horizon.

HOUSE SEVEN: HOUSE OF MARRIAGE—WESTERN SETTING

Any type of long-lasting partnership, whether in marriage, schooling, or business, appears here—from best friends to live-in lovers to future marriage prospects. This is also the house of open enemies, meaning those people who purposefully bring bad luck to your doorstep. Finally, the house of western setting lets us know what is beginning to move out of the querent's life. What is finished will show up in the next house.

HOUSE EIGHT: HOUSE OF DEATH— DESCENDING TO THE UNDERWORLD

This is by far the most interesting house in the Roman spread, as it tells us what we should have finished, what is finished (but we are too stubborn to admit it), and what we may be burying in our subconscious so that it can percolate awhile. "Cast off thy raiments" is a very good analogy for this placement. What is left when all is gone? Only your own true self, which will emerge in the second house in a later reading.

HOUSE NINE: HOUSE OF JOURNEYS— HOME OF THE GOD

Long-distance travel and higher education are found here. How the querent reacts to the laws of the land or school (or whatever) may also be discovered. One's current social class and faith, in the self and in others, might also be shown. This is the home of the God (Sun God), and in that respect speaks of any rituals, magicks, or studies that relate to this energy.

HOUSE TEN: HOUSE OF HONORS— HIGHEST ALCHEMICAL HEAVEN

This position shows where the querent has the highest influence, and who may have influence over him or her. If the querent is experiencing a psychological dysfunction, it may appear here. Career, recent and future achievements, and the dominant parent are also under the rulership of this house.

HOUSE ELEVEN: HOUSE OF FRIENDS—GOOD SPIRIT

The querent's connections to people and groups of all sorts can be found here, as well as possible hopes and dreams. Information about one's guardian angel/spirit guide might also be found. In the Roman system, one's association to Spirit and faith are also shown here.

HOUSE TWELVE: HOUSE OF ENEMIES—BAD SPIRIT

The character of enemies (open and hidden) can sometimes be discerned through the cards that fall here, or those groups or organizations that carry ill will toward the querent. Hidden physical illnesses (bad spirits) might be discovered by reading this placement. This is also the house of one's undoing—meaning it is another warning house that can let the querent know where *not* to tread in the future, or what to change to provide a better outcome of a particular situation.

Magickal Purposes and Some Suggested Tarot Cards

Carrying the magickal meditation further, you can perform complete rituals with your divination tool. First, choose which cards (runes, lots, etc.) you feel are appropriate to the situation. Cast a circle and call the quarters, then call your favorite divine energy into the circle. State the purpose of the ritual. Slowly lay out the cards, indicating aloud what each is for. Once you have placed all the cards on the white cloth, hold your hands over the cards and activate them by thinking of what you would like to occur. Be specific. Try not to let your mind wander. Some magickal practitioners like to listen to a favorite piece of music while they concentrate on the desired outcome. When you are finished, blow once lightly on the cards, visualizing the energies of the cards swirling with power, then draw an equal-armed cross in the air over the cards to seal the spell. The cards should remain untouched until the desire has manifested.

I asked my daughters to compile a general idea of what they have worked magick for during their teen years to give you a list of corresponding cards that would meet your needs. We've also included the moon phase associated with the intended magick and the best days of the week, giving you a choice if your need does not match the current moon phase. You don't need to use all the cards under any category.

Magickal Tarot Correspondences
ARTS, CREATIVITY, MUSIC

Cards: The Moon, the Star, the Sun, the Hermit, the High Priestess, the Magician, the Empress, 3 of Pentacles.

Moon phase for spell: Waxing and full.

Day of the week: Sunday (success), Monday (intuition), or Friday (love and pleasure).

BUSINESS SUCCESS, FINDING A JOB, WINNING AN ELECTION, GETTING GOOD GRADES, PASSING DRIVER'S TEST

Cards: The Sun, the Star, the World, the Empress, the Emperor, the Wheel of Fortune, the Chariot; Ace, 2, 3, or 4 of Wands; 3 or 9 of Cups; Ace of Swords; Ace, 4, 8, 9, or 10 of Pentacles.

Moon phase for spell: Waxing or full.

Day of the week: Sunday (success), Tuesday (action and to win), Wednesday (interviews and studying), Thursday (money and expansion).

CAREER SUCCESS, CHOOSING CLASSES, GRADUATION, CHOOSING AND PURCHASING A CAR, RECEIVE AN AWARD, SCHOLARSHIP

Cards: The Sun, the World, the Star, the Empress, the Emperor, the Wheel of Fortune, the Chariot, the Lovers; Ace, 2, 4, or 6 of Wands; 3 or 9 of Cups; Ace of Swords; Ace, 3, 4 6, 8, 9, or 10 of Pentacles.

Moon phase for spell: Waxing or full.

Day of the week: Sunday (success), Tuesday (action and to win), Wednesday (talking to counselor or your parents, and interviews), Thursday (money and expansion).

DATING (SUCCESSFUL EVENING)

Cards: The Sun, the Star, Ace or 2 of Cups.

Moon phase for spell: Waxing or full.

Day of the week: Sunday (success), Wednesday (communication), Friday (love).

EMOTIONAL HEALING

Cards: Use the High Priestess for a woman and the Emperor to represent the man, and a page to for a child, then add any of the following: The Star, Temperance, Strength, Justice, the Empress, the Hermit, the Magician, the Sun, the World, Judgment; 7 or 9 of Wands; Ace, 3, or 6 of Cups; 2, 4, or 6 of Swords; 2 of Pentacles.

Moon phase for spell: Waning to banish negativity; full to promote healing.

Day of the week: Saturday (to banish); Sunday (success); Friday (healing with love).

FAMILY HAPPINESS

Cards: The Empress, the Emperor, the Star, the World, Ace or 4 of Wands; 10 of Cups; 10 of Pentacles; court cards to represent the people involved.

Moon phase for spell: Waning to banish negativity in the home; full to promote happiness.

Day of the week: Sunday (success); Monday (family); Wednesday (communication); Friday (love); Saturday (to banish).

GOSSIP (TO STOP)

Cards: Emperor, High Priestess, Strength, Justice, Ace of Swords.

Moon phase for spell: Waning or dark.

Day of the week: Saturday.

LEGAL ACTION, DETENTIONS, SUSPENSIONS, DIFFICULTIES WITH TEACHERS AND THE SCHOOL ADMINISTRATION IN GENERAL, PARENTAL DIVORCE, CHILD CUSTODY MATTERS

Cards: Emperor, High Priestess, Strength, Temperance, the Star, Justice, Ace of Swords.

Moon phase for spell: Waning or dark.

Day of the week: Saturday (to banish offending issue or party); Sunday (success); Monday (child custody); Tuesday (war day);

Wednesday (open lines of fair and logical communication); Thursday (legalities); Friday (love and harmony).

LOVE

Cards: The Lovers; the Empress; the Sun; 4 of Wands; Ace or 2 of Cups; any court card that resembles the type of partner you desire but not a specific person.

Moon phase for spell: Waxing or full.

Day of the week: Sunday (success); Monday (family love); Friday (love).

MONEY

Cards: The Sun, the Empress, the Star, the Emperor, the Wheel of Fortune; 2 or 9 of Wands; 3 or 9 of Cups; Ace, 9, or 10 of Pentacles.

Moon phase for spell: Waning to lessen bills and push away poverty; waxing and full to promote prosperity.

Day of the week: Saturday to banish debt; Sunday (success); Tuesday (to take action); Wednesday (to sign contracts); Thursday (to expand prosperity).

PARTY (SUCCESSFUL)

Cards: The Sun, the Magician, Wheel of Fortune, the Star; Ace, 2, or 6 of Wands; Ace, 3, 9, or 10 Cups; Ace or 3 of Pentacles.

Moon phase for spell: Waxing or full.

Day of the week: Sunday (success), Wednesday (communication); Friday (socialization).

PHYSICAL HEALING

Cards: The Sun, Strength, Temperance, 9 of Wands; 3 of Cups; 6 of Swords. Choose a court card to represent the person, and the Strength card to represent an animal.

Moon phase for spell: Waning and dark to banish illness; waxing and full to promote healing.

Day of the week: Saturday (banish sickness); Sunday (general health); Monday (family health); Thursday (to expand good health); Friday (healing with love).

PROM

Cards: Use the Empress and the Emperor to represent you and your date, then add the Sun, the Magician, the Chariot, Wheel of Fortune, Temperance, the Star; and the Ace or 3 of Cups.

Moon phase for spell: Waxing or full.

Day of the week: Sunday (success); Friday (love).

PROTECTION

Cards: The Emperor, the Chariot, Strength; 3, 6 , 7, or 9 of Wands; Knight of Swords.

Moon phase for spell: Waning or full.

Day of the week: Saturday (to banish evil), Wednesday (to find a criminal); Thursday (to bring justice).

PSYCHIC POWERS

Cards: The High Priestess, the Moon, Tthe Hanged Man, the Hermit, the Magician.

Moon phase for spell: Waxing or full.

Day of the week: Monday (intuition); Wednesday (communication); Friday (socialization).

SPORTS

Cards: The Sun, Strength.

Moon phase for spell: Waxing or full.

Day of the week: Sunday (success); Tuesday (excellence of movement and action).

Recommended Reading

Authors I would recommend for Tarot books include Sasha Fenton, Rachel Pollack, and Janine Renée.

shadows

of

Magick

&

Enchantment

Alchemy

Alchemy is a bridge between Earth and Heaven, matter and spirit, the solid and the fluid, the visible and the invisible, bringing the horizontal and the vertical together.

—J. Ramsay[1]

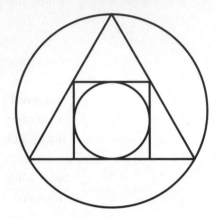

A symbol for alchemy: the void, activated by thought and purified by deity, makes the manifestation.

Alchemical Chant for Manifestation

Out of the black and into the red

out of the red and into the white

out of the white and into the gold

out of the gold and into the world.

Where my hand is laid, enchantment is made.

Out of the void and into the action

out of the action and into the spirit

out of the spirit and into the astral

out of the astral and into the world.

Where the gods' hands are laid,

magick is made.

At the threshold of the Notre Dame Cathedral in Paris, the figure of the goddess of alchemy sits enthroned beneath the figure of Christ on the central pillar of the Porch of Judgment, her feet touching the ground, her head in the heavenly waters. In ancient cultures, the sky was associated with the waters of the cosmic birth mother. In one hand, Alchemy holds a scepter, and in the other, two books—one closed, one open. Against her body rests a nine-runged ladder.[2] You may have seen this image before: She is the High Priestess of the Tarot deck, who stands for mysteries revealed and closely guarded secrets. She is the goddess of initiation. She is the transformation of the soul. Alchemy is none other than the Greek Sophia, whose name means "wisdom," and who was worshipped by early Christians.

The Word

To discover what alchemy really means we have to look at the history of the word, which, like alchemy itself, is shrouded in mystery. Some believe that its origin is Arabic: *al kimia*, sometimes translated as "the black soil art" or "the Egyptian art." This idea comes from the Egyptian word *chem*, meaning "black," and also the Greek word *chyma*, which describes the casting or fusing of metals. Others believe that the word is related to the Hebrew *chamaman*, which means "mystery" in the sense that something occult or secret is not easily revealed.[3] Since we know ancient Egyptians, Greeks, and Jews were involved in the practice of alchemy, any or all of these meanings could be correct. We also know that the idea of alchemy was present in ancient China before 2500 B.C., in India, and in areas of the Far East. What all this information tells us is that alchemy, like magick, was very much a part of the ancient world.

The History

There are two types of alchemy in the modern era, yet they are intricately related. The first kind of alchemy involves real science (think of the periodic table you learned about in school), which uses mathematical formulas and elements to create something interesting, like a chemical compound. In ancient times, the process of alchemy involved taking an element (a material thing like lead), purifying it, and then adding a bunch of stuff that turned the lead into something else entirely (like gold).[4] It is thought that the early Chaldeans, Phoenicians, and Babylonians used this kind of science and did indeed manufacture real gold, but as we know with all things historical, there is always some debate, especially since our modern scientists have not admitted whether they have accomplished this feat or not. Some people believe that the ancients did discover how to turn a base metal (like lead) into gold, but that through history, the formula was lost. This type of alchemy, the science that studies elements and compounds, was practiced until the beginning of the eighteenth century, when the term "alchemy" was replaced by the word "chemistry." Historical references also indicate that some of the first and foremost alchemists were women, specifically a "priestess of Isis" who wrote on the subject; an early scholar calling herself Cleopatra; a woman named Theosebia; Mary the Jewess (possible sister of Moses and sometimes called the Mother of Alchemy); and the female philosopher Hypatia (murdered in A.D. 415).[5]

There were quite a few alchemists running around during the Middle Ages. Some sought science, some sought faith, and others just wanted the gold. Alchemists were attached to both churches and royal courts. Since the practice was expensive and time consuming, most of them went broke unless they were doing side jobs to indulge the royalty (like spying and other interesting activities). Many times, however, royalty were slow to reimburse for services or did not bother to pay their debts at all. Did anyone ever turn metal into gold? Well, there is one that's a possibility. Nicholas Flamel (1330–1418) claimed he had done just that by following an

ancient manuscript, supposedly written by Abraham Eleazar, which contained a number of fascinating but baffling illustrations with some obscure text, possibly Greek.[6] What makes his claim more credible than any other is that not long after he reported his success, he became amazingly rich. So rich, in fact, that by the time he died, he had endowed fourteen hospitals, three chapels, and seven churches in Paris, France, alone, not to mention his work in Spain.[7]

The second form of alchemy brings real magick into play, and I'm sure you've seen movies or read stories about wizards practicing alchemy. We call this kind of alchemy an esoteric study. *Esoteric* means "for the initiated only." The word *initiated* means "to go through a special ceremony" or reach a divine truth. So, an esoteric study is a course of learning for people who are required (at some point in the learning process) to experience a unique ceremony, and from this learning and ceremony find the divine truth meant only for them. Witchcraft can be considered an esoteric study because those who practice Witchcraft often go through an initiation during their first year of study (depending on the group to which they belong) and, if they stick with it long enough, are transformed into better individuals because they have realized the divine truth as it is important to them.

Some people use the words *divine alchemy*[8] to explain esoteric study. Divine alchemy comes from the Greek word *dynamikos*, meaning "energy in motion," which says that by using different techniques we can mix our mental abilities with the energy of Spirit (creating a special light/vibration) that affects matter and causes change in the physical world. In plain English it means using your belief in god/dess with your thoughts to change the world around you, and your certainty (faith) that the change is possible.

If this is not your first book on the occult, you will have read about changing thought into form before, and that all thoughts are things. Indeed, almost every Wiccan, Pagan, New Age, or spiritual self-help book on the market today strives to teach you how to use your mind to create positive change in your world. Not exactly a religion in its own right, divine alchemy became part of various mystery traditions over the ages (teachings that weren't given to just anybody), and traces of this kind of alchemy lurked in secret societies. Moses, Roger Bacon, St. Germain, Leonardo da Vinci, Isaac Newton, and Victor Hugo, to name a few, were all considered alchemists.[9] Therefore, every magickal person who truly seeks to make themselves and the world a better place through their actions, studies, and thoughts is practicing a form of alchemy. You can tell how advanced they are by their actions and bearing—meaning that if they act like a jerk, are rude, or focus on hurting someone in thought, word, or deed, they are basically nothing but hot air masquerading as the real thing.

Unlike today, with thousands of books flooding the market on how to mentally program yourself to reap the most benefits out of life, the alchemical symbols found in old manuscripts were *not* written to inform the world how to change thought into form. They were created to help initiates of secret societies focus on the spiritual realms by giving them a visual aid—think of magickal flash cards and you're on the right track. By meditating on the symbols and using them in ritual, the students learned how to be better people. This process of self-transformation was called the Great Work or Magnum Opus. The Great Work—your spiritual rebirth—has two parts: learning to become a spiritual person, and then using what you have learned to effect change in the world. Modern Witchcraft is just such a process!

In the Craft you are expected to learn mastery over chaos (and it takes time). This chaos in alchemy is called *prima materia*, meaning "first matter." It is the essence from whence all things were born, and is the raw material from which you can create anything. It is the material of the mind. It is thought itself. It is the cosmic sea, the subquantum level. The second part of the Great Work involves taking that thought (or chaos) and fine-tuning it inward to create a pure body of light—your spiritual rebirth, from which you can transform yourself and the world around you. When a Witch Draws Down the Moon, he or she is taking part in an ancient alchemical ceremony geared to create change from within that will, in turn, change things without to match the Witch's desire. If the desire is not pure, then the process is fouled.

Studying alchemy (magick) requires practice, and the student must work slowly through several mental and physical purifying steps to reach a specific goal. Esoteric alchemical studies include breathing exercises, meditation, visualization, reading auras, astral projection, psychometry, telepathy, remote viewing, and more. The ultimate goal is to reach a mental place of pure power called the philosopher's stone, which is the key to turning thoughts into things in a controlled way. The philosopher's stone is the crossroads, the journey to the subquantum level of existence. To some, the philosopher's stone is not a real stone like you find in the ground, it is a mental key, a way of knowing *how* to think that makes things happen, literally turning thoughts into things. It is also believed that not only can you use your mind in directed, focused steps to create matter (such as gold and silver), you can also produce a universal medicine for all diseases. If you have read about quantum physics in the Magick section of this book, then right about now you are seeing a major parallel.

Gold, then, was what the alchemist strived to create, definitely mentally and in some cases physically. It was believed that if you could penetrate the mysteries of space, time, and matter by unlocking the secrets of how a substance is put together, then you could reach conscious transformation as well. The body of light was considered the root of the universe, and if we could perceive the mystery of this light, we could change anything. (Again, quantum physics revisited.) To the ancients, gold, representing this body of light, was the symbol of the eternal, radiant light of the spirit, and the transformation[10] through the colors of black (chaos), red (the dawning of information and change), white (purification), and gold (ultimate transformation) became the symbolic colors of the alchemist. Although at first we may think that the color black is bad, the symbology of the color is far from negative. Black, the color most often associated with wisdom in ancient cultures, represents the dark phase of the lunar cycle (a portion of the fourth quarter moon), where preparation is made for the coming birth of the next cycle. It is a time of looking within, of finding the wisdom one needs to build a bright future, the darkness of the womb of the Great Mother, and the place of germination of the greatest human ideas. Moving from black to red to white to gold speaks of the ultimate magickal journey. Watch a sunrise sometime and you might visually be able to understand what the alchemists were saying (depending, of course, on weather patterns and atmospheric phenomena). Every once in a while you will see a sunrise that bleeds from black to the reddening of the heavens, to pure white light, to a golden glow. This is the ceremony of the dawn.

Now do you know where Einstein got his ideas and what he was shooting for?

The hexagram, caduceus, and the pentacle (below) were among those symbols used to train these students of alchemy.[11]

Today, each of these symbols still carries part of their original meaning and you will find them discussed in various areas of this book.

If alchemy (magick) had not been for "the select few," history as we know it would not exist; indeed we, as humans, may (as a collective) have reached a more enlightened state by now. Then again, maybe not.

Although alchemy was well known in the Byzantine and Muslim worlds, Europe only experienced the practice in fragmentary form until around 1144, when Robert of Chester translated Arabic texts found in Spain to Latin. This presented the first alchemical documents to the European reader[12] as a direct result of the Crusades, which was not exactly the best of times to bring occult knowledge to his fellow Europeans, given the struggles of the Christian church for world rule. This doesn't mean Europeans didn't work with the idea, but it certainly put a cramp in their style, and by 1317 Pope John XII presented yet another papal document condemning the practice.[13] The goddess Alchemy reigned, however, moving subtly into the strength and power of the Christian Mary, and finding a seat on her very own throne in the Cathedral of Notre Dame in Paris. At the same time, a philosopher by the name of Ramon Lull introduced the words "first matter" (*argent vivre*) and related it to the four elements we find so familiar in magickal studies (earth, air, water, and fire). Lull added the fifth element, which he called "quintessence," meaning Spirit or Heaven. Unfortunately Lull was stoned to death by Moslems when he arrived in Africa, much like Hypatia, who was stoned by the Christians almost 100 years before.

Alchemy, Psychology, and Magick

Magick, in its own way, is a science of psychology because it uses the power of the mind to bring forth change in one's life. Interestingly enough, at the turn of the twentieth century, those who dabbled in psychology and matters of the mind were also those who were interested in the occult sciences (Fortune, Blavatsky, Regardi, etc.). At that time, psychology was a new, suspicious interest to the world at large. It was Carl Jung who propelled the sciences of the mind into our daily lives and forced the scientists and medical people of the times to pay attention to this amazing facet of human nature. Jung believed that alchemists were projecting or seeing their own unconscious, and he wrote reams of material on dreams, human behavioral patterns, and the mind in general in relation to his own alchemical studies. Thanks to Jung's work, psychology is here to stay.

Magick Pictures: Alchemical Symbols

Many of the symbols used in current magickal practices are linked to alchemical designs of the past. Historians have found strong links between alchemy, astronomy, astrology, and magick. For example, long ago, only five planets were proven to exist (Mercury, Mars, Venus, Jupiter, and Saturn) and two luminaries (sun and moon). I say "proven" because even in medieval astrology/astronomy there were ideograms (word pictures) that suggested there may be more planets in our solar system. Each of the five known planets were associated with an element, and each astrological sign (Aries through Pisces) spoke of an alchemical process. Sound familiar?

With the information you have already read, you now know that an alchemical process is a mental one that involves daily meditations, learning to focus (concentrate), and practicing magick and ritual regularly. Many magickal people today still use those alchemical symbols (magick pictures) to work magick. But what do all those pictures mean? In ancient alchemy, the sign of Aries, for example, meant to reduce something by the use of heat. Mixing the signs and planets together, the alchemists made symbols to represent chemical compounds and/or esoteric philosophy. On one hand, the pictures spoke of a chemical scientific formula. On the other hand, they meant a way of thinking. The symbols were a shorthand or code and, over time, the code became interchangeable between scientific alchemy (chemistry), astrology, astronomy, and divine alchemy (or magickal practices). Therefore, it isn't the symbol itself that carries the power of change, but how you *use* that symbol in your daily and magickal life. Symbols, whether scientific or magickal, represent formulas for change. Many of the symbols and philosophical ideals currently used in the Craft can be traced to the practice of alchemy, including many of the tools found on our altars.

Alchemical ideograms (symbols or drawings that illustrate an idea or concept) aren't the only signs or sigils you'll find in the Craft. Interestingly, the word *symbol* comes from the Greek word *symbolon*, and describes the practice of breaking a piece of clay into several pieces and handing a piece to each member in a group for safekeeping. Later, when the group reunited, they would match the pieces together to make sure that everyone present was actually a member of the original group. This practice was used by the ancient mystery traditions to ensure that nosy busybodies didn't sneak in with the serious students at important gatherings and rituals. Today, when we see people wearing the same symbol (cross, pentacle, Star of David), we know that they belong to a particular group of people (in this case, a particular religion). This means they belong to a group mind, and we talked about that under the section on Group Mind and the Witches' Coven in Part I.

In the Craft community, various groups may design their own symbols, or put symbols together in a specific way to show that they all belong to an organization of like mind, or share a common magickal history. A few embroider the symbol (or set of symbols) on their ritual robes, on altar cloths, or paint (or sew) the symbol on a banner that hangs in the ritual room, at a Grand Coven event, or at Pagan festivals. These symbols are often ancient ideograms, and many find their roots in alchemy.

Understanding How Alchemy Works: Alchemical Elixir of the Moon

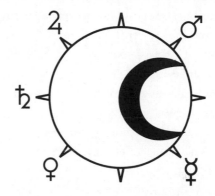

In medieval times, the word *elixir* meant "catalyst," and when we hear the word today, we expect to see some sort of potion, or at least a liquid. In ancient times, however, an elixir didn't mean a liquid at all, it simply meant a method of change—a formula not of liquid, but of words or drawings. I'm sure you've heard the words "mathematical formula" in school. See? The apple really doesn't fall far from the tree. The symbol above, thought to be designed in the fifteenth century, is an elixir—a formula written on paper. When used properly, it can be a formula for change. The picture called the Elixir of the Moon is actually a model of our solar system, with the sun and the moon as the centerpiece, and the various planets (Mercury, Venus,

Mars, Saturn, and Jupiter) on the outside, circling around the moon/sun. This particular symbol is interesting because there is room for the three planets Uranus, Neptune, and Pluto, discovered much later than the original drawing.

The eight triangles stand for the eight phases of the moon, the eight paths of Wiccan power (ritual, chanting, spells, aspecting deity, meditation, drumming, divination, and working with the dead), the eight High Holy Days (SEE PART I, WHEEL OF THE YEAR), and the eight cardinal directions (North, Northeast, East, Southeast, South, Southwest, West, Northwest), as well as the eight planets in our solar system (Mercury, Venus, Mars, Jupiter, Saturn, Uranus, Neptune, and Pluto). The sun stands for male energy (the God), and the crescent moon links to female energy (the Goddess)—or you can exchange the symbolism, tying the female energy to the sun and the male energy to the moon, as practiced by some ancient societies.

When used for magickal purposes, the symbol above is also called a talisman (SEE TALISMANS IN PART IV TO UNDERSTAND EXACTLY HOW THIS MAGICKAL OPERATION WORKS). When we use this talisman, we activate the powers of the sun (your will), the moon (your emotions), Mars (your ability to take action), Venus (your ability to love), Mercury (your ability to communicate), Jupiter (your faith), and Saturn (your ability to work within a structure without hurting anyone).

This symbol is an example of what divine alchemy (magick) is all about. Here, we will be using the picture to help us focus on our desire, and we will be using it for magick and meditation. To anyone who pages through this book and doesn't read the explanation of the picture, the symbol appears to be a simple drawing, but you just learned that the picture speaks of several different magickal ideas. Look at the picture again while you read those magickal ideas aloud. They are: the eight High Holy Days of the

Wiccan faith, the eight phases of the moon, the eight directional compass points, the dynamic energy between male and female (sun and moon), the idea of God and Goddess (Lord and Lady), the ten major celestial bodies (sun, moon, Mercury, Venus, Mars, Jupiter, and Saturn, with points for Uranus, Neptune, and Pluto)—all working together to become one.

Okay, you've started the divine alchemical process by associating thoughts and ideas to a symbol. What more do you see in that symbol? What does it mean to you? That is also part of the alchemical magick, or the process of change. Therefore, each magickal symbol you encounter can mean many things (not just what you perceive on the surface or what you are told). How you process the symbol in your mind is important too!

Any symbol, then, can be used on a variety of levels, some obvious and others not. Here, we can use the symbol of the Elixir of the Moon for any number of magickal operations, including requests for good health, healing, prosperity, protection, love, and so on. But what of the symbols in magickal writings that don't carry a full explanation of what they are for, and what you can do with them? My best advice to you is be a magickal detective! If you don't know what a symbol, or a deity, or a particular practice is for, or what its history entails, don't use it in your magickal work until you do. It is as simple as that. A guy or girl off the street doesn't walk into a hospital, boogie down to the operating room, and start cutting people open. He or she has studied the human body, learned how to use the tools of surgery, and mentally prepared him- or herself for the operation (we hope). You should think of yourself the same way. In the Craft, adults speak of being properly prepared. This is what they are talking about: think, study, learn, grow—that's all a part of the Witchcraft experience.

Gee, that sounds like a lot of work, doesn't it? Well, it is. But it's worth it. What will happen if you aren't properly prepared (meaning zapping without the study part, and being mature enough to work for positive things rather than being immature and working for negative stuff)? Honestly? The ground will not gobble you up, nor will demons dance about your bed as you try to get a good night's sleep, nor will your little sister be possessed (sorry) by the spirit of your great-aunt Milly. Nah. Spirit is incredibly forgiving about these things. Instead, you'll fail. Simple as that, over and over again, until you give up, and then you'll tell people that magick doesn't really work, or you'll hide your failures and tell others that only a chosen few should be allowed to work magick. Get it?

Spell for the Holidays

The most stressful times of the year often revolve around family holidays, regardless of the country in which you live. Expenses are high, emotions are pulled to the breaking point, and responsibilities seem greater. If we look at the Christmas/Yule season especially, we see that the sun influence rides through Sagittarius, the sign of expansion, spirituality, and excess (food, presents, etc.) right before the holiday season, but when the sun moves in to Capricorn (around December 21), the brakes go on and the panic turns to depression. At no other time in our modern lives do we see such drastic distinction between two sun signs: expansion versus contraction.

If you are a working teen and going to school, it seems like there isn't enough time in the day to get everything accomplished. The family wants you to participate in family traditions, but you have a term paper to write, you want to spend time with your boy- or girlfriend, your job wants extra hours, and if you are involved in other school activities, the advisor seems to have a "me first" attitude. It's no wonder that teens get sick or frustrated over the holidays! Whether you are in middle school, high school, or college, the demands on your time can become excruciatingly painful. Here's a wonderful spell to lessen the angst over the holiday season.

Remember to check your divination tool before using any spell, then follow one of the ritual formats provided in this book to flesh out the Elixir of the Moon.

SUPPLIES: The Elixir of the Moon, drawn in your own hand on a piece of white paper (if you can get white parchment from an art store or the art department at school, that would be even better); one black marker; a set of colored pencils; any one of the following selection of candles: bayberry (prosperity and good fortune), gold (success and prosperity), silver (psychism and success), red (to get things moving), or the all-purpose white (your candle selection is up to you. If you are not permitted to use candles, Spirit will understand). Your favorite incense; your favorite magickal oil.

TIMING: Perform on the full or new moon; on a Sunday or Monday; or in the planetary hour of the sun or moon; or when the moon is in the sign of Leo (you can find this out by looking at your magickal almanac). Don't worry if the timing information of these spells appears complicated at first. If you don't understand the planetary hours, or how the moon gets in Leo in the first place, don't despair, just pick a Sunday or Monday to work your spell. Explanations on planetary hours and moon phases are found in Part III, under Astrology and Moon, respectively.

INSTRUCTIONS: Draw the Elixir of the Moon on the piece of paper. Repeat the Alchemical Chant for Manifestation three times (ON PAGE 360) while holding your hands over the drawing. Light the incense and pass the paper and the candle through the scented smoke, saying this statement of intent: "I manifest love, luck, happiness, and serenity over the holiday season."

Rub your favorite magickal oil on the candle, and repeat the statement of intent. Light the candle, and again repeat the statement. Pass the piece of paper over the flame (not too close) and say the statement. With the colored pencils, color the sun yellow, saying: "I activate the good fortune of the sun."

Color the moon with the white colored pencil, saying:

I activate the power of the moon, and draw to-
ward myself love, luck, happiness,
and serenity over the holiday season.

With the red colored pencil, slightly shade the area around the symbol of Mars ($\male$), saying:

I activate the energy of Mars to bring myself love,
luck, happiness, and serenity
over the holiday season.

Using the blue pencil, color the area around Mercury ($\mercury$), saying:

I open the pathway between myself and Spirit so
that I may enjoy clear thinking and communicate
well over the holiday season.

Using the pink pencil, color the area around Venus ($\female$), saying:

I call forth the energy of universal love
to abide in and around me during
this holiday season, and beyond.

For Jupiter ($\jupiter$), choose the green pencil. While coloring the area around Jupiter, say:

I call upon the powers of clear vision
and expansion to bring growth to my good
fortune over the holiday season.

Use the purple pencil to color around Saturn ($\saturn$), saying:

I work well with authority figures and my efforts
will bring great rewards over the holiday season.

Take three deep breaths and hold the colored talisman in your hand, then write your name on the back of the talisman. Dot the scented oil under your name. Place both hands over the talisman and envision the holiday season you desire. Put the paper under the candle holder. Allow the paper to remain there until the candle has completely burned. Carry the paper with you in purse or wallet during the holiday season. If you feel that the energy is wearing down, repeat the statement of intent while holding the paper close to your heart. (SEE ALSO AS ABOVE, SO BELOW.)

As Above, So Below

As above, so below is called an occult maxim. The word *occult* means "hidden," and the word *maxim* means "truth," or "underlying principle." When Witches seal a circlecasting, sacred space, or a spell, they will often say the words "As above, so below. This circle (or this spell) is sealed. So mote it be." That's great, but what does this mean? The words *As above, so below* stem from the mystery traditions that we talked about under the Alchemy category, and specifically from an amazing piece of work called the Emerald Tablet.

As with all things ancient, we have an excellent mystery that goes along with the first mention of written information about alchemy. The credo of the alchemical adepts (*As above, so below*) supposedly came from an inscription found on an emerald tablet in the hands of a mummy in an obscure pit by the pyramid of

Giza, discovered by none other than Alexander the Great. The information was supposedly written on an emerald tablet with a pointed diamond.[14] The emerald was linked to Mercury, and you can see now where the Hermes-Mercury-Thoth association comes into play. The document is called the Emerald Tablet and if you read the words carefully you will slowly understand a large chunk of the mystery traditions, including Witchcraft.

The Emerald Tablet

The following translation of the Emerald Tablet is a modern translation by J. F. Ruska.[15] Remember that I told you how the Witch's Creed relates to alchemy? Do me a favor and page back to the Creed (IN PART I, WICCAN REDE/WITCH'S CREED), read it, and then read the following translation of the Emerald Tablet.

1. In truth certainly and without doubt whatever is below is like that which is above, and whatever is above is like that which is below, to accomplish the miracles of one thing.

2. Just as all things proceed from One alone by meditation on One alone, so also they are born from this one thing by adaptation.

3. Its father is the sun and its mother is the moon. The wind has borne it in its body. Its nurse is the earth.

4. It is the father of every miraculous work in the whole world.

5. Its power is perfect if it is converted to earth.

6. Separate the earth from the fire and the subtle from the gross, softly and with great prudence.

7. It rises from earth to heaven and comes down again from heaven to earth, and thus acquires the power of the realities above and the realities below. In this way you will acquire the glory of the whole world, and all darkness will leave you.

8. This is the power of all powers, for it conquers everything subtle and penetrates everything solid.

9. Thus the little world is created according to the prototype of the great world.

10. From this and in this way, marvelous applications are made.

11. For this reason I am called Hermes Trismegistus, for I possess the three parts of wisdom of the whole world.

12. Perfect is what I have said of the work of the sun.

As you can see, the tablet is a bit like a riddle. What is "it" referred to in its contents? "It" is thought.

Changing Thought Into Form

Some magickal people (and historians, too) feel that the idea of changing thought into form began in ancient Egypt during its Greek reign,[16] with a fellow named Hermes Trismegistus, who was most likely not a real person, but a collection of people involved in the study of alchemy. He may even have been Aristotle, who taught Alexander the Great and helped to conquer most of the known world at the time. Despite the fact that we have no clue who the author might be, Hermes Trismegistus (meaning "wisdom three times the greatest") is known as the father of occult wisdom (though there is now debate that the first alchemists were women). Further writings on the subject seem to be a product of Greek settlers in Egyptian territory who migrated to that area at the beginning of the reign of the Greek pharaohs (as opposed to the native Egyptian peoples). This group of Greeks recognized their own gods in the Egyptian deities, matching their god of wisdom (Hermes) with that of the Egyptians (Thoth), the divine inventor of magick, of writing, and of the spoken word.[17]

Man or woman as the creator aside, the resulting teachings were called hermetic philosophy, or hermeticism. The idea of the philosopher's stone (a legend that stated there was a material that could turn metal into gold, yet the material itself would remain unchanged—see Alchemy) might have been an allegory, meaning the mastery of mental forces could change anything. Now, at this point you might be saying, "Excuse me, Silver, but history bores me to tears. I hate it in school, and I'm certainly not too thrilled with reading about it here. I wanna do the fun stuff!" Me too! After teaching the Craft to hundreds of students over the past fifteen years, I discovered that if the student (that's me too, by the way) doesn't learn about the building blocks of any magickal study, then half the power waiting at their fingertips will be lost. Regardless of what religion or spirituality you follow, the axiom of *As above, so below* will apply, and has several meanings, depending on your idea of how the universe ticks. For some, it means *As in heaven, so it is on earth.* You've probably heard that statement if you've had any sort of Bible study or gone to Sunday school. What heaven decrees, occurs on earth. For others, it means that the invisible and visible are all manifestations of the divine. Everything is one. What happens on the visible plane (right in front of your nose) occurs on the invisible one (spiritual places of the unseen), and vice versa. There is no dividing line between "what runs the universe" and "human beings." We are God, and God is us, and the material world is an expression of the spiritual one. When Einstein shocked the world by proving that energy and mass are equal, identical, and interchangeable, the old mystery teachings of the ancients found new vigor and have continued to grow. Why? Because now science and spirituality meet on common ground. The ancient conclusion that the same laws operated in the world of Spirit and in the material world was now validated. Basically it means: What happens here, happens there; and what happens there, happens here.

The Witchcraft practiced today is, to put it bluntly, a bunch of old ideas and practices melded into a new form. It is a mixture of ancient occult philosophy, folk practices of various cultures, and a very old (but sturdy) belief that God is both male and female, not specifically one or the other. Yes, major portions of the Craft predate Christianity. Yes, the Craft is a nonviolent way of belief. Yes, the Craft does its level best to be nonjudgmental. All of these things are true, but in trying to form new dogma (uh oh), some individuals become a bit cranky when they realize modern Craft isn't exactly like it was a hundred, three hundred, or five hundred years ago, nor do they understand that a great deal of the modern "gelling processes" for this faith are direct results of archeological study, overactive romanticism, and the falsified hierarchy put forth by various Inquisitions' record keeping. The product of all this—what you practice today—is a positive one that seeks to find the best within, and then share that exciting relationship with god/dess through our words and actions involving others.

Change is necessary for the growth of spirituality. If our religion became stagnant, it would die. For example, the standard Wiccan tools on the altar were called the Four Elemental Weapons over a hundred years ago by a group called the Golden Dawn, which incorporated Christian, Pagan, and Judaic teachings, among other things, in its lodges. There is no doubt that the Golden Dawn helped preserve alchemy as a major point of reference, as well as brought alchemical language into common awareness.[18] Just as in the Golden Dawn material, we see elements of the Kabbalah, the Tarot, astrology, and various pieces of Freemasonry in today's Craft environment. To be honest, it is highly unlikely that ancient peoples set up their altars precisely the way Wiccans do today, with precisely the same tools, which accounts for the differences of tools and their placement in various Craft traditions. For example, in the Black Forest Tradition, you only use your tools through the first level of study. From the second level on, you are expected to know how to work without them, which tells you that the Wicca of today carries a great deal of the mental arts within its teachings, just as the esoteric sciences did thousands of years ago. If we have so many differences among us, how could anything possibly work? Unity through our diversity is one of the strongest elements in modern Wicca and, surprisingly enough, it was also a tune sung at the turn of the twentieth century with the Theosophical Society (the influence of Madame Blavatsky and her crew of political and bourgeois dabblers). It is *because* we are different and that we can honor those differences among ourselves that we survive. Individuals that cannot honor those differences are breaking the "An' it harm none" code, and therefore are not truly practicing the Craft of the Wise.

This doesn't mean that goddess worship didn't exist, or that there weren't matriarchal and matrifocal (women-centered) ancient religions,[19] nor does it mean that the Craft you practice today is invalid. The maxim *As above, so below* (as well as others you'll study in the future) *does* tell us that Wicca carries with it into the twenty-first century a heavy coil of very old, very ancient, golden energy.

There is another meaning that goes along with the "as above" statement, and this deals with astrology. As an astrologer myself, I can tell you that the movement of the planets and the position of the stars in the heavens do indeed reflect available energies that we can use or ignore. It is said that the stars do not compel, they impel, meaning that we have free will to use the available energy—or not. I mention astrology because many Witches are also practicing astrologers, although not all astrologers are Witches or even magickal people. Most Witches know at least the meanings of the planets and how they can be used in magick, and they can follow the phases of the moon for magickal workings. If you choose the path of a ceremonial magician, or the path of the Druid, you will find it necessary, in time, to turn your studies to astrology.

As above, so below also relates to Craft terminology that includes the words *invocation*, *raising power*, and the *cone of power*. In these three magickal operations you are focusing upward (in a spiritual sense), sending your thoughts into the spiritual realm. The change you desire occurs on the spiritual planes first, before it can settle into the material one where you are *(As above, so below)*. This is why most people experience a delay in their magickal workings. To get what you want, change must occur. Sometimes the changes are minor (adjustments, really) and so the work seems smooth and quick. Other times the changes you are asking for are much bigger, and several things must happen *above* as well as *below* for the working to reach its desired conclusion.

For example, if you want to improve your grades and cast a spell to help you do that, then you must actually study (the mind), and get enough sleep (the body), or the magick won't work. If you want a spell to be more beautiful, then you must remember that beauty begins on the inside, and your behavior and what you think has everything to do with how you appear on the outside to other people. That's the mind part. Being clean, like bathing and using deodorant and making sure your hair is clean and combed, is the body part. Working to include your belief in god/dess is the spiritual part. In anything magickal, the physical, mental, and spiritual must all run on the same race track for you to be the winner. They must all be focused on that checkered flag of success.

This is why magick is seen by some as too much work. In the beginning, when you are first learning, it is hard to focus. Let's say you did a spell for good grades, and you brought your books home with the intention of studying for a test tomorrow, but then Tom calls and since you've got the hots for him, you might spend an hour on the phone, and then that hour marches into the second one. When you look at the clock you realize that it's bedtime and you haven't studied for that test tomorrow. If you stay up and study, then you'll be exhausted tomorrow and barely pass, or you say, "The heck with it," and cram in the morning. Either way you've just taken some of the oomph (or all of it) out of your spell. You did all that work to make the changes in the spiritual realm, but you ignored the physical one. When the weekend comes, you dutifully bring all of your books home, intending to learn as much as you can, but then the family goes out to dinner, there's the football game you simply can't ignore because Tom is there and you certainly can't miss that. On Saturday you work at the convenience store from ten to six, and then Marsha picks you up to go to the movies, and after that you stop at Sandra's house for pizza. By Sunday *maybe* you have to work again, or go somewhere with your family, and then you can't possibly miss the car show over at the fairgrounds (Tom said he was going,

too)—and so ends the vicious circle, with you staring at that pile of books on Sunday night thinking, "Tomorrow, I'll do it tomorrow." You know what they say about tomorrow—it never comes. Hey, don't feel guilty, we've all done it. Procrastination on the earth plane will blow a hole in your spell or ritual faster than anything else—just ask me.

The same difficulty arises when I teach students magickal material. They get so far, then life sort of takes over and off they go, not realizing until later that they have missed golden opportunities because they have shoved their magickal studies aside.

Astral Nasties

I don't believe that angels can fall down and go boom, and I don't believe in demons, like the ones shown in medieval texts. After much contemplation on the subject, I believe that negative stuff like fallen angels, demons, or whatever, are purely the design of the human brain, although there are many people who would argue with me on this point and they have every right to do so. To understand where the concept of demons comes from, we have to look deep into history and the split between the Pagan belief system and Christian superstition used as a vehicle to control the people. For Pagans, *daimones* (Latin *daemones*) were neutral spirits, energies of plants, trees, stones, and elements, etc.[20] These energies were neither good nor evil, and could be used by both gods and people. For Christians and most Jews, due to the influence of the Arabic historical culture from which their religious beliefs find root, demons were angels who had turned against their creator. What we have here is the difference between apples and oranges, yet both fruits were thrown in the same box and labeled "rotten."

In 1904 (yes, I'm giving you a boring date), a popular magician at the time (not the illusionary, cool kind like David Copperfield) named Samuel Liddell "MacGregor" Mathers translated a few of the medieval magick books. (There were other popular occultists roaming around, and we'll touch on them throughout this book, but not right at this second.) One book in particular talked about conjuring spirits. Okay, that's enough to make the level-headed run screaming from the room. Who wants a bunch of yucky invisible things waltzing around the house, right? Maybe this is something that should best be forgotten? Maybe magick and all those elixirs, and drawings and that mumbo-jumbo should just be allowed to fade from our grasping little human hands?

Ah, you say, but maybe all is not what it seems? I'm so glad you said that, because you're right. In the introductory material of *The Lesser Key of Solomon* (a book on ceremonial magick), N. B. Foyers says,

> *I can give a rational explanation . . . the spirits are portions of the human brain . . . and* [the] *pictures* [meaning the symbols] *therefore represent methods of stimulating or regulating those particular spots . . .* [in our brains].[21]

He goes on to explain that the five senses—smell, taste, sight, touch, and hearing—can be used as a jumpstart to get your noggin moving in the direction you want it to go. *This* is basic divine alchemy. *This* is magick! Of course, there's more to it than that (isn't there always), but from what we've read so far, at least we know we're heading in the right direction.

When we are born, we are given the power to create and to destroy on many levels. We know that thoughts are things. Therefore, if you think about nasty junk, it has to go somewhere.

This takes the fear out of evil things that we can't see (if you ponder the subject) because all you might be dealing with (and I say *might be* because lots of people live their whole lives without bumping into astral nasties) are someone else's (or your) wild thoughts. In fact, German scientists have recently discovered that moods are catching. No kidding—just like the flu. Believing that these errant imaginings have any power over you is even sillier than the original thought, which is why I sometimes lose my patience with people who claim that demons (as in some sort of corporeal being) are after them. Teens (forgive me) seem to especially fall into this trap because they have excellent imaginations, far better than most adults. The answer? Just get a mental pin and pop that sucker because that's all it is, a creation of the mind. It only has the power you give it. Yucky thoughts such as these feed off your imagination and your fear, a powerful combo that has made men rich and women swoon (so to speak) but, in the end, leads only to a muddy destiny if you turn your thoughts in that direction. Trying to control anyone by using threats, violence, negative magick, or fear is a big no-no that's bound to turn around and give you a one-two punch, which you would thoroughly deserve.

Fast Folk Magicks to Combat Astral Nasties

- Cleanse the house (or room) with the four elements.

- Place mothballs in the four corners of the room (or house).

- Sprinkle the room or house once a month with holy water.

- Place crushed garlic under your bed.

- Hang a pair of child-safe open scissors over the doorway to your room or over the front and back doors to cut negativity before it enters the house.

- Burn sage or a mixture of sage and angelica in a fire-safe container.

- Place a cut onion on the windowsill to suck up negativity.

- Burn white candles.

- Place small mirrors on the front door, back door, or your bedroom door so that negativity is deflected from the room or other area.

- Wash the floor with Florida Water (SEE PAGE 414).

Astral Nasty Trap

Use this to suck up yucky energy.

SUPPLIES: One shoebox or wooden box; 2 mirrors; one lodestone or magnet; black paint; brushes; glue; holy water (SEE PAGE 413); hexagram drawing (SEE PAGE 363).

TIMING: Create during the dark of the moon.

INSTRUCTIONS: For measuring purposes, lightly tape the hexagram drawing on the outside front (the side that is facing you) of the box, ¼ inch from the bottom edge. Cut a one-inch round hole above the drawing. Remove the drawing. Paint the box, inside and out, with black paint. Allow to dry. Glue one mirror on the inside bottom of the box and one mirror on the inside top of the box. Sprinkle the picture with holy water, asking that Spirit empower the drawing to destroy all evil. After the picture dries, glue it underneath the hole on the inside of the box (this is important). Allow to dry.

Place the lodestone on your altar or magickal working surface. With your fingers, form a triangle over the lodestone, and say:

Little stone of darkest gray
work my will this very day
pull toward you all that's ill
catch it up in darkness till
it's gobbled up by pure white light
vanquished by the sigil bright
kept from harming anyone
as I say, it shall be done!

Put the lodestone on top of the mirror that you glued to the bottom of the box.

Wooden boxes can last years, where shoeboxes last only about six months. If you take shop class and your instructor asks you to make a birdhouse, you can fashion an astral nasty box that will keep on chugging for years. If your birdhouse has a slanted roof, glue a mirror on each slant as well as on the bottom. If you don't take shop class, many craft stores carry all the supplies that you will need (including the small mirrors, paint, glue, and brushes). Some stores even sell ready-to-assemble bird house kits. When you wish to discard the box, it is advised that you bury it off your property. Pour holy water inside the box before you do so to cleanse the lodestone before you give the stone back to the Earth.

Note: You can make a smaller version of this box for your locker, dorm room, a sick friend, or even your mom or dad's office if they are having a tough time at work. The fact that you have made something for them means that you understand things aren't always great for them either, and that you care about them. A gift, even a small one, for your parents made by yourself speaks volumes and helps to open the lines of communication during those tense moments we all experience. Indeed, using your magick to help people is what magickal individuals are all about!

Binding and Banishing

To bind or to banish? That is the question. For some this issue is not easily answered, where others feel that any debate is senseless. Although most magickal people will not argue the usefulness of banishing negativity, illness, or disease, there is continued discussion and differing opinions when it comes to binding and banishing people. Just so you won't feel lonely in this modern world of ours, such discussions were just as avid in Greco-Roman times among philosophers as they are today among the magickally minded. A millennium or two has not changed this emotionally charged topic.

Under our discussion on the Wiccan Rede (SEE PART I), we chatted about how social models, environment, dogma, and other interesting topics ebb and flow over, around, and in magickal practices, whether we are looking at magick in antiquity or magick here and now. What one does in magick and religion has a lot to do with one's process of self-identification, maturity, and level of spirituality. You can read lots of books, have discussions at the local Pagan hangout, and type your little fingers raw online expressing your opinion on such things; however, in the end, what you do is the loudest shout of all. The wise student carefully considers all options and possible consequences before making a magickal move. This contemplation also includes using a divination tool to check the outcome of your magickal work.

In this book we cover the "magickal norms" for most beginning Crafters, meaning what is written here represents the broadest range of magickal practitioners and what they normally do. There will be those that will not agree with everything I've written; however, what is in this book represents the general consensus for training new seekers. Therefore with no more pos-

turing, let's get into binding and banishing—two incredibly powerful practices in the world of magick—and the safest way to use them.

If we agree to use banishing and binding energies, keep the following in mind so it won't be a recipe for disaster:

• Work to create balance.

• Work through Spirit to remove personal judgment.

• Remember that all magick first changes our own perception before any other changes occur.

• Work through science, not through superstition.

If, however, we remove any of the above reminders from our workings, then we are asking for trouble and we'll probably get it.

To banish is to send something away, whether that something be illness, negative energy, or nasty people. When we create sacred space, cleanse any item for ritual or magickal use, or release negativity from our minds and bodies, we are practicing the process of banishment. We are ridding ourselves or the object of negative vibrations. Throughout this book you will find many "acts of banishment" written into the text of spells and rituals.

To bind (the most volatile of the magickal workings) renders an energy or person ineffective for a varied length of time. The problem with both, in regard to people, is the ethical questions the subject presents; however, if you keep those four rules in mind that I listed above, you shouldn't have a problem. Of the two, binding is the trickiest, for two reasons: First, if you don't handle the root of the problem, binding someone or something is worthless; and second, binding a person holds that individual or energy to you (which isn't such a hot idea). In the case of negative situations (for example, your best friend's boyfriend is treating her like trash), if Witches bind at all, it is usually an emergency measure followed by a complete banishing. Although little used in the modern Craft, the word for a binding of this kind is *defixiones*, which means to "bind down" (SEE ALSO SECTION ON TALISMANS, AMULETS, AND DEFIXIONES IN PART IV). Another word for binding used by historical scholars when speaking of magickal binding applications is *execretion*.

Bindings can also be used in healing by binding positive, recuperative energy to the person or more specifically to an open wound. Other bindings in the Craft include one's binding oath of service upon dedication or initiation, and various forms of knot or cord magick in which magick is bound for a specific length of time. This timing is stated within the body of the spell.

In recent studies of ancient world magick, scholars have finally begun looking at the importance of magick in society and the weight it carried among the people. They have realized that magickal practices were not separate from society, nor were they unusual—in fact, they were a common practice. Defixiones were used to bind and banish negativity, whether we are talking about situations of love, honor, business, sports competitions, marriage, and so on. Bindings, especially in the Greco-Roman world, grew into a cottage industry (mass production on a small scale that usually begins in the home). Although it is well known that magick and religion walked hand in hand through the ancient world, the manufacture of the defixiones gives us a historical trail that can be traced to Hoodoo, Pow Wow, root doctors, and the functional spells of Witchcraft—meaning evidence of magick removed from the political grasp of the "state" religion and practiced by the common man or woman in the privacy of their own home. Granted, those individuals who made the defixiones in Greco-

Roman times considered themselves "professionals" or "experts" of the trade, but this opinion is no different than that of the Pow Wow doctor (or the others listed) in modern times. It is not that they haven't had training, but that they are not ruled by a structured religion tied to the politics of the country. Binding and banishing spells, tablets, and figurines were used in North Africa, Egypt, Persia (Iraq), in the Jewish religion, and later in the Christian religion,[22] where they were finally rewritten and sometimes attached to saints, holy relics, and other church practices, including exorcism. In a way, if we follow the trail of defixiones through time, we follow the birth and transmutation of spellwork as it touched each and every popular religion. It is in the study of binding and banishing spells that we discover our ancestor's relationships between gods, planetary powers, angels, magickal writing, and the dead—all employed in defixiones, the oldest discovery of which dates to approximately 500 B.C.

As with all things in this world, from fire to antibiotics, the banishings and bindings could be used in a positive or negative way. If you misuse the procedure, then you are going to pay for it. If you work through Spirit and remain nonjudgmental, then you will succeed. In modern Craft, students are taught that it is unwise to banish or bind any energy without serious thought to the consequences. For example, just because you don't like the color of Tiffany's hair does not give you a solid reason to use binding or banishment. If, however, Tiffany was ill, then banishing the sickness is more than appropriate. If Tiffany has attacked you, again, binding and banishing is acceptable, though the procedure should be done in a magick circle and performed as a two-step process by binding her actions to her first, then banishing her. Regardless, you should always use your common sense, followed by your divination tool, to check what is the right thing to do—and you should never, ever act on gossip or hearsay.

Calling for Restraint Spell

There are situations in life, legal ones, where a restraining order has been set into motion because the person named has proven that he or she means to do harm to someone. In the legal system, restraining orders are normally used for abusers and stalkers. In the magickal world, Witches are known to use restraining orders too, to either protect themselves or an individual until they can legally make a move, and to strengthen the legal paperwork. The following spell is to be used in such an instance and the pipe concept comes from Greco-Roman times. Please note that this spell only works if there is a legitimate problem.

SUPPLIES: One 7-inch length of pipe; a cap for both ends (a hardware store can help you, and if you haven't got the courage to ask for the supplies, you can use a paper towel tube, cut to the correct length, and seal the openings with tinfoil, a rubber band, and candle wax); paper; a black candle; a white candle; one nail; coffee grounds; one fresh egg; a picture of the perpetrator, if you have it—if not, the person's full name, and a taglock if you can get it.

INSTRUCTIONS: During a fourth quarter moon, gather all your supplies. Follow Silver's Spellcasting ritual under the Spells section of this book (SEE PAGE 331). Place all items on the altar. Cleanse, consecrate, and empower to bind the negativity present in this situation associated with that person and then state your intent to banish that negative energy. Light the black candle, asking Sprit to banish all negativity from your life. Light the white candle, asking Spirit to bring harmony and happiness into your life. Seal one end of the pipe. Put the threatening individ

ual's name, picture, or taglock (or all three if you have them) into the tube. Say: "You have begun your descent."

Pour the coffee grounds on top. Say:

The darkness you have created is bound to you. I do not own your darkness. You own your darkness. You may no longer share this darkness with myself or others.

Place the egg on top, saying:

As this egg rots, so shall your negative energy be destroyed, and your evil shall be banished. The process begins now!

Stick the nail into the egg, saying: "This spell is sealed!" Cap the pipe. Carefully seal with wax from the black candle.

Bury off your property, preferably close to a crossroads. Many Witches believe that a crossroads provides a vortex through which energy can travel from this world to the world of Spirit. The crossroads have long been sacred to the Grecian goddess of witchcraft and magick, Hecate.

CADUCEUS

(SEE ILLUSTRATION, PAGE 363.) To the people of Sumer over 4,000 years ago, the caduceus was the emblem of life. The symbol is said to have the power over wealth, prosperity, happiness, and dreams, allowing the person who carries the rod of the double serpents to touch the magick of the heavens. In Egypt, the caduceus was carried by the Egyptian Goddess-Queen Isis and Anubis, and in pre-Hellenic Greece the caduceus was displayed on healing temples, and represented the strength and wisdom of the Greek God Hermes.[23]

In its earliest form, the caduceus appears as a forked rod, the prongs knotted or crossed to form a loop. In the Craft, the stang or forked rod is associated with the early, ancient caduceus, and was used to not only represent the dual forms of deity (male and female) but also the ability of the human to reach the gods, and for divinity to reach the human by traveling up and down the world axel or *axis mundi*. Both the stang and the caduceus were often adorned with fluttering ribbons.[24] Later, the rod was twined with two serpents, their heads turned toward each other as a symbol of settled quarrels, commerce, trade, transportation, communication, and enterprise.

In alchemy, the caduceus is still considered the symbol for the planet Mercury and the element Mercury, and meant "that which poisons can also heal"—again speaking of the duality of energy and the need for balance. In the Craft, the caduceus stands for the adage *A Witch who cannot hex, cannot heal*, meaning that we must walk in balance at all times, and it is *how* the energy is used, not the energy itself, that is important.

We find the caduceus in other parts of the world, too. In Hindu symbolism, the caduceus represents the central spirit of the human body, the twining serpents becoming the DNA pattern we now know exists—the genetic double helix. The Aztecs and the American Indian also had their own version of this symbol as well. In the Greek and Roman mystery cults, the caduceus represented the four elements: earth (rod), air (winged orb), fire, and water (the serpents with their undulating motions suggesting waves, and their darting tongues suggesting flames).[25] By this time some of you are realizing that the serpent in many ancient cultures wasn't a bad guy at all (just in Judaic/Christian mythos), and found an honorable place in thousands of religious legends.

With so many useful associations—commerce, communication, harmony, trading, joy, duality of life, health and healing, resolving quarrels, wisdom, and prosperity—there's no end to how we can use this symbol in positive ways. Under the chakra category, I show you how to use the caduceus in healing. Here, we will use it in two different spells—one to settle an argument and the other to gain wisdom.

Caduceus Spell for Resolving a Fight

SUPPLIES: Holy water; a forked branch (if you are desperate and can't find a forked branch, you can make one out of straws; however, you can't leave it outside when you are through); something small and disposable that belongs to both individuals involved in the quarrel. Choose beforehand which divinity you will use: Spirit, the angels, Isis, etc.

INSTRUCTIONS: In the dirt outside of your home (or in the woods, or in the sand at the beach), trace a circle on the ground that is large enough for you to stand in as well as roomy enough to draw in the dirt. After you have cast your magick circle, roughly sketch the caduceus symbol with the single end of the forked branch in the dirt at your feet in the center of the circle. On one side of the drawing (right or left), write the name of one person. On the other side, write the name of the other individual. Place the items matching the people under their names. (If you can't find anything belonging to the people, don't have heart failure. The spell will still work, though perhaps a bit slower.)

Point the forked end of the stick at the sky, and say:

I beseech and call upon thee, O mighty (name of divinity), in the hour of my need. It is I, (say your name), who seek the wisdom and strength of your counsel. Behold the ancient

symbol of caduceus, that which resolves the
arguments of man and beast and brings
harmony into this life. I ask thee, great
(name of divinity), to activate this symbol
and to find resolution between (say the names
of the two people) in your name.

Breathe on the drawing three times, and say: "With sacred breath I cleanse all wounds."

Point the forked end of the stick toward the drawing, chanting "The Witch, the power, the magick, the flame; no one loses, everyone gains, harmony reigns," as many times as you feel necessary. Sprinkle the holy water on both names (it doesn't matter if it washes the names away). Say: "With the power of Spirit, I break the hate."

Again point the stick at the drawing, and say:

Sun to moon, and moon to sun, the evil is
broken, and harmony won! As I will, it has
been done. May this spell not reverse
or place upon me any curse.[26]

Thank divinity and dismiss the circle. Lay the stick over the drawing with the forked end up and the pointed end down. Leave this place knowing that your work is finished.

Caduceus Spell for Gaining Wisdom

Sometimes we just can't seem to find an answer to a particular problem. Using the caduceus to gain wisdom brings opportunities or gives us a view of the bigger picture, showing us something that we may have overlooked. This spell is normally performed on Wednesday, the day of Mercury.

SUPPLIES: An empty notebook; black marker; a piece of overhead transparency paper (like you buy at an office supply store); cellophane tape; a bit of silver glitter.

INSTRUCTIONS: On the second page of the notebook, write down your problem, or what type of wisdom you are trying to reach. Just the word *wisdom* is okay, too, if you can't seem to put your desire into words. Sprinkle the word with silver glitter. Draw the caduceus symbol on the overhead transparency sheet (don't worry if you aren't a good artist, Spirit doesn't mind at all). Draw a square around the caduceus. Draw a circle around the square. In this picture the circle represents the spiritual plane and the square represents the material one. (In ritual when we cast the circle and then call the four quarters, we are doing the same thing—drawing in the wisdom and positive energy from Spirit toward yourself on the material plane.) Carefully lay the transparency over the words you wrote. Tape the ends so that the glitter will not escape.

Cast the magick circle and call the quarters. Carry the notebook to the center of the circle and ask for the divine blessing of Spirit. Then walk to each quarter, asking for wisdom from the four elements. Lay the book on your altar. Hold your hands over the drawing, and say:

North and south, east and west,
wisdom comes at my bequest.

Repeat this chant seven times. Your hands might tingle or grow warm over the drawing—that's okay. When you are finished, blow on the drawing three times, close the book, and draw an equal-armed cross in the air over the notebook. Thank deity and the elemental energies. Dismiss the quarters and take up the circle. Place the notebook someplace where it will not be disturbed. The answer you need will appear shortly, but be sure to look for it. Sometimes very ordinary occurrences are very magickally driven.

The nice thing about your wisdom book is that you can use it again and again. Just use a new page for each concern. When the book is full, and you have received answers to all your questions, burn it in the back yard (or some other safe place) and thank deity for the assistance given.

Charms

The word *charm* comes from the Old English *cyrm*, which means "hymn" or "choral song," and from the Latin *carmen*, a sacred incantation to the goddess Carmenta, mythological inventor of the alphabets and words of power. *Enchant* comes from *incantare*, "to sing over," which also means incantation.[27] The charm is a conjuration, a blessing, and a prayer all rolled into one format. The largest collection of charms is housed in the Humboldt University in Berlin, with over 250,000 entries.[28] Studying charms tells us about the people, medicine, folk practices, community, and religion of any given era. Using magickal charms with normal medical care has always been a part of American heritage, whether we are talking about the Native Americans or the Pennsylvania Dutch, and if you dig deep enough into the customs of your own ancestors, you'll find it there. In the United States, the words "pow-wowing," "trying," "to use," and "to conjure" were all a part of religious folk healing practices commonly associated with "charming."

A charm, then, is a piece of spoken or written magick—words of power that might be added to a variety of magickal practices. Most charms rhyme (easier to remember and the cadence creates an energy of its own); are short (easier—again—to remember and repeat); in some way mention the problem or situation at hand, or at least the desired end; and are said three, seven, or nine times (with three being the most prominent number). In modern Witchcraft charms are relatively short, where incantations are longer and might contain several stanzas. In Pow Wow, the magickal charm is always said three times: First, to declare and summon the spiritual assistance needed; second, then spoken to banish any unwanted energies; and third, to infuse the object or person with "the change" and to seal the spell (which is often followed by a physical motion, such as an equal-armed cross, which acts not only as a vortex [a landing pad for the positive change] but also as a seal to keep unwanted energies out).

Charms from the ancient world (Egypt, Persia, Mesopotamia, Greece, Rome, etc.) often used the vowel series (in our case, *a, e, i, o,* and *u*) intoned somewhere within the overall working. In some cases the vowels were turned into what the uninitiated considered to be nonsense and gibberish, but it is the sounds and their vibrations that formed the magickal key. You will especially see this in the traditional Crafts of Gardnerian, Alexandrian, and in ceremonial magick groups, should you choose to work in those areas. Such sounds are used not only to banish negativity, but to raise energy as well (SEE MAGICKAL VOICE, PAGE 312).

Author Donald Tyson, in his notes compiled for the Llewellyn edition of Henry Cornelius Agrippa's writings titled *Three Books of Occult Philosophy*[29] (first published in 1533), gives the reader an explanation of what sort of charms were prevalent in Agrippa's time. These include:

Adjurations: A renouncement of an oath or pact, or the commandment that evil must depart.

Breathing: Adding the sacred breath before or after the charm is spoken, such as the three-breath technique of the Pow Wow artist.

Conjurations: The binding or releasing of energy by speaking a sentence or a number of sentences.

Deprecations: Prayers for averting evil, unfortunate circumstances, or negative energy.

Imprecations: Prayers for invoking a deity or positive energy.

Invocations: Calling upon the presence or power of deities or positive energy.

Obtestations: Chargings or beseechings by sacred names in which god/dess or other spiritual agencies are called to witness.

Some of these words are no longer used in modern Wicca, though the practices themselves are apparent. We still bind things, tell things to go away, call deity, draw from nature and the elements, use sacred breath, raise power, and ask Spirit to be present at workings, etc., and many times these actions are done in poetry form, or through the use of simple sentences. One version of a German healing charm called "The Drawing" is at least eleven hundred years old, and is an adjuration:

Out of the marrow and into the bone
out of the bone and into the blood
out of the blood and into the flesh
out of the flesh and into the hair
out of the hair and into the green forest
out of the green forest and into the dry sand
as surely as god/dess made woman and man.

In my experience, this works for just about every sort of malady, from a bee sting to infection and even terminal illness. "The Goddess Charm"[30] is an imprecation, because you are specifically asking deity for assistance:

Queen of the Moon,
Queen of the Stars,
Queen of the Horns,
Queen of the Fires,
Queen of the Earth,
bring to me _____ (fill in the blank).

Repeat chant nine times.

If we were to mix an herbal recipe for a specific purpose, hold our hands over the herbs, and say:

I conjure thee, O leaf and bud of nature, in the name of the Lord and Lady, to release thy positive energy into this brew and bring forth into the world of form (your specific request).

. . . then we are practicing a conjuration.

The invocation is a magickal horse of a different color and is extremely prominent in almost every Wiccan ritual. It is where the practitioner attempts (and hopefully succeeds) to heighten his or her consciousness to reach the pure energy of deity, and this is normally done in poetry or hymnlike form. Whether you call the God and Goddess separately or alone, above all else the invocation should emotionally move you. Like the other charms listed above, there is no reason why you cannot write your own.

Invocation to the God and Goddess

I gazed upon your faces,
in the darkness and the light
I sought your wisdom in the stars
in the fabric of the night.
I looked in books both new and old,
and heard my own heart beating
I looked to find your story,
and so I kept on reading.
To think a thing and make it happen
was your gift to all.
So simple, yet so difficult,
yet you're there at beck and call
in every flower, leaf, and bud,
in cat, and snake, and bee
but what is most amazing
is that you are found in me.

Perfect love and perfect peace
will make conditions right
and from that place that's not a place
the form will come to light.
I lift my heart to touch you,
there is magick to be done
and all I need is knowing
that you and I are One.

The most famous deprecation that is used in our time throughout the world is Psalm 23 from the Bible. Now, before you panic, let's remember that most of the psalms were written by Pagans and most of the poetry was composed to entreat the assistance of the Goddess, specifically those goddesses of Sumer and Babylonia. Though the influence of Sumer, Babylon, Egypt, and Persia on the Bible has long been documented by scholars,[31] it is only recently that the implications have become widely considered, and it is the Pagan religious revival (Wicca/Witchcraft, Druidism, Goddess worshippers, etc.) that has plopped this information in mass quantities at the feet of the public.

> *For hundreds of years the transmission of this imagery from one culture to another passed unnoticed and the roots were ignored. From a reading of the Old Testament alone, one cannot currently discern the existence of the goddess culture for many thousands of years before the appearance of the monotheistic father god. Consequently, the effects of the Iron Age repression of the goddess culture, and its implications for our own culture, have not been fully evaluated.[32]*

This means that practically everything in the Old Testament of the Bible was rewritten to give credence to the creation of a new God—an all-male one. Indeed, one of the "rewritings" of the Bible occurred during the reign of James I of England and VI of Scotland, who authorized a new translation of the Bible and changed the passage "thou shalt not suffer a poisoner to live" to "though shalt not suffer a Witch to live." He also included a new government statute against Witchcraft in 1604. James, by the way, was a Calvinist.[33]

When people figure out they've been lied to by the current structured religions for thousands of years, they have a decision to make. Abandon that religion, or rework it. There is no other option. As you can see by now, when you study the Craft, not only do you study the modern practices of our faith, but you must also be willing to look at history eyeball-to-eyeball and try to understand the vast amount of information at your disposal. Knowledge is power. Knowing is power. Therefore, if we tweak the psalm a bit, don't get excited.

> *The Goddess is my guardian, I shall not want.*
> *She surrounds me with perfect love and perfect*
> *peace. She leadeth me beside still waters. She restoreth my soul. She guideth me on my spiritual*
> *path. Yea, though I walk through the valley of the*
> *shadow of death, I will fear no evil; for thou art*
> *with me. Thy love and thy protection, they comfort me. Thou preparest me with strength, courage,*
> *and knowledge in the presence of mine enemies.*
> *Thou anointest my head with oil. My cup runneth over and I am filled with an abundance of*
> *health and joy. Surely goodness and mercy shall*
> *follow me all the days of my life and I will dwell*
> *in the house of Spirit forever.*

While we are on the subject of invocations, we should probably discuss the word *evocation*, which has two distinct meanings in the Craft community, depending on who you talk to. If you are speaking to someone with a ceremonial background, they will tell you that evocation is the summoning of a spirit into a magick triangle, which is drawn outside of the circle. The triangle here is the symbol of manifestation. More confusing is that "a spirit" can mean many things to many people. For some, a spirit (in this explanation) is the "spirit of the thing," meaning the energy essence of a person, place, animal, or object. To others, the "spirit" is a named and numbered entity found in medieval occult literature. Most Wiccans do not use the triangle outside of the circle, and none of them are dumb enough (hopefully) to call an entity from medieval occult grimoires into the Wiccan magick circle, as the circle is the symbol of perfect love and perfect peace. And to be honest with you, if they did, all they would be calling up is the yucky stuff they've buried in their own subconscious. Then there are those Wiccans who teach that to evoke is to call positive energy up from within themselves, or from within an object. For example, when conjuring an herb, you would be evoking its inherent power. This type of evocation is done within the Wiccan ritual circle.

The obtestation is most seen in the quarter call. For example:

Hail, guardians of the north, element of earth, and all ye in the realm of Faery. I call ye forth to witness this rite and protect this sacred space.

Some magickal people believe that the actual words you use for any of the above-mentioned operations are not as important as the feeling you evoke within yourself as you speak aloud, where others believe that the sound and form of all words are important and carry great power and therefore should be carefully preserved (as in an old chant or charm) or selected with a great deal of consideration if you are writing a new one. The argument for using the older charms intact stems from the belief that because they have been used for hundreds, if not thousands, of years, their strength on the astral plane is greater due to the repetition. There are also magickal people who insist on saying charms and spells in a language other than their native tongue, believing that the sound of the foreign language entices the mind to consider the spell or chant exotic and magickal.

According to Dr. G. Storms, in his book *Anglo-Saxon Magic*, magickal practices by foreigners in strange languages always seemed to hold greater power than home-grown recipes:

> *The qualities, idiosyncrasies and failures of the magician residing next door lead to familiarity, and though the familiarity need not breed contempt, it makes it more difficult for him to compete with rivals whose fame is firmly based on report, whose successes are repeated and exaggerated and whose failures remain unknown.*[34]

This gives us an explanation as to why words and deeds formed in a language other than your own seem to hold more of a psychological power than what is familiar.

Finally, many charms, especially in Egyptian magick, Hoodoo, Southern Root work, and Pow Wow, contain what is called a *historyola*—a declaration of an act or a story about a person (or deity) of great worth who brought about positive radical change in society. This person can be a living/breathing one, or a personage or mythos who has accomplished great deeds. Sometimes the story lasts only a line or two, other times several lines are attributed to the amazing act. By listing the personage and the deeds in the spell, it is believed that "as they accomplished such a feat, so can I accomplish such a feat." The historyola has been used for over 4,000 years, and has been massaged and expanded by various religions, including Christianity.

For example, many Christianized chants (charms that predate Christianity and then were "remade" for the sake of sticking with the church) invoke the deeds of Christ and Mary (his mother and sometimes his consort, Mary Magdalene) rather than invoking the older gods, as they were originally spoken.

Scholars have made numerous classifications in an effort to understand the art of charming; however, until you actually do it for yourself and it works for you, you could literally categorize until doomsday because as you research and apply you will meet thousands of nuances that can enter into this practice.

- Exorcisms of diseases or removal of diseased spirits from a person, place, or thing.

- Herbal charms to invoke the powers of the vegetation (often called conjuring the plant, leaf, bud, herbal mixture, etc.)

- Charms for transferring disease (which is really an exorcism, but with flair, where you are actually taking the negative energy from one place and specifically putting it in another). For example, transferring the negativity from a person to an egg, and then from the egg to the ground.

- Amulet/talisman charms for pushing away/drawing energies.

- Charm remedies that are much like a prescription for salves, things to drink and eat, or other magickal applications, where the magick and the mundane meet on equal ground. You will continue to find this type of charm in the Pennsylvania Dutch Pow Wow medicinal usage (as well as in the above four categories).

- Historyolas—drawing the power of a certain person or deity involved in a specific past event in an effort to recapture that same type of energy.

When delving into medieval manuscripts currently available, keep in mind that many of the charms you read under specific headings should not necessarily be taken at face value. One reason why these charms have survived is because they have either been Christianized, miscategorized, or are indicative of only one purpose in an effort to protect the original intent or to mask the possibilities for which the charm could be used. For example, let's take the eleventh-century charm found in Dr. G. Storm's book *Anglo Saxon Magic*:

FOR A SWARM OF BEES

Take earth, throw it with your right hand under your right foot, and say:

> *I catch it under my foot, I have found it.*
> *Lo, earth has power against all creatures,*
> *and against malice and against ungratefulness,*
> *and against the mighty tongue of man.*

And afterward throw sand over them when they rise up to swarm, and say:

> *Settle, victorious women* (an analogy
> for the bees)*, sink down to earth.*
> *You must never fly wild to the wood*
> (meaning you cannot freely act to harm,
> or for the beekeeper's purposes,
> not get lost).
> *Be as mindful of my welfare*
> *as men are of food and home.*

This charm is wonderful if you are a beekeeper, but can also be used successfully in other situations, especially those that involve a group or organization. The bee swarm represents a group mind within its own community. If a group mind chooses to abandon its purpose, or to turn its energies on a particular person in a negative way, the charm can be employed to diffuse a nasty situation. You can substitute the sand with an all-natural magickal powder mixed with sand or dirt from the physical heart of the group mind (where they live or work) designed specifically for the intent of the spell. The powder can be thrown in a circular motion with the right hand at the place of business or residence of the group.

Cleansing, Consecrating, and Empowering (CCE)

To *cleanse* means to purify with the four elements (earth, air, water, and fire). To *consecrate* means to bless in the name of a deity (or deities). To *empower* means to activate the object for a specific magickal purpose.

To CCE a Person

This is normally done as a person steps into a magick circle or before a hands-on healing; however, if you are a "Witch alone," then you can choose whether you want to bless yourself before or after the circle has been cast. In many ceremonies the smoke of burning sage is passed lightly over the body. Then, the words of power commonly used are:

May you be cleansed, consecrated, and regenerated in the name of the Lord and Lady. Blessings upon you now as you enter this sacred space.

As the words are spoken aloud, a star or sacred spiral is drawn on the individual's head with anointing oil, followed by the sprinkling of holy water. You can also bless an animal before a healing with the same words, but omit the smoke and oil. Use the water instead.

To CCE an Object

In most cases, the four elements (earth, air, fire, and water) are used to cleanse any object. In the Craft it is believed that all things used for magickal purposes and religious reasons should be properly prepared by following this process; however, as you grow in the Craft, you'll begin to cleanse, consecrate, and empower just about everything, even stuff you use in your daily life (like your car, your bike, and even your skateboard). At first, this will seem stupid. Let's face it, when most of us begin our Craft training, the world of religion and faith is often separate from the world of work, school, and play. As your spirituality grows, the world of religion, faith, and spirituality melds with the experience of work, school, and play. This overlapping process is called walking your talk—being what you say you are rather than wearing a face that others see, but isn't the real you. This is a slow process, but it happens just the same. Those who give up the Craft and seek no other form of spirituality always live in two worlds, rather than one, making life so much more difficult than it needs to be. The choice is always yours.

To cleanse, consecrate, and empower an item, you need to make two decisions: to whom will you consecrate the item (God, Goddess, Spirit, the name of a deity), and what kind of empowerment you want the item to carry (love, harmony, peace, joy, protection, prosperity, truth, etc.). Once you have made these choices, it is a simple matter to place the item on your altar and begin.

Before you use the four elements, you must cleanse, consecrate, and bless them. Ground and center. Blow three times over the elements, then hold your hands over each element, and say:

In the name of (list your deity here).
One heart, one mind, one magick.

One truth, one body, one energy.
In perfect joy and perfect peace
in perfect love and perfect trust
I call forth the power of Spirit
and the serenity of divine order.
As above, so below.
So mote it be.

Now, hold your hands over the first item you wish to magickally prepare. Let's say we are using the necklace you want to wear for protection (which would make it an amulet). Sprinkle the necklace with holy water, and say:

Element of water. In the name of (chosen
deity), I cast out all unclean energies,
real and imagined.

As you say the words, imagine a brilliant white light surrounding the necklace. Then say:

May you be blessed in the name of (chosen
deity), and be filled with the energy of (love,
peace, joy, truth, protection, etc.).
So mote it be.

Sprinkle a little salt over the necklace, and repeat the process:

Element of earth. In the name of (deity), I cast
out all unclean energies, real and imagined. May
you be blessed in the name of (deity), and be
filled with the energy of (love, peace, joy, truth,
protection, harmony, etc.). So mote it be.

If you do not want to use salt, you can pass a crystal over the necklace—just remember that the crystal (like the water and any other element) should also have been cleansed, consecrated, and blessed before it is used on the necklace.

Using incense, pass the smoke over the necklace, saying the same words, except beginning with the words "Element of air." Finish by passing the candle flame over the necklace, calling out "Element of fire" and then finishing with the rest of the words.

Blow on the necklace three times, then draw an equal-armed cross in the air over the necklace, saying:

Thou art cleansed, consecrated, and empowered
in the name of (deity). This magick is sealed.
So mote it be.

How long does any cleansing and empowerment last? That depends on the activity around the object. If things are particularly nasty at home, on the job, or at school, you may want to perform this type of ritual once a month until things settle down.

CCE for Your First Car (or the Family Vehicle)

One of the most amusing rituals you'll perform is blessing your car without making a spectacle of yourself in public. If you have a garage, or live on a dirt road where no one ever comes knocking, this isn't a problem, but if you live in town (like we do) it's always a fun challenge to see how much magick you can do without looking too suspicious.

SUPPLIES: Holy water; your choice of magickal oil; an amulet previously prepared for protection that you will place in the car.

INSTRUCTIONS: On a sunny day (we're going to use the sun as the element of fire), take your supplies outside and set them on the ground near the car. Walk deosil (clockwise) completely around the car, whispering: "Protection, safety, bring to me. As I will, so mote it be." Walk around the car (or truck or motorcycle), sprinkling the holy water on the hood, roof, doors, etc., speaking the normal words of cleansing, consecration, and empowerment as given on page 385. Make sure you put the water on the headlights and taillights, saying: "All will see when lit you be." Next, draw pentacles on each tire with the oil, saying: "Earth, air, water, fire—protection always on this tire."

I always draw pentacles on the hood, all doors, and the back of the car with my finger for extra protection. Put your hands on the hood of the car, and recite the following:

Sun above and air around
bless this car upon the ground.
Water, earth, give power too
protective energy, stick like glue.
As the wheels move round and round
angels sing protective sounds.
Let not ill fortune come this way
keep us safe both night and day.
And should some idiot target me
send back that energy three times three.
In the name of (list your deity here),
one heart, one mind, one magick.
One truth, one body, one energy.
In perfect joy and perfect peace
in perfect love and perfect trust
I call forth the power of Spirit
the protection of the angels
and the serenity of divine order.
As above, so below.
So mote it be.

Seal the car by drawing an equal-armed cross in the air over the hood of the vehicle. Place the protective amulet you prepared inside the vehicle. Renew every six months. This spell works for cars, trucks, vans, bicycles, motorcycles, skateboards, and rollerblades—basically anything with wheels that provides transportation.

Color

Witches consider color as one of the many magickal correspondences available in their enchanted toolboxes. Ancient cultures, even into prehistory, have used color in ritual, magick, religion, and daily life to promote happiness, success, and well-being for themselves and others. The origins of healing with color in the Western world can be traced to ancient Egypt, where the diagnosis and treatment of an illness were related to corresponding colors available in the natural world. Hippocrates, who lived in the fourth century B.C.E., used ointments and different colored plasters on wounds. Aristotle worked with colored crystals, salves, minerals, and dyes as remedies around 300 B.C.E., and Aurelius Cornelius Celsus, a first-century Roman physician, extensively used color therapy in his work. The Christian church, however, put an end to all that, calling the use of color in medicine and ritual a "pagan" practice, and demanding that many of the healing techniques using color be abolished.[35] Even so, we must keep in mind that the ancient and medieval worlds were not devoid of color.

The discovery of color as light vibration entered the world with the sixteenth-century scientist Sir Isaac Newton. In 1666, Newton passed light through a prism and divided the light into the seven colors of the spectrum. He associated these colors with the seven known planetary energies of that time: sun, moon, Mercury, Venus, Mars, Jupiter, and Saturn. Yes, I know that the sun and moon aren't planets (exactly), but that's how they were classified and how astrologers still see them today.

In magick, ritual, and everyday life, Witches use color as an energy force. Much like an artist, we mix and match the vibrations of the colors to help us obtain what we desire. From the altar cloth to ritual robes, to the choice of candle colors, powders, and herbs, all have meaning to the magickal practitioner. At first, you will discover that some colors work better for you than others. This could be because a saturation of a particular color isn't good for you, as you already have all you need in that area of life and health, or you may hate a particular color because you need it. Only you can determine which colors are right for you and how you feel when using them. Colors do affect our emotional and physical health, and we should always keep this in mind when working magick. Even if a particular spell does not require a color association, you can always add color to boost the power of the operation.

Colors and Their Corresponding Magickal Properties

The following list represents cross-cultural beliefs associated with colors; therefore, you will notice that some colors may have the same associations. For example, blue and black both represent wisdom. Here, black stands for the wisdom of the unknown or what has yet to be learned, and blue is for the wisdom of Spirit.

White: The Goddess, ancient mother, purity, spirituality, devotional magick, general prayers, illumination, cycle of life, good will, initiation, feminine mystery, freedom, love, health, to symbolize a person, place, or thing.

Black:[36] Return energy to sender, divination, protection, dark goddesses, time, chaos, the first stage of a working, the beginning of creation, North, winter, rebirth, wisdom, the number 8, infinity, destroy bad habits, rest, investigation and combats hyperactivity. Use sparingly. Many practitioners follow the burning of a black candle with the lighting of a white one to bring balance to the magickal working.

Blue-Black: Use for wounded pride, for broken bones to knit properly, and angelic protection.

Violet: Intelligence, call the ancient ones, create sigils, anything to do with government, truth, justice, humility, planet Jupiter, religious devotion, and forgiveness.

Lavender: Peace, serenity, dreaming magicks, invoke Spirit when in the process of charitable works.

Blue: Truth, intelligence, wisdom, loyalty, fidelity, protect one's reputation, peace, meditation, feminine mysteries, water, Great Mother Queen of Heaven, infinity, poetry, faith, planet Venus, to defeat an enemy, and protect hearth, home, and the young. Use with white to create confusion among evil.

Green: Healing, the Green Man, god or goddess of vegetation and forest, youth, hope, happiness, new beginnings, improve the weather, financial gains (with gold and silver), agricultural magick, abundance, prosperity, immortality, spring, the planets Venus and Mercury.

Yellow: Healing, energy of the sun, prosperity, self-esteem, intellect, intuition, goodness, humility, beauty, light, life, truth, prosperity, attraction, and the God. Wear some yellow to a job interview to show that you can be trusted (brown says that you are responsible).

Orange: Opportunities, the ability to overcome challenges, break blocks, material gain, helps to seal a spell, happiness, luxury, remove feelings of abandonment.

Red: Action, passion, deep affection, courage, fire, masculine principle, festivity, strength, faith, life renewal, joy, summer, active leadership, expansion, the planet Mars.

Pink: Friendship and harmony.

Silver: Fast money, moon magick, the Charge of the Goddess, the Goddess, reality, connection to Spirit, astral travel, freedom, destroy illusions, restore balance, endurance, star magick, meditation, peace, personal illumination.

Gray: Stabilize a disturbed personality, slow down a reckless person or situation, use in some glamouries. Wear this color with some green when applying for a loan or asking for a raise.

Brown/Bronze: Soothe emotional upsets, security, support, friendship, and nature magick.

In the Craft, certain color combinations represent particular ideas. For example, the trio red, white, and black are the alchemical colors of initiation: red for your blood and your lineage (your personal history), white for the purity of Spirit, will, and intention, and black for power, protection, and that which was here at the time of creation, the void. In many traditions, the dedicant (or seeker) wears white at his or her initiation to indicate that he or she is willing to accept purity and harmony within his or her lifestyle, where those who have begun their training and are working through the levels of advancement provided by that organization wear black; however, keep in mind that traditions differ. The black, in this case, is to ward off negativity. Black also represents authority, rules, and order—time, karma, and wisdom. Rather than wearing black at a crossing (funeral), Wiccans often wear white as a symbol that the friend or family member has gone to a place of purity and will be met by emissaries of Spirit. Often, the entire ceremony will pivot on the use of only white—candles, altar cloth, clothing, statuary, and so on.

Magick done with black and white patterns (candles, cloth, drawings, etc.) promotes balance within ourselves and in the world around us. Black also stands for the night, and the white brings our focus to the moon and the light she reflects to us—we find strength in her power to overcome the darkness of human emotion or difficulties we are experiencing. I find it interesting that people outside of the Craft fear the use of black in our religious system, yet within their everyday lives and sometimes within their own religious beliefs, black is an acceptable color. Who has not seen a Catholic priest or nun in black? Who has not seen a rabbi wearing black? Who has not seen a Protestant minister in black? Yet when a Wiccan priest or priestess dons black robes, outsiders are suspicious. Go figure. In ritual, the color black is also a representation of the place between the worlds—not here, not there, but in between, where we can access the qualities and power of both to reach our desires.

Psychologists tell us that if an adult wears black all the time they are making a statement that something is missing from their lives, yet if a teen wears black they are basically saying that they are ready to change the world and have confidence in their own power[37]—since no one can see this but themselves, they subconsciously resort to black to make their point. Although black allows us to stand still and take a breather, wearing black all the time sends mixed messages to those around you, and you are stuck dealing with the various reactions you receive. When you are a teen, this can make life extremely difficult and perhaps throw more things at you than you bargained for. Adults who fear are scary animals indeed.

If you are trying to make new friends, wear pink. If your parents are going through a divorce, decorate your room in orange and indigo. If you have a friend who stammers, give them something yellow and blue. Headache? Green and violet. Is your sibling having a problem with wetting the bed? Give him or her a pink stuffed animal or blanket to hold and love. Empower the animal with lots and lots of love. First day of school (kindergarten to third grade) for your little sister or brother? Give him or her something peach colored to take along, empowered for protection. For teens, soft (not bright) yellow and turquoise are your colors, especially for studying and stress-related difficulties. Do magick with indigo to help a friend with a drug problem. Anorexia and bulimia? Rich orange and deep gold for anorexia, and yellow and violet for bulimia. Obviously just using a color isn't going to stop something like anorexia, bulimia, or drug abuse, but the colors are tools to help the person on their way to a happy, healthy lifestyle. You'll find more information on these topics under Eating Disorders in Part V. Between the color correspondences provided above and the chakra list on page 240, you'll be mixing and matching colors and magick like a pro in no time![38]

Correspondences

[Correspondences:] Magick that works by a secret sympathy or symbolic likeness between the cause and the effect.
—*J. G. Frazer*[39]

All things on the earth plane consist of energy. This energy pulsates (fast or slow) in a unique geometric pattern. A correspondence is the relationship between two patterns, either by size, shape, color, element, or historical lore. There are angelic, animal, herbal, gem, astrological, color, symbol, and deity patterns/correspondences in modern magick, to name a few. Patterns that are much like each other work well together and, when linked, build a network of energy that you can use in your spellcasting or ritual work. The patterns correspond to each other. This network of like energy is usually referred to as patterns working in sympathy.

Patterns/correspondences often fall into subcategories that relate to the elements of earth, air, fire, and water. Other categories used are those of gender. Some planets, for example, are seen as feminine, and others as masculine. It is the same with herbs, gems, and stones. Gender doesn't mean the item is "just for boys" or "just for girls"—here, it can mean active energy (male) or passive energy (female). As not all boys are active nor all girls passive, some new students have a problem at first with this qualification because they think it has to do with strength or weakness of one's sexual makeup—which it doesn't. Others see the male energy as positive and the female as negative. Again, this has nothing to do with people problems (or enhancements), but with energy pulsation. We could even say that male is a "sending" energy and female is a "receiving" energy and drop the gender bit all together.

The cataloging of correspondences began in ancient Sumer. In their view, the arts and crafts had been revealed to them by the gods above and were unchanging. Everything must have its name to assure its place in the universe, and one who knew the true name of something had a power over it. Among the earliest Sumerian documents are lists of stones, animals, and plants, classified on their outward characteristics.[40] This belief was also paralleled by the ancient Egyptians. In both societies priests busily cataloged everything! The advent of Christianity didn't change the idea of linking names and energy patterns together. Paracelsus worked out his own Doctrine of Signatures in the 1500s (SEE HERBS, PART III, FOR MORE INFORMATION ON THIS FASCINATING MAN) by studying classical Greek and Roman writings and conducting his own research. Then, in the 1800s, at the dawn of the alternative religion revolution, another fellow scientist-turned-visionary continued working on this same theory. Reflecting on the contemporary controversy about the significance of Egyptian hieroglyphics and the possibility of a universal language in 1784, Emmanuel Swedenborg[41] wrote out his theories suggesting that there are three different levels of meaning in any symbol: the natural, the spiritual, and the divine.[42] Like modern Witches, Swedenborg believed that the universe is ultimately a harmonious whole, and that sin does not exist, only human error. He believed that if people could develop intuition and imagination, then they could reach a higher level of spirituality. Swedenborg is important to our study of Witchcraft and magick because his revolutionary ideas—the theory of correspondences, the belief that one can access the Spirit world, the idea that positive change within oneself can ultimately affect world reality, and the melding of science and occult religious practices together to create a better lifestyle—represent part of the current Wiccan religious foundation. Should this information bore you to tears, take heart. Next time someone tries to tell you that the Craft is a product of deluded thinking and is ruled by the devil, you'll be able to confidently tell them that you are in excellent company, listing such greats as Kepler, Swedenborg, Paracelsus, Mesmer, and any other number of famous historical names you'll find in this book.

There are several correspondence lists in this book, including chakras, astrological symbolism, angels, herbs, gems, and colors, each listed under their own category (see individual part pages for their exact locations). Witches use the lists to design or enhance rituals and magickal operations, such as spellwork. You read about how these lists were developed under Herbs in Part III.

Designing Your Own Spell Using Correspondences

Spells are not hard to create if you remember the following:

- Each spell should have a statement of intent.

- Most spellwork should be done in the magick circle.

- All items you use in the spell should correspond to each other. There are exceptions to this rule, called spells of antipathy, where you want things to be opposite each other for a reason. Let's say you wish to bring balance into your life. If this is the case, you might choose a black candle and a white candle. Light and the absence of light (black) are in antipathy.

- You should try to get a taglock if possible, especially if you are first learning magick. A taglock is something that belongs to the person for whom you are working the magick. Although outsiders often think it's yucky that magickal people use hair and fingernails to work magick for someone, this practice isn't as weird as it sounds. Given what we know today about DNA, the ancients were right when they said these things carry your energy pattern. They certainly do! If you find this particularly repulsive or if someone in your household would go ballistic seeing stuff like this on your altar (*gee, Mom, I'm just cleaning your hairbrush so I can work prosperity magick for you—really!*), then their photograph or something they have touched frequently will do. The closer the taglock to their DNA structure, the faster the magick works. Using a picture, for example, might take longer for a healing spell than if you included a lock of hair. However, my kids have used pictures from their school yearbook to work healing magick with great success for those friends who have been in unfortunate accidents or peers who somehow met with one of life's many disasters. If you know a person's birth date, time, and place, you can get a copy of their astrological chart off the Internet and use that as a taglock as well.

- Always work for "the best possible outcome" no matter what the problem or situation. If you do this, then ethical questions will not be that big of a deal. Remember, magick is the act of creating balance.

- Research all parts of the spell thoroughly. Know what deity, colors, gems, herbs, etc. match each other through their energy patterns before you mix them together. Given the correspondence lists in this book, this shouldn't be too hard. Later, when you want to get fancy, you'll be eager to discover new information on your own.

- Try to remain focused throughout the spellwork. No blaring stereos, interruptions, telephone calls, etc.

- Don't work while you are angry or stressed. Always remember to ground, center, and breathe!

- Be honorable and honest in every magickal operation. Sometimes a spell isn't needed—an attitude adjustment is what's necessary.

- Don't forget to use your "Secret Formula" (PAGE 115).

Elements

Philippus Aureolus Paracelsus, a Swiss physician, chemist, and philosopher (1490–1541), is credited with the Doctrine of the Four Elements, from which early nineteenth-century occult practitioners drew the belief that an element (earth, air, fire, and water) is not only physical, but also contains a spiritual essence. Granted, ancient cultures around the world long before Paracelsus' time believed in this same principle; however, the condemnation of the Christian church did its best to eradicate this belief for over a thousand years. Pliny (Rome, first century A.D.), Pythagoras (Greek, 582–500 B.C.), Aristotle (382–322 B.C.), and Manilius (there is debate whether he lived in the first or ninth century A.D.) were all saying basically the same thing. To have Paracelsus renew the idea and pass it around didn't make him especially popular, therefore in the occult world he gets five gold stars.

Paracelsus defied physicians of his time by insisting that diseases were caused by agents that were external to the body, and that they could be cured by using chemistry. Many of his remedies were based on the belief that "like cures like." He could be called the father of homeopathy, which has become popular in alternative medical circles (which include practitioners of Witchcraft). Homeopathy stems from the idea that one should treat the underlying problem, rather than just try to cure the symptom, by using natural ingredients, such as herbs. He was pooh-poohed by his peers because he included magick in his scholarly writings. Witches also believe that we need to treat the problem rather than concentrate solely on the symptoms, but what does this have to do with the primary elements?

Almost everything in the Craft, from the tools we use to the herbs we employ to the sigils we design, zodiac associations, and planetary alignments we follow, fits into the ancient and medieval elemental category of the primary elements. Manilius put it this way:

> *And first the heaven, earth, and liquid plain, the moon's bright globe and stars titanian* [bright white]. *A spirit fed within, spread through the whole, and with the huge heap mixed infused a soul; hence man and beasts and birds derive their strain and monsters floating in the marbled main; these seeds have fiery vigor, and a birth, of heavenly race, but clogg'd with heavy earth.*[43]

So, about 2,000 years ago, the Roman Manilius was trying to tell people that everything—animals, humans, stars, seas, and earth—consisted of living energy. I realize that philosophy might not interest you, but then I'm sure there are those among you who will be delighted to discover that even though these old geezers are long gone, their ideas of magick, science, and philosophy continue on, right into the lap of modern Witchcraft.

According to the *Oxford English Dictionary*, the word *element* has a mysterious origin, and is first found in Greek texts meaning "complex whole" or "a single unit made up of many parts." From the ancient up to medieval times there were only four elements (earth, air, fire, and water) and if you were occult-oriented the fifth was Spirit. Cornelius Agrippa called spirit the "quintessence."

Today, although scientists list more than 100 chemical elements (with some being manmade), magickal people continue to rely on the five basic building blocks of medieval occultism—earth, air, fire, water, and Spirit—using some of the additional elements of the modern age to support the original five, depending on the spell or ritual. For example, silver (an element/metal) is used in various spells, and is a symbol of the divine Goddess, feminine mysteries, and is associated with moon magick, dreaming, and psychism. Gold, another element, stands for the God, male mysteries, success, prosperity, general well-being, and all magicks associated with the sun. Let's begin, however, with the big four—earth, air, fire, and water.

Element of Earth

Earth is the universal archetype of the divine feminine. Our planet is fondly called Mother Earth, the Great Mother, and Gaia, among many others. She represents the inexhaustible spirit of creation and is associated with abundance. When we work with earth, not only are we calling the great expanse of our planet—its mountains, caves, minerals, and deserts—but we are also invoking her support and massive strength. From her emerges hidden treasure, and she is the proof that material things can be manifested from the divine.

The earth gives all living things the space and minerals they need to grow, so when we call earth into our circle as we stand at the north quarter, we are inviting the living essence of our planet to join us in our celebrations and our magick. We are asking that this energy lend its aid to the work we are doing. When we ask for blessings from the north, we are envisioning abundance, stability, protection, and room to grow in a positive way.

Throughout the history of magick the element of earth has been associated with a variety of deities, spirits, and angels. You can use what you like, as long as you remember the underlying basic: Earth is earth is earth. We can use a lot of breath with long invocations, and draw exquisite, complicated sigils and dress it up all we want, but it's still dirt. Once you move through this book and start reading more advanced material, you'll see what I mean.

From the magickal (as well as the esoteric alchemical) viewpoint, earth has the lowest vibration of the four elements because it is solidly manifest in our world. In astrology those signs symbolized by the earth element are Capricorn (motivated earth); Taurus (rooted earth); and Virgo (changing earth). As the moon moves through each sign for approximately two and a half days each month, you have an opportunity to work with the moon's receptive energy in that sign. If you wanted to work on the structure of something, then you would choose a day when the moon is in Capricorn (see your almanac). If you wished to keep things the same or stockpile something, then moon in Taurus is a perfect time for such a spell or ritual. If you need to make changes to a structure, investigate something, or find the "bugs" in a system, then the Virgo moon is the perfect time.

Sigils of Earth and How to Use Them

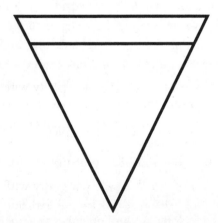

The triangle has a long spiritual history. No matter the culture or religion, its basic meaning is "three in one." From the Zoroastrian Fire-Light-Ether to the astrological significance of "the Big Three"—sun, moon, and rising sign

that make up the bulk of your personality—to the Wiccan idea of Maiden, Mother, and Crone and Father, Son, and Sage, all stand for the threefold nature of the universe. In Egyptian magick this triangle included Isis (the mother), Osiris (the father), and Horus (the manifestation of the two—the son). An upward-pointing triangle stands for the male principle, where the downward-pointing one is feminine. Remember, masculine and feminine in magick really have nothing to do with gender, and have everything to do with how energy flows and manifests. The alchemical earth symbol (pictured) draws a line across the top portion of the triangle. Fire, air, and water also have triangular symbols (which you'll see as we move along). The four triangular symbols can be used in your Book of Shadows to indicate information that deals with a particular element, and be carved into tools, painted on magickal projects, or sewn on robes and altar cloths—in essence, on anything that you want to use to draw earth energy to you.

We can also activate the sigil itself by writing a person's name that we want protected in the center of the earth symbol, asking for grounding, protection, and the gifts of the earth. Triangles, whether they stand for earth, air, fire, or water, are activation points. Don't put anything in there that you don't want to change.

Odin's Cross or the Sun Cross, above right, appeared around the beginning of the Bronze Age.[44] It materializes in ancient Egypt, China, pre-Columbian America, and the Near East. Not only does it stand for the element of earth, but also for thunder, highest power, and energy. In astrology, it is associated with the Part of Fortune, a point on every natal chart that, when activated by the movement of planets throughout one's lifetime, brings good fortune, riches, and success. Carve it on candles for that extra oomph. Use to break the negativity of another by placing the

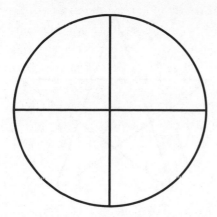

sigil with your name on it over their name or picture. Draw on the back of your own picture to add success to any personal spellcasting procedure. Carry in your wallet dressed with a little money oil for drawing extra cash your way. Don't draw it on the pavement in sidewalk chalk by the front of your house, though, because in the hobo sign system this one means *Here you will find food, work, and generous people.* Although hobo picture writing isn't used much these days in America, I highly doubt your mother would be thrilled with strangers knocking at her door. On the other hand, this symbol is also known as the Gamma Cross and is used in the inauguration of a Roman Catholic church, wherein twelve such crosses are drawn in blessed water and oil upon the walls of the establishment. Given this information, you can use the same sigil to bless the room in which you work magick.

The Wheel Cross (Sun Cross, etc.) also has another association, that of planet Earth in astrology, although it is rarely used by modern astrologers due to their use of the geocentric system. In magick, however, we can put this symbol to good use by drawing it in combination with other astrological sigils. Simply draw, paint, or write the symbols directly on candles, altars, or other magickal projects that match the intent given in the list below.

Earth/Planetary Combinations

Note: Regarding the colors—for the most part, these are ceremonial magickal associations. You can use these, or find colors that you feel would work better.

EARTH ⊕ WITH SUN ☉

Resulting action: Stability/prosperity with will.

Associated colors: Blue/orange and gold.

EARTH ⊕ WITH MOON ☽

Resulting action: Stability/prosperity with emotions.

Associated colors: Blue/silver with white/silver.

EARTH ⊕ WITH VENUS ♀

Resulting action: Stability/prosperity with socialization.

Associated colors: Blue with pink or green.

EARTH ⊕ WITH MARS ♂

Resulting action: Stability/prosperity with action.

Associated colors: Blue with red.

EARTH ⊕ WITH JUPITER ♃

Resulting action: Stability/prosperity with expansion.

Associated colors: Blue with violet.

EARTH ⊕ WITH SATURN ♄

Resulting action: Stability/prosperity with building structure or working with authority; or speed and the strength to banish.

Associated colors: Blue with black.

EARTH ⊕ WITH URANUS ♅

Resulting action: Stability/prosperity in the face of change.

Associated colors: Blue with light blue.

Invoking earth pentacle, left, and banishing, right.

EARTH ⊕ WITH NEPTUNE ♆

Resulting action: Stability/prosperity with dreaming/visionary work.

Associated colors: Blue with aqua.

EARTH ⊕ WITH PLUTO ♇

Resulting action: Stability/prosperity with radical change—to destroy to rebuild.

Associated colors: Blue/silver and black.

Invoking and Banishing Earth Pentacles

In ceremonial magick and some Wiccan groups you will find what are called the invoking pentacles of the elements. There are five of them—earth, air, fire, water, and Spirit. To invoke the energy of the earth at the north quarter, you would draw the star starting at the top and following through. To release that energy, you would start at the bottom left-hand corner and draw the sigil. Usually the symbols are drawn in the air with one's finger, wand, rod, or athame. As pictured, the invoking earth pentacle brings earth energy into the circle, and the banishing earth pentacle sends the energy back from whence it came. You might want to trace your finger over the diagrams to get the magickal

hang of the energy of this symbol. If you are trying to bring prosperity into your life, then you might at some point in your ritual or spell draw an invoking earth pentagram on your supplies. You can even use a pen or pencil and draw it right on a dollar bill, asking for the blessings of abundance. This system of invoking and banishing the elements using pentagrams is attributed to Samuel L. Mathers, who improved on the original material of the ceremonial magician Eliphas Zahed Levi.

Meditation of Earth

The best way to get to know the energy pattern of an element is to work with it and use meditation to "become" that element. For this exercise you will need a bowl of dirt or sand and a seed of some kind. Trace one of the earth sigils on the floor with your finger and sit inside. Take three deep breaths. Put your hands in the dirt. Begin by rolling the sand or dirt around with your fingers. Let your mind drift on subjects that pertain to the earth—the planet, earth goddesses, the ideas of stability and abundance. When you are through, ask for wisdom from the earth, brush off your hands, give a gentle thank you to the element, then ground and center. Hold the seed in your hand and think of a wish that you would like to grow. Think of planting that wish in the ground and visualize the result, then physically plant the seed somewhere on your property. If you like, you can bag up the dirt or sand in the bowl and use it in a spell or ritual later on. *Note:* If you have used the invoking earth pentagram then you will need to finish by tracing the banishing earth pentagram.

Earth Correspondences

ZODIAC

Capricorn: Beginning and structure.

Taurus: Saving and fixed.

Virgo: Changing (mutable) and review oriented.

COLOR ASSOCIATION

Yellow or green, depending on the tradition you practice. Yellow for ceremonial Wicca and green for shamanic Wicca.

WICCAN TOOL

Cauldron or pentacle.

ANGELS/GUARDIANS

Abundance: Barbelo

Agriculture: Risnuch

Alchemy: Och

Animals: Thegri, Mtniel, Hehiel, Hayyal

Commerce: Anauel

Creeping Things: Orifiel

Dust: Suphlatus

Earthquakes: Sui'el, Rashiel

Farming: Sofiel

Fertility: Samandiriel, Yushamin

Food: Manna

Gaia: Michael, Jehoel, Metatron, Mammon

Gardens: Cathetel

Nourishment: Isda

Forests: Zuphlas

Fruition: Anahita

Mountains: Mehabiah

Plants: Sachluph

Trees: Maktiel, Zuphlas

Vegetables: Sealiah, Sofiel

Wild Birds: Trgiaob

DEITIES[45]

African: Earth Mother, Divine Queen, Nimba, Oshun, Tenga.

Egypt: (Female) Anatha, Bast, Isis, Mehueret. (Male) Min, Geb.

Greek/Roman: (Female) Atlantia, Clonia, Flora, Hestia. (Male) Fauna, Pan.

Norse: (Female) Frigga, Holda, Nanna, She-Wolf.

Celtic: (Female) Aine, Anu, Blodeuwedd, Cailleach Beara, Magog, Rosemerta.

Working with the Earth in Magickal Operations

There are three ways to work with the elements in magick:

Mentally: Using visualization techniques.

Astrally: Using the "energy of the thing."

Physically: Using the element through the five senses—hearing, touching, seeing, tasting, and smelling.

Many times magickal people will combine all three techniques in one spell or ritual. For example, in a standard ritual, the Witch may place a bowl of salt (the physical) at the north quarter along with a green or brown candle (a physical item that helps provide a mental and astral link by the action of lighting the candle). When opening the north quarter the magickal person might use a physical action (called a trigger) by using the hands to make the motions of parting a curtain or drawing the invoking earth pentagram with a magickal tool. As the action is performed, the mind forms pictures of the earth energy (mental). The Witch might think of a big mountain, rolling fields, a deep, protective cave, etc. When he or she lights the candle, the Witch might imagine the strength and loving security of the earth (a feeling translated into moving energy touching the astral plane that now enters the circle environment).

Most magickal people have a series of keywords they have learned through practice that are associated with that element. Keywords for earth would be: strength, stability, treasure, bounty, protection, and so on. When the keyword is spoken and the picture in the mind is conjured, the link between the individual and the element is forged. Only practice can make this visualization stronger, which in turn will give you far more successes than failures in your magickal work.

Spellwork involving any element often uses all three manifestations of that element: mental, astral, and physical. For example, let's say we wanted to "unearth" a problem. We could literally dig a hole in the ground in ritual and ask that the information or problem be exposed to the right people, who will in turn assist us in solving the difficulty. With the help of the physical action of digging, the mental visualization of the "unearthing," and the request of earth's energy to move the spell along (astral work), we are using the element of earth in all three manifestations. If we need prosperity, we might call on the gnomes (earth elementals) to help bring money to us. To do this, we could find a little gnome statue, place a gold coin or paper money under him, and ask the elemental to search for and bring back the amount we need. Not only is the gnome figurine a physical representation, it is also an astral one, as on the astral plane gnomes represent the elemental manifestation of the element of earth. Again, we are using all three forms of the element. When I was very young I used a gnome finger puppet (made crudely by myself) to bring back ice cream and pretzels. My wish was granted. In this case, the ice cream and pretzels were "treasure." (At least I saw them that way.)

Many Witches bury items for the following reasons:

- As a gestation period. Seeds can be planted with an associated wish. As the plant grows, so the wish moves to completion.

- As a dispelling action. Empower an egg to "take on" a physical illness or problem, then bury it off your property. As the egg rots, so the problem disintegrates.

- As a binding action. "Deeper and longer lasting than the grave."

Burying things on your property is used to keep things, and burying something off your property sends something away. Both applications stem from folk magickal operations and can be found throughout the world in various cultures.

In spells, salt, dirt, and herbs can be added to the working to reach the desired effect. Salt (of the earth) cleanses, and is considered a general purifier. Also considered protective, you can place a circle of salt around the picture of a sick friend or a person who is in trouble to dispel any negativity that might otherwise reach them. If you are having trouble with a stalker (which is not an uncommon occurrence in the twenty-first century), you can place a circle of salt around the picture of the victim or around a picture of the victim's home. Dirt from sacred areas may be added to magickal powders, sprinkled on a symbol, or loaded into candles to boost the energy of a spell or to call ancient spiritual energies to the working. You can erect a small sand castle, placing plastic figures or stones inside to represent the people you would like to protect. Figures of people and animals made of clay (the earth) can be fashioned to represent gods, goddesses, or totems, and then empowered for assistance. Your artistic expertise does not matter. You can also use these figures to request a healing, especially if you have made the image with something belonging to the sick individual (SEE PART II, POPPETS). Clay objects and stones can also be used to multiply prosperity, especially if you collect them from all over the world, asking for prosperity to reach you from all points of the globe. As your collection grows, so does prosperity. Graveyard dirt (a Witchy favorite) is used not to curse, as so many think, but to ask for the intervention of the dead in serious situations. Dirt from a favored family member's grave does wonders when warding off a stalker, or when trying to break apart a politically corrupt situation. Here, the dirt absorbs the negativity while a link through love is established with the deceased, opening a pathway for your request to reach the loved one from whom you have petitioned assistance. Breaking clods of dirt (dried clumps) can help to break up a difficult situation into more manageable pieces. Granted, this is sympathetic magick at its lowest denomination, but it works! Jars of dirt mixed with salt and any herbs you choose can be used to remove negativity from a room (change every thirty days). Gemstones (SEE PAGE 431) have been extremely useful in all types of magickal operations, and are often used for ongoing protection and success work. Anything that moves earth can put an extra visual twist to your spellwork—spades, shovels, and small representations of earth-moving equipment such as dump trucks, bulldozers, and steam shovels work well. (And you thought you had no use for those Tonka trucks anymore!) Drumming on anything (bucket, tabletop, the floor) or using a sacred drum is one of the most powerful forms of moving earth energy in a magickal setting.

Element of Air

When we work with air we think of the divine breath of Spirit, the ability to move through space and time, and the wisdom that comes from experience and study. When we invite air into our circle at the east quarter we draw forth the sacred breath of life with vigor and clarity. Like the element of earth, air also has a long list of angelic and deity correspondences, some of which are shown in the list on page 402.

The zodiac signs for air are Libra (air in early movement), Aquarius (air as it stalls over the earth), and Gemini (air that changes direction). You can plan your magick to work with the element of air by watching your almanac. If you want to do a lot of socializing or make new friends, do a spell or ritual when the moon is in Libra. Out to do some good and take care of humanitarian concerns? Moon in Aquarius. If you need to do a thousand things at once or have to cram for a test, try the Gemini moon.

The movement of air can tell us many things. It can bring the scent of spring, letting you know if the warming season will be early or late. If it grows unusually cold in a warm area, then you may have an astral visitor. Folk legends in various cultures supported the belief that the dead could ride on the winds. Several goddesses and gods are also attributed to this skill, including the Germanic Dame Holda and the Egyptian god Shu.

Air Symbols and How to Use Them

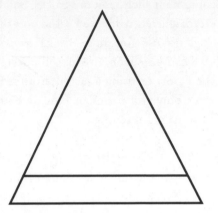

Our first symbol for air is the upright triangle with a double bottom line (as shown above). This is the alchemical sigil for air and, like the earth triangle, can be used in your Book of Shadows, etc. If you need to send a message to someone and you can't reach them the conventional way, try writing your message in the air sigil and hanging it outside where the moving air will reach it. If this isn't possible, write the person's name in the triangle and set a votive candle over the top. Sit quietly and stare at the candle, repeating your message. Keep the message brief—too many words and the meaning might get lost in the transmission. You can also try sending "pictures" in your mind instead. Run some experiments with friends and see what happens. The upright triangle puts the element of air in the active, masculine category.

Where earth magick lends itself to manifesting things in a physical form, finding treasure, creating abundance, and reaching for the strength within, air magicks are more of the mental, studious variety: sending messages, writing stories, articles, poetry, taking notes, composing music, studying anything and everything, clarity of thought, and weather magick. Wind can push or stall a weather front.

Hermes, the Greek messenger god, and his Roman counterpart Mercury are both associated with the element of air. To send a message or speed a spell, use either the symbol for Hermes, below, or Mercury (☿).

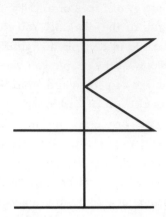

Mercury/Planetary Combinations

You can bind the symbol of Mercury to the symbols of the other planets to accomplish a variety of actions. Bind the symbols by drawing them next to, on top of, or above or below each other, with continuous lines, or by combining them together to form a unique design. *Note:* These are suggested colors only, you can change these to suit the circumstances.

MERCURY ☿ WITH SUN ☉

Resulting action: Speed/communication with will.

Associated colors: Yellow/orange and gold.

MERCURY ☿ WITH MOON ☽

Resulting action: Speed/communication with emotions.

Associated colors: Yellow/silver with white/silver.

MERCURY ☿ WITH VENUS ♀

Resulting action: Speed/communication with socialization.

Associated colors: Yellow with pink or green.

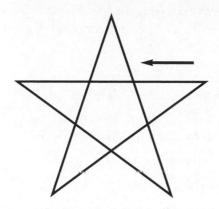

Invoking air pentacle, left, and banishing, right.

MERCURY ☿ WITH MARS ♂

Resulting action: Speed/communication with action.

Associated colors: Yellow with red.

MERCURY ☿ WITH JUPITER ♃

Resulting action: Speed/communication with expansion.

Associated colors: Yellow with violet.

MERCURY ☿ WITH SATURN ♄

Resulting action: Speed/communication with building structure or working with authority; or speed/communication to banish.

Associated colors: Yellow with black.

MERCURY ☿ WITH URANUS ♅

Resulting action: Speed/communication with change.

Associated colors: Yellow with light blue.

MERCURY ☿ WITH NEPTUNE ♆

Resulting action: Speed/communication with dreaming/visionary work.

Associated colors: Yellow with aqua.

MERCURY ☿ WITH PLUTO ♇

Resulting action: Speed/communication with radical change—to destroy to rebuild.

Associated colors: Yellow/silver and black.

Invoking and Banishing Pentagrams of Air

The element of air also has its invoking and banishing pentagrams, and are often drawn in the air with the finger, wand, rod, or athame at the east quarter.

If you are in a hurry, or just need to move your magick to a speedy conclusion, use the invoking air pentagram while calling on the spirits of air to help you. If you want a storm to move away, ring a bell three times in a succession of three (AS INSTRUCTED UNDER PART II, BELL) then draw the banishing pentagram of air in the direction of the oncoming storm. The banishing pentagram alone works well to move away heavy cloud cover, but remember, in weather magick, practice makes perfect. If you need the bad vibes brought by a letter, court summons, or other nasty legal paperwork to dissipate, draw the banishing air pentagram over the offensive message. Granted, it will probably take more on your part to make the whole thing go away, but starting with removing the negative energy on the paper is a good way to begin.

Meditation of Air

This meditation is best done outside. You will need a stick and several colorful ribbons at least thirteen inches long. Make a wish for each ribbon. Write them down so you don't forget. Draw one of the sigils listed above on the ground and sit in the center. Take three deep breaths and relax. Hold your palms open, the backs of your hands resting on your knees or your lap. Think about the element of air. Close your eyes. Do a little free association. Air moves, it is the breath of Spirit, it shifts the weather, it brings wisdom and intellect. Become the air. When you are finished, slowly open your eyes and take a deep breath. Tie each ribbon onto the stick, leaving about six inches of stick free at the bottom. As you tie the ribbons, state your wishes aloud. Blow three times on the ribbons. Set the stick upright in the ground so that the ribbons can flow free. Thank the element of air and deity. Leave the stick. If you have used the invoking air pentagram, then you will need to finish with the banishing air pentagram.

Air Correspondences

Remember to research all deity energies before you use them.

ZODIAC

Libra: Beginnings.

Aquarius: Fixed.

Gemini: Changing (mutable).

COLOR

Blue or yellow, depending upon the tradition used. Blue for ceremonial Wicca and yellow for shamanic Wicca.

WICCAN TOOL

Athame or wand.

ANGEL/GUARDIAN

Air, general: Chasan, Casmaron, Cherub, Iahmel

Altitudes: Barachiel, Gabriel, Gediel

Announcements: Sirushi

Birds: Arael, Anpiel

Communication and protection from harmful words and thoughts: Ambriel

Dawn: Hlm hml

Doves: Alphun

Dreams: Gabriel

Free will: Tabris

Grace: Ananchel

Hurricanes: Zamiel, Zaafiel

Intellectual achievements: Akriel

Inventions: Liwet

Memory and tolerance: Mupiel

Moderation: Baglis

Noonday winds: Nariel

North wind: Cahiroum

Pure wisdom, knowledge, and learning: Diana

Philosophy and meditation: Iahhel

Positive thoughts: Vohumanah

Prayers: Akatriel, Metatron, Raphael, Sandalphon, Michael

Protection for libraries, archives, places of learning and computers: Harahel

Purity: Taharial

Secrets and hidden knowledge: Satarel

Sky: Sahaqiel

Storms: Zakkiel, Zaamael

Thunder: Ramiel, Uriel

Truth: Armait (also harmony)

Twilight: Aftiel

Whirlwind: Rashiel, Zavael

Winds: Moriel, Ruhiel, Rujiel, Ben Nez

Writing: Ecanus

DEITY

General air:

> Hermes (Greek, Male); Mercury (Roman, Male); Shu (Egyptian, Male).

Education:

> *African:* (Female) Aja, Minona.
>
> *Egyptian:* (Female) Selk, Seshat, Tie; (Male) Thoth.
>
> *Greek and Roman:* (Female) Carmentis, Circe, Hecate, and Mystis.
>
> *Germanic/Norse:* (Female): Eir, Saga, Vor.
>
> *Celtic:* (Female) Cerridwen, Danu, Nath.

Intelligence:

> *African:* (Female) Ogboinba.
>
> *Egyptian:* (Female) Sphinx, Tie; (Male) Toth, Horus.
>
> *Greek and Roman:* (Female) Apollonis, Erato, Harmonia, Minerva, Mnmosyne, Muses, Urania.
>
> *Germanic/Norse:* (Female) Nat.
>
> *Celtic:* (Female) Canola, Cerridwen, Sephira.

Weather:

> *African:* (Female) All-bringing-forth; Bunzi, Oya.
>
> *Egypt:* (Female) Nebt, Nephthys, Tefnut. (Male) Shu for air; Nuit (Female for Sky and Heavens).

Greek and Roman: (Female) Aura, Dais, Dione, Erato, Hera, Tempestates.

Germanic/Norse: (Female) Aslog, Frau, Holda, Sjora, Swan Maidens.

Celtic: (Female) Becuma, Cesair, Dawen, Nair.

Using Air in Magickal Operations

Like the other elements, air has three manifestations—mental, astral, and physical—when used in magick and ritual. We can visualize (mental), request the use of the energy (astral), or physically create air associations. Mental visualization can include wind, the movement of clouds, tornados, hurricanes, small dervishes, a summer breeze over fields, the rustling sound of leaves, the whistling or moaning sounds in the eaves, the path of a hot air balloon, or the filled sails of a sailboat (to name a few). Astrally we can use the sylphs, the elemental air association, to pull things toward us or push things away or simply "feel" the movement of air in our ritual circle. Additionally we've got all sorts of physical operations that can enhance mental/astral work, including writing a message on a paper airplane and letting it go from a high or windy place, writing on ribbons and tying them onto trees, blowing on our spellwork to fill it with the sacred breath of Spirit, creating magickal banners for protection and success and hanging them inside or outside of the home, and working with bells, singing bowls, wind instruments, or wind chimes that clear and energize the air around us. Favored incantations, invocations, and singing also exercise the magick of air. Air can also tell you if the Spirits you have called have entered the area or if your spell is "working" while you are in circle. This especially occurs when you work out-of-doors.

Many Witches work magick during storms to increase the power they feel they need to accomplish a particular goal. Naturally you have to be careful because storms (as much as we love them) pose a threat to human life. Standing outside in a thunderstorm holding up a metal rod would be sheer stupidity, as would planting oneself in the path of a tornado to obtain power. But placing a seven-day candle on an enclosed back porch or by the bay window in your apartment where it can "soak up" the power of the storm works extremely well. Even gentle storms contain useful energy—a snow that blankets the earth can be used for protection or to slow things down if events are moving too fast. Strong winds whistling around windows can be harnessed into a candle or other physical object, which in turn may be useful in trying to move a stagnant situation along or breathe new life into an old project. Magickal alphabets (see that heading) also fall under the air category. Only your imagination becomes the limit.

Element of Fire

Working with the element of fire may be more difficult for some of you than for others. Those who are not permitted open flame in their rooms or other areas of the house will have to be inventive. Don't feel bad. Certain members of the armed forces (depending on their location) and adults in other specialized environments due to either employment or housing restrictions have the same problem. That doesn't mean you can't use the fire sigils or deities. If you can visualize a flame in your mind, that's really all you need.

When we invite fire into our circle at the south quarter we are visualizing the eternal flame of Spirit. It never ever dies. Fire is the sizzle of creativity and the eruption of passion. Fire is also difficult to control, so you must always be extra cautious when working with living flame. Where water consumes, fire bites and gnaws. Don't forget that. With fire we have the legend of the phoenix, where we can rise from the ashes of what was and embrace what will be with joy, looking forward to the change.

Fire is strength, power, protection, and the ability to change from one state to another. It is enlightenment and extremely potent but, like air, it can represent truth and knowledge through purification. The kindling of a fire in many cultures relates to birth and death—the cycle of life—which is why Witches call the cross-quarters fire festivals. They are Candlemas, Beltane, Lammas, and Samhain. In almost every culture, fire is the representation of manifested deity. Fire is also the great destroyer.

The three zodiac signs relating to fire are Aries (for beginnings with inspirational fire), Leo (steadfast fire), and Sagittarius (changing fire). If you wanted to begin a project with zest and zeal, start when the moon is in Aries. The only problem with this sign, unlike the others, is that its energy tires out not long after it gets going. A second ritual or spell in another sign is usually required to carry on the work. When the moon is in Leo, magicks for courage, a happy home, and defending others work well. In Sagittarius, a jolly, social energy, work for expansion and adapting to circumstances.

Fire Symbols and How to Use Them

The alchemical sigil for fire is the upright triangle, a male symbol meaning action and movement. Remember, the gender association doesn't mean only boys can use the symbol—this is just a medieval way of categorizing energy that we never quite got away from. The upright triangle is the "burning way"—the path to truth, light, and transformation through self-motivated activity. Drawn in the magick circle it can be the

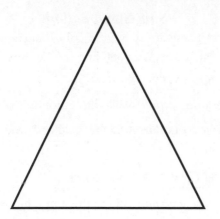

focus of manifestation, and in Greek was described as the "cosmic birth" (probably from what we now call the Big Bang Theory of universal creation). In some ceremonial circles it is called the "all-seeing eye," with nine beams of light drawn from the top point of the design. This is the eye of god/dess. In Egyptian mythology, the all-seeing eye of the God often belonged to the Goddess. Like the earth and air alchemical symbols, this one can be inscribed on candles, used in your BOS, sewn on altar cloths and robes, and activated in spells and rituals. With fire, there is no end to your creativity!

In European history, bonfires bound culture and religion together, especially on the solar holidays (eight High Holy Days). These conflagrations earned the title of "needfires" because at dawn all the fires in the home were extinguished. In a group celebration on top of a hill or elevated outdoor area, an appointed person would rub two sticks together to create the needflame, which was transferred to a large pile of wood, dried grasses, and herbs. Each person from the countryside would take a torch home to relight their own hearthfire. In some Craft traditions today, the fire candle in the altar setup is called the "needflame," and a cauldron fire, hearthfire, or bonfire is dubbed the "needfire."

Living fire in the modern circle is used in a variety of ways. The bonfires can be lit on the eight High Holy Days to invoke or banish; cauldron fires (with proper supervision, even for adults) might be the focus of dance magick, where the flame spirals to the beat of the music; or in a more sedate atmosphere as the center of petition magick. Outdoor grills or barbeque pits with hanging conveniences for pots provide a way to brew potions and notions of magickal interest. Hearthfires, should you be lucky enough to have a fireplace, can also provide a vehicle for the magick of the flame. Don't forget the ever-favorite candle or oil lamps (used historically before candles) with scented or colored oil for added effect.

Planetary Symbols of Fire

The most commonly associated celestial fire sigils are the planet Mars ($\mathrm{\male_{mars}}$) and the sun ($\odot$), both major players when it comes to natal and predictive astrology. No matter where they are, action is sure to follow. If you cannot use flame or candle, the Mars sigil will carry the magick through with the same intensity, and it gives an extra boost when inscribed on any candle. The sun represents your will and overall success and can be used in the same way. You can also focus the power of both sigils by linking their symbols with those of the other planets, or bind Mars (or the sun) with other magickal sigils of your choice.

Mars/Planetary Combinations

Note: These are suggested colors, but use what feels right to you depending upon the situation.

MARS ♂ WITH SUN ⊙

Resulting action: Action in will/success.

Associated colors: Red and orange/gold.

MARS ♂ WITH MOON ☽

Resulting action: Action in emotion/psychism.

Associated colors: Red and white or silver.

MARS ♂ WITH MERCURY ☿

Resulting action: Action in communication.

Associated colors: Red and yellow.

MARS ♂ WITH VENUS ♀

Resulting action: Action in social situations.

Associated colors: Red and pink or green.

MARS ♂ WITH JUPITER ♃

Resulting action: Action with expansion.

Associated colors: Red and violet.

MARS ♂ WITH SATURN ♄

Resulting action: Action with structure, or action to banish.

Associated colors: Red and midnight blue or black.

MARS ♂ WITH URANUS ♅

Resulting action: Action with change.

Associated colors: Red and light blue.

MARS ♂ WITH NEPTUNE ♆

Resulting action: Action in the arts or dreaming.

Associated colors: Red and aqua.

MARS ♂ WITH PLUTO ♇

Resulting action: Action to remove or banish in order to rebuild.

Associated colors: Red and black or brown.

Sun Combinations

Note: These are suggested colors, but use what feels right to you, depending on the situation.

SUN ☉ WITH MOON ☽

Resulting action: Will with emotion (balance).

Associated colors: Orange/gold and white or silver.

SUN ☉ WITH MERCURY ☿

Resulting action: Will with communication/focus.

Associated colors: Orange/gold and yellow.

SUN ☉ WITH VENUS ♀

Resulting action: Will with socialization/friendship.

Associated colors: Orange/gold and pink or green.

SUN ☉ WITH MARS ♂

Resulting action: Will with action.

Associated colors: Orange/gold and red.

SUN ☉ WITH JUPITER ♃

Resulting action: Will with expansion.

Associated colors: Orange/gold and violet.

SUN ☉ WITH SATURN ♄

Resulting action: Will with structure, will to banish.

Associated colors: Orange/gold and midnight blue or black.

SUN ☉ WITH URANUS ♅

Resulting action: Will with change.

Associated colors: Orange/gold and light blue.

Invoking fire pentacle, left, and banishing, right.

SUN ☉ WITH NEPTUNE ♆

Resulting action: Will with the arts, dreaming, transformation.

Associated colors: Orange/gold and aqua.

SUN ☉ WITH PLUTO ♇

Resulting action: Will to remove in order to rebuild.

Associated colors: Orange/gold and black/brown.

Invoking and Banishing Pentagrams of Fire

In ceremonial groups the Witch may stand at the south quarter and draw the invoking pentagram of fire to open the portal. When dismissing the quarter, the banishing pentagram of fire would follow. As with the other examples (earth and air), begin in the direction of the arrow on the figure pictured above and follow through until the drawing is completed. You might want to trace the ones in the book until you are comfortable with the idea.

When used in sigil magick, you can draw a flame in the center of the pentagram. To stop gossip, draw the banishing pentagram of fire with black indelible marker on the back of a white ceramic plate. Place the plate over the offending party's name, so that the pentagram is facing you when you look at it. If you don't know who started the rumor, write "The rumor of . . ." and then fill in the false accusation. Leave the plate on top of the rumor until circumstances fizzle.

Meditation of Fire

Although this is an outdoor meditation, you can change it to fit your circumstances if necessary. You will need your favorite powdered incense (not the self-lighting variety); sidewalk chalk (optional); a small grill; self-lighting charcoal (I don't recommend lighter fluid for anyone of any age); a grill lighter or long matches; a piece of paper on which you have written a special wish; and a selection of plain, small stones. Depending on your age, you may need your parents' permission to work with the grill. If they say no, don't sweat it, just do the ritual at noon under the sun.

First, draw a circle around yourself with the sidewalk chalk (if you can't do that, use your finger instead). Put the grill in the center of the circle. Make sure you can sit far enough away from the grill so that there is no chance of being burned. With the stones, lay out an upright triangle around the grill. Put a few pieces of charcoal in the grill (not too much, this isn't a barbeque for 100). Sprinkle your incense over the charcoal. In most magickal operations, the smoke from a fire represents your prayers moving from this plane of existence to the divine. Scented smoke is employed to draw the attention of pleasant spirits/angels who will help to move those prayers along.

Ground and center. Draw the invoking fire pentagram in the air over the grill. Take a deep breath and relax. Light the fire. As you watch the flames, think about what fire means: power, transformation, success, rising from difficulty, divine inspiration, creativity. Let your mind wander. Allow your thoughts to dance with the flames. When you have finished, repeat your wishes aloud and throw the paper into the fire. As you watch it burn, say: "Blessings and fire, higher and higher," until the paper is consumed. You might also chant the word *change*. When you are through, thank divinity and the element of fire. Wait until the fire dies down, then draw the banishing fire pentagram over the grill (not too close). *Note*: Do not leave the grill untended while it still contains the fire. You may choose to sit and simply enjoy the out-of-doors while you wait for the ashes to cool.

If you can't use fire in a literal sense, then close your eyes under the noon sun and work through the same mental associations. Hold the paper up to the sun and repeat your wish. You can use the same chant. Fold the paper and save it until you wish comes true, then dispose. Inside, you can use a tea candle in a cauldron rather than the outdoor grill idea.

Fire Correspondences

ZODIAC

Aries: Beginnings.

Leo: Fixed, Stability.

Sagittarius: Mutable.

COLOR

Red or orange.

WICCAN TOOL

Athame, wand, or sword, depending on your tradition.

ANGEL/GUARDIAN

Comets: Zikiel, Akhibel

Constellations: Kakabel, Rahtiel

Creativity: Samandriel

Divine knowledge: Zagzagel

Good causes: Nemamiah (warrior)

Fire, general: Nathaniel, Arel, Atuniel, Jehol, Ardarel, Gabriel, Seraph

Flame: El Auria, Uriel (same)

Inspiration: Hael

Light: Isaac, Gabriel, Mihr, Parvagigar, Raphael (Regent of the Sun), Uriel

Light of day: Shamshiel

Love and romance: Anael

North star: Abathur, Muzania, Arhum Hii

Song: Uriel, Radueriel, Israfel, Shemiel, Metatron

Stars: Kakabel, Kohabiel. Star of Love: Anael

Success and good fortune: Barakiel

Sun's rays: Schachlil

DEITY

African: (Female) Tsetse

Egyptian: (Female) Amit, gatekeeping goddesses, Sekhmet, Uatchet. (Male) Ra, Kephra, Atum, Toth (Inspiration).

Greek and Roman: (Female) Aetna, Hestia, Vesta. (Male) Hephaestos, Vulcan.

Germanic/Norse: (Female) Girda, Holla, Vana Mothers.

Celtic: (Female) Bried/Brigid, Tres Matres.

Fire in Magickal Operations

Under the earth and air categories we discussed the three primary uses of any element: mental, astral, and physical. Visualizations of fire (mental) are as varied as those of the other elements: candle flame, the sun, starlight, laser beam, campfire, cauldron fire, roaring inferno, the backyard grill, a chimera, leaping flames, or the steady pilot light in your stove, furnace, or water heater. Like the other elements, we can add the astral projection and the physical plane in fire magick. Astrally the salamanders, or fire elementals, can provide the energy and movement we need in that realm or you can simply "feel" the essence in the working. Physically we have the ability to make and tend a fire in a contained area, whether we're talking about a simple votive candle or lighting a ritual bonfire for a High Holiday. Although we don't create it, lightning also falls in this category, and can be used to add extra zap to holy water or other magickal projects or potions.

Fireworks can provide additional punch to any magickal working, though again, caution is mandatory and for the sake of your parents' sanity, stick with those items approved by your parents. Witches involved in ritual drama (rituals conducted like plays on stage) will use special effects such as flash paper, flash powder, flash cotton, and other illusionary marvels; however, all these items carry an element of danger that can't be discounted. Spices from the kitchen visually soup up a fire the same way without endangering anyone. Try pumpkin spice to create glorious colors in an outdoor fire. Coating logs or charcoal with sweet-smelling herbal mixtures or incenses also provide safe, interesting visual effects as well as create a pleasant, magickal atmosphere; however, read the package carefully. Some incenses contain a self-burning ingredient, which means that a charcoal brick to keep it going isn't required, and once lit it will burn on its own. You should always keep your face away from either type when burning, but use particular care with the self-burning variety. With the right conditions (which can happen all too often), fire can move faster than a cheetah.

In magick, Witches use fire to stir the passions and ignite creativity in oneself, to purify, to celebrate an event (the needfire), to actively release a magickal operation (such as burning a paper petition or using a sparkler), or to find solace and comfort in meditation by concentrating on a single flame. To light any object (candle, oil lamp, or bonfire) proclaims birth and transformation.

Like any magickal energy, each element has two sides, creation and destruction. Fire magick is used to destroy bad habits, consume negativity, and burn away those things that we no longer need in our lives. The most popular form of destructive fire involves petition magick, where-in the problem or difficulty is written on something flammable and offered to the fire for consumption. In most cases the flammable material is a piece of paper, though on occasion other things are burned such as photographs; bits of yarn, ribbon, or cloth; or images made of wood or wax. Of the four elements, fire is the most dangerous in a magick circle. Burning items can emit noxious fumes and wax images can billow into an inferno. Contained outdoor fires are recommended if you have any doubt whatsoever on how the material chosen will combust. Most Witches have castiron cauldrons (with lid) for limited indoor burning, and larger ones for out-of-doors. They may also have castiron chimeras for outdoor work. Keep in mind that these pots and other devices get very hot on the outside and you can burn yourself by touching them. Remember to place cauldrons on fire-safe tiles or cement, and always have a fire extinguisher nearby.

Many Witches place lighters under their altars so that fire is readily available. Some have pockets in their robes and keep the lighters safely tucked on their person. Few Witches use matches, believing that the sulfur on the match head contaminates the ritual circle/magickal operation.[46]

Element of Water

Water, symbolic of the Great Mother, is associated with birth and transformation. When we invite water into our circle at the west quarter, we are seeking the fountain of life and the source of all things. Water cleanses and purifies, representing our search for the secrets of life and death. In folklore, deep waters represent the depths of the human soul, the subconscious, and sometimes the realm of the dead (though earth caves have also been attributed to the cycle of death to life). Running water symbolizes the unending cascade of spiritual energy. Crossing a stream in outdoor ritual means that you wish to pass from the world of illusion into a higher spiritual state. Walking over a bridge can have the same effect. In the Greek culture, morning dew, collected as the sun rises, was thought to hold the magick of moonbeams on Earth, and was used to bless one's eyes as a medicinal aid for vision difficulties.

Looking at astrology, we have Cancer (water at its source), Scorpio (fixed or deep waters), and Pisces (water changing directions). All water signs have something in common: emotions. Cancer is nurturing, Scorpio is intense, and Pisces speaks of transformation and the visionary experience (looking at the big picture rather than losing yourself in minute detail). Each month the moon spends two and a half days in each sign of the zodiac. When she is in Cancer, you can work on emotional family issues or projects that need nurturing. When in Scorpio, the

moon gives you an extra punch of emotional intensity. Use Pisces for meditation, dream work, telepathy, and especially divination. Check your almanac to find out when the moon visits these signs this month.

Water Symbols and How to Use Them

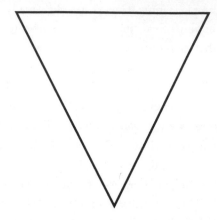

In alchemical magick the inverted triangle stands for water and the divine feminine, and takes center stage in most creation myths.

Other Water Symbols

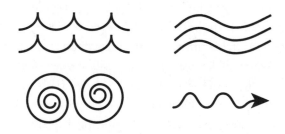

The first symbol (top left) is a standard water sigil. Studies of European antiquity tell us that moving and especially salt water could wash away all evil spirits, hence its inclusion in most recipes for holy water. The second drawing (top right) is Chinese and means "flowing water." The third (bottom left), used from the Bronze Age onward, found in Greece and Sweden, speaks of the sea and how manifestation works.

Invoking water pentacle, left, and banishing, right.

In magick, this design shows the cycle of what we do. We start with a thought (or prayer) —beginning at the center of the spiral on the left, which spirals outward to the universe, then condenses to become physical matter or our goal. This symbol is the flowing of alchemical magick. The last picture (bottom right) means "directed current" or showing the water element where to flow. The Voodoo vèvès, magickal drawings used to invoke deities/planetary powers, trace their origin back to alchemical pictures like those above. They believe that water signifies the birth seas, where all energy first "becomes," much like the teachings of the Kabbalah, where the top of the tree is the great "unmanifest" or the "great void." Both of these ideas (the Jewish mysticism and Voudon religion) begin with the sacredness of water and its ability to cleanse, purify, and move.

Invoking and Banishing Pentagrams of Water

In ceremonial Wicca, the invoking pentagram of water is traced in the air at the west quarter. Sometimes, rather than using a blade, rod, or wand, the Witch might use a small broom laced with holy water. To release the energy of water, draw the banishing pentagram of water.

If you are trying to bring rain during a drought, draw the invoking water pentacle on the ground with a broom and place a water sigil or even a bowl of water in the center. Raise your broom to the heavens as you ask Spirit for relief and the right amount of water for yourself as well as those in your community. Done in this way, you aren't putting anyone in danger by "messing with the weather" because you have asked Spirit to guide the magick in a way that will be good for all. *Caution:* Weather magick does not do well with an audience. If you are going to work it, do it in private. Water plays a prevalent role in Voodoo and Hoodoo practices not only as a cleansing device, but as a dowsing mechanism to find the correct placement of vèvès.

Meditation of Water

You will need a white ceramic bowl, a small bottle of spring water, three gold coins (if possible), and an indelible marker. This meditation can be performed either inside or outside of your house.

Draw a circle on the ground with your finger. With the black indelible marker, draw the double spiral sigil inside the bowl on the bottom. Allow to dry. Place the bowl in the center of the circle. Sit down beside the bowl and fill with the spring water. Take three deep breaths, then place your hands in the water. Close your eyes and think about the element. Let your mind do a little free association—birth, purification, emotions, the spring of life, etc. In Egypt, water was thought to wash away the sins of one's ancestors (which is probably where the idea of Christian baptism came from). You might ponder on the priestesses and priests of Isis using water in their rituals to the Queen of Heavenly Magick.

When you are finished, open your eyes, sit back, and take a few deep breaths. For many, this meditation leaves them feeling as if a crushing weight has lifted from their shoulders. You might feel that way, too. Now blow on the water and watch the spiral drawing appear to move. This is the activation of the sigil (or you could choose to draw the invoking air pentagram over the water). Pick up the three coins, and ask Spirit to provide prosperity for yourself and your family. One at a time, throw them into the water. As the water moves, think of your wish spiraling out to Spirit, and then manifesting on the earth plane. The practice of throwing coins or other valuables into a fountain or pool of water dates to early Celtic beliefs.[47]

Thank the element of water and Spirit for the abundance that will now flow toward you. Pour the water onto a deserving plant. Wipe out the bowl to use another time, either for meditation, making holy water, or other magickal purpose.

Water Correspondences

ZODIAC

Cancer: Beginnings.

Scorpio: Fixed and intense.

Pisces: Transformative (mutable).

COLOR

Green or blue, depending upon the tradition.

WICCAN TOOL

Cauldron or chalice.

ANGEL/GUARDIAN

Aquatic animals: Manakel

Baptisms and wiccanings: Raphael, Barpharanges

Beauty: Camael

Birth and conception: Gabriel

Compassion: Rachmiel, Raphael

Deep seas: Tamiel, Rampel, Rahab

Fish: Gagiel, Arariel, Azareel

Gratitude: Shemael

Hail: Bardiel, Nuriel, Yurkami

Healing: Shekinah

Intuitive powers: Sachiel

Overcome jealousy: Balthial

Liberation: Colopatiron

Longevity: Mumiah, Scheiah, Rehail

Love: Raphael, Rahmiel, Theliel, Donquel, Anael, Liwet, Mihr

Mercy: Michael, Gabriel, Rhamiel, Rachmiel, Zadkiel

Peace: Gavreel

Platonic love and friendship: Mihr

Positive, loving thoughts: Hahaiah

Protection for travel over water: Elemiah

Rain: Matarel, Mathariel Ridia, Matriel (chant these four in sequence), Dara

Rivers: Trsiel, Rampel, Dara

Running streams: Nahaliel

Science and medicine: Mumiah

Sea: Rahab

Showers: Zaa'fiel

Snow: Shalgiel, Michael

Waters: Phul

Water insects: Shakziel

DEITY

African: (Female) Abuk, Asase Yaa, Aziri, Dada, Nimm, Oshun (Rivers and Streams), Yemaya (Sea).

Egyptian: (Female) Akhet, Celestial waterer, Hast, Heqet, Meri, Nephthys, Satet, Sphinx, Uat. (Male) Tefnut, Khnum (god who controlled the Nile).

Greek and Roman: (Female) Acantha, Alcyone, Cleone, Dero, Hippo, Hypereia, Ianassa, Therma. (Male) Neptune, Poseidon.

Germanic/Norse: (Female) Atlaq, Holda, Lady Wen, Matrona, Norns (Fates who are Skuld, Verdandi, and Urd), Wave Maidens. (Male) Donar, Ull.

Celtic: (Female) Bried/Brigid (considered fire and water goddess), Boann, Danu, Eona, Lady of the Lake, Tres Mares. (Male) Condatism, Manannan.

Magickal Water Recipes

You will find several different kinds of magickal waters used in Craft practices. Although the ingredients may be different, all magickal waters are purified, blessed, and empowered within a magick circle, sacred space, or ritual environment. The water is then used to purify a person, place, or thing, as well as work some type of additional magick (depending upon the recipe).

HOLY WATER

The general all-purpose variety of magickal water, made with only two basic ingredients: three pinches of salt to a cup of water. Recipes vary per Witch as some prefer additional ingre-

dients such as rose water, a particular herb, or a drop of their favorite magickal oil. The words and motions used to banish negativity, bless and empower the water also differ from Witch to Witch. The consecration of water to extend purification and blessings does not belong to Catholicism alone—ancient Egyptian, Sumer, Hindu, Greek, and Roman (to name a few) used it too. In time you will have your own recipe for holy water, but for now, let's show you how to make holy water using some of the things we've already learned when studying the elements.

SUPPLIES: A small bowl of water, a small bowl of salt, a bell, and a container in which to save the water. Most Witches use either spring water, or water from a pure, running stream. Although the regular table variety salt works fine, you can also use sea salt (sold by your local grocer).

INSTRUCTIONS: Cast a magick circle. With your finger, draw the inverted triangle representing water on the center of your altar. Place the cup of water in the center of the triangle. Place a small bowl of salt beside it. Ground and center, then take several deep breaths and relax. Draw the banishing water pentagram over the bowl of water, saying: "I cleanse thee of all negativity in this world and all others, so mote it be." Visualize white light surrounding the bowl of water. Draw the banishing earth pentagram over the bowl of salt, and say: "I cleanse thee of all negativity in this world and all others, so mote it be." Visualize white light surrounding the bowl of salt. Again, using the banishing earth pentagram, repeat the process over the container that will eventually hold the water for storage.

Hold the water bowl in both hands, and say:

Sweet Spirit (or name a deity)*, I ask thee for your blessings upon this water. I consecrate it in your name. May it be used only for good and its power be magnified tenfold.*

Blow three times on the water, imagining that the white light is sparkling in the water. Replace the bowl of water in the triangle and draw the invoking water pentagram over the bowl. Pick up the bowl of salt and say the same thing, blow on the salt, set the bowl down, and draw the invoking earth pentagram over the bowl. Don't forget to imagine the white light infusing the salt in the same glittering way. Bless the storage container exactly as you did the salt. *Note:* If you choose to add extra ingredients, such as rose water or a drop of your favorite oil, they will need to be cleansed and blessed as well. Ring the bell three times.

Slowly add three pinches of salt to the bowl of water, stirring clockwise three times with your athame or your finger. Here is where you add any additional ingredients, three drops (or pinches), stirring clockwise three times. (If you have added an herb, be sure to add a step to strain the water before it goes into the bottle or container. This will also require that you cleanse the strainer.) If you are permitted to use an athame, hold firmly in both hands over the bowl of water. Slowly lower the athame into the water, firmly saying:

> *As the rod is to the God, so the chalice*
> *is to the Goddess, and together they are one.*
> *I empower thee for positive work in perfect love*
> *and perfect trust. So mote it be.*

(The "one," of course, being the totality of Spirit.) Imagine white sparks flying out of the water and your entire altar vibrating with positive, magickal energy. Ring the bell three times. Draw an equal-armed cross in the air over the water to seal the energies. Transfer to the storage container. Close. Repeat the equal-armed cross procedure, and say: "This container is sealed. So mote it be." Thank the elements of earth and water, thank deity, and release the circle.

No matter the kind of water you make, you can always follow the procedure above and change the words in the empowering paragraph. In the recipes below I've added a few suggestions on what the water is used for to help you.

Crystal Water: Used for healing. Cleanse a crystal, then bless it and empower it under the full moon for special gifts of the Goddess or for healing work. Add to the water before the salt.

Fire Water: Used to turn negativity away or bring love and creativity. Cleanse a taper candle of your color choice, bless it and empower it under the sun. Douse the burning candle in the water rather than using the athame. Don't forget to use the invoking fire pentagram when you light the candle, saying: "Spirits of fire, work my will by my desire!"

Florida Water: ½ gallon of 90-proof alcohol; 1 ounce of lavender; 1 ounce bergamot; 1 dram of lemon; 1 dram of cloves; 1 gallon of water. Used to cleanse homes, businesses, magickal tools, and candles. Can also be purchased at a botanica.

Love Water: Used in love spells and glamouries. You can add rose water or live rose petals. If you use the rose petals, allow the water and petals to sit for one hour before straining and bottling.

Prosperity Water: Used for creating prosperity and abundance in the home or workplace. Add three drops of juice from a freshly squeezed orange per one cup of water. You can also add a dash of cinnamon.

Thunder Water: Leave the water outside in a thunder and lightening storm during the empowerment process of the recipe. Used to ward off the baddest of the bad. Candles can also be empowered in this way for a variety of purposes. Once, to help a friend conquer writers' block, I placed several candles outside, asking that the spirits instill the candles with power, movement, and creativity. He wrote 7,000 words in two days (where normally he wrote less than 500). You can also add thunder water to any spell or ritual involving sports or action, or to ward off aggression.

Putting the Elements Together

So far we've only worked with the elements separately or, in the case of holy water, with two elements at a time. Now we have to put them together and work in a concentrated whole. In almost all sabbats, most esbats, and a variety of working rituals, most Witches cast the circle and then call the four quarters. Those with a more ceremonial taste will begin with the east, and those that prefer the shamanic energies begin in the north. Regardless, the one thing all Witches are taught is to respect the energies that they call. They are also taught to draw power from the elements and direct that energy (linking the power of the element with mind and the tool—the rod, wand, or athame) in their workings. If you practiced the element meditations I gave you, then you have experienced drawing power from that element. When you became the element, you drew its power to you. Drawing power and raising your own power are two different things. First you draw, then you raise, and when you raise you use a minimum of your own energy unless this is something really, really important. If you do it any other way, you will be exhausted and/or giddy, take your pick.

When we call the four quarters we are drawing the energy of that element into the circle. We are also asking that while the drawing process occurs, we are protected and that the opening allows only what we desire to enter the circle. As each quarter is opened, you should feel the energy pattern of that element. If you don't, keep practicing, you'll eventually get it. When we call Spirit either through statement, a motion, or stance, or through invocation and poetry, we are calling Spirit into our circle and into us. There can be no harm here because there is nothing more perfect than God. When we draw the energy of Spirit into us (such as Drawing Down the Moon), then we are completing a unified energy pattern—the elements, God, and us—working together to create something positive. In sixteenth- and seventeenth-century magickal writings (and even in some of the nineteenth-century ones), we find that many of the practitioners felt they had to coerce the "spirits" in order to get something magickally accomplished. Today with our advancements in psychology, medical science, chemistry, and yes, even spirituality, we know that we don't have to lure anything or trick it into doing what we want. There is order and there are patterns in all things. We don't have to be superstitious about manipulating energy.

The Sigils of the Combined Four Elements and How to Use Them

One of the most popular symbols in element magick is that of the hexagram, which is the fire and water triangles placed one on top of the other.

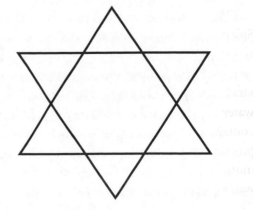

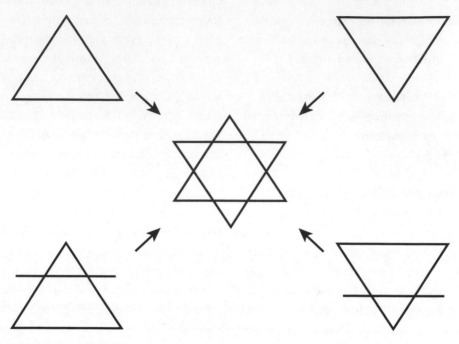

Known as the hexagram or alchemist's symbol, this symbol represents the four elements.

Uniting fire and water (Celtic), water and ice (Norse), or force and form (ceremonial), gives you a symbol representing the four elements—known as the hexagram or alchemist's symbol (see above).

Look familiar? The earliest examples of the hexagram date back to approximately 700 B.C. By 10 B.C., legend has it that the biblical King Solomon, son of David and Bathsheba, exorcised negativity with this symbol until his death. From this, the six-pointed star was known as the Solomon's Seal or *sigillum Salomnis*. It has also been called *sutum Davidis* (David's Shield).[48] Today it appears on the coat of arms of the state of Israel, who refers to the symbol as the Star of Zion or Star of David. Medieval grimoires figure various spells and seals using this sigil, which are unrelated to the currently structured religion of Judaism (depending on to whom you speak on the subject). Although the historians do not dispute Solomon's magickal expertise, they are di-

vided on what symbol he used. Many claim that it was the pentagram, not the hexagram, embossed on a magick ring with the name of his god on the reverse.[49] This is one of those cases where it appears you can believe what you want to until someone unearths additional facts. Regardless, the Jews began using the hexagram as a religious seal denoting their belief system as early as 90 B.C.[50] In medieval alchemy the hexagram also stood for the fifth element, Spirit (called *quintessence* by Agrippa).

Now that we've talked so much about it, how do we use it? The hexagram gives you command over the four elements and stands for the fifth element, that of Spirit. Therefore, if you wanted to invoke the elements and Spirit all at one time, you would draw the hexagram in the air over the object. This isn't as hard as it sounds. Draw the fire triangle first, from the point down, then over (clockwise), then back up. Second, the water triangle from the bottom point up (clockwise), then over, then down on top of the first triangle. Practice. You'll get it. To banish, draw counterclockwise.

You can also use the hexagram to invoke the powers of six of the seven classical planets. The classical planets are the sun, the moon, Mercury, Venus, Mars, Jupiter, and Saturn. They are called classical because for a long, long time no one knew that Uranus, Neptune, and Pluto were out there floating around. Therefore, magick done by the ancients until fairly recently (in magickal terms) consisted only of those mentioned. (Yes, I know that scientifically the sun and moon aren't planets, but this is acceptable in astrology and magick.)

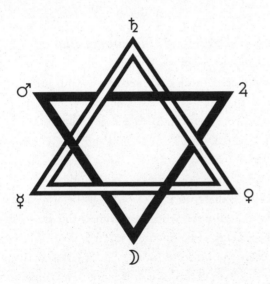

Remember the Elixir of the Moon spell earlier in this book? This one is much like it. We choose something we want to work on, let's say finding faithful friends, and then we invoke the hexagram by stating aloud what we are looking for as it matches the planets. First, cast a magick circle and call the quarters. Invite the Lord and Lady into the area. State aloud exactly what you want: a new friend that is good for you (and that the relationship will also be good for this new

person). Draw the hexagram in the air with your finger, saying:

Saturn for reliability, Venus for loving friendship, Mercury for good communication (then finish that triangle with your finger)*, I invoke my will. The moon for a positive psychic bond, Mars to bring this friend to me, and Jupiter for a faithful, spiritual companion. I invoke my emotions.*

Blow three short breaths in the air and say:

Earth, air, fire, water, I draw forth the energies needed to work this spell. No more, no less than is required. Hexagram, please work for me. Blessings of Spirit upon me. As I will, so mote it be.

If, for some reason, you need to send this person away, do the spell using the banishing hexagram. You could also draw this sigil on a piece of paper, and on the back write: "In the name of Spirit, I call the perfect friend to me." Then pass the four elements over the paper. Blow on it, then seal with an equal-armed cross in the air over the paper. As with all spells (especially those involving other people), you must be patient until the work can manifest. Don't expect to open the front door immediately after you cast the spell and trip over your new friend. This spell is best performed during a waxing moon. Oh, and be careful—sometimes Spirit thinks that the best friend you could have is a kitty or puppy, so if you want a person, you will have to be clear on that issue.

Elemental Plane

Many magickal people believe that there are several dimensions other than our own. They also believe that the dimension we live in vibrates at a lower frequency, which allows all manner of things (and people) to appear solid. Science tells us that all things are made up of energy, which moves (vibrates), and that although this book you hold in your hand appears solid and unmoving, the atoms (and their parts) are quite busy. Although magickal people have believed this all along—which is the basis for their enchantment—science has just now caught up with us.

The other dimensions, they say, vibrate at a faster rate. One of these dimensions, the one right above ours, is called the elemental plane, and it contains the energy patterns or blueprints of everything on the earth plane (the one we live in). The book is solid and physical here, but on the elemental plane the book is really a collection of elements joined together—a pattern. The book is on this plane because it has a pattern in the elemental one.

Above the elemental plane is the astral plane, with an even higher vibration. This is where our thoughts, images, desires, daydreams, themes, and concepts go when we create them.[51] Here's where things get confusing. Some people believe that your thoughts go through the elemental plane and into the astral plane, where others believe that your thoughts go directly to the astral plane, but the patterns coalesce on the elemental plane, and then return to the physical. By now you are probably scratching your head and saying, so this matters? Why should I care where they go? As long as I get what I want, who cares?

We've discussed Dion Fortune's advice of sending energy "up," working "above" to make things happen in the material realm. All humans work magick, whether they know it or not. Some seem to be able to manifest what they want faster than others. Once we realize that there is a method to manifestation through magickal study, things can happen for us a lot faster. Tie that magick to spirituality and we are more likely to live in

harmony through most of our lives *and* accomplish our missions in life at the same time. This idea of sending and receiving in magick is the basis of alchemical change and relates to our discussion on quantum physics, wherein magick occurs on the subquantum level. Let's do a few runthroughs using the astral and elemental planes that you can add to any spell, meditation, or ritual.

Exercise 1: Perfect Peace

Close your eyes and empty your mind. Now let your mind go as high as it can. Not a "place"—a feeling of perfection. Hold this feeling as long as you can. Practice this exercise every day. You will be able to keep that "perfect peace" longer each time you practice.

Exercise 2: Harmonic Planes

Complete exercise 1, and, while your eyes are still closed, think of something in your life that is not in harmony. This can be a person, place, thing, or situation. As if you are looking on from a distance, watch your mind slip down to meet that situation. This may take a few tries, maybe several until you observe this "slipping" process. Notice that you don't come all the way down. Like a climber who has reached the peak of a mountain, you slip only so far but you do not reach the bottom. Notice also that as you observe the situation, you do not "feel" like you did when you tried to reach the realm of perfect peace. You may, in your mind, see shadows of movement, cloudiness, or sense a vibration that isn't quite right. Like the climber, go back up to the top, to perfect peace. Think of that situation linked to harmony. *Become* harmony in your mind. Hold this as long as you can. You will sense movement in the planes below the perfect one. This is the reorganization of the energy patterns, which will then rearrange the situation on the earth plane. When you reach the earth plane you may sense a quick feeling of "muddiness." That's because it's denser here, and you're working to correct a problem, which you are now sensing (energy-wise) more than you did before. Take a deep breath and open your eyes. Practice this exercise every day. There is always something to fix, renew, or change. Continue to work on reaching harmony in your life in this way.

Several esoteric study programs list more levels or "planes" than just the three we've used here, but this is a good start, and for some of you, it will be all you ever need. The more you practice this exercise, the better your magickal expertise will be.

Manifestation Exercise 1: Working for Information

Finding information that you need is the easiest of the manifestation exercises, because we are dealing with thought and communication, not the density of a mountain. Close your eyes. Find the "perfect peace." Sometimes it helps if you visualize a color. Gold works for me, I have no idea why. It just came to me one day, and stuck with me, though sometimes the color mixes with an almost translucent white. State precisely what information you need. Mentally let go.

That's all there is to it. After a while you will be so accomplished at this that you need only close your eyes, state the need, and in no time at all, the information will come to you. In our example here, you reached toward perfection. Perfection searched the energy patterns on the elemental plane, and then sent that information on to you in the physical plane. Two things are required of you: that you be patient until the energy can reach you, and that you are honest in the use of that information.

This technique works especially well for research papers, finding the next subject you should study to advance your spirituality, infor-

mation on an illness and healing to help a sick person, finding a college that's right for you, or even using it in a shopping spell to find the best deal on a rental tux or dress for the prom, getting the best buy on that new stereo you want, or choosing a video game that you'll like once you open the package. You can also use this technique before reading any divination tool, followed by a request that you relay what you see correctly. Asking for other people is also okay. Let's say your father has been looking for information relating to his job and he is frustrated because he can't find it. Use the same technique, asking that the information be given to your dad. If you trust in the process, it will work for you, and the more you practice, the faster the information will come.

Manifestation Exercise 2: Working for a Physical Object

This one is a little more difficult because the energy pattern will be denser than that of pure thought. Find a picture in a magazine or newspaper that closely resembles something you would like to have. Start with a small item that you feel is a necessity. Look at the picture for a few minutes. Think about how the item will feel in your hands. Is it rough? Smooth? Hard or soft? If you had to draw its energy pattern, what kind of design do you think it might be? It's okay to use your imagination. Now close your eyes and think, "I need (name the item)." Go to perfection—that feeling of perfect peace. Project the picture in your mind of the item out into that feeling of peace. Don't fill your head with worries about how you will get it or how you will pay for it. Just project the need for the item. Now think of the projection sinking into the elemental plane and taking on its individual energy pattern, then think of the item descending to you. Remember what you thought that item would feel like in your hands. Project the idea one last time into the area of perfect peace, and you'll feel your mind move up of its own accord. Let the thought go. Open your eyes. Take a deep breath and relax.

Once you get the hang of this technique there is no end to what you can manifest; however, the longer you work, the less material things you'll want, not because you have them all, but because your inner self realizes you don't need them. If you have a problem with impulse shopping, you'll notice a distinct change in your buying pattern. This exercise works especially well if you are in need of food, clothing, shelter, or medical supplies, even if you are a beginner. Your call for the basics of life will be provided. Just trust in the process.

Manifestation Exercise 3: Healing

Go to that feeling of perfect peace and imagine yourself vibrating in total harmony—that everything wrong is fixed. Sit restfully until you can't hold that feeling any longer. Take a deep breath and open your eyes. If you are doing healing work for someone else, take a good look at their picture until you are confident that you can see them in your mind. It's okay if they appear fuzzy. If you can't see a picture of them, think about how they feel to you when you are around them. What is their personal energy pattern? Go to your perfect peace and project that person into that harmonious energy. Go down a notch and see the changes taking place in their energy pattern. Go down to the earth plane and imagine them smiling and being happy and well. Go once more to the perfect peace and envision them once again as healthy and in tune with the perfect peace. Take a deep breath and open your eyes. Practice this technique every day (three times a day if the person is really sick) until they get better.

The elemental plane is thought to hold all energy patterns for what is on Earth, including nature spirits, faeries, and devas (often referred to as "elementals").

Elementals

From the twelfth century onward, European scholars seized upon the writings of early Greek philosophers (alive at the beginning of the Common Era) to fuel their own ideas of the universe and how it ran. From this information sprang the European grimoires, the books of magick. Earlier we discussed how the Greek Pliny, Manilius, and others believed that everything was made of living energy, and that each object had its own energy pattern. Their science, however, was not as advanced as ours, so what they didn't understand took on (in some cases) fictional theories mixed with romanticism. Even those cultures before the Greeks turned things they couldn't understand into something tangible (the belief in dragons, for example, especially in the Chinese culture). When a group of people believes something exists, then puts a physical manifestation to it (a drawing, a statue, even a song or legend that is repeated often), then that thoughtform takes on a life of its own. The pattern is made. Even if it doesn't exist here in precisely the way we composed it, it can exist on the elemental plane because something that is associated with it exists here in the physical world.

If this is confusing, think of the fire dragon. Fire is fire. If a group of people choose to give the element of fire a personality (that of a dragon), that doesn't stop the basic element of fire from being here, on the earth plane. To those who do not believe, the fire will look like a bunch of flames dancing around, but to the Chinese, who see a dragon form romping through their imaginations, it isn't hard for them to bring that personality to the earth plane. They have created the pattern of the dragon, superimposed it over the element, given it a personality, and believed that this was so. The more people that believe in a thoughtform, the stronger it gets. Older Crafters (those traditionally trained) say, "We need the gods to survive, and the gods need us to continue. There is no part of us that is not of the gods."[52]

This is why leaders of religious dogmas don't want you to believe in anything but what they tell you, and is the basis for smashing the gods and goddesses of other cultures, the disposing of saints and martyrs, the outlawing of magick, the refusal to work with magick of any kind, and the murder of people who don't see things their way. They fear the power of your belief because you can take that power and turn on them when you realize that spirituality has gone out the window and the money bags are flowing in. The fewer people that believe the way they do, the weaker the dogma becomes. Hence the idea of frightening you with demons, the devil, and hell to keep you under their control. Gotta keep the followers in line, don't ya know.

Some of you are saying, "Look, I've seen fire lots of times, and it never looked like a dragon to me." Fine. You aren't cuing in on the idea of a dragon, so you won't see it. Of the four Chinese dragons, the air dragon is the easiest to see. Watch an oncoming storm and look for the dragon. You'll see it, and when you do, you will be amazed. Stare at a bonfire, and sooner or later, you'll see the Chinese fire dragon. Watch particularly big waves from the shore, and suddenly the water dragon will appear. Earth dragons sleep in the mountains and are on parade during an earthquake, but if you look very closely you can see them breathe as they snooze.

From these Greek and European renaissance thinkers came four terms that you will see in the Craft: sylphs, salamanders, undines, and gnomes. Like the Chinese dragon elementals, they are romanticized energy patterns of the elements of air, fire, water, and earth, and because they have been used frequently in magickal lodges, esoteric traditions, and Witchcraft for almost two thousand years (going back to the Greeks, at least), they are as real as the rain that falls from the sky. You just have to look for them to see them. Because the elementals are energy, they should be viewed as neither good nor bad—the same way we view the basic pattern of an element. Fire can burn you, or it can heat your home. Air can descend on a town with tornado force or gently push the sails of a boat on a brilliantly sunny day. What is made perfectly clear in occult practices, however, is that humans should never mistreat, disrespect, or lie to an elemental. For some practitioners of the Craft, working with the four elementals are part of their basic study, where other groups and traditions might recognize their existence but don't necessarily use them in magick, choosing to work with the basic element pattern rather than the romanticized version. If an elemental is constructed, it is usually something of their own design, rather than one they've read about.

Each elemental spirit embodies its own special energy. The gnomes are the "knowing ones," from the Greek *gnoma*, meaning "knowledge." Undine is from the Latin *unda*, meaning "wave," and therefore these spirits are said to control the waters of the earth. Sylph is from the Greek *silphe*, and the word means "butterfly." These spirits control all winds. Finally, the salamander comes from the Greek word *salambe*, meaning "fireplace."[52] These spirits control all manner of flame and combustion. All can be invoked through the use of the pentagram or the hexagram. Some magickal practitioners believe that the four elementals represent four worlds, each having their own reigning king.

You don't have to use any elemental thought-form that you don't want to, and you shouldn't use any that you haven't researched, especially if you are digging through old grimoires looking for material. The medieval and Renaissance minds were different (in some respects) than the mind of a twenty-first-century human being. Remember, up until the fifteenth century, they didn't believe germs existed, and many doctors in the nineteenth century thought it was an okay thing to bleed you to death with leeches if you were sick. And sterilize tools? You can thank Clara Barton and Florence Nightingale during the mid-1800s for that feat of magick. So even though that old grimoire from the sixteenth century looks perfectly yummy when it comes to playing with various elementals, do your homework first. The old saying goes: *Don't call up what you can't put down.*

Faeries and Devas

Although you may think that all faeries and devas (both nature spirits) are all cute and cuddly, they're not, and there's one thing you should never do—and that's cross one! No fibbing, cheating, or any underhanded behavior whatsoever. If you think you can't be good, don't venture into the realm of faery magick. If you will recall, even Tinkerbell had her vicious side, and the faery population of Shakespeare's *A Midsummer Night's Dream* were not particularly enamored with humans. Sir Arthur Conan Doyle, the famed author of the Sherlock Holmes adventures, literally lost his reputation over them. When it comes to faeries, tread carefully. As the story goes, if you force them to choose between one of their own kind and a human, we mere mortals are almost always toast.

Now that I've gotten your attention, let's talk faery. Faery energy is very much a part of modern Wicca, Druidism, and Norse belief systems. Faeries either like you or they don't. They'll either talk to you or they won't. They're not particularly dependable unless you can somehow prove that you're the dependable, honest, and upstanding type. If you have fey (meaning faery) blood running in your veins, you have a better chance at having some type of relationship, unusual as it may be. You think I'm kidding? Not on your life. Above all, you must have patience when dealing with the Sidhe (pronounced *shee*, of Celtic derivation). There are two types, the English ones invented by Rudyard Kipling and the Irish ones, which are the Sidhe. The English ones particularly like outdoor offerings of milk and honey, and their sacred wooded triad is the oak, ash, and thorn. Since this seems to translate well for any faery or dryad, you should be safe with these offerings. Maybe.

Historically, this faery stuff was deadly serious, to the point of very frightening things perpetrated by superstitious humans as a result of their belief in said faeries. Not only did such a belief ruin the chance of home rule in Ireland in the late 1880s (the opponents against home rule claimed that since the greater population believed in the faery folk, they could not govern themselves), some of the superstitions also led to serious injury and death, especially to rural children. Although we think it an interesting tale now, many people in medieval Ireland believed that their children could be "changlings"—a human taken by the sidhe and a sidhe put in its place—and, to get rid of the faery energy, they would use fire. Logically, this did not sit extremely well with English Parliament, who could care less about children and used such incidents to enhance their political desires. As a result of the political home rule fracas, the Church declared war on paganism in general, hoping to suck up Irish and English money while they watched the chips fall where they may. Obviously, faery stuff was very serious business, indeed.[54]

Like many nouns, the word *faery* means different things to different cultures. In England, the first mention of faeries appears in the *Anglo-Saxon Chronicles* (800 C.E.), with writings related to charms against elf-shot, and the earliest origins for the stereotypical image of the faery as a small humanlike creature with wings comes from ancient Mediterranean art in Etruscan tomb paintings dating to 600 B.C.[55] These fantastical little creatures were known as the Lasa.

A vast amount of folklore has developed from all corners of the world; however, Europe harbors more legends about faeries than any other area. The word *faery* is actually a collective term that loosely weaves several different kinds of unusual creatures together. Faeries come in all shapes, sizes, colors, and personalities, though often they are depicted as smaller than the human. There are nice ones and nasty ones, invisible ones and those you can plainly see. Some faeries are silly, some industrious, and most are mischievous. They can be loyal and helpful if treated with proper respect. In many stories, faeries are tied to the earth, nature, and the cycles of the planet. Some think they live in another dimension and the doorway to their home lies deep within the arms of the Earth Mother.

The word *faery* comes from late Latin *fata*, which is related to *fatum*, meaning "fate." The word also means enchantment, magickal inhabitants of such a land, or the collective unconscious of nature. Other words that relate to the faery are *fays* and *fees* (French).[56] Many theories have been advanced by folklorists to account for the origin of the concept of the faery. Some believe that the idea of the faery grows out of folk memories of the original inhabitants of a country conquered by the present (or a past) people, where those conquered fled and hid, attacking for as long as they could in the dead of night, giving these real people a mysterious, mythical aura. Conversely, some of these hideaways could have been helpful, working at night (as in the Girl Scout Brownie story) then stealing away before dawn. The offering of bread and cheese did not go into a faery tummy, but that of a real live person. When studying Irish folklore and learning about the Sidhe, this might be very true. The word *Sidhe* or *side* is plural for the Irish *sid* or *siod*, which means a round barrow, mound, or hill and the home of the Tuatha de Danann, the divine race of Old Irish mythology who were eventually conquered by another race of people.[57] The Irish called the land of the faeries Tir-nan-og, meaning "Land of Everlasting Youthful Ones." The Welsh labeled the faeries "the Mothers" or "the Mother's Blessing," and believed that faeryland was a place ruled by feminine compassion, a principle stemming from their original matrilineal society.[58]

Other folklorists judge that faeries are the discarded gods and goddesses of another time, whose memory lies in the tradition of a family unit, but the original meanings of rituals and magick associated with those practices has been lost. Many Pagan deities switched from god/desses to nature spirits, such as the Roman Fanus (Greek satyr Pan), who morphed into fauns, a general word for woodland spirits.[59]

The third explanation for faeries, and one held by many magickal people, dates back to the origins of the human, when all things on the planet were thought to have a living energy associated with them (called animism).

Putting this information together, we have several types of faery energy: those that constitute a race of people (such as the Sidhe of Ireland, the Lasa of Italy, and the dwarves of Germany), those that are connected with a place (such as mountains and streams), an element (earth = gnomes; fire = salamanders; water = undines; and air = sylphs), an event (such as the banshee that warns of the impending death of a family member), or nature itself (Green Man, flower faeries, tree elves, etc.). Regardless of the type of faery, time is unimportant to them, as they never grow old, get sick, or die. Some folklorists think the idea of never-never land actually belongs to Egyptian history, and comes from the ancient word *nefernefer*, the Egyptian word for "paradise" (meaning "doubly beautiful"). In magick, it is believed that faeries have control over time and that they can suspend it completely if they desire.

Occasionally you will read or hear about a faery ring or circle. These are dark green circles in the grass or weeds of a meadow, lawn, or field, caused by a fungus. Sometimes the ring is surrounded by mushrooms. Legend has it that this is the ritual circle of the faeries, a place of reverence, dancing, and merriment.[60] All legends agree that one should never disturb such a place. The faery wind (or whirling dervish) is that mini swirl of wind on a calm day that picks up bits of leaves, flower petals, and other tiny debris, dancing across the road or skipping through the meadow. If you are working outside and the wind appears close to you, it is said that these are the nature faeries lending energy to your task. Scientifically, these winds are created by air currents, downdrafts, and wind shear. Others believe that the faery host are passing through, leaving blessings in their wake. The faery fortune often discussed in many legends is not a pot of gold or a stash of gems and silver, but the abundance of living energy found in all inhabitants of earth, and the ability to work with that energy to create harmony and balance. Also related to faery are holey stones or holed stones, which are bits of smooth, circular stone with a hole through the center often found near lakes, creeks, streams, or ocean beaches where the elements or sea creatures have worn away the center to produce the hole. Some think that if you blow gently through the hole of the stone you can call nature spirits, and others believe that a nature spirit lives within the body of the stone. These stones are used in modern Witchcraft to bring good luck, prosperity, and earth-related powers, hung on bedposts to prevent nightmares, and rubbed on the body to assist in removing disease.[61]

One of the sigils for modern elven (faery) magick is the seven-pointed star, called a heptagram (below). The heptagram also relates to the days of the week, their planetary associations, and energies (SEE PAGE 184).

Gnome Spell for Prosperity

Prosperity isn't just money. You can be prosperous by having good friends, a bountiful harvest from your garden, or enjoying a harmonious atmosphere at home, school, or work. There are only three requirements for this spell to work:

1. That you believe in faery energy.

2. That you believe you deserve good fortune.

3. That you honor the faery energy by leaving an offering out-of-doors.

SUPPLIES: Three toy elves (Christmas ornaments will do) or gnomes; gold glitter; a drawing of the seven-pointed star (elven star, or heptagram); 2 gold illuminator candles; your favorite incense; a bowl of water.

INSTRUCTIONS: On the new moon, place the elven star in the center of your altar. Light the illuminator candles. Cast the magick circle. Dip your hands in the bowl of water and say: "I release any anger, unhappiness, sickness, and poverty into this water. So mote it be." Mentally think of all these negative things slipping from your body, down into your fingertips, and out into the water. Set the water aside.

Use the following quarter calls:

North: *Elven magick, I invoke thee through Spirits of the north. Gnomes from the depths of the fertile Earth, I call thee. Bring to me prosperity in thought and mind and deed.*

East: *Elven magick, I invoke thee through Spirits of the east. Sylphs, faeries of knowledge and thought among the airy breezes, I call thee. Bring to me prosperity in thought and mind and deed.*

South: *Elven magick, I invoke thee through Spirits of the south. Salamanders, beings of creative fire, I call thee. Bring to me prosperity in thought and mind and deed.*

West: *Elven magick, I invoke thee through Spirits of the west. Undines, creatures of the teeming seas, I call thee. Bring to me prosperity in thought and mind and deed.*

Walk to the center of the circle and say the Call of Nine to invoke the Goddess and the God. Hold your hands up, palms facing the heavens, and say:

I call thee forth from heavenly sky
to answer now my call of nine
from misty vale and under hill,
I turn the spokes of the magick mill!
One! I stand before thy holy throne;
two! I invoke thy power alone;
three! I hold aloft my magick blade;
four! Ascend! I am the power
of night and day.
Five! Descend! Element of Witchery—
O gracious Goddess, be with me.
Six! Enchantment! Belongs to me
from sandy beach to roiling sea!
Seven! Power! The God bestows His mystery!
Feel the pulse of energy!
Eight! Come ye now my work be done.
Nine! Your essence now and I are one!
So mote it be!

Slap your hands down on the elven star and repeat loudly: "Love, happiness, peace, patience, mercy, compassion, honesty, kindness, and self-control." Sprinkle the gold glitter over the elven star. Place the three gnomes on top. Hold your hands over the gnomes, and repeat the following:

I invoke thee and call upon thee,
O powers of prosperity.
Gentle gnomes, by elven magick
I bid thee to leave this place
And bring back (list your need here)
to my sacred space.
Ensure that I will never fear,
for food or drink or loved ones dear.
Go forth and fulfill my humble desire.

3, 7, 9, and 21;
end ye well, that's here begun!
As I will, it shall be done!

Place the gnomes, glitter, and elven star under or behind the altar (depending on the shape and size of your altar). In my experience, gnomes won't skip off your altar to fulfill your need while you are looking. They like to prowl around in privacy.

Thank deity. Thank the quarters and release them. Release the circle. Don't forget to ground and center. Set a bowl of milk along with a piece of bread, cheese, or bit of honey outside of your home as an offering of thanksgiving, then leave the gnomes to do their job. If you have asked for continued prosperity, you may not have to do this spell again for quite some time. If, on the other hand, your request was finite and is granted, gather up your gnomes (if they are still there), wash them off, and put them in a safe place. Sprinkle any leftover glitter outside. Place the paper in your Book of Shadows.

Blessing House Plants (and Reviving Dying Ones)

SUPPLIES: Spring water; your favorite incense; fertilizer (specifically made for that type of plant).

TIMING: When the moon is in Cancer, Scorpio, or Pisces.

INSTRUCTIONS: Research the needs of the plant. Does it require a lot of sunlight or not so much? Does it need a lot of water, or just a bit? What sort of history does it have (magickal, folklore, and medicinal)? By knowing all about the plant, you can better serve Mother Earth. Place the plant and all supplies on the altar, or where the plant is under direct sunlight. Clap your hands three times and say loudly: "All negative energy, seen and unseen, be gone from this place!"

Hold your hands over the altar, and say: "I invoke and call upon thee, elven magick."

Sprinkle the plant with a little water, saying: "Blessings of the undines upon thee."

Light the incense and pass lightly over the plant, saying: "Blessings of the sylphs upon thee."

Add a little fertilizer to the soil (follow the directions on the package), and say: "Blessings of the gnomes upon thee."

Hold the plant up to the sun, and say: "Blessings of the salamanders upon thee."

Set the plant on the altar. Hold your hands over the leaves/flowers, and say:

From under hill and faery glen
from darkest forest to meadow's end
from elven mound and shining sea
fill this plant with energy.
Protect it in its time of need
bless the flower and the seed.
So mote it be!

Cut Flower Blessing

Most Wiccans do not use their ritual circle knife (athame) to cut flowers or herbs. This task is reserved for the bolline, much like a small paring knife. Before any plant is cut, the Witch asks permission of the plant and holds his or her hand over the plant. If the energy is soft and loving, permission is granted. If you do not get these feelings, choose another plant or flower. As you cut, give your thanks to the plant for its gift to you. Once you have the flowers arranged (on your altar or in a vase for a gift), give a blessing of thanksgiving.

Faery magick strong and pure
King and Queen whom I adore
bless these blooms with love and grace
bring joy and peace unto this place
and as these flowers wilt and fade
return their energy to the glade.

Removing Negativity from a Room or a Home

SUPPLIES: Freshly cut flowers with long stalks, or a few branches from a willow tree; cinnamon; red, white, and black ribbons, each about 2 feet long; holy water; incense of your choice; salt.

INSTRUCTIONS: In the fourth quarter of the moon, or when the moon is in Cancer, tie the flowers or willow branches together with the three ribbons. Clap your hands three times over the flowers/branches and say: "Evil be gone!"

Sprinkle the flowers with the three elements and the cinnamon. Hold your hands over the flowers/branches, and say:

> *Power of the earth, awaken elven magick!*
> *Power of the air, awaken elven magick!*
> *Power of the fires, awaken elven magick!*
> *Power of the water, awaken elven magick!*
> *Red for the blood of life*
> *white for the Lord and Lady*
> *black to remove all negativity*
> *waken golden energy.*
> *As I will, so mote it be!*

Using the flowers/willow branches like a broom, sweep the entire area in a counterclockwise direction, starting from the center of each room outward toward the door. When you are finished, open the door and sweep the threshold in an outward motion. As you make the final sweep, throw the flowers/willow out the door, saying: "This house is clean. So mote it be."

Place the flowers off of your property with a final blessing of thanks.

In considering just what faery energy might be, I think Doreen Valiente, in her book *An ABC of Witchcraft*, puts it very well:

> *My own opinion is that the fairy creed is a composite of several factors: actual spirits of nature whose presence can sometimes be perceived, but who usually share this world invisibly with humans; souls of the Pagan dead, who take the third road that the Fairy Queen showed to Thomas the Rhymer, "the road to fair Elfland," away from either the Christian heaven or the Christian hell; and folk-memories of aboriginal races, now mostly vanished. There may be a fourth factor, the very old and apparently worldwide belief in a hidden land or underworld within the earth.*[62]

Farming by Almanac and Gardening by the Moon

Magical timing (in the case of gardens and agriculture) is a two-part process—knowing the quarters (SEE ALMANACS, PART III, for an explanation of moon quarters) and/or phases of the moon, and understanding how the moon behaves in each astrological sign. Applied together, these two facts will earn you the green thumb award. To begin, you'll need an almanac that lists the quarters and the astrological sign the moon is visiting any given day.

Let's begin by listing what type of energy you're dealing with (when discussing gardening) when the moon enters the various signs. They are *barren*, *productive*, *semi-fruitful*, and *fruitful*.

Below is a short list that tells you how the astrological signs fit into these categories.

Moon in Aries: Barren

Moon in Taurus: Productive

Moon in Gemini: Barren

Moon in Cancer: Fruitful

Moon in Leo: Barren

Moon in Virgo: Barren

Moon in Libra: Semi-Fruitful

Moon in Scorpio: Fruitful

Moon in Sagittarius: Barren

Moon in Capricorn: Productive

Moon in Aquarius: Barren

Moon in Pisces: Fruitful

You might think that you can't plant anything in the barren signs, but there is an exception to the rule: Virgo, as you will see by the following list. Below, I've created the following handy gardening table to help you with your astrological timing when growing herbs, planting a moon garden, or helping Mom or Dad harvest the backyard garden. The information even works for windowbox gardens and other indoor plants.

Magickal Planting

APPLE TREES

Quarter: First or second.

When the moon is in: Cancer, Pisces, Taurus, or Virgo.

BEANS

Quarter: Second.

When the moon is in: Cancer, Taurus, Pisces, or Libra.

BULBS

Quarter: Third.

When the moon is in: Cancer, Scorpio, or Pisces.

CACTUS

Quarter: (none.)

When the moon is in: Taurus or Capricorn.

CORN

Quarter: First.

When the moon is in: Cancer, Scorpio, or Pisces.

CROCUS

Quarter: First or second.

When the moon is in: Virgo.

CUCUMBERS

Quarter: First.

When the moon is in: Cancer, Scorpio, or Pisces.

DAFFODILS

Quarter: First or second.

When the moon is in: Libra or Virgo.

FLOWERS, GENERAL

Quarter: First.

When the moon is in: Libra, Cancer, Pisces, Virgo, Scorpio, or Taurus.

GARLIC

Quarter: Third.

When the moon is in: Libra, Taurus, or Pisces.

GOURDS

Quarter: First or second.

When the moon is in: Cancer, Scorpio, Pisces, or Libra.

HERBS, GENERAL

Quarter: First or second.

When the moon is in: Cancer, Scorpio, or Pisces.

HOUSE PLANTS

Quarter: First.

When the moon is in: Libra, Cancer, Scorpio, or Pisces.

MELONS

Quarter: Second.

When the moon is in: Cancer, Scorpio, or Pisces.

MOON VINE

Quarter: First or second.

When the moon is in: Virgo.

MORNING GLORY

Quarter: First or second.

When the moon is in: Cancer, Scorpio, Pisces, or Virgo.

ONION SETS

Quarter: Third.

When the moon is in: Libra, Taurus, Pisces, or Cancer.

PARSLEY

Quarter: First.

When the moon is in: Cancer, Scorpio, Pisces, or Libra.

PEPPERS

Quarter: Second.

When the moon is in: Cancer, Pisces, or Scorpio.

POTATOES

Quarter: Third.

When the moon is in: Cancer, Scorpio, Taurus, Libra, or Capricorn.

PUMPKINS

Quarter: Second.

When the moon is in: Cancer, Scorpio, Pisces, or Libra.

ROSES

Quarter: First or second.

When the moon is in: Cancer or Virgo.

SAGE

Quarter: Third.

When the moon is in: Cancer, Scorpio, or Pisces.

SUNFLOWERS

Quarter: First or second.

When the moon is in: Libra or Cancer.

TOMATOES

Quarter: Second.

When the moon is in: Cancer, Scorpio, Pisces, or Capricorn.

SHADE TREES

Quarter: Third.

When the moon is in: Taurus or Capricorn.

TRUMPET VINES

Quarter: First or second.

When the moon is in: Cancer, Scorpio, or Pisces.

TURNIPS

Quarter: Third.

When the moon is in: Cancer, Scorpio, Pisces, Taurus, Capricorn, or Libra.

VALERIAN

Quarter: First or second.

When the moon is in: Virgo or Gemini.

WATERMELONS

Quarter: First or second.

When the moon is in: Cancer, Scorpio, Pisces, or Libra.

You may not ever raise potatoes or turnips, but by looking at this chart, we learn something important. If we want to deal with the root of anything (onions, potatoes, and turnips are root

plants), then we plant the idea (or in this case the plant) during the waning moon phase (preferably in the third quarter) in a fruitful or productive sign, but if we wanted something to be buried and stay that way, we would pick the fourth quarter of the most barren moon signs: Leo or Sagittarius. If you want something to rot, choose the fourth quarter of a water sign. If you are forced to start something you absolutely don't want to finish, pick a fourth quarter Aries moon. Here's some more to ponder. If you want to fertilize something the natural way (say organic fertilizers), then you would make sure the moon is in a fruitful sign (Cancer, Scorpio, or Pisces) and you would begin during the third or fourth quarter of the moon. But if you want to use artificial means (such as a chemical fertilizer), then you would again use those fruitful signs, but choose the first or second quarter of the moon. Finally, if you want Mom and Dad to have a beautiful, lush lawn that all the neighbors brag about, mow it in the first and second quarters of the moon, but if it seems to be growing faster than you can cut it, mow in the third and fourth quarters to decrease the growth; however, remember that grass contains living energy and just because you are lazy is no excuse to take it out on the poor lawn. If Mom has her heart set on having you weed the garden, put your back into it during the fourth quarter when the moon is in Aries, Gemini, Leo, Virgo, Sagittarius, or Aquarius—those pesky weeds won't spring back as fast. Who knows, you might gain yourself extra time at the pool this summer.

Now, this doesn't mean that if you plant something in a barren sign, it won't grow at all. However, scientists have found that plants do up to 32 percent better in fruitful signs as opposed to the barren signs. If you can't get the right quarter (due to extenuating circumstances), concentrate on the moon sign.

Spring Blessing for the Garden

At first planting, perform the following spell when the moon is in Pisces, Cancer, or Scorpio.

At dawn, take four unbroken pretzels (Pennsylvania Dutch symbols of good fortune) and place them at the four corners of your garden, saying:

> *Fresh-turned earth filled with treasure*
> *I give this garden my love and pleasure.*
> *I walk the magick three times three*
> *to plant great joy and harmony.*
> *Bugs be gone with other pests*
> *I frighten away unwanted guests.*
> *Elven magick, weave your spell*
> *keep my plants both strong and well.*
> *As I will so now it's done*
> *by leaf and vine and rain and sun.*

Autumn Blessing for the Garden

When the last herb, fruit, or vegetable has been harvested, clear away dead plants. At dusk, stand in the center of your garden plot. With a stick, draw the elven star in the dirt. Place a single white candle in the center. Light the candle, and say:

> *Your work is done, the harvest gone*
> *I bring thee thanks for work hard won.*
> *Elven magick, fill this place*
> *bring blessed sleep and peaceful grace*
> *to soil and garden tired and worn*
> *that in the spring will be reborn.*
> *Many moons will pass till then*
> *recover quickly, my old friend.*
> *Blessings and thanksgiving upon you.*
> *So mote it be.*

Meditate on the light of the burning candle as dusk turns to night. When you are ready, extinguish the candle and bury on your property.

General Magickal Gardening Rules

Above-ground plants: Plants that will produce crops above ground should be sown the day after the new moon up until the day before the first quarter. Try to stay in a fertile or semi-fertile astrological sign.

Annuals: Begin planting the day after the new moon up until the day before the first quarter. Try to stay in a fertile or semi fertile astrological sign.

Below-ground plants: Plants that produce their crop underground should be planted during the day after the full moon. Try to stay in a fertile or semi-fertile astrological sign. This ensures a strong root system.

Biennials and perennials (including trees and shrubs): Begin planting the day after the full moon and stop on the day before the last quarter. Try to stay in a fertile or semi-fertile astrological sign. This ensures a strong root system.

Collecting seeds: Best done at the full moon or when the moon is in a fire or air sign—Aries, Leo, Sagittarius, Libra, Gemini, or Aquarius.

Harvesting: Small harvests and fresh flowers for ritual circle and immediate magickal use can be done in early evening, when the plants have maximum food reserves. Flowers and herbs intended for drying and storage should be cut midmorning when the dew has evaporated. Harvest fruit and vegetables during the waning moon (full to new) and when the moon is in the barren or semi-barren fire or air signs of Aries, Leo, Sagittarius, Libra, Gemini, or Aquarius. Always try to cut any stems on a slant if you plan to place flowers in water for ritual. This helps the plant continue to absorb water and nutrients.

Gems and Stones

Precious, semiprecious, and even ordinary stones found in sacred or daily traveled areas have served as personal adornment, a mark of one's wealth, and at different times in different cultures functioned as representations of gods, guardians, healing agents, amulets, talismans, charms, and for foretelling the future.[63] In Egyptian magick gems were worn to protect or heal, to bring wealth and success, to attract love and promote fertility, or even to curse an enemy. These magickal gems consisted of three main parts: the color of the gem, the properties of the gem, and the words or images engraved on it or wrapped around it with a bit of papyri.[64] During the mummification process, gems and stones were wrapped within the cloth-binding process in the belief that their magick would be given to the deceased on the other side and protect the body on this side of the veil. The Egyptians created an elaborate system of color symbolism that matched the gem's magickal abilities with its color. Milky white stones might be used to promote a mother's milk supply, wine-colored amethysts were used to prevent alcoholism, and so on. The combination of the gemstone and their words of power were popular all over the Roman empire and became part of an international tradition of magick, of which Egyptian sources gained high prestige.[65] It is here also that we can follow the trail of the science and art of astrology from Sumer, Babylon, and Egypt, to Greece, to Rome, and then into Europe through the Middle Ages as we study their astrological and alchemical writings. Gemstones figured prominently in those musty pages.

Even in the Middle Ages, gem magick was popular both in the royal courts and among the commoners. A grocer named Richard de Preston is known to have donated a sapphire that could cure ailments of the eyes to a local church.[66] Court chronicles inventoried stones that could detect poison (handy for royalty), bring good luck, assist in childbirth, cure a compendium of personal ailments, dispel envy and malice, reduce fever, banish terror, or promise the bearer magickal abilities. Lists that compared the powers of saints to that of preferred gemstones appeared, and relics were often set with gems to enhance their strength. Books called "lapidaries" appeared that detailed the wondrous properties of gems. It is interesting that during the time of great religious oppression, stones emerged almost unscathed as carriers of natural magick rather than of the demonic variety. Considering that one cannot rid the world of stones and that gems translated into money, it isn't any wonder that they didn't try.

In modern magickal practices (much like in Egyptian lore), the color, shape, and mineral properties of a stone or gem are used in its classification and in its magickal association, though today any carvings or inscriptions are not seen as a necessity for the stone to work. Instead, they are activated through prayer, charming, or ritual. Some feel that simply thinking about one's intention and rubbing the stone will work, and in fact I've used this simple method myself with great success. Activation, then, depends on the personality and skill of the user.

Magickal people today believe that the energies of the mineral kingdom are universal energies, and that when you are willing to receive this energy and are also willing to work with a higher purpose, that true activation of the stone begins. It is for this reason that stones and gems will only work if you are using them for a right intention—in love and light, rather than in pain or darkness.[67] In the Craft, it is believed that the Witch is the magick, and the gem or stone is a universal support energy to help us obtain our goals. The stone is a catalyst of our intentions.

Ritual to Find the Right Stones, Gems, and Minerals for You

When you first begin collecting stones, you might make a trip to your favorite metaphysical store, take a walk in the woods, or visit a rock shop. After a while you'll probably have quite a collection of stones. To help you determine what they are I've provided a suggested reading list at the end of this section. The following ritual can be used to find your initial collection, or fine-tune the choice of a specific stone for a single spellcasting purpose.

SUPPLIES: A bowl of dirt or sand; tea candle or solar light; a magnet.

INSTRUCTIONS: When the moon is in Scorpio, or during a new moon (first quarter), go outside to a private place. Sit down and set the bowl of dirt in front of you. Bury the magnet in the dirt. Light the candle and place it in the center of the dirt. Ground and center. Take a deep breath and close your eyes. In your mind, visualize what you would like to do. Find stones to begin your collection? Find a particular stone to give you courage and help solve a problem? Bring prosperity to the home? Find the truth of a matter? It's entirely up to you.

Say:

Spirits of the forests: wood and hill and dales.
Spirits of the seas: sands and waves and gales.
Steward of earth's treasures,
guardian of the vale
please draw to me the stones I need
upon your sacred trail.
As I will, desire fulfilled.
So mote it be.

Sit back and enjoy the sounds, sights, and smells of nature. Snuff out the candle. Keep the magnet in the bowl until you find the right stone, then remove the magnet and scatter the dirt to the winds, thanking the spirits for their service.

Sensing the Vibrations of Stones

How do you know if a particular stone is right for you? Go with your gut. If the stone attracts you and you feel good about it, most likely that stone is meant to work with you. If there's "just something about it" that bothers you, find a different stone. You can also test a stone by placing it in your receptive hand (if you are right-handed, this would be your left hand, as your right hand is considered dominant. If you are left-handed, then your receptive hand would be your right one). It doesn't take long to feel the vibrations of any stone or gem, even if you have never done it before. Just close your eyes and push away all events of the day, then allow the stone to talk to you through touch. Is it hot? Does it tingle? These are usually good signs. How do you feel when holding the stone? Good feelings mean the stone is right for you; bad feelings tell you that you should choose a different stone.

Cleansing and Preparing Stones

Whether you have discovered your gem or stone on the beach or found it at your favorite magickal store, stones should be cleansed in preparation for magick and ritual. There are quite a few ways to purify them. They can be washed in spring water or the running water of a creek, river, or stream, then allowed to dry in direct sunlight or moonlight. If you think the stone has been in unfortunate circumstances, you might leave it to sit in the light for up to a week. This is especially true of gems set in jewelry where you didn't know the previous owner, or unfortunate circumstances surrounded that person. If you are wary of where the gem or stone has been, a good dunking in vinegar helps to re-

move negativity. Other magickal people have been known to bury gems and stones in the ground for at least twenty-four hours before initial cleansing, asking the Earth to absorb any negativity and return the gem or stone to its natural energy state.

Charging Stones for Magick and Ritual

Before you use your gems and stones for magick, you should charge them to match your intent. Bless them with the four elements, then hold the gem or stone in your hand. Rub the stone lightly between the fingers of your dominant hand, then place the stone on your third-eye chakra (in the center of your forehead) while saying:

> *In the names of the Lord and Lady*
> *(or deity of your choice), I conjure thee,*
> *O stone of earth, to assist me in my magickal*
> *working. By the moon and the stars, may you be*
> *blessed and empowered to* (name intent here).
> *So mote it be.*[68]

Stones from Your Environment

Although many people like gemstones, I've found that stones found around your property, in the woods near your favorite sacred space, or in a place that contains a great deal of legend and lore can be extremely powerful. In Pow Wow magick, the only stones ever used are those that are near one's home and indigenous to the area, thus providing a link between the conjurer and his or her environment. These stones (that can fit in the palm of the hand) are used to draw out sickness, protect one's property, or to bring good luck to any homestead.

Therefore, if you don't have a lot of money to collect gemstones, or you must wait until you can save your money for that trip to the metaphysical store or rock shop, don't worry. You can begin working with stones right away by just going outside and collecting some. Sharp stones are normally used to push things away (like gossip, criminals, etc.), where smooth stones act to draw things to you. The only exception is the healing stone, which must be smooth because it normally touches the patient. You can also collect pebbles to put in conjuring bags for almost any purpose as well as paint or draw magickal sigils on smooth stones to match your magickal intent.

You can use a stone from someone's property in place of a personal item. Let's say your neighbor is sick and in the hospital and you'd like to say a prayer and send healing energy his or her way. Collect the stone from their property, think of the person's need, and send positive energy. If you like, you can write the person's name on the stone with a green marker. A New Year's spell for money and prosperity uses a large stone (as big as you can carry) from your property. Take the stone into the house and place it where everyone can see it (but not trip over it). Sprinkle the stone lightly with holy water, followed by cinnamon. Hold your hands over the stone and use the empowering statement above, then clap your hands three times. Replace the stone the following year.[69]

Magickal Gems for Planning by the Moon

AGATE (GENERAL)

Purpose: Strength, courage, love, healing and protection.

Element: Depends on the type of agate.

Planet: Mercury.

Most powerful when the moon is in: Virgo or Gemini.

AMBER *(a fossil, not a stone or gem)*

Purpose: Luck, healing, strength, protection, beauty and love.

Element: Fire and spirit.

Planet: Sun.

Most powerful when the moon is in: Leo or when the sun is in your sign of the zodiac.

AMETHYST

Purpose: Dreams, overcoming alcoholism, healing, psychism, peace, love, protection against thieves, and happiness.

Element: Water.

Planet: Jupiter and Neptune.

Most powerful when the moon is in: Sagittarius and Pisces (or when the moon is in the sign where your natal Jupiter or Neptune falls).

APACHE TEAR

Purpose: Protection and luck.

Element: Fire.

Planet: Saturn.

Most powerful when the moon is in: Capricorn or Aquarius.

AVENTURINE

Purpose: Mental powers, eyesight, money, peace, healing, and luck.

Element: Air and earth.

Planet: Mercury.

Most powerful when the moon is in: Virgo or Gemini.

BLOODSTONE

Purpose: Halting bleeding, healing, victory, courage, wealth, strength, legal and business success, agriculture and gardens.

Element: Fire.

Planet: Mars.

Most powerful when the moon is in: Scorpio or Aries.

CARNELIAN

Purpose: Protection, peace, saying the right thing at the right time, courage.

Element: Fire.

Planet: Sun.

Most powerful when the moon is in: Leo.

CITRINE

Purpose: Anti-nightmare, protection, psychism.

Element: Fire.

Planet: Sun.

Most powerful when the moon is in: Leo or when the sun is in your sign of the zodiac.

CORAL

Purpose: Healing, regulating menstruation, gardening, protection, peace and wisdom.

Element: Water and spirit.

Planet: Venus.

Most powerful when the moon is in: Libra or Taurus.

CROSSED STONES

Purpose: Magick, working with the elements, luck.

Element: All.

Planet: All.

Most powerful when the moon is in: All.

QUARTZ CRYSTAL *(general)*

Purpose: Healing, psychism, power, success, speaking with the deceased, spiritual attainment.

Element: Fire and water.

Planet: Sun and moon.

Most powerful when the moon is in: Leo, Cancer, or when the sun or moon are in the same signs as your natal sun and moon.

FLUORITE

Purpose: Mental agility, technology, past-life regression, healing emotional upsets.

Element: Air and earth.

Planet: Mercury.

Most powerful when the moon is in: Gemini, Aquarius, and Virgo.

FOSSILS

Purpose: Working with the elements, past-life regression, protection, longevity.

Element: Earth.

Planet: Saturn.

Most powerful when the moon is in: Taurus, Virgo, and Capricorn.

GEODES

Purpose: Meditation, helping in childbirth.

Element: Water.

Planet: Moon.

Most powerful when the moon is in: Cancer.

HEMATITE

Purpose: Healing, grounding, divination.

Element: Fire and earth.

Planet: Saturn.

Most powerful when the moon is in: Scorpio and Capricorn.

HOLEY STONES

Purpose: Anti-nightmare, protection, healing, psychism, projection of any kind, eyesight.

Element: Water.

Planet: Moon.

Most powerful when the moon is in: Cancer or when the moon is in the same sign as your natal moon.

JADE

Purpose: Love, healing, wisdom, protection, gardening, prosperity, money.

Element: Water and earth.

Planet: Venus.

Most powerful when the moon is in: Libra and Taurus.

JASPER, BROWN

Purpose: Grounding and centering especially after magick, protection from physical harm.

Element: Earth.

Planet: Saturn.

Most powerful when the moon is in: Capricorn.

JASPER, GREEN

Purpose: Healing, restful sleep and general health.

Element: Earth.

Planet: Venus.

Most powerful when the moon is in: Taurus.

JASPER, RED

Purpose: Courage, guard against poison and fevers.

Element: Fire.

Planet: Mars.

Most powerful when the moon is in: Scorpio, Leo, or Aries.

JET *(nickname: Witch's armor)*

Purpose: Protection, anti-nightmare, luck, divination, health.

Element: Earth and Spirit.

Planet: Saturn.

Most powerful when the moon is in: Capricorn.

MALACHITE

Purpose: Power, protection, love, peace, and business success.

Element: Earth.

Planet: Venus.

Most powerful when the moon is in: Taurus.

MARBLE

Purpose: Protection and success.

Element: Water.

Planet: Moon.

Most powerful when the moon is in: Cancer or when the moon is in the same sign as your natal moon.

MOONSTONE

Purpose: Love, divination, psychism, sleep, gardening, protection, youth, dieting.

Element: Water.

Planet: Moon.

Most powerful when the moon is in: Cancer or when the moon is in the same sign as your natal moon.

MOONSTONE (RAINBOW)

Purpose: Unconditional love, magick, personal power, protection, spirituality, speaking to the dead and public speaking, teaching.

Element: All.

Planet: All.

Most powerful when the moon is in: All.

OBSIDIAN

Purpose: Protection, grounding, divination, peace.

Element: Earth and fire.

Planet: Saturn and Mars.

Most powerful when the moon is in: Scorpio and Capricorn.

ONYX

Purpose: Protection, defensive magick.

Element: Fire and earth.

Planet: Mars and Saturn.

Most powerful when the moon is in: Scorpio and Capricorn.

SODALITE

Purpose: Healing, peace, meditation, wisdom.

Element: Earth and air.

Planet: Venus.

Most powerful when the moon is in: Taurus and Libra.

SUGILITE

Purpose: Psychism, spirituality, healing, wisdom.

Element: Fire and water.

Planet: Jupiter and Neptune.

Most powerful when the moon is in: Sagittarius and Pisces.

SUNSTONE

Purpose: Protection, energy, healing cancer, health in general.

Element: Fire.

Planet: Sun.

Most powerful when the moon is in: Leo or when the sun is in your natal sign.

TIGER-EYE

Purpose: Money, protection, courage, energy, luck, divination, to find the truth of a matter.

Element: Fire.

Planet: Sun.

Most powerful when the moon is in: Leo.

TURQUOISE

Purpose: Protection, courage, money, love, friendship, healing, luck, success.

Element: Water, earth, or air.

Planet: Venus or Neptune.

Most powerful when the moon is in: Libra, Taurus, or Pisces.

If You Lose Your Gems or Stones

Don't sweat it—they had someplace to go. It's not as if they don't like you anymore, but perhaps they are needed elsewhere. When one of my stones does a disappearing act, I often think of the gnomes scurrying through the house, picking them up, and delivering them to the next owner (or perhaps back to the ground where they can rest and recuperate). Although whimsical, the thought makes me feel better.

Recommended Reading

Cunningham's Encyclopedia of Crystal, Gem & Metal Magick by Scott Cunningham

Love Is in the Earth: A Kaleidoscope of Crystals by Melody

Magick

Much of magic is based upon the idea, usually
understood by all but perhaps unsaid, that the
universe is a single living conscious being
within whose body all things exist.
—*Donald Tyson*[70]

Over the last fifty years, archeologists have discovered thousands of paintings and carvings on the walls of caves and the surfaces of rocks in Europe, Africa, Australia, and North America that date from the Paleolithic era.[71] From study-ing the cultural models of the few tribes still ex-isting in various parts of the world, we learn that the cave paintings were vital to community rit-ual magic and that such a practice is called sym-pathetic magick. In studying Congo Pygmy archeological research, we learn that cave paint-ings were used as a form of prayer that involved securing the name or physical likeness of an ob-ject in order to control that object and bring about the desired result. In the case of the Congo Pygmy, this meant a successful hunt. These ritual prayers usually required the proper combination of words (chanted, sung, or spoken) and visual images and gestures such as dance—elements we still find in modern-day magick.[72] Some historians, however, feel that basing what-may-have-been on what-is-now might be a bit of a stretch. As Ronald Hutton notes,[73]

> It is still generally thought that Paleolithic cave paintings were generated for, or as parts of, rites of religion and magick, but the idea that this was specifically sympathetic magic went out in the 1970s: see Peter Ucko and Andree Rosen-feld, Paleolithic Cave Art (1967). The current favorite interpretation is that the paintings were of shamanic spirit doubles or helpers, though this is unlikely even to be proved and is controver-sial. For the classic user-friendly argument in favor, see Jean Clottes and David Lewis-Williams, The Shamans of Prehistory (Abrams, 1998).

At the dawn of time, magick, religion, and daily community functions were one. Reading through this book, you have discovered that many of the spells, incantations, and practices used today in modern magick (though changed somewhat to keep pace with the times) came to us from Egypt, Mesopotamia, and several other ancient civilizations, and it is amazing to think that the practice of magick has remained with us

(in view of recent anthropological discoveries) since the dawn of the human era.[74] Indeed, it is the investigation into magick that brought us the science of heliocentrism, the infinity of worlds, and led to the discovery of how blood circulated in the body.[75]

From the earliest times of civilization, politi-cal power was linked with spiritual power and superhuman abilities. It was believed that divine power flowed from the gods to their royal agent, who, as theocratic monarch, represented heaven's will on earth. Linking politics, magick, and reli-gion together ensured the ruler's "right" to rule.[76] This was an ancient mind-game that worked quite well for thousands of years, and unfortunately although the idea of magick as a valid practice has been shoved aside, the partner-ship of politics and religion as a vehicle to con-trol the populace still works in many parts of the world. In the thirteenth century, it was believed that the ruling monarch could touch you and, by divine power, make you well.

Over the centuries, magick was dropped be-cause it was a vehicle that the common person could employ for personal and political gain—not good for those in power should they rule unwisely (which oodles of them did and still continue to do) or who feared the loss of such power. And while they were at it, they threw out divination (can't let them know what we're up to) and astrology (what do you mean, you can see the movement of what I'm most likely going to do by looking at the heavens? Eeek! Gotta stop that.). Where the belief in magick was not destroyed, its history was rewritten to take on completely religious associations where the indi-vidual had no power, but occasionally that-which-runs-the-universe kindly did a miracle or two. The Christian Church in particular wrote canons (laws) as fast as a machine gun ejects car-tridges in hopes of destroying any known traces of magick that tried to bubble out of their historical past, and converted all acts of positive magick to miracles. Judaism took a different stance, steeping magickal practices in rabbinical teachings reserved only for the vaunted few. When history spoke of the real magicians (and they did exist), they rewrote that history to indicate the magi was really a rabbi all along. The result, especially in Europe, was a total lockdown on information. Unfortunately, there was one thing they didn't count on, and that was the fact that magickal abilities are an inherent part of every human being, to a greater or lesser degree, depending upon their life purpose. To become a great artist, one draws. To become a great musician, one plays music. To become a great magi, one practices magick. It is as simple as that.

Throughout this book we've talked about how magick managed to reassert itself in the last three hundred years. I have written about William Lilly (the sixteenth-century astrologer), Agrippa, and Paracelsus (known as the father of homeopathy). We've mentioned Dion Fortune, Madame Blavatsky (a Russian aristocrat and founder of the Theosophical Society, a movement that heralded the New Age and alternative religious beliefs), and their magickal lodges of the late 1800s and early 1900s. We touched on the Golden Dawn and Israel Regardi. We spoke of Gerald Gardner and Doreen Valiente, the birthparents of modern Craft practices. Granted, we missed a lot of history and had to gloss over a great deal of information due to the size and nature of this book, but in these discussions one thing is perfectly clear: *Magick is the ability to use one's will to create change in our environment.* How this is done, to the outside world, is a mystery. You, however, do not have this problem.

When learning modern Witchcraft, we discover that the word *magick* is used as both a noun and a verb, and many times no one bothers to differentiate between the two. On one hand, the word *magick* is used to express a way of doing something, and therefore is a system of practice—a noun. To change something through the use of magickal applications (the mental process also referred to as magick) produces the alteration we desire. That mental process, then, is the verb.

Whether we are discussing Honi the circle maker in 65 B.C.E. or what you're doing in your bedroom as you cast a spell, the constant is the ability of the human mind to reach beyond the gates and walls of disbelief and manifest your desire. Whether it's rain or a new pair of shoes, the activity remains the same, and one thing we know for sure, it is natural—not diabolical, twisted, or evil. Acts of magick are as integral to your system as breathing. Magick is nothing more than quantum physics.

I particularly like the following, written by Kurt Seligmann in his *History of Magic and the Occult*, first copyrighted in 1948:

> . . . a system that prevailed in society for thousands of years hardly needs an apology. The fact remains that magick upheld the great civilizations of the ancient world. Its predominance did not prevent man from leaving behind him works of continuing value, from tolerating his neighbor, cherishing his family, [or] doing the adequate thing at the right time. Magick was a stimulus to thinking. It freed man from fears, endowed him with a feeling of his power to control the world, sharpened his capacity to imagine, and kept alive his dreams of higher achievement.[77]

It did so then, and it does so now.

And no one has the right to take it from you.

Magick and Rules of Conduct

Over the years I've learned that the rules of magickal conduct are governed by the following circumstances:

- Your personality.

- Your past, including your environment, cultural taboos and laws, socialization skills, parental support, religious belief system, etc.

- The type of magick you are learning—folk or ceremonial (to be general), affiliations with magickal groups, contacts with online friends, and reading material you prefer.

Just looking at these three factors, we already know that every person will have their own individual way of processing and practicing any type of study, which includes magickal applications. The problems arise when confronting ego—ours, our friends, that of our parents, those who run religious organizations, those involved in magick, etc. We find that, for good or ill, not everyone's rules are the same, and not all rules apply the same way to everyone, not because one person is better than the other, but because each individual is unique and processes information in a different way and will embrace the rules of conduct most familiar to them.

In my own study I've seen lots of rules about magick and how it should be done. Some of these rules are excellent and to the point, where others seem to have grown from someone's battle with their own desires or with the dictates of their religious choice. Cultural taboos or requirements are an excellent example, where social rules have seeped into magickal ones. For example, a culture that says you "can only wear blue when practicing magick" might have sociopolitical reasons for making this rule that have nothing to do with the magick itself. It's darned hard for the new student to determine which rules should be followed, which thrown out, and which ones might be valid in a certain situation. It is also hard to understand why one rule may be okay for a ceremonial magician but not accepted by the rank and file of Witches (or vice versa).

Magick Is a System, Not a Religion

In the brief introduction I've given you on the history of magick, you learned that the ability to work magick is a natural one, and that magick, religion, science, and politics were linked together from the dawn of humankind to enhance tribal survival and flourished together during the reign of many ancient civilizations. There have always been rules (some good and some stupid) on how those experienced in the art and science of magick should behave, and how they should use their skills within the confines of the religious/political law. This tells us that some rules in magick are not a part of the system itself, but a part of the religious or political environment that encourages the use of that magickal system.

Many people turn to Witchcraft because of its stories of magick rather than its religious teachings. Others come to the Craft for the religious support (especially the belief in the Goddess), and magick is seen as secondary. This happens because Wicca is one of the few religions that overtly says magick is an okay thing to do, and encourages personal transformation through both religious and magickal practices. In Wicca, science, religion, and magick have fused back together—only politics remains the lone dog, because magick is not accepted by current political parties (who are wrapped up in other religions). Confusion arises among practitioners of the Craft because although the general consensus is that Wicca is the religion, the magickal system used within that religion may differ from person to person. For example, I may use Pow Wow (a German system of magick) quite frequently, where a friend in a Southern state may use Hoodoo, which is another magickal system. Both systems can fit comfortably into Witchcraft until we reach the discussion of ethics. As both systems do not include ethics—they are procedures, not moral dictates, sort of like stereo instructions—the student is left wondering, "What is the right thing to do?" That is what the religion is for—to guide you on those moral issues. Contrary to what other religious leaders tell you, Witchcraft does indeed have its own moral code.

Finally, Witchcraft, in some cases, has produced its own brand of magick; or should I say the Craft presents practices that fit comfortably within the belief system. In this type of teaching, a full system complete with trappings and taboos is not presented, only pieces that fit into generally accepted guidelines and encourage the student to look beyond the five senses. If an individual chooses to move deeper into magickal practices other than what is given in the Wiccan religion, they must search for a system that they feel will enhance their current magickal needs.

If, so far, you find this discussion confusing, don't feel bad. Most magickal practitioners today are more worried about getting their lives in shape rather than wrestling with categorizing what came from where and why. I know I was more worried about daily problems and how I could solve them when I first entered the Craft. I could have cared less that the Pygmies in the Congo practiced sympathetic magick or that correspondences we use originally came from the Sumerians, or that the Chaldeans (from present-day Iraq) gave us a compendium of astrological and magickal knowledge that is the foundation of what we use today. Wicca is a young religion and, because it is the fastest-growing spiritual faith in America, we would expect that a higher percentage of practitioners would be "using" it in a practical way, rather than mulling over the theory and history, or trying to quantify (define) the religion while munching on breakfast corn flakes before they dash off to work or

school. At some point, however, you will be pressed for answers to questions you may never have thought of—and the biggest question you will wrestle with deals with the validity of your magickal practices. You know they work, but trying to explain the process to another person becomes a nightmare because that other person has most likely not studied anything past his or her own field of interest, which leaves you trying to pack 10,000 years of history into a single sound bite. All this mumbling on my part leads you to the following: Contrary to what some individuals might try to tell you, Witchcraft is a religion and is not a stand-alone system of magick; therefore, if one calls themselves a Wiccan or a Witch, he or she is an adherent of the Wiccan religion—he or she is a Witch who practices an earth-centered religion. If a person practices magick, but does not follow the religion of the Craft, its rules, etc., then he or she is definitely not a Witch, he or she is a practitioner of magick, or may adhere to a different magickal religion, such as Druidism, Voodoo, Santería, or mystical Christianity.

Therefore: Witchcraft is a religion, it is not a system (or a cult, or any other such nonsense), and it definitely does not ascribe to Christian dogma (which is an entirely different religion altogether).

Knowing that magick is a system and that Wicca/Witchcraft is a religion now makes it easier for us to answer some of those rather sticky questions that have arisen within our community (and outside of it) over the last fifty-odd years, and gives us a firm foundation when trying to understand the different codes of conduct you might read about in various books on Wicca, other magickal religions, or in those books that present only a system of magick without religious overtones.

The General Rules of Successful Magick

1. **Every action has an equal reaction.** This is not a moral law, it is a scientific one, therefore the Witch should think long and hard before doing any magick. To help choose what action to take, many Witches use a divination tool before casting any spell or performing a working ritual. Within this rule lie two others: Never target the innocent, and never use magick to take something from someone else. In both cases the repercussions are vast and rightly cruel. It's just not worth it, from anyone's standpoint.

2. **The longer you practice magick, the more adept you will become.** No one is ever an instant magi. You can't read one book, do three spells, and become an expert. Practice, study, and hard work makes close to perfect. There are no exceptions.

3. **As best you can, keep your thoughts and actions pure.** Yes, everyone makes mistakes, everyone gets angry, and everyone has bad days where nothing seems to go their way—that's life. However, the purer your intentions, the more guarantee you have of success. To teach students about purity and the need for it, the Wiccan religion incorporates such practices as cleansing, consecration, empowerment, circlecasting, and sacred space. Learning how to successfully accomplish these procedures also helps you reach the purity of mind needed and enforces the focus necessary to perform fast, accurate magicks when you need them.

4. **What you think, you create.** We've talked a lot about this one already. Your mind is the key that opens the door to unlimited magickal applications. This is why the Wiccan religion urges you to release negative thoughts on a daily basis, learn to think positively rather than negatively, and teaches its students creative visualization, meditation, and energy work, and tries to concentrate on harmony rather than chaos.

5. **What you believe, you will manifest.** This rule is linked to the one above. Like my former Pow Wow teacher, Preston Zerbe, told me, "Belief is the key." You can do all sorts of magick, make petitions to that-which-runs-the-universe, and drum until your arms ache, but if you don't believe that a change can manifest, it won't. Belief is a knowing, a certainty, that what you desire will occur. If this is confusing, think about something you truly believe in or about. How do you feel when you think of those things? That millisecond of comfortability, that feeling of perfect peace is belief and your connection to the divine, and that's what you want to capture in each and every spell or ritual.

6. **Magick works better if added to a spiritual foundation.** In my experience, you will be able to manifest your desires faster if you attach magick to some sort of spiritual anchor—like Wicca, Druidism, Voodoo, Santería, Christianity, Judaism, Buddhism, Islam, etc. Some of these religions, like Witchcraft, fit well with magick, where others, like Christianity, require the seeker to wade through a tremendous amount of dogma to find sure footing. This is not to say you can't be a Christian and work magick—ceremonial magicians do it all the time. The choice is ultimately yours.

7. **Magick does not replace hard work.** You can't do a spell and expect the world to bow at your feet. If you want a good grade on your homework, then you have to do

the research, write out what is required, and hand it in on time. You can, however, use magick to persevere, find information, and remove any stress associated with that work.

8. *Do not use magick for illegal gain, and don't use anything in circle that might have been stolen.* It literally dirties the magick and will backfire on you.

Magickal Rules of the Craft

The following are the most common rules you will find in Wiccan magickal practices:

- Cast a magick circle in preparation for magick or ritual work.

- Use a divination tool before working magick.

- Always walk clockwise within the magick circle.

- Be respectful in circle. Honor the gods and those within the circle. If you are angry with someone, either solve the problem before entering the circle, put aside your argument, or simply do not stand in circle with that person.

- Never attack the innocent.

- Try your best to work for the highest good. When in doubt, ask Spirit to guide your thoughts.

- Do not mess with another person's free will. Now this one, like the "an' it harm none" rule, is also a sound-bite representation of a rather large idea. For example, if you wanted to be editor of the school newspaper and the position was open, you would compete with others for the slot. If we took this rule literally, then you could not work magick to get the editor job because other people want it, too. Your work would technically be against their free will.

However, this rule basically means that you can't work to take something away from someone (as in someone else has the job and you want them to lose it so you can have it), or make them do something they don't want to do (as in making a person love you by using magick).

- Never call anything into the circle that you have not researched first, which goes along with the adage you've also read in this book of not calling up what you can't put down.

As I mentioned earlier, you'll find lots of rules in the Craft—some that refer to ethics, some to magick, and others that relate to the government of a coven or magickal group. Regardless of the religion you use to sustain you throughout your life, if the rules make sense to you and appear to have been made to help you, then those rules are most likely sound and you can work with them. If the rules seem absurd, are against your moral judgment, or are somehow distasteful, then take a second look at these rules and try to find out where they came from and why they are in practice. Such rules may not be general ones that most adherents of that faith follow, and are simply there because of someone's folly (either in the past or present). For rules related to Wiccan magick and government, you'll find a longer discussion in my book *To Light a Sacred Flame*.

Why Magick Sometimes Fails

The most important factor you must remember about magick is this:

Magick is inherently designed to first change your perception on the issue. From that expansion of your personal viewpoint, the work can begin.

If you do not step away from narrow-mindedness, you will not succeed, simply because you do not believe, deep inside, that change is possible. This is why Witches know not to work negative magick, because by altering your perception to accept negativity you open the door to greater problems than you already have. Is this the only reason your rituals and spells may fail? No, but it is by far the biggest cause of magickal work falling short of its intended mark. Other reasons for failure can be the following:

- **You lost your focus during the spell or ritual.** This is why most Craft teachers urge their students to keep notes of all spellwork and ritual. That way, the student can look back over his or her writings to determine why a spell didn't perform in the manner expected. Questions to ask yourself are: Did you lose your focus? Did someone interrupt you during the spell? Did you miss a step? Did you remember to cast a magick circle? (Sometimes that makes a big difference.) Did you notice a positive change in the atmosphere of the circle? Did you experience any natural phenomena (the wind picking up a little is an excellent cue that you did it right, so something else must be happening with the work). Did you feel good when you finished the spell? Did you plan your spell with astrological timing in mind? (Sometimes an astrological occurrence will muck up your work, though if your intent was strong, this is rare.) Did you take time to plan your work, or did you just slap it together? (Advance planning means that you put more focus and more energy into the work, which results in smoother spellcasting abilities.) How was your mental health? Your physical health? Thumbs down on either one can affect your working. Are you subconsciously afraid that once you get what you asked for, the change will be too great to handle, or you won't really want what you asked for? Has someone beat into your head that you don't deserve

to be successful? Are you battling a self-esteem problem? This can take the gumption right out of magick.

- **You are being too impatient.** Magick doesn't make things all better in the blink of an eye. For change to occur, energy must move freely, and any blocks in the way have to go. Sometimes freeing the pathway for success is more time-consuming than we realized—I've had certain spells, especially those involving injustices that needed to be righted, take up to nine months, or even a full year! If you are nervous that "this is taking too long," you can always support the original working by doing it again at selected intervals, or by doing a different spell or ritual with the same statement of intent.

- **You received your wish, but it was so smooth and so quiet (no bells and whistles) that you didn't realize it.** Perhaps the situation has changed, but not in the way you originally hoped, or thought, it would. In this case, you asked for change, and you got it, but you were too blind to notice. New students especially have difficulty seeing the magick. Instead, they believe it was coincidence. However, if you don't like how the situation has played out, look back at your notes to see exactly what you said in the magick circle. The key to understanding may lie in your wording.

- **Magick that somehow touches groups of people takes longer than magick that is focused on a single item or person.** When you have so much energy from so many people, your work does not have a straight shot to success. It has to change quite a bit, and move through various blocks, and so on, to manifest. In this case, keep working.

- *Magick cannot replace physical action.* Sometimes it is far easier to do the "normal thing" than it is to work magick. Each has their time and place. The universe could be telling you to get off your duff and start doing some work.

- *The magick somehow interferes with your spiritual plan.* Believe it or not, there are checks and balances in the universe, and on occasion Spirit will say, "Nope. Nothing doing. You are not going there!" Yes, we have free will, but what if you've been working for three months to bring harmony into your life and then you cast a spell that would shoot the heck out of all the work you've done, but you are so angry or upset at this moment that you don't care? It is highly possible that if Spirit feels you don't need a lesson in what it is like to backslide, then the magick you've done before will override what you are doing now. This is only one example and we could probably talk about this topic all day, but you get the idea.

- *All magick strives to create balance; therefore, sometimes a situation has to get worse before it gets better.* Read Harmony in Part V for a complete explanation. Again, your perception has a lot to do with what is, and what is not, harmony in your life, and the way you view the situation may have to change before the work is completed.

Finally, as the old saying goes, *Sometimes shit happens*, which means there is no magickal or occult reasoning for failure. You bombed. Get over it. Try something else.

Magick: The Cat That Leaps Is Not the Cat That Lands

Spirits of the crossroads, show yourselves,
Let us walk the lonely mile together,
And let us share the dream of the Hidden God,
Who lies deep within my body.[78]

And we are back to holographic quantum physics. Quantum mechanics was developed early in the twentieth century to explain certain anomalous phenomena associated with light and atoms.[79] By the 1930s its mathematical structure had evolved almost to the point where it exists today as the major theoretical tool of physics and chemistry. Calculations using the mathematical formalism of quantum mechanics have been tested against countless laboratory measurements for almost a century, without a single failure. From this study we've gained lasers, transistors, computer chips, superconductors, plastics, thousands of new chemicals, computers, and nuclear power. Although we are obviously using quantum mechanics, we still don't exactly understand it, because—oh, my—the human brain might be an integral part of it, something mystery teachers the world over have been trying to tell humankind for thousands of years. Today, we know that the math is right, now we're trying to figure out the rest of it (scientifically speaking).

In the 1950s David Bohm, an eminent physicist, had several spirited discussions with Albert Einstein. From those discussions he proposed a new field of quantum physics he called quantum potential. He theorized that this potential pervaded all of space. He realized that quantum potential had a number of features that seemed at odds with the current orthodox scientific thinking. He believed that quantum physics could prove true and operated on the importance of the wholeness of the universe (just what the ancient mystery teachers were trying to say all along). Where classical science says that the interaction of the parts creates a whole, quantum theory was proving that the behavior of the parts was organized by the whole—which supports the mystical statement that we are all one and is an indicator of the possible vastness of any group mind. Bohm also felt that the things that we perceive as disordered aren't disordered at all—that there is a hidden order in all things, a sublevel that only quantum physics could prove. Bohm called this deeper level of reality the implicate order.[80] When we practice magick, we are unfolding our desire from the implicate order of quantum potential into our level of existence (called the explicate or unfolded order).

In our study of alchemy, we learn that quantum potential is known as "the void." It is a cosmic sea with attitude, that attitude being the potential to morph into anything at any time. An even more surprising feature of the quantum potential is its implications for the nature of location. At the level of our everyday lives things appear to have very specific locations (unless you move them or knock them down, of course). However, Bohm said that in the subquantum level (the void), location ceased to exist. All points in space became equal to all other points, and nothing is ever separate from anything else. Indeed, when Christ said your brother is yourself, he wasn't kidding. In physics this lack of taking up space is called *nonlocality*. This means, technically, that we can manifest anything, anywhere, anytime because everything is everywhere *all* the time. We just need the right key-code (if you will) to access it, which is what magick is all about—finding the right key-codes for each individual.

Therefore, the vibrations that a magickal action creates unlock the subquantum level, pull through the pattern that we need, activate it to stabilization, and relock the subquantum level,

allowing the manifestation to stabilize. Granted, this is a very rough view of the process and not entirely correct but it will certainly give you something to think about. That "pulling through to manifestation" is what the crossroads is all about in magick. The crossroads is the vortex of manifestation. If we throw in superimposition, the spiral spin, and holographic unfolding of patterns, the cat that leaps is not the cat that lands—it is a different cat, a successive cat, which is how Martha Raymond could have a tumor as big as her fist on Tuesday and by Tuesday three weeks the later the tumor is gone. It is how miracles have always occurred. It is how Jesus changed water into wine, how Honi was able to make it rain (or not) and cure snake bites, how Mary Magdalene turned the white egg to red, and how Moses changed his staff into a snake.

It is science.

And it is faith, but it is NOT dogma.

Every pattern, from people to events, is a series of holographic unfoldments. Quite frankly, some physicists are having heart failure over the idea that we do indeed create our own reality, and believe that current philosophers are only making a fad out of quantum physics mixed with their search for the meaning of life and making some bucks in the process. Although that very well could be true, as a magickal person you will discover that quantum physics answers a whole lot of those "why" questions that may have endlessly nagged you. If you are brave, you can study more about quantum physics and run your own experiments. What frightens some physicists is that the ability to manipulate our reality appears to be a natural phenomenon, meaning we don't realize the level of control we already have. We don't think about breathing, but we do it. It is the same with the ability to manifest all sorts of things, from that new computer we want so badly to poltergeist activity.

And, while we're on the subject, Craft teachers have always taught that time is not linear; indeed, the Celtic knot is an example of how the ancients believed time manifested. Time, as the new physics postulates, is only a series of "nows" that loops in and on itself.

Removing Magick from a Project or Item

Most spellcasting procedures use some form of material, hands-on approach to help the practitioner create the intended desire. When the goal has been reached, such items (spell bottles, coins, crystals, cords, etc.) should be cleansed and released with appropriate honor unless the spell specifically indicates the fate of the object within the procedure. The idea is to "unmanifest" the item—releasing a pattern and sending it back to the subquantum level. Sometimes we will want to keep the tools we used and other times we will want to discard them. Releasing energies is just as important as conjuring them, and shows your respect of the universal energies. A tidy Witch is a successful Witch.

If a spell does not give instructions for disposal of an item, you may wish to use the following guidelines:

Crystals and gems: Cleanse in running water after each use and place in moonlight for at least five hours.

Food and consumable liquid (such as juice): Dispose of immediately by placing outside and saying: "Blessings of the gods upon me," unless otherwise directed.

Spellcasting projects: These are items you have put together yourself, such as a conjuring bag filled with herbs and stones, a sigil on a piece of paper, etc. that you have kept until the goal manifested. Now that you have obtained your desire, you will need to dis-

pose of the item in a sacred way. Check your notes to see exactly what type of ritual you did and from what or whom you asked assistance. In ritual circle, thank those energies, then lay your hands over the item, and say:

The future has come, my desire was granted
Your work is now finished,
no longer enchanted.
Air will disperse, and fire combust.
Water joins Spirit, earth turns to dust.
Though you must depart,
your gift shall remain
blessings upon you in Goddess' name.

Break apart the project. Release your circle in the normal way. Cleanse those objects you will use again in holy water and store. Bury or burn all other items. This mini-ritual is sometimes called "License to Depart."

Tools or objects made of metal or wood: Cleanse with holy water in a magick circle and place in moonlight or sunlight for about five hours. This should be done at least once a month.

Locks, Keys, and Subquantum Crossroads

Locks and keys can be used for a variety of purposes, from unlocking a tightly bound situation to slamming the brakes on unwanted energies by locking them out of your life. The Key/Lock/Unlock correspondence gives your subconscious mind an appropriate analogy as a springboard for the conscious focus. Keeping the idea of the holographic quantum physics information you read in the last section, try this spell, not only to further your own goals but as a mental exercise to fine-tune your abilities.

Key to Success Spell

SUPPLIES: One brand-new padlock and key; one small, red, terra-cotta pottery dish (the kind that you place under plants)—the color red is important; white paint; a brush; a taglock or representation of the success you wish to achieve; herbs to match your intent; taper candle in the color that matches your intent. Write a statement of intent on a small piece of paper. I would also like you to practice saying the vowels of the English language (*a,e,i,o*, and *u*), connecting the sound of each letter to the next. Do this at least twenty or thirty times, until you are comfortable with the sound.

PREPARATION: Determine whether "success" in this instance refers to locking or unlocking the energies. If you will be unlocking something, begin with the lock closed. If you want to lock something, begin with the lock open. Plan your ritual according to this choice and the Moon quarter (SEE PAGE 24). Paint the Spirit circle (SEE PAGE 9) or a pentacle (SEE PAGE 9) on the inside of the dish. Allow to dry.

SPELL: Cleanse, consecrate, and empower all items. Whether the lock will be opened or closed, place the key in the lock. It must remain there throughout the spell. Make sure that your statement of intent is clear. Cast the magick circle and all the quarters. Breathe deeply several times, then ground and center. State your intent aloud. Begin chanting the vowel sounds you practiced in the preparation phase. Place the red dish in the center of the altar. Stare at the dish, envisioning the quantum physics idea of the crossroads between this level of reality and the subquantum level. Imagine these crossroads opening, providing you with the ability to change your reality. Keep chanting "A-E-I-O-U" until the image of the dish wavers or your eyes get a little swimmy.

Continue chanting the same sounds as you place the paper on the red dish. Sprinkle your chosen herbs on top. Continuing to chant, empower the candle and light it. Finally, add the picture, taglock, etc. on top of the herbs. Continue to stare at the dish while chanting, envisioning the pattern of what you want coming together and rising out of the vortex of the crossroads. When you feel you are ready, pick up the lock and either open it or close it with a flourish. Stop chanting. Place the lock on top of all the items in the dish. Say very loudly:

I know my wish has been granted.
May this spell not reverse or place upon me any
curse, and may all astrological correspondences be
correct for this working. So mote it be!

Allow the candle to completely burn.
Close the quarters. Take up the circle.

Twenty-four hours later, cast your circle again and call the quarters. Begin the chant again. Burn all items in the dish in a fire-safe cauldron or pot, believing that what you desire is in the process of manifestation. Visualize it rising from the vortex painted on the red dish. Stop chanting when the fire dies or when you are sure your visualization is complete. Take the key out of the lock. Wear it around your neck until your desire has manifested. Release the quarters and take up the circle. Scatter the ashes to the winds. Bury the cold candle end on or off your property, depending on whether you were drawing something to you or pushing something away. When your desire has manifested, de-magick the lock and key. You can use it again for the same type of working.

Recommended Reading

The Holographic Universe by Michael Talbot

Three Roads to Quantum Gravity by Lee Smolin

The Unconscious Quantum: Metaphysics in Modern Physics and Cosmology by Victor J. Stenger

Physics and Psychics: The Search for a World Beyond the Senses by Victor J. Stenger

The End of Time: The Next Revolution in Physics by Julian Barbour

Schrodinger's Kittens and the Search for Reality: Solving the Quantum Mysteries by John Gribbin

In Search of Schrodinger's Cat by John Gribbin

Sigils, Symbols, and Magickal Alphabets

As you study the Craft and magick, you will discover hundreds of symbols and sigils that can be used in spellcasting and ritual. We've covered several of these symbols in this book, including the pentagram, the equal-armed cross, runic glyphs, alchemical ideograms, Tarot trumps and pips, astrological symbols, elemental drawings, and the hexagram. The word *sigil* is from the Latin *sigillum*, which means "seal." Although magickal people will differ on the meanings of these symbols and sigils, all agree that they won't work for you in magick unless they are activated. Whether we discuss a Pennsylvania Dutch hex sign, a Voodoo vèvè, or ceremonial seals, the basic instructions for use are always the same.

- All symbols/sigils require research, and no symbol should be used unless you thoroughly understand what that symbol stands for, its history, why it is used, and in what kind of environment it works the best. For example, you learned in the runic section of this book that the rune symbols do not work well unless they are activated, and that they prefer deities from their own pantheon

(either Norse or Germanic). Voodoo vèvès are the same. They also prefer their own pantheon and ritual energy, and are especially partial to drumming vibrations.

- All symbols/sigils require activation to work well. Yes, the history around a symbol can impart some energy, but unless you tap into that energy, the symbol either won't work, or won't work well. Activation normally includes cleansing, consecrating, and empowering (or charging) the symbol to work in a specific way for a specific reason.

- It's better to make, carve, sew, or draw any symbol/sigil yourself rather than buying a premade one. The energy you spend in creating that symbol gives a solid foundation to the magickal operation for which that symbol is intended.

- Symbols/sigils are the keys to the subconscious and are used in magick to assist in creating your desire on the astral/material plane.

All symbols, therefore, have more than one dimension. First, they normally represent a single, basic thought. For example, the American flag is the symbol of my country (a physical thing), and most of us, when we look at the flag of our country, think: *Yeah. It's a flag. And your point being?* This flag, however, is also a symbol of something not physical: the idea of freedom. Each star on the flag represents a state (a physical thing), but they also stand for something *not* physical: the concept of unity. The flag stands for a dream—"the stars and stripes forever" (as we say in America)—a vision of the future projected by the symbolism of the flag. This, indeed, is a magickal operation, thinking the future to create it, and using a symbol as a focus for this dream.

The flag of one's country also links to the collective unconscious of the people it represents, their history, their hopes, dreams, and, yes, . . . their failures. The symbol, then, becomes a picture (a flashcard) of a bunch of thoughts all rolled up into one physical item: the flag. The idea of what that flag represents gets bigger and bigger over the years. Let's face it, hundreds of thousands of people have died for what that flag means to them. A symbol can represent the most powerful type of magick in the world, and the ancient alchemists knew it. (SEE ALSO DISCUSSION ON TALISMANS UNDER ALCHEMY.)

Finally, a symbol is the pattern of quantum physics. It is the vehicle illuminated by mind-light that jettisons the desire from the void into the world of form. It is the "pop" of nothing into something. It is the zeno effect—the link of you the observer to the desire, which allows the change from nothing to something to take place. In essence you are saying: "Let there be only this set of little dots in a specific sequence instead of lots of little dots all over the place." Upon your perception, observation, recognition, cognition, or registration of this physical recording device (the symbol), the cloud of ghostly dot possibilities evaporates and the thing you desire is born.[81]

Matching a Sigil to Your Intent

To create a sigil that you will eventually empower and add to other spellcasting techniques that match a specific intent, think carefully about what it is that you really want. As an example, let's use:

A Good Grade On
My Chemistry Exam

Now write down the first letters of each word:

A G G O M C E

You could remove one of the Gs if you like, or trace it twice in your sigil. As with the bind runes, we are going to combine these letters.

The sigil you design, depending on your own handwriting and how creative you want to be, might look like this:

At this point you will decide whether you want the symbol to stand alone, or whether you will add it to another magickal project that you have designed for the same intent. If you wish to activate the symbol to stand alone, you can use the following instructions.

Empowering a Symbol or Sigil

Choose a ritual format. At the appropriate point, place the sigil in the center of your altar. Pass the four elements over the symbol or sigil. Hold your hands over the symbol, and say:

I conjure thee, O great symbol of the art,
to combine and coalesce, to meld and unite the
universal energies necessary to obtain my goal of
(state your intention here). *Where this mark is*
made, Spirit's (or a chosen deity's) *hand is laid.*
So mote it be!

Carry the sigil with you, in pocket or purse, until your desire has manifested. You can use it again—in this case, for the next chemistry test—by repeating the ritual and empowering the sigil once again. If you will not use the sigil again, remove the magick and burn the paper. Remember to thank Spirit as you scatter the ashes.

Magickal Alphabets

Magickal writing and spoken charms, because they both deal with "the word made flesh" either by sound or letter, carry similarities. In the ancient world, written charms had one or all of the following,[82] and many of these same uses are still employed today by magickal people:

Palindrome: A word, verse, sentence, or number that reads the same backward as forward. *Palindrome* is a Greek word meaning "running back again." The repetitive nature of the word or sentence creates a magickal loop that builds power until released by the practitioner.

Astrological sigils: These are symbols of planets, stars, the signs of the zodiac, comets, and other heavenly body associations. In your studies you have learned that each of these sigils contains its own reference to a particular type of energy. In the Greco-Roman world (famous for their written charms), such symbols were called *charakteres.*

Geometric shapes: For the modern practitioner, these can include squares (four directions), triangles (sacred trinity), wings (movement), pentacles, hexagrams, etc.

Voces mysticae: These are words not immediately recognizable as the common language of the times—the "gibberish" that scholars sometimes refer to when studying ancient texts. It can be anything from the broken-down pronunciation of a "real" word, or a personally created word that acts as a keyword for the working. Such an example in modern Craft would be *Eko Eko Azarak—Eko, Eko, Zomalack.*[83] Many of the original voces mysticae have turned out to be real words borrowed and frequently distorted from other real languages, including Hebrew, Aramaic, Persian, Egyptian, and Coptic,[84] however, the Eko passage has never been (*a*) proven to be legitimate, nor (*b*) translated into something sensible. The Latin words used in the Witch's Pyramid are an example of translated voces mysticae.

Repetitive formulas: Called *logi*, which may be several voces mysticae strung together and then repeated. Common repeated phrases were then considered "formulas." Therefore, in the body of any spell, you may have a formula for addressing the gods, for addressing the dead, for the actual spellwork, etc. Modern Craft also has such repetitive formulas, including the poetry by Doreen Valiente that has permeated almost every Craft-related group in the US in one way or another. Again, *Eko, Eko, Azarak* and its successive passages would be considered an old repetitive formula used in a modern way. Other popular words found mostly in ceremonial magick are *Adonai*, which is the cosmic spirit of the Hebrews, and *Iao*, originally derived from the tetragrammaton, the holy and unpronounceable name of God.

Names ending in –el or –oth: These don't appear so much in modern Craft but they do appear prominently in ceremonial work. These names are clearly built on Jewish and Hebrew models.[85]

Another ancient technique still used today, especially in the systems of Hoodoo and Pow Wow, is the practice of either scrambling words or sentences, or writing them backward in an effort to confuse evil, muddle negative energy, and mystify bad vibrations—sort of like a magickal eggbeater for the brain. However, if you use this technique outside of the line of defense, it will come back and bite you.

ENGLISH	CELESTIAL WRITING	MALACHIM	PASSING OF THE RIVER	THEBAN	DAGGERS
A					
B					
C					
D					
E					
F					
G					
H					
I					
J					
K					
L					
M					
N					
O					
P					
Q					
R					
S					
T					
U					
V					
W					
X					
Y					
Z					

Magickal alphabets.

Using magickal sigils, symbols, and alphabets have the following advantages:

- It keeps your work hidden from prying eyes.

- The amount of time you expend translating your language into the magickal alphabet lends more power to the work.

- Pencil and paper or carving tool and knowledge of the alphabet is all that is required.

- Magickal alphabets can be turned into magickal sigils.

Magickal alphabets were carried from the ancient civilizations into the medieval occult world. Indeed, the older the alphabet, the more powerful it was thought to become. As early alphabets did not have vowels, translating one's desire could be tricky. The most popular alphabets in Agrippa's day consisted of Celestial Writing, which had a connection to astrology; Hebrew, thought to be powerful due to its association through Moses; Malachim, known as Angelic Writing, said to be channeled to man by the angelic host; and an alphabet called the Passing of the River. Theban and Arabic were also popular.[86] Some magickal practitioners create their own enchanted inks for sigil work, others sometimes purchase the inks from specialty shops and add their own ingredients, being careful not to meddle too much with the consistency of the ink.

Outdoor Spell for Juggling Your Busy Schedule

Sometimes it feels like there just isn't enough time in the day. You've got school work, maybe a job, perhaps a sport or other special interest. Then of course there are chores at home. Maybe you're stuck babysitting a younger brother or sister, or you have to help clean the house, mow the lawn—you know the drill. With all this stuff to do, just how do you fit everything together?

In the regular world, prioritizing helps. Do those things that you must first so you're not worrying about them later, then add in the things you most enjoy. Drop those things that are not serving you well. You can also learn about multitasking—doing several things at once (though not to the end of doing several things together, badly). In multitasking, you pick those things that are related and do them together. For example, let's say you have to go on the Internet and look up something for science class. You've also got a project in health, but that's not due for another week. While you are on the 'Net, find all the information you need for both categories. When you are ready to work on the health project, you will already have the information. Sometimes employers allow you to do your homework on the job when business is slow. If your employer allows this, go for it! Maybe you can do your homework while watching your little brother or sister. There are lots of ways to multitask if you just use your creativity and common sense.

You can also pull magick into daily life. Let's say your mother asked you to take out the garbage. Fine. As you take the garbage to the dumpster (or wherever), imagine that you are throwing out all the negativity you've been experiencing lately. Mowing the lawn? "Cutting away unhappiness and fear" is one idea, or putting yourself in touch with the devas on your property. Who lives in what tree? What sort of personality does it have? Can you use those grass clippings in magick? Of course you can!

Now that we've got the everyday stuff covered, let's take a look at the following spell:

SUPPLIES: One stick; soft ground or sand outside; ½ cup dried dandelion leaves; your desire, written on a piece of paper using one of the magickal alphabets in this book (or from another). In this spell, your desire would be to learn to prioritize in a positive way; however, you can use the spell for other needs if you like. Here, however, you are asking for organizational abilities and the quality to be a visionary—to look ahead to the future and plan accordingly.

INSTRUCTIONS: On a clear night or at dusk, cast a magick circle and call the quarters. Sit in the center of the circle and look up at the heavens. Draw the peace and tranquility of the stars (or setting sun) into your heart. Think about what you truly want in life. Ask Spirit for help in getting your organizational act together. Ask for clear vision. Now stand up and take a deep breath, inhaling through your nose and exhaling from your mouth. Using the piece of paper as a guide (if it is dark, you may need a candle or flashlight), copy the magickal writing from the piece of paper into the dirt or sand. Then hold your hands over the writing, and say:

Time is not linear. Past, present, and future are now. I am the Witch who makes the word become flesh.

As you say the next passage, scatter the dandelion over the writing:

I conjure thee, O magickal writing, to rise and take shape, to grow and take form, to live and bring forth the completion of your task. I know you will do this for me. So mote it be.

Clap your hands three times and say:

The magick is sealed. May this spell not reverse or place upon me any curse[87] and may all astrological correspondences be correct for this working.[88]

Sand Sigils

Sand sigils can be used as a magickal operation alone, or can be added to boost other magickal practices or rituals.

SUPPLIES: Oval bowl at least 2½ to 3 inches deep, filled with 2 inches of sand; stick incense of your choice; one cleansed crystal.

INSTRUCTIONS: Consider your intent and design your sigil ahead of time. Place the bowl of sand, crystal, and incense under the light of a full moon for at least fifteen minutes. Use one of the basic rituals in this book for the overall format. Place all supplies on the altar. Using the unlit incense stick, draw a sacred spiral in the sand, beginning at the outside rim of the bowl and working in. Draw the sigil in the center of the spiral. Light the incense stick. Pass over the sigil, saying:

I conjure thee, O magickal writing, to rise and take shape, to grow and take form, to live and bring forth the completion of your task. Where this symbol is made, the Mistress of the Universe lays her hand. I know you will do this for me. So mote it be.

Empower the crystal for your desire. Place on top of the sigil. With the incense, carefully trace the sacred spiral in the air over the drawing from the center out, visualizing your desire entering the arms of the sacred Mother. Place the burning incense stick near the center of the spiral so that it can burn freely. Be careful that it doesn't tip over. Draw an equal-armed cross in the air over the entire project. When you have received your desire, thank the Goddess, cleanse the crystal under running water, and set the sand out in the sunlight for at least a half hour. Leave what is left of the cold incense stick outside in front of your doorstep, unless your intent was to banish. If banishing, leave at a crossroads. ***Note:*** You can mix the sand with a little of your favorite herbs; however, when the desire has been met, the mixture should be given back to the earth.

Talismans, Amulets, and Defixiones

Most present-day historical scholars agree that amulets and talismans were very much a part of the ancient everyday world, regardless of religious persuasion, including those sects who overtly frowned upon such nonsense. The word *amulet* comes from Arabic, meaning "to bear" or "to carry"[89]—sounding much like the Latin *amolior*, which means "I repel or drive away." In the ancient world an amulet was called *periapta* or *periammata*, meaning "things tied around."[90] According to Pliny, the word *amulet* meant "an object that protects a person from trouble."[91] The word *talisman* comes from the Greek root *teleo*, which means "to consecrate." Most historians also agree that amulets and talismans were prepared and sold by specialists, who produced them according to traditional recipes and consecrated them through ritual acts designed to empower the object for the special needs of the client.[92]

Over the centuries, amulets and talismans have sometimes changed or shared definitions, though they have separate magickal functions. Cultures all over the world have used them in magick, adornment, and religion. Where an amulet is often considered passive (used for protection and preventative reasons), the talisman is active (made to bring something to you, like success). A third object, designed specifically to bind evil, whether it was a person, god, or animal, was called a *defixiones*, meaning "to fasten," or *katadesmoi*, "to bind down" (both are Greek)—meaning curse tablet.[93] A third meaning, sometimes added to either defixiones or to katadesmoi, is *eucha*, meaning "prayer," therefore the total meaning would be "to bind down (or fasten) a prayer." Although called "curse tablets" for lack of better terminology, not all of the tablets consisted of negative thoughts or banishing. Some were created for increased physical strength or for matters of the heart. For more information on banishing and binding, see page 375. Some historians feel that the ancient defixiones were specifically for harming, restraining, or enslaving enemies or objects of lust and thus fell (as a whole) into the cursing category.

Some magickal people will tell you that an amulet can only be of natural material (a stone from a river bed, herbs, a bone from an animal), where the talisman and the defixiones are usually a construction of some sort (jewelry, a statue, even a bumper sticker); however, this explanation doesn't bear up under archeological findings,[94] and as we move on in this section you'll see why it gets a bit confusing.

Although we tend to think of an amulet as a single object, the Egyptian words for amulet have a less restrictive meaning. The word *sa* can mean a group of objects, the cord they were strung on, or the bag that contained them, as well as the words and gestures needed to activate them.[95] Such bags have a variety of names, depending upon the culture—conjuring, gris-gris, and mojo bags, to name a few.

In most magickal symbolism, an amulet is normally a small, usually portable item that is unusual in nature, and can be worn or carried on a person, placed in a house, office, or car, and can be temporary or permanent. An amulet's job is to ward off danger and sickness—a protective device. A talisman, on the other hand, is designed to transmit energy, such as bringing success to the wearer. If you always wear the same unwashed socks before an athletic event to bring you luck, then those stinky, smelly things would be considered a talisman. The defixiones is a finishing device—binding negative energy and then banishing that energy completely from the client. Defixiones have been found all over Europe in wells, foundations, streams, pits, and cemeteries, left by the clients hundreds and thousands of years ago right where they put them for the original ceremony. The amulet pushes away, the talisman brings in, and the defixiones banishes. What is confusing to the new practitioner of magick is the fact that all three can (but not always) be used for protection. Of the three, the defixiones is the most volatile because if it is handled incorrectly it will backfire on the practitioner. Many magickal individuals do not bind or banish by name; instead, they work on breaking the negative energy and then banishing the unwanted residue.

In modern magick you will discover that everyone has an opinion on the definitions of all three items. For example, according to the Order of the Golden Dawn,[96] a talisman is a drawing or inscribed object charged with the force it is intended to represent, therefore you need to research all correspondences before activation. Studying medieval talismans from books on occult philosophy can be time consuming because each talisman contains a variety of symbolism, including heavenly hierarchies, specific colors, metals, and tools for activation, and are extremely strict on timing. These talismans can push or pull energy, depending upon your point of view.

One of the most popular ancient Egyptian amulets was the *wedja*, used to both protect the wearer and bestow desirable qualities such as health and vitality—a combination between an amulet and a talisman that both repelled and attracted.[97] The wedjat eye[98] (or protective eye of Horus), shown below, can be drawn on anything you wish to protect. Make a copy of this drawing and hang it in your locker to keep people from taking your things.

What is most amazing about the wedjat eye is that it consists of a mathematical shorthand of fractional proportions for Egyptian medical ingredient measurements, listed in six parts. The eyeball is ¼, the eyebrow is ⅛, the portion in front of the eyeball is ½, the portion behind is 1/16, the curlycue is 1/64, and the line straight down is 1/32. In total, the picture equals 63/64, with Spirit supplying the last little bit to equal 64/64.[99] Not only is the design spiritual in nature, it also links to medical and practical uses. If you wanted to write a spell of your own using the wedjat eye, as listed later in this section, then you would need a total of six ingredients, each representing one portion of the eye in the measurements listed above.

Natural amulets (wood, bone, seeds, herbs, stones, gems) depend on their association with the elements (earth, air, water, fire) and the inherent energy of the item. This kind of device bases its magick on animistic principles: the notion that things throughout nature have spirits or personalities dwelling within them.[100] For example, a wolf's tooth placed in the home for protection would connect with the energy of the wolf species (protection against attack, guarding family energy). An amulet made of garlic would work on the principle of the garlic's natural healing energy to ward off sickness. The use of amulets for protection is worldwide among almost all peoples, and they are used to protect the owner against shipwrecks, terrible storms, sickness, evil spirits, death, guarding one's possessions, gossip, warfare, and bodily attack. Amulets aren't reserved only for people, and can be found tacked on homes, barns, sheds, and even government buildings, as well as around gardens, fields, and tied onto animals.[101] The modern-day scarecrow is an amulet set in the fields to ward off negative energies that might harm the crops. Granted, the scarecrow is a mighty big amulet (and certainly human-made), but it could be considered a protective device just the same. In Egypt, as well as many other cultures, unusual natural objects such as the holey stone (a stone with a hole in it) were considered to have special powers because they were exotic. Egyptians called this special power *heka*, meaning the object contained the energy that first created life. In the Craft, we call heka Spirit. Even more interesting, the Egyptian word for *seal* sometimes means "amulet," and sealing is a standard magickal technique not only in ancient times, but in modern ones as well. In the Craft, we seal the magick circle and magickal operations so that the energy is not lost.

Human-made amulets serve the same function: to protect. Examples over the centuries are coins, horseshoes, statues, bracelets, necklaces, rings, prayer papers, pieces of the crucifixion cross, balls made from wax and herbs, even Pennsylvania Dutch testimonials (letters asking God for protection) and hex signs created for protection and warding off sickness.

From their history we can see that amulets, talismans, and defixiones are not specifically related to Witchcraft, but to magick and culture. Many people, regardless of religion, believe in the power of these items, whereas if you asked them if they believe in Witchcraft because they refused to change their socks (that lucky talisman) in an effort to make sure they win the upcoming hockey game, they might look at you as if you lost your mind. Most amulets, talismans, and defixiones are activated by charms, which are spoken words of power.

Before working the following spells, remember to check your divination tool and the correspondences throughout this book, especially those that discuss timing. Remember to cast all spells in the magick circle.

Thunderstone for Home Protection

SUPPLIES: One round, smooth stone that fits in the palm of your hand, preferably from a stream, lake, or river; several small pieces of mirror—rather than breaking a mirror, you may want to check your local handicraft store, which sells packages of tiny mirrors; glue.

INSTRUCTIONS: On the night of a full moon, cleanse, consecrate, and empower the stone, mirrors, and glue, asking for divine protection. You can petition the Lord and Lady, the angels, or the animal spirit of your choice. As you glue the mirrors on the top surface of the stone, intone the following chant:

> *To guard, to protect, to ward off evil*
> *keep my world safe from awful upheaval*
> *thunder to shatter and lightning to blast*
> *so mote it be, this magick is cast.*

Repeat chant seven times, then blow on the stone, saying: "As above, so below, this magick is sealed." Empower again in thirty days. For extra power, infuse during a thunderstorm.

Empowering Jewelry for Protection

Choose symbols that mean protection, such as the pentacle, the Goddess, the lunar crescent, or pick a gemstone that has protective correspondences. On the night of a full moon, cleanse and consecrate the piece with the four elements in a magick circle. Repeat the following chant seven times while consistently rubbing the jewelry with your fingers:

> *Formed in earth and forged in fire,*
> *Goddess blessing, lift me higher.*
> *Guard me from life's evil blows*
> *please make sure my safety grows.*
> *Goddess grant me my desire*
> *formed in earth and forged in fire.*

Empower every month (or when you are feeling particularly fearful).

Talisman to Bring Love

SUPPLIES: Pink paper; pen; pink box or bag; rose petals; perfume; pink candle.

INSTRUCTIONS: Make a copy of the above vèvè or draw by hand on a pink piece of paper (it works better if you draw it yourself). On the back of the paper, write your name three times, as well as "Please bring the right person to love me that I will also love." Rub your hand over the talisman three times, then kiss the front and back of the paper once to seal. Set aside in a pink box or pink bag that also contains several rose petals. Spray the inside of the bag three sprays or add drops of your favorite perfume. Close tightly. Place the bag in the light of the full moon for one hour before performing the spell.

Cast a magick circle. Pass the bag over the flame of the pink candle seven times (be careful not to burn the bag or box). Open the bag and remove the talisman. Pass over the flame three times, repeating: "Please bring the love that's right for me." Allow the candle to burn completely, or relight once a day for seven days, repeating the statement. Don't forget to thank deity and release the circle.

Spell works well in spellcasting ritual on page 331. Carry the talisman until you meet the right person. To reverse or break the spell, burn bag/box, talisman, and rose petals.

Wedjat Spell

SUPPLIES: One small red bag; 2 small stones, one black, one white, empowered for balance in healing; one hand-drawn wedjat eye (PAGE 456) on a small piece of paper; mortar and pestle; a picture of the sick person and something small (a taglock) that belongs to them; 6 herbs in the following proportions:

$\frac{1}{64}$ thyme

$\frac{1}{32}$ dried, crushed garlic

$\frac{1}{16}$ allspice

⅛ cinnamon

¼ dried mint

½ crushed pine needles or rosemary

Note: Herbs chosen for your ease in obtaining them. You can substitute more exotic healing herbs if you so desire.

INSTRUCTIONS: Using one of the basic rituals in this book, prepare the area, cast the circle, and call the quarters. Cleanse and consecrate all supplies. Place a picture of the sick person in the center of your altar. Grind herbs with mortar and pestle. Empower with herbal charm on page 381. Empower black and white stones for healing in balance. Place herbs, stones, and taglock in red bag. Set on top of picture. Place wedjat eye on top of photo. Hold your hands over the wedjat eye and repeat the following incantation:

I belong to the Craft of the Wise. I belong to (say patron God or Goddess name—Egyptian deity would be best. If this bothers you, say "Spirit.") *I have come from* (say where you were born) *with the Great Ones of the Great House, the Lords of Protection and the Rulers of Eternity. I come from magick with the Mother of the Gods and I am in her safekeeping. I know charms that the Almighty wrought to chase away the spell of a god, of a goddess, of a dead man, of a dead woman, a living male, a living female, and they are a part of my knowledge. It is I who shall guard the sick person,* (say name of sick person), *from his/her enemies. Our guide shall be Thoth* (main patron of physicians and healers), *who lets writing speak, who creates the books, who passes on useful knowledge to Those Who Know, that they may deliver from disease the sick person of whom a god wishes so that he/she be kept alive and healthy.*

Place the wedjat eye in the bag. Tie closed with ribbon or string. Hold bag in both hands while saying:

O Isis, great in sorcery, mayest thou remove all sickness, mayest thou deliver (person's name) *from everything evil and vicious and angry, from the spell of a god, from the spell of a goddess, of a dead man, of a dead woman, of a living male, of a living female and deliver* (person's name) *as thou delivered both Osiris and Horus. Behold! Thou hast saved* (person's name) *from all things evil, and vicious, and angry, from the spell of a god, from the spell of a goddess, from a dead man, from a dead woman, from a living male, from a living female.* (Person's name) *is one with you, one with the universe, and one with perfect health. I know you will do this for me. So mote it be.*[102]

If the ill person is magickal or will believe in your work, you may give the person the bag and tell them to keep it with them until they are well. If they do not believe, place the photo and the bag in a safe place until the healing occurs. When the individual is well, dismantle the bag, bury the stones, and burn the remainder, giving thanks to the gods, particularly Horus and Isis.

Recommended Reading

The Complete Book of Amulets and Talismans by Migene González-Wippler

Tetragram/ Tetragrammaton

Although not specifically used in this book, you will see the words *tetragram* and *tetragrammaton* in several occult writings, and I have actually seen sigils and circles in modern Wicca (specifically in the Alexandrian tradition) that have used a form of the tetragram/tetragrammaton for magick. Normally, however, you will only see it in reference to ceremonial magickal practices.

According to the *Oxford English Dictionary*, the tetragram/tetragrammaton stands for any four-letter name of God, including Zeus (Greek), Jove (Latin), Soru (Persian), Allah (Arabian), Amon (Egyptian), and a host of other words that mean "deity."[103] In Exodus 3:14, God gave Moses the classic tetragrammaton or four-letter divine name: YHWH or JHVH, pronounced *Yahweh*, or Jehovah, made up of the four Hebrew letters yod, he, vau, he, which, like other Hebrew words, is spelled without vowels.[104] YHWH meant the eternal and unknowable nature of the divine. Many medieval occultists used these divine names (often the Hebrew version) as mystical conduits to the power of God in their magickal workings, and called the tetragrammaton the "Secret Name of God." The letters without vowels become a magickal symbol/sigil that can be added to any working (usually in the making of talismans) to pull in the divine supremacy of Spirit.

If we dig deeper into history and magick, we learn that the tetragram is a geometric design of a four-pointed star formed by the interlacement of two pillars, and is symbolic of the four elements. The two pillars are force and form. This design is used in the conjuration of the elementary spirits—sylphs of the air, undines of the water, the fire salamanders, and the gnomes of the earth[105] (SEE ELEMENTS). In alchemy it represented the magickal elements, and in mystic philosophy the ideas of Spirit, Matter, Motion, and Rest—also attributed to the human, the eagle, lion, and bull (you'll find these four magickal animals on The World Tarot trump and sometimes called *tetramorphs*,[106] meaning the elemental powers).

Barbara Walker's take on the tetragrammaton is equally interesting. In her book *The Woman's Dictionary of Symbols and Sacred Objects*, she indicates that the most secret element of the tetragrammaton was its root, the radical HWH, which means "being," "life," or "woman." Latinized, the letters spell "Eve." She also indicates that there were two versions of the tetragrammaton, the usual male version as listed above, and a female version EHYH or HYH that often appeared on Samaritan amulets. The male and female versions (YHWH and HYH) were often intertwined on magickal parchments.[107]

While we're at it, let's add one more bit of trivia about YHWH/YHVH. In Hebrew lore the total numerical value of YHVH is 26. The number 26 is exactly between the numbers 13 and 52. The number is associated with the 13 lunar months (remember once-upon-a-time calendars were calculated by lunar cycles) and 52, the number of solar weeks in a year. Thus YHVH is at the center of the year and is the essence of the sun and the moon (God and Goddess), and is the essential source of all light—scientific or spiritual.[108]

At this point you are probably saying, "Gee, this is more than I need to know"; however, to increase our knowledge and raise our level of spirituality, we do need to dig into the past and see where the threads of different religions changed, merged, or separated. The tetragrammaton is a good lesson in learning precisely just that. In the seventeenth century, the tetragrammaton was condemned by the Inquisitors, who claimed that it was the symbol of the devil and a protective sigil[109] for Witches. It was Samuel Liddell Mathers who, in the late 1800s, joined the "new breed" of occultists that strengthened the process of invocation by adding the tetragrammaton to then-current occult practices and the Lords of the Watchtowers.[110] Through Mathers' rites, the Lords of the Watchtowers became a staple part of the repertoire of the Golden Dawn and its successor societies. Israel Regardie published these, and they were read by Alex Saunders and introduced into Wiccan workings, which is why they are not found in early Gardnerian Books of Shadows. The Watchtower symbology, then, contains the Alexandrian flair.

You can tell if a Craft group is ceremonial or shamanistic by their quarter calls. If they invoke the Lords of the Watchtowers with the invoking pentagram and ritual blade, then they are practicing ceremonial Wicca. If they call the winds or totems (Celtic origin) and use their hands rather than a blade, then they are shamanistic. We now know by studying history (both past and present) that the inference to the devil in relation to the tetragrammaton was outright hogwash. As to the protection of Witches? As I said, I know those who use it.

A Simple Talisman for Strength and Protection

This is one of those double-duty magickal objects I spoke about earlier. Although deceptively simple, I've known it to work quite well.

SUPPLIES: One Popsicle stick, washed in hot water and dried; a black indelible marker, fine point.

INSTRUCTIONS: Cast the magick circle and call the quarters. Ask Spirit to enter the circle, bringing strength and protection. Cleanse and consecrate the stick with the four elements. On one side of the Popsicle stick, write the Hebrew name of God: YHWH, and on the other side, write the feminine Hebrew letters for God: HYH. Hold the stick in your hand and, using your magickal voice (SEE PAGE 312), intone the names of god/dess (*yod, he, vau, he* and *he yod he*). Begin softly and slowly raise the energy and volume level of your voice. When you feel that the stick has been blessed (the stick may grow warm in your hand), say: "Ho!"

Seal the magick by pressing the stick first to your forehead, then heart, over to your left shoulder, followed by your right. Say, "As I will, protection be." Carry the stick with you or give to a friend.

Tree of Life

The ancients believed that the world hung from a silver cord attached to a fixed point in the heavens, that stable point being the North Pole Star (or the Pole Star). Neither seasons, politics, nor religion could change this fixed point. It was thought that the heavens rotated around this star with the analogy of a great mill that churned out the riches and wealth of the universe, gifts from Spirit to those deserving on Earth. The Pole Star was seen as an umbilical cord to heaven, called "Mother Bond of Heaven" by the Babylonians. Other cultures likened this silver thread to that of the World Tree, Tree of Life, Tree of Yggdrasil, or Cosmic Tree.[111] In Wicca, we find an old magickal charm (author unknown) that matches the idea of a magickal mill/pole in the following incantation, called *The Mill of Magick:*

Fire flame and fire burn
make the mill of magick turn;
work the will for which I pray,
Io Dia Ha He He Yea!

Air breathe and air blow
make the mill of magick go
work the will for which we pray
Io Dia Ha He He Yea!

Water heat and water boil
make the mill of magick toil;
work the will for which we pray
Io Dia Ha He He Yea!

Earth without and earth within,
make the mill of magick spin,
work the will for which we pray
Io Dia Ha He He Yea!

As below it is above
make the mill of magick love;
work the will for which we pray
Io Dia Ha He He Yea!

When we analyze astrology, religion, and magick, we discover that often these systems share many of the same foundational tools. Here, the elements (fire, air, water, earth, and Spirit) form a correspondence and show the primal drive of magick lies in the concept of unity between that which is without, and that which is within—that which is above, and that which is below.

Adding an even more striking association to this rhyme is the Celtic myth of Duibhne, king of Dalriadian, Ireland, who found himself in an unlikely enchantment—basically, even though he looks human, he's stuck acting like a bird. Since he doesn't want anyone to see him in this sorry shape, he runs away to contemplate how he's going to get himself out of this mess. On his

journey he meets the Hag of the Mill, who "is the Cailleach na Dudain or Old Woman of the Mill, who regulates the turning mill of life and death; and is the Gaelic counterpart of the British goddess Arianrhod of the of Caer Sidi."[112] *Arianrhod* means "Silver Wheel," and this interesting goddess has several associations, including Keeper of Time and Custodian of the Silver Wheel of Stars (the zodiac). The wheel (some say) was made by three Druidesses (the Triple Goddess). It is Arianrhod's Wheel that becomes the astrological chart you wish to interpret or the Wheel of the Year of the Wiccan High Holy Days.

Once again we see that Spirit, magick, and you are one, whether we think of a tree, a wheel, or an enchanted mill that connects us all together. Below is a brief listing of the various trees of life.

Cultures, Religions, Practices, and Their World Trees

ALCHEMY

World tree: Axis Mundi, around which the cosmos is oriented; the joining of body, mind and spirit, the three worlds.

BUDDHIST

World tree: Peepul or Bo Tree—under which Buddha attained enlightenment.

CHINESE

World tree: Pear and mulberry, beneath which oneness flows.

CHRISTIAN MYSTICISM

World tree: Tree of Life (sometimes attributed to the Virgin Mary).

DRUID

World tree: Oak, the Sacred Nemeton, Bile.

EGYPTIAN

World tree: Sycamore fig from which the goddess Hathor extended nourishment to the dead. Represents Nut, goddess of the heavens, and is sometimes called the Lady Sycamore.

HINDU

World tree: Brahman was the wood, the tree from which was shaped all heaven and earth.

ISLAM

World tree: Has several trees, including the tree of blessing and illumination, the tree of happiness, and the celestial tree at the center of paradise from which flows the four rivers of water, milk, honey, and wine. Also the world tree on whose leaves the name of every person is written.

JEWISH MYSTICISM

World tree: Kabbalah's Tree of Life, the four worlds, and the ten Sefiroth.

MAYAN

World tree: Yaxche, which supports the layers of the sky.

NORSE

World tree: Ash, Yggdrasil, from which the nine worlds can be reached.

SUMERIAN

World tree: Tammuz, vegetation god gifting the Earth through his tree of life.

WICCA

World tree: The Magick Mill; pole star.

The Tree of Yggdrasil

Perhaps the most mystical of the various Tree of Life legends is that of the Tree of Yggdrasil in Norse mythology. The story has always touched me deeply because it can be read on many levels. It's one of those legends that no matter how many times you go back to it, you'll always find something new to think about. The main character of the story is Odin (sometimes called Woden), the Father/God of the Nordic pantheon. In many ways, Odin goes beyond the simplistic way we might look at God. He is the invisible Soul of the World that animates all things and travels through the nine Nordic worlds like the wind. He rides upon a magickal steed named Sleipnir, and his deep azure cloak stretches into infinite space. He has two familiars, ravens named Huginn (meaning "thought") and Muninn (meaning "memory") that represent his soul. Each day the birds fly around the world and then report back to him, telling him everything that has taken place. Not only does he stand for the mind of God, he also has many other talents: shapeshifting, writing, inspiration, intellect, communication, magick, and seership. A white serpent (wisdom), skilled in magick, lies at his feet at all times.

The story goes that this legendary hero wanted above all to find wisdom and obtain the gift of prophecy. To do this he was required to hang upside-down on the world tree, Yggdrasil, for nine days and nights (each day and night representing one of the nine sacred worlds in Nordic lore). At the dawn of the tenth day, he reached down into the roots of Yggdrasil and withdrew the runes, the magickal alphabet of the Nordic peoples. Hanging there wasn't all he had to endure; he also had to make a sacrifice and exchange one of his human eyes for "the sight." Obviously this is a tale to teach us a lesson—that sometimes we must sacrifice those attitudes that are outdated to grow spiritually. He could not truly see until he looked within himself.

Sometimes Odin is referred to as Grom. This is an Old English term meaning "marked" or "hooded." In some Pagan circles, the Hooded Lord is either a direct reference to Odin, or to the magick and secrecy that surround "the God." The Celts also possessed a pantheon of gods known as the *Genii Cucullati*, or Hooded Ones, and there is a vague association to a Celtic horse cult wherein the practitioners could whisper magickal words to horses and the animals would do their bidding.

Odin is connected to the shamanistic mythos of our present-day Santa Claus. In Holland as late as 1920, cookies called *vrijer* were given as tokens of good fortune over the Christmas holiday. These cookies depicted a stylized Odin turned gentleman as the bringer of the sun and good fortune. The women were given the "male" cookie, and the men the "female" cookie—a stylized Freya.[113] Yggdrasil is sometimes said to be an ash and at other times a fir, the same fir tree from which the legend of the Christmas tree grew.

shadows of Magick & Real life

Acne

Whenever we deal with a medical problem, we must first research the background of the illness. According to the experts, eating too much chocolate doesn't cause acne. Our bodies produce hormones (called *androgens*) that make our skin oily. That oil can lead to acne in some people. Acne may also run in families, although dermatologists aren't sure exactly what the connection is yet.[1] The following spell is to show you how medical science and magick can work together, and how Witches in particular watch the changes in medical theory over time and adapt to those shifts in knowledge. When I was a teen, we were told that acne came from eating junk food or foods with a high grease and fatty oil content. If you wanted clear skin, you stayed away from those foods. This wasn't exactly inaccurate, but today they've discovered more about acne, including that there are several kinds of acne.

To rid your body of the teenage plague, begin by realizing that acne (as well as many other conditions) is linked to stress. Therefore, the first thing we might review is determining what is causing this stressful outbreak. Grades? Family problems? If we want to be healthy, we simply cannot retreat into denial. Something in your life is stressful. If you can't come up with anything, it's probably because you've repressed it, or you've lived with it for so long that you didn't realize that those ugly bumps you have now are caused by an energy that you've put up with since the sun first rose in the east. By mentally reviewing what is going on in your life, you are actively beginning the healing process. By recognizing the stress, you are another step ahead. And not only do we want to remove the symptom (the acne), we also want to remove the cause. If we just do magick for the symptom, then the cause may lie dormant for a while, but sooner or later, the symptom (or some other medical malady) will emerge again. Are there any adjustments that you can physically make in your daily life that will help to reduce the stress? Think about it.

Next, we want to eliminate those stressful feelings, so, at least once a day, go through the Body of Light Meditation (ON PAGE 293) or one you have designed for yourself. Granted, you won't get rid of an acne problem overnight with meditation, but this is a good, healthy practice that you should be doing daily anyway.

Now we're going to look at the physical causes of acne, which we have researched by looking on the Internet or talking to a dermatologist. The advice on this score is to keep your skin clean. Our local dermatologist recommends a mild soap rather than all those nifty-neaty ones on the market. A pharmacist can help you choose the one that is right for you. Wash the afflicted area often, especially if you are involved in sports, but try to avoid scrubbing, which only inflames and irritates your skin. Applying cool water right after strenuous activity helps to remove the oil and dirt. A benzoyl peroxide lotion from the pharmacy can help to dry the skin and reduce bacteria.

For girls, stay away from pounds of makeup, which clogs the pores. I realize that cosmetic companies won't be too thrilled with this advice, but in the case of acne, the foundation especially creates a vicious circle. You wear it to cover up the acne, which results in more acne because you are continually clogging the pores, which forces you to apply more foundation.

As an observer of four teens, I've found that the biggest enemy of healthy teen skin is time. Teens are so active they find any regular cleansing routine irritating and consequently put it off, not realizing that every time they forget to wash the skin gives that acne a firm foothold on their face, back, and chest.

Mild cases of acne can usually be conquered in about three months with a daily regime of stress reduction and proper skin care. If after three months nothing works for you, then it's time to see a dermatologist. You can find one located in your area by looking in the phone book or visiting http://www.aad.org (American Academy of Dermatologists) online (you'll also find information on acne, rashes, and insect bites under the kid's page).

Acne Removal Spell

Okay, so we've done the research. We've looked squarely at our lives and tried to pinpoint where that stress might be coming from, and we've taken the steps we think are necessary to remove that stress. We've also set our daily meditation into motion, and we've begun to do the physical things (like cleansing the skin often) in order to accomplish our healing goal: the complete removal of acne.

What's next?

I want you to draw a really horrible, awful, ugly monster on a piece of paper, and I want you to name it "My Acne." I'm not kidding (and yes, this has been known to work). Have a great time making your monster. Use colored pencils, markers, whatever. Don't worry, we're going to get rid of it, so have a blast with your creativity. However, don't put it into form until you are immediately ready to get rid of it right after you finish the drawing.

When you are done with the drawing, clearly state, while looking at the paper, "You represent my acne!"

You are now going to perform the adjuration or banishment sequence by using an Anglo-Saxon spell that is 900 years old. Light the illuminator candles on the altar. Cast the circle and call the quarters (general wording will do), then ask deity to help you banish your acne. Place the acne monster drawing on the center of your altar. Hold your hands over the paper, and say (with lots of feeling and conviction):

May you now be consumed as a coal upon the hearth. May you shrink as dung upon a wall. And may you dry up as water in a pail. May you become as small as a linseed grain, and much smaller than the hipbone of an itch-mite, and may you become so small that you become nothing, never to abide in me again![2]

With a flourish, burn the paper in a fire-safe container, saying: "By the power of the Lord and Lady, I banish thee from my life-force!" If you are not allowed to burn things in the house, then tear the picture into teeny-tiny pieces, repeating the words "I banish thee" as you work.

Now let's concentrate on healing your skin. Place an empowered quartz crystal in a bowl of clear water. Hold your hands over the water, and say:

I conjure thee, O holy liquid of earth and water, by the moon, sun, and stars, in the name of the Lord and Lady, to transmute into healing energy, so that as this water touches my body, my skin will recover and heal. So mote it be.

In your mind, see the water filling with brilliant white light. With a clean, white cloth, dab the water on the afflicted area. As you do this, envision your skin covered with the pure white light of healing energy. Take your time. There's no rush. When you are finished, close your eyes and visualize yourself without acne. I know it's hard. Try anyway.

You have just fulfilled the magickal portion of the healing process. Let's move on to the blessing part. Light a white candle (often used for blessings of any type). Then sit back, and say:

O my mother, Great Goddess of the Heavens
She who is found in the primordial waters
of the midnight sky
Who gives birth each day to the glowing sun
And lights the path before me
with the shimmering light of the moon,
stretch your protective arms over me
and enfold me with thy healing energy.
At whose feet lies eternity
and whose hand contains the Always
bless me, thy daughter/son, in thy name.
So mote it be.[3]

Take a deep breath. Ground and center. Thank deity. Release the quarters and release the circle. Throw the ashes of the defunct acne monster to the winds out-of-doors. Allow the white candle to continue burning, or put the candle out and light each night, repeating the blessing until either the acne is gone or the candle has been completely burned.

Follow through with positive self-thought. Reject any negative thoughts about yourself or your skin condition.

What happens if your acne gets worse? Shudder the thought, but let's deal with it. Review that stress level. Have you been doing your daily meditations and self-talk? Did you at least *try* to remove some of the stress in your life? If not, then you are still feeding the acne monster with your negative emotions. Let's say it was going great, then *whap!* the acne starts up again. Did you remember to keep your skin clean? If you've done everything by the magickal numbers, and you are still having a problem, then it's time to see a dermatologist (if you haven't already). He or she will most likely prescribe a cleansing cream and perhaps pills for you to take. You can't be sloppy about this, like take a pill today and then forget for a week, or lose the cream at the bottom of your dresser drawer and come up with it a month later. If you're going to tackle this beast and win, then you have to see it through.

Action

From personal empowerment comes a flow of energy; in that gentle current, the heart, the mind, and spirit work as one, and from that oneness grows contentment. No matter what the situation, the religion of Wicca urges you to take action rather than stare helplessly into the abyss. Don't stew, pout, or moan if things don't go your way. Instead, put that wonderful, creative brain of yours to work and consider solutions to whatever problem you may have encountered. Do magick! Do ritual! Actively seek to conquer and overcome. Like Einstein said, "Within every difficulty, there is a solution." Use magick, meditation, and ritual to help you find the resolution that feels right to you.

Helpful Magickal Tips to Start Anything

- If you really need to pump it up, begin a spell or do a ritual when the moon is new (to begin) or full (more power).

- Use a red candle to add a little extra *vroom* to your magickal work.

- Add drumming to your desire.

- Using your almanac, choose a day to begin your work when the moon is in the sign of Aries, or in a Mars hour (SEE PART III, PLANETARY HOURS, UNDER ASTROLOGY) or on a Tuesday (Mars' day).

- Add either of the following herbs to your magickal work: dragon's blood (for more power) or vervain (to make the work go faster).

- Start any spell at dawn to pull in the birthing energies of earth, sea, and sky.

- Inscribe the birth rune, Birca (ᛒ), on your candles or other magickal supplies.

- Place the Magician Tarot card under your altar to enhance your ability to meld thought with Spirit to enhance the manifestation of your magick.

- Cast your spell during a thunderstorm (this really works!) or on a windy day.

- Cast a spell over moving or rushing water, or to match the tides of the sea (if you are lucky enough to live by the ocean).

Sometimes it isn't the "getting moving" part that is so frustrating, but finding the right direction in which to move. Remember to perform all magick in a cast circle and check your divination tool before casting any spell.

General Spell for Action

In the Craft, Witches may call upon the natural powers of the elements (SEE PART IV, ELEMENTS) to speed the manifestation of a desire. In this spell, we are keeping the following in mind:

- Earth moves by the natural acts of decomposition.

- Air moves by the natural act of dispersion.

- Fire moves by the natural act of combustion.

- Water moves by the natural act of evaporation.

To help you learn these four basic types of movement, look through some of your spell books (or visit a local bookstore or library) and read the spells to determine what type of basic action is called for. Sometimes spell books do not include elemental associations, so it will be up to you to choose which element(s) you feel will best do the job to give your chosen spell a little more *oomph*.

SUPPLIES: A red plastic dinner plate; a tomato (earth); incense of your choice; a fan or large feather (air); red candle and lighter (fire); a red bowl filled with holy water; 4 red ribbons, 7 inches long; a piece of red paper; a black indelible marker.

INSTRUCTIONS: Think of what you want to move in your life. Spells work best if they are specific, so take the time to think about what you want, why you want it, and how you will word your intent. Write down your desire on a piece of red paper. Choose one of the three ritual formats given in this book as the outline of your spell. Follow the ritual format, then include the spell as listed below.

Place the red dinner plate in the center of your altar. Write your intent on the tomato with the black marker, and place the tomato on the center of the plate. Lay the ribbons over the tomato. Light the red votive candle and place the candle holder next to the tomato. Set the red bowl beside the plate. Light the incense. Pass the incense over all the items on your altar, saying:

> *Air disperses, moves and flows,*
> *mighty Spirits make it go.*

Pass the red candle over all items, saying:

> *Fire crackles, changing form,*
> *flame to heaven, change is born!*

Pour a little of the holy water onto the plate, saying:

> *Moonlight water moves the tides,*
> *moisture travels to the skies.*

Hold your hands over the tomato and say:

Fruit of north will rot away,
sending magick on its way.

State the intent of the spell (what you wrote on the tomato). Allow the candle to burn completely. Seal the spell by burying the candle and tomato outside. If someone would get suspicious of what you are burying (if you are on campus), place near a dumpster. Tie the ribbons to a tree. If there are no trees nearby, a bush will do. If no bushes, hang from windowsill of your room. *Note:* If you can't bury the tomato, you may wish to write your intent using a magickal alphabet (SEE PAGE 452).

Just as the elements can be used to activate a situation, they can also be used to stall, slow down, or stop something that has gotten out of control. If we view the elemental energies in this way, we have the following:

- Earth buries and seals, such as a cave-in or the grave.

- Air can stall or push down, as when a weather front stalls over an area or the wind sheer pushes down and creates a tornado.

- Fire can hold, as the burning embers in a fireplace hold the heat.

- Water can capture, as the sea ensnares her treasures in her watery depths.

Anger and Conflict Resolution

Some people just never seem to get upset by anything. It would be nice if we could live our lives without anger, but anger is an emotional outlet letting us know that we aren't happy and our needs are not being met. Anger tells us that there is something deep inside of us that should be addressed. Magickal elders teach us that we should never practice magick when we are angry, meaning that we shouldn't target a person, place, or thing just because we're mad. We can use magick, however, to work toward reducing stress, which will also (in time) turn our mental fuses into slow burn rather than a quick explosion.

Our feelings are not separate from the body. In magick, we learn that the body, mind, and soul should work together as one to create a harmonious lifestyle. When something is out of whack, our emotions let us know. When we feel good and express that nice feeling to others, then we are in tune with the universe and it is harder for people to push our emotional buttons. Sometimes anger, annoyance, frustration, or rage comes from old hurts, present fears, or even physical sickness. Occasionally we are angry because of what others do.

When you hear people talking about righteous anger, they are speaking of a moral issue that has deeply upset them—such as murder, abuse, or unsafe practices at work or play. Sometimes when righteous anger takes hold of people, they demand changes that will make our world a better place. Anger (in this case) can be a catalyst for positive change, but we should never forget that anger is as volatile as a volcano.

One of the hardest things to realize is that we manufacture our own anger. Magickal people know that we control our thoughts, therefore we can learn to harness and move through our anger in a positive way. The trick is to remember to do it before we get carried away, because emotions are quick and natural. They aren't like a delayed television feed where you have time to sort out what you will show the world and what you wish to keep private.

Not everyone behaves the same way when they are annoyed or upset. Some people hold their anger in, acting sullen or very quiet. Others scream and shout, throw their hands around, and make a terrible display. Then there are the people that are so overwhelmed by their feelings that they can't think or speak, and when they do, strange and nonsensical things pop out of their mouths, covered in globs of spit. (That's me.) Being mad every now and then is okay and even healthy because it keeps you from swallowing all that energy and getting sick. On a daily basis, however, how you express that anger is the key to your personal success. Don't be ashamed if you know you are having trouble controlling your emotions. I know adults that have never gotten the hang of it and are now too old to care about how their rage affects themselves or others; conversely, I've met lots of young adults (and full-grown ones, too) that have come to the Craft seeking positive ways to harness their fury or frustration and have succeeded magnificently.

Here are some magickal tips on how to deal with anger (or emotions in general).

Keep a Personal Journal

Journaling serves several purposes. First, your journal becomes a magickal vehicle of expression. You can draw in it, write poetry, add photos of your friends, and record important family events. It helps to sit down and write out your feelings. In fact, many college curriculums today insist that you keep some type of personal journal. Most magickal training, whether we are talking about a ceremonial lodge or a coven environment, also require journaling, and a few might ask you to keep more than one. Putting words on paper (or on your computer) becomes an exciting history of you, and even though you might not think so, your children (should you have any) will enjoy reading about your life when you were their age. Some of the most important historical records we have of life in our country have come to us not from publishing companies, newspapers, or magazines, but from the hearts and minds of everyday people explaining on a daily or weekly basis what life was like for them. These diaries, journals, and letters help us to understand that history isn't something separate from us, and that it can't be totally controlled by the media. History is happening now, and you have every right to record it. Okay, so maybe you want the journal to be totally private—that's great, too.

Keeping a personal journal also has a practical side—in my family, we've solved more arguments about what happened on what date simply by the fact that I keep a journal. When I say, "Fine, I'll go get my journal and prove it," everyone shuts up. If, in the future, you plan to study astrology, you'll find that keeping a personal journal or diary is extremely helpful in pinpointing trends that are unique to you. In this way, you can prepare for the future. So what if you're not into writing? Keep a calendar or date book (you can also record what spell you did when, which is helpful). A few notes and you're done. Time and again I've found my date book very helpful in tracing bills I've paid, phone calls I've made, or conversations I've had. You never know when you'll need to back yourself up with information.

Most magickal books contain some sort of blessing and a warning to those who would use the material therein against the author. You can use the personal journal/book blessing in Blessings (SEE PART I), written in English, or translate it using one of the magickal alphabets in Part IV (SEE PAGE 452). If you don't like this one, you can always write one of your own.

Echo's Enchanted Door Spell

My oldest daughter, Echo, created the following spell to help herself deal with anger. Not everyone at school was nice to the local Witch's kid, and she knew she needed to work out her frustrations in a positive way. It started with a chant on a three-by-five-inch card and grew into an incredible magickal masterpiece. Whenever she made a new friend, participated in a school event, or went on a trip away from home, she took pictures and then pasted them to the inside and outside of her bedroom door around the spell. She also collected her favorite quotations, wrote them on slips of paper, and stuck them around the pictures. As time marched forward, pretty cards, dried flowers, and other memorabilia showed up on that old wooden door. As she became more comfortable with herself and her place in our family, pictures of her siblings at some of their special events also joined the ranks of the door magick. After a while, you couldn't see the door but she could see her own living history, which was extremely important to her. When Echo reached adulthood she performed a personal ritual, removing some of the items from the door and asking for bright and positive future possibilities. The entrance to her room took on a new look to match her growing needs. I realize that some parents don't want you to mess up the door of your room, so you might ask them for a big bulletin board, which will work just as well.

SUPPLIES: Pictures, your favorite quotations, school memorabilia, etc.; your favorite magickal oil and incense; holy water; a white candle; a bell; salt; your favorite spell or poem written on a three-by-five-inch card (or use the spell below); tape or other parent-approved adhesive. Don't forget to check your divination tool.

TIMING: Begin on a new or full moon.

INSTRUCTIONS: Carry the four elements around your room in a clockwise direction, envisioning the area being cleansed with white or blue light. Silently pass the four elements over both sides of the door. Sprinkle the holy water on the doorknob and at the base of the door. Toss just a bit of salt at the threshold. With the oil, draw an equal-armed cross on the four corners of both sides of the door (just a bit of oil will do). Ring the bell three times. Read the spell on the card, then paste the card in the center of the door. Hold your hands over the card and repeat the spell twice more. Your hands may grow warm or tingle—that's okay.

Now, blow three deep, slow breaths on the surface of the door. Your breath carries the moisture from inside of your body (though you rarely see it) into the air. Most magickal people and occultists believe in what is called *sympathy*, wherein something from your body or worn on your body can be used to link energy from yourself to another individual, place, or thing. Your breath carries your essence all the time. It also bears your will. "Breathing life into a spell," then, becomes a literal as well as a mental function. It creates a pathway between you and something else, so that you work in sympathy.

Ring the bell three times to seal the spell. Repeat the chant three times every thirty days (to keep the energy fresh), and ring the bell three times. You can also repeat the spell whenever you are feeling angry or blue.

Enchanted Door Incantation

By oil and water, censer and light
I enchant this door with magick bright
each time it opens love will grow
each time it closes hate will go.

With pictures, words, and thoughts of life
I end unhappiness, pain, and strife
and ever when I ring the bell
I breathe new life into this spell.
Love and peace are now my names
I grow in wisdom, joy, and fame
by light of moon and might of sun
as I will it shall be done
and as above or so below
I'm in control—just so you know.

Learning to identify why you are angry or frustrated is an excellent way to understand yourself and reduce the stress of being mad, especially when the commotion in your head (and gut) is your mental response to another's words or actions. Mentally step back and ask yourself the question, "Why am I angry?" and be honest with the answer (that's the hard part, by the way). While you are doing that, take slow, deep, even breaths. Not only does full, slow breathing calmly reduce stress, it also lessens the side effects of anxiety. The biggest hurdle to overcome is controlling our anger in a social situation where you may not have time to contemplate what's making you so mad. There are people who will try to force you to be angry to satisfy their own personal agendas, firing words at you like a machine gun to give themselves an emotional high. If they do not receive the response intended, some choose to up the ante and push you harder. Their emotionally charged energy bleeds from them like real blood, washing the area around them with ugly vibrating signals. Your body will pick up these messages first on a subconscious level, moving up from the basement of your mind to let you know something is wrong. This is why your heart rate may increase, breathing becomes shallow, palms sweat, and shoulders tense the more volatile a situation becomes. Your body is doing what it can to let you know that the energy around you has changed and that you should be prepared. In fact, your whole body is actually wired for psychic reception (a psychic barometer, if you will) but we often fail to recognize the gift. If you take deep breaths and physically step back, you have consciously told your subconscious mind that you have acknowledged the signals coming at you and that you are prepared to deal with them. Your thinking will become clearer. Almost all magickal students learn to shield themselves from such negative energy once they recognize it (SEE PROTECTION, PAGE 534).

If, after a mental rundown, you believe that you have caused the problem, or that your words or actions were misunderstood, do open your mouth and try to provide an open flow of communication. Sometimes people don't realize that they made you angry. Why? Because either you misread them or they misinterpreted you. The best way to communicate with a good friend or family member is to begin by saying, "When you say (whatever) it makes me feel (and explain)."

The "Protecting Yourself from Angry People" Spell

by Ray Malbrough[4]

There's an old saying that tells us when others are angry with us, we should keep cool. This isn't always easy! In African belief, the head contains the seat of the soul. By keeping the head cool and emotions calm, you will be guided by Spirit to overcome any situation. During the times when you feel that you are about to lose control, try the following African spell:

Take two leaves of the kalanchoe plant (available in most nurseries and large supermarkets selling common house plants), and place them on the center of your altar, desk, or worktable. Rub cocoa butter and powdered eggshell on both leaves. Place them in the shape of a cross on the top of your head and cover the leaves with cotton. Cover this with a white handkerchief tied to your head, as a gypsy or pirate might tie a scarf. Write your name on a white candle, then light the taper, praying for peace in your life. Leave the leaves and scarf on your head for about eight hours. As you remove the leaves and cotton, place them in the garbage with a firm affirmation that your anger is discarded in the trash.

More Tips for Conflict Resolution

Communicating with others (including your parents) isn't always easy. Try these anger-reducing tips:

- Be honest. Look at them, and say, "When you say _____, it makes me feel _____." For example, "When you say I'm stupid, it makes me feel that you don't love me." If you are talking to a parent or guardian, they would probably say, "But I didn't mean that," and then they will probably apologize. They don't want to make you feel bad, but they are frustrated and having a hard time putting their feelings into words. State your feelings without being accusatory.

- Try not to scream and yell. When one person raises their voice, the other person will do the same. It's a natural reaction. You are using so much energy screaming that you miss the point of the discussion. If you ever take a telephone service position, one of the most useful tools is to learn to lower your voice as the other person is raising theirs. It will force them to listen to you— and to lower their voice as well.

- Don't interrupt when the other person is speaking, and don't try to finish their sentences for them. They have as much right to explain how they feel as you do.

- Concentrate on what is being said to you rather than allowing your mind to jump ahead, looking for that great comeback. It is very important to maintain eye contact.

- Ask questions to clarify what the other person is saying. Not only does this make you think about what they are saying, it makes them think about what is coming out of their mouth too.

- Repeat the other person's ideas as you understand them. For example, "Okay. Let me make sure I understand what you are saying. You said (repeat the statement). Is that right?"

- Be open to negotiation. Compromise ensures that everyone feels that their needs are being met.

- Learn to listen. When in an argument, we become so focused that we tune out the other person's point of view. Sometimes, by simply listening, we discover that the argument isn't about a surface issue at all, but about something else. For example, arguments about religion aren't about religion at all—they are about control and low self-esteem.

- Pay attention to your body language. Everyone subconsciously reads body language. If someone crosses their arms while you are having an argument, it means that you are not getting through. Try another tactic.

- Don't put the other person down during the discussion. Accusations don't help. You're looking for a resolution, not an ongoing war.

Armed Services

Boot camp is a place where your freedoms are extremely limited for a set period of time. During the boot camp and additional training phase of their service career, most installations do not have accommodations to serve the Wiccan community (although many of the armed service branches recognize Wicca as a religion in its own right). When my daughter entered Army boot camp, one of her sergeants said, "Yep, there's one in every platoon. We don't have facilities for you, private. Do you need a special tree or will any one do?" She was permitted, however, to wear her pentacle. Those nine weeks were incredibly busy for her, with little time to set aside for private workings. She resorted to doing affirmational magick and mental cleansings in the shower, talking to her grandmother while in the field (for ancestral protection), and programming herself for success during boring tasks (like night duty fire watch). The family here at home did the rest. When she finished boot camp and moved into her additional training cycle, she used my *Teen Witch Kit* as her portable altar.

The Military Shrine

When our youngest daughter chose the armed services, we knew she would be so busy the first several months that she wouldn't be able to practice Witchcraft in the way in which she was accustomed. When she left home we turned her room into "the magick room," and set up a shrine for her protection while away from us. The shrine grew to include the letters and postcards she sent home, pictures of her before and while she entered the service, a Himmelsbrief (SEE PAGE 552), talismans and amulets, a continuously burning candle matching the color of the

day she was born, a bowl of water changed every two days, and other offerings to deity. When we attended her boot camp graduation, we discovered a Catholic family that had done the same thing, proudly displaying the pictures of their home shrine dedicated to two of their children in the armed services. They topped our efforts, however, because they had two life-sized pictures of their children beside their shrine. That's dedication!

If you have a family member in the armed services or in one of the top ten most dangerous jobs in the country (which include timber milling, being a police officer, search and rescue, and so on), then you may wish to build a protection shrine just for them. Don't kid yourself—every little bit you do, even if you seem estranged or too distant, will certainly help the individual you love.

Beauty

Beauty is all about taking care of your health and the image you would like to project to the world. In the Craft, some Witches use an image projection called a *glamoury*. The glamoury has two important facets:

- It is temporary.

- It enhances what you already have.

Lots of nonmagickal people use glamouries out of habit and, somewhere along the way, the habit gets stuck for good and it's terribly hard to peel it off (if you dare) because pieces of you will come off with it. For example, Richard may seem like a great guy to your face, but when you're not around, he's constantly talking trash about you and everyone else. Richard is suffering from low self-esteem, and he's using a glamoury to your face every time he speaks to you. Denise acts tough. She brags about how many kids she can "take down." Her glamoury includes strutting, carrying her shoulders a certain way, and giving people her special "tough" look. Denise is also suffering from low self-esteem. If neither changes their behavior, although it may not seem that way right now (because they are making your life miserable), Richard and Denise are heading down the "Loser" path, and they are actively creating a rotten future life.

Being beautiful, for all of us, is a learned behavior. I'm not kidding. Beauty is not the model on the cover of your favorite magazine, it is not having the most expensive clothes, buying the "best" makeup, or going to the most popular hair salon, or having the hottest car—all those things are glamouries used by normal people because their insides may not be so great. With these people, what you see is all you get.

In the world of the Craft, we know that beauty is really your astral energy shining through, and that outer beauty, as well as mental and physical health, are all part of the same package. Think of it this way: If you are wearing fifty pounds of makeup, what are you saying to the world? If you don't take a bath, don't wear deodorant, and never brush your teeth, what are you telling people? What you wear, how you speak, who you hang out with, and how you behave (gossip, moocher, slacker, friendly, kind, loyal) are aspects of beauty (or not). All of us, from time to time, play roles—Prep, Skater, Drama Queen, Jock, Tease, Teacher's Pet, Greaser, Goth, Nerd, Loser, Perpetual Grump (whew! lots of labels, huh?)—but when we do, we're not allowing our true selves to shine through and, after a while, whether we are aware of it or not, we become the role we are playing.

Of all the situations that my children dealt with through their school years (college, too), I think the idea of role playing was the hardest for them to understand. They believed the roles they saw in others, and didn't understand the roles they played within themselves, or that you can change your role in life to bring toward you what you most desire. The hardest thing to do is to get the outer you in sync with the inner you because you are growing so fast, and life is changing so quickly, you're not exactly sure what you want. If you desire to be beautiful, then remember the words of Ralph Waldo Emerson: "What you do speaks so loud that I cannot hear what you say."

Spell for Beauty

SUPPLIES: A mirror; your favorite incense; a picture of Hathor (the Egyptian goddess of beauty); a list that includes what you would like to change (for example, "I wish to walk with grace," "I would like to be kind to others," "I would like to be able to use my musical talent to help people"); a pen; a blank sheet of paper. (Yes, the list represents all "inner beauty" stuff, and when the inner beauty comes out, you'll knock 'em dead.)

INSTRUCTIONS: Light the incense and look into the mirror. Ask yourself, "What message am I sending to the world?" Write down on the blank paper the outer things you would like to change (clothing style, haircut, posture, makeup). Now think about how you act with your parents (you can make faces, look mad, sincere, whatever). Is there anything there you would like to change? If so, write it down. Finally, think about how you act around your friends. If there is something you would like to be different, write that down, too.

Hathor, the Egyptian goddess of beauty.

Take three deep breaths and think about Hathor, the Egyptian goddess of beauty. She's not a vacant-headed beauty, either. She's smart, wise, and graceful. Close your eyes and talk to her (in your mind, if you think someone will hear and make fun of you). Tell her the inner beauty things you wrote down on the first list—what you would like to be: kind, loyal, not so critical of others, and so on. Open your eyes and draw her symbol over your list with the pen. Say:

Heaven and earth, liquid and plain
the moon's bright glow and stars maintain
that goodness grows within my soul
and spreads throughout my body whole
and with the blessing of Hathor's kiss
I become the beauty that none shall miss.

Fold the paper and hold it in both hands. Repeat the words while thinking of yourself the way you wish to be. Blow on the paper three times, then make the symbol of the equal-armed cross over your reflection in the mirror. Say: "This spell is sealed from skin to soul. So mote it be."

Beauty and the Moon

Is there any cool stuff happening where beauty and the astrological sign the moon is in is concerned? Absolutely![5]

WHEN THE MOON IS IN . . .

TAURUS, CANCER, LEO, LIBRA, OR AQUARIUS

Practice the following: Beauty treatments, skin care, massage, general beauty magick and ritual.

ARIES, TAURUS, CANCER, OR LEO

Practice the following: Cut fingernails.

ANY SIGN BUT GEMINI OR PISCES

Practice the following: Cut toenails.

THE THIRD OR FOURTH QUARTER

Practice the following: Remove corns.

THIRD OR FOURTH QUARTER IN ARIES, LEO, VIRGO, SAGITTARIUS, OR AQUARIUS

Practice the following: Begin healthy eating practices.

FIRST OR SECOND QUARTER OF CANCER OR PISCES

Practice the following: To grow out that bad hairdo—pronto! Cut during this moon cycle. Best time to cut for thicker hair (one day before the full moon, especially in the sign of Leo).

FIRST QUARTER OF TAURUS OR LEO

Practice the following: Permanents, straightening, and hair coloring.

THE FIRST AND SECOND QUARTER OF GEMINI, VIRGO, SAGITTARIUS, CAPRICORN, OR PISCES (AVOID THE FULL MOON)

Practice the following: Tooth removal.

FIRST AND SECOND QUARTER OF TAURUS, CANCER, LEO, OR LIBRA

Practice the following: Spells for romance.

Temporary Glamoury

A temporary glamoury is just that—it doesn't last. The difference between what nonmagickal people do and what you'll be doing is that the temporary glamoury in the Craft brings forth something that is already a part of you—you just want to show it off a little more than usual. Think about how you want to appear for a short period of time. Let's say you are going for your first job interview. You want to look smart, efficient, and responsible. Check your clothing and your hair before you go. Are you neat and clean? Do you look like a dependable person? Now say the following spell nine times, visualizing what you should look like:

> *The chameleon dances in the glade*
> *he blends, he shifts, and now he's shade.*
> *I change myself to meet the need*
> *I am the change they need to see.*
> *As I will, so mote it be.*

This spell also works very well for a part in the school play, giving a speech in public (especially if you have the jitters), or giving a report before your class. It also works well in karate and other sports-related tournaments; however, there

you pick up some of the dirt on the ground while you say the charm.

You can also change one of the lines for an invisibility spell. In invisibility work, you are actually pulling your aura in as far as it can go, which is why you seem to blend in with the environment. You won't go "poof" and not be there, but you can move without undue attention; however, this does not work for illegal activities.

> *The chameleon dances in the glade*
> *he blends, he shifts, and now he's shade.*
> *I change myself to meet the need*
> *my essence now they cannot see.*
> *As I will, so mote it be.*

Bullies

According to the National Education Association, 160,000 students stay home from school each year out of fear of bullies, and a bully strikes every 7.5 minutes each day, with the average attack lasting 40 seconds. An April 2001 article in the *LA Times* states that female bullies and male bullies tend to torment their victims in different yet equally painful ways, and that teachers and adults only intervene approximately 20 percent of the time, and peers only 10 percent.[6] Indeed, part of the bullying problem stems from the lack of action by those students who watch the behavior and do nothing about it, and those who join in, feeding the "pack" mindset. As Witches take an oath to Spirit and to humanity, we cannot condone such negative behavior.

When you are a teen, adults advise that you report a bully to a parental or school employee (should the problem be happening there), but you and I know that even though you do that (and it is the right thing to do), it doesn't mean that the problem will be immediately handled. Although several schools are trying to implement anti-bullying programs, not all formulas work, and not all schools have the programs. My oldest daughter remembers being chased down the hall in high school by such a bully—a girl who came from a rough family background with little supervision. As my daughter zoomed down the hall screaming for help, all the teachers closed their classroom doors, one after another. When she reached the office and tried to explain, they told her to go to class and forget about it.

Adults tend to forget that bullies grow up. There are teachers who are bullies—and stock brokers, doctors, computer techs, store clerks, and so on. Every walk of life has its own set of bullies. Parents label these people with other names, forgetting on purpose what the word *bully* means. For many of us, when we leave our childhood years behind, we try to wash away the pain and sorrow we experienced at the hands of a bully, therefore it is difficult to recognize this behavior in adults. Some adults erroneously think, "I made it through, so can you." We leave those experiences "back there" and refuse to look in our battered memory box for fear we will have to relive those painful times. For some strange reason, we believe that the bully never grew up and remains in the halls of yesterday, with the ability only to torment the ghosts of the past. Not so.

If you are being bullied, it is important that you talk to your parents or an adult whom you trust about the situation. If you are an adult, seek a trusted friend, a therapist, or counseling service. Suffering in silence is not the way to go. Do not choose someone that you instinctively know will support the bully, or support non-action (the "maybe it will go away" scenario). Choose someone strong of character and wise of thought. If the person you talk to does not see the seriousness of the situation, don't give up—find someone else who will listen to you.

In this book you have read about how ancient alchemists believed that transformation is a natural magickal art for those people who understand the connection between all forms and all life. It is the understanding that, because we are a part of all things, we can often have an effect on all things in our lives. We are part of everything, and everything is a part of us. When we wish to change things for the better in our lives, we need only understand that the change *already* exists, we just have to *accept* our belief in that change (the Knowing part of the Witch's Pyramid). In the theory of holographic quantum physics, this means that there are many paths available to us at the same time. Which path we choose determines what causal events will follow. Therefore if we need to have the strength of a warrior to get through a difficult situation, we need only transform ourselves into that warrior that is already a part of us and we will rise with confidence to the challenge.

The following information cannot take the place of asking for assistance, but can work in your favor while you are speaking to someone who will help you change the situation.

Shatter the Shadow Spell

SUPPLIES: A handful of small pebbles; a white candle; incense (your choice); salt; holy water; a picture of the bully or at least his or her full name written on a piece of white paper (yearbooks are great places to find pictures of school bullies; if you are an adult, use office newsletters, business cards, pictures from parties, etc.); one black pouch or bag to hold the stones once you have empowered them; black plate, cloth, or construction paper.

INSTRUCTIONS: Choose what type of person you would like to become in this situation. Be careful. Think of qualities like "strong" or "honorable." Write down the quality you would like to possess. On the full moon or dark of the moon, cast a magick circle, call the quarters, and cleanse and consecrate the four elements with the incense, salt, holy water, and candle flame. Hold your hands over the stones. Take a deep breath and relax. Begin by saying seven times, while envisioning the stones being filled with light, the following:

> *One magick*
> *one power*
> *one Spirit*
> *one might*
> *shatter the darkness*
> *bring only the light.*

Take another deep breath and relax. Hold the stones in your hands, and say the quality you would like to possess in this situation (for example, "strong"), then say the word out loud three times. Follow this by chanting the words "I am" until you feel lighter, happier—sort of floaty. At the end of the last time, blow on the stones, saying:

> *One magick*
> *one power*
> *one Spirit*
> *one might*
> *shatter the darkness*
> *bring only the light*
> *as I will, so mote it be.*
> *This spell is sealed.*

Draw an equal-armed cross over the stones. Set the picture of the person (or their name, if you couldn't find a picture) on a black plate, cloth, or construction paper. Repeat the above incantation every time you drop one of the small pebbles on top of the picture. Finish by saying: "You are burdened with your own negativity. You can no longer move against me."

Finish the ritual in the normal way. When you know you will see the person again, take three stones from the top of the pile and place them in a black bag or pouch. Drop them on the shadow of the individual. If you will not see the person, don't worry about it. After seven days, bundle the stones on top of the picture in a black cloth. Bury the picture, stones, and cloth off your property.

As you learn and grow in the Craft, you will eventually begin tailoring rituals and spells that meet your needs. You will also discover how to insert parts of ritual, poetry, invocations, meditations, and so on into the basic structure of spellwork and ritual that will create something brand new, just for you. This is the joy and the beauty of the Craft.

Dating

Okay, so there are a lot of "firsts" going on in your teen years, and although you may not think so, some of these "firsts" normally attributed to preteen and teen don't occur until you are in your late teens or even early twenties: your first crush (which usually doesn't last too long because they are one-sided), your first kiss, your first date, and for some, your first sexual experience. All of this is pretty emotional stuff. Truth be told, there is no "right" time to start dating and you are legally bound, at least through age seventeen (or the rules of the house, if you are older) to the desires of your parent(s) or guardian on this issue. Parents set these rules because they don't want you to get hurt, and let's face it, there is a lot that can happen in your teen years that you thought you were prepared for and found out later that you were sadly mistaken about. If mom meets your new boyfriend and she's normally the sensible sort, and later says, "I don't like him," then there may be a darned good reason. She may see (or sense—mothers are good at that) something that you do not. Your personality prefers to see, hear, and feel things that please it, and endorse what it wants, where your mind focuses on what is sympathetic to its desires and eliminates extraneous information. Your perception, then, when it comes to dating and the choice of partners, may be narrowed more than you are aware. Lump in the added hormones of the teen years and it's no wonder that people claim "love is blind."

It's best to start dating in a group, with several couples, and even if you have been dating for quite some time it's always safest to go out with a new person a few times accompanied by other couples. This cuts down on the real possibility of date rape. When she (or he) says no—it's no! Only a sick, misguided fool thinks he or she is justified if the "signals" were there. Flirting comes from a need to be acknowledged, it does not necessarily mean that the person desires a meaningful relationship, sex, or marriage. It is more a statement of "Look at me! Look at me!"

In middle school and high school, the dating scene often begins with long phone calls, notes (not a good idea—if you don't want the world to read it, don't write it), e-mails, and spending time together at parties, school events, going to movies and community-sponsored programs, and spending time at the local hangout (if you are lucky enough to have one). Come to think of it, adult dating isn't much different. Peer pressure can make or break a relationship. Don't let it get you down. If your chosen love succumbs to the shallowness of listening to his or her best friend be-

cause they are jealous and don't like you, then that guy or gal wasn't worth it in the first place.

Too often new students of magick want to meddle in the affairs of the heart by throwing magick at specific people. Don't do it. Playing god/dess with another's free will *will* come back to seriously haunt you. You can, however, do magick to ensure that you have a good time, that you are protected, that you see clearly, and that you find an agreeable companion, all without naming a specific person and still concentrating on your own needs. Now, this doesn't mean that you are supposed to be selfish in your dealings with others; you are simply working on your self-improvement and personal empowerment. In the Craft, this way of thinking is often equated to "getting your own house in order."

Safe, Great Date Spell

SUPPLIES: One empty paper towel tube; white paint; red paint; paint brushes; 3 rubber bands; normal altar setup that includes incense and a bell, scented oil or perfume, paper, and pen. Choose a ritual format.

INSTRUCTIONS: Completely paint the outside of the paper towel tube with the white paint. Allow to dry. Encircle the top and bottom with painted red hearts. Allow to dry. In a magick circle, consecrate and empower the "safe date tube," asking (in your own words) that your dating experience be fun and safe. Write on the paper exactly what you desire to occur on the date. Don't get caught up in a complete itinerary or demand that others act in a certain way. Something like, "May my trip to Washington, D.C., with my friends be filled with joy and laughter. May we be protected on our journey from all harm and sickness. May I walk with grace the entire evening," etc. If you are worried that someone will read what you have written, use a magickal alphabet (SEE PAGE 452). Blow on the paper, then seal with a star drawn with your finger in oil (or your favorite perfume or men's cologne). Roll the paper and place in the tube. Wrap the three rubber bands around the tube, repeating "For health, for safety, for joy," then, when the last rubber band is in place, say, "So mote it be." Carry the tube to the four quarters, asking for the blessings of the elements on the upcoming date. Ring the bell at the quarter over the tube. Return to the center of the circle. Thank deity, close the circle, and place the tube in a safe place. After the date, de-magick the tube by removing the rubber bands, saying: "I thank the universe for the gifts given to me and release this conjured energy." Remove the inside paper and burn. If you are not permitted to burn things in your current environment, then tear it into tiny pieces and cast to the winds. You can use the tube again for the next date. This also works well for a school fieldtrip or vacation with friends and family.

What happens if the date didn't go exactly as planned? Did your magick poop out? Not necessarily. First, who knows what might have happened if you didn't cast that spell? Could have been worse than it was, right? Second, think about what Spirit might have been trying to show you with this experience. Is there something you need to pay attention to that you didn't before? What if Spirit is trying to tell you that the people you were with aren't right for you? (It's always a possibility.) Also, take into consideration your own behavior. Were you a sterling example of humanity or did you fall into a familiar negative behavioral pattern? If so, you might have blown a hole in your own spell. Finally, if the date fell apart and you are stuck sitting at home, say a word of blessing to Spirit. Something very funky was going on either with the people involved or where you were planning to go. Be glad you aren't there.

Mummy Spell

Sometimes we are so infatuated with someone that we can't make a wise decision. Perhaps someone is telling you that John is a real jerk, but so far he's been nice to you. Or that Amanda "sleeps around" and "breaks hearts." Could be that the source of the information is usually reliable, but now you're not so sure. Although no one likes to talk about it, physical abuse in teen relationships it is just as prominent as in adult ones (where do you think the abuser first started? Probably with his or her first girl- or boyfriend.). You need to know if it is true that Mike slapped his last girlfriend around, because you know that if he was violent with one girlfriend he will (eventually) become violent with you. Don't ever fall for the line: "Oh, she made me mad, but you won't." Sometimes this behavior takes us by such surprise that we fall into the victim pattern far too easily. To stop this before it begins, this spell works double-time. Not only does it call for the truth, but it also calls for the cessation of any negativity toward you that might be woven by either the individual in question or general gossip.

SUPPLIES: One empty plastic soda or water bottle; one tiger-eye gemstone (or a smooth pebble if you can't find one); a picture of you; a roll of white medical gauze (like you buy at the pharmacy); glue; the person's name (or their picture); a paint brush. Choose a ritual format.

INSTRUCTIONS: Place your picture in the bottle. Hold the tiger-eye gem in your hand and repeat several times while rolling the stone around in your palm, "Spirit of stone, truth be known." Drop the stone into the bottle. Cap. If you can, seal with wax from a burning white candle. Allow to dry. Begin winding the gauze around the bottle, using the glue to tack it in place. Cover the bottle up to the neck. With a disposable paintbrush, lightly coat the gauze with the glue (you can add a little water to the glue to make it more pliable, but not too much). As you work with the gauze, keep repeating: "Only truth can come to me, as I will so mote it be."

Place the person's picture or name in the center of your altar. Place the mummy bottle on top. Cast a magick circle and call divinity. Hold your hands over the bottle, and in your own words address your concerns about this person. Ask for the truth and that the best thing happen for you in this situation. Thank deity and release the circle.

Now, you wait.

The most difficult part of this spell lies in the art of practicing patience. Sometimes you will get your answer immediately or so quickly that you can't believe how fast that spell worked. Other times you will need to relax and allow the universe to bring the information to you when the time is right for you to hear it. Remember, once you have asked for the truth, you will receive it. If you deny the information, then the fault lies with you. You can continue to reuse the bottle anytime you wish to know the truth of a matter. *Note:* If you need to know something extremely important, cast this spell when the moon is in Scorpio. You will need to check your almanac for that information.

Ðivorce

Parents divorce each other, not their children. Many kids experience divorce, whether it is in their own families or the family of a friend. Even as an adult, if your parents suddenly tell you that they have chosen to get a divorce, it can be shocking. Lots of painful emotions can charge through you—anger, hurt, guilt, sadness, the feeling of loss. The most important thing to remember is that you aren't to blame for the breakup of your parents' marriage, whether you are six or sixty-six. When parents divorce, we realize that what we lived with as a "unit" all our lives has now changed and we must reevaluate our perception of ourselves and how we relate to our family members. How you react to this change in family dynamics depends largely on how your parents behave. The first year is usually pretty hard, but after that tensions seem to lift as you all become more accustomed to the new living arrangements. Many times kids feel like they are betraying their parents if they listen to mom or dad's complaints. You're not. Sometimes, talking to a friend who has gone through the same experience can be really helpful. Find an adult you trust in your extended family, maybe a coach or a favorite teacher, who will listen to how you feel—someone who will respect your privacy. Keeping your emotional pain bottled up inside isn't good for you, and it's okay to share to help you work through this change in your life and how you feel about it.

Spirit always listens in times of trouble, and your choice of religion can also be a means of emotional support. While the divorce action is proceeding, cleanse the house with the four elements at least once a week (if you can). If you can't, at least take care of your own room in this manner. Burn blue and orange candles when you are feeling emotionally low.

Hex Sign for Overcoming the Pain of Divorce

With a compass and ruler, draw the hex sign below to bring harmony into your life during the difficult proceedings. Use only blue and orange colors to fill in the drawing. The hex sign won't make your parents get back together, but

Hex sign to bring harmony into your life.

it will help to relieve the stress you are feeling. The rosette design (six petals) is found all over the world, from Athens, Greece, to Pennsylvania. This single rosette is called a *blummesterne* ("flower-stars") by the Pennsylvania Germans. Three petals represent the female trinity (Maiden, Mother, and Crone) and the male trinity (Father, Son, and Sage). The rosette also looks like a fully opened tulip. These flowers were considered symbols of the Witch's cauldron. In fact, many Pennsylvania Germans called the rosette the *hexefus*, meaning "Witch's foot" or "Witch's cauldron."[7] Each day, as you gaze at the center of the flower, imagine that you are looking into a Witch's cauldron of transformation. The hearts are love rising from your drawing to you. The diamond shapes represent the assistance from the four elements and protection.

Once you have finished the drawing, pass the picture through your favorite incense to cleanse, then write all family member's names on the back. Hold your hands over the design and think of peace, love, protection, and harmony. Tap the drawing with your finger five times, once for each element (earth, air, water, fire, and Spirit). Hang where you can see the drawing every day.

Eating Disorders

Did you know that there are about 8 million people in the United States that suffer from eating disorders? Yep. And that nearly 20 percent of this 8 million are teens and young adults? Yep, again. Let's see, what is 20 percent of 8 million—that's one million, six hundred young people. These problems are not fad diseases; they are very real and very dangerous to your long-term good health. Eating disorders include anorexia nervosa, bulimia, and binge eating, and all are potentially fatal. The most important thing for you to remember is that an eating disorder is not about food. Therefore, encouraging your friend to eat or not eat is not going to solve the problem. According to doctors and other informed health personnel, eating disorders afflict a wide variety of people with all sorts of personality types. They stem from complex social, psychological, physical, and emotional roots. People who use drugs to stimulate vomiting, bowel movements, or urination are in the most danger because these practices increase the risk of heart failure.[8]

Have I scared you enough yet?

Hope so.

When the American Anorexia/Bulimia Association canvassed their members, they found that most felt their eating disorder was a way to express their feelings because they didn't know what else to do. These people talked about self-doubts, shame, rage, grief, and feelings that they weren't good enough. Many said that they felt like they were glued to the wall, that no one noticed them. Most of these people are extremely sensitive and have trouble telling others how they really feel.[9] Even when they are desperate for help and are feeling sick, they may not ask for assistance. This could be because they are in denial, or because they feel that they don't deserve the help.

There are a variety of symptoms to look for, the most basic being tingling in hands and feet, fatigue, dizziness, lightheadedness, feeling faint (all caused by malnutrition), slowed heart rate, joint pain, muscle soreness, tendency to be too hot or too cold, depression, and stressed-out behavior. A person with anorexia will not eat enough because they tell people they don't want to get fat. They will eat tiny amounts, filling their limited diet with lowfat, low-calorie foods, then overexercise and vomit. Someone suffering from bulimia eats unusually large amounts of food in short time periods, then purges using fasting, laxatives, diet pills, or overexercise. They may have an unusual swelling around the jaw. Binge eaters usually eat alone, spend a lot of money on food, and many times eat continuously. There's more, but you get the idea.

What to Do

If you think a friend is having this kind of problem, the experts say that you should express your concerns, point out the facts, and suggest that your friend visit a doctor. This isn't easy and your friend may laugh you off; however, most people will respond to concerns about their physical health, even if they deny that there's an eating problem.[10] Suggesting that they see a physician who can recommend "safe foods" (especially if they are on a diet) is reasonable, and your friend probably won't think you are out of line.

What if I've just described you? Is there a spell you can do? Yeah, pick up the phone and make an appointment with the doctor. Now, there is no spell in the world that can replace adequate health care. You are not a bad Witch because you have an eating disorder, but you will be a sick one if you don't do something about it.

Yes, there is a lot of spellwork and ritual work that you can do to support medical treatment, especially those magickal workings designed to help you with your self-esteem and goal planning for the future, but they cannot replace medical help. There are lots of great spells in this book. Just pick the ones you like—*after* you talk to the doctor.

Whether you are having the problem, or you are concerned about a friend or family member, visit these websites for more information:

The American Anorexia/Bulimia Association: http://www.aabainc.org

Eating Disorders Awareness and Prevention: http://www.edap.org

Mirror Mirror: http://www.mirror-mirror.org

About Face: http://www.about-face.org

Something Fishy: http://www.something-fishy.org

You might also want to pick up *The Unofficial Guide to Managing Eating Disorders* by Sara Dulaney Gilbert and Mary C. Commerford, Ph.D. at your local bookstore.

Enemies

There is an occult philosophy that says when we experience anger at what someone does or says, it is because we are within the vibratory range of that event—that for some reason our body, mind, and spirit allows itself to be swept up in the moment because we haven't learned something important. If an event does not affect us, then we are either above or below it, and therefore the energy does not vibrate with our own. I can think of two examples that might help you to understand this philosophy. First, let's take one of those chat rooms, newsgroups, or list serves on the Internet. You may read several posts and think, "This doesn't relate to me or my life," and switch to one that does interest you. Someone else may read the same posts and get really angry, which moves them to write something nasty. In this example, your energy pattern at this time was either vibrating above or below the information on the list, which resulted in no interest. The other person, however, due to events or situations in his or her life, immediately keyed into the negative energy of the list, and succumbed to it.

Let's look at the second example. Here, the drama unfolds at school. Horace is smaller than you, has a rotten home life (which you don't know about), and suffers from taunts from other kids. By the time Horace reaches middle school, his behavior toward others is intolerable (his way of trying to displace his unhappiness). Up to this point, Horace has never been in your class and you don't know that much about him. In fact, his face just blends in with all the others. By the time you encounter Horace (either middle school or high school), he has become monstrous. You, on the other hand, have been fairly popular. Not liked by everyone, but you have your friends, the things you like to do, and the places you like to go. This year, Horace is placed in one or two of your classes and, for the first time, rides home on your bus. For the first month or two, Horace observes you, your popularity, the clothes you wear, etc., and for whatever reason, perceives you as a threat. He then begins a personal campaign to bring you down. Since he has no friends to manipulate, he uses the teaching staff. He's been doing this for several years, so he's gotten fairly good at it. One moment you are having fun with your friends and the next moment Horace has brought the

Hounds of Teaching Hel down on your head. You are furiously blinking your eyes, trying to figure out what the heck happened. You now have an enemy where you had none before. What gives?

In this example, you haven't done anything to set Horace off. Why, then, should you be forced to deal with him? Here, it is simple growth and learning. If you react negatively the first time Horace hones in on you (falling into his negative energy pattern), then it will take awhile for you to move out of that pattern—meaning if you allow yourself to go as low as Horace, then you will feel the same anger, unhappiness, and displacement that Horace does. Horace may even have targeted you because he picked up on something in your life that you are angry about, which puts you both in the same energy vibration. So, what can you do?

Although we are using the young Horace as an example, the Horace-all-grown-up can be just as much (if not more) of a nightmare. Let's say Horace found himself a job in a collection agency, one that has the ability to affect your credit. He sits behind bullet-proof glass all day and threatens people over the phone. He delights in damaging the credit history of strangers. You don't know Horace from a hole in the wall, but there is a snafu with your truck payment because one bank has bought out another and your loan seems to be floating around somewhere out there on its own. What you think will be easy to fix becomes a nightmare, thanks to Horace. Not only does he call you daily, he swears and infers that your character is less than delightful.

In either case, preventative magick isn't going to do you any good at this stage. It's time to do something in your defense.

Ritual of the Red Pot

First, regardless of Horace, think about what, in your life, you are angry about. Write that down. Why are you angry about it? Write down your reasoning. What steps can you take to work through your personal problem? Some affirmations? Meditating? Working with your guardian angel? What can you fix in the regular world without magick? What magick can you use to help you grow away from the situation? Form a plan of action. To break the negativity in your life, add this spell to your workings.

The breaking of the red pot is of Egyptian origin and was used to remove negativity from the home, sacred area, and even the tombs of the dead. In keeping with the Egyptian flavor of the ritual you may wish to call upon Isis, the Mother of Magick, or another Egyptian deity of your choice.

SUPPLIES: Red clay; pencil or clay stylus (a tool used to inscribe symbols and pictures into the clay); a large black cloth; one large metal bucket.

INSTRUCTIONS: Fashion a clay pot with your hands. Don't worry about it being a piece of art, because you are going to destroy it. Carefully draw on the pot all the things that you want to get rid of in your life. For example, your anger, feelings of insecurity, and so on. Allow the pot to dry completely. Hold the pot in your hands and with your mind, fill it up with all the things that make you angry and unhappy. Cover the pot with the black cloth until you are ready to perform the spell.

On a dark moon night (if you can; the problem could be more immediate, so you might have to act right away) or on a Saturday, take the pot and the bucket outside (again, if you can). Cast a magick circle. Call divinity. State exactly what you want to do, like: "I want to rid my life of feelings of unhappiness," and say what is mak-

ing you sad or angry. Ask for strength and blessings. Release the circle by taking the energy into yourself (rather than just letting the circle go). Stand in the middle of where the circle was. Place the bucket at your feet. Take a firm grip on the pot with both hands. Slowly raise the pot above your head, feeling the power of divinity within yourself. At the peak, say loudly:

I release myself from all negativity.
By the power of the mighty Isis,
Mother of Magick, I break all negative
connections to me. As I will, so mote it be!

Then dash the pot into the bucket, visualizing all negativity breaking from you and dispersing where it can do no harm. Take the pottery pieces away from your home and dump them (if you can)—if not, place in an outside trash receptacle.

Ritual of the Guardians[11]

How do we know whose anger belongs to whom? The realization that the anger you are dealing with may not all be your own is the first step. If the thought, "Gee, this can't possibly be all of my own anger" makes you feel lots better, then there's your first proof. If you've done the Ritual of the Guardians, and you don't have any anger left within you afterward, just the cool, calm thinking process, then that's the final indication of just how much power displaced anger can have. Scary, huh?

SUPPLIES: A gold cord, 9 feet long; one white seven-day candle.

INSTRUCTIONS: Perform at daybreak. Make a large circle on the ground or back porch or where you will not be disturbed, but where you can face the sun with the golden cord. If you can't go outside, sit in the center of your bed, arranging the cord in a circle around you, or face a window that beholds the rising sun.

Hold the white candle in your hands and concentrate on being solution-oriented. The ritual is a bit like a play where you are acting out all the parts. Each speaker will come to your circle. You are to imagine him or her with the definitions given. Then read the speech, thinking that they are talking to you. This works best if you read aloud. Before you read the ritual, think about the problem at hand and (if you have decided) what kind of help that you think you need. It's okay if you are confused and have no idea what kind of help is best.

SPEAKER ONE IS THE GODDESS. She is dressed in white and is crowned with glittering, silver stars. As she begins speaking to you, she will place her hand on your head. Behind her is the night sky.

Seeker of Light, I have heard your call in the
darkness, and as the sun meets the new day
I come to you. I am the Mistress of the Heavens
and the Queen of the Stars. I am the Mother
who created all things from the void. I am the be-
ginning and the end of all manifestation.
I have come to protect you. I will guard you
against hunger, pain, sickness, and enemies.
You have the power to master all difficulties.
I ride on the winds of the North. I only ask
that you will try to be truthful in all things.

SPEAKER TWO IS THE GOD. He is dressed in gold, with a crown of stag antlers upon his great head. Daybreak is behind him. He, too, will place his hand upon your head during the reading. He will stand close to the Goddess, who does not leave. She remains as he speaks.

Seeker of Light, I have heard your call. I am the
Lord of the Sun and the King of the Earth. I am
the strength and power of the universe. I am the

divine partner of your Spiritual Mother. I have
come to protect you. Just as I am the master of
the force of the sun, you must be master of your
own fate. You have the ability to change your life
in positive ways. I bring the wit and the wisdom
of the east winds. May they bear you up and
speed you over your unhappiness. I have only
one request, that you do your best to
speak the truth in all things.

SPEAKER THREE IS YOUR GUARDIAN ANGEL. Only you can visualize this form. He or she will stand close to the Lord and Lady.

Seeker of Light, friend, and companion, I have
heard your cry, as have others in your heavenly
circle of learning, those who you have left behind
here in the Summerland, and those who have
passed from your world to ours. They, as I, are al-
ways ready to assist you. I have walked with you
into birth and have trodden your path, matching
you step for step. Know that you are never alone.
You have the power to change your life. I bring
you protection and solutions to your problem. I
have come on the winds of the South, and I hand
you the flaming torch of knowledge and protec-
tion—take it and rejoice! I have only one re-
quest, that you do your best to
speak the truth in all things.

SPEAKER FOUR IS YOURSELF, and you are addressing the other three.

I am the Seeker of Light, and master/mistress of
my universe. I am a Witch in thought, word, and
deed. I am a part of the Hidden Children.
I have the power to change and improve my life.
I can orchestrate my own destiny. My life will be
filled with beauty, love, and joy. I, above any,

have the ability to direct the ship of my life to
wherever I want to go, and to become whomever
I wish to be. I welcome your protection and your
gifts. Please help me to use them wisely.
I will do my best to speak the truth
in all things. So mote it be.

Meditate on the rising sun and enjoy the feeling of warmth that surrounds you. Don't be afraid to reach out and touch the divine. Spirit doesn't bite. When you are through, take three deep, cleansing breaths and leave the circle area, drawing the energy of the circle into yourself. Ground and center. Allow the candle to burn completely. Be sure to take fire-safe precautions.

You know you've hit the mark with this ritual if, in your mind, the voices of the speakers begin to take on a slight echo quality, as if they are speaking the same words you are reading. It's a rich, pleasantly vibrating experience.

Friends

I do not confuse what I seem to be
with who I really am.
—*U. S. Andersen*[12]

A friend is kind, loyal, compassionate, courageous, open-minded, loving, a good listener, and honest. This person does not whine, gossip, ask for more than you can give, treat you like dog food, throw tantrums, or expect you to obey or hang on every word he or she utters. A friend does not have a hidden agenda. Given this introduction, you might want to rethink who and what you are currently calling a friend. If they don't fit the above profile, you might want to move them into the category of acquaintance. On the other magickal hand, if you aren't showing those good traits of friendship, you might try giving yourself an attitude adjustment, because you can't draw great people to you if you act like a jerk.

When high school hits, friendships take on a brand-new meaning. Some experiences you'll have will be great, and others not so hot. This is the first time (most likely) that your parents give you a little more freedom than maybe you had in elementary or middle school. By college you're running on your own, but now you have to deal with moving from a high-school mentality to a more adult-oriented world. At college you are no longer under the microscope, and lines between groups of people begin to blur. Neither high school nor college friendships are easy for anyone, no matter how cute and perky they might be. Many therapists will tell you that the most damaging experiences in our self-esteem occur during the transition years—the first year of middle school, the first year of high school, the first year of college, and the first year you take on a full-time job. Any blows to your self-esteem that occur in those time frames dig in like a tick and munch for years on the inner you if you don't make a concerted effort to deal with the experience and then let it go.

Magick and friendships both require effort, practice, honesty, and patience. Not everyone will like you and you aren't going to adore every classmate, teacher, boss, circle member, or coworker, but there is no reason why you can't benefit from as many friends as you'd like to have. Just remember that inside everyone is a spirit body; there isn't any difference in shape, size, or color, we are all beings of light. Once you are okay with who you are and make a conscious effort to change those things about yourself that you do not like (rather than trying to fix or control everyone else around you), you'll find yourself with more friends than you know what to do with.

Spell to Gain Friends

Real friends like you because of who you are inside, not because of a face you wear, what your clothes look like, or who your parents might be. However, if you are friendless at the moment, it might be a good idea to take stock of yourself. Is your hair clean? Do you remember to brush your teeth? Are you knocking yourself over the head with negative mental programming, like "I'm stupid. People always hate me. I can't do anything right." If you are doing this to yourself, stop! (CHECK OUT PART III, AFFIRMATIONS, IF I'VE JUST DESCRIBED YOU!) Finding friends means getting to know new people. This isn't easy for a lot of folks (including me). I think everyone has a shy streak, some just hide it better than others. The first step in finding new friends is to believe that you deserve having those friends. The second step is to remember to be yourself; don't give way to the temptation of trying to behave in a manner that's not natural for you. In magick we believe that the mundane and the enchantment must work together to be successful. This means that if you want to make new friends, you're going to have to join clubs, maybe volunteer in the community, or find a local recreation center or other safe place where people your age hang out. Since it's hard to meet other Wiccans in your age group (many are still in the closet), many kids tell me that they have met some of their best spiritual friends at the local New Age or occult shop, or in the local book superstore in the Alternative Religion section. There are also several Wiccan teen-related sites on the Internet if you don't want to do the "in person" thing.

The best time to cast a spell to bring new friends toward you is during the new moon. Try to avoid the moon in Aries (friendship might fizzle out) or the Pisces moon (hallmark of the con artist). Following is a moon table designed to help you choose the right moon sign for your spell.

Note: Herbs/flowers were chosen for their planetary correspondence, safety, and your ability to buy them in the grocery store. Gemstones were chosen for their sign association as well as their spiritual properties.

Moon Table for Finding a New Friend

WHEN THE MOON IS IN . . .

ARIES

Type of person you will attract: Full of energy, but beware of temper.

Use the following herb in your spell: Ginger.

Use the following gem in your spell: Bloodstone.

TAURUS

Type of person you will attract: Dependable, but can be stubborn.

Use the following herb in your spell: Vanilla bean.

Use the following gem in your spell: Rose quartz.

GEMINI

Type of person you will attract: Intelligent, but can be scattered.

Use the following herb in your spell: Lavender.

Use the following gem in your spell: Citrine.

CANCER

Type of person you will attract: Loving, but wants to mother.

Use the following herb in your spell: Lemon rind.

Use the following gem in your spell: Moonstone.

LEO

Type of person you will attract: Loyal, but likes attention.

Use the following herb in your spell: Sun-flower seeds.

Use the following gem in your spell: Amber.

VIRGO

Type of person you will attract: Helpful, but can be critical.

Use the following herb in your spell: Celery seeds.

Use the following gem in your spell: Moss agate.

LIBRA

Type of person you will attract: Social, but can get anything out of anyone.

Use the following herb in your spell: Cinnamon.

Use the following gem in your spell: Jade.

SCORPIO

Type of person you will attract: Passionate, but possessive.

Use the following herb in your spell: Mustard seeds.

Use the following gem in your spell: Flint.

SAGITTARIUS

Type of person you will attract: Fun-loving, but has LOTS of other friends.

Use the following herb in your spell: Dande-lion.

Use the following gem in your spell: Azurite.

CAPRICORN

Type of person you will attract: Strong, but builds emotional walls.

Use the following herb in your spell: Sage.

Use the following gem in your spell: Tiger-eye.

AQUARIUS

Type of person you will attract: Humanitarian, but watch for the drama.

Use the following herb in your spell: Ivy.

Use the following gem in your spell: Amethyst.

PISCES

Type of person you will attract: Visionary, but prone to illusions.

Use the following herb in your spell: Cloves.

Use the following gem in your spell: Blue lace agate.

SUPPLIES: Two illuminator candles; a small amount of the chosen herbs; at least one gem-stone matching the moon sign; a small cloth bag (or small envelope); your favorite perfume or cologne.

INSTRUCTIONS: In the new moon (or first and second quarter) under the moon sign you've chosen, gather herbs and gems and place them on the altar. Light two white illuminator can-dles. Place the herbs and gems in a bowl. Mix with your hands while saying:

> *Moon in (sign), shine for me*
> *fill this bowl with energy.*
> *Herbs and gems, please do your work*
> *find a friend who's not a jerk.*
> *No one's perfect, this I know*
> *help us both to learn and grow*
> *with love, and joy, and dignity*
> *as I will, so mote it be!*

Add three drops of your favorite perfume or cologne to the mixture. Repeat the words of the spell again, then pour the mixture into a small cloth bag or small envelope. Tie shut or seal. Hold your hands over the packet and repeat the words a final time. Thank the Lord and Lady for their assistance. Carry the packet with you.

True Blue?

Now that you're meeting new people, how do you figure out who is going to be a real friend and who might be fooling? You may have a good feeling inside right away, or maybe you have a lot in common—computer games, sports, hobbies, or even Wicca! It's highly possible that this person may be totally different from yourself (but don't hold that against them). Your new friend(s) will respect you and listen. You're expected to do that, too. Carry a tiger-eye gemstone in your pocket if you have any doubts, and be patient. A person's real personality surfaces in time, regardless of how hard they may try to hide it.

Disagreements Among Friends

Being someone's friend means that you are willing to communicate with them in good times as well as not so good. Every friendship will have its ups and downs, especially during the high school and college years when you are maturing so fast. You may even feel a bit jealous of your friend. Actually, that's natural. If the green-eyed monster tries to bite you, think of all the good things you do for people and the accomplishments you have achieved. Your friend deserves to feel good, too, so be sure to compliment him or her on exactly the thing you were jealous about. You'll be shocked at how much better you'll feel! Being a friend also means that you can't monopolize the other person's time. If you try to cut them off from socializing with others, you'll only bring heartache to yourself. If you are having a problem with your friend, first sit down and think about what's really bothering you. Maybe you need to change your behavior patterns. Some-

times when we are angry with others, like our teachers, parents, husbands, or partners, we take it out on our friends. If you're doing that, you will need to explain why you feel the way you do and apologize for your behavior. But what if it is something else? Then what do you do? Before you talk to your friend, think of as many solutions to the problem as you can. A person always prepared with a solution can overcome anything. Once you've done this, talk to your friend. Be kind and add a little humor. Follow up magickally by using the spell below. You and your friend may like to do it together.

Best Buddy Spell

SUPPLIES: A picture of you and your friend together; the suit of hearts from a deck of cards.

INSTRUCTIONS: Lay the photograph on your altar. Surround the picture with the playing cards. Lay the Ace of Hearts on top of the photo. Hold your hands over the cards, and say:

> *Suit of hearts, friendship and love*
> *blessings from the Goddess above.*
> *Cast away our hurt and pain*
> *let us be good friends again.*
> *Help us solve all tears and woes*
> *bring us happiness, head to toes.*
> *Strengthen our bond of love and respect*
> *remove from us all pain and neglect.*
> *And when it's time for us to part*
> *let us do it from the heart*
> *filled with peace and joy and love*
> *sending blessings from above.*
> *As I will, so mote it be*
> *from sandy shore to shining sea!*

Leave your altar untouched until the conflict is resolved.

Helping a Friend Through Culture Shock

The world is an ever-changing place. It used to be that a "foreigner" was a bit unusual in the small-town environment (cities have always had a wonderful cultural mix of people), but today, with opportunities available and world unrest being what it is, almost every community is stretching to welcome those individuals from other countries. Unhappily, many have fled their previous home, hoping to escape unjust laws, human atrocities, and irrational governments. Naturally they are bringing their children with them. These young people must struggle to learn a new language and new customs, are forced to meet an entirely new set of people, deal with an unfamiliar school system, overcome slang, figure out where the general consensus stands on moral issues, and understand our laws. Their senses are assaulted with a different terrain, a different climate, billboards, television advertising, SUVs, and washing machines that are not the size of a peanut. Even if they practiced a structured religion, the customs of the church they came from will be somewhat (if not entirely) different than those in your country. Even more frightening may be the treatment of women. In America (and several other democratic countries), females are not subservient, and we don't plan to go back there anytime soon, thank you. And just try to tell a Bosnian what a Wiccan is. No clue. Tribal law does not exist in the United States, and that itself can be a major head trip.

Although many of these families filter into an already established community begun by those who have come here before them, these groupings are not insulated like they were a hundred years ago. Soon these teens and adults will begin to explore your country, and take the necessary steps toward integration. This is not easy for them.

Your mission, should you choose to help them, is to *listen*, above all else. Ask them about their culture, what's done differently, and compliment them on something that you truly like about them. Don't be insulted if they talk about how much they miss home. They already feel out of place, so jokes about their culture, religion, manners, or dress are out of line. Most of these people do not want to leave their family traditions behind (which is how America became so rich in so many holiday customs). Celebrate their holidays with as much enthusiasm as you celebrate your own. Offer to exchange recipes, music, and family history. My oldest daughter is currently attending college and working part-time. At her company, a group of people from all over the world decided to make an arbitrary day a New Year's celebration. Each person brought their favorite food dish that they felt exemplified their culture. The party was such a success that they've met together for the last three years. You may want to write a special ritual or host a dinner that merges a friend's customs and yours.

Spell to Ease Homesickness and Bring Happiness

SUPPLIES: Illuminator candles; objects from both cultures, nationalities, and faiths; flags from both countries.

INSTRUCTIONS: This spell is to be done with your foreign friend. Place the objects you both collected on your altar—your things on one side, your friend's belongings on another. Place both flags in the center of the altar, side by side. Light the illuminator candles. Have your friend teach you a favorite song in his or her language. Sing it together in his or her language, then sing it together in your native tongue. If you both know a common language that isn't your native one, sing that one, too! As you sing, move the things on the altar so that they get all mixed up on top of both flags. Try singing faster as you move the objects. I guarantee you that it will be lots of fun. When you're done laughing, hold hands over the altar, and tell each other how you feel about what you've just done. As you collect your things, exchange one token object with your foreign friend, as well as the flags. Wrap the object in the flag you received. Store it in a safe place.

When You've Grown Apart

Sometimes, in friendship (and in romance) there are relationships that for one reason or another cannot be saved. Perhaps you have simply grown apart and now have other interests, or maybe something has happened, and even though one or the other has apologized, there's no taking it back. It could be, too, that your friend has been doing things that you don't agree with, like hanging out with a bad crowd, taking drugs, or stealing. Sometimes it hurts so much to lose a friend that we have to be brave in order to end the relationship. Before you end the friendship, if you can, talk to your parents or guardian about the situation. Yeah, I know, we're over the hill, but we might be able to give you some helpful insights into the situation and give you options on how to end the friendship with the least amount of pain and upset. I will agree with you that parents tend to lecture on the subject and a few will do the I-told-you-so routine, but they also have experienced things like this. Sometimes experience can be helpful. Often a parent will relate a story of what it was like for them in the same situation. You probably heard the story before, but this time it may mean more to you. Regardless of whether you think the conversation was worthwhile (or not), you have opened the lines of communication with your parents,

made them feel like they are involved in your life and decisions, and opened the pathway for understanding your behavior and feelings during this difficult time.

There are basically two ways to end a friendship. Come right out and say something, or distance yourself, finding new activities and new friends, slowly cutting the bond between you. Unfortunately, I've found that with my own teens (as different as they may be), the second option is far more difficult than the first, especially since they attended a small high school. College, on the other hand, isn't as hard (unless you live there, and even then you can find plenty of activities and classes to keep you busy). Failed friendships that occur over the summer are far easier for both parties, as there are lots of things to do and places to go, including extended family vacations or a few weeks' visit with a relative. How you end the relationship depends on your personality. You are not a rotten coward if you choose to distance yourself, and you're not a bully if you come right out and be honest about it.

There is, of course, magick that you can do to make you feel better and help the situation along.

Peace Be with You Spell

Although you're probably feeling unhappy right about now, and maybe even angry, the best way to handle the separation of a friendship (or romance) is to do it in healing and love. Trust me on this one. I've tried several spells for myself and others, and a nonviolent attitude shines above the rest. If you remember that we are all one, it's easier. I particularly like the following quotation:

There is only one intelligence, one mind in all creation, and everyone is a part of it. Saying things at the same time, thought transference, and clairvoyance are only a few examples of the fact that we are all using one mind. Every book has been written by the same author, every building and bridge built by the same engineer, every picture painted by the same artist, every sonnet composed by the same poet, all music conceived by the same musician. You and your friend, us, everybody, one. That's the way it is.[13]

This is why they tell you to love your brother like yourself—because you ARE your brother (metaphysically speaking, of course).

Let's pick a toughie, just to make a point. Say Lucy was your best friend. You've known her since middle school and you've had a lot of great times together. Last year she practically lived at your house. Your mom says she's your adopted sister, which was cool then, but now you just can't take it anymore. She stole your boyfriend, lied about you to the Spanish Club, told one of the teachers you lifted a 99-cent plastic glove from the science room, and got your behind suspended. Is that enough for you? Obviously, the friendship is *O-V-E-R*. Either Lucy is possessed by an evil demon (which we don't believe in) or something in her life has gone totally haywire. The situation has gone too far for you to do anything constructive, and besides, Lucy is in denial about her behavior. It doesn't help that you're so mad you'd like to shapeshift into a wolf and tear her throat out, and turning the other cheek is not within your religious values. Witches are not, and never will be, doormats, and we are not playthings for the demented.

If we consider the above statement that we are all of the universal mind and that mind flows through every living being in the universe, then that would mean that a part of us (metaphysically speaking) is one sick puppy and needs a little help, but not at our expense. And that's what this spell does. It helps you. It helps our mythical Lucy. Only the gods determine the outcome of her fate, not you.

SUPPLIES: A picture of the two of you together; a pair of scissors; a black cloth; illuminator candles; a bowl of water; a box of tissues.

INSTRUCTIONS: In the fourth quarter of the moon, or when the moon is in Libra or Aquarius, or on a Saturday, place the picture, the bowl of water, and the scissors on a black cloth on your altar. Keep the tissues handy, you may need them. Light the illuminator candles, asking that the illumination of Spirit come into your life during this difficult time. Place your hands in the bowl of water and ask that all anger and unhappiness over this situation be removed from your body, soul, and mind. Allow the negativity to flow into your fingertips and then into the water. When you are finished, say: "So mote it be." Set the water aside.

Hold your hands over the picture, and say:

Once upon a time, in the land of happiness a friend and I went walking in joy and harmony. But now that time is passing, and we two are not as one; I must break the bond between us, and journey on alone. I honor the gifts we had, and wish him/her the very best, in hopes that healing comes quickly, right now at my request. It isn't easy to say goodbye, but I know the time is right to separate that bond of joy that held the sacred light. Friends will come and friends will go, like waves upon the beach. I ask that Spirit heal the wounds, may we not be out of reach of love and joy and faith and peace—the miracles of life. Upon this day I close the book, this chapter it is written; future friends await my gifts, of that I know I'm certain.

Pick up the picture and cut between the two of you so that you are on one piece and the lost friend is on the other. Place your picture on the altar between the illuminator candles. Wrap your friend's picture in the black cloth. Say:

It is done. We are separated in love and healing.

The gods alone determine his/her fate.

So mote it be.

Take the picture wrapped in black cloth to a crossroads (if you can) and say:

Go thee hence from the threshold of my life. Return nevermore. Your fate is in the hands of the gods. So mote it be!

The Spell of Selket to Remove Negativity and Stop Gossip

This spell requires no tools (as Witches need to be magickal on the go) and banishes unwanted negative energies that are building inside or around you. Egypt has the longest-running history of any culture. Deities rose and fell or were assumed into other deities over this incredible period of time. Selket (or Serket) was known as the Scorpion Goddess, and was usually depicted as entirely female (not having an animal head, or in this case, a bug head). She wore a scorpion crown. For those of you who are really into astrology, she even has her own fixed star, Cor Scorpionus (also known as Antares),[14] meaning the "Scorpion's Heart," and is located today at 9° 46' in Sagittarius. The Egyptian goddess Selket heralded the sunrise through her temples at the autumnal equinox about 3700 to 3500 B.C.E. She was also known as the Watcher of the West–Autumn Equinox Star. Some reference to her in the twenty-first dynasty does give her the head of a lion,[15] however that visage is normally given to Sekhmet (a different goddess). The incantation of this spell primarily tells you of her responsibilities in the Egyptian pantheon; I've also found her to be very helpful when traveling, especially long distances, and in turning away bad weather. She is also very helpful when the moon or sun is in the astrological sign of Scorpio, and she can be called on when other planets are in the sign of Scorpio that match your magickal intention. If you use her in this way, you will need to pay attention to your almanac; however, the following spell is for immediate action and doesn't require a vast amount of planning.

Cup your hands. Visualize a glowing ball of light growing in your palms. Whisper or think the following incantation in your mind.

Selket, Queen of Magick
sister of Mother Isis
guardian of Osiris
protector of the child-god Horus
She who binds the dead
and fashions the magick
great Scorpion Goddess of Egypt.
May foul words not sting me
may misdeeds fly from my day
may the light and enchantment
of love surround me and dispel all evil
from my heart, mind, and soul.
SMIB.

Cross your chest with your palms, visualizing positive energy entering your heart chakra. Take a deep breath and relax, then snap your fingers three times to break any remaining negative energy around you. The snapping noise will also seal the spell. When you return home, burn a stick of incense or make a small offering to represent your gratitude for her assistance.

Discriminating Friends

On more than one occasion teens (and adults) have written to me telling me that their "best" friend, boyfriend, or girlfriend has demanded that they give up their religion of Wicca. When someone (anyone) actively tries to take your chosen religion away from you, we know that the following is most likely true:

1. This is a control issue,

2. This is an issue of self-esteem (theirs, not yours), and

3. The accuser has no desire to be educated, because if they did, they wouldn't be bothering you about your religion at all.

Once we realize their behavior has everything to do with psychology and nothing to do with religious sanctity, it makes the whole situation easier to understand and overcome. If a friend or significant other leaves you because you won't "convert," then you should know in your heart that your relationship was based on what they wanted and needed, meaning that the original bond was probably extremely self-centered on their part, and that eventually a different issue would have arisen wherein their selfishness would have been exposed anyway. When people are unhappy, they tend to want to drag their friends down with them—don't go there.

You also need to understand that as your spirituality grows you will naturally push away those people who carry negative energy and look for friends and companions that have a higher level of thinking and being, and have a healthier outlook on life. They won't all be Wiccan, but they will be loving, accepting, courageous, and compassionate, to name just a few qualities. It's not the religion that declares the person, it's their behavior.

Harmony

The ultimate design of religion and magick should revolve around the creation or enhancement of harmony here on Earth as well as in other planes of existence. Whether we are talk-

ing about balancing your chakra energy, meditation, acts of magick and honor, helping a sick person to get better, situations of service (like a school club you might belong to), working within a coven environment, studying for a test at school, trying to work out relationship problems with our family or peers, finding love, living successfully, taking care of our pets and the environment, or following our talents, all, every bit, has to do with manipulating energy to build and support harmony. Even dealing with some of the heavier stuff—anger, crime, injustice, and discrimination—involves energy and harmony. Why? Because these situations arise when harmony is disrupted or disturbed. Magick, then, isn't really a selfish thing after all (something that a few people worry about), but a tool that helps us bring harmony into focus in our lives, which in turn brings harmony into the lives of others.

Conformity and harmony aren't the same thing. Conformity means you have to be like everyone else around you (and we know Witches aren't), where harmony says there is unity through diversity. Our differences can actually work together to make a better world, if we let them—and that's the key. Being willing to accept harmony is hard, especially if we somehow think that harmony is boring, weak, or, as I've heard in some Craft circles, "fluffy bunny stuff." Conformity is all those things (and worse). Harmony is actually exciting, giving us a solid foundation where we can reach to capture our goals whether we want to be the next astronaut, race car driver, or Pulitzer prize winner. Harmony doesn't mean you have to buckle under to someone else's desires, or take second best, or tolerate a bully. That's living in *dis*harmony, right? There is no reason why you must accept disharmony. Instead, work to create harmony, and you have banished the negative energy of the situation.

Harmony, then, will bring change. If things are out of whack, then working for a harmonious conclusion will make adjustments to the situation. Sometimes these changes will occur only inside of you, because that is all that is necessary. Other times the changes will be outside of yourself. How long this takes, and what changes occur, depend on what was wrong in the first place.

Many Witches work on creating harmony every day by practicing some sort of devotion, of which there are several to choose from. Those that enjoy more ceremonial magick may practice the Middle Pillar Exercise or the Lesser Banishing Pentagram.[16] Others may like working with a more shamanic energy by connecting with Earth (Gaia) and animal energies. Some individuals simply like to take a morning and evening walk, contemplating the wonder of the universe. It really doesn't matter how you connect with Spirit every day, just that you try your best to *do* it. By practicing such daily devotions, you begin building a firm foundation for future magickal work, relieving daily stress and, through conscious effort, bringing harmony into your life.

Wicca, as you have seen in this book, opens the way for practitioners to use various pantheons (SEE PART I, GODS, GODDESSES, AND PANTHEONS). For our harmony exercise we're going to use energies from the Egyptian culture, though you can substitute Celtic deities or the names of angels in the appropriate places. For now, though, we'll work with the Four Adorations in its original form. The Four Adorations is a set of prayers that come from the ceremonial study called the Golden Dawn,[17] and represents a technique of hailing the energy of Earth, Spirit, and sky, allowing your spirit to soar in the words as you say them each day. This devotion has four parts, the first to be said when you get up in the morning, the second to be recited at noon, the third at the setting of the sun, and the fourth right before you go to bed. You might want to copy them down on a piece of paper that you can keep handy. Granted, the hardest for the school student will be the noon devotion, because you may have class or be in the lunchroom surrounded by your peers. A moment of silence or reciting the words in your mind would be just fine. We can't always have the privacy we need to do what we want.

As all pantheon work requires study, I've provided the associations of each deity energy after the prayers. Read the prayers once, then read through the explanations, matching the history to the poem. You may also wish to go to the library or surf online for more detailed information. One you have worked with this format and understand how it works, you can write your own adoration that fits your chosen pantheon.

The Four Adorations

In the morning, turn to the east, touch your forehead with the first three fingers (thumb, index, and third finger) and slowly draw your hand out toward the rising sun, saying:

> *Hail unto thee who art Ra in thy rising,*
> *even unto thee who art Ra in thy strength,*
> *who travellest over the heavens in thy bark*
> *at the uprising of the sun.*
> *Tahuti standeth in his splendor at the prow*
> *and Ra-Hoor abideth at the helm.*
> *Hail unto thee from the abodes of the night!*
> *Hail unto thee in the arms of Nun.*[18]

At noon, turn to the south, making the same hand gesture on the forehead, and then slowly moving your hand out toward the south, saying:

> *Hail unto thee who art Hathor*
> *in thy triumphing,*

Even unto thee who art Hathor in thy beauty,
who travellest over the heavens in thy bark
at the mid-course of the sun.
Tahuti standeth in his splendor at the prow,
and Ra-Hoor abideth at the helm.
Hail unto thee from the
abodes of the morning!
Hail unto thee in the arms of Nun!

At sunset, turn to the west, repeating the hand gesture toward the west, saying:

Hail unto thee, who art Tum in thy setting,
even unto thee who art Tum in thy joy,
who travellest over the heavens in thy bark
at the down-going of the sun.
Tahuti standeth in his splendor at the prow,
and Ra-Hoor abideth at the helm.
Hail unto thee from the abodes of the day!
Hail unto thee in the arms of Nun.

Before you go to bed, turn to the north, use the hand gesture, and say:

Hail unto thee who art Khephra
in thy hiding,
even unto thee who art Khephra
in thy silence.
Who travellest over the heavens in thy bark
at the midnight hour of the sun.
Tahuti standeth in his splendor at the prow
and Ra-Hoor abideth at the helm.
Hail unto thee from the abodes of the evening!
Hail unto thee in the arms of Nun!

This devotion invokes five Egyptian deities, who (if we check our history) have multiple spellings, according to which expert you talk to, and are linked to a particular theme: the sun as a representation of Spirit and enlightenment. Egyptian names are spelled differently because the original language was a series of pictures (re-member our discussion on alchemy?) and are therefore subject to the translator's interpretation.

Re (or Ra) is considered a sun god, his name meaning "the creator" or "creative power." He rose to prominence in Egyptian history in the fifth dynasty. The Egyptians believed that the sun was fire and the heaven water. The sun could not travel through water unless it was in a boat, which is where the reference to the "bark" (or boat) comes into play in the adoration.

Ra-Hoor is a combination of Ra/Re and Horus, the god who represented the heights of the skies. These two, Ra and Horus, stood for the united Solar Force (or Spirit). Horus is called the "divine child." Isis, the prominent Egyptian female divinity, was often represented in statuary holding the divine sun/son, Horus. The statues made their way through Europe and were a part of the cult of the Black Madonna.

Tahuti is another name for Thoth, the god of wisdom and learning. Although not mentioned in the poem, his lady friend (for those who would like to work with them in pairs) is Ma'at. Her name means "truth." Therefore, if you would like to find truth, wisdom, or learning, then you would call on this duo in spell or ritual, but be careful—to ask for truth must mean that you wish to give it in return. In some myths, both Tahuti and Ma'at stand on either side of Ra-Hoor in his boat as he travels across the sky on his daily journey, and they are responsible for keeping the Sun on course. The Tarot deck is often associated with the magickal and hermetic arts (SEE PART III, ALCHEMY), and is sometimes called the Book of Thoth. Tahuti (Thoth) is also associated with the moon, and as Ra traveled across the sky, Tahuti gave light to the moon to dispel the darkness in the waters of the night, which is why he is located at the back of the boat, casting the light upon the midnight skies that fall behind the sun's passing.

Hathor's history, like so many of the deity legends, touches on more than one persona. Hathor is linked to Nun (or Nut, as she was sometimes called), who was considered the cosmic mother. In early Egyptian legend, Nun was the queen of the heavens, and gave birth to the sun, the moon, and the stars. Later she was associated with the journey to the underworld. In time she would be partnered with Hathor. In early legend, Hathor is also Sekhmet, goddess of the afternoon sun, and destroyer of bad guys. As Hathor, she is the goddess of happiness, dancing, music, and women, and she wears a solar disk on her horned headdress. If you know someone who is pregnant, you can always call on Hathor to help protect mom and baby through those nine months and at the birth of the baby. At one time, Hathor was known as the mother of Horus, and is said to have the powers of divination, prophecy, and the knowledge of a person's destiny. All this good stuff gets her a seat in the boat, and associates her with the midday sun. Hathor, if you forget the details, is a goddess of many faces and energies.

Tum (also known as Tem, Temu, Tum, Atem) is considered to be one of the oldest gods of ancient Egypt. Originally an Earth god, he eventually became associated with the sun. He was thought to be the first god to emerge from the waters of heaven (Nun) and will return to those waters at the end of time. Atum was also a first in that he wasn't considered male or female, but both. He was called the "Great He-She" and his name meant the "complete one." Because he would someday return to Nun, he was associated with all sunsets. Of all the Egyptian gods, Tum may be the closest to the modern-day mindset in Wicca of the God and Goddess being one, yet also being able to operate separately if necessary.

Khephra (Khepera, Khepri, Khopri) is also a form of the sun god, Ra, and is associated with the scarab beetle. Legend has it that as a beetle he pushes the moon through the sky. He stands for self-generation and renewal, the dawn, and the beginning of all things.

Read through the adorations while you are outside (the time of day doesn't matter). Look to the heavens as you say some of the lines of the poem. Can you visualize Nut, the cosmic waters of the universe? Do you see the difference that research makes? It is one thing to read through a magickal book, but it is something else altogether different when you have researched the history and then apply that information to your life in a pleasant or practical way. The words begin to mean something special to you, rather than just marching across the page or tumbling out of your mouth without a thought to where they might have originated. Cool, huh? Try standing outside at dawn and saying the first adoration. If you can't remember the whole thing, simply start by looking up as the soft, liquid light streams over the horizon, and say: "Hail to thee who art Ra in thy rising." The power you will touch is indescribable.

Many magickal individuals perform some sort of daily devotion such as the one listed above. These devotions might be done out-of-doors, at a family altar, or in the privacy of one's room and can include prayers, the lighting of incense, an offering to deity, meditation, or other spiritual activity. You'll find more information on daily devotions in my book *To Stir a Magick Cauldron*.

The Stress of Change

As we work to change our behavior patterns and our way of life, we will encounter various stresses that result from our needs to meet the new structure we have created for ourselves. Students who work a great deal of magick have found that after a flurry of magickal practices they may feel "out of wack" or that events are happening so fast they weren't prepared to deal with the emotional upheavals. Although daily devotions help to make this transition smoother, we can also add "riders" to our spellwork and ritual that include an effortless flow from one type of structure to another. For example, you may wish to add any of the following to the body of your spellwork:

"Change will flow with ease and love, blessed by Goddess from above."

"My transition to my new life will be effortless and natural."

"I will easily find success and happiness." You may also find that you will go through periods of enforced rest, meaning you just don't feel like doing magick or ritual because that's precisely the way you're supposed to feel. Sometimes these breathers can last up to a full year and they are a direct result of the germination process required by the spellwork and ritual you have done in the past. Rather than worry about your lack of desire to zap the world fantastic, sit back, relax, and take the changes in stride, one day at a time. Here again, daily devotions or meditation will be very helpful. After a while you will feel that familiar excitement that precedes a magickal working and then you'll be off again, working toward obtaining your goals.

Recommended Reading

Celtic Devotional: Daily Prayers and Blessings by Caitlin Matthews

Hearth and Home

When a person eighteen or over enters the Craft requesting formal training from a specific teacher, group, or tradition, one of the requirements often explained to the student is that they must have a stable hearth and home—meaning a job that can support them and a secure place to live. Even if the student is in college, they must show that they have a means of supporting themselves, because it is felt that if they practice self-reliance in their everyday life they have the maturity to seriously begin studying the occult sciences. *Hearth and home*, in Craft lingo, means that your personal life is established.

If you are a teen moving into adulthood, you are experiencing many "firsts"—first job, what college or trade school you might like to attend, and where (eventually) you would like to live. Some teens are able to stay home and live with their families during these years, while others find themselves (sometimes unexpectedly) searching for a place to live, or perhaps your family has been looking for a new home or apartment. The following table is designed to help you choose the most auspicious moon phase and moon sign as they relate to your hearth and home. You can use this table in a practical way, or as a guideline for choosing the best time to cast a spell for the matter listed. *Note:* For the herbal combination, use a combination of three ingredients, or choose your own.

Spell Planning Guide

BANISHING NEGATIVITY

Moon quarter: Fourth/waning.

Astrological sign: Aquarius, Leo, Taurus, or Scorpio.

Herbal combination for conjuring bags: Angelica, basil, clove, lilac, mint, pine, rosemary, sage.

BIRTH/WICCANING

Moon quarter: First and second/waxing.

Astrological sign: When the moon is in the child's natal sun sign.

Herbal combination for conjuring bags: Cedar, frankincense, rosemary, lavender, honeysuckle, sage, lilac, mint.

BUYING A CAR

Moon quarter: First and second/waxing.

Astrological sign: Gemini, Sagittarius, Aquarius, Taurus, Leo, and Scorpio.

Herbal combination for conjuring bags: Ginger, African violet, basil, cactus, cinnamon, ginseng, lime peel, willow, marjoram, nutmeg.

BUYING A HOUSE

Moon quarter: First and second/waxing.

Astrological sign: Taurus for security, Leo for family unity, Aquarius for the social family.

Herbal combination for conjuring bags: Gardenia, lavender, myrtle, vervain, violet, alfalfa, nuts, tulips, allspice, clover, oak, rice, tea, wheat.

CAR REPAIR

Moon quarter: Third and fourth.

Astrological sign: Taurus, Leo, Aquarius, or Virgo.

Herbal combination for conjuring bags: Cedar, fennel, lemon peel, peppermint, rosemary, cotton, heather, rose petals, oak, lavender, maple, bay, ivy.

CLEANING

Moon quarter: Third and fourth/waning.

Astrological sign: Scorpio and Capricorn.

Herbal combination for conjuring bags: Angelica, allspice, dried apple peels, dried lemon peels, dried orange peels, pine, sage.

CROSSING CEREMONY (DEATH)

Moon quarter: Full moon.

Astrological sign: When the moon is in the deceased's sun sign.

Herbal combination for conjuring bags: Angelica, frankincense, lilac, birch, clove, clover, myrrh, sandalwood.

ERECTING HOME ALTAR OR SHRINE

Moon quarter: First and second/waxing.

Astrological sign: When the moon is in your natal sun sign or natal moon sign.

Herbal combination for conjuring bags: Lavender, violet, cinnamon, frankincense, myrrh, sandalwood, clover, ginger, cedar, fennel, iris, thyme, lemon.

FAMILY TREE RESEARCH

Moon quarter: Third and fourth/waning.

Astrological sign: Scorpio, Virgo, or Cancer.

Herbal combination for conjuring bags: Crocus, cinnamon, clover, ginger, dandelion, marigold, rose, fern, moss, straw.

FINDING RENTAL PROPERTY

Moon quarter: First and second/waxing.

Astrological sign: Cancer, Leo, or Aquarius.

Herbal combination for conjuring bags: Catnip, lavender, lily of the valley, marjoram, oak, mint, rose, pine, daffodil, marigold, sunflower, hyacinth, orchid, tulip, willow.

HOLIDAY BAKING

Moon quarter: First and second/waxing.

Astrological sign: Cancer is best—Aries, Libra, or Capricorn.

Herbal combination for conjuring bags: Allspice, cloves, nutmeg, rosemary, vanilla, orange or lemon peel, brown sugar, ginger, rose petals.

HOME REPAIR

Moon quarter: First and second/waxing.

Astrological sign: Capricorn.

Herbal combination for conjuring bags: Cinnamon, clover, ginger, mugwort, tea, thistle, bay, mulberry, birch, ash, bamboo, clover, moss, honeysuckle, hyssop, mimosa, mustard, oak, pine, rose, sage.

HOUSE HUNTING

Moon quarter: First and second/waxing.

Astrological sign: Cancer.

Herbal combination for conjuring bags: Catnip, lavender, lily of the valley, dogwood, sage, walnuts, ginseng, dandelions, marjoram, oak, mint, rose, pine, daffodil, marigold, sunflower, hyacinth, orchid, tulip, willow.

INTERIOR DECORATING

Moon quarter: First and second/waxing.

Astrological sign: Taurus, Cancer, Leo, Libra, or Aquarius.

Herbal combination for conjuring bags: Cinnamon, eyebright, honeysuckle, marigold, rose, yarrow, lemon, catnip, morning glory, and violet.

MOVING HOUSE

Moon quarter: First and second/waxing.

Astrological sign: Taurus, Leo, Scorpio, or Aquarius.

Herbal combination for conjuring bags: Allspice, angelica, apple peels, barley, bay, cedar, cinnamon, eucalyptus, gardenia, ginseng, hops, ivy, lime, mint, myrrh, oak, peppermint, pine, rose, rosemary, spearmint, violet.

PAINTING ROOMS

Moon quarter: Fourth quarter.

Astrological sign: Taurus, Leo, or Aquarius.

Herbal combination for conjuring bags: Fern, oak, walnuts, marjoram, nutmeg, lavender, maple, sage.

POURING CONCRETE OR LAYING FOUNDATIONS

Moon quarter: Full moon.

Astrological sign: Taurus, Leo, or Aquarius.

Herbal combination for conjuring bags: Bay, plantain, tea, mugwort, oak, carnation, thistle.

REMOVING NEIGHBORS

Moon quarter: Fourth/waning.

Astrological sign: Scorpio, Capricorn, or Aquarius.

Herbal combination for conjuring bags: Bamboo, chili pepper, black pepper, thistle, angelica, basil, beans, clove, clover, fern, frankincense, horseradish, lilac, mint, myrrh, onion, rosemary, snapdragon, yarrow.

SELLING A HOUSE

Moon quarter: Third and fourth/waning.

Astrological sign: Capricorn or Virgo.

Herbal combination for conjuring bags: Alfalfa, basil, blackberry, cashew, cedar, chamomile, clove, dill, ginger, grape, jasmine, maple, marjoram, mint, nutmeg, oak, orange, pecans, pine, pineapple, rice, tea, wheat.

SECURITY AND PROTECTION

Moon quarter: Any.

Astrological sign: Capricorn or Scorpio.

Herbal combination for conjuring bags: African violet, aloe, alyssum, amaranth, angelica, anise, ash, bamboo, barley, basil, bay, bean, birch, broom, cactus, caraway seeds, carnation, cedar, celandine, clove, clover, moss, coconut, curry, dill, dogwood, fern, garlic, ginseng, gourds, holly, mint, onion, turnip, willow.

SETTLING FAMILY DISPUTES

Moon quarter: Third and fourth/waning.

Astrological sign: Libra.

Herbal combination for conjuring bags: Gardenia, lavender, morning glory, vervain, catnip, hyacinth, marjoram.

WEDDING

Moon quarter: First and second/waxing.

Astrological sign: Taurus, Leo, or Libra. Avoid the full moon or waning moon.

Herbal combination for conjuring bags: Clover, magnolia, nutmeg, rhubarb, passionflower, sweet pea, lavender, maple, sage, crocus, daffodil, daisy, jasmine, orchid, rose, sugar cane.

The following spells are designed to help you work toward a stable home environment. All spells require casting a magick circle, calling the quarters, and invoking deity, even though it is not specifically listed in the instructions.

Spell for Finding a New Home

SUPPLIES: One small brown paper bag; crushed mint; a picture of your family, including all pets; a lodestone or magnet; a list of everything you would like to have that applies to the new house (number of rooms, yard space, location, school system, etc.). *Optional:* white candle.

INSTRUCTIONS: When the moon is in the chosen sign (check your almanac) or during a first or second quarter moon (new and waxing), draw a picture of a house on the paper bag. If you like, you can cut out the top half of the bag in the shape of the roof of a house, so that when the bag is open, it looks like a paper house. Place the picture of your family, the list of what kind of house you would like, the lodestone or magnet, and the crushed mint in the bag. Place the

white candle (if you are using one in this spell) by the bag (but not so close that it might catch fire). Cast the magick circle and call the quarters. Hold your hands over the bag, and say:

> *A home is filled with joy and love*
> *with blessings fashioned from above.*
> *A house I seek to call a home*
> *where peace is found and joy is known.*
> *We'll find a place to call our own.*

Light the candle, saying:

> *Earth, air, water, fire, please bring to me*
> *the house I/we desire.*

Hold your hands over the bag, repeating the chant three times. Take a deep breath and relax. Close your eyes. Visualize your family happy and smiling, moving into your new house, trailer, or apartment. Take another deep breath and clap your hands, saying: "It is done!" Draw an equal-armed cross in the air over the candle and bag. Allow the candle to burn completely. Keep the cold candle and the "house bag" together until you have moved into the new house. On the night of the full moon, thank deity, light another white candle, and ask for blessings on your family and new home. Bury the candle ends and "bag house" in the yard.

Spell for if You've Been Thrown Out of the House

SUPPLIES: Candle; small bowl of spring water.

INSTRUCTIONS: Cast a circle. Hold the bowl of water in your left hand and the lit candle in your right hand. Bring the candle close to the bowl so that the reflection of the candle is cast upon the water. Carry the bowl and candle to each quarter, making sure that the reflection of the candle remains in the water. As a part of your invocation to the quarters, at each quarter ask that the guardians of those portals make way for the path between yourself and a place to live that is affordable, loving, save, and secure. Walk to the center of the circle and hold the bowl and candle a little above eye level, and repeat your request, then plunge the candle into the water, saying: "It is done!" Thank deity, release the quarters, and release the circle.

Home Repair Spell

When you would like to fix up your room, or your family would like to do renovations, add this spell to your fixer-upper plans.

SUPPLIES: Cantaloupe; 2 yellow votive candles; 10 marigold blossoms.

INSTRUCTIONS: Cut the cantaloupe in equal halves. Clean out the seeds with a spoon. Place one votive candle in each half. Surround the candles with marigold blossoms, arranging them so that the blooms are not right on top of the flame to keep them from burning. Cast a circle, call the quarters, and invoke deity. Hold your hands over the melon and unlit candle. Visualize the room or object as you would like it to look when the repair is completed. In your mind, add the sounds it might make (stereo, air conditioner, etc.). Light the candle, visualizing Spirit entering your house, bringing happiness, harmony, love, and joy. Allow the candle to burn completely. *Note:* You will have to watch this spell as it is possible, depending on the circumstances, that the flowers might ignite. Although I have never had this problem, there's always a first time. Carry the melon to an area where the candle can safely burn. When the candle goes out, offer the melon, candle, and flowers to the four quarters outside, then leave outside on your property.

Finding the Right Roommate Spell

Perhaps you're going off to college and are worried about what sort of dorm mate you'll get, or circumstances have unfolded in a way that you must leave home and find a roommate to shoulder some of the apartment expenses. In either case, finding a compatible roommate may not be as simple as you first thought. Here's a simple spell to draw toward you the right person to fit the circumstances.

SUPPLIES: One small apple with long, strong stem; 2–3 bags of medium-sized red sequins; sequin pins (straight pins sold at the arts and crafts store); a small magnet; a piece of paper; a black marker; one red ribbon, 13 inches long.

INSTRUCTIONS: Cleanse, consecrate, and empower all supplies. Carefully insert the magnet into the bottom of the apple. (You may have to use a knife or apple corer to do this.) Carefully cover the apple with the sequins. This will take about one hour to an hour and a half, depending on the size of the apple. Write on the paper exactly what you want for the ideal roommate—be specific! Fold the paper, then punch a hole through it. Thread the ribbon through the paper. Tie the ribbon to the apple stem. Cast a magick circle and call the quarters, then stand in the center of the circle and hold the apple high in the air with both hands. Say:

Blessings from the east
blessings from the south
blessings from the west
blessings from the north
gifts of the Lord and Lady
water and earth
fire and air
the heartbeat of companionship
all will be there!

Read aloud the list on the paper. Place the apple on your altar and leave it there until you find the roommate that is right for you. If you have any doubts, remember to use your divination tool. Don't forget to thank divinity, close the quarters, and release the circle.

Getting Rid of a Bad Roommate or Unwelcome House Guest Spell

On occasion it's time for a person to move on to a better place. The welcome mat at your house dried up and blew away a year ago.

SUPPLIES: One skein of red yarn; a cast-off item belonging to the unwanted guest; red pepper (to get them moving); crushed onion skin; crushed eggshells; one carnation; one broom; one small red felt bag.

INSTRUCTIONS: When the moon is in the third or fourth quarter (waning), mix the onion skin, eggshells, and red pepper with mortar and pestle until finely ground. Use the herbal conjuring chant on page 381. Pour mixture into red bag, add carnation and cast-off item, and tie closed. Wrap the red yarn around the red conjuring bag until you have a small ball three inches in diameter. Tie so that the yarn will not unravel. As you are winding the yarn, think of your guest happily leaving, going on to something more fulfilling for him or her.

Take the broom and the ball of yarn to the room in which the individual sleeps. Begin pushing the yarn around with the broom, saying:

Earth, air, fire, water, cleanse this place
from top to bottom. Remove, remove, remove

(and then say the person's name).

Bat the yarn around in every room, repeating the chant. Finish at the back door. Say the chant one more time and give the ball of yarn a mighty whack out the door. Bury off your property.

Note: If it would be obvious that you are playing soccer with the ball of yarn, do the following: Put the cast-away item in a clean bag used by your vacuum cleaner. Place the bag in the vacuum cleaner. Prepare the magick powder. Vacuum up one teaspoon of the powder. Cut seven pieces of red yarn one inch long. Vacuum those. Clean the entire house with the vacuum while repeating or humming the chant. At the back door, remove the bag and take the bag outside. Draw the banishing pentagram with holy water on the bag. Bury the bag off your property.

Spell for Protecting Your Home, Apartment, or Dorm Room

Almost any everyday item can be empowered to protect your home, property, or those who live within the household. Here are some ideas:

- Find a stuffed animal that matches your totem animal. Empower the animal in your own ceremony to protect your home and loved ones.

- Fill a clear glass bell jar, Christmas ball, or unique canister with protective herbs. Empower and place by the front and/or back doors.

- Hang a pair of open scissors over the front and back doorways to cut all negativity before it enters the home.

- Each night, in your mind, cast a protective circle around your home by intoning the circlecasting and envisioning the circle completely encompassing your property.

- Find a painting or poster that depicts protective, warrior energy to you. Hang on the door of your bedroom. Empower for protection.

These ideas should be used along with standard protection procedures, such as remembering to lock your doors and windows, putting expensive possessions out of sight, keeping blinds and drapes drawn in the evening, and never telling anyone how much cash you have or how much money you've saved in your bank account. Certain items have a very bad habit of disappearing, especially at college. These items are laptop computers, bank and credit cards, stashed cash, expensive jewelry, and stereo systems.

Homework

Teens aren't the only one with homework requirements anymore. Many adults are choosing to further their education by taking night courses, weekend classes, Internet college courses, or taking the plunge and going back to school full time. Try turning your homework into magick with these great ideas!

- Translate your spells and rituals into the foreign language you are currently taking. Saying spells in a foreign tongue adds mystery and power!

- Turn any math-oriented homework, including economics, calculus, geometry, or algebra homework, into talisman magick.

- Research what was happening in the history of magick during the time period you are expected to study in school. For example, did you know that Alexander the Great was Aristotle's student? Did you know that Aristotle taught Alexander how to make favorable war proclamations by using astrology?[19] Considering Alexander the Great conquered more countries than I have pentacles in my magickal cabinet (and I have a slew, let me tell ya), this should let us know that magickal astrological timing is no joke.

Did you also know that Benjamin Franklin was into astrology? He better have been, because he produced *Poor Richard's Almanac*, which was an astrological publication used by many of his day. It is highly likely that he used astrology to select the date of the signing of the Declaration of Independence, because the United States had the strongest chart of all the nations of the world. (England was number two.)[20]

Jail or Detention Center

If this is where you find yourself, you are not a lost cause, but you do have more work ahead of you than others your age. Although many youth facilities will allow you to have this book (and others like it on the Craft), others will not, and it is a fair assumption that you won't be able to work with what modern Craft considers the standard tools of the trade; however, that doesn't mean you can't change your life, work magick, or do ritual. The Witch is the magick, after all, and the work takes place in the mind and culminates in your actions. Thoughts and choices require only your mind.

The most difficult hurtle to overcome at this point is the question: Where is your head at? Although considering what choices put you in this predicament are important, despairing over your fate is not the way to go, and there is one glaring fact: For things to get better, it is absolutely necessary that you *want* them to get better, and that anything you do from this point on supports that desire! If you plan to work with this book, you've already put positive energy in motion, but you will have to follow up in thought, word, and deed. Here are some suggestions:

- Practice some sort of mental morning devotion. Try the four adorations (PAGE 500) or make up your own.

- Work with your chakra system, mentally opening and closing them (PAGE 242).

- Practice nightly meditation using the Body of Light Meditation (PAGE 293). Tailor to your own needs.

- Remove negative self-talk from your mind and replace with positive affirmations.

- Make positive goals for your future. Visualize yourself attaining those goals.

- Sprinkle holy water around your area nightly. Don't make a big deal out of it.

- Practice grounding and centering daily (PAGE 238).

- Practice shielding (SEE PROTECTION).

- Try your best to be positive in word and deed.

- If you are permitted, put your mind and hands to work with something artistic—painting, sewing, composing music, drawing, poetry, journaling, writing stories, etc.

- Read—not just this book, but books on all subjects. Ignorance is not bliss.

- Practice penmanship. You think I jest? Nope. The clearer your writing, the clearer your mind and the easier it will be to express yourself.

- Connect with Spirit daily in your own way.

- Pray with positive words. No whining or being mad at the universe. No groveling.

- If your counselor tells you that you are in denial, he or she is probably right. At least give them the courtesy of thinking about it, and ask them for what their definition of denial is (in a nice way, please).

As you can see, none of the above require magickal tools, and all of the above require the exercise of your mind, yet these are the basics that all Wiccan students must learn if they wish to reach their goals.

Magick for the Incarcerated

The first thing you must remember is that all magick balances and seeks to bring harmony. This means that if the situation is truly in the toilet, Spirit may hit the flush button, which appears to cause chaos (at first) and makes things look worse than they are. The old adage *This, too, shall pass* is important here. Psychologically, most mental crises take six weeks to bounce around in the mind like a red rubber ball. After that, mentally, emotionally, and physically, the journey will begin to smooth out. During those six weeks, keep your head up and your brain working in a positive direction. This is not the time to cop out. Yes, I know this takes courage, but I also know that you can do it!

Incarceration magick requires that you acknowledge and understand that every action you do has an equal reaction. There is no way around this, yet not all "crimes" committed are morally wrong and what one culture may deem a criminal act (based on its social model), another culture may find acceptable. When talking about karma, then, we can't always rely on the cultural model to tell us what is right and what is wrong. In karma, however, all nasty acts must be paid for and all acts of good will must be returned in kind. No matter how hard our social model tries to get it right, there are people who are jailed unjustly, or those whom we feel the punishment may not fit the crime. When working magick in these situations, it is not our place to judge. Our mission is to ask for balance and allow the universe to work for the good of all. Now, as an aside, the "good of all" may not be so hot for the criminal. It doesn't mean he or she is going to skate out of the mess he or she created. It does mean, however, that the checks and balances of the universe will be put into motion without hindrance of our pushing something where, karmically, it should not be going. It also means that if someone is not guilty, energy will be released to rectify the problem, if it is within that individual's spiritual plan. The following spells, then, are designed for both sides of this sticky karmic coin. The first is to find favor when faced with unjust incarceration and the second is to catch a criminal.

Unjust Incarceration Spell

SUPPLIES: A handful of white feathers (or if it is summertime, you can use dandelion heads that have gone to seed); a short, brittle stick; clay; a pencil or stylus.

INSTRUCTIONS: When the moon is in Aquarius, fashion the clay into a thin tablet. Write the incarcerated individual's name on the tablet with the stylus, along with his or her birth date, current age, and the place where he or she is jailed. Allow to dry. ***Note:*** If you have purchased slow-drying clay, you may wish to fashion the clay tablet a few days before.

Find a place outside where you will not be disturbed. Cast the magick circle and call the quarters. Invoke Spirit. Stand in the center of the circle, and say: "In the name of (say deity name), I break the bonds of (name of jailed individual)."

Snap the stick in two. Hold up the clay tablet, and say: "I release him/her from unjust confinement." Break the clay tablet over your knee, and allow the pieces to drop freely to the ground.

Hold up the feathers and say, "May the winds of change bring you your freedom!" Release the feathers.

Very loudly proclaim, "As I will, so mote it be. This spell is sealed!" Thank deity, close the quarters, and release the circle. Leave the stick, clay shards, and feathers to the forces of nature.

Note: This spell will not work if the person is guilty, or if the punishment karmically fits the crime.

Spell to Catch a Criminal

SUPPLIES: Bird cage or small animal cage; small, red clay flower pot; dirt; water; marigold seeds; white parchment paper; a black marker.

INSTRUCTIONS: When the moon is in Scorpio, cast a magick circle and call the quarters. Invoke Spirit. Cleanse, consecrate, and empower all supplies. With the black marker, write down your intention; for example, *To catch and bring to justice the person who slashed the tires of my car.* Place the dirt in the pot, then plant the marigold seeds, and say:

As these flowers grow, so I will the universe
to spread its blanket of justice upon you.

Pour a little water over the ground, and say:

As Spirit cleanses my Spirit,
so will my life be cleansed of your evil.

Place the pot in the cage. As you shut the door to the cage, say:

As I have caged these seeds,
so you shall be caged by your own actions.

Tap each side of the cage, and then the top and bottom, and say:

Justice from the east, justice from the south,
justice from the west, justice from the north,
as above and so below, you have sealed your own
fate. The gods sit in judgment of you now.

Place the cage in sunlight, saying:

Thou who art in the heavens, smile upon my request. Bring light to this mystery so that harmony may come to pass. So mote it be.

Thank deity, close the quarters, and release the circle. Be sure to care for the plant. When the criminal has been caught, and the season and time are right, transplant the marigold to the out-of-doors. Sometimes you will not know that justice has been rendered; for example, the person who sliced your tires may be jailed for an entirely different reason and you didn't hear about it. When doing criminal magick you must learn to let go of what you feel is justice and allow Spirit to balance the scales. You won't always get a front-row seat.

Jobs

Applying for and getting your first job is an exciting experience. It means that you are reaching a level of independence and taking your first steps into the world of personal finance, economics, and (gulp) budgeting. It also means that you will learn about a new social model different, perhaps, than the one you experience at home—the world of work ethics.

A place of employment is not much different than school. There are rules to be followed and a specific type of behavior is expected of you; however, rather than working for grades and peer approval, you are working for cold, hard cash. There are also governmental rules that affect how many hours you can work per day and per week until you are eighteen years of age, and there are additional new rules about how many hours an employer can expect you to work as an adult.

With your first job you will also discover that part of the money comes right out of your check and is funneled into local, state, and federal taxes. In some states there is also a one-time fee per year called the occupation tax (about ten bucks). So, if they tell you that you will be earning $6.50 an hour, and your check reflects much less than that according to your math, it's probably because of the taxes. If someone hires you and tells you that you are an independent contractor, be careful. This means that you must do all the tax work and the business is not responsible for taking the taxes out of your check. They still must report what you earn to the government, so you can't get away without paying taxes.

The following spells are designed to help you get a job and, once you have it, help you work through some of the difficulties you might experience in this new environment. Each spell requires a magick circle, calling the quarters, and invoking divinity, although these steps are not specifically listed in the instructions.

Part I: Spell to Get a Job

First, you should sit down and think about what type of work you would like to do. Yes, I know you need money, so maybe you don't care what it is as long as it coughs up dough, but there is no reason why we can't tailor your magick to moving you toward work that you think is personally fulfilling. On a piece of paper write:

1. The salary you need (be realistic in relation to your skills, but don't cut yourself short).

2. What type of job you would like to do.

3. What kind of environment you would like to work in.

4. What kind of people you would like to work with.

5. What kind of supervisor you would like to have.

6. What location you are looking for (within 5, 10, or 15 miles of your home).

7. What kind of transportation you need. Some of you will need to think about this. You might not have a car. How will you get to work? If you say, "A friend," just how reliable is this friend? Be very honest with yourself in answering this question. Be careful if you choose to work with a friend. If that person is not reliable, his or her actions will affect you once you are on the job, especially if you have an argument and you suddenly discover you don't have a ride to work. Perhaps you would like a job close enough to home so that you can walk. Fine, but then watch the hours. It may not be safe to walk home alone after dark. If this is the case, is there someone that can take you home if you must work after dark?

8. How long you want this job to last (please never say forever, life has a habit of changing too often for this request). Is this a summer job, something to take up your time and earn a little money until you start high school or college?

Once you have answered these questions, you are ready to look at the career by the moon table below. Cast your spell during the corresponding moon-in-sign. If you must work before that time, cast the spell at the new moon or during the first quarter. In looking at the list you will notice that some occupations are shared by two or more signs, which definitely gives you more to choose from. This list is only a guideline. If you feel comfortable working in a different moon sign that what is shown, that's fine, too. Remember, to know the sign that the moon is in, you must consult an almanac (SEE PART III).

Part II: Jobs and Careers by the Moon

When the moon (new or first quarter) is in the signs listed below, work for the following type of employment:

ARIES

Selling sports equipment; finding a sponsor for your favorite sport; coaching a sport; helping out at a local sports center or dojo; automobile industry such as mechanics or a gas station; racing and ambulance driver; any kind of mechanical engineering or jobs dealing with new technology or ideas for the future.

TAURUS

Banking industry (Capricorn is also good for this one); biologist; cashier at a store; musician and music; working in an orchard; selling or making holiday ornaments; gardening; interior designing; farming; horticulture; creating luscious desserts; forestry; camp counselor; working with wildlife habitats; construction.

GEMINI

Working with the media; secretarial; writing for newspapers or magazines; working part-time at a college or a job sponsored by the school district; telephone service; audio-visual equipment operator; working at a convenience store; announcing events; courier or dispatcher; illustration; working in a library; manicurist; reading palms; driving truck; copy services or printing; forecasting the weather; working with elementary school children.

CANCER

Home repair services; working in a real estate office; food service; child care services; the marine and fishing industry; coast guard; making home-crafted goods for sale; plumbing; property caretaker.

LEO

Hotel industry; athletics (a bit more stable than Aries energy); cheerleading; working in daycare; the stock market; cosmetics and hair; any kind of artistic pursuit; leadership positions; movie theaters.

VIRGO

Accounting; carpentry; data processing; health care industry; janitorial; working with metals; mechanical engineering; any type of public service position, such as police officer, EMT, state, local, or county positions; secretarial; waitress or waiter; catering; pet stores; proofreading; investigative services; working at a zoo.

LIBRA

Music; entertainment and the arts; anything to do with weddings or parties; planning and facilitating large events; business services; dating services; engraving; graphic arts; hairdresser; host or hostess positions; modeling; house painting; pottery; social director; sculpting; referee for sports; charity functions; weaving; working with stone (masonry).

SCORPIO

Analyst; archaeology; babysitting; bill collector; biochemist; working in a cemetery; criminologist; detective agency; diving; excavation; fortunetelling; guard; hypnotherapy; insurance occupations; junkyards; laboratory technician; magician; pathology; police force; research companies; secret service; mining; psychology; ghost buster; scientist; Navy Seal; Army Special Forces; tax collector; union work; career counseling.

SAGITTARIUS

Academic studies; archery; attorney; advertising; broadcasting; clergy; diplomatic services; editor; teaching night classes for adults; fireman; grocery stores; animal grooming; horse training; hunting supplies and activities; interpreter of foreign languages; judge; jockey; lawyer; philosophy; college professor; publishing; sales person (general); scholarship; skateboarding; jobs located in foreign countries; travel agencies; x-ray technicians.

CAPRICORN

Astronomy; banking and financial services; dentistry; executive position; foreman; geologist; manager; mountain climbing; physicist; valedictorian; any leadership position.

AQUARIUS

Advocate; airline industry; astrology; consultant; electrical work; clubs such as country clubs or other private clubs as well as nightclubs; high-tech equipment; inventions; mechanic (dealing with electrical components) navigation; politics; power industry (such as gas, oil, electricity, water); sociologist; space exploration; setting trends.

PISCES

Addiction counseling; tending bar; working in a brewery; charity work; chemistry; working with the disabled; ghost writing; magician (as in illusion); working in a jail; photography; oil refinery; shipping; podiatrist; shoe repair; social work; game warden.

SUPPLIES: An old embroidery hoop; green tissue paper; your list; glue; a roll of new pennies; your favorite incense.

INSTRUCTIONS: On a new moon, cleanse, consecrate, and empower all supplies. Carefully stretch a few layers of green tissue paper over the embroidery hoop and secure. Glue your list of job requirements to the center of the hoop. Set the hoop down flat. Arrange the pennies around the outside of the hoop so that the spacing is pleasing to your eye. Now, glue the pennies, clockwise, on the flat edge of the hoop. As you glue each penny, say:

> *The circle is unending,*
> *from birth to death to birth,*
> *and life is but a pattern*
> *I weave upon this Earth.*
> *This spell is for employment,*
> *to meet my needs and more*
> *the energy I raise this eve*
> *will open fortune's door.*

Note: You can use this charm for other prosperity magick as well.

When the glue has dried, repeat the charm three times, then blow on the hoop, imagining that the circle is a vortex drawing employment and prosperity to you. Hang in a window, facing north. Once you land the job, put the hoop in a safe place. Later, if you wish to leave that job, dismantle the hoop on a full moon at midnight, saying:

> *I honor the work you did for me*
> *but now I must move on*
> *a better job awaits me*
> *at the coming of the dawn.*
> *The fire will release the pact*
> *the air sends magick home*
> *I'm very pleased that in this job*
> *I've learned a lot and grown.*
> *But now the north will open up*
> *new treasures come to me*
> *therefore this Witch releases you*
> *as I will, so mote it be.*

Note: This part of the charm can be used to release you from any job.

Burn the green tissue and the job list. Scatter to the winds. Bury the hoop and the pennies, asking that a new and better job grow in place of the old one.

Helpful Job Hints

- Dress nicely for your interview.

- Never go for an interview when the moon is void of course; likewise, do not sign any important papers (college loan, employee statements, tax forms, etc.) when the moon is void or when Mercury is retrograde.[21]

- Don't take your personal life into the job, and don't bring the job life home. Try to keep them separate.

- Always try to be at work on time.

- If you are between sixteen and eighteen, there are special labor laws to protect you. Your place of employment should have those laws posted.

- If you are fired, take a parent or other adult with you to finish business and hand in uniforms, keys, etc. Ask for a receipt indicating you have returned these items. Do not sign anything, no matter what that manager or supervisor says to you. They cannot legally withhold your paycheck for a signature. Take your case immediately to the Bureau of Unemployment Compensation and/or hire an attorney.

- It is illegal for an employer or a company employee to sexually harass you. Know your rights.

Leaving a Job or Getting Fired

There are lots of reasons to leave a job. Regardless of why you've decided to move on (or someone has decided for you), the experience is, in its own way, a loss. The daily pattern you've been experiencing for some time will cease to exist, and you will no longer be active in the group mind of the business. If you are not moving immediately to another job, the loss of this one can be more stressful than you anticipated. The world of business is not a fair one and situations will arise where you feel you have been treated unfairly or been downright cheated. If you have been fired, you will be wrestling with feelings of inadequacy and negative emotions connected to issues of self-worth.

It is at this point that you must be absolutely honest with yourself. If you were fired, did you deserve it? Did you frequently call in sick, come in late, disobey the rules, etc.? If the answer is yes, then consider why you did these things. Perhaps once you got into the job you realized it wasn't the right place for you. Maybe you didn't like your coworkers or supervisor. Rather than quitting, you played it out as far as you could. Was it worth it? Teens have a particularly rough time because they are trying to juggle an extremely heavy schedule—school, homework, socializing with friends, sports or other interests, family—and a part-time job can leave them exhausted, cranky, and unhappy. Statistics tell us that of all the age groups, teens suffer the most from sleep deprivation, which leads to accidents, emotional trauma, and other unfortunate side effects. Were you trying to cram too many activities into too little time? If so, you might want to revamp your schedule before finding a new job.

Regardless of why or how you left this job, it is healthy to do some type of closure ritual. This helps us to release any negativity or fear and open the pathway to a new, fulfilling experience. You can use the second half of the spell listed above, or you can perform the following:

Laying a Job to Rest Spell

SUPPLIES: Items from the old job that you did not have to return to your place of employment; bowl filled with spring water; fresh mint; a stick or rod (SEE PAGE 149); black cloth; white candle; incense of your choice.

INSTRUCTIONS: During the third or fourth quarter moon (waning), lay the black cloth on the altar. Place items from your old job on the cloth. Crush the mint and float in the bowl of spring water. Light the white candle, asking for the light of deity to enter your heart. Pass the candle flame over all items, saying:

Light and darkness meld this night, from under the pond and over the head. The light of the night, and the light of the day, banish impurity and send it away. Stars, air, water— spirit, soul, body—the fire above, the fire below, as I wish, this will be so.

Breathe the incense over all items, saying:

Stars, air, water—spirit, soul, body—the air above, the air below, as I wish, this will be so.

Sprinkle the items on the black cloth with the spring water, repeating:

Stars, air, water—spirit, body, soul—the water above, the water below, as I wish, this will be so.

Gather up the four corners of the cloth and tie. Hold your hands over the cloth, and say:

Guardians of the crossroads, release me from the bonds of (say the place of employment). *Sever all negative connections between myself and* (say the place of employment and anyone there who was unkind or cruel to you), *and anyone who worked against me. Prepare for me a new employment pathway, filled with light, love, and happiness. So mote it be.*

Bury the bundle off your property, preferably as close as you can to a crossroads. Pour the water on the ground in front of your house. Allow the candle to burn, or light every day for seven minutes until it has burned completely.

The Nasty Customer Spell

As many teens find their first jobs in the service industry, they learn very quickly that some people believe the word *service* means "you are my verbal punching bag," especially if the customer is older than the teen. This also happens to young adults in their twenties, and sometimes in their thirties wherein an older individual feels it is their right to treat the younger person unfairly. Hopefully your place of employment will have guidelines on how to handle the difficult customer, but a little magick goes a long way to ease the stress, and works like . . . oh, yes . . . a charm.

If you can, use your finger to trace a counter-clockwise spiral on a flat surface, while staring impassively at the spot between the screaming person's two eyes. In your mind, keep repeating "Evil be gone." Continue to trace the spiral until either the person stops ranting and decides to be a reasonable human being or simply goes away. You can also spin a long necklace in a counter-clockwise motion, though this is more obvious.

Outdoor Bad Boss Spell

There is a warning that goes along with this spell. If you are misbehaving on the job, and the supervisor or manager is only doing what he or she is supposed to do, then this spell will not work. This spell is reserved for the truly scummy boss. In most cases, I've noticed that when an employee is targeted, it is time to get out and find a new place of employment. It is as if Spirit is using this bad management as an example, and is saying to you: "Gee, you don't want to end up like that guy or gal. Don't you think it's time to bail? Weren't you just saying the other day how much you hate this job? So why are you still here?" If, however, you want to hang in there, or you feel that this person's behavior is hurting other people, then your best plan of action is to create harmony. Yes, I know, doesn't sound quite like the sweet taste of revenge, but it certainly gets the job done—sort of like playing "The Sound of Music" until they go insane.

SUPPLIES: Items from the job that are disposable (these items cannot be stolen, they must be cast-offs); a small piece of white paper with the boss's name written on it; holy water in a bowl; a broom; a white candle; a bowl of cooked white rice; and a stuffed snake (the snake here stands for wisdom; if you don't have a stuffed or rubber snake, you can make one out of paper. Some Witches have a staff with a carved snake that they can use for this purpose.). One egg; black marker; thin wire or masking tape; a square of white cloth; a spade; a plastic resealable bag; a drum (a bucket turned upside-down will do if you don't own a drum).

INSTRUCTIONS: With the black marker, write carefully on the egg exactly what you want, then draw a snake underneath; for example, *Harmony at (name the place of employment) for the good of all*. Set carefully aside. Tape or wire the snake around the broom so that it looks like it is crawling up toward the bristles. Dig a small hole in the ground so that the broom can stand, bristles up, in the hole and not fall over. Tightly pack the ground around the broom handle. Scatter the white rice around the base of the broom. (You can support the broom with stones if it just won't stand up straight.)

Note: You are not worshipping the snake. You are using the broom and snake as a visualization key. Your thoughts move up the broom to deity, and your request is answered by the energy coming back down the broom.

Draw a large circle in the dirt around the broom. Fold the white cloth so it is shaped like a triangle and lay the cloth on the ground in front of the broom. Place the item(s) from work on the triangle of cloth. Put the egg on top. Cast a magick circle. Call the quarters. Invoke deity. Sprinkle the items in the triangle with the holy water. Place the bowl of water on top of the work items beside the egg in the triangle. Light the white candle and place in front of the triangle. With your athame or your hand, salute the broom. Lay your hands on the egg and repeat the intent of this ritual. Be specific. Imagine that the egg is surrounded by white or blue light. Begin drumming as you chant (definitions are in brackets):

Spirit of the drum
[the voice of deity]
spirit of the serpents
[wisdom of the Lord and the Lady]
spirit of the waters
spirit of the fires
mystery of the places
where the waters meet.

Spirit of the drum
spirit of the serpents
spirit of the waters
spirit of the fires.
Where the spirit travels
on the sacred crossroads.

Spirit of the drum
spirit of the serpents
spirit of the waters
spirit of the fires.
Rise O mighty serpent
[wisdom]
from the void of darkness.

[This does not mean darkness as in evil, but the darkness of the Great Void where the formula for all life is contained.]

Spirit of the drum
spirit of the serpents
spirit of the waters
spirit of the fires.
Birth your mighty wisdom
emerge from time and space!

Repeat as many times as necessary, until you feel the circle fill with energy and the drum beat becomes naturally faster. When you reach the last line of the last stanza ("Emerge from time and space") say it loudly, point to the egg, then smash the egg. Say: "The birthing is done! "

Pick up the three corners of the white triangle and place the cloth with its contents in the plastic resealable bag. Pour the water at the base of the broom, thanking deity for swift action in this matter. Snuff the candle, saying, "Blessed be." Release the quarters and the circle. Now here is the tricky part. Littering is against the law and bad for the environment, therefore you can't just throw this bag onto the employment property (as your ancestors would have done before you). You will have to dump the biodegradable contents on the property and place all other non-biodegradable items in the property dumpster.

Legal Undertakings

Every family at some point in time finds themselves in need of legal assistance. The following spells can be used to help in these matters.

Cutting Through the Red Tape Spell
In our highly technological society we manufacture an amazing intangible called red tape. This

is when the system (whether legal, school, or otherwise) gets so bogged down with paperwork, passing the buck, personal agendas, and other nonsense that nothing gets done and the entire situation stalls, drawing out negativity and creating stress. Unlike a one-on-one situation with limited variables, red tape vibrates, draws, and binds enough dirty energy together to make what our ancestors called a "haint"—a hulking energy thing that affects many people on several levels. Here's a spell to get rid of that red tape and get things moving!

SUPPLIES: One skein of red yarn; a picture of the outside of the offending business; a pair of scissors; 13 nails; a hammer; an old piece of board; holy water; a black indelible marker; one clear quartz crystal.

INSTRUCTIONS: On the dark of the moon, draw a large spiral with the black marker from the outer edge of the board into the center. Place the picture of the business on the center of the board. Hammer the thirteen nails into the picture about an inch apart from each other, leaving the very center of the picture free (you will place the crystal there). As you hammer, use the following alchemical chant:

> *Out of the black void*
> *and into the red action*
> *out of the red action*
> *and into the white Spirit*
> *out of the white Spirit*
> *and into the gold world*
> *force and form unite*
> *negativity be bound*
> *and what I need be free to come to me!*

Place the crystal, empowered for exactly what you need, in the center. Tie one end of the yarn to one nail, then slowly wind the red yarn around the nails, repeating the alchemical chant.

Take your time. Visualize strongly what you need. When you feel you have finished, use the scissors and cut the yarn from the skein, saying: "What I need be free to come to me." Tie that loose end onto a nail.

Hold your hand over the crystal and repeat the entire alchemical chant one more time, then snatch up the crystal. Carry the crystal with you until your desire is granted. When you have received what you need, sprinkle the board, nails, and yarn with holy water and throw in the trash, saying: "All negativity be gone!" Cleanse the crystal for use another time.

The Void Box Spell

If your family is being unfairly sued, is battling a large corporation for benefits due (but not forthcoming), or finds itself in some type of legal mess, try this spell.

SUPPLIES FOR BOX: One small paper box (you can buy these at arts and craft stores in various sizes) about 3 inches by 3 inches; black acrylic paint; paint brush; 12 small mirrors that will fit on and in the box, 1 inch by 1 inch or 2 inches by 2 inches; glue; business card, letterhead, picture, or name of the corporation. ***Note:*** Box preparation takes approximately two hours. Box should dry completely for twenty-four hours before use. Total cost of supplies is around $11.

BOX PREPARATION: Apply two to three coats of black paint to inside and outside of box. Allow box to dry between coats. Glue mirrors as follows, one at a time, allowing each mirror to dry before turning the box (if you don't, the mirrors will slide): top of lid, under lid, outer bottom of box, four outer sides of the box, four inner sides of the box, and inside bottom of the box. ***Hint:*** When gluing mirrors to outside of box, be sure that the mirrors are at the upper edge, as the box won't close.

ADDITIONAL SUPPLIES: Two white candles. Two flat gray stones that fit in the palm of your hand.

ADDITIONAL PREPARATION: Paint a black snake on one stone and a white snake on the other stone.

SPELL INSTRUCTIONS: When the moon is in Capricorn, Aquarius, or Sagittarius, or full, cast the circle and call the quarters. Cleanse, consecrate, and empower the box to consume all negativity on the part of your opponent. (This is assuming, of course, that your side of the fence is being honest.) Let the universe be the judge. Open the lid of the box and place the business card, court summons, or names of those against you in the box. Hold the stones over the open box and strike them rhythmically together as you say:

> Power of the universe
> air and sky and sea
> holy breath of sacred verse
> I remove all negativity.
> By the drumming of my hands
> and the rhythm of my soul
> my mind will move in sacred trance
> to help me reach my goal.
> As the beat transcends the sky
> the sound rings loud and clear
> the stones of wisdom send the cry
> that magick moves through here.
> On this day I'll overcome
> all hate and pain and fear
> and nevermore will you trod down
> my family oh so dear.
> Snared and caught, the world will know
> the evil that you are
> you cannot hide, or lie, or show
> false faces to the bar. [the legal bar]

> My magick dances pure and strong
> it echoes on the wind
> the beat will haunt you all night long
> it's time for this to end
> and every move you try to make
> reflects upon your sin.
> Your days are numbered this you'll see.
> As I will, so mote it be!

Close the box and tap on the lid three times, saying: "Buried deep inside this box, all your deeds will now be caught." Draw an equal-armed cross in the air over the box to seal the spell. If you used the white candles, allow them to burn completely. Leave the offending parties in the box until the case is fairly cleared. Once the situation is over, remove the paper from the box and burn. Cleanse the box with sage smoke.

Locker Spells

These days there isn't much room in your locker, and with regular searches for drugs, having herbs in baggies in there won't earn you any medals from the administration, so here are some low-profile ideas you might want to try. If you've been to boot camp or your job requires a locker to keep your possessions, you know how small that locker can be! Feel free to use your own imagination, too. Here are some quick and easy spells to turn your locker into a power-house of magickal energy!

- Empower a comb and tape onto the door of your locker to comb away any negativity that your books or clothes might collect during the course of the day.

- Add a little holy water to your perfume. Spray on pulse points before that dash to lunch to keep your shielding strong.

- Place a piece of smoky quartz at the back of your locker to ward off theft.

- Knot seven red strings together in the name of the Seven Hathors to ward off sickness. Tape to the back of your locker, where clothing hangs.

- Empower an old watch to always ensure you are on time for class or aren't late when returning to work from break or lunch. Tape or place at the bottom of the locker near where shoes are kept.

- Empower a blank, black notebook to ensure that you never forget any homework or other scheduling requirements. Keep in the locker at all times, and don't use for anything else.

- Fill a salt shaker with salt, red pepper, black pepper, and gold glitter, then draw a spiral on the cap from the outside to the center of the cap to catch and destroy negativity.

Empowerment Charm

Mistress/Master of the Universe.

I, (state your name), *your Wiccan son/daughter, do ask you to instill in this object* (state your desire) *so that it will function for me in the best way possible, and carry your essence and power to the end of its days. I know you will do this for me. So mote it be!*

Love and Romance

In the Craft, as in all things, there are rules, and then there are rules. Magick for love and romance is especially fickle because you are dealing with the volatile energy of passion, which makes the heart go pitter-pat and the blood pressure soar. Here, then, are the magickal rules for love spells:

- People cannot be owned. They are not your personal property. Therefore, spells limiting the freedom of any individual are against the rules, and will eventually backfire on you, should you choose to mess with their free will.

- A relationship with anyone does not stand still. All relationships change as we mature and encounter new experiences. Over time, the energy of any relationship moves, grows, changes, and sometimes dies. Trying to prevent such growth through magickal means will backfire.

- People are human. Although you may seek someone who is perfect, you will never find perfection. Not every relationship you experience will contain the commitment that you think you need. Learn to respect the feelings of others.

- Every relationship you enter requires responsibility and effort to keep it healthy. Magick alone cannot hold the love you desire.

- You can't force someone to love you, with or without magick.

- True love has more definitions than you can count. Each person thinks of love in a different way. You may think true love is moonlight and roses, and your girlfriend may think that true love is spending a Sunday afternoon playing a game of baseball.

- Do all love magick in a magick circle. You don't want just anyone waltzing into your life.

- Always cleanse, consecrate, and empower all supplies used in love magick.

- Always double-check your divination tool to make sure you are doing the right magick for you.

- Magickally work on yourself, rather than flinging magick at someone else.

When learning how to cast spells, my teachers gave me two very important pieces of advice on the nature of love magick:[22]

1. It's temporary. Love itself goes through too many phases in a relationship for a one-spell-fits-all scenario. Love magick is to get you going in the right direction, and is not intended to overpower another. Consider love spells being like lighter fluid and, like this combustible material, handle such magick responsibly. If you don't, then expect the work to blow up in your face. Love magicks should simply kindle nature's natural fire. You are required to put forth the mental and physical effort (as in any relationship) to reach ultimate success.

2. The good love spells, those that could lead to a lasting relationship, are slow workers. The energy must age a bit, working subtly to create ultimate satisfaction. If patience is a problem for you, you may wish to work on that aspect of yourself before you go zapping the universe for a soulmate.

Seven-Knot Love Spell

The symbol of the knot relates to tying something together, or to keeping something stable. Stability in astrological magick would include the fixed signs of Aquarius (air); Leo (fire); Taurus (earth); and Scorpio (water). With this in mind, you could cast this spell when the moon is in any of these signs (check your magickal or planetary almanac), or you could fine-tune your enchantment by considering the nature of the sign. Air speeds, fire encompasses, water cleanses, and earth roots. Call on the four elements to ensure success.

SUPPLIES: Four ribbons, 17 inches long, in red, white, green, and blue (red for passion, white for purity, green for growth, and blue for wisdom); 2 small bells to thread on the ends of the ribbons; perfume or aftershave; a lock of your own hair.

INSTRUCTIONS: Cleanse, consecrate, and empower all items. Take the ribbons and place one on top of the other, ends matching. Recite the following as you tie each knot, beginning in the center of the ribbon bunch and working outward on each side:

With knot of one, this love's begun.
With knot of two, love shines through.
With knot of three, love comes to me.
With knot of four, my heart will soar.
With knot of five, this spell's alive.
With knot of six, the love is fixed.
With knot of seven, by blood and kin,
this spell is cast and love comes in!
Force and form attend to me,
as I will, so mote it be!

Thread a bell on each end of the ribbon bunch. Attach your lock of hair. Spray ribbon with perfume or aftershave, saying:

The breath of Goddess sparks the flame.
True love lives and knows my name.

Tie ribbon bunch around ankle, wrist, onto your purse, or place in your pocket. Each night for seven nights, repeat "The breath of Goddess" charm seven times while swinging the ribbons in a clockwise direction. On the eighth night, hang the ribbons over your bed and leave them there. Anytime you lose confidence, ring the bells. Don't forget, love magick requires patience!

Orange Love Spell

SUPPLIES: *For the drawings*—One smooth board; a box of new cornmeal; a butter knife; a pencil. *For the spell*—One firm orange; allspice; one red rose; one aspirin; spring water; one pink candle; love oil or perfume.

INSTRUCTIONS: First, draw the seven symbols of the planets on the board with the cornmeal. This will take about two hours. Take your time. Use the knife and pencil to help push the cornmeal into the shape of the symbols. Set aside until you are ready to complete the spell. The symbols are:

⊙ Your will.

☽ Your emotions.

☿ Your ability to communicate.

♀ Your ability to socialize and see beauty.

♂ Your ability to take action.

♃ Your faith and your ability to expand.

♄ Your ability to work with structure and listen to inner wisdom.

As you draw the symbols, repeat what they are for.

When the moon is new, cast a magick circle. Cleanse, consecrate, and empower all supplies. Cut the orange in half. With a spoon, scoop out the pulp of one half of the orange. Sprinkle this half with the allspice. Fill ¾ with water. Crush the aspirin and sprinkle in the water. Float the rose on top. Place the hollowed orange with rose in the center of the seven-planet drawing on the previously prepared flat board. Rub love oil or spray candle with perfume. Place candle beside orange. Light the candle, saying: "Love enters this place."

Hold your hands over the rose, and say:

> *From the sun, love will come.*
> *From the moon, love's sweet tune.*
> *From Mercury, thoughts of clarity.*
> *From Venus, honesty.*
> *From Mars, passion be.*
> *From Jupiter, faith to love.*
> *From Saturn, wisdom from above.*
> *Force and form at my command*
> *fulfill my will as I demand.*
> *So mote it be.*

Allow the candle to burn completely. Release the circle. Take the other half of the orange and place it outside at a crossroads, saying:

> *Vortex of energy, as I will, so mote it be.*
> *Love will find a pathway and quickly*
> *come to me.*

Let the love altar remain in place for seven days. On the eighth day, dump the cornmeal from the drawings, the orange, rose, water, and any end remaining from the pink candle into a plastic bag. Take the bag to the same crossroads and empty, repeating the "Vortex of energy" portion of the charm.

It's Over Spell

Love comes, grows, and sometimes dies. If it is time to release a past love, consider using this spell.

First, remove all items given to you by that person. If you desire to hold on to keepsakes, douse them with holy water and place them in a black box that remains unopened for three months. This includes all photographs. If the relationship ended in a particularly nasty way, get rid of everything, including those photos.

Next, cleanse your home of any unwanted energies left behind by that person by performing a house cleansing.

Finally, cast the following spell on the dark of the moon.

SUPPLIES: One black candle; one white candle; one black ribbon, 3 feet long; one pair of scissors; one large piece of black construction paper; one white crayon; 2 metal tent stakes or long metal nails; one bowl of spring water; one large piece of disposable black cloth.

INSTRUCTIONS: Cleanse, consecrate, and empower all supplies. Cast a magick circle. Place the white and black candle on the altar. Light the black candle, saying: "I dispel all negativity, as I will, so mote it be." Light the white candle, saying:

> *From the void I pull forth the light of Spirit*
> *surrounding myself with love and protection.*
> *As I will, so mote it be.*

Circle the bowl of water three times over the altar, saying: "Sweet release, unhappiness cease."

On the black paper with the white crayon, slowly draw an equal-armed cross, saying:

> *Guardian of the crossroads, bringer of the vortex,*
> *lend me your ear, activate the powers of the*
> *pathways, the cross between the veil, the road*
> *of left and right, the center of heart and sight, at-*
> *tend my wishes from dusk to light.*

Bang the tent stakes together three times over the cross.

Gather the ribbon in both hands, and say:

> *As I cut this ribbon, so I will be released from*
> *(say the person's name), and in that release,*
> *healing energy shall grow. All negative energy*
> *will be removed by the Guardian of the Vortex.*

Slowly begin cutting one-inch pieces off the ribbon, allowing them to fall directly in the center of the white cross on the black paper. With each cutting, say: "Sweet release, unhappiness cease."

When all the pieces are in the center of the paper, say: "It is done. Force and form attend my will!" Then cross the tent stakes over the ribbon pieces to match the drawing and let them lie there. Cover with the black cloth. Pass the bowl of spring water over the cloth, again saying: "Sweet release, unhappiness cease." Allow the candles to burn completely. Wrap everything, including candle ends, in the black cloth. Release the magick circle. Throw everything in a dumpster off your property, repeating the release charm one last time, then stomp your foot on the ground and walk away. Do not look back.

Money

Over the years you will learn that various magicks have their own set of rules. If we put magick into categories, we'd come up with love, health, money, protection, spirituality, and "other" (magicks that don't fit under any particular title). So far we've covered the general rules (under "Magick") as well as those guidelines that relate to love and health, under their respective categories. Here, then, are the general rules for money magicks:

- Past mental programming has a lot to do with the success or failure of magicking for money. If you believe you will always be poor, if your relatives have told you that you will never have anything, if your parents tell you working for money with magick is stupid, if you constantly think about "not" having, then you must learn to accept that abundance is possible for you before you work for money. If you are wrestling with a negative money attitude, try meditating on positive abundance and concentrate on creative visualization relating to prosperity for at least a week before working any money magick.

- Always work both sides of monetary issues: (1) Work on pulling money toward you during the first and second quarters of the moon; and (2) work on debt reduction during the third and fourth quarters of the moon.

- Make a concerted effort to release bad money habits while practicing money magicks. For example, if you have trouble with impulse buying (where you visit a store and just have to buy something because you are there), leave your money or bank card at home. Better yet, lock up your bank card! If you have a particular friend that loves to go to the mall and shop till she drops, and encourages you to do the same so she won't feel alone in blowing her budget, either politely refuse or suggest going somewhere else (like a walk on the beach). Some people spend money to alleviate depression. Better to get to the root of what's making you feel bad rather than adding to that unhappiness with money worries.

- Never tell anyone how much you spent for anything.

- Never show off things you've bought.

- Never tell anyone you are working magick for money.

- Never steal or cheat (your life will go in the toilet).

- Try never to borrow money, and if you do, pay it back promptly. The longer you wait to pay a debt you owe, the more negativity you allow to grow.

- Never substitute money magick for hard work.

I know some of these rules may sound silly to you, but these are the ones I've found to work most consistently in magicks relating to money and overall prosperity.

Saving Money

If you are a teen, you have to be particularly aware that YOU are the targeted age group for what is called "discretionary income." Statistics show that you have more money to blow than any other age group, therefore every company on the face of the planet that can lure you in with marketing ploys will try their best to get you to cough up your hard-earned cash in their direction. Always beware of the word *free*—there ain't no such animal. My children had a really hard time understanding that the word *free* in marketing is a smoke-and-mirrors ploy to encourage you to spend money. Remember the old adage, *If it sounds too good to be true, it is too good to be true.* Teen buying power has become an extremely important factor in the fight for supremacy in American economics, and companies pay big bucks for marketing surveys that tell that company all about you—your likes and dislikes, how you are feeling, and what you think you want out of life. Every time you fill out a survey form from any company, you are telling them where to hit you with future advertising. Although you may think this is cool, think again. Once you leave your teen years and acquire responsibilities (like car payments, house payments, utility bills, etc.), it may be difficult for you to learn to limit your spending.

For some teens and adults, saving money is particularly difficult, as they may subconsciously see their money as a type of freedom. With that money, they can buy what they want, when they want it—where in their earlier years purchases were made at their parents' discretion. Shopping is also a way to get out of the house and still appear to have some sort of purpose. Sometimes we are so excited about this new freedom that we forget it is important to try to save our money. Other teens and adults go on buying sprees because spending money is a subconscious way of letting go of fears and worries. Here are some easy ways to save money:

- Use the public library rather than buying books and magazines. They even lend out CDs, cassette tapes, DVDs, and videos.

- Go to the movies during the twilight or matinee shows. If you must go at night, remember to ask about your student discount. You can also have a movie night with friends and rent movies with a three-for-one discount, or pool your movies together, or borrow a movie from the library.

- Pack your lunch (it'll probably taste better).

- It's okay to take your friends somewhere, but if it becomes a habit, like transportation to and from work or school, you have every right to ask for gas money. If you are always the designated driver for the fun stuff, where you constantly cart around your friends because they don't have a car, it's only fair that everyone either chip in money for gas, pay for your entrance into wherever you are going, or cover your meal. If they refuse to do this, close your taxi service.

- If you must go to the mall because you are bored, take only enough money to get you there and have to call home for emergencies. Leave your savings and your bank card at home.

- Don't lend money. Some friends can nickel-and-dime you to death.

- Don't blow every penny when you are on vacation. Determine ahead of time how much money is okay to spend on one or two souvenirs rather than carting half the beach home with you and then losing interest in what you bought two weeks later.

- Mend clothes and use your own creativity to make dull clothes cool again rather than constantly buying new ones. My mother used to tell me that the only important name that was on my clothes was my own.

- Find discount stores when it's time to shop. What most people don't know is that clothing made carrying their favorite hot label is also sold to discount stores under a different, cheaper label.

- Buy generic, over-the-counter products.

- Learn comparison shopping techniques—this is where you look for the best deal possible on the item you want. Especially comparison shop when buying a car or auto insurance. Ask an adult for help because salespeople often take one look at your young face and think "sucker." I overheard a teenage boy just yesterday who was bragging about his new stereo system. The salesman had skinned him alive but, as yet, the boy hadn't figured it out.

- Have someone knowledgeable go over your cell phone plan with you, or better yet take someone experienced with cell costs with you when you get your own phone. Check your bills every month for plan changes or other strange costs. If you are in doubt, call the company promptly. If you are not satisfied with the answer, ask to speak to a supervisor, or have someone older than yourself get on the line with you. In some states you can actually go to jail for the nonpayment of a cell phone bill.

- Watch hidden costs at garages. At any age you are susceptible to dishonest practices. When you take your car to be serviced or repaired, ask an adult to ride along. Insist on the following:

  1. That they call you with the total amount of the bill BEFORE they fix your car.

  2. That you be given an exact date and time when you can retrieve your vehicle.

  3) ALWAYS get a receipt for work done and make sure that the receipt fully covers the type of work completed. Make sure that receipt is dated and is marked "paid" before you leave the premises.

- Delinquent bills: In most cases you DO NOT have to pay a collection agency fee if you go back to the source and pay the bill from there. However, the collection agency will still report your default and you must contact the credit bureau to add your side of the story to the file. I agree that this isn't fair, but it is how it works.

- If you have credit cards or personal loans and are in trouble paying your bills or just want to learn how to budget, visit http://www.debtorsanonymous.org.

Debt Reduction Spell

Save all receipts from everything you spend. Keep the important ones (like for the stereo or computer) in case something goes wrong. Put the receipts for those little purchases (sodas, candy, fast food, batteries, etc.) into a black box

until the fourth quarter moon. Burn them, saying the following prayer:

> *Dark moon enchantment*
> *banish debt and woe*
> *feelings of insecurity, I order you to go!*
> *Expenses now grow smaller*
> *and debt you must depart*
> *and in your place, by Goddess' grace*
> *I learn the saving art.*

Scatter the ashes to the wind. Practice this for at least three months, more if you can. If you do this spell once a month for a full year you'll notice a big reduction in those miscellaneous receipts. ***Note:*** If you have credit cards, the companies may decide to cut your limit, as this is part of debt reduction work. Don't be surprised if it happens to you.

Paycheck Spell

Say the following spell over your paycheck before you put it into the bank. If you have direct deposit, use the deposit ticket.

> *Black moon and white, red moon and gold*
> *the fullness of harvest brings riches untold.*
> *Energy to matter and force to form*
> *my prosperity grows and savings are born.*
> *Silver and mercury, knowledge and thought*
> *go into each purchase before it is bought.*
> *Con men can't see me, and thieves shy away,*
> *prosperity comes to me each night and each day.*

Spell to Bring Money Into the Home

SUPPLIES: One 3-inch by 3-inch square of black cloth (or paper); silver pen; a rubber band; old jar or flower pot; dirt from your back yard; dried or fresh mint leaves; a pencil or small maple twig; water in a small white or silver bowl (real silver, not imitation).

INSTRUCTIONS: On the new moon (or when you really need money), with the silver pen draw the symbol of Mercury (☿) on one side of the black cloth (or paper) and the symbol for the Earth (⊕) on the other.

Hold your hands over the bowl of water and imagine that your entire body receives spiritual cleansing, then old your hands over both symbols (one at a time) and empower for prosperity. Using the herbal chant on page 381, empower the mint leaves. Sprinkle or lay mint leaves over the symbol of the Earth, saying your name nine times. Roll the cloth/paper and leaves around the barrel of the pencil. Secure with rubber band. Carry in pocket, book bag, or purse until the money you need comes to you. You can re-empower the symbol again on the following new moon. Remember to scatter the old mint leaves to the winds, thanking the Spirits, and replace with freshly empowered leaves.

Note: If you need someone to pay up on a debt, then choose the full moon and use a gold pen to draw the symbol of the sun (☉) beside that of Mercury. Place the symbol of Earth on the other side of the cloth/paper. Say the person's name who owes you the money seven times. Keep the remainder of the spell the same.

Coughing Up the Dough Spell

Let's say, for the sake of argument, that you know the school project will require supplies that your family cannot afford. Hey, it's happened. Not every mom or dad can waltz out to the store and spend over two hundred bucks on supplies for a project. You think I'm kidding? I can recall two projects that were that expensive (and several more that were about half that). The first was a miniature fort that my youngest son built in middle school, and the second project involved making masks for a theater production that my daughter had to do for her first semester at col-lege. How many of you have experienced parental angst when it comes to shelling out money for something you are told at school you must have? It certainly isn't your fault and your parents don't mean to hurt your feelings when they whine, but it happens all the same.

So! The project requires supplies, and supplies are bought with money. Therefore, a little prosperity magick thrown in here won't hurt a bit, will it? Take out your magickal calendar and keep an eye on that circled green date—the one that tells you it's time to have all the supplies together for your project. Time to do a bit of hunting in the house. Find a small, empty bottle (a little water bottle will do) and one teaspoon of cough medicine. Parents often monitor the medicine in the home, so if necessary you will have to ask your parent or guardian for the cough medicine—don't sneak it. Put the cough medicine in the bottle, then fill the bottle with water. Make a list of the supplies that you need. Put the bottle on top of the list and ask the universe to "cough up" the supplies or the money needed to buy them. Shake the bottle every morning before you go to school and ask for the same thing.

Take the opportunities you are given, don't overlook them. Magick follows the path of least resistance, which means that you are never aware of all the opportunities any request might have attached to it. There's always, in any event or situation, an unknown factor. I believe that life is constructed this way to keep it interesting. If you knew everything, you'd be bored silly.

Now what do I mean by grabbing opportunity? Let's say (and this has happened) that your parents do not have enough money for school supplies. You know this, so you are going to work magick to get the supplies, which you do. The next day, your friend Jane tells you that her parents bought her too many notebooks; would you like some? If you say no because you are embarrassed to receive the gift, then you just cut off the opportunity presented to you. Result? Another opportunity may not arise. Let's say you said, "Yes, thank you," and took the notebooks home. At this point, you should thank the universe for providing what you asked for (after thanking Jane, of course). The thank-you to the universe could be in a prayer, by reading a poem, by lighting a white candle, or however you see fit. What if you needed more than the notebooks that Jane gave you? Don't give up. Work the spell again (if you like) or allow more opportunities to come into your life. Often, magick doesn't happen with a snap of your fingers—time is needed for your will to take form.

I think that magick is a lot like a spiritual smoke signal. You send out the request, it goes into the air, and Spirit picks up the message and sends the signal elsewhere, to the person, place, or thing that can best help you. It takes time for that "help" to happen. If the goal is little, it doesn't take much time, but if it is a much bigger goal, you may have to be patient. Sometimes Spirit needs to direct several people to help you accomplish a single success.

Let's go back to those supplies you needed. Let's say that it is the beginning of the school year. Jane, if you remember, provided the notebooks. You also needed a backpack, a gym bag, sneakers, and a calculator. In the following week, Grandma may bring you the gym bag or offer to take you shopping, your mother may receive a small bonus on her check and be delighted that she can buy you the shoes you need. Okay, so not all parents are delighted to spend money, but you get the picture. Your father brings home a used calculator because he remembered that you said you needed one. The next-door neighbor asks if you will cut her lawn for twenty bucks and then pays you extra to clean out her base-

ment. Now you can get the backpack. And that's basically how physical things of any kind manifest when spellwork is the root of your activities. Sometimes it is money, sometimes gifts, and sometimes it is an offer of one thing (mowing the lawn) to get something else (buying the backpack). With magick, you may find what you are looking for in the strangest places—that's the mystery, after all!

Once you receive all the things on your list, you need to de-magick that spell. Why bother? Think of it as a spiritual cleanup. You've created something, you have used it with success, and now you need to put it away. If you drink a soda, you don't litter with the bottle. The same thing goes with magick. No littering allowed. Place your hands over the bottle, thank the universe, then pour the contents of the bottle down the drain. Wash out the bottle (so you can use it next time, perhaps for something else). Burn the paper (if you are allowed to burn things). If you aren't permitted to burn the paper, tear it into tiny pieces, thanking the universe, and then re-cycle it.

Parents

This is a tough one. Since my *Teen Witch* book came out in 1998, I've gotten thousands of letters from teens. Some of these letters and e-mails despaired at the attitude of their parents in regard to magickal studies and Wicca. In these letters teens ask me how to "make" their parents understand. Opening a closed mind is an incredibly difficult task, especially if to open that mind someone must re-educate themselves on information they thought, up until the present, was correct. Add to this fact (and sadly so) that the issue of religion in the home is sometimes used as a negative control factor—meaning religion isn't the issue at all, there are other psychological dynamics brewing—and an argument over religious choice is just the tip of the problem. Some parents "get religion" because something very terrible has happened to them in the past, and the religion they found helps to take away their fear of the future (or helps to obliterate the past). Others don't want you to look at different religions because the tradition of their own religion is very important to them—it makes them feel grounded and it also makes them feel that they are giving you good practices to help carry you through adulthood. Neither of these two positions on religion are wrong, they are simply different. A third position, and slightly more distasteful, is that some parents are struggling with control issues themselves—the more out of control they feel, the tighter they try to manage others. Don't jump to this explanation, however, just because your parents are exerting their authority—you may have done something to deserve their need to pull in the reins. As Witchcraft does not permit self-denial, you know whether or not you have legitimately earned their angst.

The best way to handle the fear that your parents exhibit in regard to Witchcraft is to carefully monitor your own behavior, as well as study other religions and why people believe and behave the way they do as much as possible. If this sounds like a lot of work—it is; however, you are the next generation. If you don't learn as much as you can and keep an open mind, then you too in the future may become too settled and behave in the same closed way. By keeping up your school work, socializing with your friends in a positive way, staying away from drugs, alcohol, and crime, and helping the adults around the house, most adults (in time) will see that your new choice in spirituality is not harm-

ful either to yourself or to the family unit. On top of this, studying all the major religions of the world, past and present, will not only help you to understand what has made the world tick for so many thousands of years, it will also influence your parents because they will want to look at your reading material and many times talk about it. Having a family "history night" is not as corny as it sounds. Everybody benefits.

As a parent of four children, I can certainly understand how and why parents sometimes overreact. Kids don't come with instruction manuals. As a parent, you learn as you go and you are always in the spotlight. Parents must try to set a good example at all times, and that isn't easy because we aren't perfect and we do make mistakes. Many times a situation that is a "first" for you is also a "first" for your parents. Believe it or not, many of them lay awake at night worrying about whether or not they have done the right thing in decisions that involve you. They realize that your childhood and young adulthood are a one-time shot. They don't want to mess up, either.

In the book of Tao there is a saying: "Once a statue is finished, it is too late to change the arms. Only with a new block of stone are there possibilities."[23] The story that goes along with this bit of wisdom will probably sound familiar to you. In the tale, a young boy is telling his father that he thinks it is unfair that the father always says, "Do as I say, not as I do." Where the child feels that his father is being a hypocrite, the father says, "Oh, no. This is wisdom." Of course, the son says, "So how do you figure that? If it is okay for you, why isn't it okay for me?" The father takes his son to an artist that carves statues. There are lots of haunting stone people in the display area. The father points to the statues and says, "I'm like those statues. I am many years into my life, and I am set in my ways. My mistakes are carved into my soul, and I am the product of all my actions." He then takes the son into the workshop out back and says, "But you—you are like those blocks of stone. You have not completely taken shape. I do not want you to make the same mistakes that I did. There is still time for you to learn, and it is my hope that you will become more beautiful than I."

Puts a whole new twist on the "Do as I say, not as I do" routine, doesn't it?

Peer Pressure (Adults Included)

Now that you know the basic building blocks of the group mind, I'd like you to think about that dreaded dis-ease called peer pressure. Often, people want to be accepted by their peers, to feel like they are a part of something bigger than themselves, that they belong. For some of us, being born was traumatic enough; the idea of total ostracism by our friends is more than the subconscious mind can bear. The conscious mind, then, overrides what we know to be right or wrong behavior, and says, "I'll move with the group because then I will not be alone," never realizing that it cannot be disconnected in any way from the collective unconscious. This is when we mistake the group mind (the temporary microcosm) for the macrocosm of the collective unconscious.

The other thing we tend to forget is that although the collective unconscious lasts forever, the group mind does not. It begins, grows, changes, and eventually disintegrates. Sometimes this happens quickly, and other times it takes awhile, but especially through the teen years the lifespan of the group mind is very limited and it will change radically from one season to the

next. In this case you must ask yourself, "Is this decision I am about to make worth it?" As a magickal person, you are expected to step back and be a visionary before you charge along with the pack, because you know that the pack has a limited history (even if they have no clue).

There's also something else I should add here, before you go further. In the magickal world, once you've been informed of a particular occult maxim (or rule), then you are considered responsible, whether you like it or not. Spirit feels that when you have been educated on any subject, then you have to own up to your choices. This is why, throughout history, different cultures have used the snake to represent wisdom and knowledge. Once you know the truth, it will bite you if you don't honor it. When Witches say "Honor is the law; love is the bond," this is what they are talking about.

The Dreaded Cupcake Story

Let's take an example. From studying Witchcraft you now know that the universal mind creates harmony and abundance in all things. You need never want, and there are ways to tap into that universal abundance that harms no one. This is knowledge. Granted, waiting for things to work in our favor sometimes takes patience, but you're learning how to handle that. Let's say that you have two dollars in your pocket, plenty to pay for that cupcake in the school lunchroom. Your friends, however, have decided that stealing that cupcake out from underneath the lunch lady's nose is great fun. You want to be one of the guys. You don't want to be left out. One of your friends goes first, and he gets away with it. Now you try, and bingo! You're tagged. Before when kids were caught taking cupcakes, the lunch lady made them pay double, so you thought that this time, if you were caught, it would be no big deal, the risk would be minimal. You had the money in your pocket to pay double, so you thought you had all bases covered. The universe, however, says, "Yo, kid. I'm an abundant place. You knew that already. Stealing is wrong. So guess what? I made sure the principal was standing there, and you're busted." Much to your surprise, you are suspended from school. However, this isn't the end of the story, and your greatest challenge has yet to occur.

When a group mind has condoned a negative behavior pattern (whether it consists of children, teens, or adults) and it is affected by the laws of the universe, it closes ranks and congratulates you on a job well done or at least tries to convince you that your treatment was unfair. You can either choose to buy into this false sense of belonging, or you can own up to what you did wrong. Accepting responsibility for your actions is by far the biggest challenge.

All of us, at some point, have had to handle peer pressure, and some of it is no big deal, but when that pressure moves into stuff like shoplifting, drugs, alcohol, violence, or destroying property, it's time for you to step back and think about what sort of energy you're going to reap should you ride along with the group mind. Since the group mind of the teen years is very limited, and the consequences for actions such as these are great, aren't the stakes too high? Don't beat yourself over the head because you wanted to go along with the group. Everyone is presented with lots of challenges in his or her lifetime. It's the choice that's important.

Teens aren't the only ones who have to deal with peer pressure. When you reach adulthood (whenever that is), it doesn't go away. Some of the worst mistakes in history are the result of a poorly functioning group mind and pressure from that mind. A family can also exert negative pressure if the group mind is infected with drug abuse, alcoholism, or constant negative behavior

patterns. Whether you are twenty-one or one-hundred-and-one, a smart cookie knows when to bail out.

So how do you handle peer pressure? In high school and college, I tried to take the humorous way out first. I made a joke, and lightened the energy, so to speak, with laughter. Usually this was enough to get me out of the danger zone. With that I'd change the subject, or hail a friend walking by, or find a good reason to disengage from the group. If this didn't work, I resorted to honesty. Rather than judging the group, which they wouldn't like, I usually said something like, "If you want to do that, it's cool, but I'm not into it." If they pushed, then I'd add why—and that "why" had a lot to do with what "I" wanted. With younger kids, the statement "My parents would kill me" goes a long way, but with the older teens, especially those who for whatever reason are rejecting authority, this statement will get you ridiculed. Better to be honest and firm in your own goals rather than indicate you are afraid of condemnation. Don't vacillate and act like they can convince you. Be confident and assertive, which isn't too hard because you are stating the truth, and the truth alone carries great power.

Amulet for Discernment Spell

This amulet is designed to protect you and help you make wise choices when you feel that you may be influenced by peer pressure in a negative way.

SUPPLIES: A small amount of clay (of your choice); sharp pencil or pen.

INSTRUCTIONS: Flatten the clay into a disk the size of a fifty-cent piece. Inscribe your initials on one side with the pen or pencil. Write the words *Karma* and the name of Spirit or your patron deity on the other side. Follow the instructions on the clay package—some clays can air dry, others require baking—to harden the clay. In a magick circle, cleanse, consecrate, and bless the amulet, asking that protection and wisdom surround you whenever you carry it in pocket or purse. Follow this by saying:

I let go of time and space
and connect with love and infinite grace
the perfection of (name God or Goddess).
I join with Spirit
I am part of the One!
I conceive the form [wisdom]
I remove error
I accept success [wise choices]
with the power of unlimited creativity
my word is done.
So mote it be.

You can change the words in parentheses to match any spellcasting intent. This was just one example. Use your own creativity to tailor the spell just for you.

Physically Handicapped Practitioners

In the words of Lord Rowan, one of our Black Forest high priests who has a congenital deafness condition:

The number-one point to remember is that I have found that the words handicapped *and* disabled *don't carry as much weight in the Craft community as they do in the outside world. Wicca is about spirituality and accessing your inner power and wisdom. You should have absolutely no problems raising power, and then*

releasing it toward your desired goal. However, if you are expecting the Lady and Lord to cut you some slack because of your handicap, don't count on it. Deity expects you to grow, and to develop your powers, along with the other practitioners of the Craft. You will be pleasantly surprised by the gifts Spirit may bestow on you for your hard work.

Magick and religion only require the use of your mind. Therefore, no matter what your handicap, physical challenge, and so forth, you can always find ways to accomplish your goal. Yes, you may have to use a little ingenuity to master some rituals, or find a totally different way to do something, but the Craft is fluid enough to support the changes that you must necessarily make.

If you are working in a group, make sure that the facilitator knows of your special needs. For example, in Rowan's case, the coven always worked in low lighting so that he could read lips. Frequently he was given rituals ahead of time so that he could review them before the ceremony. He never got frustrated if the high priest got carried away and forgot to face him. Rowan simply moved with the flow of the energy and was rewarded by Spirit with the information he needed to be a part of the ritual. Other Black Forest covens have also worked with "special needs" individuals. The Texas groups made audiotapes of all our lessons for our sight-impaired members. Dyslexic individuals were given additional time to complete written tasks and many times were given the opportunity to take oral examinations rather than written ones. Because the Craft is all about making a better you, and not following a hard-line dogma, special needs individuals can flourish and grow in the same manner as anyone else.

Protection

There are two types of protection magick:

Preventative: Learning to set up wards and boundaries around yourself and your home to keep negativity out.

Defensive: Where you have been physically or verbally attacked and move to protect yourself in mundane and magickal ways.

Preventative Magick

One of the first methods of protection magick that the new student learns is that of shielding or warding one's body or environment. Two books that you may find extremely helpful are:

Practical Guide to Psychic Self-Defense and Well-Being by Denning and Phillips

Psychic Self-Defense by Dion Fortune

Although you might first think that protective magicks are geared only to combat someone coming at you with fists or angry words, that's just part of it. Protection magicks also work for situations that we don't think much about, or those minor irritations in which we believe little can be done—putting a lid on your impulse buying when you are teased by flashy advertisements and other marketing gimmicks, the kid who keeps bugging you to borrow money, the friend who borrows CDs and never gives them back, the friend of your older brother who tries to convince you that drugs are okay (which they aren't), that girl that got your phone number from a supposed friend and now calls your house every day and then hangs up before someone can answer, the football player that keeps moving your stuff at the lunch table, the bill collector who is harassing your mom, that sleazy guy at your dad's work who is always coming over to the house and looking at you

funny, that friend of your dad's that keeps trying to get him into bad financial deals, the nasty aunt that blows in and out of your family life leaving unhappiness and emotional pain in her wake, or the friend who despite her good intentions always seems to get you into hot water with your other friends . . . whew! Have I missed anything? As Carl Llewellyn Weschcke, owner and publisher of Llewellyn, says:

> [Psychic self-defense] *is a matter of strength, of confidence, of success and fulfillment coming to you through the use of some simple and perfectly natural psychic techniques.*[24]

The biggest problem I've found in training students is not that they can't learn defensive techniques, but that as the years go by and their lives improve, they forget them. Granted, some of the things they learn become very much a part of their everyday lives and continue to work subconsciously, but if the student moves to a new environment (from high school to college, from an old job to a new one, from an old home or apartment to a different one), they sometimes forget to rework some of the original techniques they learned years ago. I have also seen difficulties arise exponentially with a person's public identity. Let's say in your freshman year at high school you didn't know too many people, you weren't in many school clubs or activities—you basically kept to yourself. But over the summer you blossomed, matured, and gained more self-confidence. In your sophomore year, with that new-found inner strength, you began joining things, becoming more active in your community. In your junior year you find yourself surrounded by lots of friends, enjoying popularity, and finding yourself extremely active in school. Suddenly where no one paid attention before, now eyes are turning toward you, and some of those eyes are jealous, vindictive, and spiteful. The small minds behind these eyes plot to take you down. To be hit unprepared with this negative energy is a shock. This happens to adults, too, and can rattle anyone right down to the bone.

This doesn't mean that you should be afraid or look for a boogie-teen around every corner. Indeed, psychic self-defense techniques teach you to deal with and eliminate fear, but the above example (which really happened) is to remind you that psychic self defense techniques are important throughout your life, not just when you face something upsetting, like a bully or jealous ex-friend, and should be practiced even when everything is going great and no black clouds loom on the horizon. If you begin experiencing difficulties, and you've been working with magick for a year or two (or even more), you might want to remember to "get back to basics" by going over those techniques you learned early on in the Craft—grounding and centering, meditation, daily devotions, and psychic self-defense techniques. Yes, these are all mental activities, yet they form the strong foundation of your magickal work.

Web of Stars Psychic Protection Meditation

This meditation, practiced every day alone or with other meditations, exercises your ability to protect yourself from negativity, relieves stress, and urges you to think about the divine. Sometimes we call this activity "shielding" or "warding." This meditation takes only a few moments, so it's easy to fit into your busy day.

Find a place where you will not be disturbed. Sit comfortably in a chair. You can play soft music if you like. Close your eyes. Ground and center. Take three nice, deep breaths. Count down from ten to one. Imagine that you are surrounded by white light. Allow that white light

to grow stronger. The light becomes a solid shield around your body. Now surround the white light with a web of stars. This web is like an electrical force field. When any negativity touches the web, it disintegrates. The waves that result from these tiny explosions turn into positive energy, clinging to the net, thereby reinforcing the original web. If you have trouble visualizing this, think of a bug light. The bug hits the light, and there is a zapping sound as the light grows brighter. Hold this visualization as long as you can. Then take a deep breath. Reach out with your heart and feel the presence of Spirit, allowing that peaceful feeling to flow through your body. Take another deep breath. Count from one to five and open your eyes. Practice at least twice a day, every day. You can also use this visualization when you feel sick, upset, sad, or think you are in danger.

When you have practiced at least two weeks, you can begin to use the same meditation to protect pets, friends, and family members. Follow the instructions above, then visualize the person surrounded by white light, covered by the web of stars. Hold the visualization as long as you can. Practice every day until you feel the threat is over, or practice as a part of your daily prayers that include pets, friends, and family members.

Protecting Inanimate Items

Hold the object in your hands, or lay hands on the item if it is too large to hold. Close your eyes. Ground and center. Take three deep breaths. Imagine a bright, white light surrounding the object. Now add the web of stars as in the previous examples. Hold the visualization as long as you can. Take a deep breath and then open your eyes.

Defensive Magicks

Defensive magicks are performed when you have been attacked, either physically or verbally. If you have come under physical attack it is vitally important that you tell someone who can help you—parents, teachers, close family friends, or the police. Verbal threats can be just as bad, and you need to share what is happening to you with someone you trust. Don't bottle it up inside and suffer through alone. On a lesser scale, small things such as gossip, intolerance to the way you feel about something, or ignoring how you feel can also put you on the defensive. It isn't always easy to see the other person's point of view when your feelings have been hurt. Sometimes we just want to come out fighting no matter what!

While an event occurs (or has just happened) that makes you feel bad, it is really important to consider doing some (or all) of the following:

- Remember to breathe properly. Taking several deep breaths throughout the day when you feel very stressed is important. It helps you capture some semblance of order in your brain and releases nervous tension, which can make you irritable, snappish, and downright yucky to be around.

- Get plenty of sleep. Sleep deprivation not only turns your brain to mush and makes you useless physically, it also tinkers with your magick in unpleasant ways.

- Practice a cleansing visualization every morning and evening. Keep up with the basics of daily meditations, devotions, and grounding and centering. I know it's hard, especially when you are upset, but these exercises give you something to do so that you don't focus on the negative.

- Add physical exercise to your daily life. In times of crisis, keeping busy through physical exercise helps you to heal faster mentally.

- Physically and magickally cleanse the area of your home or apartment where you spend the most time. For most teens and young adults, this will be your bedroom or dorm room. During times of great crisis, magickally cleanse the area every day with any of the following: incense, sage, holy water, drumming, bells, or rattles. You may not feel like doing it, but allowing the negativity to grow around you while you sit there and stew will make any magick you attempt difficult to accomplish. You want the area to be as pure as possible when you decide on the best course of action.

- Crying is okay. If we weren't supposed to cry, we wouldn't have tear ducts. Crying allows you to vent those wild emotions.

So far, most of the above suggestions don't seem particularly magickal, but all of them open the mental pathway for sound decision-making in times of crises. Here are some simple, immediate protective magicks to keep the situation from getting any worse than it already is:

- Mix a large quantity of salt and protective herbs of your choice together. Walk around your home and scatter the mixture, uttering your own protective prayer. Be careful, however, as salt kills grass and other plants, so be sure to watch where the mixture falls. If you live in an apartment, scatter the mixture under the front doormat and under the rug near the fire escape.

- Draw pentacles with holy water on al windows and access doors to keep negativity out.

- Burn a black candle to dispel negativity and send evil back to its source.

- Use your magickal voice whenever you feel it is necessary to cleanse body, mind, and area.

Letters to the Ancestral Dead Spell

When someone passes away, many people mistakenly think that they cannot hear us, nor do many individuals believe that they can help us if we are in trouble. Granted, they cannot take the place of your spiritual source, but they can work with that source to assist you. Where prayers to honor the dead are intoned to keep the connection open between us and are said to help them continue to work on their own karma, prayers for assistance are used to bridge the gap between the worlds and draw the protection we need on this plane around us with their help.

SUPPLIES: A purple candle; paper; pen; an envelope; 3 stones.

INSTRUCTIONS: Light the purple candle, intoning prayers for the deceased. For example, you can say:

I honor my grandmother and grandfather,
who have passed beyond the veil.
May the light of perfect love and perfect peace always surround them.

Write a letter to one of the people you honored in your prayer. Detail the problem. Ask for their assistance. Place the letter in the envelope and seal with a kiss. Release the circle by drawing the energy into the letter. Take the letter outside and place on top of three stones arranged like a pyramid. Put the letter on top. Repeat the prayer of honor. Burn the letter. Let the cool ashes escape in the wind. Know that help is on the way. Leave the stones the way you have placed them.

You will find many spells and rituals in this book on protection. Check the index if you can't find them right away.

School Difficulties

This is probably, by far, the most controversial area of this book. No kidding. When I wrote *Teen Witch*, I put a magickal working in there called the Bad Bus Driver Spell. Needless to say, a lot of people weren't too thrilled with it, because I was, in essence, kicking at the base of the ivory tower that we call your school system. Granted, it was just little kick and it came from an experience I had at sixteen. I remember telling my father that if my school bus was ever involved in an accident, that he should immediately sue and take it as far as he could go. My statement, I felt, was justified. Every morning my bus driver pulled out onto a four-lane highway and he never looked. Never. He just moseyed on out there, thinking that because the bus was bigger than most cars, and because drivers would not want to hit a school bus if their lives depended on it (which they did), that they wouldn't hit the bus. We were lucky. Granted, this was the behavior of one bus driver in thousands, and not all bus drivers are grumpy or disobey the rules of the road—still, there was that one.

Teens are not stupid, and above all, they expect honesty from their parents and the school system, from writers like me, from their pastors at church, and from society in general. They expect this because this is what they have been taught. Honesty, as the sages put it, is the best policy, and this is not an inaccurate assumption. But what teens expect and what some adults are willing to give, in many cases and for a variety of reasons, are two entirely different things, and there comes a point in every teen's life when they are smacked in the face with this realization: Not all adults are good, honest, hardworking people. Some of them are nasty, others are just strange, and a few are downright monsters and, like it or not, these dregs of society occasionally manage to squirrel their way into the school system. There they are protected by the sugar-coated belief that such a place would never harbor an unstable individual, coupled with the unions and attorneys who protect them.

So, let's be blunt. There are good teachers who do their very best to bring you the finest education possible, and there are those who look the other way when trouble starts, turning a blind eye to your problem, or who create unbearable situations for you because they have unfulfilled lives, suffer from personality disorders, or are just downright dysfunctional. There are good coaches and there are those that should never be anywhere near children. There are good principals and administrative employees who strive to make the system work in your favor, and there are really crappy ones that care more about power, prestige, and that paycheck. A school is a business and an industry. And, as many parents have discovered, this industry is not above doing just about anything to protect itself. When the people involved in the school system are great, we should support them and help them as much as we can, but when their behavior is unacceptable, we need to do something about it, to protect ourselves and others like us. This, let me tell you, can get extremely complicated, messy, downright nasty, and expensive.

Many student versus school difficulties arise because of discrimination, and we're not talking about just race, your income level, your religion, who your parents know in the system, or all sorts of things that fall into this category. Discrimination is a disease. It knows no color, no sex, no age, and no religion; it is vile energy that sweeps into homes, schools, jobs, and churches. It is a plague unlike any other, and it can and does destroy lives. It brings a slow and painful death. Since the dawn of man it has been the number one killer of human beings. It works on an archaic social system known in tribal societies as "honor and shame," and uses this system to its best advantage. Most schools participate in the honor and shame scenario every day. You are either put on the honor roll or you are shamed by ostracism, detention, suspension, or expulsion. You are rewarded with a school party, or you are publicly defamed in front of your peers and classmates.

As you can tell, this social system is considered a bad one, yet we participate in it all the time. Street gangs also use the honor and shame model. Although the general populace rejects the gang behavior, they support the exact same social model in the school system, in churches, and in businesses. Why? Because most of us are too busy living to worry about social models and human behavioral patterns, until, unfortunately, the model blows up in our faces and even then people are not always moved to make changes, especially radical ones that may involve time and expense. Instead, they are more inclined to spend their time in the process of finger pointing, until the situation "blows over." Because many of the present school systems work on a "yearly" basis—nine months in the trenches and three months out, with students ever-moving from one building to another in the march toward graduation from one level to the next—situations that normally would demand resolution in the outside world can be stalled, ignored, or even hidden for a very long time in the hopes that they will never become an issue, and many times that is precisely what happens.

When it comes to school issues, the most powerful magick in the world lies, for most of you, in the hands of your parents. They love you and want the best for you. It is to your parents, then, that you should turn to immediately when problems at school arise. Don't hide that infraction, detention, or (Goddess forbid) suspension notice. Sure, they're going to be mad at first, especially if up till this point you've never had a problem at school, and suddenly you seem to be on the wrong end of the educational stick. If you have done something to deserve that suspension (like stealing a cupcake), then it's far better for you in the long run to 'fess up and deal with your own actions. Your friends did not make you steal that cupcake (and if you say that, then you are playing right into the honor/shame model and you know better).

What if, however, this is something far more insidious? Teachers, I've found, are not above trying to build a case against a student because he or she is different than the rest, and because the teacher is an adult who has been entrusted with the care of children, they can practice their personal brand of discrimination for many years. Threats, belittling students in public, nitpicking, and temper tantrums are all signs of an unstable personality and emotional immaturity in a teacher. These are people who have definite personality dysfunctions, yet they remain protected by the teachers' union, a system called tenure, and the school system in general. Some are never caught due to the constantly turning wheel of students, and some are shuffled from school to school in hopes of diffusing angry parents. A few are quietly forced to leave, but only after the involvement of your parents. If you feel that you have suffered or are suffering from this type of abuse from a teacher or a school official, you must talk to your parents or a trusted advisor.

As far as discrimination against your religion, or your interest in Witchcraft and Paganism goes, your school system cannot take this book away from you. Some will try. They cannot force you to give up your pentacle necklace, but some will attempt to suspend you if you wear it. There are school systems in the United States that don't know the law and are spitting in the face of the Constitution that they claim to uphold, and are using their honor/shame social model to try to control your religious behavior—which, last time I checked, is against the law in this country. When outrageous events like this occur, it is your parents who must step up to the plate and join the fight, and in cases like these, the system is weighing the odds of whether or not your parents want to spend the time, energy, and money it takes to beat them. They are also hoping that your parents are too busy with their own lives, and they will use the honor/shame scenario on your parents just like they use it on you. Most school systems, I will tell you, are not so stupid as to blatantly discriminate against your religion because, when taken to court, they will always lose. Unfortunately, especially in rural America, there are (on occasion) those who will be dumb enough to try.

Finally, there are teens and young adults who will use the rules and regulations of the school against you. These are the devious ones, and you might as well admit that they exist because you are going to run into these people in adulthood (and they won't have changed much). They will set you up for a fall by accusing you of something that you haven't done. Often they are a teacher's pet who feels they are not getting enough attention. Again, the strongest magick is the bond and communication you have with your parents. You aren't being a wuss if you ask them to help you. In fact, in all my examples under this section, those who oppose you are counting on your silence.

Tempest Smith[25]

At the beginning of this book you may have seen the dedication. It says: "To Tempest Smith, gone but not forgotten."

On February 20, 2001, a young girl named Tempest Smith killed herself in Lincoln Park, Michigan, USA. Her suicide was directly caused by the taunting of other students at the Lincoln Park Middle School who mocked her because she was "different" and because she was Wiccan. This is a dramatic and extreme example of hundreds of everyday cases of prejudice based on religion. Even those who would never make a racial or gender-based slur may still discriminate based on religion, because many faiths teach that their religion is the only true religion. We know that change is made one person at a time. So in memory of Tempest Smith and millions of victims of religious discrimination worldwide, we at the Pagan Pride Project ask you to pledge the three things at the bottom of this page:

THE PLEDGE

I remember Tempest Smith.

I remember that it's never right to make fun of someone's beliefs.

I remember that sticks and stones can break my bones, but names are words of power that can wound the soul.

I remember that many mocked—and one died.

I remember Tempest Smith.

I remember that it takes all types to make a world.

I remember that nature likes biodiversity. This is true of beliefs and ideas as well.

I remember that I make a better witness to my own beliefs by simply living them, not belittling others.

I remember Tempest Smith.

And I remember that another person's belief (or nonbelief) is just as sincerely held as my own.

I remember to have the courage to say, "Hey, that's not right," when I see someone being ridiculed.

And the next time I am tempted to go along with the crowd and tease someone who is "different," I will remember Tempest Smith, and I will remember my pledge.

Because what is remembered lives.[26]

- I pledge my word and my honor to accept that another's belief, or nonbelief, is just as sincerely held as my own.

- I pledge that when I see prejudice based on religion, be it taunting on a playground or whispered in a board meeting, I will stand and say, "No. This is wrong."

- I pledge that to the best of my ability, I will respect practitioners of other spiritual paths and treat them with kindness and courtesy.

All this said, is there anything you can do magickally to ease the situation? Absolutely, but never forget that your greatest ally in situations such as these is a loving parent or guardian. The following spells combat negativity at school or on campus.

Wisdom Lamp Spell

SUPPLIES: One white fire-safe bowl; 8 ounces vegetable oil; one package of gel wicks (found at arts and craft stores for about $3); one chamomile tea bag; one mint tea bag; ⅛ teaspoon ground cloves; ⅛ teaspoon angelica (or herbs of your choice that break up negativity); 3 quarters; one small red felt bag (which you can sew yourself, or use a red cloth whose four corners you will tie together with a black ribbon); one plastic baggie; the name of your school on a small piece of paper; salt.

INSTRUCTIONS: Cast a circle. Cleanse and empower all supplies. Open tea bags, mix contents, and pour all but ¼ teaspoon in the plastic baggie. Set aside. Place the name of your school in the bottom center of the white bowl.

Carefully place the wick at the bottom of the bowl so that it stands vertically. We use a gel wick because this type of wick will stand straight and self-trims, meaning as it burns the used wick disappears and the flame won't get too high. Use the quarters to weight the bottom of the wick so that the wick will not move. Be sure the wick stands straight in the center of the bowl.

Mix cloves, angelica, and the ¼ teaspoon of tea leaves together. Grind with mortar and pestle, saying:

The belief makes the Witch, the Witch
makes the Spirit, the Spirit makes the magick.
What I wish will come to pass.

Pour this mixture in the white bowl. Then slowly pour the oil into the bowl. Place the bowl in the center of your altar. Be sure that the area around the bowl is clear of papers or any ignitable articles. Slowly pour a circle of salt around the outside of the bowl.

Hold your hands over the bowl and repeat:

The belief makes the Witch, the Witch
makes the Spirit, the Spirit makes the magick.
What I wish will come to pass.

Now, state your wish in very clear and specific terms. For example, "May all negativity be removed from the Northern York County School System and may any negativity be replaced with only light and wisdom. As I will, it shall be done."

Light the wick, repeating the incantation and your desire as many times as you feel necessary. Take the leftover tea mixture, pour in the center of the red cloth, repeat the incantation, tie up the ends, and secure with the black ribbon. Place inside last year's school yearbook. It doesn't mat-

ter if you don't go to that school anymore. Close circle, and allow the wisdom lamp to burn. Depending upon the circumstances, the area in which you burn the lamp, and the type of oil used, the wisdom lamp may keep its flame for two to three days. When it has extinguished, repeat the incantation one more time. Take the remaining contents of the bowl to a crossroads and dump, saying: "My will be done!" Leave tea mixture in the yearbook until school ends for this year.

Note: Because this spell contains an open flame that burns over a long period of time, please take every precaution against accidental fire. You can place the white bowl with flame in a large turkey pan, sturdy fire-safe cauldron, or other large pot to ensure home safety. Keep away from all animals.

Locker/Desk Drawer Feather Web Spell

SUPPLIES: A package of black feathers; several yards of gold cord; 13 small bells (all can be purchased at your local arts and crafts store); glue; perfume. *Optional:* White candle.

INSTRUCTIONS: The night before school starts, sit quietly in your room and think about what you want to accomplish this year. Form a picture in your mind of how you want the year to progress for you. Cast a magick circle. Cleanse and empower all supplies. Tie the string around individual feathers and add the bells where you like. Use glue to secure the knots around the feathers. Make the garland as long or as short as you desire. Say the following chant while working on your web of protection:

The Witch is the magick, the web
is the protection, the bells clear the air,
the feathers brush away danger.

When the garland is finished, repeat the incantation seven times, spray with perfume or aftershave, then clap your hands over the project. Hang at the back of your locker. Re-empower every thirty days by spraying lightly with perfume or aftershave. Burn on the evening of the last day of school, thanking Spirit for the protection you received during the school year.

Locker/Desk Drawer Combat Jar Spell to Prevent Theft or for the Return of Items Stolen at School

SUPPLIES: A small, clean canning, jelly, or other glass jar with seal and lid; a picture of your school with the full name of the school written on the back; a black indelible marker; a small rubber snake (for wisdom) that will fit in the jar; one black feather symbolizing the power of the raven (discernment, protection, knowledge, etc.); 3 nails.

INSTRUCTIONS: On a full moon, cast a magick circle. Take the picture of the school and roll it as tightly as possible, then place it in the jar with the feather, nails, and the snake. Hold your hands over the jar, and say:

> *From the void to the action*
> *from the action to the Spirit*
> *from the Spirit to the manifestation.*
> *All evil is caught and replaced by light*
> *force and form unite*
> *there is no escape.*
> *So mote it be!*

Seal the jar. Repeat the chant seven times while slowly drawing a spiral from the outside of the lid to the center. Place the jar in the back corner of your locker. Throw in the garbage at home on the evening of the last day of school.

Focus Rattle Spell

The focus rattle can be used anytime, but it seems particularly helpful when you must solve a problem, are dealing with fears where you need to clear your mind, or when you are just having trouble concentrating on schoolwork.

SUPPLIES: One-half ounce of unpopped popcorn kernels, beads, dried beans or collection of seeds (your choice); one plastic or glass spice jar with smooth sides; ¼ teaspoon dried mint.

INSTRUCTIONS: Cast a magick circle. Cleanse and empower all supplies. Pour mint and kernels into jar. Hold your hands over the jar and concentrate on the jar filling with pure, white light. Cap the jar tightly.

TO USE: Ground and center. Roll the jar back and forth lightly between your palms, allowing your mind to drift with the rhythmic sound. Chant:

> *The magick is the Witch, the Witch is the*
> *magick, I am the Witch. I rise above my*
> *problems, and my problems dissolve.*

The more you practice with the rattle, the faster you will experience future results.

Sex

The word *sex* is linked to a wide territory of behavior in the American culture, which is confusing to lots of teens as well as adults. Sometimes they think that "everybody's doing it," when really it's all a bunch of bragging. Magazines and the media geared for adults don't help in eliminating teen confusion on the issue, and quite frankly lots of adults are befuddled on the subject too!

Let's get the most important issue out of the way first: Nobody can tell you what to do with your body. That's your decision and it should be a private one. Having sex won't make you cool, grown up, or raise your self-esteem (no matter how old you are). How do you know when you're ready? If you feel pressured in any way, nervous or frightened, you are definitely not ready. Don't fall for the old line, "But if you loved me, you'd have sex with me." If this person tells you that he or she won't see you anymore, or will break up with you because you won't have sex, then they aren't worth your time. You're too good for them! Be glad you found out how shallow they are now rather than later, when the breakup would be more painful. Sex should be a beautiful, loving experience between two people, not done on a dare because you think it will increase your popularity (it won't—just the opposite will happen), because your friend did it, because you think it will show your prowess and make you look cool, or because your partner thinks you should do it. If in doubt, you might want to talk to an older person whom you can trust about how you feel on this issue.

Sex and Risk

There are physical and emotional risks to any sexual encounter. For example, girls who start having sex before the age of eighteen tend to have more health problems, including a higher chance of contracting cervical cancer. Catching a sexually transmitted disease (STD) like chlamydia, herpes, lice, trichomoniasis, genital warts, gonorrhea, syphilis, and AIDS is also a very real danger, and you need to know that herpes, genital warts, and AIDS cannot be cured—ever— and if you don't catch those diseases that can be treated right away, the consequences to your long-term health can be very serious, even

deadly. According to one recent study, one out of every eight teenagers contracts STDs. If you think you have contracted an STD, don't be embarrassed to find medical help. Get treatment right away; don't wait. There is also the risk of pregnancy, which is a very real consequence of sexual activity. A baby is a very big responsibility. If you aren't ready for that, think twice. Finally, people have sex for different reasons and emotions, and self-esteem issues play a large part in sexual activity, including later feelings of self-worth. There's always a chance that your feelings may be hurt because of a misunderstanding. The difference between sex and love is volatile ground. With all these risks, many young people do choose to wait. This is called abstinence.

Safe Sex

Naturally the safest sex is no sex at all, but that's not particularly logical, bearing in mind that sexual desire and the actions thereof are naturally wired into the human process, and seem to be especially rampant when your hormones fire during the teen years (and possibly early twenties, depending upon your physical makeup). To protect yourself and your partner, you should use a lubricated latex condom and a spermicide with nonoxynol-9 (read the label to make sure it has this ingredient). These products are not 100 percent safe, but they will help lower the risk of contracting an STD or getting pregnant. Even if you are on the pill (drug used to inhibit pregnancy), there is still the risk of an STD. Also, some antibiotics can make the pill totally ineffective. Always check with your doctor if you are on the pill and taking other medications. You may not be as safe as you think. Be sure to read all packages and instructions that accompany birth control devices to ensure their proper use. If you don't understand the directions, talk to a health care professional or visit a clinic.

To Learn More about STDs

National STD Hotline: 800-227-8922

National AIDS Hotline: 800-342-2437 (English); 800-344-7432 (Spanish)

http://www.iwannaknow.org: Answers to questions about teen's sexual health.

Or browse through the FDA website: http://www.fda.gov

Shopping

Styles sometimes change drastically from year to year, so you can't always count on borrowing a dress from a friend or relative for that special party, homecoming, or the prom. Tuxes are so expensive that most guys decide to rent them rather than pay an astronomical price for one night of dinner and dancing. Just as there is a "run" on dresses right before the big evening, so, too, tuxes get picked over rather quickly. Graduation can also be a pain. Some schools require that you wear a specific color of outfit under your graduation gown, and finding that color isn't always easy. Between the shoes, jewelry, clothing, limo rental (should you decide to go that way), hair appointments, and the realization that you are leaving childhood behind (in the case of graduation), the stress level is high prior to these three events. To ease part of the strain, think timing. Normally, you'll experience shopping success if you buy (or make rental arrangements) for clothing and accessories during the following two moon quarters:

- First quarter to day before second quarter: Value for your money.

- Day after second quarter to day before fourth quarter: Best sales.

I say "normally" because astrology is fluid and doesn't depend on a single planet when it comes to timing. If you are really into astrology, good aspects to Venus, the sun, and Jupiter are also great for shopping, but guard against overspending. Use the Moon School and Shopping Table below to help you match the flavor of the moon to the type of school, educational, or personal beauty aid purchase that you'd like to make. Even if you can't buy during those days, you can work magick to obtain the things you desire.

Moon School and Shopping Table

MOON IN ARIES

Buy or focus on: Sports clothing and supplies; products new on the market; gifts for coaches or players on your team; hats; temporary hair dye; supplies and tools for industrial arts class; metal shop, wood shop, a mechanics course, American history, or any class that deals with the history of war; camping supplies. Watch impulse buying.

MOON IN TAURUS

Buy or focus on: Designer label clothing; cosmetics; permanent hair dye; supplies for 4-H and FFA, horticultural class, and earth science; bed linens (home or dorm); beds; sleeping bags; potted plants for gifts; chocolates for your girlfriend; expensive jewelry; things you want to last a long time because what you buy, you're stuck with.

MOON IN GEMINI

Buy or focus on: Books for courses (college and high school required reading); magazines; all writing materials (pens, notebooks, pencils, paper); computer supplies (paper, toner, software, disks); gift cards and personal stationary; stamps; telephones and telephone service; answering machines; cell phones; beepers; radios; two-ways; calculators; dictionaries; encyclopedias; fun gadgets and small toys; definitely supplies for English literature or creative writing classes; the debate team, class yearbook, and school newspaper; finding a tutor or signing up to be a tutor for others.

MOON IN CANCER

Buy or focus on: Researching family and local history; general history classes; supplies for cooking class; buying classmates, friends, and family gifts or cards; food shopping; things for your personal space at home; lock for your locker or dorm room; wrapping paper and ribbon; supplies for marine biology; joining a swim team; volunteering at the concession stand for home games; sewing your own clothes and sewing supplies; choosing the school mascot.

MOON IN LEO

Buy or focus on: Anything with flash and dash; child-care courses; offering babysitting services; tickets for the movies, concerts, rodeos, theme park, or other forms of entertainment; things associated with your favorite hobbies, or a new hobby; choosing pleasurable electives; reading about leadership; buying gold jewelry or items made of silk; making flags; renting a limo for the prom; pet supplies.

MOON IN VIRGO

Buy or focus on: Buying personal care items, medicines, and vitamins; exercise equipment; joining a gym; self-defense, karate, or first-aid class; working out a budget and any type of organizational supply (date books, journals, diaries, report covers, page protectors, index cards and boxes,

etc.); supplies for any sort of math class or health class; books and materials for research projects; volunteering for community service, including sponsored organizations such as the Red Cross, inner city projects, etc.; work on school planning committees including the prom and graduation committees and dinner reservations for any of those functions; asking for help with homework; writing an agenda for a meeting; buying supplies to repair things.

MOON IN LIBRA

Buy or focus on: Clothing for parties, proms, graduation, and dates; perfume; tapes and CDs; ordering corsages and boutonnieres; food for parties; having your nails done; buying party supplies, including those purchased to help decorate for homecoming, the prom, general school dances, and other school social activities; arrange a sleep-over; speech class; debate team. Buy stickers, decorative items for notebooks and lockers, incense, school spirit items, presents for your girlfriend or boyfriend, supplies for art or music class, romance novels. Have your hair done.

MOON IN SCORPIO

Buy or focus on: Occult supplies; photographic equipment; taking pictures for any report or course; video cameras and tape or film; darkroom supplies; making a movie for any subject; classes involving self-defense, military, or police training; ROTC functions; sex education; archeology; collecting news clippings for class; studying the stock market; information for psychology and sociology; studying economics; throwing a Halloween party and choosing Halloween decorations; studying social issues; buying undergarments; working on your bug collection for science class. Buying crime and mystery novels, or books on the occult.

MOON IN SAGITTARIUS

Buy or focus on: Gag gifts and humorous books or movies; ordering imported items; translating your spells into a foreign language; any supplies or reports related to foreign language studies, the law, geography, social studies, politics, or comparative religion; visiting second-hand shops; planning a trip; buying and studying maps; bartering with friends; choosing classes; buying souvenirs; preparing for field trips and trips abroad and the supplies you will need while there; doing research at the library; writing or learning the school pledge.

MOON IN CAPRICORN

Buy or focus on: Gifts for your grandparents; thinking about your goals in life; gathering information about various colleges and your major; supplies and studies for astronomy; buying calendars and watches; buying school uniforms or items with a school or club insignia; skin lotions or oils; working on speeches for public speaking class or issues involving the student council. *Note:* Capricorn is not the best shopping moon.

MOON IN AQUARIUS

Buy or focus on: Buying computers, zany stuff, supplies for clubs or group efforts, and anything electrical. Setting trends at your school; working for political changes in your school system; booking an airline flight; studying astrology; becoming an advocate; joining the band or school chorus; joining a sorority or fraternity; studying social models.

MOON IN PISCES

Buy or focus on: Buying or renting movies; dream books; shoes; nylons; swimwear; art supplies that require thinning with liquid such as watercolors, acrylics, and oils; designing report covers; working creatively; enhancing psychic abilities; buying clothing, accessories, and masks for costume parties; studying chemistry and buying supplies for chemistry class; collecting charitable contributions.

Stalkers

These days stalking is against the law, but that doesn't mean people don't do it. If you are being stalked you should obtain legal advice immediately. Don't be embarrassed because the stalking may be a result of a love relationship gone bad (which often happens). Stalking is wrong, no matter the reasoning. Your next step is to follow through with whatever legal action is recommended, which usually involves some kind of official restriction being placed on the stalker. Don't drop the ball. And after you have dealt with the mundane reality, it's time to let Witchcraft step in.

Before I go any further, there are going to be times in your life where you just can't be a wimpy, wishy-washy Witch. This is one of those times. If you (or a friend) are being stalked or threatened in any way, there is no compromise—this behavior must cease.

Anti-Stalker Spell

SUPPLIES: Graveyard dirt, preferably from an ancestor's grave; dirt from a jail or prison; dirt from a courthouse. Mix with equal parts of mullein and wormwood. Pulverize. This is Justice Powder. A picture, handwriting, or description of the stalker, including the full name if you have it; a small cage; a paper plate with a large pentacle drawn on it; The World Tarot card that depicts the lion, the serpent, the eagle, and the bull; a small padlock and key.

TIMING: Midnight on a Saturday, on the dark moon, or when the moon or sun is in Scorpio, or the hour of Saturn, or when Scorpio is rising—however, if immediacy is required, so be it.

INSTRUCTIONS: If you can swing it, outside is best, in the dark of the night. Cast the circle and use the following alchemical quarter calls:[27]

Beginning in the east:

Soaring eagle, great ruler of the tempest,
storm, and whirlwind, tornado and hurricane
master of the starry vault
great being of the powers of air
attend this circle, I pray thee
and guard this sacred space
from all perils seen and unseen
in this reality and the next!

Move to the south, and say:

Courageous she-lion! Princess of lightning
Goddess of the Fire
bringer of spark and flame
mistress of conflagration
great being of the powers of fire
attend this circle, I pray thee
and guard this sacred space
from all perils seen and unseen
in this reality and the next!

Move to the west, and say:

O thou Serpent of Old, ruler of the void
guardian of the sweet and bitter sea
mistress of transformation
great being of the powers of water

attend this circle, I pray thee
and guard this sacred space
from all perils seen and unseen
in this reality and the next!

Move to the north, and say:

Black bull of the north, Horned One
dark ruler of the mountains and valleys
master of all that lies beneath them
great being of the powers of earth
attend this circle, I pray thee
and guard this sacred space
from all perils seen and unseen
in this reality and the next!

Lift athame or sword to the heavens, and say:

Lady of the Night,
Horned Lord of the Dark Forest
attend me now!
(Shout it if you can,
or at least say it reverently.)

Repeat the following chant three times while administering the next portion of the spell:

Everyone knows you reap what you've sown
captured and caught, your folly is known
the dead have arisen
the hound's at your door
the Horned Lord is coming to settle the score!
Pester me not from the earth nor the sea
I've locked you away and I'm tossing the key!

Place the cage on the pentacle plate. Put the picture of the stalker in the cage. Cover with Justice Powder. Place the Tarot card facedown on the powder. Lock the cage. Thank deity. Close the quarters and release the circle. Bury the cage off your property. Toss the key far away from your home and miles from the cage.

Suicide

Few Craft books talk about suicide, but we're going to get into it here. In the Craft view, suicide is not an option. Most Crafters believe in reincarnation—that you lead many lives and the one you are in at the moment is only one of them. Each life is a stepping-stone toward ultimate spirituality. We also believe that before you got to this life, you chose your parents, your body type, your environment, and some of the main experiences you will have during the present lifetime. If you decide to cave in on this one, then you will be required to come back and live the same experiences over again, with the same amount of angst, and the same amount of emotional pain that you might be encountering right now. I don't know about you, but once is enough for me! With that in mind, it is far better to look at more positive options to combat our problems.

If you've been contemplating suicide, you need to know that people do get through these awful feelings you are having. *There is no typical victim.* These thoughts happen to the young, the old, the rich, and the poor, to people of all colors and religions, and it's true that just about everyone at one point or another in their lives has contemplated suicide, even though most people won't admit it, or have conveniently forgotten. To survive suicidal feelings you can do either one of two things—find a way to reduce your pain in a positive way or find a way to increase your coping resources. Both are entirely possible, and you are capable of one or both of these options. If you have been thinking about ending it all, give yourself some distance. Say to yourself, "I will wait twenty-four hours before I do anything," or one week, or longer. Even another five minutes. If you wait even a few minutes, then you are already on the way to taking charge of the situation!

People often turn to suicide because they are looking for a way out of the pain. To feel relief, however, you have to be alive. Being dead doesn't make it all go away. Those who think about committing suicide believe that they can't stop the pain. They have trouble thinking clearly and can't seem to make a decision on anything. Their vision of the future is closed, as if a muzzy, dark fog has filled their brains. They might have trouble sleeping. Feelings of the whole world being out of control are prominent. They might feel that they aren't worthwhile, and that sadness haunts them like a sickness determined to eat away their soul. You need to know that there is a way out and that there truly is a way to find the balance you so desperately need. Suicide is not the way out. It's just another cage.

In Witchcraft, we believe that you are never, ever alone. Even when you are sitting in your room all by yourself listening to music or reading a book, there are quite a few "beings" present. Your guardian, for one. Call it an angel, call it a totem, call it whatever you like. It is with you from the moment you entered this world and will stay with you the entire time you are here. Loved ones who have passed through the veil to the other side also check up on you from time to time, especially when you are sad, upset, or hurt. They are there, right with your guardian, trying very hard to send you loving energy. Spirit is also with you, as well as your connection to the collective unconscious. Yep. That room of yours is a pretty busy place, you just have to reach out and ask for help when you need it. (All these energies are very polite, you see, and won't intrude unless you ask them to.) Like a harp whose strings must be plucked to hear the sound, your personal support tapestry of energy has to be activated. Three little words will do: "Please help me." And then you must support this request by believing that they will. You can't ask and then shut the door in their faces.

If you are contemplating suicide, I have two things I want you to try for me. I'd like you to say the prayer below and believe that I'm right there with you, holding your hand, because my spirit will be. I want you to live. And then I want you to pick up the phone and call the number listed below. I know you can do this.

Gracious Mother, I am in desperate need of Your assistance. The pain inside of me is more terrible than words can allow and I am very afraid. Please banish all the negative energy around me and in me. Help me get through this time of awful hurt. Please cover me with Your cloak of love and peace. Fill me with the warmth of Your divine love. Send me the support I so urgently need. I know You will do this for me!

Now, pick up the phone and call.

1–800–Suicide (in the US)

The Goddess has already alerted the right person for you to call. She's trying to help you, preparing the way for you to receive immediate help. It doesn't matter if you're not a Witch yet, or a Witch-in-Training, or don't ever plan to be one at all. The Goddess listens to ALL the children, whether you are eight years old or eighty-eight.

Other options are:

- Look in the front of your phone book for a crisis line.

- Call a psychotherapist.

- Call your family physician.

- Carefully choose an adult who is a close friend, someone who is likely to listen.

Spotting Suicidal Behavior in Your Friends

As you read earlier, there is no typical victim. There are, however, some common warning signs that, if acted on, can save the person's life. Your friend may talk about committing suicide—sometimes seriously, but sometimes as a frequent joke. He or she may have trouble eating or sleeping. You might see a drastic change of behavior and wonder, "What's up with her/him?" People tend to lose interest in hobbies, work, school, etc.—and you'll notice that what they loved to do before, they have little interest in now. Sometimes people make out a will or spend a lot of time talking about final arrangements, give away objects that meant a lot to them, or seem too preoccupied with death and dying. They may take unnecessary risks or lose interest in their personal appearance. An increase in drug and alcohol use is another sign. He or she may withdraw from social activities, shut out their best friends, and spend long hours by themselves.

As a caring and magickal person, there is a lot you can do. Don't mince your words if they talk about suicide. Be direct, but most of all, be caring and willing to listen. Allow them to express their pain. The worst thing you can do is cop a judgmental attitude. Debating whether suicide is right or wrong isn't going to help them. The last thing they need is a lecture. What they do need is help. Don't act shocked or wimpy and don't accept a secrecy pact. Offer alternatives that you know are available. If you don't know—find out! If you are over twenty-one and the person lives in your house, you must immediately take action, removing stockpiled drugs, guns, or other means by which they can harm themselves. And, whether you are under or over twenty-one, you should immediately seek outside assistance. You can call the hotline above, or visit any of the websites listed below. If you are at a party where a suicide attempt is in progress, don't debate with other friends who are trying to be helpful yet seem to be stalling for time because they will get in trouble for illegal or other types of behavior. The death of a human being is not worth the selfish desires of some idiot. Call for help right away, no matter the consequences. Okay, so maybe there is underage drinking there, or even drugs, but your friend's life is more important.

What Else You Can Do

Real magick can never override real help, but there are spells and rituals that you can do to help your friend, loved one, or maybe yourself recover. Suicidal feelings are traumatic. Even after they go away, we have to continue caring for ourselves—therapy is important and helpful. Add to this daily meditation, devotions, prayers, self-empowering rituals, and the enjoyment of communing with nature to help with the recovery process.

Spell for a Suicidal Friend or Family Member

This spell cannot replace outside help or assistance.

SUPPLIES: A picture of the friend or family member and something very small he or she owns or has touched recently for at least five minutes (even a piece of clothing will do); a metal hanger; one clothespin; a piece of black construction paper; anything you consider holy—pentacle, amulet, the name of a god or goddess, etc.—doesn't matter what it is as long as you feel it is a sacred object; cellophane tape; a strong tissue, dinner napkin, or white handkerchief; one spice jar of rosemary from the grocery store.

INSTRUCTIONS: Tape the object belonging to the person on the back of the picture. Wrap the picture in the black construction paper and tape, saying:

Nothing can harm you. All negativity will leave you. You will find the help you need in the strength of the Mother and those she brings to your aid.

Lay the tissue out flat. Place the black packet on the white tissue. Conjure the rosemary for love and protection (SEE PAGE 381) and sprinkle over the black packet. Place the holy object on top. Tie the corners of the tissue or napkin together (or tape them if you think the ply is too weak). Hold your hands over the bundle, and say:

Greatest Mother up above, send Your aid to the one I love. Please make peace in his/her perception and banish his/her doubt. Don't let her/him give away their power and help him/her to discover the simple pleasures in life. Remove his/her fear and pain. Make the way clear for his/her healing and recovery and let him/her recognize help when it comes, no matter the will or the way. I know You will do this for me. As I will, so shall it be done!

Clip the healing bundle to a wire hanger, then hang in a safe place where it will not be disturbed until the crisis is over and healing is complete (this means that the healing bundle will be around for awhile). Every week, take the hanger out and repeat the prayer. That way you will be sending continuous healing energy to your friend or family member. Remember, however, that the choice to accept that healing energy is ultimately theirs. You can't control anyone but yourself.

Helpful Websites

These two are excellent sites with lots of helpful information, including recovering from those feelings you may have as a result of a friend- or family-related suicide.

Recommended Reading

Out of the Nightmare: Recovery from Depression and Suicidal Pain by David L. Conroy, Ph.D.

Suicide: The Forever Decision by Paul G. Quinnett, Ph.D.

War

No one likes to think about war. For many of us, war is something our parents or grandparents may have experienced, but it isn't something in which we directly participated. Sure, we hear stories, but hearing about war isn't like living through it. War brings out the best and the worst in human beings. Stories of gallantry and human courage are matched step for step with stories of horror and atrocity.

Occult practices including astrology, divination, and the raising of energy for protection have played a large part in thousands of wars, from those tribally waged to WWII. From Witches who raised storms to protect the English fleet during medieval times, to energy workers in the states chanting long hours for days at a time to protect the American shores during the Second World War, to a wolverine ritual to bring karma to bear on the enemies of England during the Second World War, Witches have historically done their part to help their countrymen and women.

We can thank Ronald Hutton and Doreen Valiente for researching and finding as much accurate information as possible on the activities of a particular group run by Dorothy Clutterbuck (yes, she actually existed) during the Second World War (though whether or not they were Craft-related and not merely a "magickal group" from various lodges is not clear, historically speaking). Given the fact that I know American magickal lodges were also working ritual at the time, the story is plausible. As the following has been circulated in the Craft community for about sixty-odd years, we should share it here, though it is dubious to many, given Gerald Gardner's penchant for romanticism if it did, indeed, occur.

> When France fell in 1940 and the invasion of Britain seemed imminent, old Dorothy called up covens right and left; although by Witch law they should not be known to each other. The result was "Operation Cone of Power" in which a Great Circle was cast at night in the New Forest and a cone of magickal energy raised and directed against the enemy, as one had according to tradition been sent against the Spanish Armada and Napoleon. This was repeated four times until the coven elders called a halt; the strain of the work upon those present was severe, and many died a few days later. This dramatic episode became Gardner's favorite story about the coven. He provided many extra details to Doreen Valiente, including the vital one that the power was raised by frenetic dancing and chanting, and that it was these exertions which had proved fatal to many of the older people. Although others tried to capture credit for the story (including the infamous Aleister Crowley) historians have since proven Crowley had no part in the night of allied magick.[28]

To double-check, I asked Raymond Buckland at dinner one night if the story of Lammas Night (as this occurrence has been often called) was indeed true. He replied in the affirmative.

Regardless whether this particular story is true, I do know that Witches across the United States went immediately to work minutes after it

Letter of Protection for

_____

In the names of the Lord and Lady
Whoever beareth this letter upon
the self shall not dread the enemy,
nor be overcome, nor suffer injury,
nor misfortune, nor fear flood,
fire, weapons, chemicals, poison,
nor be affected in any way by self
same, nor be captured, face torture,
nor fear weather nor war,
nor suffer mental anguish.
Whoever beareth this letter will be
filled with strength, mental acuity,
protection, and love. They shall
sense unseen dangers and respond accordingly. They shall persevere where
others fall. They shall
return home victorious and
live a full and active life.

So mote it be!

The Black Forest Himmelsbrief. The design above was created by Silver RavenWolf and cannot be sold in any form. It is her gift to American service personnel, firefighters, emergency workers, and police officers of our nation in this time of political unrest. If you make copies, you must give them freely, without sale of any kind.

was realized that the World Trade Center was attacked on September 11, 2001. Covens across the country worked into the evening and on successive days and months to provide continued protection for American citizens.

Generally, Wiccans do not have a religious position on acts of war and are patriotic to one degree or another. Many shy away from politics for a variety of reasons, where others march right into the thick of things. In our community, personal choices range from conscientious objectors to hawks. Many Wiccans serve proudly in the armed services (my daughter being one of them). In March 2001, Neopagans in the Air Force won their right to inscribe the religious choice of Pagan, Shaman, Druid, Wicca, Dianic Wicca, Gardnerian Wicca, or Seax Wicca on their dog tags, with that category recognized by the military's Personal Data System.[29] The chaplain's manual for the military service includes instructions for Wiccan ceremonies. Hopefully you will never have to deal with war; however, I've included some helpful information should you be forced to live it up close and personal. War doesn't have to be a conflict between countries—many people suffer from criminal acts, therefore these spells can also be used in reference to the war on crime. One final note of warning before we continue: Wartime spells must follow the rules of the Witch's Pyramid to succeed. If you don't understand this concept, please flip to Part I and read about it before you continue.

The Black Forest Himmelsbrief

The Himmelsbrief was a type of letter or testament carried on a person or hung in the home for protection against evil people and deeds. These magickal papers were also known as "Letters of Protection" or "Letters from Heaven." The Pennsylvania Germans thought this paper to be as powerful as an invocation. In 1918, the Aurand Press out of Lancaster, Pennsylvania, received an order for printing copies of such a "Letter of Protection." It was later learned that the copies were distributed to members of the National Guard and to draftees departing from several south-central Pennsylvania counties and heading for World War I. The Himmelsbrief came in a variety of forms, from a self-penned version to stuff in one's pocket to more elaborate documents complete with handpainted art and ornate borders. Some included Christian symbolism while others were more paganized versions with magickal designs.[30]

Instructions for Activating BFC Himmelsbrief

1. Copy the Himmelsbrief and cut excess paper.

2. Fill in the name of the person who is to be protected on the corresponding line on the Himmelsbrief.

3. In a magick circle, cleanse and consecrate paper with the four elements. Add any additional symbols of your choice on the paper. If you have the facilities, you can copy a picture of your loved one and scan it on the back of the paper.

4. If you have not scanned the picture onto the paper, place the loved one's picture on top of the paper.

5. Carry the paper and the picture to the four quarters, beginning with the north, and ask each quarter energy for divine protection for the person named on the paper.

6. Call down the Lord and Lady (or your idea of Spirit) and ask for blessings and protection for the individual listed on the paper.

7. Repeat the prayer on the paper three times, beginning with the person's full name each time.

8. Hold your hands over the paper and picture, and allow protective energy from the divine to flow through your fingertips. Envision the paper and the picture filled with glaring white light. Hold this visualization as long as possible.

9. Hold the paper and picture, and close your eyes. See the paper on your loved one. See the paper as a shield that grows and covers them. Hold this visualization as long as possible. Finish by saying: "I know you will do this for me. So mote it be."

10. Draw an equal-armed cross of the picture to seal the work.

11. Thank divinity. Thank the quarters.

12. Release divinity. Release the quarters. Release the circle.

13. Give the paper to your loved one and tell him or her to keep it on them at all times.

Note: You can reduce the Himmelsbrief on a copy machine and laminate it. If you used a separate photo, place in a frame and put on your altar. Keep it there as long as your loved one is in danger. You can also burn a white candle every week to continue putting energy into the spell.

Additional Note: Parents—Change step 9 to the following: The mother puts the paper on her chest. The father holds the mother, chest to chest. The parents breathe together until their breath is synchronized for at least one full minute, visualizing the safety of the child. Finish by saying: "I know you will do this for us. So mote it be."

Spell for Protecting Your Town or Area of the City

SUPPLIES: Use the spellcasting ritual on page 331 for the format. You will need a mortar and pestle; 3 protective herbs (SEE PAGE 276 FOR AN HERBAL LISTING) of your choice; salt; a local map that shows the boundaries of your town or city; glue; a black cord, 2 feet long; a small piece of paper; black marker; a clean notebook with a black cover; one white candle; one black candle.

INSTRUCTIONS: Make a sigil on a piece of paper following the instructions on page 552 using the following words: "Protection for (name of the town) and all who reside therein." Inscribe this sigil on the black and white candles. The black and white association is to repel negativity and bring harmony to your area. Follow the spellcasting ritual instructions. At the appropriate point, grind the salt and herbs together with mortar and pestle. Empower using the herbal charm on page 381. Lay the map out on your altar. Draw the protective sigil you made directly onto the center of the map. Empower the map, asking for protection and harmony for all who reside within the town. Trace the outline of the border with the glue. Sprinkle glue with the protective mixture. Light the black and white candles using your favorite magickal chant. Place the candles on either side of the map. Allow the map to dry. When completely dry, place the map inside a clean notebook with a black cover. Put the sigil you drew on the separate piece of paper inside the front cover. Tie the notebook shut with a black cord. Put in a safe place. Do not remove until the conflict is over.

Note: This spell also works if your town or city block has a high crime risk or has been inundated with criminals and drug dealers.

Spell to Remove the Enemy and Promote Harmony

SUPPLIES: Follow any of the basic rituals given in this book for the format. You will need one piece of braided rope (a new large pull-toy made for dogs works very well); 7 black feathers; 7 white feathers; a stone at least 2 inches wide; a small plastic toy person or a poppet you have purchased or made yourself. If you are truly in the midst of a terrible war, add one cup of graveyard dirt—but this is only to combat a great atrocity and will not work otherwise. The ability to get to a lake, a stream, river, or the ocean.

INSTRUCTIONS: Begin the ritual. At the appropriate point, lay out all your supplies on the altar. Connect the poppet to the negative energy emitted by the enemy using the instructions on page 148. Untie one of the ends of the dog toy. Separate the strands of rope. Begin tying first a black feather into the rope (to banish the enemy), followed by a white feather (to bring peace and harmony). As you tie all the feathers, use your favorite chant to build power. Tie the poppet into the strands last. Weight the work by tying the stone into the rope. If you are truly in the center of an act of war, sprinkle the rope with graveyard dirt. Take the work to a flowing stream, river, lake, or the ocean. Throw the work into the water with as much strength as you can, saying:

> *O gracious lady, bring to me*
> *peace and acts of harmony.*
> *Banish evil—make it flee*
> *as I will, so mote it be!*

Note: This spell will not work unless you are legitimately in fear for life and limb or you have been attacked.

One final piece of advice. Wartime can mean rationing of all sorts of things. Don't let that hold you back. Use what you have handy. Witches have always been known for their creativity.

Witch's Tree of Power

This is a system of meditation and magick that I designed especially for Wiccan students using familiar Craft symbology. Each "point" represents:

- A cosmic force.
- A living system of spiritual development.
- The eight paths of power utilized by Witches.
- The eight sabbats.
- The eight phases of the moon.
- The seven classical planets.
- The five elements.

If you are more ceremonially inclined, you can match the seven archangels to the seven planets:

> Sun = Michael
>
> Moon = Gabriel
>
> Mercury = Raphael
>
> Venus = Uriel
>
> Mars = Camael
>
> Jupiter = Sachiel
>
> Saturn = Cassiel

However, you should study a bit of angelology before you use them.

As a meditation tool, you might wish to spend at least one month working with each path. Study the element, the moon phase, and the holiday. Do as much research as necessary. Meditate on the symbolism and consider why each was chosen as a path to power. Keep a short journal of your personal discoveries. In time you will see connections that are not written on the diagram. That's the purpose of the tool, to urge

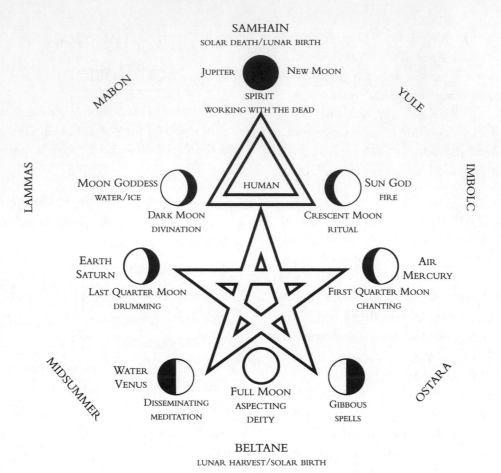

SAMHAIN
SOLAR DEATH/LUNAR BIRTH

JUPITER   NEW MOON
SPIRIT
WORKING WITH THE DEAD

MABON   YULE

MOON GODDESS   SUN GOD
WATER/ICE   FIRE
HUMAN
DARK MOON   CRESCENT MOON
DIVINATION   RITUAL

LAMMAS   IMBOLC

EARTH   AIR
SATURN   MERCURY
LAST QUARTER MOON   FIRST QUARTER MOON
DRUMMING   CHANTING

WATER
VENUS
DISSEMINATING   FULL MOON   GIBBOUS
MEDITATION   ASPECTING   SPELLS
               DEITY

MIDSUMMER   OSTARA

BELTANE
LUNAR HARVEST/SOLAR BIRTH

The Witch's Tree of Power. ©2001 Silver RavenWolf.

you to expand your mind and work toward total spirituality and a deep understanding of magick and Witchcraft.

As a divination tool you can scatter runes over the drawing and relate the diagram to the runic influence, or you can lay out your Tarot cards in the Witch's Tree of Power spread. The moon phases will give you excellent timing information, and can suggest what type of power to raise on any given situation.

Planetary points and moon phases can be activated either by tapping on the diagram within the body of the spell or laying out candles, gems, or herbs to match the eight points.

Conclusion

Solitary Witch: The Ultimate Book of Shadows for the New Generation took me over two years to write and was highly influenced by teens and young adults who are currently learning and practicing Witchcraft, both in America and abroad. When information was hard to find and I thought I would never finish the project, their letters and e-mails of encouragement and support kept the light of creativity going. I am deeply indebted to the youth of the Pagan community, and it is my sincerest desire that this book serves them well in the present as well as throughout their adult lives.

pagan pride

In darkness you paint us, but we will not hide.
We're the light of the country in which you abide,
we're fearless and strong, the protectors of life
hidden in shadows, we conquer all strife.

We come from the Old Ones, our lineage secure.
We rise from the ashes, we always endure.
It's time you remembered that we were here first.
We healed your sick, yet suffered your worst.

From time immemorial we've woven our lore
cunning folk, healers, benandanti—there's more.
We're black and we're white, we're brown and we're yellow.
We're women and children, and mighty fine fellows.

We're Her hidden children, the angels of light,
our task is to teach and to help set things right.
We conjure and cast, and whisper and pray
so you can enjoy your freedom each day.

We've long been your army, protecting your back
when you are in trouble, in secret we act.
The Mother is watching—She hasn't missed much.
She's gathered Her magick and given the touch
to Witches and Pagans and Druids and such!

The times are a' changing and one thing is clear
the Lord and the Lady have now reappeared.
Two pillars, three points, four quarters extend
five is the number of magickal blend.
By moon and by sun, by earth and by stars
realize this day that the power is ours!

Pagan pride—
Live it, breathe it, be it.

Notes for the Preface

1. Hutton, R. *The Triumph of the Moon: A History of Modern Pagan Witchcraft*. Oxford, England: Oxford University Press, 1999. p. 3.

Notes for Part 1

1. Crossan, J. D. *The Historical Jesus: The Life of a Mediterranean Jewish Peasant*. San Francisco, Calif.: HarperCollins, 1992. pp. 142, 143.

2. Honi's story is taken from Ibid., p. 145.

3. *Standard Dictionary of Folklore, Mythology, and Legend,* ed. M. Leach. New York, N.Y.: Harper & Row, 1984. p. 235.

4. If you like variety, you will find a large selection of circle castings and quarter calls in my book *To Stir a Magick Cauldron.*

5. "So mote it be" was first noted in Masonic rites in the 1700s.

6. Biedermann, H. *Dictionary of Symbolism: Cultural Icons & The Meanings Behind Them*. New York, N.Y.: Meridian, 1989. p. 71.

7. Smolin, L. *Three Roads to Quantum Physics*. New York, N.Y.: Basic Books, 2001. p. 231.

8. Walker, B. *The Woman's Dictionary of Symbols and Sacred Objects.* New York, N. Y.: HarperCollins Publishers, 1998. p. 41.

9. Lady MorningStar is an elder of the Black Forest Clan, Coven of the Pale Horse.

10. Grimassi, R. *Encyclopedia of Wicca & Witchcraft*. St. Paul, Minn.: Llewellyn, 2000. p. 55. Gimbutas, M. *The Language of the Goddess*. New York, N.Y.: HarperCollins, 1991. pp. 147–149.

11. It is believed that Gerald Gardner's method of the consecration of the liquid comes from the sixth-degree initiation of the OTO, in which a man dips the point of the blade in a cup of wine held by a woman—however, in the Wiccan rite in group format, this is reversed. The man holds the cup and the female holds the athame (Hutton, R. *The Triumph of the Moon*, p. 231. Valiente, Doreen, *Rebirth of Witchcraft*, p. 60.) In the modern Craft tradition, holy water is made the same way, where the athame is dipped into the liquid; however, in most cases this is a solitary process where the chalice of water sits on the center of the altar.

12. Biedermann, H. *Dictionary of Symbolism: Cultural Icons & The Meanings Behind Them*, p. 362.

13. Walker, B. *The Woman's Encyclopedia of Myths and Secrets*. New York, N.Y.: HarperCollins Publishers, Inc., 1983. p. 268.

14. Gimbutas, M. *The Language of the Goddess*, p. 316.

15. Leeming, D. M. *A Dictionary of Creation Myths*. Oxford, N.Y.: Oxford University Press, 1994. p. vii.

16. Grimassi, R. *Encyclopedia of Wicca & Witchcraft*, p. 121.

17. Bartel, P. *Spellcasters: Witches & Witchcraft in History, Folklore & Popular Culture*. Dallas, TX: Taylor Publishing Company, 2000. p. 151.

18. If this format is unclear to you, you may want to refer to my book *Teen Witch*, where I've provided a complete walk-through of an esbat and sabbat ritual. You will find additional information on ritual in my New Generation Witchcraft series: *To Ride a Silver Broomstick, To Stir a Magick Cauldron,* and *To Light a Sacred Flame.*

19. Fortune, D. *Aspects of Occultism*, ed. G. Knight. York Beach, Maine: Samuel Weiser, Inc., 1962, 2000. p. 35.

20. Hutton, R. *The Triumph of the Moon*, p. 16.

21. Ibid., p. 32.

22. Ibid., pp. 391, 392.

23. Hutton, R. *The Pagan Religions of the Ancient British Isles: Their Nature and Legacy*. Blackwell Publishers Ltd., 1991. p. 150.

24. Fiero, G. K. *The Humanistic Tradition: The First Civilizations and the Classical Legacy*. Third ed., vol. I. The McGraw-Hill Companies, Inc., 1998. p. 6.

25. Ibid., p. 8.

26. Chambers, E. K. *The Medieval Stage, vol. I.* Oxford: Oxford University Press, 1903. p. 9. Hutton, R. *The Triumph of the Moon*, p. 36.

27. From private correspondence, 9 August 2002.

28. Hutton, R. *The Triumph of the Moon*, p. 41.

29. Interested in the story? Here's your chance to do some research.

30. Gibons, P. E. *Pennsylvania Dutch and Other Essays*. Philadelphia, Penn.: J. B. Lippincott & Co., 1882. p. 427.

31. Anderson, W. *Green Man: Archetype of Our Oneness with Earth*. San Francisco, Calif.: Harper Collins, 1990. p. 14.

32. Ibid., p. 34.

33. The poet Shelly's *Song of Proserpine* (1820).

34. You will find complete information on quarter calls and energies in my book *To Stir a Magick Cauldron* (Llewellyn).

35. This section written by Lady MorningStar, Elder of the Black Forest Clan, Coven of the Pale Horse.

36. See my book *To Light a Sacred Flame* for complete information on Healing Circles.

37. Both in Celtic lore and Roman astrological literature (*Ancient Astrology Theory and Practice—Matheseos, Libri VIII* by Firmicus Maternus, translated by Jean Rhys Bram, edited by David McCann, published by Ascella, Spica & JustUs Publications, written approximately A.D. 346; translation 2001), the winds were associated with cardinal directions and astrological signs. To the north wind were ascribed the signs of Aries, Leo, and Sagittarius; to the south wind Taurus, Virgo, and Capricorn; to the east wind (*Afeliotes,* meaning wind of the sun), Gemini, Libra, and Aquarius; and to the west wind Cancer, Scorpio, and Pisces, which the Greeks call *libs* (meaning wind from Libya) (p. 34). Notice that in western Wicca by the year 2001, sign placements changed between north and south.

38. RavenWolf, S. *Halloween: Customs, Spells, and Recipes.* St. Paul, Minn.: Llewellyn, 1999. p. 209.

39. Hutton, R. *The Stations of the Sun.* Oxford: Oxford University Press, 1996.

40. Ibid., pp. 6, 7.

41. McNeill, M. F., *The Silver Bough, Vol. 2: A Calendar of Scottish National Festivals, Candlemas to Harvest Home.* Glasgow, Scotland: William Maclellan, 1959. p. 132.

42. Ibid., p. 20.

43. Currently debated by scholars. Definitely of Germanic derivation, but the meaning is still considered unclear. Hutton, R. *The Stations of the Sun,* p. 180.

44. McNeill, M. F. *The Silver Bough, Vol. 2,* p. 49.

45. Hutton, R. *The Stations of the Sun,* p. 203.

46. First recorded mention of the maypole and ribbons is called "the May" and was found under the expense category in the East Cornish market town of Launceston, Briton. Ibid., p. 226.

47. McNeill, M. F. *The Silver Bough, Vol. 2,* p. 75. The Floral Games of the Romans began on April 28 and ended on May 3 with a battle of flowers.

48. Ibid., p. 58.

49. Ibid., pp. 56, 57.

50. Ibid., p. 89.

51. Hutton, R. *The Stations of the Sun,* p. 314.

52. This does not refer to Satan or to Satanic practices. The Dark Lord is the representation of Saturn, authority, organization, and master of the crossroads between this world and the world of magick.

53. Hutton, R. *The Stations of the Sun,* p. 333

54. McNeill, M. F. *The Silver Bough, Vol. 2: A Calendar of Scottish National Festivals, Candlemas to Harvest Home,* p. 199.

55. You will find instructions on how to make a harvest doll in my book *Halloween: Customs, Spells, and Recipes.*

56. Hutton, R. *The Triumph of the Moon,* p. 97.

57. Levi, E. C. (Alphonse Louis). *The History of Magic.* York Beach, Maine: Samuel Weiser, Inc., 2000. p. 384.

58. Regardie, I. *The Golden Dawn.* 6th ed. St. Paul, Minn.: Llewellyn, 1971. p. 807.

59. Graf, F. *Magic in the Ancient World.* Cambridge, Mass.: Harvard University Press, 1997. p. 117.

60. Flint, V. I. J. *The Rise of Magic in Early Medieval Europe.* Princeton, N.J.: Princeton University Press, 1991. p. 103.

61. Grimassi, R. *Encyclopedia of Wicca and Witchcraft,* p. 394. *Decorative Symbols and Motifs for Artists and Craftspeople,* Dover Publications, 1986.

62. Earliest historical documentation of the Witch's Sabbat appears in trial records from Toulouse and Carassone, circa 1335. (Grimassi, p. 310.)

63. "Her book *The Witch Cult in Western Europe* rested upon a small amount of archival research, with extensive use of printed trial records in nineteenth-century editions, plus early modern pamphlets. . ." Hutton, R. *The Triumph of the Moon,* p. 195.

64. Bartel, P. *Spellcasters: Witches & Witchcraft in History, Folklore & Popular Culture.* Dallas, Texas: Taylor Publishing Company, 2000. p. 173.

65. In the late 1800s the infamous Aleister Crowley coined "Do what thou wilt shall be the whole of the law"; "love under will" applies to many twentieth-century interpretations of Egyptian material, including esoteric renditions of The Book of the Dead, better known as the Coffin Texts, with the date of origin approximately 3000 B.C. Pinch, G. *Magic in Egypt.* Austin, Texas: University of Texas Press, 1995. p. 175.

66. Valiente, D. *Witchcraft for Tomorrow.* Custer, Wash.: Phoenix Publishing, Inc., 1978. p. 44.

67. Z. Budapest.

68. As exposed by Raven Grimassi in *Encyclopedia of Wicca and Witchcraft.*

69. Valiente, D. *Witchcraft for Tomorrow,* pp. 172–174 and Grimassi, R. *Encyclopedia of Wicca and Witchcraft,* pp. 436, 437.

70. Valiente, D. *An ABC of Witchcraft.* Custer, Wash.: Phoenix Publishing, Inc, 1973. p. 150.

Notes for Part II

1. Walker, B. *The Woman's Dictionary of Symbols and Sacred Objects,* p. 82.

2. Ridpath, I. *Stars and Planets.* New York, N.Y.: Dorling Kindersley, 2000. p. 68.

3. You will find more diagrams of altar setups in my book *To Stir a Magick Cauldron.*

4. Hugh Ross Williamson's novel *The Silver Bowl* (1948) portrayed a seventeenth-century Witch cult based on the theories of Margaret Murray and described by members as "the Craft of the Wise," an expression Gerald Gardner subsequently used for his religion that officially became known as modern Witchcraft in the 1950s. Hutton, R. *The Triumph of the Moon,* p. 233.

5. Valiente, D. *An ABC of Witchcraft,* p. 23.

6. Grimassi, R. *Encyclopedia of Wicca & Witchcraft,* p. 468.

7. Pinch, G. *Magic in Egypt,* pp. 78, 79.

8. Valiente, D. *Witchcraft for Tomorrow,* pp. 78, 79.

9. Hutton, R. *The Triumph of the Moon,* p. 230.

10. Valiente, D. *Witchcraft for Tomorrow,* p. 78.

11. Cooper, J. C. *An Illustrated Encyclopaedia of Traditional Symbols.* New York and London: Thames and Hudson Ltd., 1978. p. 166.

12. Fortune, D. *What Is Occultism?* ed. G. Knight. York Beach, Maine: Samuel Weiser, Inc., 1967, 2001. p. 73. Dione Fortune (1891–1946) was the founder of The Society of the Inner Light and is recognized as one of the most luminous and significant figures of twentieth-century esoteric thought. A pioneer in psychology and the occult, she has left a legacy that continues today.

13. A line most likely taken from the poetry of Doreen Valiente.

14. Walker, B. *The Woman's Dictionary of Symbols and Sacred Objects,* p. 120.

15. *Standard Dictionary of Folklore, Mythology, and Legend,* p. 133.

16. Pinch, G. *Magic in Egypt,* p. 9.

17. Ibid., p. 61.

18. Frazer, J. G. *Folklore in the Old Testament, vol. 1.* London: MacMillan, 1918. p. 143.

19. Savedow, S. *Sepher Rezial Hemelach: The Book of the Angel Rezial.* York Beach, Maine: Samuel Weiser, Inc., 2000. p. 11.

20. Kieckhefer, R. *Magic in the Middle Ages,* 2nd ed. Cambridge, U.K.: Cambridge University Press, 1989, 2000. pp. 3–9.

21. Grimassi, R. *Encyclopedia of Wicca & Witchcraft,* p. 47.

22. Drury, N. *The History of Magic in the Modern Age: A Quest for Personal Transformation.* New York, N.Y.: Carroll & Graf Publishers, Inc., 2000. p. 304.

23. Hutton, R. *The Triumph of the Moon,* pp. 232, 233.

24. Walker, B. *The Woman's Dictionary of Symbols and Sacred Objects,* p. 123.

25. Biedermann, H. *Dictionary of Symbolism: Cultural Icons & The Meanings Behind Them,* p. 50.

26. Cunningham, S. and D. Harrington. *The Magickal Household: Empower Your Home with Love, Protection, Health and Happiness.* St. Paul, Minn.: Llewellyn, 1983. p. 114.

27. *Standard Dictionary of Folklore, Mythology, and Legend,* p. 165.

28. Walker, B. *The Woman's Dictionary of Symbols and Sacred Objects,* p. 123.

29. Grimassi, R. *Encyclopedia of Wicca & Witchcraft,* p. 49. The main theme of goddess symbolism, from Paleolithic times into the present, holds tightly to the mystery of birth and death, and the continuous renewal of life on the planet. From Iraq to Scotland, paintings of birds mixed with female anatomy have been found in Proto-Neolithic tombs, indicating the connection between the Goddess, birth, death, and renewal. Vultures with awesome wingspans painted in red (the color of life), their wings shaped like brooms on various cave paintings tell us of the belief in the power of the Death Goddess (Gimbutas, M. *The Language of the Goddess,* p. 189) and may give us an explanation as to why the broom figures so prominently

in the modernday Craft. The transformation of the Goddess into bird form is well known from Egypt through Greece, on into the Celtic belief system with the Morrigan, and even the Germanic Valkyrie is identified with the raven, the dark bird of the dead that assists great warriors to the other side. Rather than something (or someone) to be feared, the Death Goddess is symbolic of hope for continued renewal on Earth as well as in other realms.

30. Drury, N. *The History of Magic in the Modern Age,* p. 175.

31. Pinch, G. *Magic in Egypt,* p. 77.

32. Cunningham, S. *The Magickal Household,* p. 115.

33. Malbrough, R. T. *The Magical Power of the Saints.* St. Paul, Minn.: Llewellyn, 1998. p. 68.

34. Walker, B. *The Woman's Dictionary of Symbols and Sacred Objects,* p. 123.

35. Malbrough, R. T. *The Magical Power of the Saints,* p. 68.

36. Spitzer, K. D. "Candle Dipping." *1999 Lewellyn's Moon Sign Book and Gardening Almanac,* pp. 4, 83, 84.

37. Malbrough, R. T. *The Magical Power of the Saints,* p. 2.

38. Ibid., pp. 11, 14, 21, 27.

39. Matthews, C. J. *The Encyclopedia of Celtic Wisdom.* Boston, MA: Element Books, 1996. p. 219.

40. Hutton, R. *The Pagan Religions of the Ancient British Isles: Their Nature and Legacy.* Malden, Mass.: Blackwell Publishers Ltd, 1991. p. 150.

41. Matthews, C. J. *The Encyclopedia of Celtic Wisdom.* Boston, Mass.: Element Books, 1996. p. 219.

42. Cooper, J. C. *An Illustrated Encyclopaedia of Traditional Symbols,* p. 31.

43. This church tradition was thrown out in 1960. Walker, B. *The Woman's Dictionary of Symbols and Sacred Objects,* p. 125.

44. Seligmann, K. *The History of Magic and the Occult.* New York, N.Y.: Pantheon Books, Random House Division, 1948. p. 32.

45. Gager, J. G. *Curse Tablets and Binding Spells from the Ancient World.* New York, N.Y.: Oxford University Press, 1992. p. 15.

46. Ibid., p. 15.

47. Pinch, G. *Magic in Egypt,* p. 91.

48. Ibid., p. 99.

49. You will find instructions on how to make a corn dolly, as well as its cultural history, in my book *Halloween.*

50. Pinch, G. *Magic in Egypt,* p. 41.

51. Kieckhefer, R. *Magic in the Middle Ages,* p. 49.

52. Valiente, D. *An ABC of Witchcraft,* p. 50 under Bune Wand entry.

53. Pinch, G. *Magic in Egypt,* p. 87.

54. Valiente, D. *An ABC of Witchcraft,* p. 38.

Notes for Part III

1. Llewellyn produces several yearly almanacs for the magickally minded, including the Sun Sign Book, the Moon Sign Book, the Witches Date Book, and the Daily Planetary Guide.

2. Manilius. *Astronomica.* Loeb Classical Library, ed. G. P. Goold. Cambridge, Mass.: Harvard University Press, 1977. p. 386.

3. A classical system of study taken from the *Picatrix* wherein each astrological sign is broken into parts, called mansions. Each mansion has its own attributes related to various life circumstances. Each mansion is broken into magickal activities that can be practiced for either waxing or waning cycles.

4. Carr-Gomm, P. and S. *The Druid Animal Oracle.* New York, N.Y.: Fireside, Simon and Shuster, Inc., 1994. p. 7.

5. Renault, D. *Principles of Native American Spirituality.* Hammersmith, London: Thorsons, 1996. p. 24.

6. Although most people think of the Inquisition as a single horrific occurrence, it was an institution that experienced development and change, in terms of organization, procedures, and definitions of the law throughout a long period of history. There were several periods of inquisition, including the Medieval European Inquisition, the Roman Inquisition, and the Spanish Inquisition. Ginzburg, C. *The Cheese and the Worms: The Cosmos of a Sixteenth-Century Miller,* 3rd ed. The Johns Hopkins University Press, 1992. p. ix.

7. Renault, D. *Principles of Native American Spirituality,* p. 6.

8. The Witch's Garter in traditional groups is commonly worn by the Queen or Mother of several covens. A bell or charm is affixed to the garter to represent each hived coven. A female Witch can only be considered a "Queen" if she has seven active covens under her direction. Naturally, this is true only for certain sects in the Craft—others will have their own titling system.

9.   Webster, R. *Astral Travel for Beginners: Transcend Time and Space with Out-of-Body Experiences.* St. Paul, Minn.: Llewellyn, 1998. p. xi.

10. Myers, F. W. H. *Human Personality and Survival of Bodily Death.* London, England, Longmans Green and Company, 1903. p. 252.

11. Webster, R. *Astral Travel for Beginners*, p. xiii.

12. Ibid., p. 3.

13. Ibid., p. 5.

14. Walker, B. *The Woman's Encyclopedia of Myths and Secrets*, p. 71.

15. Smith, C., and J. Astrop. *The Moon Oracle.* New York: St. Martins Press, an Eddison-Sadd Edition, 2000. p. 13.

16. Seligmann, K. *The History of Magic and the Occult.* New York, N.Y.: Gramercy Books. 1948, 1997. p. 58.

17. Whitfield, P. *Astrology: A History.* New York, N.Y.: Harry N. Abrams, Inc., 2001. p. 96.

18. Walker, B. *The Woman's Dictionary of Symbols and Sacred Objects*, p. 76.

19. Ridpath, I. *Stars and Planets.* New York, N.Y.: Dorling Kindersley, 2000. p. 224.

20. Ibid.

21. Ibid.

22. Ibid.

23. Information gathered from my own experience and information found in Mathers, S. *The Key of Solomon the King.* York Beach, Maine: Samuel Weiser, Inc., 1888, 1972. pp. 12, 13.

24. Table research done using my own experience and the following references: Hand, R. *Planets in Transit: Life Cycles for Living.* Atglen, Pa.: Whitford Press, 1976. p. 528. Ramesy, W. *Astrologia Restaurata or Astrologie Restored.* Modern ed. vol. 1–4. 1653, Issaquah, Wash.: JustUs and Associates, 1653. p. 356.

25. Webster, R. *Aura Reading for Beginners: Develop Your Psychic Awareness for Health and Success.* St. Paul, Minn.: Llewellyn, 1998. 185.

26. Ibid.

27. Mercier, P. *Chakras: Balance Your Body's Energy for Health and Harmony.* New York, N.Y.: Sterling Publishing Company, 2000. 6.

28. Smith, M. *Auras: See Them in Only 60 Seconds!* St. Paul, Minn.: Llewellyn, 2000.

29. Ibid., 139.

30. Mercier, P. *Chakras,* p. 6.

31. Jones, B. *Chakra Workout for Body, Mind, and Spirit.* 2nd ed. St. Paul, Minn.: Llewellyn, 1999. p. 3.

32. Talbot, M. *The Holographic Universe.* New York, N.Y.: HarperCollins Publishers, 1991. p. 28.

33. Dr. Fred Alan Wolf is an award-winning theoretical physicist who believes the human mind can leap around the future (holographic quantum physics). This quote is from a paper presented at the Vigier conference called The Timing of the Conscious Experience. Geller, U. *ParaScience Pack.* Abbeville Publishing Group, 2000. p. 12.

34. Thomas, K. *Religion and the Decline of Magic.* New York: Oxford University Press, 1971. p. 664.

35. Geller, U. *ParaScience Pack*, p. 65.

36. There is sporadic reference to the cult of Diana, especially in France, that was not restricted to women throughout the early Middle Ages; however, much of the information gathered was done so under the torture of the Inquisitions. Flint, V. I. J. *The Rise of Magic in Early Medieval Europe*, p. 122. Other dream goddesses included Hecate (Greek) and Holda (German). Saint Kilian met his death when attempting to convert the East Franks from the cult of Diana.

37. Ginzburg, C. *The Night Battles: Witchcraft and Agrarian Cults in the Sixteenth and Seventeenth Centuries.* Baltimore, Md.: Johns Hopkins University Press, 1983.

38. Flint, V. I. J. *The Rise of Magic in Early Medieval Europe*, p. 125.

39. Thomas, K. *Religion and the Decline of Magic*, p. 120.

40. Silverthorn, J. M. O. *Dreaming Realities: A Spiritual System to Create Inner Alignment Through Dreams.* Carmarthen, U.K.: Crown House Publishing Limited, 1999. p. 14.

41. Ibid., p. 18.

42. Talbot, M. *The Holographic Universe*, p. 63.

43. Kieckhefer, R. *Magic in the Middle Ages*, pp. 64, 65.

44. Thomas, K. *Religion and the Decline of Magic*, p. 259.

45. Ibid., page 647.

46. Chants are from Storms, Dr. G. *Anglo-Saxon Magic.* The Hague: Martinus Nijhoff, 1948.

47. Verner-Bonds, L. *The Complete Book of Color Healing: Practical Ways to Enhance Your Physical and Spiritual Well-Being.* New York, NY: Sterling Publishing Company, 2000. p. 119.

48. Baring, A. C. *The Myth of the Goddess*. London, England: Penguin Books, Ltd., 1991. p. 567.

49. Leek, S. *How to Be Your Own Astrologer*. New York, N.Y.: Cowles Book Company, Inc. 1970. p. 145.

50. York, U. *Living by the Moon*. Woodside, Calif.: BlueStar Communications, 1997. p. 125.

51. Some astrologers feel that Aries includes the nose, where others do not.

52. York, U. *Living by the Moon*, p. 106.

53. Ibid., p. 129.

54. Leek, S. *How to Be Your Own Astrologer,* p. 106.

55. The fifteenth century also gave birth to Michelangelo, Leonardo da Vinci, Kepler, Copernicus, and other geniuses.

56. Paracelsus. *Paracelsus: Selected Writings*, ed. J. Jacobi. Princeton, N.J.: Princeton University Press, 1951. p. 43.

57. Seligmann, K. *The History of Magic and the Occult*, p. 218.

58. Lord Byron, 1788–1824, "She Walks in Beauty."

59. RavenWolf, S. *Silver's Spells for Love*. St. Paul, Minn.: Llewellyn, 2001. p. 63.

60. Scoble, G. *The Meaning of Flowers: Myth, Language, and Lore*. 1998, San Francisco, Calif.: Chronicle Book, 1998.

61. Potently fragrant, the flower was once thought capable of warding off the Black Death (plague). Ibid., p. 58.

62. Associated with the Roman Juno and Middle Eastern Goddess Astarte. Ibid., p. 26.

63. There are over 25,000 species of orchid, more than any other flower. Ibid., p. 17.

64. Pinch, G. *Magic in Egypt*, p. 80.

65. Pavlov believed that all behavior is learned. Therefore, if it is learned, he said, it can be unlearned. To prove this he began experiments in which he "conditioned" some dogs. First, he rang a bell, then he produced food. Upon smelling the food, the dogs would salivate. He repeated this method over and over again, and each time the dogs salivated. The dogs learned to associate the sound of the bell with the smell of the food. After a while, Pavlov did not produce the food when the bell rang, but the dogs still salivated, proving the power of the mind.

66. Geller, U. *Mind Medicine*. Boston, Mass.: Element Books Limited, 1999. p. 184.

67. Valiente, D. *An ABC of Witchcraft,* p. 244.

68. Parker, J. D. *KISS Guide to Astrology*. London, England: Dorling Kindersley Publishing, 2000. p. 96.

69. Agrippa, H. C. *Three Books of Occult Philosophy*. Llewellyn's Sourcebook Series, ed. D. Tyson. St. Paul, Minn.: Llewellyn, 1533, 2000. p. 938. Ovid. *The Metamorphoses*. trans. Henry T. Riley. London: George Bell and Sons, 1884. (provided by D. Tyson under Notes, page 220.)

70. Barrett, F. *The Magus or Celestial Intelligencer*. London: Lackrington, Allen and Co., 1801.

71. Donald Tyson in *Three Books of Occult Philosophy*.

72. Agrippa, H. C. *Three Books of Occult Philosophy*. p. 938. Smith, C. *The Moon Oracle: Let the Phases of the Moon Guide Your Life*. New York:New York: St. Martin's Press, 2000. p. 128. The writings of Bic Thomas at http://www.renaissanceastrology.com. Ramesy, W. *Astrologia Restaurata or Astrologie Restored*. Modern ed., vol. 1-4. Issaquah, Wash.: JustUs and Associates, 1653. p. 356.

73. Richard Webster (New Zealand) is a highly respected writer on many New Age topics, and has written books on palmistry, astral travel, dowsing, feng shui, and many other metaphysical topics.

74. Liungman, C. G. *Dictionary of Symbols*. New York, N.Y.: W. W. Norton and Co., 1991. p. 298.

75. Ibid.

76. Pythagoras was a Greek philosopher who traveled widely in Egypt and the East acquiring occult knowledge. Said to possess the gift of prophecy, he believed in reincarnation and taught that the divine might be approached through the mystic power of numbers. Agrippa, H. C. *Three Books of Occult Philosophy*. p. 827 in Biographical Dictionary written by Donald Tyson.

77. Liungman, C. G. *Dictionary of Symbols,* p. 298.

78. Ibid., p. 334.

79. Regardie, I. *The Golden Dawn*, p. 280.

80. Valiente, D. *An ABC of Witchcraft*, p. 266.

81. Hutton, R. *The Triumph of the Moon,* p. 71.

82. Geller, U. *ParaScience Pack*. Introduction, page 1.

83. Ibid., p. 72.

84. Autumn Ayla Craig (Colchester, CT) is a Holistic Facilitator, Reiki Master, and teacher who believes that there is no one correct way to do things, that everyone has a unique path to follow, and who hopes to learn from her students as they learn from her. She is a certified practitioner and

instructor in various energy healing modalities, including Traditional Usui, Karuna Reiki, Essential Reiki, Shamballa Multidimensional Healing and Magnified Healing. She began her holistic studies in herbology and holistic healing, is an American Naturopathic Medical Association Board Certified Naturopath, and co-owns and operates Dolphin Heart, a holistic center. She is an Elder in the Black Forest Clan Circle and Seminary and has been involved in magical studies since the early 1980s.

85. Runic introduction reprinted from Jackson, N. *The Rune Mysteries*. St. Paul, Minn.: Llewellyn, 1996. p. xi.

86. Grimassi, R. *Encyclopedia of Wicca & Witchcraft*, p. 105, Divination.

87. *The Oxford English Dictionary*, 2nd ed. New York, N.Y.: Oxford University Press, 1999. p. 417, plate 513. Other words associated are ascry, descry, espy, and scry.

88. Pinch, G. *Magic in Egypt*, p. 88.

89. Valiente, D. *An ABC of Witchcraft*, p. 301.

90. Although some magickal practitioners have dropped the circle, our statistics show that your work has a better chance of completion matching your desire if you continue to use the circle environment. It is highly possible that some magickal systems have dropped the circle due to faulty recording of data during medieval times.

91. Gager, J. G. *Curse Tablets and Binding Spells from the Ancient World*, p. 278.

92. Ibid., p. 243.

93. Ibid., p. 221—from Mesopotamia, fourth to sixth century B.C.

Notes for Part IV

1. Ramsay, J. *The Art of Alchemy*. Hammersmith, London: Thorsons (an imprint of HarperCollins Publishers), 1997. p. 8.

2. Baring, A. C. *The Myth of the Goddess*. London, England: Penguin Books, Ltd., 1991. p. 647.

3. Ramsay, J. *The Art of Alchemy*, p. 10.

4. Hall, Manly P. *The Secret Teachings of All Ages*. Los Angeles: Philosophical Research Society, 1977. p. CLIII.

5. Seligmann, K. *The History of Magic and the Occult*, p. 80.

6. Ramsay, J. *The Art of Alchemy*, p. 25.

7. Seligmann, K. *The History of Magic and the Occult*, pp. 123, 124.

8. Price, J. R. *The Alchemist's Handbook*. Carlsbad, Calif.: Hay House, Inc., 2000.

9. Ibid.

10. Baring, A. C. *The Myth of the Goddess*, p. 650.

11. Biedermann, H. *Dictionary of Symbolism*, p. 465.

12. Kieckhefer, R. *Magic in the Middle Ages*, p. 134.

13. Ramsay, J. *The Art of Alchemy*, p. 21.

14. Levi, E. C. (Alphonse Louis). *The History of Magic*, p. 79.

15. Tabula Smaragdina, Heidelberg, 1926, quoted in Titus Burckhardt's *Alchemy*, (Stuart & Watkins, 1967, Element Books, 1986, pp. 1966-197), quoted from *Alchemy, The Art of Transformation* by Jay Ramsay, Element Books, 1999, pp. 11–12.

16. A little history for you. Egypt was the longest-running civilization in the world. It began somewhere around the year 3032 B.C. and ran under its own steam until Greek rule from 332 B.C. to 30 B.C. (when Cleopatra was overthrown by the Romans). Roman rule lasted from 30 B.C. to A.D. 313 (about 343 years), and then the great Egyptian civilization as the world understood it was no more.

17. Seligmann, K. *The History of Magic and the Occult*, p. 84.

18. Ramsay, J. *The Art of Alchemy*, p. 41.

19. Gimbutas, M. *The Language of the Goddess*, p. 388.

20. Kieckhefer, R. *Magic in the Middle Ages*, p. 38.

21. Mathers, S. L. M. *The Goetia*. 2nd ed. Red Wheel/ Weiser, 1995.

22. Gager, J. G. *Curse Tablets and Binding Spells from the Ancient World*, p. 13.

23. Walker, B. *The Woman's Encyclopedia of Myths and Secrets*, p. 131.

24. Biedermann, H. *Dictionary of Symbolism*, p. 54.

25. Grimassi, R. *Encyclopedia of Wicca & Witchcraft*, p. 55.

26. The phrase "May this spell not reverse, or place upon me any curse" is attributed to Sybil Leek.

27. Walker, B. *The Woman's Encyclopedia of Myths and Secrets*, p. 162.

28. Yoder, D. *Discovering American Folklife: Essays on Folk Culture & the Pennsylvania Dutch*. Mechanicsburg, Pa.: Stackpole Books, 2001. p. 88.

29. Agrippa, H. C. *Three Books of Occult Philosophy,* p. 217.

30. Bell, J. W. *The Grimoire of Lady Sheba.* St. Paul, Minn.: Llewellyn, 1972. p. 175.

31. Baring, A. C. *The Myth of the Goddess,* p. 428.

32. Ibid.

33. Russell, Jeffrey B. *A History of Witchcraft, Sorcerers, Heretics, and Pagans.* London, England: Thames & Hudson, Ltd., 1980 with reprint in 1997, p. 97.

34. Storms, Dr. G. *Anglo-Saxon Magic.* The Hague: Martinus Nijhoff, 1948.

35. Verner-Bonds, L. *The Complete Book of Color Healing: Practical Ways to Enhance Your Physical and Spiritual Well-Being.* New York, N.Y.: Sterling Publishing Company, 2000. p. 10.

36. Theoretically, black is not a color—it is the absence of light.

37. Verner-Bonds, L. *The Complete Book of Color Healing,* p. 70.

38. Ibid., pp. 88–91.

39. Fraser, Sr. James G. *The Golden Bough,* 3rd ed. London: Macmillan, 1913. p. 54.

40. Starr, C. G. *A History of the Ancient World.* New York, N.Y.: Oxford University Press, 1991. p. 36.

41. Emmanuel Swedenborg (1688–1772) was the child of a Swedish royal chaplain, thirty year professional in the mining industry, and student of science, mathematics, philosophy, and religion. He established Sweden's first scientific journal, and also published treatises on cosmology, lunar measurement, chemistry, physics, the circulation of the blood, and sensory perception. Washington, P. *Madame Blavatsky's Baboon—A History of the Mystics, Mediums, and Misfits Who Brought Spiritualism to America.* New York, N.Y.: Schocken Books Inc., 1993. p. 13.

42. Ibid., p. 14.

43. Manilius. *Astronomica.*

44. Liungman, C. G. *Dictionary of Symbols.* New York, N.Y.: W. W. Norton & Company, 1991. p. 328.

45. There are hundreds of pantheons and thousands of deities. These are just to get you started. Remember, you must research a deity energy before you call on it.

46. When I make statements like "Most Witches or many magickal people . . ." keep in mind that I don't know everyone, everywhere, although I have traveled all over the US and visited many magickal groups and spoken to thousands of Wiccans (both traditional and eclectic). It is from my own traditional Wiccan, Druid, Hoodoo, Pow Wow training, and personal interviews conducted on my travels that I learn the "consensus" of the community.

47. Biedermann, H. *Dictionary of Symbolism,* p. 375.

48. Ibid., p. 173.

49. Cotterell, A. *The Ultimate Encyclopedia of Mythology.* London, U.K.: Lorenz Books, 1999. p. 320.

50. Liungman, C. G. *Dictionary of Symbols,* p. 300.

51. Grimassi, R. *Encyclopedia of Wicca & Witchcraft,* p. 115.

52. Attributed to Greek philosophy.

53. Valiente, D. *An ABC of Witchcraft,* p. 107.

54. For more information, read *The Cooper's Wife is Missing* by Joan Hoff and Marian Yeates (Basic Books, New York, N.Y., 2000). In the mid- to late 1800s, in addition to cleaning its own clerical house, the church launched a major campaign to wipe out the last vestiges of Pagan practices among the peasants who, for centuries, cherished their Pagan Celt traditions—naturalism, sympathetic magic, attachment to ancestral ground, communal involvement, gaiety, and abandon. One strategy used to eliminate Paganism was to impose stricter discipline and reemphasize Romanized rituals, such as Sodalities, Confraternities, and the Stations of the Cross, which had not attracted the Irish before the Famine. To erase vestiges of Pagan Goddess worsihip, the church fostered more traditional, male-oriented rituals directed from Rome, administered by a growing army of priests. Cardinal Paul Cullen, Ireland's first Cardinal, threw his weight behind the war on Paganism and introduced jubilees, triduums, pilgrimages, shrines, processions, and retreats designed to replace seasonal Pagan agricultural pageants, holy wells, charms, effigies and wakes. By 1875 they had beaten back many older forms of paganism.

55. Grimassi, R. *Encyclopedia of Wicca & Witchcraft,* p. 124.

56. *Standard Dictionary of Folklore, Mythology, and Legend,* p. 363.

57. Ibid., page 1010.

58. Walker, B. *The Woman's Encyclopedia of Myths and Secrets,* p. 298.

59. I have seen this type of information loss in the Pennsylvania Dutch community in regard to Pow Wow and the use of astrology in farming and

household affairs too. In all but a few cases, individuals still practicing Pow Wow have no clue as to how a specific superstition came about, nor do farm wives understand the concept of the phases of the moon—speaking solemnly, however, of what should be done when the horns of the moon are up, and what should be done around the farm when the horns of the moon are down. Although these practices originated in solid science, they became nothing more than practiced superstition.

60. *Standard Dictionary of Folklore, Mythology, and Legend*, p. 364.

61. Cunningham, S. *Cunningham's Encyclopedia of Crystal, Gem & Metal Magick*. St. Paul, Minn.: Llewellyn, 1988. p. 101.

62. Valiente, D. *An ABC of Witchcraft*, p. 123.

63. *Standard Dictionary of Folklore, Mythology, and Legend*, p. 444.

64. Pinch, G. *Magic in Egypt*, p. 165.

65. Ibid., p. 166.

66. Kieckhefer, R. *Magic in the Middle Ages*, p. 102.

67. Melody. *Love Is In the Earth—A Kaleidoscope of Crystals (Updated)*, 2nd ed. Wheat Ridge, Co.: Earth-Love Publishing House, 1995. p. 32.

68. Wording taken from a fourteenth-century magickal charm. Kieckhefer, R. *Magic in the Middle Ages*, p. 84.

69. Parts of this spell taken from Cunningham, S. *Cunningham's Encyclopedia of Crystal, Gem & Metal Magick*. St. Paul, Minn.: Llewellyn, 1988. p. 61.

70. From Appendix II, written by Donald Tyson, in Agrippa, H. C., *Three Books of Occult Philosophy*, p. 713.

71. Fiero, G. K. *The Humanistic Tradition: The First Civilizations and the Classical Legacy*, 3rd ed. vol. I. The McGraw-Hill Companies, Inc., 1991.

72. Ibid.

73. Hutton, R. From private correspondence, 9 August 2002.

74. Early in the twentieth century, anthropologists discovered the first fossil remains of the proto-human, who lived five million years ago. This Paleolithic culture, called the Old Stone culture, lasted from 5 million to 10,000 B.C.E. and evolved during a period of great climactic change, called the Ice Age. Important to our studies of magick, we learn that the roots of humankind, begun in the Paleolithic Age, flow from the heart of Africa, and it is from this area that the great magickal cultures, Egypt and the neighboring Mesopo-tamia, arose around 4000 B.C.E.

75. Thomas, K. *Religion and the Decline of Magic*. Oxford: Oxford University Press, 1971. p. 644.

76. Fiero, G. K. *The Humanistic Tradition*.

77. Seligmann, K.

78. *Doktor Snake's Voodoo Spellbook—Spells, Curses and Folk Magick for All Your Needs*. New York, N.Y.: St. Martin's Press, 2000. p. 62.

79. Stenger, V. J. *The Unconscious Quantum*. Amherst, N.Y.: Prometheus Books, 1995. p. 20.

80. A condensed version of *The Holographic Universe* by M. Talbot, HarperCollins, 1991, pp. 36–49.

81. Wolf, Fred Alan, Ph.D. *Mind into Matter: A New Alchemy of Science and Spirit*. Portsmouth, N.H.: Moment Point Press, 2001.

82. Gager, J. G. *Curse Tablets and Binding Spells from the Ancient World*, pp. 7, 8.

83. Appears in a 1926 article written by J. F. C. Fuller, who used these two sentences as an incantation in which he claimed them to be a "sorcerer's cry in the Middle Ages," of which this has not been proven. *The Occult Review* 43 (1926), p. 231—Hutton, R. *The Triumph of the Moon*, p. 232.

84. Gager, J. G. *Curse Tablets and Binding Spells from the Ancient World*, p. 10.

85. Ibid., p. 9.

86. Agrippa, H. C. *Three Books of Occult Philosophy*, pp. 561–570.

87. Attributed to Sybil Leek.

88. Attributed to Laurie Cabot.

89. Schueler, G. and B. *Egyptian Magick: Enter the Body of Light & Travel the Magickal Universe*. St. Paul, Minn.: Llewellyn, 1989. p. 59.

90. Gager, J. G. *Curse Tablets and Binding Spells from the Ancient World*, p. 219.

91. González-Wippler, M. *The Complete Book of Amulets & Talismans*. St. Paul, Minn.: Llewellyn, 1991. p. 1.

92. Gager, J. G. *Curse Tablets and Binding Spells from the Ancient World*, p. 219.

93. *Witchcraft and Magic in Europe: Ancient Greece and Rome. Witchcraft and Magic in Europe*, ed. B. and C. Ankarloo, Stuart. Philadelphia, Pa.: University of Pennsylvania Press, 1999. Ogden, Daniel. *Binding Spells: Curse Tablets and Voodoo Dolls in Greek and Roman Worlds*, p. 3. Note: More than 1,100 of these tablets have been found, of which most are Greek in origin—the earliest from a colony in Sicily dating from fifth century B.C.

94. Pinch, G. *Magic in Egypt*, pp. 104–119.

95. Ibid., p. 108.

96. Regardie, I. *The Golden Dawn*.

97. Pinch, G. *Magic in Egypt*, p. 191.

98. Walker, B. *The Woman's Dictionary of Symbols and Sacred Objects*, p. 563. Egypt's sacred eye symbol, sometimes called *utchat*, was at various times the eye of Maat, of Horus, of Thoth, and of Ra. Probably the male gods came later chronologically, since Maat was the original All-Seeing Eye and Mother of Truth, her name based on the verb "to see."

99. Majno, G. M. D. *The Healing Hand: Man and Wound in the Ancient World.* Cambridge, Mass.: Harvard University Press, 1975. p. 118.

100. Kieckhefer, R. *Magic in the Middle Ages*, p. 13.

101. *Standard Dictionary of Folklore, Mythology, and Legend*, pp. 51–52.

102. Text paraphrased from an original Egyptian healing incantation. Majno, G. M. D. *The Healing Hand*, pp. 126, 127.

103. *The Oxford English Dictionary,* 2nd ed. New York, N.Y.: Oxford University Press, 1999. p. 2033, plate 842.

104. Kieckhefer, R. *Magic in the Middle Ages,* p. 149.

105. Spence, L. *An Encyclopedia of Occultism: The Comprehensive Treasury of Occult Knowledge from All Times and Places.* New York, N.Y.: Carol Publishing Group Edition, 1960, 1996. p. 261. (Interesting book, but dated, meaning that not all the research is accurate.)

106. Cooper, J. C. *An Illustrated Encyclopaedia of Traditional Symbols*, p. 170. In Christianity the tetramorphs are Matthew, Mark, Luke, and John and the four corners of Paradise; in Egypt they are the four Sons of Horus; and in Hinduism they are the four heads of Brahma.

107. Walker, B. *The Woman's Dictionary of Symbols and Sacred Objects*, p. 223.

108. Berenson-Perkins, J. *Kabbalah Decoder: Revealing the Messages of the Ancient Mystics.* Hauppauge, N.Y.: Barron's Educational Series, Inc., 2000. p. 96.

109. Walker, B. *The Woman's Dictionary of Symbols and Sacred Objects*, p. 223.

110. Mathers, S. L. M. M. *The Key of Solomon the King.* York Beach, Maine: Samuel Weiser, Inc., 1888, 1972.

111. Brady, B. *Brady's Book of Fixed Stars.* York Beach, Maine: Samuel Weiser, Inc., 1998. p. 1

112. Matthews, C. & J. *The Encyclopedia of Celtic Wisdom.* Dorsett, England: Element Books, 1994. p. 163.

113. Jackson, N. and S. RavenWolf. *The Rune Mysteries.* St. Paul, Minn.: Llewellyn, 1996. Last two paragraphs from p. 13.

Notes for Part V

1. American Academy of Dermatology: Kids Connection, 2001.

2. Storms, G. *Anglo-Saxon Magic*, p. 155. And in case you are wondering, I chose this charm because no one likes acne, so I felt the dung association was extremely relevant. This spell was used for cysts, acne, and other strange growths.

3. Adaptation taken from an Egyptian prayer to the Goddess Nut. Baring, A. C. *The Myth of the Goddess,* pp. 259–260.

4. Author of *Charms, Spells and Formulas* and *The Magickal Power of the Saints* (Llewellyn).

5. General guide only, more detailed information can be found in Llewellyn's annual Moon Sign Book.

6. Mestel, R. "When Push Comes to Shove," in *Los Angeles Times,* 2001.

7. RavenWolf, S. *American Folk Magick: Charms, Spells & Herbs.* St. Paul, Minn.: Llewellyn, 1995. p. 242.

8. Gilbert, S. D. *The Unofficial Guide to Managing Eating Disorders.* Foster City, Calif.: IDG Books Worldwide, Inc., 2000. p. xxi.

9. The American Anorexia/Bulimia Association, Inc., 165 W. 46th Street, New York, NY 10035. 212-575-6200; http://wwwaabainc.org

10. Gilbert, S. D. *The Unofficial Guide to Managing Eating Disorders*, p. 120.

11. This ritual is a parody of one found in *Egyptian Magick: Enter the Body of Light & Travel of the Magickal Universe* by Gerald & Betty Schueler.

12. Andersen, U. S. *Three Magic Words*, 2nd ed. Hollywood, Calif.: Melvin Powers Wilshire Book Company, 1954. p. 220.

13. Ibid., p. 21.

14. Due to what is called the Precession of the Equinoxes, the position of the stars has moved in our relation to viewing them. When Egyptian rule was at its height, this star fell in the sign of Scorpio.

15. Lesko, B. S. *The Great Goddesses of Egypt*. Norman, Okla.: Oklahoma University, 1999. p. 273.

16. See *Modern Magick* by Donald Michael Kraig (Llewellyn) or the work of Israel Regardie.

17. The Golden Dawn, once a secret order, was one of the most prestigious groups flourishing at the turn of the nineteenth century. Membership included such notables as W. B. Yeats, Dion Fortune, S. L. MacGregor Mathers, A. E. Waite, Evelyn Underhill, and many others. The influence of the Golden Dawn on twenty-first century Wicca is enormous and can especially be seen in the more ceremonial rites of the Gardnerian and Alexandrian traditions.

18. Added to honor the cosmic mother, birth and death energy, and the realm of the dead.

19. Society, T. M. *Astrology Really Works!* Carlsbad, Calif.: Hay House, 1995. p. 247.

20. Ibid., p. 250.

21. Mercury goes retrograde approximately three times a year for three weeks at a time. Check your planetary guide or other astrological almanac to keep an eye on these time frames.

22. RavenWolf, S. *Silver's Spells for Love*. St. Paul, Minn.: Llewellyn, 2001. pp. 4–7.

23. Ming-Dao, D. *365 Tao Daily Meditations*. San Francisco, Calif.: HarperCollins Publishers, 1992. p. 281.

24. Phillips, D. *Practical Guide to Psychic Self-Defense & Well-Being*. Second ed. St. Paul, Minn.: Llewellyn, 1980. p. x, Introduction.

25. Written by Cecylyna Dewr, Executive Director Pagan Pride Project, PMB 119, 133 W. Market St., Indianapolis, IN 46203 http://www.paganpride. org, and distributed throughout the Internet for public domain use.

26. "What is remembered lives" line is from the litanies created for the very first Spiral Dance Samhain ritual in San Francisco in 1979. It supposedly has been used every Samhain since then. Line attributed to Lauren Liebling and Starhawk.

27. The original version of these quarter calls can be found in Huson, pp. 160, 161.

28. Hutton, R. *The Triumph of the Moon*, p. 208. Bracelin, Gerald Gardner, pp. 166–167, and Valiente, D., *Rebirth of Witchcraft*, pp. 45, 46.

29. To learn more, visit http://www.milpagan.org/

30. Excerpt from *American Folk Magick: Charms, Spells & Herbals* by Silver RavenWolf, 1995, 1998.

Bibliography

Adler, Margot. *Drawing Down the Moon*. Revised and expanded ed. New York, N.Y.: Penguin, 1997.

Agrippa, H. C. *Three Books of Occult Philosophy*. Llewellyn's Sourcebook Series, ed. D. Tyson. St. Paul, Minn.: Llewellyn, 1533, 2000.

American Academy of Dermatology: Kid's Connection, 2001.

Andersen, U. S. *Three Magic Words*. 2nd ed. Hollywood, Calif.: Melvin Powers Wilshire Book Company, 1954.

Anderson, W. *Green Man: Archetype of Our Oneness with Earth*. San Francisco, Calif.: Harper Collins, 1990.

Andrews, Ted. *Animal-Speak*. St. Paul, Minn.: Llewellyn, 1993.

———. *Animal-Wise: The Spirit Language and Signs of Nature*. Jackson, Tenn.: Dragonhawk Publishing, 1999.

Aswynn, Freya. *Leaves of Yggdrasil*. St. Paul, Minn.: Llewellyn, 1990.

Barbour, Julian. *The End of Time: The Next Revolution in Physics*. Oxford UP, 2001.

Baring, A. and J. Cashford. *The Myth of the Goddess*. London, England: Penguin Books, Ltd., 1991.

Barrett, F. *The Magus or Celestial Intelligencer*. London: Lackrington, Allen and Co., 1801.

Bartel, P. *Spellcasters: Witches & Witchcraft in History, Folklore & Popular Culture*. Dallas, TX: Taylor Publishing Company, 2000.

Bell, J. W. *The Grimoire of Lady Sheba*. St. Paul, Minn.: Llewellyn, 1972.

Berenson-Perkins, J. *Kabbalah Decoder: Revealing the Messages of the Ancient Mystics*. Hauppauge, N.Y.: Barron's Educational Series, Inc., 2000.

Biedermann, H. *Dictionary of Symbolism: Cultural Icons & The Meanings Behind Them*. New York, N.Y.: Meridian, a division of Penguin Books, USA, Inc., 1989.

Buckland, Raymond. *The Complete Book of Witchcraft*. St. Paul, Minn.: Llewellyn, 1986.

———. *The Witch Book: The Encylopedia of Witchcraft, Wicca and Neo-Paganism*. Canton, MI: Visible Ink Press, 2002.

Campanelli, Pauline and Dan. *Ancient Ways: Reclaiming Pagan Traditions*. St. Paul, Minn.: Llewellyn, 1991.

———. *Wheel of the Year*. St. Paul, Minn.: Llewellyn, 1989.

Carr-Gomm, P. and S. *The Druid Animal Oracle*. New York, N.Y.: Fireside: Simon and Shuster, Inc., 1994.

Conroy, David L., Ph.D. *Out of the Nightmare: Recovery from Depression and Suicidal Pain*. New Liberty Press, 1991.

Conway, D. J. *Flying Without a Broom*. St. Paul, Minn.: Llewellyn, 1995.

———. *Magickal Mystical Creatures*. St. Paul, Minn.: Llewellyn, 1996.

Cooper, J. C. *An Illustrated Encyclopaedia of Traditional Symbols*. New York, N.Y.: Thames and Hudson Ltd, London, 1978.

Cotterell, A. and R. Storm. *The Ultimate Encyclopedia of Mythology*. London, UK: Lorenz Books division of Annes Publishing Limited, 1999.

Crossan, J. D. *The Historical Jesus: The Life of a Mediterranean Jewish Peasant*. San Francisco, Calif.: Harper-Collins, 1992.

Cunningham, S. and D. Harrington. *The Magickal Household: Empower Your Home with Love, Protection, Health and Happiness*. St. Paul, Minn.: Llewellyn, 1983.

Cunningham, S. *Cunningham's Encyclopedia of Crystal, Gem & Metal Magic*. St. Paul, Minn.: Llewellyn, 1988.

———. *The Truth About Witchcraft Today*. St. Paul, Minn.: Llewellyn, 1994.

———. *Wicca: A Guide for the Solitary Practitioner*. St. Paul, Minn.: Llewellyn, 1988.

Drury, N. *The History of Magic in the Modern Age: A Quest for Personal Transformation*. New York, N.Y.: Carroll & Graf Publishers, Inc., 2000.

Fiero, G. K. *The Humanistic Tradition: The First Civilizations and the Classical Legacy*. 3rd ed., vol. I. The McGraw-Hill Companies, Inc., 1998.

Fitch, Ed. *Magickal Rites from the Crystal Well*. St. Paul, Minn.: Llewellyn, 1984.

Flint, V. I. J. *The Rise of Magic in Early Medieval Europe*. Princeton, NJ: Princeton University Press, 1991.

Fortune, D. *Aspects of Occultism*, ed. G. Knight. York Beach, Maine: Samuel Weiser, Inc., 1962, 2000.

———. *What Is Occultism?*, ed. G. Knight. York Beach, Maine: Samuel Weiser, Inc., 1967, 2001.

Franklin, Anna, and Paul Mason. *Lammas*. St. Paul, Minn.: Llewellyn, 2001.

Franklin, Anna. *Midsummer*. St. Paul, Minn.: Llewellyn, 2002.

Frazer, J. G. *Folklore in the Old Testament*. Vol. 1. London: MacMillan, 1918.

Gager, J. G. *Curse Tablets and Binding Spells from the Ancient World*. New York, NY: Oxford University Press, 1992.

Geller, U. and M. Ron. *ParaScience Pack*. Abbeville Publishing Group, 2000.

Geller, U. *Mind Medicine*. Boston, Mass.: Element Books Limited, 1999.

Gibons, P. E. *Pennsylvania Dutch and Other Essays*. Philadelphia, Pa.: J. B. Lippincott & Co., 1882.

Gilbert, S. D., and Mary C. Commorford, Ph.D. *The Unofficial Guide to Managing Eating Disorders*. Foster City, Calif.: IDG Books Worldwide, Inc., 2000.

Gimbutas, M. *The Language of the Goddess*. New York, N.Y.: HarperCollins, 1991.

———. *The Goddesses and Gods of Old Europe: Myths and Cult Images*. University of California Press, 1990.

Ginzburg, C. *The Cheese and the Worms: The Cosmos of a 16th-Century Miller*. 3rd ed. The Johns Hopkins University Press, 1992.

———. *The Night Battles: Witchcraft and Agrarian cults in the Sixteenth and Seventeenth Centuries*. Baltimore, Maryland: Johns Hopkins University Press, 1983.

González-Wippler, M. *The Complete Book of Amulets & Talismans*. St. Paul, Minn.: Llewellyn, 1991.

Graf, F. *Magic in the Ancient World*. Cambridge, Mass.: Harvard University Press, 1997.

Gribbin, John. *In Search of Schrodinger's Cat: Quantum Physics and Reality*. Bantam Doubleday Dell, 1985.

———. *Schrodinger's Kittens and the Search for Reality: Solving the Quantum Mysteries*. Little Brown & Co., 1996.

Grimassi, R. *Encyclopedia of Wicca and Witchcraft*. St. Paul, Minn.: Llewellyn, 2000.

———. *Beltane*. St. Paul, Minn.: Llewellyn, 2001.

Hutton, R. *The Pagan Religions of the Ancient British Isles: Their Nature and Legacy*. Malden, Mass.: Blackwell Publishers Ltd., 1991.

———. *The Stations of the Sun*. Oxford: Oxford University Press, 1996.

———. *The Triumph of the Moon: A History of Modern Pagan Witchcraft*. Oxford, England: Oxford University Press, 1999.

Jackson, N. and S. Ravenwolf. *The Rune Mysteries*. St. Paul, Minn.: Llewellyn, 1996.

Jones, B. *Chakra Workout for Body, Mind, and Spirit*. 2nd ed. 1999, St. Paul, Minn.: Llewellyn, 1999.

K, Amber. *Coven Craft*. St. Paul, Minn.: Llewellyn, 1998.

K, Amber, and Azrael Arynn K. *Candlemas: Feast of Flames*. St. Paul, Minn.: Llewellyn, 2001.

Kempton-Smith, Debbi. *Secrets from a Stargazer's Notebook: Making Astrology Work for You*. Topquark Press, 1999.

Kieckhefer, R. *Magic in the Middle Ages*. 2nd, 2000 edition ed. Cambridge, UK: Cambridge University Press, 1989.

Leek, S. *How to Be Your Own Astrologer*. 1970, New York, N.Y.: Cowles Book Company, Inc. 264.

Leeming, D. M. *A Dictionary of Creation Myths*. Oxford, New York: Oxford University Press, 1994.

Lesko, B. S. *The Great Goddesses of Egypt*. 1999, Norman, OK: Oklahoma University. 319.

Levi, E. C. (Alphonse Louis). *The History of Magic*. York Beach, Maine: Samuel Weiser, Inc., 2000.

Liungman, C. G. *Dictionary of Symbols*. New York, N.Y.: W. W. Norton & Company, 1991.

Maddon, Kristin. *Mabon*. St. Paul, Minn.: Llewellyn, 2002.

Majno, G. M. D. *The Healing Hand: Man and Wound in the Ancient World*. Cambridge, Mass.: Harvard University Press, 1975.

Malbrough, R. T. *The Magical Power of the Saints*. St. Paul, Minn.: Llewellyn, 1998.

Manilius. *Astronomica*. Loeb Classical Library, ed. G.P. Goold. Cambridge, Mass.: Harvard University Press, 1977.

March, Marion D. and Joan McEvers. *The Only Way to Learn Astrology* (series of 5 books). San Diego, Calif.: ACS Publications, 1981.

Mathers, Samuel L. MacGregor. *The Key of Solomon the King.* York Beach, Maine: Samuel Weiser, Inc., 1888, 1972.

———. *The Goetia: The Lesser Key of Solomon the King (Clavicula Salomonis Regis)*. York Beach, Maine: Samuel Weiser, 1995.

Matthews, C. J. *The Encyclopedia of Celtic Wisdom*. Boston, Mass.: Element Books, 1996.

Matthews, Caitlin. *Celtic Devotional: Daily Prayers and Blessings.* Harmony Books, 1996.

McCoy, Edain. *Ostara*. St. Paul, Minn.: Llewellyn, 2002.

McNeill, F. M. *The Silver Bough, vol. 2. A Calendar of Scottish National Festivals: Candlemas to Harvest Home.* Glasgow, Scotland: William Maclellan, 1959.

Melody. *Love Is in the Earth: A Kaleidoscope of Crystals* (Updated). 2nd ed. Wheat Ridge, Co.: Earth-Love Publishing House, 1995.

Mercier, P. *Chakras: Balance Your Body's Energy for Health and Harmony*. New York, N.Y.: Sterling Publishing Company, 2000.

Mestel, R. "When Push Comes to Shove," in *Los Angeles Times*, 2001.

Ming-Dao, D. *365 Tao Daily Meditations*. San Francisco: HarperCollins Publishers, 1992.

Morrison, Dorothy. *Yule*. St. Paul, Minn.: Llewellyn, 2000.

Myers, F. W. H. *Human Personality and Survival of Bodily Death*. Vol. 2. London, England: Longmans Green and Company, 1903.

Newton, Michael. *Destiny of Souls*. St. Paul, Minn.: Llewellyn, 2000.

———. *Journey of Souls*. St. Paul, Minn.: Llewellyn, 1994.

Paracelsus. *Paracelsus: Selected Writings*, ed. J. Jacobi. Princeton, N.J.: Princeton University Press, 1951.

Parker, J. and D. *KISS Guide to Astrology*. London, England: Dorling Kindersley Publishing, 2000.

Phillips, D. *Practical Guide to Psychic Self-Defense & Well-Being*. 2nd ed. St. Paul, Minn.: Llewellyn, 1980.

Pinch, G. *Magic in Egypt*. Austin, Texas: University of Texas Press, 1995.

Pottenger, M. *Easy Astrology Guide*. San Diego, Calif.: ACS Publications, 1996.

Quinnett, P. G., Ph.D. *Suicide: The Forever Decision*. Crossroad/Herder & Herder, 1997.

Ramesy, W. *Astrologia Restaurata or Astrologie Restored*. Modern ed. vol. 1–4. Issaquah, Wash.: JustUs and Associates, 1653.

Ramsay, J. *The Art of Alchemy*. Hammersmith, London: Thorsons, 1997.

RavenWolf, S. *Halloween: Customs, Spells, and Recipes.* St. Paul, Minn.: Llewellyn, 1999.

———. *American Folk Magick: Charms, Spells & Herbs.* St. Paul, Minn.: Llewellyn, 1995.

———. *Teen Witch Kit*. St. Paul, Minn.: Llewellyn, 2000.

———. *Teen Witch*. St. Paul, Minn.: Llewellyn, 1998.

———. *Silver's Spells for Love*. St. Paul, Minn.: Llewellyn, 2001.

———. *To Ride a Silver Broomstick*. St. Paul, Minn.: Llewellyn, 1993.

Regardie, I. *The Golden Dawn*. 6th ed. St Paul, Minn.: Llewellyn, 1971.

Renault, D. and F., Timothy. *Principles of Native American Spirituality*. Hammersmith, London: Thorsons, 1996.

Ridpath, I. *Stars and Planets.* New York, N.Y.: Dorling Kindersley, 2000.

Rogers-Gallagher, Kim. *Astrology for the Light Side of the Brain*. San Diego, Calif: ACS Publications, 1995.

———. *Astrology for the Light Side of the Future*. San Diego, Calif: ACS Publications, 1998.

Savedow, S. *Sepher Rezial Hemelach: The Book of the Angel Rezial*. York Beach, Maine: Samuel Weiser, Inc., 2000.

Schueler, G. and B. *Egyptian Magick: Enter the Body of Light & Travel the Magickal Universe*. St. Paul, Minn.: Llewellyn, 1989.

Scoble, G. *The Meaning of Flowers: Myth, Language, and Lore.* San Francisco, Calif.: Chronicle Books, 1998.

Seligmann, K. *The History of Magic and the Occult.* New York, N.Y.: Pantheon Books, Random House Division, 1948.

Silverthorn, J. M. and J. Overdurf. *Dreaming Realities: A Spiritual System to Create Inner Alignment Through Dreams.* Carmarthen, UK: Crown House Publishing Limited, 1999.

Simms, Maria K. *The Witches' Circle.* St. Paul, Minn.: Llewellyn, 1996.

———. *A Time for Magick.* St. Paul, Minn.: Llewellyn, 2001.

Smith, C. and A. John. *The Moon Oracle: Let the Phases of the Moon Guide Your Life.* New York, N.Y.: St. Martin's Press, 2000.

Smith, M. *Auras: See Them in Only 60 Seconds!* St. Paul, Minn.: Llewellyn, 1997.

Smolin, L. *Three Roads to Quantum Physics.* New York, N.Y.: Basic Books, 2001.

Society, T. M. *Astrology Really Works!* Carlsbad, Calif.: Hay House, 1995.

Spence, L. *An Encyclopedia of Occultism: The Comprehensive Treasury of Occult Knowledge from All Times and Places.* New York, N.Y.: Carol Publishing, 1960, 1996.

Spitzer, K. D. "Candle Dipping," in *Lewellyn's 1999 Moon Sign Book and Gardening Almanac*, p. 4.

Standard Dictionary of Folklore, Mythology, and Legend, ed. M. Leach. New York, N.Y.: Harper & Row, 1984.

Starr, C. G. *A History of the Ancient World.* New York, N.Y.: Oxford University Press, 1991.

Stein, Diane. *Essential Reiki.* Crossing Press, 1995.

Stenger, Victor J. *Physics and Psychics: The Search for a World Beyond the Senses.* Amherst, N.Y.: Prometheus Books, 1990.

———. *The Unconscious Quantum: Metaphysics in Modern Physics and Cosmology.* Amherst, N.Y.: Prometheus Books, 1995.

Storms, G. *Anglo-Saxon Magic.* The Hague: Nijhoff, 1948.

Talbot, M. *The Holographic Universe.* New York, N.Y.: HarperCollins, 1991.

The Oxford English Dictionary, 2nd ed. New York, N.Y.: Oxford University Press, 1999.

Thomas, K. *Religion and the Decline of Magic.* New York, N.Y.: Oxford University Press, 1971.

Tyson, D. *Rune Magic.* St. Paul, Minn.: Llewellyn, 1988.

Valiente, D. *An ABC of Witchcraft.* Custer, Wash.: Phoenix Publishing, Inc., 1973.

———. *Witchcraft for Tomorrow.* Custer, Wash.: Phoenix Publishing, Inc., 1978.

Verner-Bonds, L. *The Complete Book of Color Healing: Practical Ways to Enhance Your Physical and Spiritual Well-Being.* New York, N.Y: Sterling Publishing Company, 2000.

Walker, B. *The Woman's Dictionary of Symbols and Sacred Objects.* New York, N.Y: HarperCollins Publishers, 1998.

———. *The Woman's Encyclopedia of Myths and Secrets.* New York, N.Y: HarperCollins Publishers, 1983.

Washington, P. *Madame Blavatsky's Baboon: A History of the Mystics, Mediums, and Misfits Who Brought Spiritualism to America.* New York, N.Y.: Schocken Books, Inc., 1993.

Webster, R. *Astral Travel for Beginners: Transcent Time and Space with Out-of-Body Experiences.* St. Paul, Minn.: Llewellyn, 1998.

———. *Aura Reading for Beginners: Develop Your Psychic Awareness for Health and Success.* St. Paul, Minn.: Llewellyn, 1998.

———. *Palm Reading for Beginners.* St. Paul, Minn.: Llewellyn, 2000.

Webster's New Collegiate Dictionary, 6th edition. Springfield, Mass.: G. & C. Merriam Co., 1979.

Weinstein, Marion. *Positive Magic.* Phoenix, 1985.

Witchcraft and Magic in Europe: Ancient Greece and Rome. Witchcraft and Magic in Europe, ed. B. and Stuart C. Ankarloo. Philadelphia, Pa.: University of Pennsylvania Press, 1999.

Yoder, D. *Discovering American Folklife: Essays on Folk Culture & the Pennsylvania Dutch.* Mechanicsburg, Pa.: Stackpole Books, 2001.

York, U. *Living by the Moon.* Woodside, Calif.: BlueStar Communications, 1997.

Index

Note: Page numbers in bold type indicate where the primary reference of the entry is located.

Teen Witch

Wicca for a New Generation

SILVER RAVENWOLF

Teenagers comprise a growing market for books on Witchcraft and magick, yet there has never been a book written specifically for the teen seeker. Now, Silver RavenWolf, one of the most well-known Wiccans today and the mother of four young Witches, gives teens their own handbook on what it takes and what it means to be a Witch. Humorous and compassionate, *Teen Witch* gives practical advice for dealing with everyday life in a magickal way. From homework and crabby teachers to parents and dating, this book guides teens through the ups and downs of life as they move into adulthood. Spells are provided that address their specific concerns, such as the "Call Me Spell" and "The Exam Spell."

Parents will also find this book informative and useful as a discussion tool with their children. Discover the beliefs of Witchcraft, Wiccan traditions, symbols, holidays, rituals, and more.

1-56718-725-0
288 pp., 7 x 10   **$16.99**

TO ORDER, CALL 1-877-NEW-WRLD
Prices subject to change without notice

A Witch's Notebook
Lessons in Witchcraft

SILVER RAVENWOLF

What if you could peek inside the journal of a skilled and powerful Wiccan and read all about her exciting forays into the Craft? What if that Witch was the ever-popular Silver RavenWolf?

Silver's own pearls of wisdom gained along the bumpy road to spiritual enlightenment can be found in *A Witch's Notebook*. This hands-on guide is designed to work from moon to moon—leading students through five months of spiritual advancement. In discussing cleansing, sacred symbols, renewed spirituality, and magickal ingredients, Silver urges Wiccans to step outside the usual confines of Witchcraft and explore other belief systems. This book also includes exercises, spells, and herbal information to assist in forging one's own unique spiritual path.

0-7387-0662-0
264 pp., 6 x 9   **$14.99**

TO ORDER, CALL 1-877-NEW-WRLD
Prices subject to change without notice

To Ride a Silver Broomstick
New Generation Witchcraft

SILVER RAVENWOLF

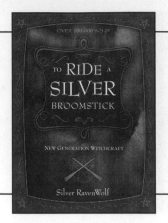

Throughout the world there is a new generation of Witches—people practicing or wishing to practice the craft on their own, without an in-the-flesh magickal support group. *To Ride a Silver Broomstick* speaks to those people, presenting them with both the science and religion of Witchcraft, allowing them to become active participants while growing at their own pace. It is ideal for anyone: male or female, young or old, those familiar with Witchcraft, and those totally new to the subject and unsure of how to get started.

Full of the author's warmth, humor, and personal anecdotes, *To Ride a Silver Broomstick* leads you step-by-step through the various lessons with exercises and journal writing assignments. This is the complete Witchcraft 101, teaching you to celebrate the Sabbats, deal with coming out of the broom closet, choose a magickal name, visualize the Goddess and God, meditate, design a sacred space, acquire magickal tools, design and perform rituals, network, spell cast, perform color and candle magick, divination, healing, telepathy, psychometry, astral projection, and much, much more.

0-87542-791-X
320 pp., 7 x 10, illus.   **$17.99**

To Stir a Magick Cauldron

A Witch's Guide to Casting and Conjuring

SILVER RAVENWOLF

The sequel to the enormously popular *To Ride a Silver Broomstick: New Generation Witchcraft*. This upbeat and down-to-earth guide to intermediate-level witchery was written for all Witches—solitaries, eclectics, and traditionalists. In her warm, straight-from-the-hip, eminently knowledgeable manner, Silver provides explanations, techniques, exercises, anecdotes, and guidance on traditional and modern aspects of the Craft, both as a science and as a religion.

Find out why you should practice daily devotions and how to create a sacred space. Learn six ways to cast a magick circle. Explore the complete art of spellcasting. Examine the hows and whys of Craft laws, oaths, degrees, lineage, traditions, and more. Explore the ten paths of power, and harness this wisdom for your own spellcraft. This book offers you dozens of techniques—some never before published—to help you uncover the benefits of natural magick and ritual and make them work for you—without spending a dime!

Silver is a "working Witch" who has successfully used each and every technique and spell in this book. By the time you have done the exercises in each chapter, you will be well trained in the first level of initiate studies. Test your knowledge with the Wicca 101 test provided at the back of the book and become a certified Witch! Learn to live life to its fullest through this positive spiritual path.

1-56718-424-3
320 pp., 7 x 10, illus.   **$17.99**

To Light a Sacred Flame
Practical WitchCraft for the Millennium

SILVER RAVENWOLF

Silver RavenWolf continues to unveil the mysteries of the Craft with *To Light a Sacred Flame*, which follows her best-selling *To Ride a Silver Broomstick* and *To Stir a Magick Cauldron* as the third in the "New Generation WitchCraft" series, guides to magickal practices based on the personal experiences and successes of a third-degree working Witch.

Written for today's seeker, this book contains techniques that unite divinity with magick, knowledge, and humor. Not structured for any particular tradition, the lessons present unique and insightful material for the solitary as well as the group. Explore the fascinating realms of your inner power, sacred shrines, magickal formularies, spiritual housecleaning, and the intricacies of ritual. This book reveals new information that includes a complete discussion on the laws of the Craft, glamouries, and shamanic Craft rituals, including a handfasting and wiccaning (saining).

1-56718-721-8
320 pp., 7 x 10 $17.99

TO ORDER, CALL 1-877-NEW-WRLD
Prices subject to change without notice